Lecture Notes in Computer Science 3689

Commenced Publication in 1973
Founding and Former Series Editors:
Gerhard Goos, Juris Hartmanis, and Jan van Leeuwen

Gary Geunbae Lee   Akio Yamada
Helen Meng   Sung Hyon Myaeng (Eds.)

Information Retrieval Technology

Second Asia Information Retrieval Symposium, AIRS 2005
Jeju Island, Korea, October 13-15, 2005
Proceedings

 Springer

Volume Editors

Gary Geunbae Lee
Pohang University of Science and Technology (POSTECH)
Department of Computer Science and Engineering
San 31, Hyoja-Dong, Nam-gu, Pohang, 790-784, South Korea
E-mail: gblee@postech.ac.kr

Akio Yamada
Media and Information Research Laboratories, NEC Corp. Shimonumabe 1753
Nakahara-ku, Kawasaki 211-8666, Japan
E-mail: a-yamada@da.jp.nec.com

Helen Meng
The Chinese University of Hong Kong
Human-Computer Communications Laboratory
Department of Systems Engineering and Engineering Management
Shatin, NT, Hong Kong SAR, China
E-mail: hmmeng@se.cuhk.edu.hk

Sung Hyon Myaeng
Information and Communications University (ICU)
Munji-dong, Yuseong-gu, Daejeon, 305-714, South Korea
E-mail: myaeng@icu.ac.kr

Library of Congress Control Number: 2005933614

CR Subject Classification (1998): H.3, H.4, F.2.2, E.1, E.2

ISSN   0302-9743
ISBN-10   3-540-29186-5 Springer Berlin Heidelberg New York
ISBN-13   978-3-540-29186-2 Springer Berlin Heidelberg New York

Springer is a part of Springer Science+Business Media

springeronline.com

© Springer-Verlag Berlin Heidelberg 2005
Printed in Germany

Typesetting: Camera-ready by author, data conversion by Scientific Publishing Services, Chennai, India
Printed on acid-free paper   SPIN: 11562382   06/3142   5 4 3 2 1 0

Preface

Asia Information Retrieval Symposium (AIRS) was established in 2004 by the Asian information retrieval community after the successful series of Information Retrieval with Asian Languages (IRAL) workshops held in six different locations in Asia, starting from 1996. The AIRS symposium aims to bring together international researchers and developers to exchange new ideas and the latest results in the field of information retrieval (IR). The scope of the symposium covers applications, systems, technologies and theoretical aspects of information retrieval in text, audio, image, video and multi-media data.

We are very pleased to report that we saw a sharp and steady increase in the number of submissions and their qualities, compared with previous IRAL workshop series. We received 136 submissions from all over the world including Asia, North America, Europe, Australia, and even Africa, from which 32 papers (23%) were presented in oral sessions and 36 papers in poster sessions (26%). We also held a special session called "Digital Photo Albuming," where 4 oral papers and 3 posters were presented. It was a great challenge and hard work for the program committee to select the best among the excellent papers. The high acceptance rates witness the success and stability of the AIRS series. All the papers and posters are included in this LNCS (Lecture Notes in Computer Science) proceedings volume, which is SCI-indexed.

The technical program included two keynote talks by Prof. Walter Bender and Prof. Eduard Hovy respectively, and a total of 10 oral sessions with two in parallel including one special session and also two poster sessions.

The technical and social programs, which we are proud of, were made possible by the hard working people behind the scene. In addition to the Program Committee members, we are thankful to the Organizing Committee, Poster Chair (Helen Meng), Demo/Exhibition Chair (Myung-Gil Jang), Publicity Chairs (Hsin-his Chen, MunChurl Kim, Mun-kew Leong, Tetsuya Sakai, Bing Swen, Robert Luk), Sponsor Chair (Hee Suk Lim), Treasurer/Secretary (Bo Yeong Kang), and Qing Li for conference website management.

We also thank the sponsoring organizations Toshiba Corporation, Japan; LexisNexis, USA; INEK, Korea; and Daum Soft, Korea for their support, as well as the Information and Communication University and the Korea Institute of Science and Technology Information for hosting the conference, and Springer for publishing these proceeding in their LNCS series.

We believe that this conference has already set a very high standard for a regionally oriented conference, especially in Asia, and hope that you enjoyed the conference as well as the beautiful scenery of Jeju island.

August 2005

Gary G. Lee and Akio Yamada
Sung Hyon Myaeng and Dong In Park

Organization

General Conference Chairs
Sung Hyon Myaeng (ICU, Korea)
Dong In Park (KISTI, Korea)

Program Chairs
Gary G. Lee (POSTECH, Korea)
Akio Yamada (NEC, Japan)

Poster Chair
Helen Meng (Chinese University of Hong Kong, China)

Demo/Exhibition Chair
Myung-Gil Jang (ETRI, Korea)

Publicity Chairs
Hsin-hsi Chen (National Taiwan University, Taiwan)
MunChurl Kim (ICU, Korea)
Mun-kew Leong (I2R, Singapore)
Tetsuya Sakai (Toshiba, Japan)
Bing Swen (Peking University, China)
Robert Luk (Hong Kong Polytechnic University, China)

Sponsor Chair
Hee Suk Lim (Hansin University)

Treasurer/Secretary
Bo Yeong Kang (ICU, Korea)

Steering Committee
Jun Adachi, National Institute of Informatics, Japan
Hsin-Hsi Chen, National Taiwan University, Taiwan
Lee-Feng Chien, Academia Sinica, Taiwan
Gary Geunbae Lee, POSTECH, Korea
Mun-Kew Leong, Institute for Infocomm Research, Singapore
Helen Meng, The Chinese University of Hong Kong, China
Sung Hyon Myaeng, Information and Communication University, Korea
Hwee Tou Ng, National University of Singapore, Singapore

Tetsuya Sakai, Toshiba, Japan
Kam-Fai Wong, The Chinese University of Hong Kong, China
Ming Zhou, Microsoft Research Asia, China

Organization Committee
Bo Yeong Kang (Information & Communications University)
Munchurl Kim (Information & Communications University)
Myung-Gil Jang (ETRI)
Pyung Kim (KISTI)
Qing Li (Information & Communications University)
Hee Suk Lim (Hansin University)
Dong-Chul Lee (Cheju National University)
Youngjoong Ko (Dong-A University)
Hanmin Jung (KISTI)
Kyung Soon Lee (Chonbuk National University)

Hosted by
Information and Communications University
Korea Institute of Science and Technology Information

Program Committee

Hani Abu-Salem, DePaul University, USA
Terumasa Aoki, University of Tokyo, Japan
Kohtaro Asai, Mitsubishi Electric, Japan
Ricardo Baeza-Yates, ICREA-UPF, Spain & CWR, Univ. of Chile
Hsin-Hsi Chen, National Taiwan University, Taiwan
Lee-Feng Chien, Academia Sinica, Taiwan
Tat-Seng Chua, National University of Singapore, Singapore
Fabio Crestani, University of Strathclyde, Scotland, UK
Jianfeng Gao, Microsoft Research Asia, China
Tetsuya Ishikawa, University of Tsukuba, Japan
Min-Yen Kan, National University of Singapore, Singapore
Noriko Kando, National Institute of Informatics, Japan
Christopher Khoo, Nanyang Technological University, Singapore
Munchurl Kim, ICU, Korea
Hoi-Rin Kim, ICU, Korea
Juntae Kim, Dongguk University, Korea
Kazuaki Kishida, Surugadai University, Japan
Kui-Lam Kwok, Queens College, City University of New York, USA
Wai Lam, Chinese University of Hong Kong, China
Gary Geunbae Lee, POSTECH, Korea
JaeHo Lee, University of Seoul, Korea

Jae Sung Lee, Chungbuk National University, Korea
Jong-Hyeok Lee, POSTECH, Korea
Mun-Kew Leong, Institute for Infocomm Research, Singapore
Gina-Anne Levow, University of Chicago, USA
Hang Li, Microsoft Research Asia, China
Ee-Peng Lim, Nanyang Technological University, Singapore
Chin-Yew Lin, University of Southern California, USA
Robert Luk, Hong Kong Polytechnic University, China
Helen Meng, The Chinese University of Hong Kong, China
Hiroshi Murase, Nagoya University, Japan
Hiroshi Nakagawa, University of Tokyo, Japan
Hwee Tou Ng, National University of Singapore, Singapore
Jian-Yun Nie, University of Montreal, Canada
Sam Gyun Oh, Sungkyunkwan University, Korea
Jon Patrick, University of Sydney, Australia
Fuchun Peng, BBN Technologies, USA
Hae-Chang Rim, Korea University, Korea
YongMan Ro, ICU, Korea
Tetsuya Sakai, Toshiba Corporate R&D Center, Japan
Shin'ichi Satoh, National Institute of Informatics, Japan
John R. Smith, IBM T. J. Watson Research Center, USA
Padmini Srinivasan, University of Iowa, USA
Masaru Sugano, KDDI R&D Laboratories, Japan
Aixin Sun, University of New South Wales, Australia
Maosong Sun, Tsinghua University, China
Ulrich Thiel, Fraunhofer IPSI, Germany
Takenobu Tokunaga, Tokyo Institute of Technology, Japan
Hsin-Min Wang, Academia Sinica, Taiwan
Kam-Fai Wong, CUHK, China
Ross Wilkinson, CSIRO, Australia
Lide Wu, Fudan University, China
Seong-Joon Yoo, Sejong University, Korea
ChengXiang Zhai, University of Illinois, Urbana Champaign, USA
Min Zhang, Tsinghua University, China
Ming Zhou, Microsoft Research Asia, China
Justin Zobel, RMIT, Australia

Additional Reviewers

Yee Seng Chan, Tee Kiah Chia, Yunbo Cao, Jie Tang, Jun Xu

Table of Contents

Session 2B: Enabling Technology

Session 3A: Web IR

Session 3B: Question Answering

Session 4A: Document/Query Models

Session 4B: Special Session: Digital PhotoAlbum

Session 5A: TDT/Clustering

Session 5B: Multimedia/Classification

Poster and Demo Session 1

Poster and Demo Session 2

The Reliability of Metrics
Based on Graded Relevance

Tetsuya Sakai

Toshiba Corporate R&D Center, Kawasaki 212-8582, Japan
tetsuya.sakai@toshiba.co.jp

Abstract. This paper compares 14 metrics designed for information retrieval evaluation with graded relevance, together with 10 traditional metrics based on binary relevance, in terms of reliability and resemblance of system rankings. More specifically, we use two test collections with submitted runs from the Chinese IR and English IR tasks in the NTCIR-3 CLIR track to examine the metrics using methods proposed by Buckley/Voorhees and Voorhees/Buckley as well as Kendall's rank correlation. Our results show that AnDCG$_l$ and nDCG$_l$ ((Average) Normalised Discounted Cumulative Gain at Document cut-off l) are good metrics, provided that l is large. However, if one wants to avoid the parameter l altogether, or if one requires a metric that closely resembles TREC Average Precision, then Q-measure appears to be the best choice.

1 Introduction

After a decade of TREC evaluations based on *binary* relevance, the importance of information retrieval (IR) evaluation based on *graded* relevance is receiving attention [4,5,6,7,8]. Graded relevance metrics based on *(discounted) cumulative gain* ((d)cg) [4,5] are particularly popular.

Although several (d)cg-based graded relevance metrics exist for IR, none of them is as widely-used as traditional binary relevance metrics such as TREC Average Precision (AveP) at present. For example, even though the NTCIR CLIR track series [2] uses graded relevance (S, A and B in decreasing order of relevance), "Relaxed" AveP (which treats S-, A- and B-relevant documents as just "relevant") and "Rigid" AveP (which ignores B-relevant ones) are used for ranking systems, thereby wasting the rich relevance data. The objective of this paper is to improve such situations by clarifying which of the (d)cg-based metrics are reliable and useful. To this end, we use two test collections with submitted runs from the Chinese IR and English IR tasks in the NTCIR-3 CLIR track to examine a variety of (d)cg-based metrics using methods proposed by Buckley/Voorhees [1] and Voorhees/Buckley [12] as well as Kendall's rank correlation [3,5,7,8]. We test 14 graded relevance metrics plus 10 binary relevance ones from the viewpoint of reliability and resemblance of system rankings. Our experiments suggest that graded relevance may give more stability and discrimiation power than binary relevance, and show that some graded relevance metrics such as *Q-measure* [7,8] are more reliable and useful than others.

G.G. Lee et al. (Eds.): AIRS 2005, LNCS 3689, pp. 1–16, 2005.

Section 2 defines the metrics examined, and Section 3 describes the methods we used for comparing the reliability of metrics. Section 4 presents the results of our analyses, and Section 5 provides discussions. Section 6 compares previous work with the present study, and Section 7 concludes this paper.

2   Effectiveness Metrics

We first define TREC Average Precision (AveP), R-Precision (R-Prec), Precision at document cut-off l (PDoc$_l$), Q-measure and R-measure:

$$AveP = \frac{1}{R} \sum_{1 \leq r \leq L} isrel(r) \frac{count(r)}{r} \; . \tag{1}$$

$$R\text{-}Prec = \frac{count(R)}{R} \; . \tag{2}$$

$$PDoc_l = \frac{count(l)}{l} \; . \tag{3}$$

$$Q\text{-}measure = \frac{1}{R} \sum_{1 \leq r \leq L} isrel(r) \frac{cg(r) + count(r)}{cig(r) + r} \; . \tag{4}$$

$$R\text{-}measure = \frac{cg(R) + count(R)}{cig(R) + R} \; . \tag{5}$$

Here,

R: number of relevant documents;
$count(r)$: number of relevant documents in top r of the ranked output;
L: size of the ranked output;
$isrel(r)$:   1 if the document at Rank r is relevant and 0 otherwise;
$cg(r)$:   *cumulative gain* [4] at Rank r of the system's output, obtained by accumulating the *gain values* ($gain(X)$) for each retrieved X-relevant document (where $X \in \{S, A, B\}$ for NTCIR CLIR);
$cig(r)$:   cumulative gain at Rank r of the *ideal* ranked output (obtained by listing up S-, A-, and B-relevant documents in this order in the case of NTCIR CLIR [7,8]).

As discussed fully in [7,8], the *blended ratio* $(cg(r) + count(r))/(cig(r) + r)$ of Q-measure inherits the properties of both precision and *weighted precision* $cg(r)/cig(r)$. Using weighted precision instead of the blended ratio in Equation (4) is *not* good because $cig(r) = cig(R)$ holds for $r > R$: That is, $cig(r)$ *freezes* after Rank R, and therefore weighted precision cannot penalise late arrival of relevant documents. Q-measure solves this problem by using $cig(r) + r$ as the denominator. The following are some properties of Q-measure and R-measure:

- If the absolute gain values are small, Q-measure (R-measure) behaves like AveP (R-Prec);
- Q-measure is equal to one iff a system output (s.t. $L \geq R$) is an ideal one;

- R-measure is equal to one iff all of the top R documents are (at least partially) relevant;
- With binary relevance, R-measure reduces to R-Prec.

Just like AveP and R-prec, Q-measure and R-measure use R as the basis for cross-topic normalisation. In contrast, Järvelin and Kekäläinen [4] have proposed graded relevance metrics that are somewhat akin to PDoc$_l$. Their *Normalised Cumulative Gain* and *Average Normalised Cumulative Gain* at l are given by:

$$nCG_l = \frac{cg(l)}{cig(l)} \; . \tag{6}$$

$$AnCG_l = \frac{1}{l} \sum_{1 \leq r \leq l} \frac{cg(r)}{cig(r)} \; . \tag{7}$$

If the above cumulative (ideal) gains are replaced with *discounted* cumulative (ideal) gains, which are based on gains divided by the logarithm of each rank, we have *(Average) Normalised Discounted Cumulative Gain* (nDCG$_l$ and AnDCG$_l$).

It is clear from the definition that nCG$_l$ is *not* a good metric when l is much larger than R, because of the aforementioned freezing problem: Let $gain(S) = 3, gain(A) = 2, gain(B) = 1$ (which are the default values used in this paper), and consider a topic such that $R = R(B) = 5$, where $R(X)$ denotes the number of X-relevant documents and $R = \sum_X R(X)$ in general. The sequence of $cig(r)$ for this topic is $(1, 2, 3, 4, 5, 5, 5, \ldots)$, so that $cig(1000) = 5$. Suppose that System A retrieves only one relevant document at Rank 5, while System B retrieves one at Rank 1000. Then, with System A, $cg(r) = 1$ for $r \geq 5$, while, with System B, $cg(r) = 1$ for $r \geq 1000$. Thus, for both systems, $nCG_{1000} = cg(1000)/cig(1000) = 1/5 = 0.2$. There are at least three ways to avoid this problem: (a) Use *discounting* as nDCG$_l$ and AnDCG$_l$ do; (b) Average across document ranks as AnCG$_l$ and AnDCG$_l$ do; or (c) Use Q-measure instead [7,8].

One may argue that using l instead of R as the basis for normalisation better models user behaviour. However, the choice of l is arbitrary, and this may seriously affect system ranking, as is the case with PDoc$_l$ [1]. Later, we shall show that the choice of l is in fact crucial for these (d)cg-based metrics. (nDCG$_l$ and AnDCG$_l$ depend on another parameter: namely, the logarithm base for discounting [4,5]. We use base 2 throughout our experiments.)

The *unnormalised* versions of Järvelin and Kekäläinen's metrics such as $CG_l = cg(l)$ are out of the scope of this paper as these metrics are not even bounded by one: They do not average well.

3   Methods

This section describes our adaptation of two existing methods for assessing the reliability of test collections and effectiveness of metrics.

for each pair of runs $x, y \in S$
    for each trial from 1 to 1000
        select $Q_i \subset Q$ at random s.t. $|Q_i| == c$;
        $margin = f * \max(M(x, Q_i), M(y, Q_i))$;
        if($|M(x, Q_i) - M(y, Q_i)| < margin$)
            $EQ_M(x, y) + +$
        else if($M(x, Q_i) > M(y, Q_i)$)
            $GT_M(x, y) + +$
        else
            $GT_M(y, x) + +$;

Fig. 1. The algorithm for computing $EQ_M(x, y)$, $GT_M(x, y)$ and $GT_M(y, x)$

The Buckley/Voorhees method [1] works as follows: Let S denote a set of runs submitted to a particular task, and let x and y denote a pair of runs from S. Let Q denote the entire set of topics used in the task, and let c be a constant. Let $M(x, Q_i)$ denote the value of metric M for System x averaged over a topic set $Q_i(\subset Q)$. Then, after counting $GT_M(x, y)$, $GT_M(y, x)$ and $EQ_M(x, y)$ as shown in Figure 1, the minority rate and the proportion of ties of M, given a *fuzziness value* f, can be computed as:

$$MinorityRate_M =$$

$$\frac{\sum_{x,y \in S} \min(GT_M(x, y), GT_M(y, x))}{\sum_{x,y \in S}(GT_M(x, y) + GT_M(y, x) + EQ_M(x, y))} . \tag{8}$$

$$PropTies_M =$$

$$\frac{\sum_{x,y \in S} EQ_M(x, y)}{\sum_{x,y \in S}(GT_M(x, y) + GT_M(y, x) + EQ_M(x, y))} . \tag{9}$$

The minority rate is an estimate of the chance of reaching a wrong conclusion about a pair of runs using a given metric, while the proportion of ties reflects its discrimination power. From the algorithm, it is clear that $GT_M(x, y) + GT_M(y, x) + EQ_M(x, y) = 1000$ holds for each run pair, and that a larger fuzziness value yields larger $EQ_M(x, y)$ values, and therefore a larger proportion of ties and a smaller minority rate. As a fixed fuzziness value may imply different trade-offs for different metrics, we vary the fuzziness value ($f = 0.01, 0.02, \ldots, 0.10$) and draw *minority-rate / proportion-of-ties curves* for comparing the stability of different metrics [9].

The Voorhees/Buckley method [12] works as follows. Let d denote a performance difference between two runs. We first prepare 21 *performance difference bins*, where the first bin represents performance differences such that $0 \leq d < 0.01$, the second bin represents those such that $0.01 \leq d < 0.02$, and so on, and the last bin represents those such that $0.20 \leq d$. Let $BIN(d)$

for each pair of runs $x, y \in S$
    for each trial from 1 to 1000
        select $Q_i, Q_i' \subset Q$ s.t.
            $Q_i \cap Q_i' == \phi$ and $|Q_i| == |Q_i'| == c$;
        $d_M(Q_i) = M(x, Q_i) - M(y, Q_i)$;
        $d_M(Q_i') = M(x, Q_i') - M(y, Q_i')$;
        $counter(BIN(d_M(Q_i)))++$;
        if(($d_M(Q_i) * d_M(Q_i') < 0$) or
           ($d_M(Q_i) == 0$ and $d_M(Q_i') \neq 0$) or
           ($d_M(Q_i) \neq 0$ and $d_M(Q_i') == 0$))
           $swap\_counter(BIN(d_M(Q_i)))++$;
for each bin b
    $swap\_rate(b) = swap\_counter(b)/counter(b)$;

Fig. 2. The algorithm for computing the swap rates

denote a mapping from a difference d to one of the 21 bins where it belongs. The algorithm shown in Figure 2 calculates a *swap rate* for each bin. (Our test is stricter than the original one by Voorhees/Buckley, in that our "swaps" include cases in which only one of $d_M(Q_i)$ and $d_M(Q_i')$ is zero. This is because Voorhees/Buckley's original test, which increments the swap counter only when one of the differences is positive and the other is negative, tends to underrate the swap rates for near-zero bins as the differences are actually quite often zero. We have verified that this modification gives graphs that look more stable, but do not affect our conclusions.)

Because Q_i and Q_i' must be disjoint, they can only be up to half the size of the original topic set Q. (Voorhees/Buckley have used *extrapolation* for larger topic set sizes, but we stick to the statistics actually measured in our study as our objective is to compare the sensitivity of different metrics under the same condition.) By plotting swap rates against the performance difference bins, one can discuss the performance difference required in order to conclude that a run is better than another with a given confidence level, e.g. 95%.

Recently, the Voorhees/Buckley method has been criticised as *overestimating* swap rates due to the use of disjoint subsets Q_i and Q_i'. However, the objective of the method is to *guarantee* a given confidence level by considering the worst case in which the properties of the two topic sets are completely different, and *not* to obtain accurate estimates of the *true* swap rates which would be obtained by sampling topics directly from the population of real topics P, where $P >> Q$. In fact, we have verified that using *topic sampling with replacement* (with possible overlaps between Q_i and Q_i') instead of the original Voorhees/Buckley method does not affect our general conclusions regarding the relative sensitivity of different metrics. (This alternative topic selection method has been studied earlier by Ian Soboroff at NIST [11].) Thus, this paper presents results using the original Voorhees/Buckley method, and we will discuss the effect of using alternative topic sampling methods elsewhere [10].

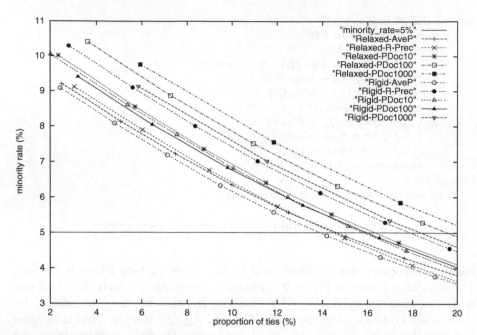

Fig. 3. Minority-rate / Proportion-of-ties curves for the binary relevance metrics (Top 30 C-runs; 42 topics; $c = 20$)

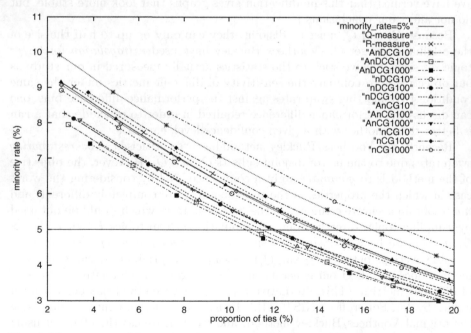

Fig. 4. Minority-rate / Proportion-of-ties curves for the graded relevance metrics (Top 30 C-runs; 42 topics; $c = 20$)

Table 1. The proportion of ties for binary/graded relevance metrics at 5% minority rate

%ties	binary relevance metrics	graded relevance metrics
(a) Top 30 C-runs; 42 topics; $c = 20$		
10-12%		Q-measure $AnDCG_{100,1000}$ $nDCG_{100,1000}$ $AnCG_{100,1000}$
13-15%	Relaxed/Rigid-AveP Relaxed-R-Prec	R-measure $nDCG_{10}$ $AnCG_{10}$ $nCG_{10,100}$
16-18%	Rigid-R-Prec Relaxed/Rigid-$PDoc_{10}$ Rigid-$PDoc_{100,1000}$	$AnDCG_{10}$ nCG_{1000}
19% and over	Relaxed-$PDoc_{100,1000}$	
(b) Top 20 E-runs; 32 topics; $c = 15$		
10-12%	Relaxed/Rigid-AveP	Q-measure $AnDCG_{10,100,1000}$ $nDCG_{10,100,1000}$ $AnCG_{10,100,1000}$ nCG_{1000}
13-15%		
16-18%	Rigid-R-Prec Rigid-$PDoc_{10}$	$nCG_{10,100}$
19% and over	Relaxed-R-Prec Relaxed-$PDoc_{10,100,1000}$ Rigid-$PDoc_{100,1000}$	R-measure

4 Experiments

4.1 Data

For our experiments, we used the Chinese IR and English IR data from NTCIR-3 CLIR [2], containing 45 "C-runs" and 24 "E-runs" [7,8]. As there are 42/32 topics for the C/E-runs, respectively, we let $c = 20$ for the C-runs and $c = 15$ for the E-runs throughout our experiments in order to obtain disjoint topic sets for the swap rate calculation [12]. We use the top 30 C-runs and the top 20 E-runs for calculating minority rates and swap rates, and the full sets of runs for calculating rank correlations. Since our C-run experiments use more runs and more topics than our E-run ones, the results of the former are probably more reliable.

4.2 Minority Rates

Figures 3 and 4 show the minority-rate / proportion-of-ties curves of 10 binary relevance metrics and 14 graded relevance metrics, based on the C-runs. Table 1 provides a summary by slicing the graphs (and ones for the E-runs, not shown here due to lack of space) at 5% minority rate and roughly grouping the metrics according to the proportion of ties. The C-run results suggest that the use of graded relevance may stabilise evaluation: Figures 3 and 4 together (and Table 1(a)) show that, at 5% minority rate, metrics such as $(A)nDCG_{1000}$ and Q-measure have smaller number of ties than Relaxed and Rigid AveP. (R-Prec and R-measure appear to be relatively unstable for the E-runs, probably because R is generally small for the NTCIR-3 English test collection [2].)

4.3 Swap Rates

Based on graphs that plot swap rates against the 21 performance difference bins, Tables 2 and 3 show the discrimination power of metrics at 95% confidence level (i.e. 5% swap rate) for the C- and E-runs. For example, Table 2(a) shows that when 20 topics are used for ranking the C-runs with Relaxed AveP, an absolute difference of at least 0.11 (or 20% in terms of relative difference) is required in order to conclude that a run is better than another with 95% confidence. Of the 435,000 comparisons (30*29/2=435 system pairs, each with 1000 trials), 23.7% actually had this difference. The metrics have been sorted by this measure of discrimination power (Column (iv)). We can observe that:

- In terms of discrimination power, the best graded relevance metrics appear to be Q-measure, R-measure and (A)nDCG$_l$ ($l = 100, 1000$). Thus, gain discounting appears to be beneficial, but using a small value of l may hurt discrimination power.
- As was mentioned in Section 2, nCG$_{1000}$ is not useful: it cannot even guarantee 95% confidence for the C-runs (Table 2(b)).
- The use of graded relevance may enhance discrimination power. For the C-runs, Q-measure appears to be slightly more sensitive than Relaxed AveP. For the E-runs, (A)nDCG$_l$ ($l = 100, 1000$) and Q-measure appear to be slightly more sensitive than Relaxed AveP.

4.4 Rank Correlations

Sections 4.2 and 4.3 discussed the stability and discrimination power of each metric. We now examine how the system rankings produced by different metrics resemble each other.

Tables 4 and 5 compare graded relevance metrics with binary relevance metrics in terms of Kendall's rank correlation [3,5,7,8], based on the C- and E-run rankings. Correlations higher than 0.9 are shown in bold. We can observe that:

- Q-measure is more highly correlated with Relaxed/Rigid AveP than any other metric. It is also highly correlated with Relaxed R-Prec.
- R-measure is more highly correlated with Relaxed R-Prec than any other metric. It is also highly correlated with Relaxed AveP.
- AnDCG$_{1000}$, nDCG$_{100}$ and nDCG$_{1000}$ are also highly correlated with Relaxed AveP.

Tables 6 and 7 compare pairs of graded relevance metrics in terms of Kendall's rank correlation, based on the C- and E-run rankings. For example, Row (A) Column (B) shows the rank correlation between Q-measure and R-measure. We can observe that:

Table 2. The sensitivity of binary relevance and graded relevance metrics at 95% confidence level (Top 30 C-runs; 42 topics; $c = 20$) (i): Absolute difference required; (ii): Maximum performance observed; (iii): Relative difference required ((i)/(ii)); (iv): %comparisons with the required difference

	(i)	(ii)	(iii)	(iv)
(a) binary relevance metrics				
Relaxed-AveP	0.11	0.5392	20%	23.7%
Relaxed-R-Prec	0.11	0.5554	20%	20.8%
Rigid-AveP	0.10	0.4698	21%	20.6%
Rigid-PDoc$_{100}$	0.05	0.2860	17%	15.4%
Relaxed-PDoc$_{10}$	0.17	0.7400	23%	14.6%
Rigid-PDoc$_{10}$	0.16	0.5900	27%	10.5%
Rigid-R-Prec	0.12	0.4660	26%	9.2%
Rigid-PDoc$_{1000}$	0.01	0.0628	16%	5.7%
Relaxed-PDoc$_{100}$	0.09	0.3940	23%	5.3%
Relaxed-PDoc$_{1000}$	0.02	0.1009	20%	1.4%
(b) graded relevance metrics				
Q-measure	0.10	0.5490	18%	25.4%
R-measure	0.11	0.5777	19%	21.8%
AnDCG$_{1000}$	0.12	0.7067	17%	21.0%
AnDCG$_{100}$	0.13	0.6237	21%	19.8%
nDCG$_{1000}$	0.12	0.7461	16%	19.6%
nDCG$_{100}$	0.13	0.6440	20%	17.9%
nCG$_{10}$	0.14	0.5967	23%	17.1%
nDCG$_{10}$	0.15	0.6262	24%	16.3%
AnCG$_{100}$	0.14	0.6662	21%	15.8%
AnCG$_{10}$	0.17	0.6613	26%	13.2%
AnDCG$_{10}$	0.19	0.6869	28%	10.7%
nCG$_{100}$	0.16	0.7377	22%	10.5%
AnCG$_{1000}$	0.15	0.8770	17%	10.1%
nCG$_{1000}$	-	0.9632	-	-

Table 3. The sensitivity of binary relevance and graded relevance metrics at 95% confidence level (E-runs; 32 topics; $c = 15$) (i): Absolute difference required; (ii): Maximum performance observed; (iii): Relative difference required ((i)/(ii)); (iv): %comparisons with the required difference

	(i)	(ii)	(iii)	(iv)
(a) binary relevance metrics				
Relaxed-AveP	0.14	0.6743	21%	31.1%
Rigid-AveP	0.16	0.6591	24%	26.5%
Rigid-R-Prec	0.15	0.6198	24%	26.2%
Rigid-PDoc$_{10}$	0.13	0.4933	26%	16.0%
Relaxed-PDoc$_{10}$	0.18	0.6533	28%	11.8%
Relaxed-R-Prec	0.19	0.6378	30%	9.4%
Relaxed-PDoc$_{1000}$	0.01	0.0358	28%	2.5%
Relaxed-PDoc$_{100}$	0.15	0.2567	58%	0.0%
Rigid-PDoc$_{100}$	0.11	0.1700	65%	0.0%
Rigid-PDoc$_{1000}$	-	0.0228	-	-
(b) graded relevance metrics				
nDCG$_{1000}$	0.12	0.8314	14%	36.7%
AnDCG$_{1000}$	0.13	0.8164	16%	34.9%
AnDCG$_{100}$	0.14	0.7689	18%	34.6%
nDCG$_{100}$	0.14	0.8009	17%	33.6%
Q-measure	0.13	0.6865	19%	33.0%
R-measure	0.13	0.6641	20%	29.8%
AnCG$_{100}$	0.13	0.8399	15%	28.9%
nDCG$_{10}$	0.17	0.7484	23%	28.1%
AnDCG$_{10}$	0.20	0.7747	26%	25.3%
nCG$_{10}$	0.16	0.7371	22%	25.3%
AnCG$_{10}$	0.19	0.7483	25%	23.8%
AnCG$_{1000}$	0.10	0.9647	10%	23.0%
nCG$_{100}$	0.16	0.9361	17%	16.8%
nCG$_{1000}$	0.12	1.0000	12%	8.4%

Table 4. Kendall's rank correlations: binary relevance vs graded relevance metrics (45 C-runs)

Relaxed	AveP	R-Prec	PDoc$_{10}$	PDoc$_{100}$	PDoc$_{1000}$
Q-measure	**.9798**	**.9232**	.8303	**.9051**	.8424
R-measure	**.9293**	**.9616**	.8485	.8828	.8242
AnDCG$_{10}$	.7737	.7778	.6768	.7556	.7333
AnDCG$_{100}$	.8747	.8828	.8263	.8404	.7859
AnDCG$_{1000}$	**.9172**	.8929	.8566	.8505	.8202
nDCG$_{10}$	.8141	.8141	.7535	.7798	.7939
nDCG$_{100}$	**.9030**	.8828	.8303	.8687	.8020
nDCG$_{1000}$	**.9091**	.8929	.8202	.8505	.8485
AnCG$_{10}$	.7838	.7758	.7313	.7657	.7515
AnCG$_{100}$	.8768	.8687	.8081	.8263	.7596
AnCG$_{1000}$	.8848	.8566	.8242	.8343	.8525
nCG$_{10}$	.8303	.8465	.8020	.8000	.7616
nCG$_{100}$	.8990	.8949	.8182	.8364	.8101
nCG$_{1000}$	.8283	.7919	.7919	.7899	.7636

Rigid	AveP	R-Prec	PDoc$_{10}$	PDoc$_{100}$	PDoc$_{1000}$
Q-measure	**.9192**	.8929	.8182	.8545	.8323
R-measure	.8848	.8828	.7960	.8404	.8061
AnDCG$_{10}$	.7333	.7232	.7131	.7212	.7313
AnDCG$_{100}$	.8747	.8525	.7859	.7939	.7758
AnDCG$_{1000}$	.8889	.8909	.7879	.8444	.8061
nDCG$_{10}$	.7576	.7717	.8141	.7293	.8000
nDCG$_{100}$	**.9071**	.8848	.7697	.8263	.7798
nDCG$_{1000}$	.8768	.8949	.7515	.8242	.8182
AnCG$_{10}$	.7475	.7455	.8121	.6990	.7616
AnCG$_{100}$	.8687	.8788	.7879	.8081	.7859
AnCG$_{1000}$	.8606	.8586	.7838	.8364	.7859
nCG$_{10}$	.7899	.8040	.7899	.7374	.7838
nCG$_{100}$	.8788	.8768	.8263	.8101	.8242
nCG$_{1000}$	.8162	.8384	.7636	.7960	.7859

Table 5. Kendall's rank correlations: binary relevance vs graded relevance metrics (24 E-runs)

Relaxed	AveP	R-Prec	PDoc$_{10}$	PDoc$_{100}$	PDoc$_{1000}$
Q-measure	**.9783**	**.9203**	.7971	.6449	.5652
R-measure	**.9348**	**.9638**	.7971	.6014	.5942
AnDCG$_{10}$	**.9130**	.8986	.7754	.5797	.5290
AnDCG$_{100}$	**.9348**	.8913	.8116	.6304	.5362
AnDCG$_{1000}$	**.9348**	.8768	.8406	.6304	.5652
nDCG$_{10}$	**.9275**	.8986	.8188	.6812	.5725
nDCG$_{100}$	**.9420**	.8841	.8188	.6232	.5580
nDCG$_{1000}$	**.9203**	.8478	.8116	.5870	.5507
AnCG$_{10}$	**.9203**	.8913	.8406	.6449	.5797
AnCG$_{100}$	.8406	.8116	.7899	.5942	.5580
AnCG$_{1000}$	.7536	.7101	.7319	.6522	.5580
nCG$_{10}$	.8913	.8768	.7971	.5870	.5362
nCG$_{100}$	.7899	.7174	.7391	.5725	.4928
nCG$_{1000}$	.6812	.6377	.6159	.5652	.4130

Rigid	AveP	R-Prec	PDoc$_{10}$	PDoc$_{100}$	PDoc$_{1000}$
Q-measure	**.9638**	**.9130**	.8478	.5942	.5435
R-measure	.8913	**.9275**	.7899	.5507	.5725
AnDCG$_{10}$	.8696	**.9203**	.7971	.5870	.5362
AnDCG$_{100}$	**.9203**	**.9130**	.8333	.6087	.5435
AnDCG$_{1000}$	**.9203**	.8986	.8043	.5652	.5435
nDCG$_{10}$	**.9275**	.8913	.8551	.6014	.5797
nDCG$_{100}$	**.9275**	.8913	.8406	.5870	.5652
nDCG$_{1000}$	.8913	.8696	.8188	.5797	.5290
AnCG$_{10}$	.8913	.8986	.8188	.5652	.5725
AnCG$_{100}$	.8116	.8333	.7971	.6304	.4928
AnCG$_{1000}$	.7391	.7464	.6957	.5435	.5072
nCG$_{10}$	.8623	.8551	.8478	.5942	.5145
nCG$_{100}$	.7899	.7391	.8043	.6087	.4855
nCG$_{1000}$	.6667	.6739	.6522	.6014	.4493

Table 6. Kendall's rank correlations: graded relevance vs graded relevance metrics (45 C-runs)

	(B)	(C)	(D)	(E)	(F)	(G)	(H)	(I)	(J)	(K)	(L)	(M)	(N)
(A) Q-measure	**.9253**	.7778	.8747	**.9051**	.8101	**.9030**	**.9010**	.7838	.8768	.8768	.8303	.8909	.8162
(B) R-measure	1	.7879	.8768	.8788	.7879	**.9091**	.8828	.7737	.8545	.8505	.8444	.8808	.7818
(C) AnDCG$_{10}$	-	1	.7657	.7475	.7455	.7576	.7717	.7919	.7273	.7232	.7657	.7253	.6586
(D) AnDCG$_{100}$	-	-	1	.8808	.7818	.8869	.8525	.8000	.8687	.8242	.8222	.8626	.7556
(E) AnDCG$_{1000}$	-	-	-	1	.8364	.8687	**.9071**	.7778	.8747	.8586	.8323	.8687	.8182
(F) nDCG$_{10}$	-	-	-	-	1	.7374	.7919	.8687	.7596	.7879	.8424	.7939	.7596
(G) nDCG$_{100}$	-	-	-	-	-	1	.8768	.7556	.8687	.8323	.8061	.8465	.7798
(H) nDCG$_{1000}$	-	-	-	-	-	-	1	.7576	.8424	.8788	.8162	.8525	.7899
(I) AnCG$_{10}$	-	-	-	-	-	-	-	1	.7253	.7414	.8202	.7515	.7091
(J) AnCG$_{100}$	-	-	-	-	-	-	-	-	1	.8263	.8202	.8970	.8182
(K) AnCG$_{1000}$	-	-	-	-	-	-	-	-	-	1	.7919	.8606	.7939
(L) nCG$_{10}$	-	-	-	-	-	-	-	-	-	-	1	.8343	.7556
(M) nCG$_{100}$	-	-	-	-	-	-	-	-	-	-	-	1	.8081
(N) nCG$_{1000}$	-	-	-	-	-	-	-	-	-	-	-	-	1

Table 7. Kendall's rank correlations: graded relevance vs graded relevance metrics (24 E-runs)

	(B)	(C)	(D)	(E)	(F)	(G)	(H)	(I)	(J)	(K)	(L)	(M)	(N)
(A) Q-measure	**.9130**	.8913	**.9130**	**.9275**	**.9203**	**.9348**	**.9130**	.8986	.8333	.7609	.8696	.7971	.6884
(B) R-measure	1	**.9058**	.8841	.8841	.8913	.8913	.8696	.8986	.8043	.7319	.8696	.7246	.6449
(C) AnDCG$_{10}$	-	1	**.9203**	.9058	.8841	**.9275**	.9058	**.9203**	.8261	.7391	**.9058**	.7899	.6812
(D) AnDCG$_{100}$	-	-	1	**.9275**	**.9348**	**.9638**	**.9420**	**.9130**	.8478	.7319	.8696	.8261	.6884
(E) AnDCG$_{1000}$	-	-	-	1	.9058	**.9348**	**.9565**	**.9275**	.8333	.7609	.8841	.8116	.6449
(F) nDCG$_{10}$	-	-	-	-	1	**.9275**	.8768	**.9638**	.7971	.7246	.8768	.7754	.6522
(G) nDCG$_{100}$	-	-	-	-	-	1	**.9493**	**.9203**	.8406	.7536	.8913	.8188	.6957
(H) nDCG$_{1000}$	-	-	-	-	-	-	1	.8986	.8478	.7754	.8841	.8551	.6739
(I) AnCG$_{10}$	-	-	-	-	-	-	-	1	.7899	.7319	.8986	.7536	.6159
(J) AnCG$_{100}$	-	-	-	-	-	-	-	-	1	.7246	.8333	.7464	.7101
(K) AnCG$_{1000}$	-	-	-	-	-	-	-	-	-	1	.7174	.7899	.6812
(L) nCG$_{10}$	-	-	-	-	-	-	-	-	-	-	1	.7536	.6594
(M) nCG$_{100}$	-	-	-	-	-	-	-	-	-	-	-	1	.7319
(N) nCG$_{1000}$	-	-	-	-	-	-	-	-	-	-	-	-	1

- Q-measure, R-measure, AnDCG$_{1000}$, nDCG$_{100}$ and nDCG$_{1000}$ are highly correlated with one another.
- For the metrics that rely on l, changing the value of l can affect the system ranking considerably. For example, in Table 6, Rows (C)-(E) Columns (C)-(E) show that the correlations among AnDCG$_l$ ($l = 10, 100, 1000$) are only .7475-.8808; Rows (F)-(H) Columns (F)-(H) show that those among nDCG$_l$ ($l = 10, 100, 1000$) are only .7374-.8768.

Figure 5 visualises how the C-run ranking according to each metric differs from that based on Relaxed AveP. As the 45 C-runs were numbered after sorting by Relaxed AveP, an increase in a curve represents an inconsistency with Relaxed AveP. While the Q-measure curve appears to be a smooth blend of the Relaxed and Rigid AveP curves [7,8], AnDCG$_{1000}$ and nDCG$_{1000}$ give quite different rankings, even at top ranks. For example, nDCG$_{1000}$ declares that System 4 outperforms System 3, disagreeing with all other metrics in this figure. One could argue that Q-measure is "conservative", while AnDCG$_{1000}$ and nDCG$_{1000}$ are "novel".

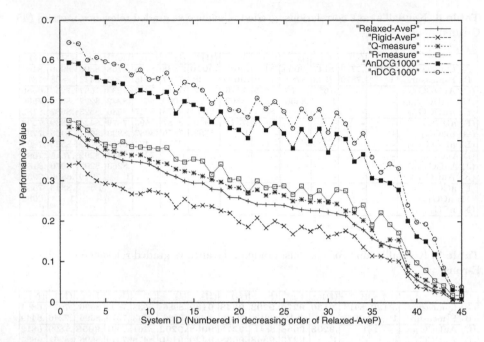

Fig. 5. System ranking by Relaxed Average Precision vs other metrics (45 C-runs)

4.5   Changing Gain Values

The previous sections used the *default* gain values, namely, $gain(S) = 3$, $gain(A) = 2$ and $gain(B) = 1$. This section examines the effect of using different gain values with the graded relevance metrics, using the C-runs only. The "flat" assignment uses $gain(S) = gain(A) = gain(B) = 1$, i.e. binary relevance. The "steep" assignment uses $gain(S) = 10$, $gain(A) = 5$, $gain(B) = 1$, thus emphasising the relevance levels. The third option, which we call "adjust", uses the per-topic gain value adjustment proposed in [6]: Starting with the default assignment, the gain values are automatically modified *for each topic* according to the proportion of X-relevant documents in the entire set of relevant documents:

$$gain'(X) = gain(X) - \frac{R(X)}{R}(gain(X) - gain(Y)) \tag{10}$$

where Y is the relevance level that is one level lower than X. (If X is the lowest relevance level, then $gain(Y)$ is taken to be zero. Moreover, the above transformation is not applied if $R(X) = R$.) This was proposed based on the observation that the ratio $R(S) : R(A) : R(B)$ differs considerably across topics for the NTCIR CLIR test collections. For example, if there are very few S/A-relevant documents and many B-relevant documents, $gain'(B)$ is set to a very small value compared to $gain'(S)$ and $gain'(A)$.

Table 8. The discrimination power at 95% confidence level with different gain value assignments (Top 30 C-runs; 42 topics; $c = 20$)

	default (3:2:1)	flat (1:1:1)	steep (10:5:1)	adjust
Q-measure	**25.4%**	**20.6%**	**22.6%**	**24.7%**
R-measure	**21.8%**	**20.8%**	19.2%	**22.1%**
AnDCG_{10}	10.7%	-	7.7%	10.2%
AnDCG_{100}	19.8%	**20.9%**	18.1%	19.4%
AnDCG_{1000}	**21.0%**	**20.1%**	19.8%	**20.9%**
nDCG_{10}	16.3%	12.2%	16.9%	18.6%
nDCG_{100}	17.9%	17.5%	16.8%	17.8%
nDCG_{1000}	19.6%	18.6%	18.5%	19.5%
AnCG_{10}	13.2%	12.0%	13.9%	15.1%
AnCG_{100}	15.8%	17.7%	15.8%	16.1%
AnCG_{1000}	10.1%	11.7%	16.9%	16.3%
nCG_{10}	17.1%	15.2%	14.3%	16.2%
nCG_{100}	10.5%	9.4%	14.6%	14.1%
nCG_{1000}	-	-	-	-

Table 9. Kendall's rank correlations with metrics based on default gain values (45 C-runs)

	flat (1:1:1)	steep (10:5:1)	adjust
Q-measure	.9798	**.9636**	.9899
R-measure	.9677	.9333	.9778
AnDCG_{10}	.7172	.7051	.7071
AnDCG_{100}	.8929	.8444	.8444
AnDCG_{1000}	**.9212**	.8444	.8808
nDCG_{10}	.8848	.7596	.8545
nDCG_{100}	.8949	**.9071**	**.9354**
nDCG_{1000}	.8626	.8606	.8667
AnCG_{10}	.8040	.6949	.7657
AnCG_{100}	**.9172**	.8606	**.9030**
AnCG_{1000}	.8828	.8727	.8727
nCG_{10}	.7919	.7939	.7677
nCG_{100}	.8626	.8869	.8929
nCG_{1000}	.8182	.7838	.8040

Figure 6 shows the minority-rate / proportion-of-ties curves for Q-measure with default, flat, steep and adjusted gain value assignments, which are denoted by Q3:2:1, Q1:1:1, Q10:5:1 and Qadjust, respectively. It can be observed that "flattening" the gains hurts stability, but otherwise the different gain value assignments do not affect it significantly. Similar trends were observed for other graded relevance metrics such as AnDCG_l as well.

Table 8 shows the discrimination power of graded relevance metrics with different gain value assignments at 95% confidence level. (The "default" column has been duplicated from Table 2(b).) Values higher than 20% are shown in bold. The table shows that Q-measure, R-measure and AnDCG_{1000} have high discrimination power regardless of the gain value assignment.

Table 9 compares the system rankings according to the flat, steep and adjusted gain value assignments with the default assignment for each metric using Kendall's rank correlation. It can be observed that the Q/R-measure rankings are very robust to the changes in gain values. Other metrics appear to be less robust.

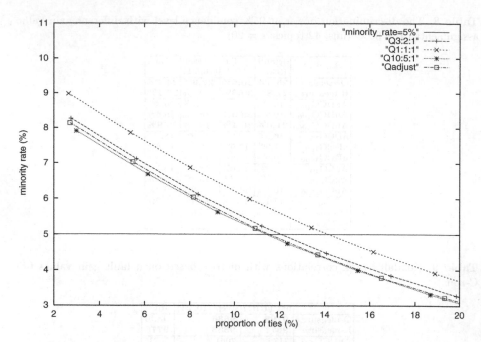

Fig. 6. Minority-rate / Proportion-of-ties curves for Q-measure with different gain value assignments (Top 30 C-runs; 42 topics; $c = 20$)

Table 10. Kendall's rank correlations for the ranking of run pairs (435 run pairs using the top 30 C-runs)

	Relaxed-AveP	Q-measure	AnDCG$_{1000}$
(a) sign vs minority	.1686	.1561	.2013
(b) sign vs swap	.2302	.2421	.1778
(c) minority vs swap	.2299	.2831	.2184

5 Discussions

Our minority rate experiments suggest that Q-measure, AnDCG$_l$, nDCG$_l$ and AnCG$_l$ (with large l) are more stable than other graded relevance metrics (Table 1). Whereas, our swap rate experiments suggest that Q-measure, R-measure, AnDCG$_l$ and nDCG$_l$ (with large l) are the most useful (Tables 2 and 3). How are these results related to statistical significance tests?

We address the above question as follows. For each of the 435 pairs of C-runs, a statistical significance test was conducted based on the sign test, and the run pairs were sorted by the p-value. Then, we created two more sorted lists of the 435 pairs, one sorted by $\min(GT_M(x, y), GT_M(y, x))$ (See Equation 8) and the other sorted by the swap counters summed across the 21 bins for each run pair x and y (See Figure 2). Thus, the first list represents the confidence ranking in terms of the sign test, which uses the *complete* topic set Q and counts the number of topics with which System x outperformed System y and vice versa. The second lists represents the confidence ranking in terms of the minority rate, which uses 1000 topic subsets for each run pair. The third list represents that in terms of the swap rate, which uses 1000 disjoint pairs of topic subsets (i.e. 2000 subsets). These ranked lists of run *pairs* can also be compared using Kendall's rank correlation.

Table 10 shows the Kendall's rank correlations among statistical significance, the minority and the swap rates for Relaxed AveP, Q-measure and $AnDCG_{1000}$. The sign test ranking, minority/swap rate rankings are represented by "sign", "minority" and "swap", respectively. It can be observed that the correlation values are surprisingly low. (The table shows weak positive correlations: note that rank correlations lie between -1 and 1.) It appears that the minority/swap rate calculation methods themselves require further studies.

On the other hand, our rank correlation experiments based on system rankings have shown that Q-measure is very highly correlated with both Relaxed and Rigid AveP, and that R-measure, $AnDCG_l$ and $nDCG_l$ (with large l) are also highly correlated with Relaxed AveP (Table 4). AveP is known to be a very reliable binary relevance metric [1], so this is good news. Moreover, by using different gain value assignments, we have shown that Q-measure may be more robust to the choice of gain value assignment than others (Tables 8 and 9).

Judging from all of our results, it appears that $AnDCG_l$ and $nDCG_l$ are the best graded relevance metrics that are based on the document cut-off l, provided that a sufficiently large value is used for l. However, if one wants to avoid the parameter l, or if one wants a "conservative" metric that closely resembles AveP, then Q-measure is probably the best choice.

6   Related Work

Järvelin and Kekäläinen [4] discussed the advantages of (d)cg-based metrics over other graded relevance metrics. More recently, Kekäläinen [5] investigated the rank correlations among $(n)(D)CG_l$ and $PDoc_l$ using TREC data with their own graded relevance assessments. Whereas, Sakai [7,8] investigated the rank correlations among AveP, R-Prec, Q-measure and R-measure using NTCIR data. This paper extends these studies in that (a) It covers more metrics; (b) It examines the reliability of metrics in addition to resemblance among metrics.

Average Distance Measure (ADM) was proposed for evaluation with *continuous* relevance [3], but ADM is not suitable for traditional document ranking tasks as it simply accumulates the absolute differences between User Relevance Scores (URSs) and System Relevance Scores (SRSs): Suppose that the URSs for documents A, B and C are 0.3, 0.2 and 0.1 for a topic, and the SRSs for these documents are 0.5, 0.4 and 0.2 acccording to System x, and 0.1, 0.2 and 0.3 according to System y. In terms of document ranking, Systems x is perfect, while System y is not. However, in terms of ADM, System y (sum of differences: 0.4) is better than System x (sum of differences: 0.5).

7   Conclusions

This paper compared 14 metrics designed for IR evaluation with graded relevance, together with 10 traditional metrics based on binary relevance, in terms of reliability and resemblance of system rankings using two different sets of data from the NTCIR-3 CLIR track. Our results suggest that graded relevance may provide more reliability than binary relevance. More specifically, we showed that $AnDCG_l$ and $nDCG_l$ are good metrics provided that a large value of l is chosen; However, if one wants to avoid the parameter l altogether, or if one requires a metric that closely resembles traditional Average Precision, then Q-measure appears to be the best choice. We plan to repeat these experiments with other graded relevance test collections, hopefully with larger topic sets.

References

1. Buckley, C. and Voorhees, E. M.: Evaluating Evaluation Measure Stability. ACM SIGIR 2000 Proceedings (2000) 33–40
2. Chen, K.-H. *et al.*: Overview of CLIR Task at the Third NTCIR Workshop. NTCIR-3 Proceedings (2003)
3. Della Mea, V. and Mizzaro, S.: Measuring Retrieval Effectiveness: A New Proposal and a First Experimental Validation. Journal of the American Society for Information Science and Technology **55-6** (2004) 530–543
4. Järvelin, K. and Kekäläinen, J.: Cumulated Gain-Based Evaluation of IR Techniques. ACM Transactions on Information Systems **20-4** (2002) 422–446
5. Kekäläinen, J.: Binary and Graded Relevance in IR Evaluations – Comparison of the Effects on Ranking of IR Systems. Information Processing and Management **41** (2005) 1019-1033.
6. Sakai, T.: Average Gain Ratio: A Simple Retrieval Performance Measure for Evaluation with Multiple Relevance Levels. ACM SIGIR 2003 Proceedings (2003) 417–418
7. Sakai, T.: New Performance Metrics based on Multigrade Relevance: Their Application to Question Answering. NTCIR-4 Proceedings (2004) http://research.nii.ac.jp/ntcir/workshop/OnlineProceedings/OPEN/NTCIR4-OPEN-SakaiTrev.pdf
8. Sakai, T.: Ranking the NTCIR Systems based on Multigrade Relevance. AIRS 2004 Proceedings (2004) 170–177 Also available in Myaeng, S. H. et al. (Eds.): AIRS 2004, Lecture Notes in Computer Science **3411**, Springer-Verlag (2005) 251–262
9. Sakai, T.: A Note on the Reliability of Japanese Question Answering Evaluation. IPSJ SIG Technical Reports **FI-77-7** (2004) 57–64
10. Sakai, T.: The Effect of Topic Sampling in Sensitivity Comparisons of Information Retrieval Metrics. IPSJ SIG Technical Reports **FI-80/NL-169** (2005) (to appear)
11. Soboroff, I. and Voorhees, E.: private communication (2005)
12. Voorhees, E. M. and Buckley, C.: The Effect of Topic Set Size on Retrieval Experiment Error. ACM SIGIR 2002 Proceedings (2002) 316–323

Improving Weak Ad-Hoc Retrieval
by Web Assistance and Data Fusion

Kui-Lam Kwok, Laszlo Grunfeld, and Peter Deng

Computer Science Department, Queens College,
City University of New York, New York, U.S.A.
kwok@ir.cs.qc.edu

Abstract. Users experience frustration when their reasonable queries retrieve no relevant documents. We call these weak queries and retrievals. Improving their effectiveness is an important issue in ad-hoc retrieval and will be most rewarding for these users. We offer an explanation (with experimental support) why data fusion of sufficiently different retrieval lists can improve weak query results. This approach requires sufficiently different retrieval lists for an ad-hoc query. We propose various ways of selecting salient terms from longer queries to probe the web, and define alternate queries from web results. Target retrievals by the original and alternate queries are combined. When compared with normal ad-hoc retrieval, web assistance and data fusion can improve weak query effectiveness by over 100%. Another benefit of this approach is that other queries also improve along with weak ones, unlike pseudo-relevance feedback which works mostly for non-weak queries.

1 Introduction

Ad-hoc retrieval is the fundamental operation in IR (information retrieval). Given a few-word query representing an information need, an IR system is expected to select, or rank to the top, the set of all relevant documents from a target collection. Ad-hoc retrieval also serves as a pre-processing step of reducing a huge collection into a small, signal-rich set for other NLP-intensive tasks such as question-answering, summarization, etc. Improving ad-hoc retrieval has important ramifications not only for normal searching, but also for other processing downstream.

Over the history of TREC ad-hoc experiments, one finds some queries that give good to excellent results while others return irrelevant answers. We call them strong and weak queries respectively. Generally, if the query words are precise in meaning like TREC topic #312 (hydroponics), it has no ambiguity and documents containing it have high probability of satisfying user needs. However, one like #379 (mainstreaming) is vague; returned results are unsatisfactory. There are also other factors such as topic aspects, requirements in a query, etc. that contribute to poor effectiveness. What makes a query easy or difficult is elusive and an unsolved issue. Since 2003, TREC initiated the Robust Track [1] that explicitly focuses on how to improve the poor performers of a query set. New effectiveness measures were introduced to observe effects on these weak queries. This paper explains how data fusion can improve weak query effectiveness, together with experimental results. It introduces our approach of

G.G. Lee et al. (Eds.): AIRS 2005, LNCS 3689, pp. 17–30, 2005.

exploiting the web to define alternate queries for enhancing ad-hoc retrieval, and proposes SVM classification to select salient terms from longer queries to probe the web. There are many retrieval activities on closed collections or private intranets that TREC experiments simulate. They may in particular benefit from this study. The paper is organized as follows: Section 2 discusses some factors that make queries weak. Section 3 compares the WWW to other external resources that may aid retrieval. Section 4 details our method of web-assisted ad-hoc retrieval. Section 5 reviews methods to select words from longer ad-hoc queries to probe the web, and Section 6 introduces a new method based on classification, and its outcome. Section 7 discusses how data fusion can help weak queries. Section 8 has our conclusion.

2   Weak Queries

What makes a query weak and difficult for retrieval? Two major causes are (see also [2,3]): 1) retrieval models generally do not account for word relationships or semantic inferences from free texts. This bag-of-words approach causes irrelevant retrievals because of wrong interpretation or unsolved ambiguities; 2) short queries (one or few words) do not capture the particular aspects of a topic that a user has in mind: e.g. a single-word query, even if it has precise meaning, is adequate only if the requirement is anything concerning the word. Within the bag-of-words approach synonyms cause term mismatch while homographs meaning mismatch, leading to retrieval difficulties. Also, hyponyms in queries such as 'weather-related accidents' are difficult because documents usually report instances of such general concepts in specific wordings: e.g. 'tornadoes'. The bottom line is that many retrieval failures may be attributed to inadequate user need representation.

Since weak queries are the focus, two new measures were introduced in TREC2003 to study effects on them [1]: '#0p10' is the number of queries that have zero precision at top 10 retrieved, and 'area', is a weighted sum of the average precision of the 25% weakest queries in a set (e.g. 12 out of 50). The weight is calculated as $\Sigma_{k=r}^{x}$ 1/k, where r = query rank (weakest has rank 1) and x = size of set. This weighs the weaker ones heavier. *The weak queries in a set are not constant.* They may change for different retrieval methods.

In Table 1, we show some results of retrieval using our PIRCS system [4]. The acronym stands for Probabilistic Indexing and Retrieval – Components – System, and is based on the probabilistic model of [5], but applied to document components (content words) using document self-relevance. The rows 'd-ini' and 'd-prf' (d means 'description' query; t means 'title') show respectively initial and pseudo-relevance feedback (PRF) retrieval results respectively for three topic sets: 'hard50', '601-50' and '651-49'. 'hard50' consists of 50 selected from TREC #301-#450 topics that are known to be more difficult. '601-50' and '651-49' are topic sets (sizes 50 and 49) introduced in the robust track of TREC2003 and 2004. Retrievals are done on TREC-8 collections. Since our objective is to improve weak queries, we generally will emphasis the 'hard-50' 'area' results. Table 1 shows that 'hard50' is indeed more difficult than the other two sets, having an 'area' measure of only .0063 and #0p10=7 for d-ini. Also, PRF procedure (d-prf) does not work for these new measures: 'area' drops to .0049 compared to d-ini, while #0p10 more than double to 15 (although overall MAP improves to .1524 from .1182). For a weak query, an initial retrieval usually does not obtain any (or only few) good documents and hence defeats the assumption of PRF (which was recently studied in [6]). Query set '601-50' shows the best 'area' value .0839 (d-prf) among the three, and improves over its d-ini. Apparently queries in this set are sufficiently strong for PRF to work. Data rows t-ini and t-prf show results using the short 'title' section of TREC topics. They behave similarly to 'description' but generally at lower effectiveness.

3   External Resources for Enhancing Query and Retrieval

Investigators in the past have sought external resources to help improve query representation, such as: domain-specific thesaurus or synonym lists [7], WordNet [8] in order to alleviate mismatch or missing terms, or collection enrichment [9] to aid in PRF. The general experience seems to be that thesaural aid can be useful when it matches the topical domain of a query; otherwise results may not be consistent. External resources employed so far appear limited in scale or scope. When the concepts/topics of a query are inadequately covered, one may result in noisy rather than helpful assistance. The Web has been in existence for over a decade. It is vast, dynamic, up-to-date, and for practical purposes an all-domain thesaurus that may remedy the shortcomings of the other types and be useful to help ad-hoc retrieval. The Web has been employed in other tasks, such as question-answering [e.g. 10] or crosslingual IR [e.g. 11]. In [12] we introduced a general method of web-assisted ad-hoc retrieval (including weak queries) that, unlike other schemes [13,14], does not need identifying which query is weak. This is discussed in the next section.

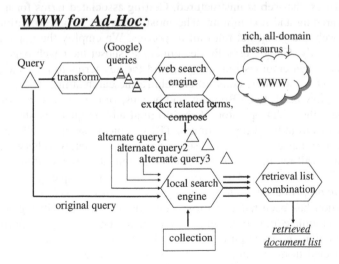

Fig. 1. Web-Assisted Ad-Hoc Retrieval

4 Exploiting the Web to Form Alternate Queries

Our web-assisted ad-hoc retrieval procedure is shown in Fig.1 and listed below as four steps:

1. Given an ad-hoc query, define associated web queries for a specific search engine;
2. Probe the web for relevant/related snippets or pages;
3. From the returned web items, define alternate queries for target collection retrieval;
4. Perform data fusion of retrieval lists from the original and alternate queries, and form final result.

Steps 2 and 3 are straight-forward, similar to steps for PRF. Here we employ the terms to create alternate queries rather than for query expansion. A fixed number of terms are chosen based on occurrence frequencies (> 10) in the web output. The use of multiple queries for an information need has been previously discussed in [15] as 'intentional redundancy as the principle of polyrepresentation'. Step 3 may involve web page structure for mining terms but will not be investigated here. Step 4, data fusion of sufficiently different retrieval lists, is very useful for weak queries, and will be discussed in Section 7. In an effort to have sufficiently different retrieval lists, we *aim at composing differing alternate queries from the web using differing web probes and web output.* Step 1, selecting appropriate terms (from longer queries) to serve as keys to probe the web, is not trivial, and will be the focus of the next two sections.

5 Salient Term Selection from Longer Queries for Web Probing

Unlike a thesaurus, the web is unstructured. Getting associated terms for a query requires web searching and text mining. The most important step is to define suitable key terms as web query and get relevant responses. We employ the popular Google engine for this study. Google uses Boolean query to subset their web page store to a manageable size, then employs link analysis and the key terms to rank the pages for output (see http://www.google.com/intl/en/help/refinesearch.html). Thus, for Step 1 (Sec.4) a web query needs to be Boolean, and because of the noisy nature of the web, we employ only the AND operator. If the original ad-hoc query is short (e.g. <=6 terms, like queries from the 'title' section of TREC topics), one just AND all terms. If it is long, like a sentence, one needs to select terms appropriately, otherwise the long AND expression will return null. This situation is simulated by the 'description' section (varying 2-20 terms) of a TREC topic used as an ad-hoc query. Our concern is how to *select appropriate salient terms from longer queries for web probing.*

Term selection has occurred in various contexts and is difficult: e.g. in [16] researchers try to mimic editors in forming headlines for a news story. Its purpose is for human consumption and its requirements may be different from ours. In PRF, terms need to be selected from an initial retrieval to expand a query. Current common approach is to use scores of terms. The technology to select precisely a few terms may not be reliable [6]. In [17], investigators compare query term distributions in documents-with-query-terms and in a general collection via KL divergence to identify important terms and evaluate a clarity score for a query. This requires the equivalence of an initial retrieval. Since web-probing already incurs a time penalty, we like to explore methods of term selection without relying on an initial retrieval. The following lists some possibilities.

5.1 Manual Selection: Title Terms

Each TREC topic contains multiple sections such as: 'title', 'description', 'narrative'. The 'title' section (mostly 2-4 words composed manually) is a succinct representation of users' needs. They may be considered as *manual selection* from the 'description' (although for a few queries there are words in the titles that do not appear in the description). Title words are used directly without modification for web probing. Alternate queries are then formed and employed for target retrieval. The result is very good as shown in Table1 last row. An average of four runs (using web pages for creating alternate queries, snippets only, and whether phrases are used - or not - during web probing) attains a 'hard50' 'area' value of .0129, more than double that 't-ini' value of .0063. Lesser improvements are also observed for other query sets (except '601-50' #0p10). Moreover, MAP improves over both t-ini and t-prf, showing that web assistance can be effective for both weak and non-weak 'title' queries.

Table 1. Original Ad-hoc & Alternate Query Results

	'hard50'		'601-50'		'651-49'	
	MAP	**Area/#0p10**	**MAP**	**area/#0p10**	**MAP**	**Area/#0p10**
DESCRIPTION Queries: original ad-hoc results						
d-ini	.1182	.0063/7	.3503	.0638/2	.3166	.0409/1
d-prf	.1524	.0049/15	.4044	**.0839/2**	.4717	.0404/5
Alternate Query Results: Term Selection by Weight & Web Probing						
w4 (avg. 2)	.1437	.0018/11	.3466	.0229/7	.3745	.0354/3
w5 (avg. 2)	.1435	.0014/12	.3267	.0165/7	.3672	.0417/5
Alternate Query Results: POS-based Web Probing						
Avg. of 5	.1383	.0036/16	.2997	.0214/7	.3556	.0470/3
TITLE Queries: Original Ad-hoc						
t-ini	.1074	.0062/8	.2871	.0332/4	.2825	.0259/6
t-prf	.1332	.0036/13	.3496	.0439/4	.3408	.0209/10
Alternate Query Results: title word-based web probing						
Avg. of 4	.1761	**.0129/7**	.3582	.0527/5	.3779	**.0525/4**

5.2 Term Selection by Term Weight

A simple automatic term selection method is by term weight w. We have experimented with selecting 4 or 5 (w4, w5) best weighted terms from the 'description' queries. Selecting less will miss many good terms when compared with 'title' as model. It is found that the normal 'tf*idf' weight (good for retrieval) does not provide as good result as the average term frequency 'avtf' weight introduced in [18]. This is defined as: $w_k = (F_k/D_k)^{1.5}/[\log(\max\{2000,D_k\})]$, where F_k, D_k are the collection and document frequency of term k respectively.

In Fig.1, 'w4', 'w5' rows show that alternate queries resulting from them attains average 'area' values of only .0014-.0018, far from t-ini. MAP however improves over t-ini. Selection by term weight seems to favor strong queries.

5.3 Term Selection by Part-of-Speech (POS) Tagging

Another approach for term selection is based on POS for each 'description' word, such as tagging via MINIPAR [19]. For example, TREC query #310: 'Evidence that radio waves from radio towers or car phones affect brain cancer occurrence' is parsed by MINIPAR with the output:

```
E2      (()        U          *        )
1       (Evidence~            N        E2      subcat)
E0      (()        fin        C        E2      )
2       (that      ~          COMP     E0      c        (gov fin))
3       (radio     ~          U        4       lex-mod  (gov "radio wave"))
4       (waves     "radio wave"  N     11      s        (gov affect))
5       (from      ~          Prep     4       mod      (gov "radio wave"))
6       (radio     ~          A        7       mod      (gov tower))
7       (towers    tower      N        5       pcomp-n  (gov from))
9       (car       ~          N        10      nn       (gov phone))
10      (phones    phone      N        7       conj     (gov tower))
11      (affect    ~          V        E0      I        (gov fin))
E3      (()"radio wave"       N        11      subj     (gov affect)      (antecedent 4))
12      (brain     ~          N        14      nn       (gov occurrence))
13      (cancer    ~          N        14      nn       (gov occurrence))
14      (occurrence~          N        11      obj      (gov affect))
```

In one method, 6 words are chosen in order of: words from phrases ("radio wave"), nouns, verbs, or adjectives. This produces a 6-word web query in backward order: (radio ^ wave ^ occurrence ^ cancer ^ brain ^ car). 'Phone' is assigned lower priority than the first of the conjuncts. After web probing and terms in returned output filtered by an occurrence threshold, the following alternative query is formed with integral values denoting proportional weights derived from frequencies: "cell 7, phone 6, phones 4, cancer 4, research 3, radio 3, brain 2, radiation 2, health 2, exposure 2 .." plus 44 other frequency two and one words.

Other ways of selecting terms from the parse are possible [12], like considering the government 'gov' relationship to form phrases, or use MINIPAR's semantically tagging capability. This approach has certain limitations. First, POS tags may not include the important words among the 5 or 6 selected. For example, adjectives like 'hydroelectric' (query #307) and 'teenage' (#658) contain the main concepts of those queries, yet are ranked below less important nouns. MINIPAR gives quite accurate POS tags on the whole, but also have occasional errors such as: 'launched' (#303), 'salvaging' (#411) tagged as punctuation. They may cause the formation of less effective alternate queries.

Table 1 data row 5 shows average result of five different alternate queries based on POS-defined web queries. 'hard50' 'area' value .0036 is worse than that of d-ini .0063. It also performs worse for '601-50' set, but improves for '651-49'. Selecting terms via POS for web probing and alternate query retrieval works for certain queries but not for others. *However, they are still useful during data fusion as discussed later in Section 7.*

6   Term Selection Based on SVM Classification

Since manually-created 'title' terms can lead to alternate queries with good results, we propose to use the 'title' words as model and train an SVM classifier to automatically select 'description' query terms. SVM classification has been shown to be effective for text categorization (e.g. [20] though a different problem), supports non-linear classification and easily available. The classifier we used is the v-SVM (Support Vector Machine) which is available from the LIBSVM program [21].

A hyperplane classifier attempts to separate input attributed vectors x into two classes by the decision function: $sgn(wx + b)$. The parameters w and b can be trained from sample labeled vectors: $\{(x_1,y_1), .. (x_i,y_i),.. (x_p,y_p)\}$ $1<=i<=p$, based on finding the unique hyperplane $(sgn(wx+b)=0)$ that gives maximum margin of separation between classes. Here, x_i is a vector with attributes that characterizes a 'description' query term, and $y_i = 1/-1$ depending on whether this term is in the corresponding 'title' section or not. SVM classifier maps the input and training vectors x_i to higher dimension feature space $\varphi(x_i)$ and trained on the same above requirement with only the support vectors. This results in the decision function: $sgn(\Sigma_i \ y_i\alpha_iK(x_i,x) +b)$, where K is a kernel such that $K(x_i,x) = \varphi(x_i)'\varphi(x)$ is dependent only on the dot product of x_i and x, and α_i are Lagrangian multipliers of the dual problem. The v-SVM [22] deals with non-separable problems by using soft margins, i.e. allowing some errors in the training samples with v a parameter interpreted as an upper bound on the fraction of margin errors. We used the default radial basis function as kernel.

For training, all terms from 550 TREC ad-hoc topics accumulated since TREC-1 minus the test set under consideration are used, similar to cross-validation procedures. The three test sets are the terms from the 'hard50', '601-50' and '651-49' topic sets. Training data excludes twelve topics because the 'description' does not contain any of the 'title' words. Terms appearing in a 'title' but not in corresponding 'description' are also discarded. In practice, the query terms are obtained from our retrieval index file, and include some two-word phrases. This leads to the following statistics for (training/testing): 'hard50' set (4440/425), '601-50' (4432/433), '651-49' (4537/328).

Each term needs to be characterized by a set of attributes that may describe its salience for web probing. After some experimentation, the following four attributes for a term k are used: query-focused term weight w_{qk}, cf_k/df_k (average term frequency in documents that contain term k), q_k, (query term frequency), and 'idf-ratio' defined as follows:

attribute-1: $w_{qk} = \log [q_k/(L_q - q_k)*(N_w - F_k)/F_k]$
attribute-2: $cf_k/df_k = (1 + \alpha*q_k)* F_k/D_k$
attribute-3: q_k
attribute-4:   idf-ratio $= \log(N_d/\min_q\{D_k\})/\log(N_d/D_k)$

q_k = frequency of term k in query, L_q query length, N_w , N_d are respectively the number of terms and documents in the target collection, F_k,, D_k are the collection and document frequencies of term k. w_{qk} is a query term weight used for our PIRCS retrieval and we assume that good weight for retrieval may also be good for web probing. cf_k/df_k is an average term frequency factor [18] that is useful as term importance indicator; here we weighted it with a function of q_k. q_k is used by itself also because of Luhn's observation that repeated use (in document/query) of a content term indicates its importance. Since training data has no query identity, idf-ratio may restore some indication of a term's relation with others in a query. These attributes are used successively as sets of 2, 3 and 4 for characterizing terms. Their results will be denoted as classification with two attributes c2, c3 and c4 respectively.

A test 'description' query, after term selection by classification, may end up empty, or just 1 or 2 terms (because most terms may be classified as -1). We augment these queries by the terms from w4 (Sec.5.2) before doing web probing. If the classification query has >6 terms, it is also truncated to six.

6.1   Classification-Based Term Selection: Alternate Query Results

In Table 2, rows characterized by c2 for example mean using the first two attributes during classification. c2‖d, c3‖d and c4‖d mean concatenating the selected terms with original 'description' (equivalent to double-weighting the selected terms) and lead to enhanced initial retrieval using 'description'. For 'hard50', the effectiveness order is c2‖d > c4‖d ~ d-ini > c3‖d. c2‖d exceeds d-ini and hints that some important terms are being selected by the procedure. Using only the selected terms for retrieval (not shown) is worse than d-ini however.

Rows c2fpg and c2snpt denote alternate query (formed by web probing with selected terms only and employing full page or snippets) results. The 'hard50' 'area' values for c2fpg (.0069), and c2snpt (.0094) improve over d-ini value of .0063, but less than 'titles' (.0129, Table 1) which can be considered as manually-selected 'alternate queries'. It appears that learning from the 'titles' does help in focusing the enhanced query (c2‖d), or defining better web queries (c2fpg, c2snpt) for the weak set. The same is true for the '651-49' set. For '601-50', d-ini still has the best area value.

The best 'fpg' and 'snpt' results of the three query sets (Table 2) via classification are highlighted. c4fpg and c4snpt are good for 651-49 set, but overall c2fpg and c2snpt seem to perform best. It is surprising that using only first two features is superior. One could consider these results as disappointing compared with the original d-ini. However, much better improvements can be obtained by combining these retrieval lists. This is discussed in the next section.

Table 2. Effectiveness of Alternate Queries via Classification-Based Term Selection

	'hard50'		'601-50'		'651-49'	
	MAP	area/#0p10	MAP	area/#0p10	MAP	area/#0p10
d-ini	.1182	.0063/7	.3503	.0638/2	.3166	.0409/1
2-Attribute Classification						
c2lld	.1140	.0071/8	.3347	.0519/3	.2952	.0498/3
c2fpg	.1671	**.0069/5**	.3072	.0141/9	.3616	.0412/4
c2snpt	.1451	**.0094/6**	.3568	**.0257/3**	.3709	.0542/4
3-Attribute Classification						
c3lld	.1242	.0054/9	.3506	.0621/2	.3188	.0378/3
c3fpg	.1746	.0054/8	.3201	.0182/6	.3750	.0461/3
c3snpt	.1373	.0031/12	.3686	**.0303/3**	.3809	.0500/4
4-Attribute Classification						
c4lld	.1109	.0065/8	.3340	.0418/3	.2825	.0445/3
c4fpg	.1750	.0036/11	.3075	.0157/9	.3683	**.0600/3**
c4snpt	.1506	.0027/11	.3596	.0189/3	.3689	**.0577/3**
An Alternate/Web Query defined from Term Selection via POS						
pos	.1380	.0031/11	.3012	.0186/9	.3545	.0539/3

7 Data Fusion of Retrieval Lists

Assume that one uses two different algorithms or representations for a query and results in two retrieval lists R_1 and R_2. When linearly combined into one $R=C(\alpha,R_1,R_2) = \alpha*R_1+(1-\alpha)*R_2$ with $0<\alpha<1$, the average precision of R, prec(R), may improve above prec(R_1) and prec(R_2). The intuitive explanation for this is that different methods are more likely to retrieve the same core relevant documents, than the same non-relevants. Combining retrievals may synergistically yield better results than the components [23, 24]. When this does not materialize, prec(R) tends to lie around the average of prec(R_1) and prec(R_2) if extreme values of α are avoided. This phenomenon is observed from past data fusion experiments. For weak queries, combination may have special enhancing effect as the following shows.

Consider a set of n=5 queries Q_i. Assume that Method 1 produces an average precision value sequence of (Q_1 .0; Q_2 .0; Q_3 .2; Q_4 .2; Q_5 .2). If one considers the lowest performing 2 queries, one gets an 'area' value of .0. Suppose a *sufficiently different* Method 2 produces another sequence like: (Q_3 .0; Q_1 .0; Q_4 .2; Q_2 .2; Q_5 .2). Combining corresponding retrieval lists of the two with α tend to produce a sequence qualitatively like (Q_1 0; Q_3 1; Q_2 1; Q_4 2; Q_5 3). Q_5 gets a synergistic boost. Q_2 (Q_3) is weak in Method 1(2) but stronger in Method 2(1); we assume they average out and receive no boost. This sequence results in an 'area' value > .0 for the worst 2 queries and combination improves on the component methods. If Method 2 is not much different, Q_1, Q_2 may both retain .0 precision, with little change in 'area' after combination. When one employs several *sufficiently different* methods, the probability of queries remaining weak and close to .0 precision for all methods (like Q1) diminishes, and 'area' will have reasonable probability of getting improvement after combination. This is also the reason why initial and PRF retrieval lists should not be combined because the same weak queries during initial retrieval will generally remain weak during PRF. For example in Table 1, the worst performing 12 'hard50' queries for d-ini differ from those of d-prf by only 2 in our system. When they are combined as $C(.6, R_{d\text{-}ini}, R_{d\text{-}prf})$ the resultant 'area' value remains weak at .0056, mid-point between that of d-ini and d-prf.

We simulate sufficiently different retrievals by using various alternate query results: e.g. alternate queries via term selection by POS, by classification with different parameters, and making use of the enhanced initial retrievals c2‖d. The following illustrates how one can employ combination to improve the 'area' for 'hard50' via training from '601-50' and '651-49' sets. Specifically, the area-sum('601-50','651-49') is used as an objective for choosing combination coefficients.

In Table 2, last row 'pos' denotes an alternate query based on POS with 5-term selection ordered by phrases and nouns. In addition, we assume the three different types of classification-based queries ('‖d', 'fpg', 'snpt') will lead to sufficiently different retrievals. 'c2‖d', c4fpg, 'c3snpt' are chosen for data fusion because they have the highest area-sum('601-50','651-49'): .1017, .0757, .0803 respectively for its type.

The progress of data fusion is shown partially in Table 3. Combinations $C(\alpha, R_{c2\|d}, R_{c3snpt})$ and $C(\alpha, R_{c4fpg}, R_{pos})$ for all α in steps of 0.1 are done independently, and the run with α that maximizes area-sum('601-50','651-49') is chosen. For $C(\alpha, R_{c2\|d}, R_{c3snpt})$ it is seen that we have missed the best $\alpha=0.7$ which will give 'hard50' 'area' of .0098 instead of .0079 at $\alpha=0.5$. However, 'hard50' values are unknown during predictive processing. Figure 2 shows the average precision of the worst 12 queries before and after data fusion. The top plot shows enhanced initial retrieval c2‖d combines with alternate queries c3snpt and improves only from position

Table 3. Example of Data Fusion For Weak Queries

	hard50		601-50		651-49	
α	MAP	area/#0p10	MAP	area/#0p10	MAP	area/#0p10
$C(\alpha, R_{c2\|d}, R_{c3snpt})$ Results						
.4	.1389	.0069/8	.3898	.0514/1	.3794	.0742/2
.5	**.1373**	**.0079/8**	**.3911**	**.0542/1**	**.3738**	**.0833/1**
.6	.1335	.0087/7	.3845	.0564/1	.3643	.0810/1
.7	.1294	.0098/6	.3710	.0584/1	.3514	.0755/1
$C(\alpha, R_{c4fpg}, R_{pos})$ Results						
.5	.1534	.0076/7	.3491	.0477/2	.3948	.0748/2
.6	**.1645**	**.0086/7**	**.3522**	**.0540/3**	**.4005**	**.0814/2**
.7	.1722	.0085/7	.3455	.0455/4	.3990	.0798/2
$C(\alpha, C(.5, R_{c2\|d}, R_{c3snpt}), C(.6, R_{c4fpg}, R_{pos}))$ Results						
.3	.1644	.0119/5	.3927	.0746/2	.4101	.0941/2
.4	**.1624**	**.0129/4**	**.3976**	**.0749/2**	**.4084**	**.0965/2**
.5	.1585	.0126/4	.4012	.0737/2	.4047	.0973/2

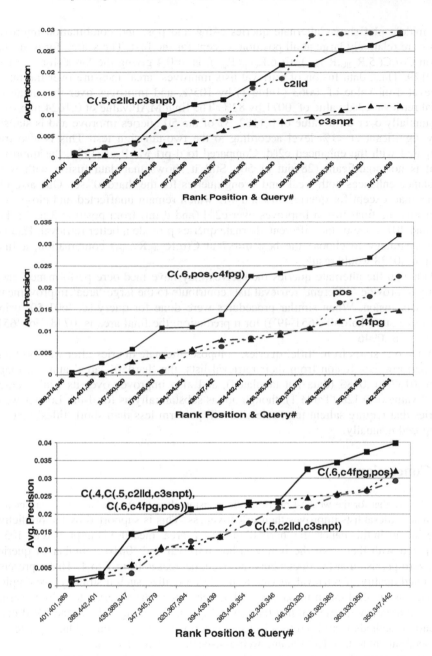

Fig. 2. Average Precision at 12 Weakest Positions before and after Data Fusion

3 to 8 over the components, because c2‖d has much better effectiveness than c3snpt. The outermost series of query numbers on the x-axis belong to the combined result. It is seen that queries like 401, 442 remain weak and not affected much by combination.

The middle plot shows alternate queries c4fpg and pos, and combination improvements are relatively large at all positions except for the first. The search for α in final fusion $C(\alpha, C(.5, R_{c2||d}, R_{c3snpt}), C(.6, R_{c4fpg}, R_{pos}))$ is $\alpha = 0.4$ giving the 'area' for 'hard50' as .0129. Thus, data fusion of retrieval lists improves 'area' measure over the initial retrieval d-ini value of .0063 (Table 1) by 105%, and improves over the enhanced initial retrieval c2||d value of .0071 by 82%. The final MAP value of 0.1624 improves substantially over d-ini value of 0.1182. 37 of the 50 queries improve and is statistically significant at <1% level according to the two-tail sign test. This is also true compared with the enhanced c2||d. Compared to d-prf MAP of .1524, the improvement is not significant (28 out of 50). Still it shows that data fusion with web-assistance enhances both weak and strong queries for the 'hard50' set. One also observes that, except for queries 389 and 401 which remain unaffected and close to .0 precision, the final fusion improves over c2||d (and d-ini) from position 3 to 12. For 389 and 401, none of the different alternate queries provide a better retrieval. Had we have a strategy to choose the best $\alpha = 0.7$ at $C(\alpha, R_{c2||d}, R_{c3snpt})$ combination, a final 'area' of .0138 would result.

Although the alternate queries themselves may have mediocre performance, their ability to provide 'different' retrieval lists contribute to the large 'area' improvements after data fusion. When similar procedures were done for query set '601-50' using max (area-sum('hard50','651-49')) for α prediction, the final area is .0748. For '651-49' set, it is .0946.

When one starts from 'title' queries, compose alternate queries after web probing, and perform data fusion from their retrieval lists, the 'hard50' 'area' attained range from .0137 to .0185 (data not tabulated), and also improves over its t-ini average 'area' value of 0.129 (Table 1), though not as substantially as for d-ini. Longer weak queries that require salient term selection still perform less than short 'titles' that are composed manually.

8 Conclusion

We observe that for the weakest queries with precision close to .0, data fusion of 'sufficiently different' retrieval lists improves their effectiveness. This is supported by the predictive experiments in this paper: the 'hard50' query set 'area' measure is improved by 105% compared with that from the initial ad-hoc retrieval and '0p10', number of queries with zero precision at ten documents retrieved, decreases from 7 to 4. This represents improved quality of retrieval service to users. To realize such a strategy, we employ the web as an all-domain thesaurus, and search it for related terms to help construct different alternate queries. When the original queries are longer, POS and SVM classification methods were used to select salient terms for web probing. Short queries do not need salient term selection, and web-assistance is also effective.

Our approach of web-assistance and data fusion is applied to all queries in a set. It would be useful to have a method to identify which query is weak (or strong) with respect to a retrieval environment. One can then target specific queries with this or other specific method in a more individual fashion. It would also be useful to study other ways of improving salient term selection for web probing.

Acknowledgments

This work is partially supported by a contract from the U.S. Government and any opinions, findings, conclusions, or recommendations expressed in this material are those of the authors and do not necessarily reflect the views of the U.S. Government. We like to thank the anonymous reviewers for their helpful comments and suggestions.

References

1. Voorhees, E.M. Overview of the TREC 2003 Robust Retrieval Track. Proc. of the Twelfth Text Retrieval Conference (TREC 2003). National Institute of Standards and Technology Special Publication 500-255, Gaithersburg, MD. (2004) 69-77
2. Buckley, C. Why current IR engines fail. Proc.27th Annual International ACM-SIGIR Conference on Research & Development in IR. (2004) 584-5
3. Arampatzis, A.T, van der Weide, T.P, van Bommel, P & Koster, C.H.A. Linguistically-motivated information retrieval. Information Processing & Management. 34 (1998) 693-707
4. Kwok, K.L. A network approach to probabilistic information retrieval. ACM Transactions on Office Information System, 13 (1995) 324-353
5. Robertson, S.E. & Sparck Jones K. Relevance weighting of search terms. Journal of American Society for Information Science, 27 (1976) 129-146
6. Harman, D. and Buckley, C. The NRRC reliable information access (RIA) workshop. Proc. 27th Annual International ACM-SIGIR Conference on Research & Development in IR. (2004) 528-9
7. Rada, R & Bicknell, E. Ranking documents with a thesaurus. J. of American Society for Information Science. 40 (1989) 304-310
8. Voorhees, E.M. Query expansion using lexical-semantic relations. Proc.17th Annual International ACM-SIGIR Conference on Research & Development in IR. (1994) 61-69
9. Kwok, K.L & Chan, M. Improving two-stage ad-hoc retrieval for short queries. Proc.21st Annual International ACM-SIGIR Conference on Research & Development in IR. (1998) 250-256
10. Lin, J, Fernandes, A, Katz, B, Marton, G & Tellex, S. Extracting answers from the Web using knowledge annotation and knowledge mining techniques. Proc. of the Eleventh Text Retrieval Conference (TREC 2002). National Institute of Standards and Technology Special Publication 500-251, Gaithersburg, MD. (2002) 447-456
11. Nie, J-Y. Simard, M., Isabelle, P & Durand, R. Cross-language information retrieval based on parallel texts and automatic mining of parallel texts from the web. Proc. 22nd Annual International ACM-SIGIR Conference on Research & Development in IR. (1999) 74-81
12. Grunfeld, L, Kwok, K.L., Dinstl, N. & Deng, P. TREC 2003 Robust, HARD and QA Track Experiments using PIRCS. Proc. of the Twelfth Text Retrieval Conference (TREC 2003). National Institute of Standards and Technology Special Publication 500-255, Gaithersburg, MD. (2004)510-521.
13. Yom-Tov, E, Fine, S, Carmel, D, Darlow, A and Amitay, E. Improving document retrieval according to prediction of query difficulty. In Working Notes of Text Retrieval Conference (TREC 2004) Gaithersburg, MD. November 16-19, 2004, 393-402
14. Amati, G., Carpineto, C. and Romano, G. (2004). Query difficulty, robustness and selective application of query expansion. In: Proc.25th European Conference on IR. (2004) 127-137

15. Ingwersen, P. Polyrepresentation of information needs and semantic entities: elements of a cognitive theory for information retrieval interaction. Proc.17th Annual International ACM-SIGIR Conference on Research & Development in IR. (1994) 101-110

16. Google B., Zajic, D & Schwartz, R. Hedge Trimmer: A Parse-and-Trim Approach to Headline Generation. Proceedings of HLT-NAACL 2003 Text Summarization Workshop, (2003) paper W03-0501

17. Cronen-Townsend, S., Zhou, Y. and Croft, W.B. Predicting query performance. Proc.25th Annual International ACM-SIGIR Conference on Research & Development in IR. (2002) 299-306.

18. Kwok, K.L. A new method of weighting query terms for ad-hoc retrieval. Proc.19th Annual International ACM-SIGIR Conference on Research & Development in IR. (1996) 187-195

19. Lin, D. PRINCIPAR – an efficient, broad-coverage, principle-based parser. Proc of COLING-94. (1994) 482-488.

20. Joachims, T. Learning to Classify Text using Support Vector Machines. Kluwer, NJ, 2002

21. Chang, C-C and Lin C-J. LIBSVM: a Library for Support Vector Machines. Available at: http://www.csie.ntu .edu.tw/~cjlin/libsvm (2004)

22. Scholkopf, B., Smola, A., Williamson, R.C. and Bartlett, P.L. New support vector algorithms. Neural Computation. 12 (2000) 1207-1245

23. Lee, J.H. Analysis of multiple evidence combination. Proc.20th Annual International ACM-SIGIR Conference on Research & Development in IR. (1997) 267-276

24. Vogt. C.C & Cottrell, G.W. Fusion via a linear combination of scores. Information Retrieval. 1 (1999) 151-173

Query Expansion with the Minimum Relevance Judgments

Masayuki Okabe[1], Kyoji Umemura[2], and Seiji Yamada[3]

[1] Information and Media Center, Toyohashi University of Technology,
Tempaku 1-1, Toyohashi, Aichi, Japan
okabe@imc.tut.ac.jp
[2] Information and Computer Science, Toyohashi University of Technology,
Tempaku 1-1, Toyohashi, Aichi, Japan
umemura@tutics.tut.ac.jp
[3] National Institute for Informatics, Chiyoda, Tokyo, Japan
seiji@nii.ac.jp

Abstract. Query expansion techniques generally select new query terms from a set of top ranked documents. Although a user's manual judgment of those documents would much help to select good expansion terms, it is difficult to get enough feedback from users in practical situations. In this paper we propose a query expansion technique which performs well even if a user notifies just a relevant document and a non-relevant document. In order to tackle this specific condition, we introduce two refinements to a well-known query expansion technique. One is to increase documents possibly being relevant by a transductive learning method because the more relevant documents will produce the better performance. The other is a modified term scoring scheme based on the results of the learning method and a simple function. Experimental results show that our technique outperforms some traditional methods in standard precision and recall criteria.

1 Introduction

Query expansion is a simple but very useful technique to improve search performance by adding some terms to an initial query. While many query expansion techniques have been proposed so far, a standard method of performing is to use relevance information from a user [1]. If we can use more relevant documents in query expansion, the likelihood of selecting query terms achieving high search improvement increases. However it is impractical to expect enough relevance information. Some researchers said that a user usually notifies few relevance feedback or nothing [2].

In this paper we investigate the potential performance of query expansion under the condition that we can utilize little relevance information, especially we only know a relevant document and a non-relevant document. To overcome the lack of relevance information, we tentatively increase the number of relevant documents by a machine learning technique called *Transductive Learning*. Compared with ordinal inductive learning approach, this learning technique works

G.G. Lee et al. (Eds.): AIRS 2005, LNCS 3689, pp. 31–42, 2005.

even if there is few training examples. In our case, we can use many documents in a hit-list, however we know the relevancy of few documents. When applying query expansion, we use those increased documents as if they were true relevant ones.

The point of our query expansion method is that we focus on the availability of relevance information in practical situations. There are several researches which deal with this problem. Pseudo relevance feedback which assumes top n documents as relevant ones is one example. This method is simple and relatively effective if a search engine returns a hit-list which contains a certain number of relative documents in the upper part. However, unless this assumption holds, it usually gives a worse ranking than the initial search. Thus several researchers propose some specific procedure to make pseudo feedback be effective [3,4]. In another way, Onoda [5] tried to apply one-class SVM (Support Vector Machine) to relevance feedback. Their purpose is to improve search performance by using only non-relevant documents. Though their motivation is similar to ours in terms of applying a machine learning method to complement the lack of relevance information, the assumption is somewhat different. Our assumption is to utilizes manual but the minimum relevance judgment.

Transductive leaning has already been applied in the field of image retrieval [6]. In this research, they proposed a transductive method called the manifold-ranking algorithm and showed its effectiveness by comparing with active learning based Support Vector Machine. However, their setting of relevance judgment is not different from many other traditional researches. They fix the total number of images that are marked by a user to 20. As we have already claimed, this setting is not practical because most users feel that 20 is too much for judgment. We think none of research has not yet answered the question. For relevance judgment, most of the researches have adopted either of the following settings. One is the setting of "Enough relevant documents are available", and the other is "No relevant document is available". In contrast to them, we adopt the setting of "Only one relevant document is available". Our aim is to achieve performance improvement with the minimum effort of judging relevancy of documents.

The reminder of this paper is structured as follows. Section 2 and 3 describe two fundamental techniques for our query expansion method. Section 4 explains a technique to complement the smallness of manual relevance judgment. Section 5 introduces a whole procedure of our query expansion method step by step. Section 6 shows empirical evidence of the effectiveness of our method compared with two traditional query expansion methods. Section 7 investigates the experimental results more in detail. Finally, Section 8 summarizes our findings.

2   Basic Techniques

2.1   Query Expansion

The main objective of query expansion is to select additional terms of achieving better search results. From where and how to choose such terms differentiate many query expansion techniques which have been proposed so far. For example, a method for domain specific search prepares documents in a certain domain and pick up terms from them as a batch procedure [7,8]. In another case, a method for ad-hoc search usually selects terms from documents at the head of an initial search result. This approach further branches off to the utility of manual or automatic feedback. Anyway, most of the methods first score each term in a certain set of documents and then choose some best scored terms for expansion.

Our method belongs to the latter approach - query expansion for ad-hoc search with manual feedback. In this approach, there is a well-known query expansion method called the Robertson's *wpq* method [1] which is used in many researches [3,4]. Our method is based on this one. The *wpq* selects expansion terms using the following scoring function.

$$score(t) = \left(\frac{r_t}{R} - \frac{n_t - r_t}{N - R}\right) * \log \frac{r_t/(R - r_t)}{(n_t - r_t)/(N - n_t - R + r_t)} \qquad (1)$$

where r_t is the number of seen relevant documents containing term t. n_t is the number of documents containing t. R is the number of seen relevant documents for a query. N is the number of documents in the collection. The second term of this formula is called the Robertson/Spark Jones weight [9] which is the core of the term weighting function in the Okapi system [10]. This function is originated in the following formula.

$$score(t) = (p_t - q_t) \log \frac{p_t(1 - q_t)}{q_t(1 - p_t)} \qquad (2)$$

where p_t is the probability that a term t appears in relevant documents. q_t is the probability that a term t appears in non-relevant documents. If we estimate p_t with $\frac{r_t}{R}$ and q_t with $\frac{n_t - r_t}{N - R}$, we can get fomula (1). Since the number of non-relevant documents can be prepared easily, $\frac{n_t - r_t}{N - R}$ is likely to be a good estimation for q_t. In contrast, it is not so easy to give a good estimation for p_t. Since users in practical situations do not give much feedback, R tends to be very small and this fact produces two problems. One is the lack of term variety. Candidates for expansion terms are limited. The other is the scoring ability of $\frac{r_t}{R}$. Since r_t is small if R is small, many terms come to have the same score. The challenge is to increase the number of R. Although pseudo feedback which automatically assumes top n documents as relevant is one solution, its performance heavily depends on the quality of an initial search. As we show later, pseudo feedback has limited performance.

Unlike pseudo feedback approach, our method tries to compensate for the smallness of R with a transductive learning technique, which is used to find documents possibly being relevant based on a set of training examples[1]. Because we want to consider an assumption not far from practical situations, we restrict the number of training examples to the minimum - a relevant document and a non-relevant document. Of course, manual judgment is an advantage to the pseudo one. However this minimum information has no utility for the *wpq* method. Performance improvement depends on the accuracy of the judgment assigned by the learning to each document with no manual judgment.

---

[1] documents with manual judgments.

2.2 Transductive Learning

Transductive learning is a machine learning technique based on the transduction which directly derives the classification labels of test data without making any approximating function from training data [11]. This learning technique is based on an assumption that two similar data are likely to have the same class label. If we can define a reasonable similarity between each element of a data set, this learning works well even if the number of training examples is small.

The learning task is defined on a data set X of n points. X consists of training data set $L = (x_1, x_2, ..., x_l)$ and test data set $U = (x_{l+1}, x_{l+2}, ..., x_{l+u})$; typically $l \ll u$. The purpose of the learning is to assign a label to each element in U under the condition that the label of each element in L are given.

Recent researches about transductive learning have proposed several algorithms which are based on the solution for graph cutting problems [12,13,14]. According to the experimental results in [14], these algorithms do not have so much performance difference that we select an algorithm called "*Spectral Graph Transducer* (SGT)" for our query expansion method. The SGT formalizes a learning task as an optimization problem of the constrained ratiocut. By solving the relaxed problem, it produces an approximation to the original solution.

When applying it to query expansion, X corresponds to a set of top n ranked documents in a hit-list. Because the number of documents in a collection is usually too huge[2], n should be set to a moderate number. L corresponds to two documents with manual judgments, a relevant document and a non-relevant document. Furthermore, U corresponds to the documents of $X \cap \overline{L}$ whose relevancy is unknown. In the learning process, first SGT makes an undirected graph where a vertex corresponds to a document in X and an edge represents similarity between vertices. For each vertex, edges to most k similar vertices are created in the graph. The problem here is how to partition it to two parts where one part includes only positive examples (relevant documents) and the other includes only negative examples (non-relevant documents). SGT formalizes it as the following constrained ratiocut problem.

$$max_y \quad \frac{cut(G^+, G^-)}{|\{i : y_i = 1\}||\{i : y_i = -1\}|} \tag{3}$$

$$s.t. \quad y_i = 1, \quad if\ i \in Y_l\ and\ positive \tag{4}$$

$$y_i = -1, \quad if\ i \in Y_l\ and\ negative \tag{5}$$

$$y \in \{+1, -1\}^n \tag{6}$$

This problem is based on a mincut problem. $cut(G^+, G^-)$ in the formula (3) represents a cut of a k-nearest graph described above. Although we can solve the learning task as a simple mincut problem, there is a risk that an unbalanced label assignment is produced as Joachims points out. Because such an assignment is not likely to be a good solution, SGT introduces a constraint in the denominator of the formula (3) to produce a more balanced label assignment.

---

[2] Normally it is more than ten thousand.

This new problem is hard to solve as it is, thus SGT gives an approximation to the solution by solving its relaxed problem. We omit the details about its concrete solution (See more details in [12]). At final stage of SGT, it assigns a value around $\hat{\gamma}_+ = +\sqrt{\frac{1-\hat{p}}{\hat{p}}}$ for examples possibly being positive and $\hat{\gamma}_- = +\sqrt{\frac{\hat{p}}{1-\hat{p}}}$ for examples possibly being negative. Here $\hat{p}$ is an estimate for the fraction of positive examples in X. According to Joachims, SGT has several parameters which give large influence to its learning performance. In particular, performance of our query expansion method is very sensitive to $\hat{p}$. We next explain how to relax this sensitivity.

3   A Modified Term Scoring Scheme

If we use the scoring function in the formula (1), we have to assign a binary label (1 for a relevant document and 0 for a non-relevant) to each document based on a value assigned by SGT. This means that it is necessary a certain threshold to make hard class assignment. SGT now tentatively use a threshold $\theta = \frac{\hat{\gamma}_+ + \hat{\gamma}_-}{2}$. However, $\hat{\gamma}_+$ and $\hat{\gamma}_-$ are sometimes not reliable because $\hat{p}$ is difficult to estimate in our setting. Accordingly, instead of binary labels, we use a scoring function in formula (2) with another estimation of $\hat{p}_t$. SGT finally assigns a value $z_i = \hat{\gamma}_+ - \theta$ or $\hat{\gamma}_- - \theta$ which distributes around 0 to each document d_i. If z_i is positive, the corresponding document seems to be relevant with strong possibility. Similarly, if the value is negative, the corresponding document seems to be non-relevant with strong possibility.

Our method quantifies the possibility using a simple function which assigns a real number of less than 1.0 to each example in X. Because it is important to make a loose threshold allowing examples to which SGT acutually assigns negative values, following functions are tested as representatives in our research. Figure 1 show the shape of each function.

1. Step function (SGT-step)

$$f(x) = \begin{cases} 1 & x \geq \alpha \\ 0 & \text{otherwise} \end{cases} \tag{7}$$

2. Partially Linear function (SGT-linear)

$$f(x) = \begin{cases} 1 & x \geq 0 \\ 1 + x & -1 \leq x < 0 \\ 0 & \text{otherwise} \end{cases} \tag{8}$$

3. Partially normal distribution function (SGT-ndist)

$$f(x) = \begin{cases} 1 & x \geq 0 \\ \exp(-2x^2) & -1 < x < 0 \\ 0 & \text{otherwise} \end{cases} \tag{9}$$

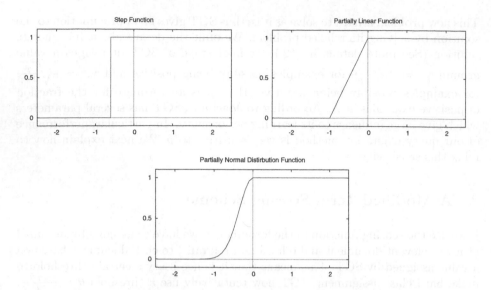

Fig. 1. Simple functions for the estimation of p_t

The first function just shifts the original threshold. The second and the third ones set a loose threshold which includes some examples assigned negative values by SGT. Using values produced by one of these functions, our method estimates p_t in the following way.

$$p_t = \sum_{i:t \in d_i} f(z_i) / \sum_{i=1}^{n} f(z_i) \tag{10}$$

The difference As described before, we estimate q_t with $\frac{n_t - r_t}{N - R}$ where R is a set of documents d_i whose z_i is positive.

4   Expansion Procedures

We here explain a whole procedure of our query expansion method step by step.

1. **Initial Search**: A retrieval starts by inputting a query for a topic to an IR system.
2. **Relevance Judgment for Documents in a Hit-List:** The IR system returns a hit-list for the initial query. Then the hit-list is scanned to check whether each document is relevant or non-relevant in descending order of the ranking. In our assumption, this reviewing process terminates when a relevant document and a non-relevant one are found.
3. **Finding More Relevant Documents by Transductive Learning:** Because only two judged documents are too few to estimate p_i and $\bar{p}_i$ correctly, our query expansion tries to increase the number of relevant documents for

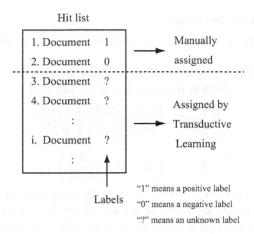

Fig. 2. Label Assignment to some Top-Ranked Documents in a Hit-List by Transductive Learning

the *wpq* formula using the SGT transductive learning algorithm. As shown in Figure2, SGT assigns a value of the possibility to be relevant for the topic to each document with no relevance judgment (documents under the dashed line in the Fig) based on two judged documents (documents above the dashed line in the Fig).

4. **Selecting Terms to Expand the Initial Query:** Our query expansion method calculates the score of each term appearing in relevant documents (including documents judged as relevant by SGT) using *wpq* formula, and then selects a certain number of expansion terms according to the ranking of the score. Selected terms are added to the initial query. Thus an expanded query consists of the initial terms and added terms.

5. **The Next Search with an Expanded Query:** The expanded query is inputted to the IR system and a new hit-list will be returned. One cycle of query expansion finishes at this step.

In the above procedures, we naturally introduced transductive learning into query expansion as the effective way in order to automatically find some relevant documents. Thus we do not need to modify a basic query expansion procedure and can fully utilize the potential power of the basic query expansion.

The computational cost of transductive learning is not so much. Actually transductive learning takes a few seconds to label 100 unlabeled documents and query expansion with all the labeled documents also takes a few seconds. Thus our system can expand queries sufficiently quick in practical applications.

5   Experiments

This section provides empirical evidence on how our query expansion method can improve the performance of information retrieval. We compare our method with other traditional methods.

5.1 Environmental Settings

We use the Okapi [10] as a retrieval system and a data set for the TREC-8 adhoc task [15].

We select the BM25 as a weight function in Okapi. It calculates the score of each document in a collection based on the following formula.

$$\sum_{T \in Q} w^{(1)} \cdot \frac{(k_1 + 1)tf(k_3 + 1)qtf}{(K + tf)(k_3 + qtf)} \tag{11}$$

$$K = k_1 \left((1 - b) + b \frac{dl}{avdl} \right) \tag{12}$$

where Q is a query containing terms T, tf is the frequency of occurrence of the term within a document, qtf is the frequency of the term within the topic from which Q was derived. K is calculated by (12), where dl and $avdl$ denote the document length and the average document length measured in some suitable unit, such as word or sequence of words. In our experiments, we set $k_1 = 1.2, k_3 = 1000, b = 0.75$, and $avdl = 135.6$. $w^{(1)}$ is the Robertson/Spark Jones weight introduced in section 2. When doing an initial search for each topic, this weight is calculated by the following formula.

$$w^{(1)} = \log \frac{N - n_t + 0.5}{n_t + 0.5} \tag{13}$$

The data set consists of a document collection, 50 topics (No.401-450) and a list of manual relevance judgment. The document collection contains about 520,000 news articles. Each document is preprocessed by removing stopwords and stemming. Query terms for an initial search are nouns extracted from the **title** tag in each topic's description. Some topics have few relevant documents or too much relevant documents. We remove such topics having none of relevant or non-relevant document within top 10 documents because we cannot apply our query expansion method for such topics. There are 8 such exceptive topics in our experiments.

5.2 Query Expansion Methods to Compare

We compared our query expansion method with the following two others.

Normal : This method simply uses only one relevant documents judged by hand. This is called *incremental relevance feedback* [16,17,18].

Pseudo : This method is called *pseudo relevance feedback*, which assumes top n documents as relevant ones. we set 30 for n in our experiments. 30 is the best value in our preliminary experiments.

According to the difference of term scoring scheme, we test four types of SGT-based query expansion methods. They are represented by **SGT-step-0, SGT-step-α, SGT-linear** and **SGT-ndist** respectively. **SGT-step-0** and **SGT-step-α** differs in each value of α. $\alpha = 0$ for the former, and α in the latter is the 30th largest value in all of z_i. The latter is another kind of Pseudo method mixed by SGT.

Table 1. 11 Points Average Precision

Number of terms added	5	10	15	20
Normal	0.191	0.175	0.164	0.162
Pseudo	0.213	0.210	0.206	0.206
SGT-step-0	0.230	0.230	0.220	0.215
SGT-step-α	**0.245**	0.241	0.240	0.231
SGT-linear	0.238	**0.249**	**0.257**	**0.240**
SGT-ndist	0.246	0.248	0.245	0.239

5.3 Results

We evaluated the results in two ways. One is 11 points average precision (in Table 1). The other is precision-recall curve (in Fig 3). The number of expansion terms we tested are 5,10,15 and 20. Precision and recall are calculated on residual collection where documents with manual judgment (2 documents in our case) are removed from an original collection. The value in the table is averaged over 42 topics. The number of documents used for SGT is 100. Since 2 documents are given as training examples, the rest 98 documents are used as test examples. SGT has several parameters to be set such as fraction of relevant documents, number of nearest neighbor in a graph, number of eigen values to use and so on. Although a default value or an automatic calculation procedure is prepared for each parameter, the parameter of fraction of relevant documents does not work well without manual setting because the number of training examples is too few. We set this parameter 0.1 for all topics based on our preliminary test.

Table 1 shows average precisions. All the SGT-based methods achieved higher precision compared with Normal and Pseudo methods. As for the usefulness of functions for the estimation of p_t, SGT-step-0 is slightly less than the other three SGT-based methods. Thus we can say that the functions are effective. However any distinctive advantage could not be seen among three functions. Since the number of expansion terms did not affect retrieval performance, we only make precision-recall curves when 5 expansion terms are added as shown in Figure 3. Curves of SGT based methods did not across over other curves at any point. This indicates the superiority of our query expansion method.

6 Discussion

Figure 4 shows a bar graph of difference of 11 points average precision between SGT-step-α and Pseudo for each topic when 5 expansion terms are added. SGT-step-α is superior to Pseudo if the difference is positive, and vice versa. As shown in the figure, there are some topics for which SGT-step-α gives worse performance than Pseudo. Because this result is related to the number of relevant documents used for query expansion, we also investigated a difference of the number of relevant documents used for query expansion in Figure 5. When

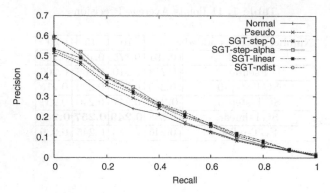

Fig. 3. Precision-Recall Curve

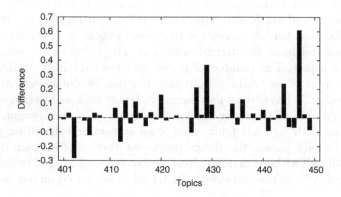

Fig. 4. Difference of 11 Points Average Precision between SGT-step-α and Pseudo

SGT-step-α has less relevant documents than Pseudo, the performance is also less than Pseudo except for some topics. The reason SGT-step-α has less relevant documents than Pseudo is a miss setting of the fraction of relevant documents which is a parameter of SGT. It is better to set a correct value for the fraction of relevant documents to SGT, however estimating the value is not so easy.

We have investigated that our query expansion methods are superior to other traditional methods from several points of view. However we have another question that query expansion procedure is necessary because SGT can re-order documents by itself. In order to answer this question, we compare recall of top n ($n = 10 \sim 100$) documents in a hit-list re-ordered by SGT itself and SGT-based query expansion method (SGT-step-α) as shown in Table 2. As shown in the table, recall rates of SGT itself is lower than the SGT-based query expansion method. This shows that SGT itself cannot work well. Under the condition of the minimum relevance judgment, SGT is effective if being mixed with our specific procedure.

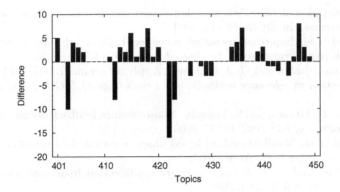

Fig. 5. Difference of the number of relevant documents in top 30 between SGT-step-α and Pseudo

Table 2. Recall at nth rank

n	SGT only	SGT-based QE
10	0.042	0.129
20	0.083	0.185
30	0.117	0.226
40	0.155	0.257
50	0.188	0.282
60	0.214	0.294
70	0.258	0.314
80	0.297	0.331
90	0.309	0.345
100	0.346	0.363

7   Conclusion

In this paper we proposed a novel query expansion method which only use the minimum manual judgment. To complement the lack of relevant documents, this method utilizes the SGT transductive learning algorithm to predict the relevancy of unjudged documents. Since the performance of SGT much depends on an estimation of the fraction of relevant documents, we introduced a modified term scoring scheme which actually changes the thresholding procedure of SGT. The experimental results showed our method outperforms other traditional methods in the evaluations of precision and recall criteria. Though our modified term scoring scheme could relax SGT's parameter sensitivity described above in some degree, we have more chance to improve the performance by removing more SGT's parameter dependencies.

References

1. I. Ruthven. Re-examining the potential effectiveness of interactive query expansion. In *Proceedings of SIGIR 2003*, pages 213–220, 2003.

2. S. Dumais and et al. Sigir 2003 workshop report: Implicit measures of user interests and preferences. In *SIGIR Forum*, 2003.
3. S. Yu and et al. Improving pseud-relevance feedback in web information retrieval using web page segmentation. In *Proceedings of WWW 2003*, 2003.
4. A. M. Lam-Adesina and G. J. F. Jones. Applying summarization techniques for term selection in relevance feedback. In *Proceedings of SIGIR 2001*, pages 1–9, 2001.
5. T. Onoda, H. Murata, and S. Yamada. Non-relevance feedback document retrieva. In *Proceedings of CIS 2004*. IEEE, 2003.
6. J. He and et al. Manifold-ranking based image retrieval. In *Proceedings of Multimedia 2004*, pages 9–13. ACM, 2004.
7. G. W. Flake and et al. Extracting query modification from nonlinear svms. In *Proceedings of WWW 2002*, 2002.
8. S. Oyama and et al. keysword spices: A new method for building domain-specific web search engines. In *Proceedings of IJCAI 2001*, 2001.
9. S. E. Robertson. On term selection for query expansion. *Journal of Documentation*, 46(4):359–364, 1990.
10. S. E. Robertson. Overview of the okapi projects. *Journal of the American Society for Information Science*, 53(1):3–7, 1997.
11. V Vapnik. *Statistical learning theory*. Wiley, 1998.
12. T. Joachims. Transductive learning via spectral graph partitioning. In *Proceedings of ICML 2003*, pages 143–151, 2003.
13. X Zhu and et al. Semi-supervised learning using gaussian fields and harmonic functions. In *Proceedings of ICML 2003*, pages 912–914, 2003.
14. A. Blum and et al. Semi-supervised learning using randomized mincuts. In *Proceedings of ICML 2004*, 2004.
15. E. Voorhees and D. Harman. Overview of the eighth text retrieval conference. 1999.
16. I. J. Aalbersberg. Incremental relevance feedback. In *Proceedings of SIGIR '92*, pages 11–22, 1992.
17. J. Allan. Incremental relevance feedback for information filtering. In *Proceedings of SIGIR '96*, pages 270–278, 1996.
18. M. Iwayama. Relevance feedback with a small number of relevance judgements: Incremental relevance feedback vs. document clustering. In *Proceedings of SIGIR 2000*, pages 10–16, 2000.

Improved Concurrency Control Technique with Lock-Free Querying for Multi-dimensional Index Structure[1]

Myung-Keun Kim and Hae-Young Bae

Dept. of Computer Science & Information Engineering, INHA University,
Younghyun-dong, Nam-ku, Inchon, 402-751, Korea
kimmkeun@dblab.inha.ac.kr
hybae@inha.ac.kr

Abstract. This paper proposes the improved concurrency control technique with lock-free querying for multi-dimensional index structure. In highly concurrent workloads due to frequent updates for storing location of moving object, the variants of R-tree structure cannot provide the real-time response. Because query processing is frequently blocked by node-split or region propagation as the locations of objects change. This paper improves the query performance by using the new versioning technique. It does not physically modify data, but creates new version for compensating data intactness. Search operation can access data without any locking or latching by reading old version. In the performance evaluation, it is proven that search operation of the proposed tree is at least two times faster than a previous work.

1 Introduction

The rapid growth of the wireless communications techniques such as global positioning systems and location determination technique have opened up various location based services. Location-based services support useful and convenient services based on the user's location such as emergency service, driving direction, and buddy finding. Users are continuously moving and send queries via WWW or wireless communication. Applications for location based services must store the current location of the large number of moving user and process the location based query in real-time manner [13, 14].

Traditional R-tree structure [4] may be used to index moving objects. However, Use of traditional R-tree structure cannot provide the real-time response since the query processing is frequently blocked by node-split or region propagation as the locations of objects change. During the last decade a number of index methods, which modified the basic structure of R-Tree, have been proposed to maximize concurrent efficiency of updating and querying, such as Rlink-Tree [6], CGiST[7], and [2],[9],[12]. They have tried to improve the query performance by minimally using

[1] This research was supported by the MIC (Ministry of Information and Communication), Korea, under the ITRC (Information Technology Research Center) support program supervised by the IITA (Institute of Information Technology Assessment).

G.G. Lee et al. (Eds.): AIRS 2005, LNCS 3689, pp. 43–55, 2005.

the lock or by linking the sibling nodes like in Rlink-tree. In highly concurrent environments, those index methods are not suitable for indexing moving objects since the query processing should be blocked even though they have tried to improve the query performance.

This paper proposes the improved concurrency control technique with lock-free querying by using the new versioning technique. It is called as "the instant versioning technique". It does not physically modify the original data, but rather make a new version for compensating the data intactness. Unlike the traditional versioning technique [11], this technique does not keep multiple versions, but it instantly keeps the original data only until the creation of new version is done. That is, the original data remains intact not for further operations but for operations that are currently accessing it. The old data is removed when no other operations are accessing it anymore. According to the instant versioning technique, an entry or a node is versioned. The proposed technique make lock-free search operations by reading old version even though an entry or a node is being modified. It requires additional work to reclaim the versioned data due to the data intactness. However the space reclamation does not require heavy overhead since the versioned entries are reused and the versioned nodes are reclaimed by an independent process without disturbing the normal operations. Experiments show better performance in search operation at least twice as fast as compared to Rlink-Tree.

The remainder of this paper is organized as follows. Section 2 describes related works and section 3 describes the proposed concurrency technique. Section 4 presents consistency and Section 5 presents experiments compared to Rlink-Tree. Finally section 6 makes a conclusion.

2 Related Works

In this section we present a problem of concurrent operations in the R-Tree. And we explain how the previous techniques solve this problem. Fig. 1 presents the problem of wrong path.

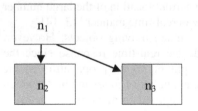

(1) - o_1 waiting to acquire lock on node n_2
    - o_2 is splitting node n_2

(2) - o_1 copies to n_2 the half of n_2 entries, and reflect pointer to n3 on parent node

(3) - o_2 releases lock on n_2

(4) - o_1 only visit the half of n_2

Fig. 1. The problem of wrong path

In Fig. 1, let's assume that o_1 is search operation that is waiting for acquiring lock on node n_2, and o_2 is insert operation that is splitting node n_2. When o_1 acquires the lock on node n_2 after node-split finishes, it only searches the half of n_2 since the other half of n_2 has been moved to n_3 by o_2.

The previous concurrency control techniques are classified into the pessimistic solution [2, 9] and the optimistic solution [6, 7, 12] to solve the problem of wrong path. The pessimistic solution does not allow node-splits in their path, and the optimistic solution allows the problem of wrong path but it corrects the wrong path by applying some special action.

The representative technique of the pessimistic solution is the lock-coupling [2, 9]. When descending the tree a lock on a parent node can only be released after the lock on the child node is granted, also when ascending the tree (node-splits or region propagation) locks on ancestor nodes should be hold until ascending step is terminated. This technique decreases concurrent efficiency since minimum of two nodes are kept locked at a time. The optimistic solution needs special method to correct the wrong path and to judge if the visiting node has been modified. The representative technique for the optimistic technique is Rlink-Tree [6]. Rlink-Tree uses LSN (Logical Sequence Number) to judge if visiting node has been split, and it corrects the wrong path by maintaining the link between sibling nodes. LSN is in charge of same roles as the maximum key of Blink-tree [10] due to the fact that R-Tree has the property that the entries of nodes are not linearly ordered. Each entry in a non-leaf node consists of a key, a pointer, and the expected LSN that it expects the child node to have. If the expected LSN taken from the parent node is different from the actual LSN of child node, a process, moves right via sibling link until the node having the expected LSN is found, is carried out.

Searching process of the previous works may be blocked since they require the shared mode lock for retrieving the consistent data against update operations. This situation over the lock-based technique cannot be avoided. This paper proposes the version-based technique which enables the search operation to progress without blocking it.

3   RIV-Tree

This section introduces the modified structure of R-Tree, called RIV-Tree, for applying the instant versioning technique, and describes internal and external operations of RIV-Tree. Finally, this section discusses the reclamation of garbage space due to the instant versioning technique.

3.1   Structure

In order to implement the instant versioning technique, timestamp is an adaptable choice like the traditional versioning technique. But the technique using timestamp imposes search operations to compare timestamps of them with that of garbage versions. Moreover, when splitting a node it needs a complex mechanism to distribute entries since it cannot decide easily which entries are the latest versions. So, the timestamp is not suitable for the instant versioning. In this paper, the linked list style is used. It is not for sorting entries, but it is for preventing operations from accessing old versions. Basically, RIV-Tree has a standard structure of R-Tree, but the traditional R-Tree structure is extended for implementing the instant versioning technique.

First, the entry structure is extended by adding two pointers for linking between sibling entries. Each entry in a node consists of a key rectangle, a pointer to the child node or indexed object, a pointer *nxtActive* to the next sibling active entry, and a pointer *nxtFree* to the next sibling free entry. Also, the node structure is extended by adding two pointers, *fstActive* and *fstFree*, for completing the instant entry versioning. *fstActive* is a pointer that points to the first among the active entries. And *fstFree* is a pointer that points to the first among the unused entry. Search operations firstly take *fstActive*, and then they move right via *nxtActive*. They visit only the latest entries since there are only the latest entries in the active link. And update operations take new entry from *fstFree*.

Second, the node structure does not need additional pointers for applying the instant node versioning technique since nodes in the tree are already linked between parent node and child node. Just, the traditional splitting algorithm is modified according to the instant node versioning. A node is instantly versioned only when it is split. In Fig. 3, let's assume that n_2 is splitting. First, new nodes, n_3 and n_4 are created unlike the traditional splitting (that only creates one new node), then entries of n_2 are distributed onto n_3 and n_4, then pointer of existing n_2 from parent node is removed, finally the pointers of n_3 and n_4 are inserted to n_1. This technique does not cause any modification on the splitting node n_2, so that the search operations can traverse subtree of n_2 without any locking and latching. However, if insert operation is waiting for acquiring lock on n_2, it may insert a new key to the wrong node n_2 (versioned node). This is the problem of wrong path as mentioned above in the related works. In order to solve this problem, the basic node structure of RIV-Tree is extended as described in the following paragraph.

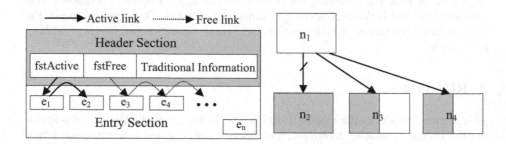

Fig. 2. The basic node structure of RIV-Tree   **Fig. 3.** The instant node versioning

Third, two pointers p_1, p_2 and a version bit v are added to the basic node structure of RIV-Tree. The variables are used to solve the problem of wrong path. That is, operations check v to detect the fact that the node has been split, and use p_1, p_2 to correct the wrong path. v is marked during the split process, and it indicates the fact that the node is versioned. If a version bit v of visiting node is true, update operations can judge that the node has been split by another operation while they were waiting. p_1, p_2 are pointers that point to the two new nodes derived from the original node.

If the visiting node is a versioned node, a process moves right via version pointers until meeting the latest nodes. Fig. 5 presents the scenario to correct the wrong path. The version bit v of node n_2 is true, and p_1, p_2 are pointing node n_3 and n_4 respectively. The update operation confirms the fact that n_2 has been versioned by checking the version bit v, and fixes the wrong path by moving to n_3 and n_4 through p_1 and p_2.

These pointers may point to another versioned node since the non-versioned node that was derived from versioned node can still be versioned again by subsequent splits, but continued moving via version pointers can guarantee that non-versioned nodes (latest nodes) are found.

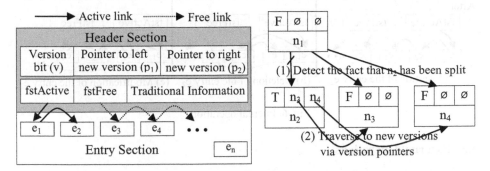

Fig. 4. The extended node structure of RIV-Tree   **Fig. 5.** Correction of wrong path

This technique requires additional work to reclaim the versioned node or the versioned entry that does not need to be accessed any more. The details are discussed in subsection 3.4.

3.2 Internal Operations

RIV-tree has four internal operations, such as insertion, deletion, modification of entry, and search operation. They are limited to a node.

Insertion and deletion of entry are very simple. A new entry, allocated from the free link, is appended to the end of the active link. It is linked only after it becomes consistent. If it does not, search operations may access the inconsistent entry. Deletion of entry is done by unlinking from the active link. In Fig. 6 (b), an entry e_2 is deleted by assigning the *nxtActive* of e_1 to e_3. And then it is linked into the free link. The active link of e_2 should not be cut because of search operations that are accessing e_2. If it is cut, they cannot move to the next active entry, e_3. The deleted entries are reused by further operation. It should carefully be reused because of search operations that are still accessing it. In order to simplify the procedure of internal operations, this issue is discussed in subsection 3.4.

Entry modification is a combination of the insertion and deletion of entry. It should be atomically done since search operations could access both entries, the original entry and the entry derived from the original entry. Fig 6 (c) describes modification of the entry e_2. The entry e_2 is atomically modified by assigning the *nxtActive* of e_1 to e_4. Especially, when splitting a node according to the instant node versioning, entry modification requires insertion of two entries unlike simple entry modification. It is also done in the same manner.

Internal search operations visit entries by taking *nxtActive*. They do not require any locking and latching due to the atomic linking of update internal operations.

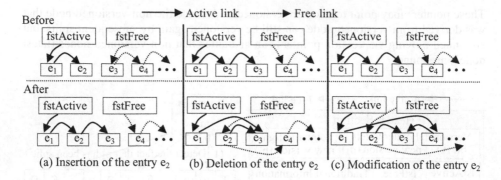

(a) Insertion of the entry e_2 (b) Deletion of the entry e_2 (c) Modification of the entry e_2

Fig. 6. Internal operations

3.3 External Operations

This subsection describes external operations such as search and insert operation. These operations are interactively invoked by the external component above the index, such as "cursor". In this subsection, delete operation is not described since it is a combination of the search and insert operation. Deletion of empty node is discussed in subsection 3.4.

3.3.1 The Search Operation

Search operation finds all entries that belong in the range of query condition. Searching starts by pushing the root node pointer to the stack. The stack is used to remember pointers of nodes or objects that need to be tested. The root node pointer will be the first to be popped from the stack. If the popped one is the pointer that indicates the node, all entries qualifying the query conditions in it are pushed to the stack. If it is the pointer that indicates objects, it is returned with the stack to caller who has invoked search operation. In next time, *findNext* procedure is invoked with the returned stack as shown in Fig. 7 (line 6). This process is repeated until the stack becomes empty.

```
1   findFirst(STACK s, RECT r)        13    if(p is pointer to indexed tuple)
2     push(s, root)                    14      return p
3     return findEntry(s, r)           15    Else
4   end                                16      for(all entries e of p)
5                                      17        if(e is intersecting r)
6   findNext(STACK s, RECT r)          18          push(s, NODE(e))
7     return findEntry(s, r)           19      End
8   end                                20      end
9                                      21    end
10  findEntry(STACK s, RECT r)         22    end
11    while not empty(s)               23  end
12      p = pop(s)
```

Fig. 7. The Search operation

3.3.2 The Insert Operation

The insert operation progresses in three steps. The first step is the descending step. This step finds the optimal leaf node that is fit to insert the new key by moving down the tree. The second step inserts the new key to the found leaf node, and the last step is the ascending step. It moves up the tree to modify the ancestor nodes in two cases: when the region of node has changed or a node should be split due to the lack of space.

```
1    insert(STACK s, RECT r)                        24    w-lock(n)
2      findLeaf(s, root, r)                          25    else
3      n = pop(s)                                    26      s-lock(n)
4      if(n is not full)                             27    end
5        insert r to n                               28    if(n is versioned)
6        if(MBR(n) has changed)                      29      pop(n); unlock(n)
7          updateParent(s, n, MBR(n))                30      n = node leading to optimal node
8        end                                                       from new versions of n
9        unlock(n)                                   31      push(s, n);
10     else                                          32      if(n is leaf node)
11       s-lock(n)                                   33        w-lock(n)
12       n1, n2 = create new node                    34      else
13       distribute n's entries to n1 and n2         35        s-lock(n)
14       insert a new entry with r to optimal node   36      end
15       set p1 and p2 to p's version pointers       37    end
16       mark the version bit of p as true           38    if(n is non-leaf node)
17       splitNode(s, n, n1, n2)                      39      e = entry on n leading to
18     end                                                        minimal MBR with r
19   end                                             40      n = NODE(e)
20                                                   41      findLeaf(s, n, r)
21   findLeaf(STACK s, NODE n, RECT r)               42    end
22     s-lock(n); push(s, n)                         43   end
23     if(n is leaf node)
```

Fig. 8. The insert operation (descending step)

When descending the tree the visited nodes are pushed to the stack. Its saved path will be used in the further ascending step. When descending the tree, the versioned node is maybe found since the insert operation does not use lock-coupling to heighten concurrent execution. That is, the child node could be split by another insert operation after taking the child node pointer from its parent node. In this case, the non-versioned nodes can be found by moving right via the version pointers. The version pointers points to each derived nodes that have been created due to node-split, so that all nodes derived from the original node can be visited by moving right. Before a process moves right, the pushed node is popped as shown in Fig. 8 (line 29). If a process finds non-versioned node leading to geometrically optimal node, it is pushed to the stack. Finally, only non-versioned nodes are in turn pushed to the stack, and if a process reaches to a leaf node, it returns.

```
1    updateParent(STACK s, NODE n, RECT r)    33    distribute p's entries to p1 and p2
2      if(s is not empty)                      34    insert entries(n1, n2) to optimal node
3        p = pop(s); w-lock(p)                 35    set p1 and p2 to p's version pointers
4        if(p is versioned)                    36    mark the version bit of p as true
5          p = findVersion(p, n)               37    splitNode(s, p, p1, p2)
6        end                                   38    else
7        unlock(n)                             39    insert entries(n1, n2) to p;
8        e = entry containing n's pointer in p  40    if(MBR(p) has changed)
9        update e with r                       41      updateParent(s, p, MBR(p))
10       if(MBR(p) is changed)                 42    else
11         updateParent(s, p, MBR(p))          43      unlock(p)
12       else                                  44    end
13         unlock(p)                           45   end
14       end                                   46  end
15     else                                    47
16       unlock(n)                             48  NODE findVersion(NODE p, n)
17     end                                     49    if(p is versioned)
18   end                                       50      unlock(p); w-lock(p.leftVersion)
19                                             51      p = findVersion(p. leftVersion, n)
20   splitNode(STACK s, NODE n, n1, n2)        52      if(p is not null)
21     if(s is empty)                          53        return p
22       p = root                              54      end
23     else                                    55      w-lock(p.rightVersion)
24       p = pop(s); w-lock(p)                 56      return findVersion(p.rightVersion, n)
25       if(p is versioned)                    57    end
26         unlock(p)                           58    if(p has the entry that contains n)
27         p = findVersion(p, n)               59      return p
28       end                                   60    end
29       unlock(n)                             61    unlock(p)
30       if(p is full)                         62    return null
31         s-lock(p)                           63  end
32         p1, p2 = create new node
```

Fig. 9. The insert operation (ascending step)

If there is space to insert the new key to the found leaf node, a new key is simply inserted. If region of the node is changed due to the key insertion, the region propagation occurs to reflect this change to the parent node. The region propagation moves up the tree until the region of ancestor nodes do not need to be changed any more. It may meet a versioned node during the region propagation. However, this case is little different to the wrong path correction of the descending step. The descending step fixes the path by finding a geometrically optimal node among all non-versioned nodes that have been derived from the versioned node. That is, all non-versioned nodes derived from the versioned node should be visited. But the ascending step only moves right via version pointers until the non-versioned node, that contains the pointer to the corresponding child node, is found.

A node is split if there is no space to insert the new key to the leaf node. Unlike the traditional node-split, the splitting process does not physically modify the splitting node, but rather marks it as "versioned", then two other nodes are created for compensating its intactness. Finally, the pointers of newly created two nodes are reflected on parent node. If there is no space to insert them in the parent node, the split process moves up to its parent node again.

3.4 Space Reclamation

According to the instant versioning technique, the garbage space, such as versioned entries and versioned nodes, is essentially created. This subsection discusses how to reclaim garbage space and who collects it.

The garbage space is reclaimed only when no other operations access it anymore, so that the reclamation needs the simple comparison between timestamp of garbage space and those of currently active operations. That is, if timestamp of garbage space is smaller or equal to the smallest one among those of active operations, it can be reclaimed. In order to implement the timestamp, a logical version number is used.

The versioned entries are not returned to system, but they are reused by internal update operations. Each node keeps a logical entry version number (*levn*) in their header section. When versioning an entry, *levn* is increased and the new value is assigned to the versioned entry. The internal operations memorize *levn* before they visit the node. If *levn* of the versioned entry is smaller or equal to the smallest one among the internal operations that are currently visiting the node, the versioned entry can be reused.

The reclamation of versioned nodes is similar to that of versioned entries. That is, tree globally keeps another logical version number, a logical node version number (*lnvn*), and the external operations memorize *lnvn* before they start. When versioning a node, *lnvn* is increased and the new value is inserted into the collector queue with the node. Garbage collector is activated on a regular basis, and pops a node from the queue. If *lnvn* of the popped node is smaller or equal to the smallest one among the active external operations, it is returned to system.

Actually, the space reclamation does not require heavy overhead since the versioned entries are reused and the versioned nodes are reclaimed by an independent process without disturbing the normal operations.

4 Consistency

This section discusses the phantom problem that is a common requirement of database systems. It is difficult to avoid the phantom problem by index itself. One simple way to avoid the phantom problem is to hold the lock on every node (leaf nodes and non-leaf nodes) that search operations visit until transaction finishes. But in this way, the concurrent execution is severely decreased. Rlink-Tree introduces a simplified form of predicate locks [3], where exclusive predicates consist of a single rectangle and shared predicates consist of query range. Insert operations check shared predicates with their single rectangle, and if they conflict, they suspend until the conflicted shared predicate is released. The main advantage of the predicate locking is to isolate the concurrency technique on index from the phantom problem. That is, when an operation is passed the predicate locking manager, it can freely access any nodes on the tree without considering the phantom problem. The predicate locking could be employed with RIV-Tree. However, it does not utilize the advantage of this paper, non-blocking search operation, since search operations could be blocked before entering to the index by the predicate locking.

A more effective solution for RIV-Tree is to cooperate with the multi-version record manager. Read transaction gets a candidate object qualifying their search condition from the index, and then the candidate object is compared with multiple versions in record manager. If the timestamp of the candidate object is greater than that of read transaction, it is ignored since the candidate object has been created after read transaction has installed, and the next candidate object is got from the index. This approach needs to consider a delete operation on index. If a key is deleted after search operation scan the tree, the number of objects got from rescan operation is maybe smaller than that of previous scan. So, the key deletion is not done by the currently delete transaction, but it is lately done by a garbage record collector like "ager" in [5]. The ager is an independent process that reclaims garbage records. When reclaiming the garbage records the corresponding keys are deleted from the index.

5   Experiments

This section proves the excellence of this technique through comparison to Rlink-Tree. It explains experimental environment, and estimates the proposed technique by increasing insert and search process.

5.1   Experimental Environment

Rlink-Tree and RIV-Tree were implemented in C under GMS [10] which is a spatial database management system. GMS run on Solaris equipped with 8 CPUs of 1.2GHz and main memory of 1G bytes.

The size of node is 4K. The fan-out of non-leaf node and leaf node is each 98 and 81 for Rlink-Tree, 89 and 75 for RIV-Tree. This experiment does not consider the phantom problem since Rlink-Tree does not mention in detail. And the quadratic split algorithm is applied to both indexes.

Initially, the data sets with 10000 rectangles (10 X 10 size) were preloaded in the 20000 X 20000 area. It was equally distributed in total domain area. In actual experiments, each insert process inserts objects with size of 10x10 randomly extracted from total area into the tree. Also, each search process searches with size of 2000x2000 (1% of entire area) randomly extracted. The response time and throughput of search and insert operation is estimated by dynamically increasing the number of insert and search process.

5.2   Experimental Results

Fig. 10 and Fig. 11 are the results of estimating response times and throughputs by increasing number of insert processes to measure insert-workload. It shows that RIV-Tree has slightly bad performance even though it tries to improve the concurrent efficiency of the update operations. This is due to the fact that RIV-Tree is more split than

Rlink-Tree since the fan-out of RIV-Tree is smaller than Rlink-Tree. That is, the overhead caused by correction of wrong path or blocking due to node-split, is increased.

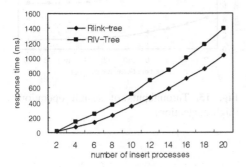

Fig. 10. Response times of insert-workload

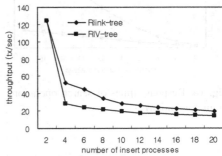

Fig. 11. Throughputs of insert-workload

Fig. 12, Fig. 13, Fig. 14, and Fig. 15 are the results of estimating average response times and throughput of search operations by increasing search operations under the low-contention (4 insert processes) and high-contention (20 insert processes). RIV-Tree is showing better performance than Rlink-Tree under the low-contention as shown in Fig. 12 and Fig. 13. This is due to the fact that search operations of RIV-Tree traverse the tree without any locking. In contrast, those of Rlink-Tree are blocked by concurrent insert operations. The difference in performance of both indexes is more severe under the high-contention. Rlink-Tree performs poorly as contention is increased. Notice that response times of RIV-Tree achieve nearly similar results in two cases, low-contention and high-contention. Consequently, response times of RIV-Tree is shown within expected time even though the contention is increased since search operations of RIV-Tree are not require any locking or latching.

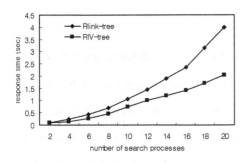

Fig. 12. Response times of search operations (low-contention)

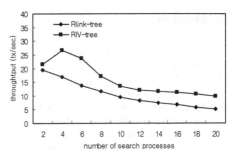

Fig. 13. Throughputs of search operations (low-contention)

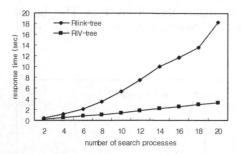

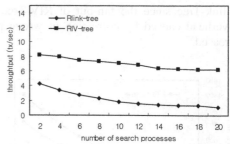

Fig. 14. Response times of search operations (high-contention)

Fig. 15. Throughputs of search operations (high-contention)

6 Conclusions

This paper has designed the modified R-Tree structure with lock-free querying, and implements it on existing spatial database management system. In order to achieve the goal, the instant versioning technique is introduced. This technique has not physically modified data, but rather new version has been created for compensating data intactness. Search operation could access data without any locking or latching by reading old version. This approach has made garbage data due to compensating action, but the reclamation task has not conflicted with the normal operation of index since it has been executed by an independent process. Experiments have showed better performance in search operation at least twice as fast as compared to Rlink-Tree.

The further work for this paper is the study of recovery. The reclamation of garbage nodes are executed independently of transactions. If system is crashed after creation of garbage node, it is never returned to system even though transaction has committed.

References

1. R. Bayer and M. Schkolnick.: Concurrency of Operations on B-Trees, *Acta Inf.*, Vol. 9, (1977) 1-21
2. J.K. Chen and Y.F. Huang.: A Study of Concurrent Operations on R-Trees, *J. Information Sciences*, Vol 98, (1997) 94-162
3. K. Eswaren, J. Gray, R. Lorie and I. Traiger.: On the Notions of Consistency and Predicate Locks in a Database System, *Comm. ACM*, Vol. 19, No. 11 (11 1976) 624-633
4. A. Guttman.: R-trees: A dynamic index structure for spatial searching, *Proc. ACM SIGMOD Int. Conf. on Management of Data*, (1984) 47-57
5. H.V. Jagadish, Dan Lieuwen, Rajeev Rastogi, Avi Silberschatz, and S. Sudarshan.: Dali: A high performance main-memory storage manager, *Proc. of the Int. Conf. on Very Large Data Bases* (1994)
6. M. Kornacker and D. Banks.: High-Concurrency Locking in R-Trees, *Proc. of the Int. Conf. on Very Large Data Bases*, (9 1995) 134-145

7. M. Kornacker, C. Mohan, and J. Hellerstein.: Concurrency control and recovery in GiST, *Proc. ACM SIGMOD Int. Conf. on Management of Data* (1997)
8. P. Lehman and S. Yao.: Efficient Locking for Concurrent Operations on B-Trees, *ACM TODS*, Vol 6, No. 4 (12 1981)
9. V. Ng and T. Kamada.: Concurrent Accesses to R-Trees, *Proc. Symp. Large Spatial Databases* (1993) 142-161
10. S. Park, W. chung, and M. Kim GMS: Spatial database management system", *Proc. of the KISS Spring Conf* (4 2003)
11. R. Rastogi, S. Seshadri, P. Bohannon, D. Leinbaugh, A. Silberschatz, and S. Sudarshan.: Logical and Physical Versioning in Main Memory Databases, *Proc. of the Int. Conf. on Very Large Data Bases* (8 1997)
12. K.V. Ravi Kanth, Divyakant Agrawal, and Ambuj K. Singh.: Improved concurrency control techniques for multi-dimensional index structures, *Technical Report, Univ. of California at santa Barbara* (1998)
13. A. Prasad Sistla, U. Wolfson, S. Chamberlain, and SonDao.: Modeling and querying moving object, *Proc. of the IEEE Int. Conf. on Data Engineering* (4 1997) 422-432
14. O. Wolfson, B. Xu, S. Chamberlain, and L. Jiang.: Moving objects databases: Issues and solutions, *Proc. of the Int. Conf. on Statistical and Scientific Database Management* (6 1998) 111-122

A Color-Based Image Retrieval Method Using Color Distribution and Common Bitmap

Chin-Chen Chang[1,2] and Tzu-Chuen Lu[2]

[1] Department of Information Engineering and Computer Science,
Feng Chia University, Taichung, Taiwan, 40724, R.O.C.
ccc@cs.ccu.edu.tw
[2] Department of Computer Science and Information Engineering,
National Chung Cheng University, Chiayi, Taiwan, 621, R.O.C.
ltc@cs.ccu.edu.tw

Abstract. Image retrieval has emerged as an important problem in multimedia database management. This paper uses the color distribution, the mean value and the standard deviation, of an image as global information for image retrieval. Furthermore, this paper uses the common bitmap to represent the local characteristics of the image. The performance of the method is tested on three different image databases consisting of 410, 235, and 10,235 images. The third database has been partitioned into 10 categories for exploring the category retrieval ability. According to the experimental results, we find that the proposed method can effectively retrieve more similar images than other methods and the category ability is also higher than others. In addition, the total memory space for saving the image features of the proposed method is less than other methods.

1 Introduction

The field of color image retrieval has been an interesting research area for several decades. Early researchers annotated each image in an image database that used keywords for similar image retrieval, called text-based image retrieval. However, the text-based retrieval methods are impractical for modern image databases, since the size of the databases has become larger and larger and different people may give the same image different keywords.

Beyond the typical text-based image retrieval methods, content-based image retrieval (CBIR) methods were proposed to automatically extract primitive features from an image. In CBIR, images are automatically indexed by summarizing their visual contents through automatically extracted features, such as color, shape, texture, size, distance, and so on. Color feature is one of the features widely used for CBIR. Many researchers used it to represent image contents for similarity searches, region matching, semantic categorization, and so on, for example, QBIC, ImageRover, Quicklook and so on [3, 14]. Nevertheless, the retrieval accuracy of a CBIR system based purely on color distribution is weak when the database is large. In order to improve the performance of CBIR based on color features, several extended methods are proposed to analyze the distribution of pixels' colors in an image [5, 6, 9, 18]. For

G.G. Lee et al. (Eds.): AIRS 2005, LNCS 3689, pp. 56–71, 2005.
© Springer-Verlag Berlin Heidelberg 2005

example, Gong split an image into nine equal sub-images and represented each sub-image by a color histogram for modeling the color spatial information [1, 7].

Stricker and Dimai split a color image into an oval central region and four corner sub-images. They evaluated and combined the color feature similarity of each of these sub-images. The central region gained more weight when a similarity was noted [16]. Gagliardi et al. integrated different color information descriptions and similarity measurements to enhance the CBIR system's effectiveness. They described the image in the CIELAB color space with two palettes [8]. Kuo et al. used the mean, standard deviation, and skewness of pixels' colors from each bin in a color histogram as the features of an image [12]. However, CBIR system only based on color cannot suffice to index large and constancy image databases. We need to combine color with other features to handle modern databases [11, 14, 15]. Chan and Liu, then, proposed a CBIR system based on CDESSO features [4]. The system used color differences among adjacent objects as the local features of a color image to increase the retrieval accuracy of the image retrieval method.

In this paper, we adopt another local information -- bitmap (BM), which is obtained from an image compression method, Block truncation coding (BTC), as a feature for similar image retrieval. BTC is a lossy compression technique applicable for images that has been used in various applications, such as image processing, progressive transmission, image processing, and so on. The BTC method uses the properties, the mean value, the standard deviation and BM, of an image for image compression. In this paper, the retrieval technique is based on these properties instead of a lot of image features. The organization of the paper is shown as follows. Section 2 briefly presents the related image retrieval techniques. Section 3 introduces the BTC method. Section 4 describes the proposed method in more detail. Section 5 presents the experimental results obtained, and finally, Section 6 provides the conclusions.

2 Related Works

Chan and Liu proposed the CDESSO-based method in 2002 [2, 4]. They used CDESSO feature to characterize the principal pixel colors, color complexity, and color differences among adjacent objects in a 24-bit full color image. Each pixel in a full color image needs 24 bits to state the color value. Hence, there are 2^{24} different kinds of color spaces of a pixel. In order to reduce the color spaces, the method first used the K-mean algorithm to divide all pixels of database images into 64 clusters. Then, each pixel was reduced into the most similar cluster. Then, the color reducing image was scanned in the spiral order, which is shown in Fig. 1, and the difference between any two continued pixels was computed. Let each cluster have its own bin to record the difference.

The scanning process begins from the central pixel of the image in a spiral direction pixel by pixel. When the current scanning pixel is different from the next scanning pixel, the color difference between two pixels would be added to the corresponding bin. The difference is given by

$$D = \left[\left(R_i - R_{i+1} \right)^2 + \left(G_i - G_{i+1} \right)^2 + \left(B_i - B_{i+1} \right)^2 \right]^{1/0.9}.$$

For example, assume an image of size 7×7, and the first pixel in the image is (6, 7, 7) in the central part of the image that is different from the next pixel (43, 78, 67).

26	27	28	29	30	31	32
49	10	11	12	13	14	33
48	25	2	3	4	15	34
47	24	9	1	5	16	35
46	23	8	7	6	17	36
45	22	21	20	19	18	37
44	43	42	41	40	39	38

Fig. 1. The scan order to extract the features

Hence, the different value of these two pixels is about 3984.7, since $[(6-43)^2 + (7-78)^2 + (7-67)^2]^{1/0.9} \approx 3984.7$. Then, they add the difference to the corresponding bin (6, 7, 7). After the scanning process, the final values of the 64 bins are the CDESSO features of the image. The main weakness of the CBIR methods is lack of spatial information. Hence, Chen and Liu used the CDESSO features as local information to enhance the limited descriptive capacity of color distributions. In this paper, we use another feature – common bitmap (CBM) as the local information to enhance the image retrieval method's effectiveness.

3 The BTC Method

The BTC is an efficient image lossy compression method that has been adapted to obtain the statistical properties of the block in image retrieval. In the BTC method, an image is firstly divided into blocks of the same size. Next, compute the mean value and the standard deviation for each block. Then, quantify the block into a tow-level bitmap (BM). That is, store a 0-bit for the pixels, which have pixel values smaller than the mean value of the block, and the rest of the pixels are represented by a 1-bit. For example, assume a gray-level image is divided into several blocks each with 4×4 pixels. One of the blocks is shown in the figure below.

123	91	81	82
140	124	89	91
115	102	147	50
170	150	144	120

Fig. 2. An example block

First, we compute the mean value for this block. The mean value of the block is approximately equal to 113, and the standard deviation is about 32. Next, compare each pixel value with the mean value to construct the BM, which is shown in Fig. 3.

The BTC method uses the BM, the mean and standard deviation to represent and reconstruct an image. We can see that the mean and the standard deviation properties, called color distribution, can be used to state the primary color and the condition of pixel color variation in an image, respectively. Besides, the BM describes the local variation of pixels. These properties depict the characteristics of an image that can be treated as image features. Therefore, this paper uses these features to construct a similar image retrieval method.

1	0	0	0
1	1	0	0
1	0	1	0
1	1	1	1

Fig. 3. The bitmap of the block

4 Proposed Method

In this section, we shall present the proposed method, which uses color distribution and BM of an image as features to represent an image.

4.1 The Color Distribution Feature

Each image in an image database may be different from all the others, but at the same time all images may share certain common characteristics. Hence, we need the statistical description of images to capture these common characteristics and use them to represent an image with fewer bits. The statistical descriptions used in this paper are the means and the standard deviations of images. Suppose P is a digital image of size M×N in an image database. The image is written as

$$
P = \begin{bmatrix}
p(0,0) & p(0,1) & \cdots & p(0,N-1) \\
p(1,0) & p(1,1) & \cdots & p(1,N-1) \\
\vdots & \vdots & \ddots & \vdots \\
p(M-1,0) & p(M-1,1) & \cdots & p(M-1,N-1)
\end{bmatrix} \tag{1}
$$

where p(i, j) is the pixel value of the coordinate (i, j), $0 \le i \le M-1$ and $0 \le j \le N-1$.

In this paper, each image is represented in RGB color space. That means each pixel can be interpreted as a vector by primary colors red (R), green (G), and blue (B). Let c represent a vector in RGB color space

$$
c(x, y) = \begin{bmatrix} c_R(x, y) \\ c_G(x, y) \\ c_B(x, y) \end{bmatrix} = \begin{bmatrix} R(x, y) \\ G(x, y) \\ B(x, y) \end{bmatrix} \tag{2}
$$

where the components of c (x, y) are the RGB components of a color image at the coordinate (x, y). In RGB color mode, the pixel of P is represented by p (i, j) = c (x = i, y = j) = c (i, j). The mean value (μ) and the standard deviation (σ) of a color image are determined as follows

$$
u = \frac{1}{M \times N} \sum_{i=0}^{M-1} \sum_{j=0}^{N-1} p(i, j) \tag{3}
$$

$$
\sigma = \left[\frac{1}{M \times N - 1} \sum_{i=0}^{M-1} \sum_{j=0}^{N-1} (p(i, j) - \mu)^2 \right]^{\frac{1}{2}} \tag{4}
$$

respectively. In the above equation, $\mu = \begin{bmatrix} \mu_R \\ \mu_G \\ \mu_B \end{bmatrix}$ and $\sigma = \begin{bmatrix} \sigma_R \\ \sigma_G \\ \sigma_B \end{bmatrix}$, where the components

of μ are the mean values of the RGB components of a color image. Meanwhile, the components of σ are the standard deviations.

These two statistical descriptions μ and σ are the global color distribution features of an image that can be computed easily and quickly. However, the feature only describes the global characteristics of images. If we only use the color distribution feature to retrieve similar images, two absolutely different images, which share the same color distribution, may be treated as similar images. Therefore, we need another feature to enhance retrieval accuracy.

4.2 The Common Bitmap (CBM) Feature

We consider another feature, common bitmap (CBM), for enhancement purpose. The first step for creating CBM of an image is to partition the image into m×n non-overlapping blocks. Let $B = \{B_1, B_2, ..., B_{m \times n}\}$ be a set of blocks, where each block is represented as

$$B_x = \begin{bmatrix} b(0,0) & b(0,1) & \cdots & b(0, w-1) \\ b(1,0) & b(1,1) & \cdots & b(1, w-1) \\ \vdots & \vdots & \ddots & \vdots \\ b(h-1,0) & b(h-1,1) & \cdots & b(h-1, w-1) \end{bmatrix} \qquad (5)$$

In the above equation, $1 \leq x \leq m \times n$, $b(i, j)$ is the pixel value at the corresponding coordinate (i, j) of B_x, $b(i, j) \in p(x, y)$, h is the height of the block that is computed by $h = \dfrac{M}{m}$ and w is the width of the block computed by $w = \dfrac{N}{n}$. The second step is to compute the mean value for each block. Let μ_{B_x} denote the mean value of B_x that is computed using the expression

$$\mu_{B_x} = \frac{1}{h \times w} \sum_{i=0}^{h-1} \sum_{j=0}^{w-1} b(i, j) \qquad (6)$$

where $\mu_{B_x} = \begin{bmatrix} \mu_{B_x R} \\ \mu_{B_x G} \\ \mu_{B_x B} \end{bmatrix}$. The components of μ_{B_x} are the mean values of the RGB

components of the block. Finally, compute CBM for the image. Let $T = \begin{bmatrix} T_R \\ T_G \\ T_B \end{bmatrix}$ be the

CBM of the image. Each component in T be expressed as:

$$T_R = (T_{1R} \; T_{2R} \; \cdots \; T_{m \times n R}), \; T_G = (T_{1G} \; T_{2G} \; \cdots \; T_{m \times n G}), \text{ and}$$

$T_B = (T_{1B} \; T_{2B} \; \cdots \; T_{m \times n B})$, respectively. In which, T_{xR}, T_{xG}, and T_{xB} are respectively given by

$$T_{xR} = \begin{cases} 1, & \text{if } \mu_{B_x R} \geq \mu_R \\ 0, & \text{otherwise} \end{cases} \tag{7}$$

$$T_{xG} = \begin{cases} 1, & \text{if } \mu_{B_x G} \geq \mu_G \\ 0, & \text{otherwise} \end{cases} \tag{8}$$

$$T_{xB} = \begin{cases} 1, & \text{if } \mu_{B_x B} \geq \mu_B \\ 0, & \text{otherwise} \end{cases} \tag{9}$$

The overall features used to represent an image are (μ, σ, T).

4.3 An Example

Fig. 4 shows an example image F of size 8×8 in RGB mode. The first step is to extract the color distribution feature of F. The mean value μ and standard deviation s

of F are $\mu = \begin{bmatrix} 56.16 \\ 63.84 \\ 62.97 \end{bmatrix}$ and $\sigma = \begin{bmatrix} 73.99 \\ 72.38 \\ 70.69 \end{bmatrix}$, respectively. Next, we divide F into 2×2

blocks, with each block having 16 pixels, where m = n = 4. Then, compute the mean

values for these blocks. We have $\mu_{B_1} = \begin{bmatrix} 50.3 \\ 94.63 \\ 72.56 \end{bmatrix}$, $\mu_{B_2} = \begin{bmatrix} 80.63 \\ 67.06 \\ 84.56 \end{bmatrix}$, $\mu_{B_3} = \begin{bmatrix} 73.63 \\ 56.38 \\ 64.88 \end{bmatrix}$ and

$\mu_{B_4} = \begin{bmatrix} 20.06 \\ 37.31 \\ 29.88 \end{bmatrix}$. Finally, the CBM for the image F is $T = \begin{bmatrix} T_R \\ T_G \\ T_B \end{bmatrix} =$

$\begin{bmatrix} (T_{1R} \; T_{2R} \; T_{3R} \; T_{4R}) \\ (T_{1G} \; T_{2G} \; T_{3G} \; T_{4G}) \\ (T_{1B} \; T_{2B} \; T_{3B} \; T_{4B}) \end{bmatrix} = \begin{bmatrix} (0\,1\,1\,0) \\ (1\,1\,0\,0) \\ (1\,1\,1\,0) \end{bmatrix}$, where $T_{1R} = 0$, since

$\mu_{B_1 R} = 50.3 < \mu_R = 56.16$, $T_{2R} = 1$, since $\mu_{B_2 R} = 80.63 > \mu_R = 56.16$, and so on.

Therefore, the features of F are $(\mu, \sigma, T) = (\begin{bmatrix} 56.16 \\ 63.84 \\ 62.97 \end{bmatrix}, \begin{bmatrix} 73.99 \\ 72.38 \\ 70.69 \end{bmatrix}, \begin{bmatrix} (0\,1\,1\,0) \\ (1\,1\,0\,0) \\ (1\,1\,1\,0) \end{bmatrix})$.

(6, 7, 7)	(4, 134, 220)	(214, 244, 2)	(23, 2, 23)	(88, 3, 215)	(58, 58, 44)	(3, 2, 221)	(227, 7, 8)
(5, 95, 16)	(9, 210, 189)	(253, 127, 29)	(19, 88, 3)	(20, 4, 65)	(4, 1, 15)	(4, 231, 21)	(128, 69, 55)
(56, 6, 12)	(9, 100, 121)	(11, 22, 222)	(12, 23, 44)	(208, 235, 71)	(43, 66, 161)	(166, 15, 113)	(224, 77, 45)
(9, 44, 12)	(43, 185, 179)	(34, 5, 77)	(98, 222, 5)	(47, 61, 7)	(3, 119, 169)	(66, 123, 77)	(1, 2, 66)
(20, 199, 112)	(221, 33, 16)	(55, 23, 65)	(21, 23, 2)	(35, 3, 32)	(43, 78, 67)	(6, 6, 20)	(8, 5, 17)
(21, 188, 220)	(240, 77, 23)	(40, 123, 123)	(222, 23, 234)	(86, 1, 25)	(19, 9, 4)	(66, 5, 15)	(6, 20, 3)
(7, 9, 1)	(5, 15, 32)	(123, 88, 45)	(89, 21, 42)	(2, 57, 89)	(25, 199, 3)	(4, 66, 1)	(5, 7, 11)
(4, 6, 7)	(8, 15, 22)	(3, 54, 88)	(99, 5, 6)	(2, 8, 6)	(9, 123, 156)	(2, 2, 9)	(3, 8, 20)

Fig. 4. An example image F of size 8×8

4.4 The Similarity Measure of the Features

In this paper, two different similarity measures for different features are used to evaluate the similarity between two images. The first one is Euclidean distance, which is used for comparing μ and σ, and the second is hamming distance, which used for comparing CBM. The overall similarity is obtained by linearly combining of these two similarity values. Before linearly combining the similarity values, we need to normalize the features of the same range. Otherwise, the linear combination will become meaningless because the magnitude similarity value may dominate the others. For this reason, the features should be normalized before applying the similarity measure. In this paper, we use the Gaussian normalization to normalize the features. The features μ and σ of an image are respectively normalized as follows

$$\hat{\mu} = \frac{\mu - \alpha}{3 \times \gamma} \qquad (10)$$

$$\hat{\sigma} = \frac{s - \beta}{3 \times \tau} \qquad (11)$$

where $\hat{\mu}$ is the normalized mean value and $\hat{\sigma}$ is the normalized standard deviation. In addition, the symbol α in Eq. 10 is the mean value of whole μ in the image database that is given by

$$\alpha = \frac{\sum_{i=1}^{|D|} \mu^i}{|D|} \qquad (12)$$

where |D| is the total number of images in the image database, μ^i is the mean value of the ith image. Another symbol γ is the standard deviation value of whole μ that is given by

$$\gamma = \left[\frac{1}{|D|} \sum_{i=1}^{|D|} (\mu^i - \alpha)^2 \right]^{\frac{1}{2}} \qquad (13)$$

Further, the symbol β in Eq. 11 is the mean value of whole σ in the image database that is given by

$$\beta = \frac{\sum_{i=1}^{|D|} \sigma^i}{|D|} \tag{14}$$

where σ^i is the standard deviation of the ith image. Another symbol τ is the standard deviation value of whole σ that is given by

$$\tau = \left[\frac{1}{|D|} \sum_{i=1}^{|D|} (\sigma^i - \beta)^2 \right]^{1/2} \tag{15}$$

Hence, the similarity measure between two images A and B is calculated as follows:

$$d(A, B) = \frac{H(T^A, T^B)}{3 \times m \times n} + \sqrt{\sum_{k \in \{R, G, B\}} (\hat{\mu}_k^A - \hat{\mu}_k^B)^2 + \sum_{k \in \{R, G, B\}} (\hat{\sigma}_k^A - \hat{\sigma}_k^B)^2} \tag{16}$$

In the above equation, function H is used to compute the hamming distance between images A and B that is defined as $H(T^A, T^B) = \sum_{k \in \{R, G, B\}} \sum_{i=1}^{m \times n} \| T_{ik}^A - T_{ik}^B \|$.

The symbol T_{ik}^A is the ith component of the common bit map T in k color of image A and $k \in \{R, G, B\}$. In addition, the symbol $\hat{\mu}_k^A$ is the normalized mean value of A in k color, meanwhile, the symbol $\hat{\sigma}_k^A$ is the normalized standard deviation of A in k color. The images in the database are ordered by their similarity to the user's query image. The image with the smallest distance is the image most similar to the query image. For example, assume that there is another image E as shown in Fig. 5. The features of E are ($\begin{bmatrix} 78.05 \\ 83.61 \\ 80.14 \end{bmatrix}$, $\begin{bmatrix} 66.73 \\ 65.74 \\ 66.60 \end{bmatrix}$, $\begin{bmatrix} (0\,1\,0\,1) \\ (0\,1\,1\,1) \\ (1\,1\,0\,0) \end{bmatrix}$).

After being normalized, the final features of E and F are ($\begin{bmatrix} 0.22 \\ 0.38 \\ 0.28 \end{bmatrix}$, $\begin{bmatrix} -0.25 \\ -0.35 \\ -0.26 \end{bmatrix}$, $\begin{bmatrix} (0\,1\,0\,1) \\ (0\,1\,1\,1) \\ (1\,1\,0\,0) \end{bmatrix}$) and ($\begin{bmatrix} -0.44 \\ -0.21 \\ -0.23 \end{bmatrix}$, $\begin{bmatrix} 0.45 \\ 0.29 \\ 0.13 \end{bmatrix}$, $\begin{bmatrix} (0\,1\,1\,0) \\ (1\,1\,0\,0) \\ (1\,1\,1\,0) \end{bmatrix}$), respectively. The distance between images F and E is computed as

$$d(F, E) = \frac{H(T^F, T^E)}{3 \times 2 \times 2} + \sqrt{\sum_{k \in \{R, G, B\}} (\hat{\mu}_k^F - \hat{\mu}_k^E)^2 + \sum_{k \in \{R, G, B\}} (\hat{\sigma}_k^F - \hat{\sigma}_k^E)^2} = \frac{5}{12} + 2.20 \approx 2.62 \cdot$$

(155, 110, 89)	(121, 120, 222)	(93, 33, 99)	(11, 3, 12)	(18, 52, 12)	(23, 112, 44)	(3, 2, 221)	(227, 75, 89)
(43, 22, 15)	(45, 12, 241)	(93, 88, 87)	(52, 33, 125)	(112, 88, 78)	(48, 64, 15)	(4, 231, 21)	(128, 10, 155)
(125, 45, 4)	(71, 88, 31)	(12, 44, 15)	(48, 65, 188)	(20, 99, 224)	(66, 77, 161)	(166, 325, 74)	(224, 47, 145)
(33, 35, 35)	(36, 41, 85)	(75, 15, 65)	(63, 48, 17)	(214, 91, 154)	(57, 77, 85)	(74, 44, 44)	(100, 245, 166)
(6, 154, 58)	(85, 128, 46)	(8, 23, 74)	(125, 12, 174)	(251, 37, 21)	(89, 156, 4)	(6, 100, 20)	(51, 225, 147)
(21, 228, 66)	(126, 56, 35)	(4, 44, 15)	(111, 97, 165)	(222, 158, 33)	(155, 77, 55)	(66, 5, 15)	(55, 125, 111)
(68, 124, 7)	(15, 123, 18)	(65, 64, 123)	(45, 54, 185)	(241, 17, 74)	(189, 48, 3)	(4, 15, 1)	(5, 123, 55)
(89, 68, 48)	(78, 44, 78)	(21, 52, 56)	(85, 85, 6)	(28, 67, 165)	(31, 178, 156)	(2, 78, 57)	(88, 145, 40)

Fig. 5. An example image E of size 8×8

5 Experiments

In order to test the performance of our proposed method, three existing algorithms are used to benchmark the proposed method. The first one is color histogram. The second is color moment. The third is CDESSO-based method [4]. In this paper, we performed two different experiments to compare the performance of the three algorithms and our proposed method. The first one is to test the retrieval accuracies of the methods, and another is to test the category query ability of the methods.

5.1 The Retrieval Accuracy

Two image databases were used to test the retrieval accuracies of the methods. The first image database used in this experiment contained two image databases D_1 and Q_1, where each database contains 410 full color animations [4]. Each image in Q_1 has a corresponding image in Q_1 in pairs. Fig. 6 shows example images from D_1 in (a) and its corresponding image from Q_1 in (b).

The second image database contained two image databases D_2 and Q_2, where each database contains 235 full color images [4]. Each image in Q_2 has a corresponding image in Q_2. Fig. 7 shows example images from D_2 in (a) and its corresponding image from Q_2 in (b). Each image in set Q_i was used as a query image to retrieve N_{RT} images in D_i with the smallest distances according to the similarity measure, Eq. 16, and their rank values determined from all those distances arranged in ascending order, where $i \in [1, 2]$ and N_{RT} is the number of images the user wants to retrieve. If the corresponding target image in D_i is one of these N_{RT} images, we say it accurately retrieves the desired image.

The retrieval accuracy (R) of the method is given by the expression

$$R_i = \frac{C_i}{|Q_i|} \qquad (17)$$

where C_i is the total number of query images which can correctly retrieve the desired image in Q_i and $|Q_i|$ is the total number of images in Q_i. In order to determine the proper number of block sizes for partition of an image, we perform difference block sizes to explore the retrieval accuracies of our proposed method. The influence resulting from different block sizes in our method is measured by setting block size ($m \times n$) equal to 5×5, 10×10, or 15×15. The experimental results are shown in Table 1. As indicated in the experimental results, when block sizes are 5×5 and 10×10, the proposed method would have approximate results that are better than 15×15. Therefore, in the following experiments, the block sizes were assigned as 5×5 and 10×10. Table 2 shows the experimental results of the first experiment. According to the experimental results, when the number of blocks is 100 ($m \times n = 10 \times 10$), the proposed method would have better retrieval accuracy than other methods in both Q_1 and Q_2 databases.

In the second experiment, a large database D_3 contains 10,235 full color images, which were collected from [10, 13, 17] and were used to explore the retrieval accuracies of the methods in large databases. The 235 images in D_2 also were embedded into D_3. When using an image from Q_2 as a query, the goal was to retrieve the corresponding image, which is the target image in D_2, from D_3.

The experimental results are shown in Table 3. For $N_{RT} = 10$, the proposed method with 10×10 blocks has better result than others. In other words, the retrieval accuracy is 55.32%, while the retrieval accuracy of the color histogram and color moment are 0.0% and 46.46%, respectively. When $N_{RT} = 100$, the retrieval accuracy of the proposed method with block size of 10×10 is 76.6%, which is higher than that of the color histogram (3.03%) and the color moment (70.71%). It is seen that the average rank of our proposed method is higher than others. The average retrieval accuracy performances of the methods are shown in Fig. 8.

(a) Example images in Q_1 (b) Corresponding target images of (a) from D_1

Fig. 6. Example images of the 410 animations in databases Q_1 and D_1

(a) Example images from Q_2 (b) Corresponding target images of (a) from D_2

Fig. 7. Example images of the 235 images in databases Q_2 and D_2

Table 1. The retrieval accuracies of various block sizes in Q_1

Rank \ $m \times n$	5×5	10×10	15×15
$N_{RT} = 1$	93.17	93.17	93.66
$N_{RT} = 2$	97.32	97.32	97.32
$N_{RT} = 3$	98.05	98.05	98.29
$N_{RT} = 4$	98.54	98.54	98.54
$N_{RT} = 5$	99.02	99.02	98.78
$N_{RT} = 10$	99.76	99.76	99.76
$N_{RT} = 20$	99.76	99.76	99.76

Table 2. The experimental results of the first experiment

N_{RT} \ Method	CDESSO-based method		Our method $m \times n = 5 \times 5$		Our method $m \times n = 10 \times 10$	
Q	Q_1	Q_2	Q_1	Q_2	Q_1	Q_2
$N_{RT} = 1$	93.72	40.00	93.17	59.57	93.17	61.70
$N_{RT} = 2$	97.09	47.23	97.32	65.53	97.32	71.49
$N_{RT} = 3$	97.09	51.49	98.05	71.49	98.05	75.32
$N_{RT} = 4$	97.76	52.77	98.54	76.60	98.54	77.87
$N_{RT} = 5$	97.98	54.47	99.02	78.72	99.02	81.28
$N_{RT} = 10$	99.33	60.43	99.76	85.96	99.76	86.38
$N_{RT} = 20$	99.55	70.21	99.76	91.06	99.76	91.06

Table 3. The experimental results of the second experiment

Method \ N_{RT}	≤ 10	≤ 100	≤ 500	≤ 1000	>1000
Color histogram	0.00	3.03	8.08	12.12	87.88
Color moment	46.46	70.71	85.86	88.89	11.11
Our method (5×5)	52.34	73.19	89.36	93.19	6.81
Our method (10×10)	55.32	76.60	89.79	94.47	5.53

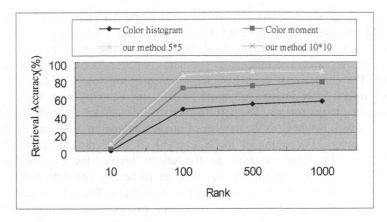

Fig. 8. Average retrieval accuracy performances of the methods

5.2 The Category Retrieval Precision

In this example, we divided the color images in D_3 into 10 categories, where images of the same theme can be regarded as belonging to the same category. The ten

Architecture   City   Dog   Eagle   Elephant

Leopard   Model   Mountain   Pyramid   Royal

Fig. 9. Example images from the ten categories in the D_3

Query: dog

Fig. 10. Retrieved images by query image: dog

categories are architecture (A), city (C), dog (D), eagle (E), elephant (El), leopard (L), model (M), mountain (Mt), pyramid (P), and royal (R). Each category contains 100 images. Examples of these images are shown in Fig. 9. The objective of this example was to retrieve images belonging to the same category as query images from a database. Therefore, every image from these ten categories was used as query images. For each query, other images belonging to the same category were regarded as the corresponding target images. The performance of the category ability (P) is measured by: $P = C_r / N_{RT}$, where C_r is the number of images belonging to the same category as the query image. For example, for $N_{RT} = 30$, if there are 16 retrieved images belonging to the same category as the query image, the category ability P $= 16/30 \approx 53\%$. In this experiment, N_{RT} was set to be 30. The performances of the proposed method and other methods are shown in Table 4. The column Cr in the table shows the average number of Cr in each category. For example, for category City, the proposed method found 12 relevant images while the color histogram did not find any relevant images, and color moment scheme only found 2 relevant images, for $N_{RT} = 30$. The corresponding precisions are 40%, 0%, and 6%, respectively.

Fig. 11. Retrieved images by query image: royal

Table 4. The experimental results on the ten categories for $N_{RT} = 30$

Category	Color histogram		Color moment		Our method (10×10)	
	Cr	P (%)	Cr	P (%)	Cr	P (%)
Architecture	1	3	2	6	7	23
City	0	0	2	6	12	40
Dog	1	3	1	3	7	23
Eagle	0	0	3	10	21	70
Elephant	0	0	2	6	16	53
Leopard	0	0	2	6	18	60
Model	1	3	1	3	8	27
Mountain	0	0	2	6	15	50
Pyramid	0	0	2	6	11	37
Royal	1	3	2	6	16	53

Fig. 10 shows the query image for the retrieval of images containing a dog in the center of the image. The retrieved images closely match the content of the supplied query image. Fig. 11 shows a query image containing royals of red and black colors. Most of the retrieved images match closely in content to the corresponding supplied query images. Fig. 12 shows the aggregated results over all ten categories. According to the results, we can see that our proposed scheme is better than others in terms of the category ability in most cases.

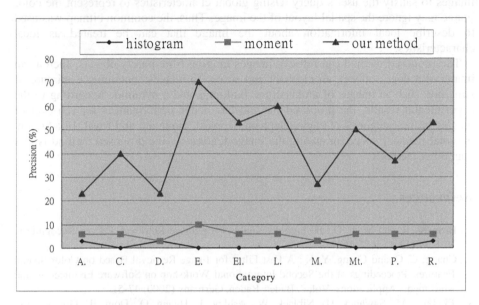

Fig. 12. Aggregated results over all ten categories

5.3 Memory Space Analysis

Let |D| be the total number of images in a database. The memory space of a color histogram for storing the features of database images is |D| × 64 (clusters) × 3 (RGB) × 3 (μ, σ, S_k) × 4 bytes (a floating point). The memory space of CDESSO-based method is |D| × 64 (clusters) × 4 bytes (a floating point). However, the memory space of our proposed method is |D| × [$\dfrac{3 \times m \times n (T_R, T_G, T_B)}{8}$ + 6 ($\mu_R, \mu_G, \mu_B, s_R, s_G, s_B$) × 4 bytes (a floating point)]. For example, the memory space of a color histogram method in D_1 is 410 × 64 × 3 × 3 × 4 = 944,640 (bytes), meanwhile, CDESSO-based method is 410 × 64 × 4 = 104,960 (bytes). However, the memory space of our method with block sizes 10×10 only takes 410 × [$\dfrac{3 \times 10 \times 10}{8}$ + 6 × 4] = 25,215 (bytes).

6 Conclusions

Content-based image retrieval has become one of the most active research areas in the recently decade. In this paper, we introduced a method for content-based image retrieval via the color distribution and common bit map. The color distribution can be seen as the global characteristic of an image. The global characteristics are associated with the entire image, and are contrasted with local characteristics, which are associated with pixels. An image retrieval system heavily relies on the global image characteristics, such as color and texture histograms, often fails to capture correct images to satisfy the user's query. Using global characteristics to represent the color image may ignore the spatial layout of the image. Thus, the common bitmap was used to describe local information about the image that can be treated as local characteristics.

The proposed method can retrieve images ranging from purely objects, such as an image of a dog, a model, an elephant and so on, to images containing a mixture of structure, such as images of architecture, buildings and a pyramid. According to the experimental results, the proposed method has better performances for retrieval of images in the categories of eagle, elephant, leopard, mountain and royal. In addition, the total memory space for saving the image features of the proposed method is less than other methods.

References

1. Brunelli, R. and Mich, O.: Histograms Analysis for Image Retrieval. Pattern Recognition. Vol. 34 (2001) 1625-1637.
2. Chang, C. C. and Chang, Y. K.: A Fast Filter for Image Retrieval Based on Color-Spatial Features. Proceedings of the Second International Workshop on Software Engineering and Multimedia Applications. Vol. 2, Baden-Baden, Germany (2000) 47-51.
3. Flickner, M., Sawhney, H., Niblack, W., Ashley, J., Huang, Q., Dom, B., Gorkani, M., Hafner, J., Lee, D., Petkovic, D., Steele, D. and Yanker, P.: Query by Image and Video Content: the QBIC System. IEEE Computer. Vol. 28, No. 9, (1995) 23-32.
4. Chan, Y. K. and Liu, Y. T.: An Image Retrieval System Based on the Image Feature of Color Differences on Edges in Spiral Scan Order. International Journal on Pattern Recognition and Artificial Intelligence. Vol. 17, No. 8, (2003) 1417-1429.
5. Du, Y. P. and Wang, J. Z.: A Scalable Integrated Region-Based Image Retrieval System. Proceedings of the International Conference on Image Processing, Vol. 1, Thessaloniki, Greece (2001) 22-25.
6. Fuh, C. S., Cho, S. W. and Essig, K.: Hierarchical Color Image Region Segmentation for Content-Based Image Retrieval System. IEEE Transactions on Image Processing. Vol. 9, No. 1 (2000) 156-162.
7. Gong, Y., Chuan, C. H. and Xiaoyi, G.: Image Indexing and Retrieval Using Color Histograms. Multimedia Tools and Applications. Vol. 2 (1996) 133-156.
8. Gagliardi, I. and Schettini, R.: A Method for the Automatic Indexing of Color Image for Effective Image Retrieval. The New Review of Hypermedia and Multimedia. Vol. 3 (1997) 201-224.
9. Hsieh, J. W., Grimson, W. E. L., Chiang, C. C.and Huang, Y. S.: Region-Based Image Retrieval. Proceedings of the International Conference on Image Processing, Vol. 1, Vancouver, BC, Canada (2000) 77-80.
10. Iqbal, Q. and Aggarwal, J. K.: CIRES: A System for Content-based Retrieval in Digital Image Libraries. Proceedings of the Seventh International Conference on Control, Automation, Robotics and Vision, Singapore (2002) 205-210.

11. Kankanhalli, M. S., Mehtre, B. M. and Huang, H. Y.: Color and Spatial Feature for Content-Based Image Retrieval. Pattern Recognition. Vol. 22, No. 3-4 (2001) 323-337.

12 Kou, W. J.: Study on Image Retrieval and Ultrasonic Diagnosis of Breast Tumors. Dissertation, Department of Computer Science and Information Engineering, National Chung Cheng University, Chiayi, Taiwan, R.O.C, (2001).

13. Li, J. and Wang, J. Z.: Automatic Linguistic Indexing of Pictures by a Statistical Modeling Approach. IEEE Transactions on Pattern Analysis and Machine Intelligence. Vol. 25, No. 10 (2003) 1075-1088.

14. Schettini, R., Ciocca, G. and Zuffi, S.: A Survey of Methods for Colour Image Indexing and Retrieval in Image Databases. Color Imaging Science: Exploiting Digital Media, (MacDonald, L. W. and Luo, M. R. Eds.), Wiley, J. & Sons Ltd., Chichester, England (2001).

15. Stehling, R. O., Nascimento, M. A. and Falcao, A. X.: An Adaptive and Efficient Clustering-Based Approach for Content-Based Image Retrieval in Image Databases. Proceedings of the International Database Engineering and Applications Symposium, Grenoble, France (2001) 356-365.

16. Stricker, M. and Dimai, A.: Spectral Covariance and Fuzzy Regions for Image Indexing. Machine Vision and Applications. Vol. 10 (1997) 66-73.

17. Wang, J. Z., Li, J. and Wiederhold, G.: SIMPLIcity: Semantics-Sensitive Integrated Matching for Picture Libraries. IEEE Transactions on Pattern Analysis and Machine Intelligence. Vol. 23, No. 9 (2001) 947-963.

18. Wang, J. Z. and Du, Y. P.: Scalable Integrated Region-Based Image Retrieval Using IRM and Statistical Clustering. Proceedings of ACM/IEEE Joint Conference on Digital Libraries, Roanoke, Virginia, USA, (2001) 268-277.

A Probabilistic Model for Music Recommendation Considering Audio Features

Qing Li[1], Sung Hyon Myaeng[1], Dong Hai Guan[2], and Byeong Man Kim[3]

[1] Information and Communications University, Korea
{liqing, myaeng}@icu.ac.kr
[2] Harbin Engineering University, China
[3] Kumoh National Institute of Technology, Korea
bmkim@se.kumoh.ac.kr

Abstract. In order to make personalized recommendations, many collaborative music recommender systems (CMRS) focused on capturing precise similarities among users or items based on user historical ratings. Despite the valuable information from audio features of music itself, however, few studies have investigated how to directly extract and utilize information from music for personalized recommendation in CMRS. In this paper, we describe a CMRS based on our proposed item-based probabilistic model, where items are classified into groups and predictions are made for users considering the Gaussian distribution of user ratings. By utilizing audio features, this model provides a way to alleviate three well-known challenges in collaborative recommender systems: user bias, non-association, and cold start problems in capturing accurate similarities among items. Experiments on a real-world data set illustrate that the audio information of music is quite useful and our system is feasible to integrate it for better personalized recommendation.

1 Introduction

A recommender system has an obvious appeal in an environment where the amount of on-line information vastly outstrips any individual's capability to survey. It starts being an integral part of e-commerce sites such as Amazon, Yahoo and CDNow.

At the initial stage, a recommender system mostly relied on a content-based filtering (CBF) mechanism. It selects the right information for a user by matching the user preference against databases, which may be implicit or explicit. For example, a search engine recommends web pages whose contents are similar to a user query [22]. Despite the efficiency of a CBF in locating textual items relevant to a topic, it is a little difficult for such a system to be directly applied to multimedia without any textual descriptions such as a music genre, title, composer, or singer. In addition, representing a user preference or query for non-textual features is also a big challenge for a music recommender system (MRS). Some researchers [6] suggested a method of querying an audio database by humming. Not all users, however, have a gift of humming the melody of their favorite songs for searching.

Collaborative filtering (CF), as in GroupLens [16] and Ringo [19], has been considered a mainstream technique for recommender systems for a long time until now.

G.G. Lee et al. (Eds.): AIRS 2005, LNCS 3689, pp. 72–83, 2005.

CF uses opinions of others to predict the interest of a user. A target user is matched against the database of user histories to discover other users, called neighbors, who have historically similar tastes. Items that the neighbors like are then recommended to the target user. For instance, the GAB system [22] recommends web pages based on the bookmarks; Jeter system recommends jokes [7]; MovieLens recommends movies; and Flycasting recommends online radio. Most of prevalent CF systems focus on calculating the user-user similarity to make predictions, which is so called user-based CF. However, Sarwar [17] has proved that item-based CF is better than user-based CF on precision and computation complexity.

Despite the popularity of CF techniques, researchers also realized that the content information of items did help providing a good recommendation service. The idea of a hybrid system capitalizing on both CF and CBF has been suggested. Examples include Fab[2], ProfBuilder[21] and RAAP[4] systems.

The Fab [2] system uses content-based techniques instead of user ratings to create user profiles. Since the quality of predictions is fully dependent on the content-based techniques, inaccurate profiles result in inaccurate correlations with other users, yielding poor predictions. ProfBuilder [21] recommends web pages using both content-based and collaborative filters, each of which creates a recommendation list separately to make a combined prediction. Claypool [3] describes a hybrid approach for an online newspaper domain, combining the two predictions using an adaptive weighted average. As the number of users accessing an item increases, the weight of the collaborative component tends to increase. However, the authors do not clearly describe how to decide the weights of collaborative and content-based components. RAAP[4] is a content-based collaborative information filtering system that helps the user classify domain specific information found on the WWW, and also recommends those URLs to other users with similar interests. To determine the similarity of interests among users, a scalable Pearson correlation algorithm based on the web page category is used.

Clustering is the key idea of CF and a hybrid system that relies on CF. The idea of clustering is implemented in various ways explicitly or implicitly in most CF techniques. A pioneering CF method called Pearson correlation coefficient method aims at grouping the like-minded users for an active user. It first calculates the similarities between the active user and others, and then clusters users into groups with similar tastes.

Probabilistic models exploit explicit clustering to model the preferences of the underlying users, from which predictions are inferred. Examples include the Bayesian clustering model [1], the Bayesian network model [1], and the Aspect model [10]. The basic assumption of the Bayesian clustering model is that ratings are observations of the multinomial mixture model with parameters, and the model is estimated by using EM. The Bayesian network model aims at capturing item dependency. Each item is a node and dependency structure is learned from observables. The aspect model is based on a latent cause model that introduces the notion of user communities or groups of items.

Besides the above methods where clustering is integrated into some probabilistic or memory-based techniques, some researchers also apply a data clustering algorithm to the process of rating data in CF as an isolated step. O'Conner [11] uses existing data clustering algorithms to do item clustering based on user ratings, and then predictions are calculated independently within each partition. SWAMI [5] applies the meta-user mechanism for recommendation by first grouping users to create the profile for each cluster as a meta-user, and then predictions are calculated with a Pearson correlation method where only meta-users are considered as potential neighbors. Li [12, 14] suggests applying a clustering method to include content information for CF.

While the aforementioned systems and methods cluster users or items, most of them fail to handle well-known problems in CF, non-association, user bias, and cold start. Since those three problems occur on both item-based and user-based CF, we address them in the context of item-based CF.

The first challenge is non-association. For instance, if two similar items have never been wanted by the same user, their relationship is not known explicitly. In pure item-based CF, those two items can not be classified into the same community.

The second one is user bias in the past ratings. For example, as shown in Table1, Music 3 and 4 have the same history in ratings. In item-based CF and thus have the same opportunity to be recommended to the user Jack by the system. If the system knows that Music 1 and Music 2 fall into the Rock category and Music 3 into the Rock category, however, it can recommend Music 3 to Jack with a higher priority, provided that he is known to like Rock music in the past.

The third one is the cold start problem. It is hard for pure CF to recommend a new item where there is no history and hence no user opinions on it. Music 5 in Table 1 is an example.

Table 1. Rating Information

Item ID	Jack	Oliver	Peter	Tom	Rock	Country
Music 1	5	4	3		Y	N
Music 2	4	4	3		Y	N
Music 3		4	3		Y	N
Music 4		4	3		N	Y
Music 5					Y	N
Music 6				4	Y	N

In this paper, we describe a collaborative music recommender system (CMRS) based on our proposed item-based probabilistic model, where items are clustered into groups and predictions are made using both the item cluster information and user ratings. This model provides a way to directly apply the audio features of music objects for a personalized recommendation, alleviating the three problems in similarity calculation of CF. This method can be easily extended to recommend other items such as movies, books and etc.

2 Probabilistic Model

It is usual that rating information in a real-world recommendation system is quite sparse. As a result the three problems mentioned in the previous section occur quite often and negatively affect the clustering result and hence recommendation. As shown in Table 1, the attributes of items such as their genre would help us alleviate those problems. For the non-association case, for instance, the relationship between Music 6 and others is unknown. However, with the help of the music genre information, we can partially infer that Music 6 has a close relationship with other music pieces except Music 4. Other two challenges are similarly handled by the virtue of genre information.

The probabilistic model we propose for our CMRS can adopt various clustering algorithms to estimate the parameters. Although some advanced methods such as an incremental clustering algorithm can be potentially applied for a better performance and flexibility, we use a simple k-Medoids[1] [8] clustering method in the current work. The K-Medoids algorithm makes each cluster to be represented by one of the objects in the cluster, whereas a cluster is represented by the center in the well-known K-means algorithm. Thus it is less influenced by outliers or other extreme values than a mean. Both ratings and item attributes such as genre are used as features for clustering items in our approach.

Observing the ratings of each user in an item community that in item-based CF satisfy a Gaussian distribution, we propose a method of probabilistic model estimation for CF, where items are classified into groups based on both content information and ratings together, and predictions are made considering the Gaussian distribution of ratings.

The domains we consider consist of a set of users $U = \{u_1,...u_n\}$, and a set of items $Y = \{y_1,...y_m\}$ and a set of possible ratings $V = \{v_1,...v_k\}$. In CF, we are interested in the conditional probability $P(v|u,y)$ that a user u will rate an item y with a value v. If the rating v is based on a numerical scale, it is appropriate to define the deterministic prediction function $g(u,y)$ that indicates the user's rating on the item y as follows:

$$g(u,y) = \int_v vp(v|u,y)dv$$

where $p(v|u,y)$ denotes a probability mass function (discrete case) or a conditional probability density function (continuous case) dependent on the context. We introduce a variable z which can be treated as a group of items with similar features or attributes. Therefore, $p(v|u,y)$ can be calculated as:

$$p(v|u,y) = \sum_z p(z|y)p(v|u,z)$$

Since items sharing similar preferences from users are clustered into one item community, most of the ratings from one user in the community will fall into the same rating range. We assume that the ratings from a certain user on all items in the community satisfy a Gaussian distribution:

$$p(v|u,z) = p(v;\mu,\sigma) = \frac{1}{\sqrt{2\pi}\sigma}\exp[-\frac{(v-\mu)^2}{2\sigma^2}]$$

Therefore, the deterministic prediction function $g(u,y)$ that predicts the user's rating on item y can be computed as:

$$g(u,y) = \int_v v p(v\,|\,u,y)\,dv = \int_v \sum_z p(z\,|\,y) p(v\,|\,u,z) v\,dv$$

$$= \sum_z p(z\,|\,y) \int_v p(v\,|\,u,z) v\,dv = \sum_z p(z\,|\,y) \mu_{u,z}$$

The user's rating on item y can be regarded as the sum of the product of $\mu_{u,z}$ (the average rating of user u in community z) and the posteriori probability $p(z|y)$ which depends on the relationship between item y and item community z.

3   Parameter Estimation

There are various ways to estimate the parameters. One of the ways to estimate the posteriori probability $p(z|y)$ is to use Bayes' rule.

$$p(z\,|\,y) = \frac{p(y\,|\,z)p(z)}{\sum_{z'=1}^{k} p(y\,|\,z')p(z')} = \frac{ED'(V_y,V_z)^{-1}\frac{|C_z|}{|C_Y|}}{\sum_{z'=1}^{k} ED'(V_y,V_{z'})^{-1}\frac{|C_{z'}|}{|C_Y|}} = \frac{ED'(V_y,V_z)^{-1}\,|C_z|}{\sum_{z'=1}^{k} ED'(V_y,V_{z'})^{-1}\,|C_{z'}|}$$

where V_y denotes the rating vector of item y and V_z denotes the centre vector of variable z. C_z and C_y are the set of the community z and the set of all items, respectively. $ED'(.)$ is a function of adjusted Euclidean distance between items. $p(z)$ is computed as the ratio of the items falling into the community z over all items. We assume that the relationship between the item y and the item community is determined by the Euclidean distance. A shorter distance represents a closer relationship. We found it helpful to adjust the Euclidean distance of two items based on ratings made by the same user; if the number of common ratings made by the same user was below a certain threshold β:

$$ED'(V_y,V_z) = \frac{\max(|V_y \hbar V_z|, \beta)}{\beta} ED(V_y,V_z)$$

where $|V_y \hbar V_z|$ is the number of common ratings made by the same user. By doing this, the items with more common ratings in calculating Euclidean distance have a high credit.

3.1   Creation of Aggregate Features

In order to get V_z, we should create the item community z. A data clustering method obviously plays an important role in creating such a community. To deal with the three challenges in CF in general and clustering in particular, we group items not only based on user ratings but also on the attributes of items. Our CMRS is developed for recommending ring tones for cell phone users. Most of ring tones are not tagged with abstract attributes such as genre information. It is also time-consuming and tedious to manually tag the genre information for each ring tone. Therefore, we cluster items (ring tones) based on the physical features such as timbral texture, rhythmic content and pitch content features to create some aggregate features, which can be treated more or less as the genre attribute. The clustering method to transfer physical features into aggregate features is derived from K-means Clustering Algorithm [8], which is extended in such a way that we apply the fuzzy set theory to represent the affiliation of objects with cliques (aggregate features). The probability of one object j (here one object denotes a piece of music) assigned to a certain clique k is

$$\Pr o(j,k) = 1 - \frac{DS(j,k)}{MaxDS(i,k)}$$

where the $DS(j,k)$ denotes the Euclidean distance between object j and the centre of clique k ; $Max\ DS(i,k)$ denotes the maximum Euclidean distance between an object and the centre of clique k .

3.2 Item Community Creation

After getting the aggregate features of items, we attach those aggregate features to the user-rating matrix as shown in Fig 1. As a result, we are able to build the item community z based on both ratings and aggregate features.

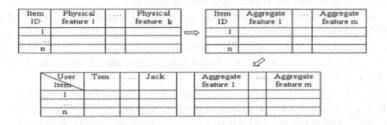

Fig. 1. Procedure to extend the user-rating matrix

Our clustering method for building community z is derived from the well-known k-Medoids clustering algorithm [8]. Informally, our algorithm creates a fixed number k , which is the number of communities, and then creates a composite object profile for each community as the representative of a community. The representative is a composite item that is the average of corresponding user ratings from the members of the community. The measure we use to compute the similarity between objects is the Pearson correlation coefficient. In effect, we are computing the extent to which two items are similar based on the extended rating matrix as shown in Fig.1, which contains both user ratings and aggregate features. In addition, we do not consider the effect of negative correlations, because the clustering algorithm considered is not designed to handle negative similarities. Following is the detail of our clustering algorithm:

1. Select k items at random to serve as initial cluster centers.
2. Assign each object to the ``best" cluster. An object's best cluster is defined to be the one whose center is best correlated with the object. The new center is the object that has the best overall correlation with all the other objects in the cluster. The Pearson correlation between an item and all of its other cluster members is applied as our measure of "best.

$$COR_z(k) = \sum_{l \in z \wedge k \neq l} sim'(k,l) = \sum_{l \in z \wedge k \neq l} \frac{Max(|I_k \cap I_l|, \gamma)}{\gamma} sim(k,l)$$

where $COR_z(k)$ denotes the correlation between the object k and its cluster z; $sim(k,l)$ is the Pearson correlation between object k and l; $|I_k \cap I_l|$ is the number of common ratings made by the same user; γ is the threshold.

3. Repeat steps 2 and 3 until the clusters are stabilized, i.e. no objects are assigned to new clusters.
4. Create a representative of each cluster.

3.3 Feature Extraction

Audio physical features extracted to create aggregate features should be helpful to distinguish music pieces. They can express some aspects of audio such as genre and rhythm. Our CMRS is designed for recommending ring tones for cellphone users, who usually select a ring tone by its rhyme. In this case, the aggregate features obtained from the vivid rhythmic, timbral and pitch content physical features are more meaningful to users than the textual description of genre.

Many of the previous reports on audio features are based on the retrieval of data from MIDI (Musical Instrument Digital Interface) corpora, where the files are symbolized by musical scores. However, considering the popularity of MP3 (MPEG Layer 3) digital music archives, we build our system based on audio features extracted from a MP3 music corpus.

Musical genre classification of audio signals has been studied by many researchers [20], which gave us some hints in selecting audio features to distinguish music objects in our CMRS. Three feature sets for representing timbral texture, rhythmic and pitch content were proposed, and the performance and relative importance of the proposed features was examined by our system using real-world MPEG audio corpus.

Timbral Texture Features. are based on the standard features proposed for music-speech discrimination [20] as follows.

- Mel Frequency Cepstral Coefficients (MFCC): They are a set of perceptually motivated features and provide a compact representation of the spectral envelope such that most of the signal energy is concentrated in the first coefficients. The feature vector for describing timbral texture consists of the following features: means and variances of spectral Centroid, RollOff, Flux, SSF and first five MFCC coefficients over the texture window.
- Spectral Centroid: It is the balancing point of the subband energy distribution and determines the frequency area around which most of the signal energy concentrates.
- Spectral rolloff point: It is used to distinguish voice speech from unvoiced music, which has a higher rolloff point because their power is better distributed over the subband range.
- Spectral Flux: It determines changes of spectral energy distribution of two successive windows.
- Sum of scale factor (SSF): the loudness distribution for whole duration.

Rhythmic Content Features. for representing rhythm structure are based on detecting the most salient periodicities of the signal. Gorge's method [20] is applied to construct the beat histogram, from which six features are calculated to represent rhythmic content.

- A0, A1: relative amplitude of the first and second histogram peak;
- RA: ratio of the amplitude of the second peak divided by the amplitude of the first peak;
- P1, P2: period of the first, second peak in bpm;
- SUM: overall sum of the histogram (indication of beat strength).

Pitch Content Features. describe the melody and harmony information about music signals and are extracted based on various pitch detection techniques [20]. Basically the dominant peaks of the autocorrelation function, calculated via the summation of envelopes for each frequency band obtained by decomposing the signal, are accumulated into pitch histograms and the pitch content features are then extracted from the pitch histograms. The pitch content features typically include: the amplitudes and periods of maximum peaks in the histogram, pitch intervals between the two most prominent peaks, the overall sums of the histograms. Because the different magnitude of features, we mapped all audio features into [0 1].

4   Experimental Evaluation

Experiments were carried out to observe the recommendation performance of our approach, especially in comparison with other methods, and to determine the parameter values in our approach. Experimental data came from a real-word music corpus that consists of sample files of mobile phone ring tones for campus users of Harbin Engineering University. It has 760 pieces of music and 4,340 integer ratings ranging from 1~5 made by 128 users. The music is stored as 22050Hz, 16-bit, mono MP3 audio files. Each piece of music lasts for about 10~20 seconds which is extracted from its corresponding entire song. The entire music data is categorized into 9 genres (Classical, Jazz, Rock, Hip-Hop, Country, Disco, Metal, Chinese Popular, and Chinese Traditional Classical).

4.1   Evaluation Metrics

MAE (Mean Absolute Error) has widely been used in evaluating the accuracy of a recommender system. It is calculated by averaging the absolute errors in rating-prediction pairs as follows:

$$MAE = \frac{\sum_{j=1}^{N} | P_{i,j} - R_{i,j} |}{N}$$

where $P_{i,j}$ is system's rating (prediction) of item j for user i, and $R_{i,j}$ is the rating of user i for item j in the test data. N is the number of rating-prediction pairs between the test data and the prediction result. A lower MAE means a greater accuracy. Allbut1 [1] protocol was applied to evaluate the obtained prediction accuracies. More precisely, we randomly left out exactly one rating for every user who possesses at least two ratings. Notice that this uses somewhat less data than required, but allows us to use a single model to evaluate the leave-one-out performance averaged over all users. We have repeated the leave-one-out procedure 25 times with different random seeds. The reported numbers are the mean performance averaged over those runs.

4.2 Community Size

The item community is the representative of music with the similar patterns. In our clustering phase, we classify the objects into k groups. In the case that k equals to 1, it means that all objects are treated as one community. In figure 2, it is observed that the number of communities affects the quality of prediction to a great extent, and the optimal performance is achieved with k=50.

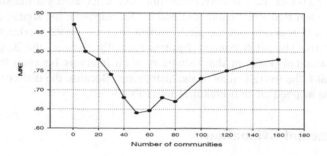

Fig. 2. Sensitivity of the community size

4.3 Audio Features

The performance of our CMRS rests on the valuable information extracted from audio features. In our approach, we integrate this information by creating aggregate features. Another factor that had to be determined was the number of aggregate features which might be also sensitive to the performance. However, we found that the recommendation performance is not very sensitive to the number of aggregate features. It only makes the performance difference of less than 0.02, as shown in Figure 3. In our experiments, we set it to 40.

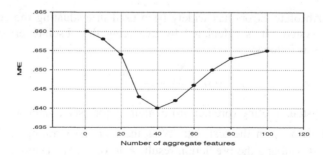

Fig. 3. Sensitivity of the aggregate features

4.4 Overall Performance

In order to observe the contribution of content information of music objects, we implemented a standard memory-based method, a Simple Pearson method [1], and a standard item-based CF [17] method to be compared with our approach. As shown in Table 2, our approach has a better performance than the others, which indicates we can get useful information from audio features of music.

Table 2. Comparison

Method	MAE	% Improvement
Pearson Method	0.78	-
Item-based CF	0.69	11.5%
Our approach	0.64	17.9%

How Do the Audio Features Affect Performances? In order to observe the performance and relative importance of the proposed features, we carried out a series of experiments. In other words, we constructed the aggregate features by individual audio physical features. As shown in Figure 4, it is clear to observe that MFCC, Centroid and RollOff are a little more effective than other feature sets.

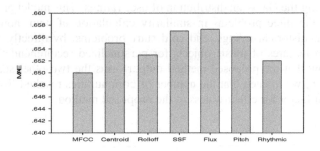

Fig. 4. Individual contributions of audio features

We then carried out a series of experiments with a combination of two audio features to construct the aggregate features. From these experiments, we find that the combination of MFCC and Rhythm achieve a better performance than other combinations. We further carried out our experiments using the combination of three audio features to construct the aggregate features. The conclusion is that the combination of MFCC, RollOff and Rhythm shows the best performance over all other combinations of three audio features, as shown in Figure 5, where No. 1, 2and 3 refer to MFCC, RollOff and Rhythm accordingly. In Figure 5, the word "Genre" represents that using the textual genre description for recommending the ring tone instead of the aggregate features of audio pieces. The aggregate features obtained from the physical features of audio pieces shows a better performance than the textual genre description. It reveals that mobile phone users select their preference not based on the genre information but on other physical features such as rhythm, timbre and pitch. By realizing this, our CMRS is designed to apply both physical features of music and user ratings for better personalized recommendation.

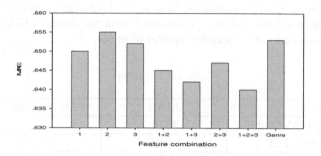

Fig. 5. Contribution Comparison of Audio features

5   Conclusion

In this paper, we described a collaborative music recommender system for online mobile phone ring tones. It is based on our proposed item-based probabilistic model, where items are classified into groups or communities and predictions are made for users considering the Gaussian distribution of user ratings. This model provides a way of alleviating the three problems in similarity calculation of item, non-association, user bias from historical ratings, and cold start problems, by directly applying the physical audio features of music objects for personalized recommendation. Our experiments show that the proposed method outperforms the two other standard methods. In addition, we learned that the number of communities resulted from clustering is an important factor for effectiveness of the proposed method.

References

1. Breese, J. S., D. Heckerman, and C. Kardie: Empirical Analysis of Predictive Algorithms for Collaborative Filtering. In Proc. Of the 14th Conference on Uncertainty in Artificial Intelligence, pp.43-52, (1998).
2. Balabanovic, M. and Shoham, Y.: Fab: Content-Based, Collaborative Recommendation. Communications of the ACM, 40(3), pp.66-72. (1997).
3. Claypool, M., Gokhale, A., Miranda, T., Murnikov, P., Netes, D. and Sartin, M.: Combining content-based and collaborative filters in an online newspaper. In Proc. ACM-SIGIR Workshop on Recommender Systems: Algorithms and Evaluation. (1999).
4. Delgado, J., Ishii, N. and Ura, T.: Content-based Collaborative Information Filtering: Actively Learning to Classify and Recommend Documents. In Proc. Second Int. Workshop, CIA'98, pp.206-215 (1998)
5. Fisher, D., Kris Hildrum, Jason Hong, Mark Newman, Megan Thomas, Rich Vuduc: SWAMI: a framework for collaborative filtering algorithm development and evaluation. In Proc. of ACM SIGIR-00, (2000).

6. Ghias, A., Logan, J., Chamberlin, D., and Smith, BC.: Query By Humming Musical Information Retrieval in An Audio Database. ACM multimedia, (1995).
7. Gupta, D., Digiovanni, M., Narita, H. and Goldberg, K.: Jester 2.0: A New Linear-Time Collaborative Filtering Algorithm Applied to Jokes. In Proc. ACM-SIGIR Workshop on Recommender Systems, (1999).
8. Han, J., and Kamber, M.: Data mining: Concepts and Techniques. New York: Morgan-Kaufman, (2000).
9. Hauver, D. B.. Flycasting: Using Collaborative Filtering to Generate a Play list for Online Radio. In Int. Conf. on Web Delivery of Music, (2001).
10. Hofmann,T.: Collaborative Filtering via Gaussian Probabilistic Latent Semantic Analysis. In Proc. SIGIR'03,(2003).
11. O'Conner, M. and Herlocker, J.: Clustering items for collaborative filtering. In Proc. ACM-SIGIR Workshop on Recommender Systems, (1999).
12. Qing Li, Byeong Man Kim: Clustering Approach for Hybrid Recommender System. In Proc. of the 2003 IEEE Web Intelligence (WI 2003), pp. 33-38, (2003).
13. Qing Li, Byeong Man Kim, J.W. Kim, J. Kim: A New Collaborative Recommender System Addressing three Problems. Lecture Notes in Artificial Intelligence, Volume 3157, Springer, (2004).
14. Qing Li, Byeong Man Kim: Constructing User Profiles for Collaborative Recommender System. In Proc. of Apweb2004, Lecture Notes in Computer Science (LNCS) Volume 3007, p100-110, Springer, (2004).
15. Qing Li, B.M. Kim, G. D. Hai, D.H Oh: A Collaborative Music Recommender based on Audio Features. In ACM SIGIR-04, Sheffield, UK,(2004).
16. Resnick, P., Iacovou, N., Suchak, M., Bergstorm, P. and Riedl, J.: GroupLens: An open architecture for collaborative filtering of Netnews. In Proc. ACM Conf. on Computer-Supported Cooperative Work. pp.175-186, (1994).
17. Sarwar, B. M., Karypis, G., Konstan, J. A. and Riedl, J.: Item-based Collaborative Filtering Recommendation Algorithms. In Proc. Tenth Int. WWW Conf. 2001, pp. 285-295, (2001).
18. Salton, G. and McGill: Introduction to Modern Information Retrieval, McGraw-Hill, New York, (1983).
19. Shardanand, U. and Maes: Social information filtering: Algorithms for automating "word of mouth". In Proc.of CHI'95 , pp 210-217, (1995).
20. Tzanetakis, George and Perry Cook: Music Genre Classification of Audio Signals. IEEE Transactions on speech and audio processing, Vol.10 No.5, (2002).
21. Wasfi, A. M. A.: Collecting User Access Patterns for Building user Profiles and Collaborative Filtering, In Int. Conf. on Intelligent User Interfaces. pp.57- 64 (1999).
22. Wittenburg, K., Das, D., Hill, W. and Stead, L.: Group Asynchronous Browsing on the World Wide Web. In Proc. of the 4th WWW, pp.51-62, (1995).

VisMed: A Visual Vocabulary Approach for Medical Image Indexing and Retrieval

Joo-Hwee Lim[1] and Jean-Pierre Chevallet[2]

[1] Institute for Infocomm Research,
21 Heng Mui Keng Terrace, Singapore 119613
joohwee@i2r.a-star.edu.sg
[2] Image Processing and Application Lab (IPAL),
French National Center for Scientific Research (CNRS),
21 Heng Mui Keng Terrace, Singapore 119613
Jean-Pierre.Chevallet@imag.fr

Abstract. Voluminous medical images are generated daily. They are critical assets for medical diagnosis, research, and teaching. To facilitate automatic indexing and retrieval of large medical image databases, we propose a structured framework for designing and learning vocabularies of meaningful medical terms associated with visual appearance from image samples. These VisMed terms span a new feature space to represent medical image contents. After a multi-scale detection process, a medical image is indexed as compact spatial distributions of VisMed terms. A flexible tiling (FlexiTile) matching scheme is proposed to compare the similarity between two medical images of arbitrary aspect ratios.

We evaluate the VisMed approach on the medical retrieval task of the ImageCLEF 2004 benchmark. Based on 2% of the 8725 CasImage collection, we cropped 1170 image regions to train and validate 40 VisMed terms using support vector machines. The Mean Average Precision (MAP) over 26 query topics is 0.4156, an improvement over all the automatic runs in ImageCLEF 2004.

1 Introduction

Medical images are an integral part in medical diagnosis, research, and teaching. Medical image analysis research has focused on image registration, measurement, and visualization. Although large amounts of medical images are produced in hospitals every day, there is relatively less research in medical content-based image retrieval (CBIR) [1]. Besides being valuable for medical research and training, medical CBIR systems also have a role to play in clinical diagnosis [2]. For instance, for less experienced radiologists, a common practice is to use a reference text to find images that are similar to the query image [3]. Hence, medical CBIR systems can assist doctors in diagnosis by retrieving images with known pathologies that are similar to a patient's image(s).

Among the limited research efforts of medical CBIR, classification or clustering driven feature selection and weighting has received much attention as

G.G. Lee et al. (Eds.): AIRS 2005, LNCS 3689, pp. 84–96, 2005.

general visual cues often fail to be discriminative enough to deal with more subtle, domain-specific differences and more objective ground truth in the form of disease categories is usually available [3,4].

In reality, pathology bearing regions tend to be highly localized [3]. Hence, local features such as those extracted from segmented dominant image regions approximated by best fitting ellipses have been proposed [5]. A hierarchical graph-based representation and matching scheme has been suggested to deal with multi-scale image decomposition and their spatial relationships [5]. However, it has been recognized that pathology bearing regions cannot be segmented out automatically for many medical domains [1]. As an alternative, a comprehensive set of 15 perceptual categories related to pathology bearing regions and their discriminative features are carefully designed and tuned for high-resolution CT lung images to achieve superior precision rates over a brute-force feature selection approach [1].

Hence, it is desirable to have a medical CBIR system that represents images in terms of semantic local features, that can be learned from examples (rather than handcrafted with a lot of expert input) and do not rely on robust region segmentation. In this paper, we propose a structured learning framework to build meaningful medical terms associated with visual appearance from image samples. These *VisMed* terms span a new feature space to represent medical image contents. After a segmentation-free multi-scale detection process, a medical image is indexed as compact spatial distributions of VisMed terms. A flexible tiling (FlexiTile) matching scheme is also proposed to compare the similarity between two medical images of arbitrary aspect ratios.

Indeed, the US National Cancer Institute has launched a cooperative effort known as the Lung Image Database Consortium (LIDC) to develop an image database that will serve as an international research resource for the development, training, and evaluation of computer-aided diagnostic (CAD) methods in the detection of lung nodules on CT scans. One of the key efforts is to create a visual nodule library with images of lesions that span the focal abnormality spectrum and the subset nodule spectrum [6]. All lesions have been characterized by a panel of experienced thoracic radiologists based on attributes that include shape, margin, internal structure, and subtlety. The library is intended to serve as a standard for the development of a practical radiologic definition of nodule as radiologists believe that "the expertise of the interpreter lies in a vast experience of seeing many thousands of radiologic patterns and sythesizing them into a coherent, organized, and searchable mental matrix of diagnostic meaning and pathologic features" [7].

In this paper, we evaluate the VisMed approach on ImageCLEF 2004 medical retrieval task. Based on 2% of the 8725 CasImage data, we cropped 1170 image regions to train and validate 40 VisMed terms using support vector machines [8]. The Mean Average Precision over 26 query topics is 0.4156, an increase over all the automatic runs in ImageCLEF 2004. We detail the VisMed framework and evaluation in the next two sections respectively.

2 VisMed: A Structured Learning Framework for Medical CBIR

In this paper, we aim to bridge the semantic gap between low-level visual features (e.g. texture, color) and high-level semantic terms (e.g. brain, lung, heart) in medical images for content-based indexing and retrieval. At the moment, we focus on visual semantics that can be directly extracted from image content (without the use of associated text) with computer vision techniques.

In order to manage large and complex set of visual entities (i.e. high content diversity) in the medical domain, we propose a structured learning framework to facilitate modular design and extraction of medical visual semantics, VisMed terms, in building content-based medical image retrieval systems.

VisMed terms are segmentation-free image regions that exhibit semantic meanings to medical practitioners and that can be learned statistically to span a new indexing space. They are detected in image content, reconciled across multiple resolutions, and aggregated spatially to form local semantic histograms. The resulting compact and abstract representation can support both similarity-based query and compositional visual query efficiently. In this paper, we only report evaluation results for similarity-based retrieval (i.e. query by image examples). For the unique compositional visual query method and its evaluation based on consumer images, please refer to another regular paper in the same proceeding [9]. We have also performed the semantic-based query based on the compositional visual query method for ImageCLEF 2005 queries and dataset. We will report this work elsewhere in the near future.

2.1 Learning of VisMed Terms

VisMed terms are typical semantic tokens with visual appearance in medical images (e.g. X-ray-lung, CT-head-brain, MRI-abdomen-liver, mouth-teeth). They are defined using image region instances cropped from sample images and modeled based on statistical learning.

In this paper, we have adopted color and texture features as well as support vector machines (SVMs) [8] for VisMed term representation and learning respectively though the framework is not dependent on a particular feature and classifier. The notion of using a visual vocabulary to represent and index image contents for more effective (i.e. semantic) query and retrieval has been proposed and applied to consumer images [10,11].

To compute VisMed terms from training instances, we use SVMs on color and texture features for an image region and denote this feature vector as z. A SVM $\mathcal{S}_k$ is a detector for VisMed term k on z. The classification vector T for region z is computed via the softmax function [12] as

$$T_k(z) = \frac{\exp^{\mathcal{S}_k(z)}}{\sum_j \exp^{\mathcal{S}_j(z)}}. \tag{1}$$

That is, $T_k(z)$ corresponds to a VisMed entry in the 40-dimensional vector T adopted in this paper.

In our experiments, we use the YIQ color space over other color spaces (e.g. RGB, HSV, LUV) as it performed better in our experiments. For the texture feature, we adopted the Gabor coefficients which have been shown to provide excellent pattern retrieval results [13].

A feature vector z has two parts, namely, a color feature vector z^c and a texture feature vector z^t. We compute the mean and standard deviation of each YIQ color channel and the Gabor coefficients (5 scales, 6 orientations) respectively [11]. Hence the color feature vector z^c has 6 dimensions and the texture feature vector z^t has 60 dimensions. Zero-mean normalization [14] was applied to both the color and texture features. In our evaluation described below, we adopted RBF kernels with modified city-block distance between feature vectors y and z,

$$|y - z| = \frac{1}{2}(\frac{|y^c - z^c|}{N_c} + \frac{|y^t - z^t|}{N_t}) \qquad (2)$$

where N_c and N_t are the numbers of dimensions of the color and texture feature vectors (i.e. 6 and 60) respectively. This just-in-time feature fusion within the kernel combines the contribution of color and texture features equally. It is simpler and more effective than other feature fusion methods that we have attempted.

2.2   Image Indexing Based on VisMed Terms

After learning, the VisMed terms are detected during image indexing from multi-scale block-based image patches without region segmentation to form semantic local histograms as described below.

Conceptually, the indexing is realized in a three-layer visual information processing architecture. The bottom layer denotes the pixel-feature maps computed for feature extraction. In our experiments, there are 3 color maps (i.e. YIQ channels) and 30 texture maps (i.e. Gabor coefficients of 5 scales and 6 orientations). From these maps, feature vectors z^c and z^t compatible with those adopted for VisMed term learning (Equation (2)) are extracted.

To detect VisMed terms with translation and scale invariance in an image to be indexed, the image is scanned with windows of different scales, similar to the strategy in view-based object detection [15,16]. More precisely, given an image I with resolution $M \times N$, the middle layer, Reconciled Detection Map (RDM), has a lower resolution of $P \times Q, P \leq M, Q \leq N$. Each pixel (p, q) in RDM corresponds to a two-dimensional region of size $r_x \times r_y$ in I. We further allow tessellation displacements $d_x, d_y > 0$ in X, Y directions respectively such that adjacent pixels in RDM along X direction (along Y direction) have receptive fields in I which are displaced by d_x pixels along X direction (d_y pixels along Y direction) in I. At the end of scanning an image, each pixel (p, q) that covers a region z in the pixel-feature layer will consolidate the classification vector $T_k(z)$ (Equation (1)).

In our experiments, we progressively increase the window size $r_x \times r_y$ from 20×20 to 60×60 at a displacement (d_x, d_y) of $(10, 10)$ pixels, on a 240×360 size-normalized image. That is, after the detection step, we have 5 maps of detection of dimensions 23×35 to 19×31, which are reconciled into a common RDM as explained below.

To reconcile the detection maps across different resolutions onto a common basis, we adopt the following principle: If the most confident classification of a region at resolution r is less than that of a larger region (at resolution $r + 1$) that subsumes the region, then the classification output of the region should be replaced by those of the larger region at resolution $r + 1$. For instance, if the detection of a face is more confident than that of a building at the nose region (assuming that both face and building (but not nose) are in the visual vocabulary designed for a particular application), then the entire region covered by the face, which subsumes the nose region, should be labeled as face.

To illustrate the point, suppose a region at resolution r is covered by 4 larger regions at resolution $r + 1$ as shown in Figure 1. Let $\rho = max_k max_i T_i(z_k^{r+1})$ where k refers to one of the 4 larger regions in the case of the example shown in Figure 1. Then the principle of reconciliation says that if $max_i T_i(z^r) < \rho$, the classification vector $T_i(z^r)$ $\forall i$ should be replaced by the classification vector $T_i(z_m^{r+1})$ $\forall i$ where $max_i T_i(z_m^{r+1}) = \rho$.

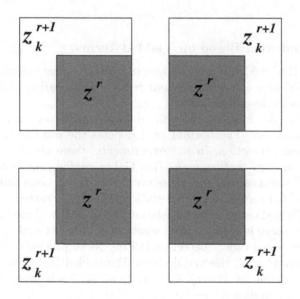

Fig. 1. Reconciling multi-scale VisMed detection maps

Using this principle, we compare detection maps of two consecutive resolutions at a time, in descending window sizes (i.e. from windows of 60×60 and 50×50 to windows of 30×30 and 20×20). After 4 cycles of reconciliation, the detection map that is based on the smallest scan window (20×20) would have consolidated the detection decisions obtained at other resolutions for further spatial aggregation.

The purpose of spatial aggregation is to summarize the reconciled detection outcome in a larger spatial region. Suppose a region Z comprises of n small equal regions with feature vectors $z_1, z_2, \cdots, z_n$ respectively. To account for the size of detected VisMed terms in the spatial area Z, the classification vectors of the reconciled detection map are aggregated as

$$T_k(Z) = \frac{1}{n} \sum_i T_k(z_i). \tag{3}$$

This is the top layer in our three-layer visual information processing architecture where a Spatial Aggregation Map (SAM) further tessellates over RDM with $A \times B, A \leq P, B \leq Q$ pixels. This form of spatial aggregation does not encode spatial relation explicity. But the design flexibility of s_x, s_y in SAM on RDM (the equivalent of r_x, r_y in RDM on I) allows us to specify the location and extent in the content to be focused and indexed. We can choose to ignore unimportant areas (e.g. margins) and emphasize certain areas with overlapping tessellation. We can even have different weights attached to the areas during similarity matching.

To facilitate spatial aggregation and matching of image with different aspect ratios ρ, we design 5 tiling templates for Eq. (3), namely $3 \times 1, 3 \times 2, 3 \times 3, 2 \times 3$, and 1×3 grids resulting in 3, 6, 9, 6, and 3 $T_k(Z)$ vectors per image respectively. Since the tiling templates have aspect ratios of 3, 1.5, and 1, the decision thresholds to assign a template for an image are set to their mid-points (2.25 and 1.25) as $\rho > 2.25, 1.25 < \rho \leq 2.25$, and $\rho \leq 1.25$ respectively based on $\rho = \frac{L}{S}$ where L and S refer to the longer and shorter sides of an image respectively. For more details on detection-based indexing, readers are referred to [11].

2.3 FlexiTile Matching

Given two images represented as different grid patterns, we propose a flexible tiling (FlexiTile) matching scheme to cover all possible matches. For instance, given a query image Q of 3×1 grid and an image Z of 3×3 grid, intuitively Q should be compared to each of the 3 columns in Z and the highest similarity will be treated as the final matching score. As another example, consider matching a 3×2 grid with 2×3 grid. The 4 possible tiling and matching choices are shown in Fig. 2.

The FlexiTile matching scheme is formalized as follows. Suppose a query image Q and a database image Z are represented as $M_1 \times N_1$ and $M_2 \times N_2$ grids respectively. The overlaping grid $M \times N$ where $M = \min(M_1, M_2)$ and $N = \min(N_1, N_2)$ is the maximal matching area. The similarity λ between Q and Z is the maximum matching among all possible $M \times N$ tilings,

$$\lambda(Q, Z) = \max_{\substack{m_1=1, n_1=1}}^{\substack{m_1=u_1, n_1=v_1}} \max_{\substack{m_2=1, n_2=1}}^{\substack{m_2=u_2, n_2=v_2}} \lambda(Q_{m_1, n_1}, Z_{m_2, n_2}), \tag{4}$$

where $u_1 = M_1 - M + 1, v_1 = N_1 - N + 1, u_2 = M_2 - M + 1, v_2 = N_2 - N + 1$ and the similarity for each tiling $\lambda(Q_{m_1, n_1}, Z_{m_2, n_2})$ is defined as the average similarity over $M \times N$ blocks as

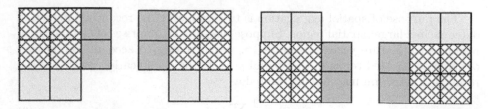

Fig. 2. Example to illustrate FlexiTile matching

$$\lambda(Q_{m_1,n_1}, Z_{m_2,n_2}) = \frac{\sum_i \sum_j \lambda_{ij}(Q_{m_1,n_1}, Z_{m_2,n_2})}{M \times N}, \tag{5}$$

and finally the similarity $\lambda_{ij}(Q_{m_1,n_1}, Z_{m_2,n_2})$ between two image blocks is computed based on L_1 distance measure (city block distance) as,

$$\lambda_{ij}(Q_{m_1,n_1}, Z_{m_2,n_2}) = 1 - \frac{1}{2} \sum_k |T_k(Q_{p_1,q_1}) - T_k(Z_{p_2,q_2})| \tag{6}$$

where $p_1 = m_1 + i, q_1 = n_1 + j, p_2 = m_2 + i, q_2 = n_2 + j$ and it is equivalent to color histogram intersection except that the bins have semantic interpretation as VisMed terms.

There is a trade-off between content symmetry and spatial specificity. If we want images of similar semantics with different spatial arrangement (e.g. mirror images) to be treated as similar, we can have larger tessellated block in SAM (i.e. the extreme case is a global histogram). However in applications such as medical images where there is usually very small variance in views and spatial locations are considered differentiating across images, local histograms will provide good sensitivity to spatial specificity. Furthermore, we can attach different weights to the blocks to emphasize the focus of attention (e.g. center) if necessary. In this paper, we report experimental results based on even weights as grid tessellation is used.

3   Experimental Evaluation

As part of the Cross Language Evaluation Forum (CLEF), the ImageCLEF 2004 track [17] that promotes cross language image retrieval has initiated a new medical retrieval task in 2004. The goal of the medical task is to find images that are similar with respect to modality (e.g. Computed Tomography (CT), Magnetic Resonance Imaging (MRI), X-ray etc), the shown anatomic region (e.g. lung, liver, head etc) and sometimes with respect to the radiologic protocol (e.g. T1/T2 for MRI (contrast agents alter selectively the image intensity of a particular anatomical or functional region)).

The dataset is called the CasImage database and it consists of 8725 anonymized medical images, e.g. scans, and X-rays from the University Hospitals of Geneva (visit www.casimage.com for example images). Most images are associated with case notes, a written English or French description of a previous diagnosis for an illness the image identifies. The case notes reflect real clinical data in that it is incomplete and erroneous. The medical task requires that the first query step has to be visual (i.e. query by image example). Although identifying images referring to similar medical conditions is non-trivial and may require the use of visual content and additional semantic information in the case notes, we evaluate the VisMed approach on the medical task without using the case notes in this paper.

In the ImageCLEF 2004 medical retrieval task, 26 topics were selected with the help of a radiologist which represented the database well. Each topic is denoted by a query image (Fig. 3). An image pool was created for each topic by computing the union overlap of submissions and judged by three assessors to create several assessment sets. The task description of the 26 topics given to the assessors is listed in Table 1. The relevance set of images judged as either relevant or partially relevant by at least two assessors is used to evaluate retrieval performance in terms of uninterpolated mean average precision (MAP) computed across all topics using trec_eval. The sizes of the relevance sets for each topic are listed in the rightmost column in Table 1.

We evaluate the VisMed approach on the medical retrieval task of the ImageCLEF 2004 benchmark. We designed 40 VisMed terms that correspond to typical semantic regions in the CasImage database (Table 2). While the first 30 VisMed terms are defined on grey-level images, the last 10 VisMed terms are for the minority of color images. Note that "print-sketch" and "print-slide" refer to drawing and text in presentation slides respectively. With a uniform VisMed framework, dark background in the scan images (e.g. CT, MRI) and empty areas in drawing etc are simply modeled as dummy terms instead of using image preprocessing to detect them separately.

Based on 172 (approx. 2%) of the 8725 image collection, we cropped 1170 image regions with 20 to 40 positive samples for each VisMed term (Table 2). For a given VisMed term, the negative samples are the union of the positive samples of all the other 39 VisMed terms. The 172 images are selected to cover different appearances of the 40 VisMed terms. We ensure that they do not contain any of the 26 query images though Q06, Q15, Q16, and Q22 have a total of 7 duplications in the database.

The odd and even entries of the cropped regions are used as training and validation sets respectively (i.e. 585 each) to optimize the RBF kernel parameter of support vector machines. The best generalization performance with mean error 1.44% on the validation set was obtained with $C = 100, \alpha = 0.5$ [18]. Both the training and validation sets are then combined to form a larger training set to train a new set of 40 VisMed SVM detectors.

Both query and database images are indexed and matched using the framework as described in the previous section (Eq. (1) to (6)). However, to avoid spurious matching between very different grids (e.g. 3×1 and 1×3), we set the similarity to zero if the difference in a grid dimension between two image indexes is more than one. That is, two images are considered dissimilar if they exhibit

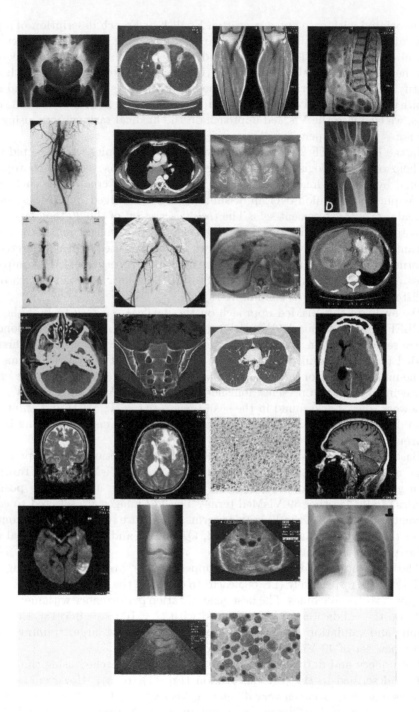

Fig. 3. Query images for the 26 topics

Table 1. Topic description for assessors and relevant set sizes

Query	Task Description	#
Q01	Frontal/Radiography/Pelvis	235
Q02	Axial/CT/Lung	320
Q03	Coronal/MRI/Legs	72
Q04	Sagittal/MRI/Abdomen & Spine	43
Q05	Arteriography/Contrast Agent	84
Q06	Abdominal CT Mediastin	252
Q07	Mouth photos showing Teeth	48
Q08	Radiography/Wrist	117
Q09	Szintigraphy/almost entire body	43
Q10	Arteriography/Contrast Agent	79
Q11	Axial/MRI/Liver	9
Q12	Abdominal CT/Liver	179
Q13	Axial/CT/Head with facial bones	95
Q14	Oblique cut/CT/Sacrum	11
Q15	Axial/CT/Lung	252
Q16	Horizontal/CT/Head, Cerebral	141
Q17	Coronal/MRI/Head/T2	31
Q18	Axial/MRI/Brain/T2	78
Q19	Histology/Cells/Color/Size	114
Q20	Sagittal/MRI/Head	27
Q21	Horizontal/MRI/Head/Diffusion	90
Q22	Frontal/Radiography/Knee Joint	171
Q23	Ultrasound/No colored parts	74
Q24	Frontal/Radiography/Thorax	409
Q25	Ultrasound/With colored parts	64
Q26	Hematology/Similar colors, size	53

very different aspect ratios. The MAP over 26 query topics is computed using the same `trec_eval` program used in ImageCLEF 2004.

Table 3 compares the MAPs of the automatic VisMed run with those of the top 5 automatic runs as reported in ImageCLEF 2004 [17] where the percentages of improvement are shown in brackets, "RF" stands for the use of pseudo relevance feedback and "Text" means the case notes were also utilized. The group "Buffalo", "imperial", and "aachen-inf" refer to State Univ. of New York (USA), Imperial College (UK), and Dept. Medical Informatics, RWTH, Aachen (Germany) respectively. All these systems used low-level visual features for image indexing and matching. Details are given in their working notes at `http://clef.isti.cnr.it/`. The best run in ImageCLEF 2004 was a manual run with a MAP value of 0.4214 by the University Hospitals of Geneva.

From Table 3, we conclude that the VisMed approach is very promising. It has attained a MAP of 0.4156, clearly an improvement over all the automatic runs in ImageCLEF 2004. the average precisions at top 10, 20, 30 and 100 retrieved

Table 2. VisMed terms and numbers of region samples

VisMed Terms	#	VisMed Terms	#
arteriography-agent	40	xray-face	40
xray-neck-spine	30	xray-lung	40
xray-pelvis	40	xray-bone	40
xray-finger	30	xray-joint	40
xray-implant	30	ct-head-brain	20
ct-head-bones	20	ct-thorax-lung	30
ct-abdomen-mediastin	30	ct-abdomen-liver	30
ct-abdomen-intestine	20	ct-abdomen-sacrum	30
mri-head-brain	40	mri-head-bones	20
mri-head-face	30	mri-head-diffusion	30
mri-abdomen-spine	40	mri-abdomen-liver	30
mri-pelvis-tissue	40	mri-legs-coronal	40
ultrasound-grey	30	print-scintigraph	40
print-sketch	30	print-slide	20
print-blank	20	print-dark	20
pathology-pink	20	pathology-blue	20
pathology-purple-big	20	pathology-purple	40
pathology-brown	20	pathology-dark	20
ultrasound-color	20	mouth-teeth	20
mouth-tissue	20	mouth-lesion	30

Table 3. Comparison of the VisMed approach with the top 5 automatic runs of ImageCLEF 2004

Group	Run ID	MAP (% up)	RF	Text
VisMed	vismed40	0.4156		
Buffalo	UBMedImTxt01	0.3488 (19.2)		X
imperial	ic_cl04_base	0.3450 (20.5)		
aachen-inf	i6-025501	0.3407 (22.0)		
aachen-inf	i6-qe02555010	0.3323 (25.1)	X	
Buffalo	UBMedImTxt02	0.3309 (25.6)		X

images of the VisMed approach are 0.70, 0.65, 0.60, and 0.41 respectively (similar results for the runs of ImageCLEF 2004 are not available), which we consider reasonable for practical applications.

Representing a medical image as compact spatial distributions (i.e. regular grids of 40 dimensional vectors) of semantically meaningful terms, the VisMed approach also has the following advantages: enables efficient matching, provides explanation based on VisMed terms that are detected and matched, and supports new compositional queries expressed as spatial arrangement of VisMed terms [11].

4   Conclusion

Medical CBIR is an emerging and challenging research area. We have proposed a structured framework for designing image semantics from statistical learning. Using the ImageCLEF 2004 CasImage medical database and retrieval task, we have demonstrated the effectiveness of our framework that is very promising when compared to the current automatic runs [17]. Indeed our adaptive framework is scalable to different image domains [11,19] and embraces other design choices such as better visual features, learning algorithms, object detectors, spatial aggregation and matching schemes when they become available.

We reckon that a limitation of the current VisMed approach is the need to design the VisMed terms manually with labeled image patches as training samples. We have begun some work in a semi-supervised approach to discover meaningful visual vocabularies from minimally labeled image samples [20]. In the near future, we would also explore the integration with inter-class semantics [19] and other source of information such as text. Last but not least, we would also work with medical experts to design a more comprehensive set of VisMed terms to cover all the essential semantics in medical images.

Acknowledgments

We would like to thank Mun-Kew Leong and Changsheng Xu for their feedback on the paper. We also thank T. Joachims for making his SVM^{light} software available.

References

1. Shyu, C., Pavlopoulou, C., Kak, A., Brodley, C.: Using human perceptual categories for content-based retrieval from a medical image database. Computer Vision and Image Understanding **88** (2002) 119–151
2. Muller, H., Michoux, N., Bandon, D., Geissbuhler, A.: A review of content-based image retrieval systems in medical applications – clinical benefits and future directions. Intl. J. of Medical Informatics **73** (2004) 1–23
3. Dy, J., Brodley, C., Kak, A., Broderick, L., Aisen, A.: Unsupervised feature selection applied to content-based retrieval of lung images. IEEE Trans. on PAMI **25** (2003) 373–378
4. Liu, Y., et al.: Semantic based biomedical image indexing and retrieval. In Shapiro, L., Kriegel, H., Veltkamp, R., eds.: Trends and Advances in Content-Based Image and Video Retrieval. Springer (2004)
5. Lehmann, T., et al.: Content-based image retrieval in medical applications. Methods Inf Med **43** (2004) 354–361
6. Armato III, S., et al.: Lung image database consortium: developing a resource for the medical imaging research community. Radiology **232** (2004) 739–748
7. Wood, B.: Visual expertise. Radiology **211** (1999) 1–3
8. Vapnik, V.: Statistical Learning Theory. Wiley, New York (1998)
9. Lim, J., Jin, J., Luo, S.: A structured learning approach to semantic photo indexing and query. In: Proc. of AIRS 2005. (2005) (accepted)

10. Lim, J.: Building visual vocabulary for image indexation and query formulation. Pattern Analysis and Applications **4** (2001) 125–139
11. Lim, J., Jin, J.: A structured learning framework for content-based image indexing and visual query. Multimedia Systems Journal (2005) to appear.
12. Bishop, C.: Neural Networks for Pattern Recognition. Clarendon Press, Oxford (1995)
13. Manjunath, B., Ma, W.: Texture features for browsing and retrieval of image data. IEEE Trans. on PAMI **18** (1996) 837–842
14. Rui, Y., Huang, T., Mehrotra, S.: Content-based image retrieval with relevance feedback in mars. In: Proc. of IEEE ICIP. (1997) 815–818
15. Sung, K., Poggio, T.: Example-based learning for view-based human face detection. IEEE Trans. on PAMI **20** (1998) 39–51
16. Papageorgiou, P., Oren, M., Poggio, T.: A general framework for object detection. In: Proc. of ICCV. (1998) 555–562
17. Clough, P., Sanderson, M., Muller, H.: The clef cross language image retrieval track (imageclef) 2004. http://clef.isti.cnr.it/ (2004)
18. Joachims, T.: Making large-scale svm learning practical. In Scholkopf, B., Burges, C., Smola, A., eds.: Advances in Kernel Methods - Support Vector Learning. MIT-Press (1999) 169–184
19. Lim, J., Jin, J.: Combining intra-image and inter-class semantics for consumer image retrieval. Pattern Recognition **38** (2005) 847–864
20. Lim, J., Jin, J.: Discovering recurrent image semantics from class discrimination. EURASIP Journal of Applied Signal Processing (2005) to appear.

Object Identification and Retrieval
from Efficient Image Matching: Snap2Tell
with the STOIC Dataset

Jean-Pierre Chevallet[1], Joo-Hwee Lim[2], and Mun-Kew Leong[2]

[1] IPAL-CNRS Laboratory, 21 Heng Mui Keng Terrace, Singapore 119613
viscjp@i2r.a-star.edu.sg
[2] Institute for Infocomm Research, 21 Heng Mui Keng Terrace, Singapore 119613
joohwee, mkleong@i2r.a-star.edu.sg

Abstract. Traditional content based image retrieval attempts to retrieve images using syntactic features for a query image. Annotated image banks and Google allow the use of text to retrieve images. In this
paper, we studied the task of using the content of an image to retrieve information in general. We describe the significance of object identification
in an information retrieval paradigm that uses image set as intermediate
means in indexing and matching. We also describe a unique Singapore
Tourist Object Identification Collection with associated queries and relevance judgments for evaluating the new task and the need for efficient
image matching using simple image features. We present comprehensive
experimental evaluation on the effects of feature dimensions, context,
spatial weightings, coverage of image indexes, and query devices on task
performance. Lastly we describe the current system developed to support
mobile image-based tourist information retrieval.

1 Introduction

The primary difference between text and non-text IR is that text IR attempts
to retrieve relevant documents based on "semantic" content whereas traditional
non-text IR (e.g., content based image retrieval (CBIR)) attempts to retrieve
images based on "syntactic" (i.e. low-level) features. If we considered, for the
sake of illustration, that an image is analogous to a printed page of a document,
on such an analogy, traditional CBIR which is feature based, would roughly be
similar to retrieving text documents based on their font size, their layout, the
colour of the ink, etc. (i.e., physical characteristics of the document) rather than
on their meaningful content.

In general, image retrieval systems are only of the following types: using
image to retrieve images, using non-image (usually text) to retrieve images, or
using image to retrieve non-images (information in general). Traditional CBIR
is of the first variety, annotated image banks and Google are of the second, and
there are only a few efforts in the third. In this paper we explore the possibility
of non-image retrieval based on the content of images. Such an approach roughly

G.G. Lee et al. (Eds.): AIRS 2005, LNCS 3689, pp. 97–112, 2005.

requires an *object identification* phase to generate[1] the semantic content followed by whatever suitable actions based on those semantics.

There are many applications for successful object identification systems. We are particularly interested in two of them. The first is for homeland security or image monitoring in general. In our discussions with intelligence agencies, they tell us that they need a way to filter images in the same way that text is filtered. Traditional CBIR does not work for their scenario which needs to work at the semantic object level and not at the syntactic feature level. Another strong reason is that it is easy to give a codeword to replace a name or definite description. So terrorists may use *FOO* in email and chat to refer to, say, the *Subic Bay Naval Base* thus defeating keyword spotting algorithms, but if they were to exchange an image, it would be very difficult to code it. Note that they cannot just encrypt their conversations or images since encrypted data is a red flag in monitoring scenarios.

The second application follows an important trend in mobility; this is the increasing prevalence of cameras on mobile phones. During an industry panel at the Consumer Electronics Show in Jan 2005[2] it was estimated that 700 million mobile handsets will be sold in 2005 and 2/3 of them will have cameras. A significant number of pictures taken on such cameras are likely to be "'throw-away"' images, i.e., pictures taken to serve a function and which has no value once that function is served. Scenarios mooted include taking a picture of a dress to get an opinion from a friend, or as an illustration to a message. But the scenario which we are interested in, is taking a picture to find out more information. So a tourist takes a picture of an unknown landmark, sends it to a server, and gets back useful information. Or a health-conscious consumer takes a picture of his dinner, sends it to a server and gets back nutritional information.

In the next section, we emphasize the significance of a few aspects in our work including the task, the indexing and retrieval paradigm, a unique image dataset, and the requirement for fast query processing. Then we describe important applications related to the object identification task followed by related approaches. Section 4 is devoted to the description of the current prototype on mobile image-based tourist directory. Our experimental evaluation on our unique STOIC dataset is given in Section 5.

2   Significance

There are four key aspects in our work. First, we look at object identification as an important genre of image search. Second, images are used as intermediate means to retrieve information about an object or location. Third, we introduce a new type of image dataset with associated queries and relevance judgments. Conventional image datasets are not designed or evaluated at the semantic level. Last

---

[1] We use the term *generate* rather than *extract* since the semantics we want is often not intrinsic to the image.
[2] See   "'DH: Digital   Cameras   Get   Competition"',   5th   Jan   2005, http://www.cesweb.org

but not least, we show that simple image feature matching is sufficient for good object identification if we provide a sufficient image set for object description. Such efficient techniques are necessary for very large scale critical applications such as homeland security monitoring or the limited processing capacity of the ubiquitous camera phones.

2.1 Object Identification

The object identification task may be described as follows: given an image, determine the referent[3] for the most salient object in the image. For example, all three images in Figure 1 are of the same object, albeit from different perspectives, scales, and colour. The referent is the Merlion statue in One Fullerton in Singapore. The most salient object in the image may be the image in its entirety, e.g., the skyline image in Figure 2 but which also includes the Merlion in it.

Fig. 1. Three images of the same referent

Once the object has been successfully identified, any appropriate follow-up based on the referent of the object can be activated. For example, you may be a tourist looking at the Merlion but not knowing what it is. You snap a picture using your mobile phone and send to a Tourist Information server (via multimedia messaging). The system identifies the object as the Merlion and sends back information about it. The link to the information is through what the object *is* and not what the object *looks like*. We describe such a system prototype known as *Snap2Tell* below.

Incidentally, face recognition in an image is a special sub-genre of object detection in images. This is a more constrained task as there is an implicit normalization of the face. However there are also clear limitations, e.g., a picture of the back of a person's heard is not a candidate for face recognition. More generally for an object, however, we should be able to identify it from any angle. This paper will not be considering face recognition but landmarks recognition.

---

[3] Different words or phrases may be used to described objects or experiences. The *referent* is that which is designated by those words. So, "'George Washington"' and "'the first president of the United States"' both have the same referent.

Fig. 2. Less salient object

2.2   Image Set as Index

In our image-to-information task, images that capture varying appearances of an object are used as an intermediate means in indexing and matching for retrieving the final information for a given query image. That is, in our mobile tourist information application, we index text and audio description of landmarks by a set of images of this landmark. We know that content access using image is still a difficult task for a computer, because low level features are often not enough to describe the intrinsic semantics depicted in an image content. Some meaningful image annotation can be automatically obtained like in [1], but they are only useful for categorizing a set of images by a few image content description (sand, sea, sky) and not very useful for the selection of one particular building, or sculpture. To overcome this problem, we propose to describe one item image using a set of representative images that are taken with different viewing perspective, distances, and lighting conditions.

As in text retrieval, a short text is hard to be retrieved as one needs additional information like synonyms or ontology or linguistic features. (Ex: in answering definitional question [9], one can use prototypal linguistic expressions). Long texts are better retrieved because of augmented probability of world concurrency related to the query. In our case, we think that increasing the amount of related relevant images to an object in the database will improve the chance of identifying this object.

2.3   The STOIC Dataset

Traditional CBIR efforts have often started from fairly arbitrary collection of images, i.e., those which are easily available to the researchers, rather than designed specifically for research. The Singapore Tourist Object Identification Collection (STOIC) dataset is designed to explore new possibilities in image search, specifically in the genre of object identification from images.

STOIC is a work in progress and currently[4] comprises 1650 pictures taken at or of tourist spots in Singapore. There are 120 different spots[5]. Figure 3 shows the current distribution of number of spots for a given set size of index images. We can see that a majority of scenes (43) have an image index set between 5 and 9, the rest have various amount of images up to 190. Images are taken with eight different imaging devices, with different resolutions, from different perspectives, at different times, under different weather conditions, and by different people. Imaging devices include low and high end digital cameras, PDA cameras and phone cameras. In particular, the images taken by the PDA and phones are of much lower resolution, often colour shifted, with poor contrast and uneven saturation. Each image is tagged with metadata to identify the referent and to provide context information for experimentation. Context information includes location (GPS and phone cell id), author, date, and device.

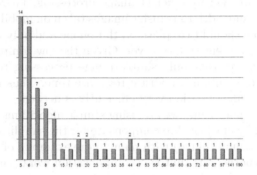

Fig. 3. Scene per image set size

The dataset can support many types of queries. For the object detection task, the query set are images of the tourist spots or objects in the tourist spots. Each image in the query set has an unambiguous referent.

Since the task is object detection, there are various ways of evaluating the success of a retrieval or a match of the query image. In particular, the idea of a ranked list (with traditional precision and recall measures) does not help at all (see 5.1). Instead, we have to use the following evaluations:

strict for a given query image, if the retrieved first image has the same referent, then it is successful. Otherwise not. This corresponds to successful object identification.

loose for a given query image and a ranked list of retrieved images, what is the position of the first image with the same referent as the query image.

---

[4] We have currently much more pictures, but we use only those related to interesting landmarks, and also landmarks associated with at least 5 images

[5] Again, only 68 are in use for the moment because we impose a minimum of 5 images per scene

While this is meaningless to the object identification task since any result other than first position is not successful, it provides an artificial non-binary measure of performance which is useful for training and evaluating changes.

Assessments of relevance, i.e., that an image has the same referent as a query image, were done by several assessors. The operational criteria for saliency was according to the intuitions of assessors. Thus if a Merlion image was the query, it would match the image in Figure 1 but not Figure 2 even if few pixels represent it in Figure 2. The complete test collection, comprising the STOIC dataset, queries and relevance judgments, are freely available at http://ipal.imag.fr/snap2tell/.

2.4 Efficient Image Processing

We are motivated in this research by the applications mentioned above. They have the same requirement for efficient image processing. There is still a limitation on the carrier bandwidth to transfer images taken on mobile phones. Ideally, the image processing should take place on the phone and only a proxy (e.g., image feature vectors) be sent to the server. Given the low compute capability on the phone, this requires that only simple image processing techniques can be applied if we are to maintain a realistic response time. Thus a program which can do scene/object identification very efficiently is needed.

In these initial experiments, we are using simple algorithms because they are more computationally efficient. We compensate for the simplicity by loading the server side (the matching engine) with many more examples of the objects to be recognized. Our hypothesis is that this compensation works sufficiently well for the object identification task.

3 Related Work

The touring machine [2] is an example of augmented reality in urban environment. This is an early version of digital help to orientation and access to information with mobile devices. The system Infoscope [3] is a good example of what can be Multimedia Mobile Information Retrieval. This is mainly an information augmentation system for foreign travelers, which superimposes new information like text translation into an actual picture of a scene. The system is composed by a PDA client associated with GPS for location, liked with a phone for communication. The communication with a server is required due to processing power limitations of small devices like PDA. The second application they proposed, *Information Augmentation in the City*, add information to an actual picture such as details about a flat for rental house hunting.

From the technological point of view, obtaining location-based information is already possible with the GPS devices or the GSM cellular network infrastructure. However, knowing the location of a mobile phone user is not sufficient to determine what he or she is interested in (or looking at). The location-based information certainly helps to refine the user's context, but fails to capture his or her intention. Hence, image-based query is complementary to the context localization information.

Another mobile tourist information system is described in [4]. The client device used is a PDA system connected to internet through WLAN. It supposes that this wireless access point is installed in the area in which the system is going to work. The system includes an iPAQ 3870, a NexiCam PDA camera, an orientation sensor, and a GPS receiver. The position detection is ensured by a GPS attached to the PDA. However, the direction and tilt sensor is connected to the PDA via a laptop computer due to technical difficulty. The camera is integrated into the communication device and localization is provided by the telecommunication operator.

In the PDA prototype [4], the image taken from the connected camera together with GPS and orientation data are sent to a server. The server then runs the 3DMax program to generate a reference image from the same position and angle in a 3D model built in advance based on the GPS and orientation data. The matching is performed using detected line features. Only one building model has been constructed and tested in the paper though color segmentation has been explored for future experimentation.

We believe that a camera phone is a better choice for communication than a PDA. In Snap2Tell, we have chosen a camera mobile phone which is a lighter and more ubiquitous device. The camera is integrated into the communication device and localization is provided by the telecommunication operator. Moreover, our approach of scene recognition is different. Instead of unnatural matching between a real image and a synthesized image from 3D model, our server will match the query image with different images of a scene, taken using different angles and positions. We think that 3D model construction is costly and not applicable to all kinds of scenes. The PDA system [4] requires a GPS device, orientation sensor, and WLAN connection. We think this solution is not realistic.

The IDeixis system [8] also adopted camera-phone as the query device and MMS as the communication infrastructure. However the image database was constructed from 12,000 web-crawled images where the qualities are difficult to control. The 50 test query images were centered around only 3 selected locations. The evaluation was still based on conventional image retrieval paradigm using the percentage of attempts their test subjects found at least one similar image among the first 16 retrieved images. In Snap2Tell, we consider a more comprehensive set of locations for both database and queries. The evaluation was carried out using object identification paradigm with the use of contextual cues such as location priming and with investigation into the effect of poor quality query images produced by mobile devices.

4   Snap2Tell: A Mobile Image-Based Tourist Directory

Imagine you are at a tourist spot looking at a beautiful lake or interesting monument. Instead of searching through your travel guide books to learn more about the scene, you snap a picture of the scene using your camera phone and send it to a service provider. Short time after, you receive an audio clip or a text message that provides you more information about the scene. You can continue to enjoy the scene while your fingers carry out this information retrieval task. As the saying goes "A picture is worth thousand words", a tourist can forget about the hassle of looking up scene description in a travel guide that distracts him/her from enjoying the scene or recalling the right name for the scene (assuming he/she knows what the scene is) to access a text-driven information directory. Moreover the charging of the on-demand service is more fine-grained and hence can tailor to the need of each tourist. Service providers can charge a fee for using this fun, easy-to-use and convenient picture-driven information directory, independent of the MMS charges.

4.1 System Architecture

The Snap2Tell framework is realized as a typical three-tier client/server architecture. The client is a mobile phone with built-in camera that supports MMS, and GPRS such as the Nokia 7650 model used in our development and test. With the camera phone, a user can launch the Snap2Tell application to send a request to the application server. The request is a picture of a real scene or object that information is sought.

After receiving the query, the application server obtains the location information from the mobile network operator. With the location identified, the Snap2Tell server sends a SQL query to the database to retrieve the image meta-data for the scenes related to the location. The image meta-data of the query image is extracted and compared with image meta-data of the scenes by image matching algorithm. If the best matching score is above a certain threshold, scene descriptions of this best matched image is extracted from the scene database. Otherwise, a no match situation has occurred.

The Nokia 7650 mobile phone is used with the Nokia Series 60 platform (powered by Symbian OS v6.1), and is one of the earliest all-in-one device that combines mobile phone, digital camera and PDA functions. Figure 4 displays a sequence of screen shots for a running Snap2Tell client which is written in C++ programming language. Following a top-down, left-to-right order, the first three screen shots shows the invocation of the Snap2Tell application on Nokia 7650 phone. After the Snap2Tell application is active, the user can start the camera to take a picture or open an existing image stored on the phone to used as the query as shown in the fourth screen shot. In this illustration, the user has chosen to select a stored image "SupremeCourt-16.jpg" as query (fifth screen shot on the second row) which is displayed in the sixth screen shot. Note that if the user has decided to take a picture instead, the video camera will be turned on to allow the user see what the camera is focused at.

Once the user has selected or created a query image, he or she can scroll to the "Get Description" option to initiate a query. As described above, the query will be sent as a MMS to the Snap2Tell application server. Once a MMS reply is received from the Snap2Tell application server, the user can play the MMS. As illustrated in the last screen shot in Figure 4, the description is shown as

Fig. 4. Sample Snap2Tell screens on Nokia 7650

text or/and audio. The Snap2Tell application server is the functional core of the system and is developed in Java.

4.2 Scene Database

Using Singapore in our tests, we have set up an original data set of image and descriptions which is a subset of the STOIC dataset. We have divided the map into zones. A zone includes several locations, each of which may contain a number of scenes. A scene is characterized by images taken from different viewpoints, distances, and possibly lighting conditions. Besides a location ID and image examples, a scene is associated with a text description, an audio description which is send to the user as answer to his query. Figure 5 shows relationships among zone, location, scene, and category with examples. For Location 11: Chinatown in Zone 4, two scenes "Chinatown" and "Thian Hock Keng Temple" are shown.

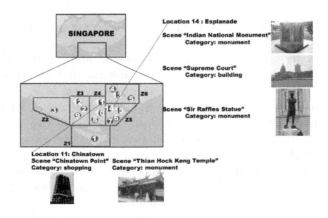

Fig. 5. Locations and scenes in the database

Three scenes labeled as "Indian National Monument", "Supreme Court", and "Sir Raffles Statue" are located in Location 14 of Zone 5.

5   Experimental Evaluation

As the STOIC Dataset is an ongoing task, we have set up a first experimentation with only 535 images, 2 devices (cameras) and 103 locations. This first version of STIOC gives us the opportunity to test the usefulness of location based context and impact of simple image structure using blocks. For this initial study, we have adopted color histograms [7] to characterize and index the images. They are known to be invariant to translation and rotation about the viewing axis and change only slowly under change of angle of view, change of scale, and occlusion.

We have experimented with both global and local color histograms. There is a trade-off between content symmetry and spatial specificity. If we want images of similar semantics with different spatial arrangement (e.g. mirror images) to be treated as similar, we can have histograms of larger blocks (i.e. the extreme case will be a single block that covers the entire image, similar to the effect of a global histogram). However, spatial locations are sometimes important for discriminating more localized objects. Then local histograms will provide good sensitivity to spatial specificity. Furthermore, we can attach different weights to the blocks to emphasize the focus of attention: in our case we have emphasized the center. That is, the similarity λ between a query q (with m local blocks Z_j) and an image x (with m local blocks X_j) is defined as:

$$\lambda(q, x) = \frac{\sum_j \omega_j \cdot \lambda(Z_j, X_j)}{\sum_k \omega_k}, \tag{1}$$

where ω_j are weights, and $\lambda(Z_j, X_j)$ is the similarity between two image blocks defined as

$$\lambda(Z_j, X_j) = 1 - \frac{1}{2} \sum_i |H_i(Z_j) - H_i(X_j)|. \tag{2}$$

Note that this similarity measure is equivalent to histogram intersection [7] between histograms $H_i(Z_j)$ and $H_i(X_j)$.

We use color histograms in the Hue, Saturation, and Value (HSV) [6] color space as it is found to be perceptually more uniform than the standard RGB color space [5]. The number of bins of a color histogram is b^3 where b is the number of equal intervals in each of the H, S, and V dimensions. We have tested from 2 to 14 bins. We have also partitioned an image in identical blocks in both X-Y dimensions (i.e. $K \times K$ grid). When two images are compared, we only compare the two local histograms of the corresponding blocks (Eq. (2)) with equal weights (eq. (1)). We have tested a maximum of $K = 8$ in each dimension. That is, images are split into 64 blocks, and 64 histograms are computed in this case. Note that $K = 1$ refers to global color histogram.

For experimentations with the dataset, we have adopted the leave-one-out methodology for evaluation. In all tests, each image of the test collection is considered as a query and is removed from the collection. This image is tested for histogram similarity matching against the rest of the collection: we compute histogram similarity between this query image and all other images, and we sort the similarities in descending order. The *strict mean precision* is the percentage of success in object identification for the whole collection.

5.1 Influence of Bins and Blocks

Results of this first experimentation is shown in Figure 6. In this figure we see the percentage of strict identification. A strict identification arises when the most similar image to the query image belongs to the same scene. In that case, the system has recognized the correct scene.

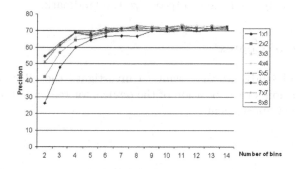

Fig. 6. Bin and blocks influence

When the number of histogram bins increases, the discrimination power increases and hence the quality of the results increases too. At some point, more histogram bins may result in mismatch of the bins when slight change in the color distribution can cause shifts of pixel counts in adjacent bins. Without using any location information, the overall best precision is found at 11 bins using 3×3 blocks with a mean of 73.4% precision. Using block provides some improvement which shows the importance of image structure. We can see that 3×3 block seems to be the minimum for a noticeable improvement. More blocks leads to more computation and not much improvement. Also, after 6 bins, the improvement is to very noticeable.

We have computed the precision at 100% of recall *as if we were considering an image retrieval task* like in traditional CBIR. It is in fact the ratio of images in the correct scene, on the total of images retrieved when all images of this scene are retrieved. The distribution of best performance is not the same: figures are much lower. Excluding low bins and low blocks number, we obtain precision between 18% and 25%. The distribution of the results depends on the content of actual images. For some scenes, the image set is very homogeneous, and the whole set is retrieved at the top of the list. As for other scenes, the set is very heterogeneous because the pictures are taken differently with varying distances or view angles, hence this image set is less consistent and reduce the precision at full recall. Clearly in these situations, the color histogram approach is not discriminative enough. But, even if this measure is very common in Information Retrieval, in our case, it is not important at all because we only need that the first image retrieved to be correct to have a correct answer. Moreover, if we want our system to work in a lot of situations, the picture set that describes an object has to cover as much different situations as possible. For example, we can plan to take 4 or 8 pictures in circle around one landmark, and select also different circle sizes: the more different images we have of the object, the more chances we have to be close to an image query. In that sense, a good indexing image set is expected to have very low recall at full precision because the variety of this data set is related to its quality. We really expect in the image database, to have a lot of different images for the same object in order to maximize the chance to find the correct image and then to recognize the landmark.

5.2   Influence of Context

In this empirical study, we also want to investigate the effect of context as location information, or the position of the device, for reducing the search space and performance improvement.

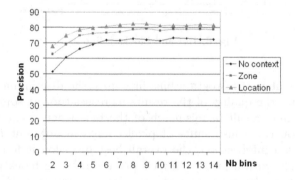

Fig. 7. Context influence (3 × 3 blocks)

Figure 7 shows the strict precision when using context information. That is, we select the best matching image from the images that share the same context as the query image. Contexts are: zone or location information (see 5.2). This figure shows only the mean precision at 3 × 3 blocks. Clearly, we notice the enhancement when context information is used. We reach 82.4%, and this follows intuition. As before, partitioning the images into smaller blocks for matching is useful, and we notice little variation with context information. Using zone the overall best precision it at 79.6% with 5 × 5 blocks and 14 bins; using location, the overall best precision is at 82.6% with 4 × 4 blocks and 11 bins.

5.3   Influence of Structure

The role of the query image is to indicate the information need. Hence we make the hypothesis the center of the image should be more relevant than the edges. Thus we propose to weight blocks according to their position at the matching process.

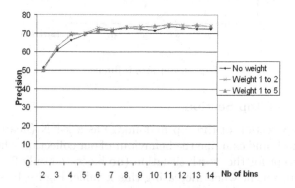

Fig. 8. Block structure influence (3 × 3 blocks)

The Figure 8 shows the results using a linear block weighting from the center to the edge of the pictures, using two weightings: from 1 (edge) to 2 (center) and from 1 to 5. The results shows that for our collection, doubling the center with 3 × 3 blocs with 11 bins, is the best choice (74.9%) compared to the table 6. We have the same behavior using contextual information. Hence, we have a small improvement using weighted blocks.

5.4   Influence of Set Size

For this test, we enlarge the STOIC collection to reach 1650 images with 68 scenes and 8 cameras. The new set of cameras has been chosen so to reflect diversity of camera quality in term of pixel size, sharpness and color consistency. With this new set we imposed a minimum of 5 images for each scene, so we can have at least 4 images do describe an object, during the leave one out process. We notice a positive change in Figure 9. The curves labeled as "small" refers as the small set of image and is a partial copy of the curves in Figure 6. Thus, it tends to prove the *variety hypothesis* for this sort of dataset: the quality in term of strict retrieval is related to the variety of the set associated to objects.

Moreover, the precision at full recall is now only 8% compared with the previous value of 18 − 25%. Thus, it is worth to mention that the full recall is reduced when the diversity of the image set associated to the object increases. Of course, this reduction depends on the matching algorithm itself, but even with a very good image matching process, if the side of one landmark is very different for one other side, it could be impossible to link semantically these two images to the same object only on a visual basis.

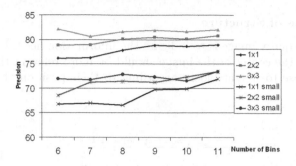

Fig. 9. Set size influence

5.5   Influence of Top Section

We can view our section of the top first image as a k-NN (nearest neighbour) classifier with k=1, and examine the behaviour of our collection when we increase the k value. Except for the worth situation (no blocs and only 2 bins), we never notice any improvement when increasing this k value. Figure 10 shows the best and worst situation with every k from 1 to 30. Notice that in case of identical value for two scenes, we choose the set of images with the overall closer total added distance.

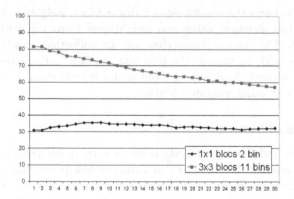

Fig. 10. k NN classification test

Usual behaviour of k-NN classifier is first an increase with k and then a decrease. One possible explanation of our results is the too small size of image set per scene.

5.6   Influence of Device Quality

With 8 different cameras, we can test the influence of the device itself. The results[6] in table 1 are computed by eliminating from the dataset all images that

---

[6] For Trademark reason, we cannot give the exact brands and models of the devices we have used. This information can be obtained on demand only.

has been taken by the same device. In that way we test the compatibility of one device among all other devices on the whole image collection.

Table 1. Device influence

Model	CCD size	Year	Strict precision
Hand phone	0.01 Mp	2004	46.1%
Pocket PC	0.3 Mp	2004	16.4%
Camera 1	2.1 Mp	2004	72.4%
Camera 2	3.2Mp	2003	15.3%
Camera 3	3.3 Mp	2000	22.2%
Camera 4	3.3 Mp	2001	16.9%
Camera 5	5.2Mp	2002	60.0%
Camera 6	6.3Mp	2003	46.7%

This results shows a clear drop (from 80% to maximum 60% and 15% minimum) in the strict precision. This can be explained by shift of device's color characteristics. The size of the CCD in mega pixel or the year of marketing, does not seem to be very important. When one looks at actual images, we can clearly notice that the Pocket PC and the phone produce very low quality images. Hence we are surprised by the relative good results of the hand phone compared to those of the Pocket PC. It is also surprising that the best results belong to a chip camera (camera 1). We can conclude that we will need either device dependent color calibration or low lever feature extraction less sensitive to camera characteristics.

6   Conclusion

Concerning our Snap2Tell prototype, our approach deals with real situation and real access device in order to measure the feasibility of such a system. It turns out that we have stretched the limit of currently available wearable technology, but we are convinced that ubiquitous computing is going to have rapid development in the very near future. We are also convinced that mobile information access, in particular context-aware image-based information access, will be a hot research and development topic.

The results we obtained using our original STOIC image database has shown us that simple matching, based on color histograms, combined with localization information, seems powerful enough to solve this object identification problem thought image matching mainly, because of task we have: retrieving among a set of images describing one object, the only one that is closed to image query. It is not a usual IR querying task, and the poor value of the precision at full recall is not that significant in this case. We also know that even if the prototype is functional and that these results are encouraging, results are not good and stable enough to be used for a real commercial product and relying only on color distribution is for sure too weak in many other real situations as it is shown by our test on the 8 different cameras. We are about to investigate this aspect and adding more discriminative image features extractions. The complete test collection is freely available at http://ipal.imag.fr/snap2tell/. This work has been done under a IPAL CNRS France and I2R A-STAR Singapore common funded research action.

References

1. J. Fan, Y. Gao, H. Luo, and G. Xu. Automatic image annotation by using concept-sensitive salient objects for image content representation. In *SIGIR '04: Proceedings of the 27th annual international conference on Research and development in information retrieval*, pages 361–368. ACM Press, 2004.
2. S. Feiner, B. MacIntyre, T. Hllerer, and A. Webster. A touring machine: Prototyping 3d mobile augmented reality systems for exploring the urban environment. In *Proceedings ISWC '97 (First IEEE Int. Symp. on Wearable Computers)*, volume 1(4) of *Personal Technologies*, pages 208–217, October 13-14 1997.
3. I. Haritaoglu. Infoscope: Link from real world to digital information space. In G. Abowd, B. Brumitt, and S. Shafer, editors, *Ubicomp 2001: Ubiquitous Computing: Third International Conference Atlanta, Georgia, USA,*, volume 2201/2001 of *Lecture Notes in Computer Science*, pages 247–255. Springer-Verlag Heidelberg, September 30 - October 2 2001.
4. W. Mai, G. Dodds, and C. Tweed. Mobile and ubiquitous information access: Mobile hci 2003 international workshop, udine, italy. In *Lecture Notes in Computer Science*, volume 2954 / 2004, pages 143–157. Springer-Verlag Heidelberg, Sept 2003.
5. G. Paschos. Perceptually uniform color spaces for color texture analysis: an empirical evaluation. In *IEEE Trans. on Image Processing*, volume 10 (6), pages 932–937, 2001.
6. A. R. Smith. Color gamut transform pairs. In *SIGGRAPH '78: Proceedings of the 5th annual conference on Computer graphics and interactive techniques*, pages 12–19. ACM Press, 1978.
7. M. Swain and D. Ballard. Color indexing. *Intl. J. Computer Vision*, 7(1), 1991.
8. K. Tollmar, T. Yeh, and T. Darrell. Ideixis searching the web with mobile images for location-based information. In S. Brewster and M. Dunlop, editors, *Mobile Human-Computer Interaction MobileHCI 2004: 6th International Symposium*, volume 3160/2004 of *Lecture Notes in Computer Science*, pages 288 – 299. Springer-Verlag Heidelberg, September 13 - 16 2004.
9. J. Xu, R. Weischedel, and A. Licuanan. Evaluation of an extraction-based approach to answering definitional questions. In *SIGIR '04: Proceedings of the 27th annual international conference on Research and development in information retrieval*, pages 418–424. ACM Press, 2004.

Extracting the Significant Terms from a Sentence-Term Matrix by Removal of the Noise in Term Usage*

Changbeom Lee[1], Hoseop Choe[1], Hyukro Park[2], and Cheolyoung Ock[1]

[1] School of Computer Engineering & Information Technology, University of Ulsan,
Ulsan 680-749, South Korea
{chblee1225, hoseop, okcy}@mail.ulsan.ac.kr
[2] Department of Computer Science, Chonnam National University,
300 Youngbong-dong, Buk-gu, Kwangju 500-757, South Korea
hyukro@chonnam.ac.kr

Abstract. In this paper, we propose an approach to extracting the significant terms in a document by the quantification methods which are both singular value decomposition (SVD) and principal component analysis (PCA). The SVD can remove the noise of variability in term usage of an original sentence-term matrix by using the singular values acquired after computing the SVD. This adjusted sentence-term matrix, which have removed its noisy usage of terms, can be used to perform the PCA, since the dimensionality of the revised matrix is the same as that of the original. Since the PCA can be used to extract the significant terms on the basis of the eigenvalue-eigenvector pairs for the sentence-term matrix, the extracted terms by the revised matrix instead of the original can be regarded as more effective or appropriate. Experimental results on Korean newspaper articles in automatic summarization show that the proposed method is superior to that over the only PCA.

Keywords: Significant Terms; Removal of Noise; Singular Value Decomposition; Principal Component Analysis; Automatic Summarization.

1 Introduction

Traditional information retrieval systems usually use a noun which has some meaning of its own as an index term or a representative word for a logical view of the documents [1]. However, all of the nouns in the document may not always be the representatives. For instance, consider a document about fruit with its nouns, "apple", "banana", "pear", "strawberry", "fruit" and "basket", and suppose only four words are selected for the respresentatives; i.e., apple, banana, pear and basket. Here the word, "basket", might appear at the phrase like "a

---

* This research was supported by the MIC(Ministry of Information and Communication), Korea, under the ITRC(Information Technology Research Center) support program supervised by the IITA(Institute of Information Technology Assessment).

G.G. Lee et al. (Eds.): AIRS 2005, LNCS 3689, pp. 113–120, 2005.

fruit basket". When "basket" is removed from the selected list and "strawberry" or "fruit" is added to, this revised word list can be more informative or effective to illustrate the example.

In order to make an effect on removal of the noise in term usage like the above example and to extract the representative words or significant terms in the document, the [6] makes use of the principal component analysis (PCA) which is to reduce dimension of data by eigenvalue-eigenvector pairs [5]. In [6], however, performing PCA over the original sentence-term matrix which might have the noise of variability in term usage. Consequently, the unnecessary terms might be selected for the significant terms (called thematic words in [6]) by the only PCA.

In this paper, we propose the way to remove the noisy data which might probably be involved in the orginal sentence-term matrix. The particular technique used is the singular value decompostion (SVD) [1,3,8]. Computing SVD of the original sentence-term matrix can be removed the noisy data by the proprotion of the singular values. As a result, the new or revised sentence-term matrix can be obtained, whose number of rows and columns is exactly equal to that of rows and columns of the original matrix. However, this matrix can have the smaller amount of the noise than the original. In contrast to [6], the PCA is performed over the revised matrix instead of the original. Actually the proposed methed is applied to the summarization for the evaluation.

This paper is organized as follows. Section 2 describes how to remove the noise in term usage by SVD, and 3 briefly illustrates the way to extract the significant terms by PCA (more details in [6]). Section 4 reports experimental results. A brief conclusion is given in Section 5.

2   The Removal of the Noise of Variability in Term Usage by SVD

2.1   SVD Overview

We will give an outline of SVD adapted from [3,8] and how to apply to remove the noise.

Let A be any rectangular matrix, for instance an $s \times t$ matrix of sentences and terms as shown in the next subsection. The matrix A can be written as the product of an $s \times r$ column-orthogonal matrix U_0, an $r \times r$ daigonal matrix W_0 with positive or zero elements (i.e., the singular values), and the transpose of a $t \times r$ orthogonal matrix V_0. Here, r is the rank of the matrix A ($r \leq min(s,t)$). The SVD decompositon is shown in Eq. (1).

$$A = U_0 \cdot W_0 \cdot V_0^T \tag{1}$$

where $U_0^T U_0 = I$, $V_0^T V_0 = I$, and W_0 is the diagonal matrix of singualr values.

Actually the reduced dimensionality can be used instead of the full rank, r, by the cumulative ratio of the singular values. The cumulative ratio, σ_k, can be calculated by Eq. (2). When the σ_k is more than 90%, k can be selected for the reduced dimensionality which can be large enough to capture most of the important underlying structure in association of sentences and terms, and also small enough to remove the noise of variability in term usage.

$$\sigma_k = \frac{\sum_{i=1}^{k} w_i}{w_1 + w_2 + \ldots + w_r}, \quad k = 1, 2, \ldots, r \tag{2}$$

In this regard, the matrix A can be rewrited by the revised matrix $\hat{A}$ whose dimension is euqal to that of A, $s \times t$, without much loss of information. That is, we can write

$$A \approx \hat{A} = U \cdot W \cdot V^T \tag{3}$$

where U is an $s \times k$ matrix, W is a $k \times k$ martix, and V^T is a $k \times t$ matrix. Consequently we can use $\hat{A}$ instead of A for performing PCA to remove the noise of frequency distribution of the original sentence-term matrix, while keeping the significant structure of the orginal.

2.2   The Creation of the Revised Sentence-Term Matrix

Now we will illustrate the way to create the revised sentence-term matrix by the sample article, and this matrix will be regarded as being removed the noise of variability in term usage in the document. Table 1 shows the extracted term list from one of the Korean newspaper articles composed of 8 sentencens and 61 unique nouns, and this article is about giving a prize on the protection of environment. Since we assume that the candidates of the significant terms are confined only to nouns occurred more than twice in the document, there are 10 terms in Table 1. Particularly, the term, X_4, is not a correct noun resulted from the malfunction of our Korean morphological analyzer. Actually this term was not included in the list of the significant terms by both methos, that is, the only PCA and the proposed.

The matrix A shows the original sentence-term matrix whose value is the frequency of each term within each sentence. For instance, the first column shows

Table 1. Term List

Term (Noun)	Notation	Remark
hwan-gyeong (Environment)	X_1	
UNEP (United Nations Environment Program)	X_2	
se-gye (world)	X_3	
i-ran (called or named)	X_4	extraction error
sang (prize)	X_5	
cheong-so-nyeon (young people)	X_6	
ta-im (TIME magazine)	X_7	
go-ril-ra (gorilla)	X_8	
ja-yeon (nature)	X_9	
il-bon (Japan)	X_{10}	

that X_1 was occurred twice in the first sentence, once in the second and twice in the fifth.

$$
\mathbf{A} = \begin{pmatrix}
2 & 1 & 1 & 1 & 1 & 0 & 0 & 0 & 0 & 0 \\
1 & 0 & 1 & 0 & 1 & 0 & 0 & 0 & 0 & 0 \\
0 & 1 & 0 & 0 & 1 & 2 & 0 & 0 & 0 & 0 \\
0 & 0 & 0 & 0 & 0 & 0 & 1 & 0 & 0 & 0 \\
2 & 0 & 1 & 0 & 0 & 0 & 1 & 0 & 0 & 0 \\
0 & 0 & 1 & 0 & 0 & 0 & 0 & 2 & 1 & 0 \\
0 & 0 & 0 & 1 & 1 & 1 & 0 & 0 & 1 & 2 \\
0 & 0 & 0 & 0 & 1 & 0 & 0 & 0 & 0 & 0
\end{pmatrix}
$$

The matrix $\hat{A}$ is the result of computing SVD of the matrix A by using Eq. (3), i.e., $U \cdot W \cdot V^T$. The values of these four matrices is rounded to two decimal places as shown below. Actually U_0 is 8×10 matrix, W_0 is 10×10 and V_0 is 10×10. However, by using σ_k like Eq. (2), the dimension of these ones can be reduced without much loss of information on the frequency distribution in the sentence-term matrix. In our sample article, k is six, since the cumulative ratio of the singular values is more than 0.9 at the first six as shown Table 2. It is said that around ten-percent noise can be removed by using this cumulative ratio.

Table 2. Singular values and their cumulative ratio

singular value	4.01	3.07	2.43	1.92	1.46	1.06	0.76	0.24	0.00	0.00
cumulative ratio	0.27	0.47	0.64	0.76	0.86	**0.93**	0.98	1.00	1.00	1.00

$$
\hat{A} = \begin{pmatrix}
2.08 & 0.88 & 1.08 & 0.87 & 0.93 & 0.10 & -0.16 & -0.05 & 0.00 & 0.05 \\
1.00 & 0.09 & 0.82 & 0.09 & 1.09 & -0.10 & 0.13 & 0.09 & 0.02 & -0.06 \\
-0.02 & 1.03 & -0.02 & 0.03 & 1.02 & 1.97 & 0.04 & 0.01 & 0.00 & -0.01 \\
0.17 & -0.22 & 0.08 & -0.25 & -0.12 & 0.19 & 0.71 & -0.06 & 0.02 & 0.09 \\
1.90 & 0.10 & 1.00 & 0.11 & 0.04 & -0.08 & 1.13 & 0.01 & -0.01 & -0.04 \\
0.01 & -0.02 & 1.02 & -0.02 & -0.01 & 0.02 & -0.02 & 1.99 & 1.00 & 0.01 \\
-0.01 & 0.02 & -0.02 & 1.02 & 1.01 & 0.98 & 0.03 & 0.01 & 1.00 & 1.99 \\
-0.01 & -0.07 & 0.18 & -0.08 & 0.92 & 0.09 & -0.12 & -0.09 & -0.02 & 0.05
\end{pmatrix}
$$

$$
\mathbf{U} = \begin{pmatrix}
-0.65 & 0.20 & -0.17 & 0.00 & 0.41 & 0.43 \\
-0.37 & 0.14 & -0.02 & -0.04 & 0.25 & -0.59 \\
-0.28 & -0.49 & -0.27 & -0.72 & -0.28 & 0.06 \\
-0.03 & 0.05 & -0.01 & 0.06 & -0.52 & -0.26 \\
-0.45 & 0.44 & -0.04 & 0.16 & -0.59 & -0.03 \\
-0.18 & 0.02 & 0.93 & -0.31 & 0.00 & 0.04 \\
-0.34 & -0.70 & 0.15 & 0.59 & -0.09 & 0.02 \\
-0.11 & -0.10 & -0.06 & -0.06 & 0.26 & -0.63
\end{pmatrix}
$$

$$\mathbf{W} = \begin{pmatrix} 4.01 & & & & & \\ & 3.07 & & & & \\ & & 2.43 & & & \\ & & & 1.92 & & \\ & & & & 1.46 & \\ & & & & & 1.06 \end{pmatrix}$$

$$\mathbf{V^T} = \begin{pmatrix} -0.64 & -0.23 & -0.41 & -0.25 & -0.44 & -0.22 & -0.12 & -0.09 & -0.13 & -0.17 \\ 0.47 & -0.09 & 0.26 & -0.16 & -0.31 & -0.55 & 0.16 & 0.01 & -0.22 & -0.46 \\ -0.18 & -0.18 & 0.29 & -0.01 & -0.16 & -0.16 & -0.02 & 0.77 & 0.44 & 0.12 \\ 0.14 & -0.38 & -0.10 & 0.31 & -0.12 & -0.44 & 0.11 & -0.32 & 0.15 & 0.62 \\ -0.07 & 0.09 & 0.05 & 0.22 & 0.38 & -0.44 & -0.76 & 0.01 & -0.06 & -0.12 \\ 0.19 & 0.46 & -0.15 & 0.42 & -0.67 & 0.14 & -0.27 & 0.07 & 0.05 & 0.04 \end{pmatrix}$$

When comparing the $\hat{A}$ to the A, they are different. In the first column of the $\hat{A}$, for instance, the first value, 2.28, increased by 0.28, but the fifth, 1.90, decreased by 0.1. Consequently, the matrix $\hat{A}$ can be regarded as one removed the noise in term usage of the original matrix, A, by using SVD. And thus, the extracted significant terms by the revised matrix like $\hat{A}$ can be more reasonable.

3   Extracting the Significant Terms by PCA

3.1   PCA Overview

PCA is concerned with explaining the variance-covariance structure through a few linear combinations of the original variables [5]. PCA uses the covariance matrix instead of the obsevation-variable matrix (sentence-term matrix like A or $\hat{A}$ above). An eigenvector and its corresponding eigenvalue can be obtained by applying PCA on the covariance matrix– in other words, the covariance matrix can be decomposed into a series of eigenvalue-eigenvector pairs (λ_1, e_1), (λ_2, e_2), ..., (λ_p, e_p) where $\lambda_1 \geq \lambda_2 \geq \ldots \lambda_p$. The cumulative proportion of total population variance due to the kth principal component(PC), ρ_k, is

$$\rho_k = \frac{\sum_{i=1}^{k} \lambda_k}{\lambda_1 + \lambda_2 + \ldots + \lambda_p} \quad , where \quad k = 1, 2, \ldots, p \tag{4}$$

If most (ρ_k is $0.8 \sim 0.9$) of the total population variance, for large p, can be attributed to the first one, two, or three components, then these components can "replace" the original p variables without much loss of information [5].

Since the PCA makes good use of the variance-covariance structure, the significant terms can be extracted by the pattern of statistical cooccurrence of the sentence-term matrix [6].

3.2   Comparing the Extracted Significant Terms

In this subsection, we will compare the significant terms by using only PCA [6] to those by using the proposed method. In order to extract the significant terms,

Table 3. Eigenvector and corresponding Eigenvalue of the original matrix A

term \ PC	PC_1	PC_2	PC_3	PC_4	PC_5	PC_6	PC_7	PC_8	PC_9	PC_{10}
X_1	-0.67	-0.39	0.29	0.07	0.25	-0.15	-0.48	0.00	0.00	0.00
X_2	0.00	-0.28	-0.09	0.45	0.15	0.54	0.16	-0.04	0.26	-0.55
X_3	-0.36	0.10	0.26	0.28	0.03	-0.37	0.76	0.00	0.00	0.00
X_4	0.06	-0.24	0.44	0.00	-0.03	0.58	0.19	0.04	-0.26	0.55
X_5	0.16	-0.37	0.06	0.21	-0.54	-0.21	-0.06	0.66	0.11	-0.01
X_6	**0.44**	-0.32	-0.18	0.37	0.58	-0.32	-0.01	0.02	-0.13	0.27
X_7	-0.16	0.06	-0.18	-0.44	0.48	0.16	0.19	0.66	0.11	-0.01
X_8	0.02	**0.61**	0.24	**0.46**	0.12	0.10	-0.28	0.22	0.38	0.24
X_9	0.19	0.23	0.41	0.05	0.14	-0.03	-0.12	0.22	-0.64	-0.50
X_{10}	0.37	-0.16	**0.59**	-0.36	0.15	-0.15	0.04	-0.14	0.52	-0.16
eigenvalue(λ_i)	1.39	0.95	0.62	0.47	0.26	0.10	0.01	0.00	0.00	0.00
cumulative ratio(ρ_k)	0.36	0.62	0.78	**0.90**	0.97	1.00	1.00	1.00	1.00	1.00

Table 4. Eigenvector and corresponding Eigenvalue of the revised matrix $\hat{A}$

term \ PC	PC_1	PC_2	PC_3	PC_4	PC_5	PC_6	PC_7	PC_8	PC_9	PC_{10}
X_1	-0.66	-0.38	0.28	0.06	0.23	-0.04	-0.46	-0.17	0.00	-0.20
X_2	-0.01	-0.30	-0.07	**0.49**	0.21	0.28	-0.02	0.28	-0.22	0.64
X_3	-0.35	0.11	0.23	0.26	0.00	-0.31	0.48	0.60	0.17	-0.17
X_4	0.05	-0.26	0.48	0.06	0.04	0.33	0.60	-0.46	0.07	-0.02
X_5	0.15	-0.38	0.08	0.23	-0.52	-0.64	-0.02	-0.21	-0.08	0.17
X_6	**0.45**	-0.30	-0.22	0.32	0.54	-0.20	0.01	-0.01	0.16	-0.44
X_7	-0.17	0.04	-0.14	-0.40	0.52	-0.47	0.28	-0.20	-0.12	0.40
X_8	0.02	**0.61**	0.24	0.48	0.15	-0.14	-0.20	-0.34	0.31	0.20
X_9	0.19	0.23	0.41	0.06	0.14	-0.10	-0.07	0.06	-0.81	-0.20
X_{10}	0.37	-0.15	**0.58**	-0.36	0.13	-0.06	-0.27	0.33	0.34	0.22
eigenvalue(λ_i)	1.39	0.95	0.62	0.47	0.26	0.04	0.00	0.00	0.00	0.00
cumulative ratio(ρ_k)	0.37	0.63	0.79	**0.92**	0.99	1.00	1.00	1.00	1.00	1.00

there are two steps in [6]. In the first step, the PCs are selected by Eq. (4), i.e., the first k where $\rho_k \geq 0.9$. In the second step, the selected PCs are represented by using their coefficients (≥ 0.5 or highest), i.e., their corresponding eigenvector.

We use the same method to extract the significant terms, but exploit the revised sentence-term matrix like $\hat{A}$ instead of the original like A for PCA. Table 3 and 4 show the eigenvector and its corresponding eigenvalue of the orginal matrix A and the revised $\hat{A}$, respectively.

In Table 3 and 4, the first four PCs are selected by ρ_k, 0.90 and 0.92, respectively. This means that variance of the A and $\hat{A}$ can be summarized very well by these four PCs, and the data from eight observations (sentences) on ten variables (terms) can be reasonably reduced to one from eight obsevations on 4 PCs. However, the degree of explanation of sample variance is slightly different between them–in other words, the selected PCs by the proposed method are more informative or reasonable.

For the significant terms, X_6, X_8 and X_{10} are the same ones that are extracted from the original matrix, A, but X_2 is added to them by the revised matirx, $\hat{A}$. Since the content of our sample article is concerned with the protection of environment, by adding the X_2, "UNEP", the degree of information on its content can be increased.

Consequently, the removal of the potential noise in term usage by SVD can be more helpful to extract the significant terms concerned with the content of the document.

4 Experiments

For performance evaluation, the proposed approach was applied to the document summarization based on the occurrence of the extracted significant terms. The proposed method was compared to that of only PCA proposed in [6] which noted that the mothod by using PCA was to be preferred over term frequency[4,7] and lexical chain[2] for the document summarization.

To extract the siginificant sentences by using the terms like [6], we first computed the score of each sentence by repeatedly summing 1 for each occurrence of terms, and second extracted the sentences by their scores in descending order, depending on compression rate.

We used 127 documents of Korean newspaper articles which were compiled by KISTI[1] for the evaluation. Each document consists of orginal article and manual summary amounting to 30% of the source text. And this manually extracted summary is regarded as the correct one.

Table 5. Evaluation result

	Matrix used	
Measure	Original	Revised
Average Precision	0.386	0.407
Average Recall	0.451	0.502
F-Measure	0.416	0.449

To evaluate the methods, we measured precision, recall, and F–measure which are defined respectively as follows.

$$Precision = \frac{\#\ of\ the\ correct\ summary\ sentences\ that\ the\ system\ extracts}{\#\ of\ the\ sentences\ that\ the\ system\ extracts}$$

$$Recall = \frac{\#\ of\ the\ correct\ summary\ sentences\ that\ the\ system\ extracts}{\#\ of\ the\ manually\ extracted\ summary\ sentences}$$

$$F-Measure = \frac{2*Precision*Recall}{Precision+Recall}$$

[1] Korea Institute of Science & Technology Information.

Table 5 shows that, by means of F-measure, the proposed method has improved the performance by around 3.3% over the method using the orginal sentence-term matrix for PCA.

5 Conclusion

In this paper, we have proposed the way to extract the representative or significant terms of the text documents by SVD and PCA.

In the first step, the noisy data in term usage of the orginal sentence-term matrix is removed by using the cumulative ratio of the singular values by computing SVD of the original matrix. In the second step, the signifcant terms are extracted by performing PCA with the revised one. Consequently, the SVD is efficient to remove the noisy data of the frequency distribution, and the PCA to extract the significant terms by eigenvalue-eigenvector pairs. The experimental results on Korean newspaper articles show that the proposed method, SVD and PCA, is to be preferred over only PCA when the document summarization is the goal.

We expect that the proposed method can be applied to information retrieval for indexing, document categorization for feature selection, and automatic summarization for extracting terms and so on.

References

1. Baeza-Yates, R., Ribeiro-Neto, B.: Modern Information Retrieval. New York: ACM Press (1999)
2. Barzilay, R., Elhadad, M. : Using Lexical chains for Text Summarization. In: Mani, I., Maybury, M. T. (eds.): Advances in automatic text summarization. Cambridge, MA: The MIT Press (1999) 111–121
3. Deerwester, S., Dumais, S. T., Harshman, R.: Indexing by latent semantic analysis. Journal of the American Society for Information Science, 41 (6). (1990) 381–407
4. Edmundson, H. P.: New Methods in Automatic Extracting. In: Mani, I., Maybury, M. T. (eds.): Advances in automatic text summarization. Cambridge, MA: The MIT Press (1999) 23–42
5. Johnson, R. A., Wichern, D. W.: Applied Multivariate Statistical Analysis. 3rd edn. NJ: Prentice Hall (1992)
6. Lee, C., Kim, M., Park, H.: Automatic Summarization Based on Principal Component Analysis. In: Pires, F.M., Abreu, S. (eds.): Progress in Artificial Intelligence. Lecture Notes in Artificial Intelligence, Vol. 2902. Springer-Verlag, Berlin Heidelberg New York (2003) 409–413
7. Mani, I.: Automatic Summarization. Amsterdam/Philadelphia: John Benjamins Publishing Company (2001)
8. Press, W. H., Teukolsky, S. A., Vetterling, W. T., Flannery, B. P.: Numerical recipes in C++. 2nd edn. New York: Cambridge University Press (1992/2002)

Cross Document Event Clustering Using Knowledge Mining from Co-reference Chains

June-Jei Kuo and Hsin-Hsi Chen

Department of Computer Science and Information Engineering,
National Taiwan University,
Taipei, Taiwan
jjkuo@nlg.csie.ntu.edu.tw, hhchen@csie.ntu.edu.tw

Abstract. Unification of the terminology usages which captures more term semantics is useful for event clustering. This paper proposes a metric of normalized chain edit distance to mine controlled vocabulary from cross-document co-reference chains incrementally. A novel threshold model that incorporates time decay function and spanning window utilizes the controlled vocabulary for event clustering on streaming news. The experimental results show that the proposed system has 16% performance increase compared to the baseline system and 6% performance increase compared to the system without introducing controlled vocabulary.

1 Introduction

News, which is an important information source, is reported anytime and anywhere, and is disseminated across geographic barriers through Internet. Detecting the occurrences of new events and tracking the processes of the events (Allan, Carbonell, and Yamron, 2002; Chieu and Lee, 2004) are useful for decision-making in this fast-changing network era. The research issues behind event clustering include: how many features are used to determine event clusters, which cue patterns are employed to relate news stories in the same event, how the clustering strategies affect the clustering performance using retrospective data or on-line data, how the time factor affects clustering performance, and how cross-document co-references are resolved.

Several studies, for example, text classification (Kolcz et al., 2001) and web-page classification (Shen et al., 2004), suggest that even simple summaries are quite effective in carrying over the relevant information about a document. They showed that if a full-text classification method is directly applied to those documents, it will incur much bias for the classification algorithm, making it possible to lose focus on the main topic and important content. Moreover, for deeper document understanding, the co-reference chains (Cardie and Wagstaff, 1999) of documents capture information on co-referring expressions, i.e., all mentioned of a given entity. As the co-reference provides important clues to find text fragments containing salient information, various practical tasks including, for example, text summarization (Azzam, Humphreys and

G.G. Lee et al. (Eds.): AIRS 2005, LNCS 3689, pp. 121–134, 2005.
© Springer-Verlag Berlin Heidelberg 2005

Gaizauskas, 1999; Chen, et al., 2003), question answering (Morton, 1999; Lin, et al., 2001) and event clustering (Kuo and Chen, 2004), can be done more reliably. On the other hand, during producing summaries from multiple documents, cross-document co-reference analyses (Bagga and Baldwin, 1998; Gooi and Allan, 2004) consider further if mentions of a name in different documents are the same.

In this paper, we will show that using summarization as pre-processing in event clustering is a viable and effective technique. Furthermore, we will integrate co-reference chains from more than one document by unifying cross-document co-references of nominal elements. Instead of using the traditional clustering approaches, we will propose a novel threshold model that incorporates time decay function and spanning window to deal with on-line streaming news. The rest of the paper is organized as follows. Section 2 reviews the previous work and shows our architecture. Section 3 describes a document summarization algorithm using co-reference chains. Section 4 tackles the issues of mining controlled vocabulary. A normalized chain edit distance and two algorithms are proposed to mine controlled vocabulary incrementally from cross-document co-reference chains. Section 5 proposes an algorithm for on-line event clustering using dynamic threshold model. Section 6 specifies the data set and the experimental results, using the metric adopted by Topic Detection and Tracking (Fiscus and Doddington, 2002). Section 7 concludes the remarks.

2 Basic Architecture

Kuo and Chen (2004) employed co-reference chains to cluster streaming news into event clusters. As the co-reference chains and event words are complementary in some sense, they also introduced the event words (Fukumoto and Suzuki, 2000). Their experimental results showed that both the two factors are useful. Furthermore, they presented two approaches to combine the two factors for event clustering, which are called *summation model* and *two-level model*, respectively. However, the best performance in terms of detection cost was improved 2% only compared to the baseline system. One of the reasons is that the nominal elements used in cross-document co-reference chains may be different. The goal of this paper is to mine controlled vocabulary from co-reference chains of different documents incrementally for event clustering on streaming news.

Figure 1 shows the architecture of event clustering. We receive documents from multiple Internet sources, such as newspaper sites, and then send them for document pre-processing. Pre-processing module deals with the sentence extraction, the language idiosyncracy, e.g., Chinese segmentation, and co-reference resolution. Document summarization module analyzes each document and employs the co-reference chains and the related feature words, such as event words, to produce the respective summaries. Mining controlled vocabulary module integrates the co-reference chains to generate controlled vocabulary automatically, which will be used for weight computation in event clustering module. Finally, event clustering module utilizes weights of word features, and similarity function to cluster the documents.

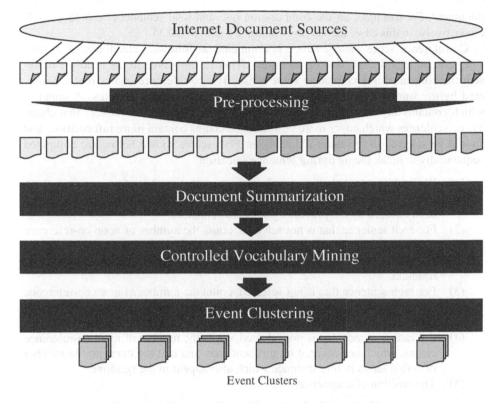

Fig. 1. Architecture of Event Clustering for Streaming News

3 Document Summarization Using Co-reference Chains

Kuo and Chen (2004) considered the event words only to be features for clustering. The basic hypothesis is that an event word associated with a news article appears across paragraphs, but a topic word does not. Take China Airlines air accident as an example. Each related news article has different event words, e.g., "body recovery", "set up", "17:10PM", "CKS airport", "Commander Lin", "stock market", "fly right negotiation", and so on. Extracting such keywords is useful to understand the events, and distinguish one document from another. Nevertheless, due to the strict decision thresholds there are only a few event words extracted and may lose some important feature words. Thus, this paper further introduces the higher *tf-idf* words to be our document features. Document summarization module extracts the event words and the 20 highest tf-idf words from each document. Then, the score of each sentence in a document is computed by adding three scores, i.e., the number of event words, the number of the highest tf-idf words, and the co-reference scores shown in the following paragraphs. Rather than using fixed number of sentences to generate summary, the sentence selection procedure is repeated until a dynamic number of sentences is retrieved. This number is equal to the compression rate multiply total sentences in a document. For example, let the compression rate and total sentences be 0.35 and 15, respectively. In this case, the length of summary is 5, i.e., 0.35 *15.

Co-reference score of a sentence is computed as follows. Headlines of a news story can be regarded as its short summary. That is, the words in the headline represent the content of a document in some sense. The co-reference chains that are initiated by the words in the headlines are assumed to have higher weights. A sentence which contains any words in a given co-reference chain is said to "cover" that chain. Those sentences which cover more co-reference chains contain more information, and should be selected to represent a document. Five scores shown below are computed sequentially to break the tie during sentence selection.

(1)   For each sentence that is not selected, count the number of noun co-reference chains from the headline, which are covered by this sentence and have not been covered by the previously selected sentences.
(2)   For each sentence that is not selected, count the number of noun co-reference chains from the headline, which are covered by this sentence, and add the count to the number of verbal terms in this sentence which also appear in the headline.
(3)   For each sentence that is not selected, count the number of noun co-reference chains, which are covered by this sentence and have not been covered by the previously selected sentences.
(4)   For each sentence that is not selected, count the number of noun co-reference chains, which are covered by this sentence, and add the count to the number of verbal terms in this sentence which also appear in the headline.
(5)   The position of a sentence.

Score 1 only considers nominal features. Comparatively, Score 2 considers both nominal and verbal features together. Both scores are initiated by headlines. Scores 3 and 4 consider all the co-reference chains no matter whether these chains are initiated by headlines or not. These two scores rank those sentences of the same scores 1 and 2. Besides, they can assign scores to news stories without headlines. Scores 1 and 3 are recomputed in the iteration. Finally, since news stories tend to contain more information in the leading paragraphs, Score 5 determines which sentence will be selected according to position of sentences, when sentences are of the same scores (1)-(4). The smaller the position number of a sentence is, the more it will be preferred.

4   Creating Controlled Vocabulary from Individual Co-reference Chains

Streaming news are disseminated from different sources and written by different conventions and styles. The expression of an entity in a document may be different from the expression of the same entity in another document. Figure 2 shows an example of four short co-reference chains in four different documents DOC1-DOC4.

Considering the co-reference chain in DOC1, "總統喬治・布希" (President George W. Bush) and "布希總統" (President Bush) denote the same person. There are two identical words "總統" (President) and "布希總統" (President Bush) between the chains in DOC1 and DOC2, so that word matching tells us these two chains have the same denotation. However, direct word matching between two co-reference chains may suffer from the following two problems.

DOC1: 總統(President) → 總統喬治‧布希(President George W. Bush) → 布希總統 (President Bush) → 小布希(Bush junior)
DOC2: 總統(President) → 布希總統(President Bush) → 他(he) → 他(he) → 布希(Bush junior) → 布希總統(President Bush) → 布希總統(President Bush) → 布希(Bush junior)
DOC3: 總統布希(President Bush) → 布希(Bush junior)
DOC4: 總統柯林頓(President Clinton) → 總統(President) → 他(he) → 柯林頓總統(President Clinton)

Fig. 2. Sample Co-Reference Chains

(1)   Because streaming news is disseminated from different sources anytime, the arrival sequence of documents will affect the quality of controlled vocabulary. For example, when DOC3 arrives before DOC2, the two chains in DOC1 and DOC3 will denote two different named entities due to no word matching between the two co-reference chains. In this case, a resolution algorithm may miss some correct cross-document co-references.

(2)   Because there are two matching words "總統" (President) and "他" (he) between the co-reference chains DOC2 and DOC4, they may be mis-regarded as the same person in spite of different person entities, i.e., "布希總統" (President Bush) and "總統柯林頓" (President Clinton). In this case, a resolution algorithm may produce incorrect cross-document controlled vocabulary.

4.1 Normalized Chain Edit Distance

Instead of using word matching, the concept of normalized chain edit distance is proposed. The edit distance of two strings, s1 and s2, is defined as the minimum number of edit operations, i.e., insertions, deletions and substitutions, needed to transform strings s1 to s2. Consider an example. Let strings s1 and s2 be defined as AAABB and BBAAA, respectively. The edit distance between s1 and s2, called $edit\_distance(s1, s2)$, is 4. The smaller the edit distance is, the more similar the two strings are. Here, the edit distance is extended to determine whether two given co-reference chains are similar or not. Assume there are two co-reference chains – say, *Given* and *Incoming*. Algorithm 1 computes the chain edit distance of *Incoming* and *Given* co-reference chains. If the score is smaller than a predefined threshold, the *Incoming* co-reference chain denotes the same entity as the *Given* co-reference chain, and will be merged into *Given* chain in Algorithm 1. Otherwise, they are regarded as different entities.

Consider the sample co-reference chains shown in Figure 2. Assume DOC1 and DOC2 are *Given* and *Incoming* co-reference chains, respectively. The normalized chain edit distance between these two co-reference chains is (0+0+1+1+1/3+0+0+ 1/3)/8=0.33. Similarly, the edit distance between the *Given* chain in DOC1 and the *Incoming* chain in DOC4 is (3/5+0+1+3/5)/4=0.55. Let the threshold value be 0.45. The two co-reference chains in DOC1 and DOC2 are deemed the same entity. Meanwhile, the co-reference chain in DOC4 denotes a different entity from that in DOC1. On the other hand, although there is no matching word between the chains in DOC1 and DOC3, their normalized chain edit distance is low enough, i.e., (3/7+1/3)/2=0.38 (<0.45). Thus, these two chains can also be deemed to denote the same entity. In summary, the above two issues can be tackled in Algorithm 1.

Algorithm 1. *Compute the normalized chain edit distance of Incoming and Given co-reference chains*

1. Let *len1* and *len2* be the length (i.e., number of words) of *Incoming* and *Given* co-reference chains, respectively.
2. Let *word1[i]* and *word2[j]* be the *ith* and the *jth* elements in *Incoming* and *Given* co-reference chains, respectively.
3. Initialize *score* to be 0.
4. for i = 1 to len1 {
    min = ∞ ;
    j = 1 to len2 {
        (1) let d = *edit_distance*(word1[i], word2[j])
        (2) d = d/max(length(word1[i]),
                    length(word2[j]))
        (3) if d < min then min = d
    }
  socre += min; }
5. Compute *score* = *score* / *len1* and output the *score*.

Pronouns (e.g., "他" (he)) and title words (e.g., "總統" (President)) are less specific in a co-reference chain, so that they contribute less information and are prone to incur errors in creating cross-document controlled vocabullary. DOC2 and DOC4 show an example. ((3/5+0+0+3/5)/4=0.30 < 0.45) In such a case, an alternative solution may be: pronouns and title words are excluded from cross document co-reference chains during mining controlled vocabulary.

4.2 Creating Controlled Vocabulary

As temporal reference denotes a specific time or date, it is not meaningful to unify cross document temporal references into controlled vocabulary. Thus, we ignored the temporal references in our approach. Algorithm 2 specifies how to mine controlled vocabulary incrementally. Figure 3 shows some examples in controlled vocabulary. The term in bold font is a header (canonic form) of a unified co-reference chain.

Algorithm 2.   Mining Controlled Vocabulary

1. Set the threshold value to be α .
2. Get the first news document and the accompanying co-reference chains.
3. Initialize the controlled vocabulary to be the co-reference chains.
4. Get the next news document and its co-reference chains until all are processed.
   a. Check each word in the document sequentially if it is covered in any co-reference chain A.
   b. Check whether the co-reference chain A is temporal expression or not. If yes, go back to step 4a. Otherwise, continue.
   c. Employ Algorithm 1 to compute the normalized chain edit distance between the co-reference chain A (called *Incoming* co-reference chain) and each chain (called *Given* co-reference chain) in controlled vocabulary.
   d. If there is a normalized chain edit distance whose score is lower than α , the elements in chain A are merged into the corresponding chain in the controlled vocabulary.
   e. If all the scores are larger than α , chain A is new and a new entry is created in the controlled vocabulary. The longest term is regarded as a header, which will be used in clustering to uniform the term usages.

(a)   中華航空公司**(China Airlines)**, 華航, 中華航空, 華航公司, China Airlines, China Air-lines, China-Airlines, 台灣最大的航空公司

(b)   澎湖**(Peng-Hu)**, 澎, 澎湖縣, 菊島

(c)   澎湖外海**(Sea around Peng-Hu)**, 外海, 澎湖馬公外海, 失事地點, 飛機失事海域, 出事現場

(d)   行政院**(The Executive Yan)**, 政院, 中央

(e)   交通部**(The Ministry of Transportation and Communications)**, 交部

(f)   交通部民用航空局**(Civil Aeronautics Administration Ministry of Transportation and Communications)** 民航局, 交通部民航局, 民航總局

Fig. 3. An Example of Controlled Vocabulary

4.3 Evaluation

We adopted the B-CUBED metric (Bagga and Baldwin, 1998) shown below to measure the precision and recall of the created controlled vocabulary.

$$\text{Precision }_i = \frac{\text{number of correct elements in the output chain containing entity i}}{\text{number of elements in the output chain containing entity i}} \tag{1}$$

$$\text{Recall}_i = \frac{\text{number of correct elements in the output chain containing entity i}}{\text{number of elements in the true chain containing entity i}} \qquad (2)$$

The final precision and recall rates are the average precision and recall rates of all entities. Besides the direct evaluation, we also employed the created controlled vocabulary to the event clustering system proposed in Section 5 to evaluate the performance indirectly.

4.3.1 Data Set

In our experiment, we used the knowledge base provided by the United Daily News (http://udndata.com/), which has collected 6,270,000 Chinese news articles from 6 Taiwan local newspaper companies since 1975/1/1. To prepare a test corpus, we first set the topic to be "華航空難" (Air Accident of China Airlines), and the range of searching date from 2002/5/26 to 2002/9/4 (stopping all rescue activities). Total 964 related news articles, which have published date, news source, headline and content, respectively, are returned from search engine. All are in SGML format. After reading those news articles, we deleted 5 news articles which have headlines but without any content. The average length of a news article is 15.6 sentences. Besides, all the above articles have been manually tagged with co-reference chains. Furthermore, we asked three research assistants to merge the related co-reference chains into controlled vocabulary separately, and then we used majority rule to create the gold answer.

4.3.2 Experimental Results

Pronouns and title words occur frequently in co-reference chains. To verify if they have significant discrimination among chains, two alternatives are experimented. M1 used the original co-reference chains to create controlled vacabulary. In contrast, M2 excludes pronouns and title words in co-reference chains. The related F-scores are shown in Figure 4. The threshold is the α value in Algorithm 2. The baseline system uses the word matching only. Normalized chain edit distance is superior to word matching no matter which kinds of co-reference chains are adopted. The experimental results also verify that pronouns and title words in a co-reference chain contribute little information no matther word matching or edit distance approaches are employed. When the approach of edit distance using M2 with threshold 0.33 is adopted, the best performance, i.e., precision 96.49%, recall 96.67%, and F-score 96.58%, is achieved.

Analyzing the created controlled vocabullary using M2, we found that there are three major types of errors shown below.

(1) Ambiguous abbreviation problem, e.g., "澳門" (Macau) and "澳洲" (Australia) have the same abbreviation (i.e., "澳"), so that they were merged incorectly.
(2) Lack of semantic information, e.g., "南部地區" (southern area) and "東部地區" (eastern area) were merged incorrectly.
(3) Word order problems, e.g., "雷馬遜颱風" (Remason Typhoon) can not be merged with chain "颱風雷馬遜" (Typhoon Remason).

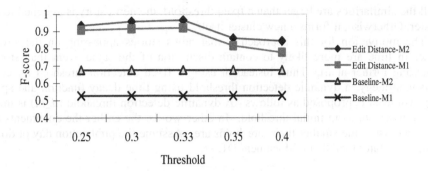

Fig. 4. F-measure Using B-CUBED

5   Event Clustering

A single-pass complete link clustering algorithm incrementally divides the documents into several event clusters. Initially, the first document d_1 is assigned to cluster t_1, and the co-reference chains of d_1 form initial controlled vocabulary (refer to Steps 2-3 of Algorithm 2). Assume there already are k clusters when a new article d_i is considered. That is, clusters t_1, t_2, ..., t_k ($k < i$) have been detected. Document d_i may belong to one of k clusters, or it may form a new cluster t_{k+1}. That is determined by the similarity measure defined below.

At first, we mine new controlled vocabulary from current controlled vocabulary and the incoming news story. The procedure refers to Step 4 of Algorithm 2. Then we compute the similarities of the summary of the incoming news story with each summary in a cluster. The newly-mined controlled vocabulary is global to each similarity computation. Let V_1 and V_2 be the vectors for the two summaries extracted from documents D_1 and D_2. Event clustering module used the headers of the mined controlled vocabulary to replace the related terms in the processing summary. Each term is represented as a vector of normalized *TF-IDF* weights shown as follows.

$$w_{ij} = \frac{tf_{ij} \times \log \frac{N}{df_j}}{\sqrt{s_{i1}^2 + s_{i2}^2 + \cdots + s_{in}^2}} \qquad (3)$$

where tf_{ij} is frequency of term t_j in summary i,
N is total number of summaries in the collection being examined,
df_j is number of summaries that term t_j occurs, and
s_{ij} denotes the TF-IDF value of term t_j in summary i.

The similarity between V_1 and V_2 is computed as follows.

$$Sim(V_1, V_2) = \frac{\sum_{common \ term \ t_j} w_{1j} \times w_{2j}}{\sqrt{\sum_{j=1}^{n} w_{1j}^2} \sqrt{\sum_{j=1}^{m} w_{2j}^2}} \qquad (4)$$

If all the similarities are larger than a fixed threshold, the news story is assigned to the cluster. Otherwise, it forms a new cluster itself.

The motivation for this approach is that news stories appearing on the stream closer in time are more likely to contain discussion of the same event than stories appearing further apart. Thus, instead of using a fixed detection threshold for comparison strategy, a dynamic detection threshold using time decay function and spanning windows is proposed as follows. A dynamic detection threshold (d_th) is introduced, where th is an initial threshold. In other words, the earlier the documents are put in a cluster, the smaller their thresholds are. Assume the publication day of document D2 is later than that of document D1.

$$d\_th(D_1, D_2) = \sqrt{\frac{dist(D_1)/w\_size+1}{dist(D_2)/w\_size+1}} \times th \tag{5}$$

where $dist$ (denoted as day distance) denotes the number of days away from the day at which the event happens, and w_size (denoted as window size) keeps the threshold unchanged within the same window.

6 Experimental Results

6.1 Data Set

The same data set described in Section 4.3.1 is used in this experiment. First, we identify thirteen focus events, e.g., rescue status. Meanwhile, two annotators are asked to read all the 959 news articles and classify these articles into 13 events. If a news article can not be classified, the article is marked as "other" type. A news article which reports more than one event may be classified into more than one event cluster. We compare the classification results of annotators and consider those consistent results as our answer set. The distribution of the 13 focus events are Fly right negotiation between Taiwan and Hong Kong (20), Cause of air accident (57), Confirmation of air accident (6), Influence on stock market (27), Influence on insurance fee (11), Influence on China Airlines (8), Influence on Peng-Hu archipelagoes (26), Punishment for persons in charge (10), News reporting (18), Wreckage found (28), Remains found (57), Rescue status (65), Solatium (34) and others (664), respectively. The number in the parentheses is the document number.

6.2 Evaluation Metric

We also adopt the metric used in Topic Detection and Tracking (Fiscus and Doddington, 2002). The evaluation is based on miss and false alarm rates. Both miss and false alarm are penalties. They can measure more accurately the behavior of users who try to retrieve news stories. If miss or false alarm is too high, users will not be satisfied with the clustering results. The performance is characterized by a detection cost, C_{det}, in terms of the probability of miss and false alarm:

$$C_{Det} = C_{Miss} \times P_{Miss} \times P_{target} + C_{FA} \times P_{FA} \times P_{non-target} \tag{6}$$

where C_{Miss} and C_{FA} are costs of a miss and a false alarm, respectively, P_{Miss} and P_{FA} are the conditional probabilities of a miss and a false alarm, and P_{target} and $P_{non-target}$ ($=1- P_{target}$) are the prior target probabilities. Manmatha, Feng and Allan (2002) indicated that the standard TDT cost function used for all evaluations in TDT is $C_{Det} = 0.02P_{Miss} + 0.098P_{FA}$.

6.3 Experimental Results

For comparison, the centroid-based approach and single pass clustering is regarded as a baseline model. Conventional *tf-idf* scheme selects 20 features for each incoming news articles and each cluster uses 30 features to be its centroid. Whenever an article is assigned to a cluster, the 30 words of the higher *tf-idf*s are regarded as the new centroid of that cluster. On the other hand, we used the algorithm described in Section 3 to study the effects of document summarization using co-reference chains, which selected four sentences to represent the corresponding document. Their experimental results with various thresholds are shown in Table 1. The best results are *0.012990* and *0.013137*, respectively when the threshold is set to 0.05.

Table 1. Detection Cost of Baseline System for Event Clustering

Fixed Threshold	Centroid	Document Sumamrization
0.01	0.024644	0.015960
0.05	*0.012990*	*0.013137*
0.10	0.013736	0.015309
0.15	0.014331	0.016507
0.20	0.015480	0.016736
0.30	0.015962	0.017360

Although the performance using document summarization is lower than the centroid approach, we further study the effects of dynamic thresholds described in Section 5. Table 2 shows the results using various window sizes. The best detection cost, i.e., 0.012647, is achieved under window 2. Moreover, it also shows efficiency of dynamic threshold and window size, i.e., 0.012647 < 0.012990. For comparison, the best experimental results using the summation model (Kuo and Chen, 2004) are also shown in Table 2.

Table 2. Detection Cost of with Various Window Sizes (Initial Threshold =0.05)

Model	1	2	3	4
Coref only	0.12657	**0.012647**	0.012809	0.012942
Coref + Event words	0.112233	**0.011603**	0.013109	0.013109

Next, we consider the length of summary. Dynamic lengths with different compression rates are adopted. The experimental results are shown in Table 3. The detection cost using compression rate 0.35 is *0.011496*, which is better than the above baseline system, i.e., a fixed length summary (< 0.011603). We conclude that the flexible length summary conveys more information than the fixed length.

Table 3. Detection Cost of Baseline System using Dynamic Length Summary

Compression Rate	0.25	0.3	**0.35**	0.4	0.45
C_{det}	0.12074	0.012074	**0.011496**	0.011709	0.12181

Besides summary length issue, we used the summarization module in Section 3 to select sentences under different window sizes. Here, compression rate is 0.35 and threshold value is 0.04. The experimental results are shown in Table 4. The case of window size 2 achieves better detection cost, i.e., *0.011083* (< 0.011496). It shows the approach of using the 20 highest *tf-idf* words can select more informative sentences in document summarization.

Table 4. Detection Cost of Baseline System Using Proposed Summarization Module

Window Size	1	**2**	3	4
C_{det}	0.011828	**0.011083**	0.011817	0.011842

Finally, we introduce controlled vocabulary mined from co-reference chains incrementally. Table 5 and Table 6 show the experimental results without and with removing duplications in the co-reference chains, respectively. It is out of our expectation that the detection cost without duplication removal is better than that with duplication removal. It seems that occurrences play important roles to some degree. That is, the more occurrences in a co-reference chains a word has, the more important it is. In the last experiments, we kept the occurrences of topic elements except pronouns and title words, and mined controlled vocabulary from the resulting chains. As the quality of the controlled vocabulary is improved, the experiments show that the performance of the model is further improved to *0.010915*. Comparing with the best detection costs of the baseline system (*0.012990*) and the summation model (*0.011604*), the best results have 16% and 6% performance gain, respectively.

Table 5. Detection Cost of a System without Removing Duplications

Threshold	0.25	0.3	**0.33**	0.35
C_{det}	0.011237	0.011183	**0.010966**	0.011084
Controlled vocabulary size	2143	2030	**2021**	1785

Table 6. Detection Cost of a System with Removing Duplications

Threshold	0.25	0.3	**0.33**	0.35
C_{det}	0.011415	0.011407	**0.011407**	0.011554
Controlled vocabulary size	2023	1959	**1896**	1719

7   Concluding Remarks

This paper proposes a normalized chain edit distance to mine controlled vocabulary from cross-document co-reference chains incrementally, and utilizes the results to uniform the features used in event clustering on streaming news. Time decay function and spanning window capture the specific characteristics of on-line news. The experiments show that occurrences of discriminative elements in a chain are useful, and pronouns as well as title words may introduce errors. The best model demonstrates 16% and 6% improvement compared to the baseline and the summation model, respectively. In the future, we will introduce linguistic information, e.g., Chinese prefix or suffix, or word senses, to improve the performance of controlled vocabulary construction. Besides, we will also extend the results to construct multilingual controlled vocabulary for multilingual event clustering.

Acknowledgments

Research of this paper was partially supported by National Science Council, Taiwan, under the contracts NSC93-2752-E-001-001-PAE and NSC94-2752-E001-001-PAE.

References

1. Allan, James; Carbonell, Jaime and Yamron, Jonathan (Eds) (2002) Topic Detection and Tracking: Event-Based Information Organization, Kluwer.
2. Azzam, Saliha; Humphreys, Kevin; and Gaizauskas, Robert (1999) "Using Coreference Chains for Text Summarization," Proceedings of the ACL Workshop on Coreference and Its Applications, Maryland.
3. Bagga, Amit and Baldwin, Breck (1998) "Entity-Based Cross-Document Coreferencing Using the Vector Space Model," Proceedings of the 36th Annual Meeting of ACL and the 17th International Conference on Computational Linguistics.
4. Cardie, Claire and Wagstaff, Kiri (1999) "Noun Phrase Co-reference as Clustering," Proceedings of the Joint Coreference on EMNLP and VLC.
5. Chen, Hsin-Hsi; Kuo, June-Jei; Huang, Sheng-Jie; Lin, Chuan-Jie and Wung, Hung-Chia (2003) "A Summarization System for Chinese News from Multiple Sources," Journal of American Society for Information Science and Technology, **54**(13), November 2003, pp. 1224-1236.
6. Chieu, Hai Leong and Lee, Yoong Keok (2004) "Query Based Event Extraction along a Timeline," Proceedings of the 27th ACM SIGIR Conference, pp. 425-432.
7. Fiscus, Jonathan G. and Doddington, George R. (2002) "Topic Detection and Tracking Evaluation Overview," Topic Detection and Tracking: Event-Based Information Organization, James Allan, Jaime Carbonell, and Jonathan Yamron (Eds), Kluwer, pp. 17-32.
8. Fukumoto, F. and Suzuki, Y. (2000) "Event Tracking based on Domain Dependency," Proceedings of the 23rd ACM SIGIR 2000 Conference, pp. 57-64
9. Gooi, Chung Heong and Allan, James (2004) "Cross-Document Coreference on a Large Corpus," Proceedings of Human Language Technology conference / North American chapter of the Association for Computational Linguistics annual meeting, Boston.
10. Kolcz, Aleksander, Prabakarmurthi, Vidya and Kalita, Jugal (2001) "Summarization as Feature Selection for Text Categorization," Proceedings of Tenth International Conference on Information and Knowledge Management, pp 365-370.
11. Kuo, June-Jei and Chen, Hsin-Hsi (2004) "Event Clustering on Streaming News Using Co-reference Chains and Event Words," Proceedings of the ACL Workshop on Coreference and Its Applications, Barcelona, Spain, pp. 17-23.
12. Lin, Chuan-Jie; Chen, Hsin-Hsi; Liu, Che-Chia; Tsai, Ching-Ho and Wung, Hung-Chia (2001) "Open Domain Question Answering on Heterogeneous Data," Proceedings of ACL Workshop on Human Language Technology and Knowledge Management, Toulouse France, pp. 79-85

13. Manmatha, R.; Feng, A. and Allan, James (2002) "A Critical Examination of TDT's Cost Function," Proceedings of the 25th ACM SIGIR Conference, pp. 403-404.
14. MUC (1998) Proceedings of 7th Message Understanding Conference, Fairfax, VA, 29 April - 1 May, 1998, http://www.itl.nist.gov/iaui/894.02/related_projects/muc/ index.html.
15. Morton, Thomas S. (1999) "Using Coreference for Question Answering," Proceedings of the ACL Workshop on Coreference and Its Applications, Maryland, pp. 85-89.
16. Shen, Dou; Chen, Zheng; Yang, Qiang; Zeng Hua-Jun; Zhang, Benyu; Lu, Yuchang; and Ma, Wei-Ying (2004) "Web-page Classification through Summarization," Proceedings of the 27th ACM SIGIR Conference, pp. 242-249.

Filtering Contents with Bigrams and Named Entities to Improve Text Classification

François Paradis and Jian-Yun Nie

Université de Montréal, Canada
{paradifr, nie}@iro.umontreal.ca

Abstract. We present a new method for the classification of "noisy" documents, based on filtering contents with bigrams and named entities. The method is applied to *call for tender* documents, but we claim it would be useful for many other Web collections, which also contain non-topical contents. Different variations of the method are discussed. We obtain the best results by filtering out a window around the least relevant bigrams. We find a significant increase of the micro-F1 measure on our collection of call for tenders, as well as on the "4-Universities" collection. Another approach, to reject sentences based on the presence of some named entities, also shows a moderate increase. Finally, we try combining the two approaches, but do not get conclusive results so far.

1 Introduction

Text classification techniques rely heavily on the presence of a good *feature set*, or indexing terms, and the selection of discriminant features with regards to the classes. This task to the "cleanliness" of the documents: the presence of non-relevant or repetitive contents, as is often found on the Web, will degrade their performance. In our work, we are especially interested in a particular kind of Web documents, *call for tenders*, in which a contracting authority invites contractors to submit a tender for their products and/or services. These documents can be found on the contracted organisation Web site, or on dedicated tendering sites. In earlier work [1] we hypothesized that the noise in such documents was caused by the use of a *sublanguage* [2,3] that describes the procedural aspects of the tenders submission, rather than their topic.

While feature selection undoubtedly brings a significant improvement to some classification methods [4], it is not clear whether it is adequate to filter such "procedural" noise. Indeed in our experiments with call for tenders we have found it difficult to extract either the procedural language (i.e. non-relevant features), or the tenders topic language (i.e. relevant features). There seems to be a significant overlap between the two vocabularies. However certain patterns or constructs of the procedural language can immediately be seen in the documents, and their presence should be an indication of the relevance of the surrounding context.

In this paper we propose to combine feature selection by *vocabulary*, with a *contextual* approach to filter out words or passages in the documents. That is, we first select some n-grams features or named entities, and accept or reject

G.G. Lee et al. (Eds.): AIRS 2005, LNCS 3689, pp. 135–146, 2005.

passages based on their presence or absence. Our aim is to improve classification removing the "noise" from documents.

First, we briefly review related work and the context of our study. We present our first approach to content filtering based on filtering out a passage around the least relevant n-grams. We obtain a significant increase of the micro-F1 measure by using bigrams and a window passage: +11% on our collection of call for tenders, and +3.6% on the 4 Universities dataset. Our second approach, filtering around named entities, gives a moderate increase (+2.6%). We have also tried combining the two approaches, but with little success to report so far.

2   Related Work

The search for a better feature set for classification is hardly new. It has been demonstrated that feature selection is central to some algorithms such as Naive Bayes [4], and therefore several techniques have been proposed, the most popular being *InfoGain*. In early work by Lewis [5] the use of *phrases*, i.e. terms syntactically connected, was considered as a replacement for single-term features. The results were discouraging, which could be partly explained by the fact that there were too many index terms, with low frequency and high redundancy. Still, the idea was revisited by many. More recently Tan et al. [6] find an improvement on the classification of Web pages, by using a combination of bigrams and unigrams selected on the merits of their InfoGain score. However the same technique applied to the Reuters collection did not yield the same gain, mostly because of its over-emphasis on "common concepts". Since their method favours recall, the authors conclude it was harder to improve Reuters because it already had high recall.

The traditional use of the term *filtering* in classification refers the selection of documents relevant to a user profile. There has been much interest lately with spam filtering [7]. Content filtering, such as discussed in this paper, is also not a new idea, although it has not often been linked with classification. Early work with filtering based on character n-grams met with surprising success [8]. In [9] the notion of non-relevant passages in a document is exploited: a document is classified based on the relevance of its passages and their sequence as modeled with Hidden Markov Models. The area of automatic summarisation [10] is also related, since one of its subgoals is also to identify the most meaningful sentences. For example, the relevancy of a sentence can be defined based on its position, length, the frequency of the terms and its similarity with the title [11].

Text classification is often used in the process of named entity extraction [12] but rarely the other way around. Its use in classification is mostly restricted to replacing common strings such as dates or money amounts with tokens, to increase the ability of the classifier to generalise.

3   Classification of Call for Tenders

3.1   The MBOI Project

This study is part of the MBOI project (Matching Business Opportunities on the Internet), which deals with the discovery of business opportunities on the

Internet [13]. The project aims to develop tools for business watch, including spidering, information extraction, classification, and search. The aspect of interest here, classification, consists of classifying call for tenders by industry type, according to one of the existing norms: SIC (Standard Industrial Classification), NAICS (North American Industry Classification System), FCS (Federal Supply Codes), CPV (Common Procurement Vocabulary), etc.

A difficulty in the classification of call for tenders is to identify the relevant information amongst submission instructions, rules, requirements, etc. Sometimes the notice posted on the Web will have all relevant information to determine the subject, sometimes very little, and in some extreme cases none. Often the contracting authority will have the applicant pay to get a full description of the call for tender.

Furthermore, since we are spidering very different sites, the style and format of the documents vary a lot. Although a given organisation will tend to reuse the same patterns, it would not be feasible to manually define filters based on these patterns, without falling into a maintenance nightmare.

3.2   The Test Collection

For our experiments, we created a collection of call for tenders documents by downloading the XML daily synopsis from the FedBizOpps Web site (tenders solicited by American government agencies, available at http://www.fedbizopps.gov/). The XML documents have the same contents as the HTML documents found on the same site. The period downloaded ranged from September 2000 to October 2003. We kept only one document per tender, i.e. chose a document amongst pre-solicitations and amendments. Our collection (thereafter called FBO) is available at http://iro.umontreal.ca/~paradifr/fbo/.

An example of call for tender is shown in figure 1. It includes some meta-data such as the date of publication ("21 May 2001"), classification codes (NAICS "424120" and FCS "75"), the contracting authority ("Office of Environmental Studies"), etc. The body of the document is composed of the subject line and the description; only these fields will be used for classification. Only a portion of the body is indicative of the tender subject (shown in bold). The rest concerns dates and modalities for submission.

We considered only documents with two classification codes, FCS and NAICS (although FCS will not be used here). Since the NAICS codes were not tagged in XML at the time (as they now are), they were extracted from the free text description. This resulted in 21945 documents (72Megs), which were splitted 60% for training, and 40% for testing.

The NAICS codes are hierarchical: every digit of a six-digit code corresponds to a level of the hierarchy. For example, for industry code 424120 (Stationery and Office Supplies Merchant Wholesalers) the sector code is 424 (Merchant Wholesalers, Nondurable Goods). Each of the three participating countries, the U.S., Canada and Mexico, have their own version of the standard, which mostly differ at the level of industry codes (5th or 6th digit). We reduced the category space by considering only the first three digits, i.e. the corresponding "sector".

This resulted in 92 categories (vs. 101 for FCS). We did not normalise for the uneven distribution of categories: for NAICS, 34% of documents are in the top two categories, and for FCS, 33% are in the top five.

Our baseline for this collection is a Naive Bayes [14] classifier trained and tested on the unfiltered documents. Naive Bayes is a common choice in the literature for baseline, and it is known to be sensitive to feature selection, which makes it appropriate to our study. Furthermore, some of the better performing but costlier techniques, such as SVM, do not scale up to our project requirement of handling more than 100K documents.

The 8,000 top terms were selected according to their InfoGain score. The following thresholds were applied: a rank cut of 1 (*rcut*), a fixed weight cut of 0.001 (*wcut*), and a category cut learnt after cross-sampling 50% of the test set over 10 iterations (*scut*). More details about these thresholding techniques can be found in [15,16].

The rainbow software [17] was used to perform our experiments. The results for our baseline classifier are shown in table 1, under the label "unfiltered". The next line, "unfiltered bigram", is provided as an indication of the effect of bigrams alone on classification. It is again unfiltered contents, but using only bigrams as features (see our definition of bigram below). Since the feature space is much larger, we have selected 64,000 features this time. Surprisingly, there is a great drop in the micro-F1 measure. A quick look at the bigrams shows that many were actually part of the procedural language. It is difficult to filter them out, because when we select less features, we also remove "good" features and decrease the micro-F1 measure further.

4   Passage Filtering

Two levels of passage filtering will be considered, depending on the unit being filtered: sentences or *windows* (i.e. sequence of words). Window filtering is appealing on our collection, because sentences can be long, and relevant and non-relevant information is often mixed in a sentence. Also, segmenting into sentences is not trivial in this collection, because it is not well formatted: for example the end-of-sentence period could be missing, or a space could appear inside an acronym (e.g. "U._S.").

4.1   Supervised Filtering of Sentences

In a first experiment we manually labeled 1000 sentences from 41 documents of FBO. The label was "positive" if the sentence was indicative of the tender's subject, or "negative" if not. Sentences with descriptive contents were labeled positive, while sentences about submission procedure, rules to follow, delivery dates, etc. were labeled negative. In the example of figure 1, only the first sentence would be labeled positive. Overall, almost a quarter of the sentences (243) were judged positive.

Intuitively, one would think that the first sentence(s) would often be positive, i.e. the author would start by introducing the subject of the tender, and then

```
<PRESOL>
<DATE> 0521
<YEAR> 01
<CLASSCOD> 75
<NAICS> 424120
<OFFADD> Office of Environmental Studies; 1323 Y Street, Washington, DC 22030
<SUBJECT> Office supplies and devices
<SOLNBR> N00140-04-Q-4555
<ARCHDATE> 07131999
<CONTACT> Mary Ann Deal, Contract Specialist
<DESC> The office of Environmental Studies intends to procure printer toner
cartridges and supplies for the Naval Inventory Control Point in Mechanicsburg, PA.
Request for Quotation (RFQ) N00140-04-Q-4555 contemplates an indefinite delivery
type firm fixed price order. This is a combined synopsis/solicitation for commercial
items prepared in accordance with the format in FAR Subpart 13.5, Test Program for
Certain Commercial Items, as supplemented with additional information included in
this notice. This announcement constitutes the only solicitation; proposals are being
requested, and a written solicitation will not be issued. This is a 100% Total Small
Business Set-Aside. etc.
<URL> http://www.oes.gov
<EMAIL>
<ADDRESS> johndoe@usa.gov
<SETASIDE> Total Small Disadvantage Business
<POPZIP> 22030
<POPCOUNTRY> US
</PRESOL>
```

Fig. 1. A Call for Tender

Table 1. FBO classification with passage filtering

method	macro-F1	micro-F1
unfiltered	.3297	.5498
unfiltered-bigrams	.2622 (-20%)	.4863 (-12%)
trained	.3223 (-2.2%)	.5918 (+7.6%)
sent-unigram	.3323 ($\approx$)	.5701 (+3.7%)
sent-bigram	.3585 (+8.7%)	.5891 (+7.1%)
sent-trigram	.3394 (+2.9%)	.5866 (+6.6%)
window-bigram	.3787 (+14.9%)	.6101 (+11%)
window-trigram	.3497 (+6%)	.5927 (+7.8%)

explain the rules and requirements. This is not always the case. In *combined*
tenders, the text often starts with background information, and then define each
item. In some cases, the subject is scattered amongst negative sentences.

We trained a Naive Bayes classifier on the 1000-sentence collection, for the
positive and negative classes. The task seems to be relatively simple, since when
we tested the classifier on a 40/60 split we obtained a micro-F1 measure of 85%.

We thus filtered the whole collection with this classifier, keeping only the positive sentences. The collection size went from around 600,000 sentences to 96,811. The new, filtered documents were then classified with another Naive Bayes classifier.

Table 1 shows that this classification ("trained") gives an increase of the micro-F1 measure, 7.6% over the baseline ("unfiltered"). Although this result in itself is interesting, our real aim is to achieve unsupervised filtering, i.e. not requiring a training collection and labeled sentences. We propose in the next section a technique to select sentences based on the presence of vocabulary.

4.2   Unsupervised Filtering of Sentences

Our approach to unsupervised filtering of sentences is to build a list of n-grams from the collection, and then filter out either a sentence or a window of terms around each of their occurences in the documents. We define an n-gram as a consecutive sequence of n words, after removal of stop words. For example, we have found the following top 5 n-grams in FBO:

- unigrams: "commercial", "items", "acquisition", "government" and "information"
- bigrams: "items-commercial", "business-small", "conditions-terms", "fedbizopps-link" and "document-fedbizzopps"
- trigrams: "link-fedbizopps-document", "supplemented-additional-information", "additional-information-included", "information-included-notice", "prepared-accordance-format".

We have tried two metrics for the selection of n-grams: the InfoGain measure and the frequency of the n-gram. Although one would expect the InfoGain measure to be a better discriminant, it turns out that the high-frequency terms in FBO are uniformly distributed in the classes, so the simpler frequency works as well if not slightly better. Also, since we are trying to select non-relevant features, i.e. features with low InfoGain, we will also capture the unfrequent features, whether they are distributed evenly or not.

Table 1 shows results of sentence filtering with unigram, bigrams and trigrams (i.e. "sent-unigram", "sent-bigram" and "sent-trigram"). Only the most frequent 1,500 n-grams in the collection were kept (this parameter was determined manually). The criterion for a sentence to be filtered out was the following: a sentence was rejected if $1/8$ of its n-grams were in the reject list (again this parameter was determined empirically).

The best result is obtained with bigrams (0.5891, or an increase of 7.1% over our baseline), which is quite similar to the results obtained with the trained classifier in the preceding section.

4.3   Window Filtering

As mentioned before, although the sentence seems like a good logical unit to perform filtering, it is a bit problematic in our collection because it is not so well delimited, and it is not guaranteed to have the right granularity (i.e. sentences can contain both relevant and non-relevant information). Another approach is to ignore punctuation and sentence markers, and to filter a window around a term.

We select n-grams as above, and filter out a region of m words preceding, up to m words after the n-gram. Additionaly, two regions to be filtered out are connected if "close" enough.

Table 1 shows the results for bigrams and trigrams ("window-bigram" and "window-trigram", respectively). of window filtering for bigrams and trigrams, using term frequency. A window of size 2 was used, i.e. the region filtered out started with the two terms preceding the n-gram, up to the two succeeding terms. Two regions to be filtered out were "connected" if less than 6 terms apart. The window-bigrams filter gives our best results: a micro-F1 of 0.6101 micro-F1 (+11%) and a macro-F1 of .3787 (+14.9%).

Note that to avoid any bias, the term distribution was computed over the training set only. Slightly higher figures can be reached by calculating term frequency over both the training and the test set (the default in rainbow). This is possible in a real scenario, if we constantly update the term distribution with new documents.

Also, we have presented results of filtering *out* sentences or windows, based on non-relevant features. We have also tried the opposite, i.e. selecting relevant features and keeping only those sentences or windows where they appeared. The results are similar.

5   Named Entities

5.1   Entities as Indicators of Relevance

Named entities are expressions containing names of people, organisations, locations, time, etc. These often appear in call for tenders, but are rarely indicative of the subject of the tender. Therefore, we hope that by identifying these expressions, we can either filter out passages that contain them, or reduce their impact on the classifier.

We take a somewhat broad definition of named entities, to include the following:

- *geographical location.* In a call for tender, this can be an execution or delivery location. A location can also be part of an address for a point of contact or the contracting authority (although these are often tagged as meta-data in FBO, they often appear in the text body).
- *organisation.* Most often the organisation will be the contracting authority or one its affiliates. For pre-determined contracts it can be the contractor.
- *date.* This can be a delivery date or execution date (opening and closing dates are often explicitly tagged as meta-data, and therefore do not need to be extracted).

Table 2. Named entities in 1000 sentences

type	accuracy	type	accuracy
-location	72% (252/348)	-person	82% (351/429)
-organisation	75% (357/479)	-date	95% (59/62)
-time	98% (42/43)	-money	100% (18/18)
-URL & email	100% (38/38)	-phone number	98% (39/40)
-FAR	100% (56/56)		
+CLIN	80% (4/5)	+dimensions	100% (8/8)

- *time.* A time limit on the delivery date, or business hours for a point of contact.
- *money.* The minimum/maximum contract value, or the business size of the contractor.
- *URL.* The Web site of the contracting authority or a regulatory site (e.g. a link to CCR - Central Contract Registry).
- *email, phone number.* The details of a point of contact.

Although these entities have a particular use in our collection, they are generic in the sense that they also apply to many other domains. We have also considered the following entities, specific to our collection:

- *FAR* (Federal Acquisition Rules). These are tendering rules for U.S. government agencies. A call for tender may refer to an applicable paragraph in the FAR (e.g. "FAR Subpart 13.5").
- *CLIN* (Contract Line Item Number). The line item define a part or subcontract of the tender. Line items usually appear as a list (e.g. "CLIN 0001: ...").
- *dimensions.* In the context of a tender, a dimension almost always refers to the physical characteristics of a product to deliver (e.g. "240MM x 120MM").

All entities except CLIN and dimensions are *negative* indicators: their presence is an indication of a negative passage or sentence, i.e. not relevant to the subject of the tender. CLIN and dimensions on the other hand are *positive* indicators, since they introduce details about the contract or product.

The entities were identified in the collection using a mix of regular expressions and *Nstein NFinder*, a tool for the extraction of named entities. Table 2 shows the accuracy of the entities as positive/negative indicators on the 1000 training sentences. For example, dates (a negative indicator) appeared in 62 sentences, 59 of which were labeled negative. Dimensions (a positive indicator) appeared in 8 sentences, all of which were labeled positive.

Locations, persons and organisations are the most problematic entities, with an accuracy around or lower that of an "always-negative" classifier (which would be correct 75.7% of the time on our 1000 sentences). That is partly because they often appear along with the subject in an introductory sentence. For example in figure 1 the first sentence contains an organisation, "Office of Environmental

Studies", a location, "Mechanicsburg, PA", as well as the subject, "toner cartridges and supplies". Furthermore, these entities are inherently more difficult to recognise than date and time, which only require a few simple patterns, and can achieve near-perfect recognition accuracy. To make matters more difficult, some documents are all in capital letters, which make the task more difficult because there are no clues to distinguish proper and common nouns. Some examples of errors were: "Space Flight" as a person, "FOB" as an organisation, or "184BW Contracting Office" as a location.

5.2   Classification with Entities

As noted above, a common use of named entities in text categorisation is to replace each instance in the text with a generic token. That strategy does not seem to pay off on FBO, as shown in table 3, under the label "tokens". The micro-F1 measure does not change and the macro-F1 decreases by 1.5%. We have tried different combinations of entities, especially leaving out locations and organisations, all with similar results.

Organisation names sometimes provide valuable clues to the tender's subject. For example, knowing that the contracting authority is the USDA (U.S. Department of Agriculture) increases the likelihood of a tender to be relevant to agriculture. This information is already taken into account by the classifier if the full name appears in the text. However if the acronym alone appears, only limited inference is possible (unless the acronym systematically appeared in all tenders of its kind).

We have tried to expand acronyms based on information collected from the training collection. Firstly we have built an acronym list from all organisation entities of the form: "full name (acronym)". We thus collected 1068 acronyms, excluding two-letters acronyms, which were deemed too ambiguous, especially since our collection includes many two-letter state abbreviations. We then expanded acronyms in the documents (except when they appeared inside brackets), and used the window-bigrams selection. Unfortunately, as shown in the last line of table 3, "acronym", this approach yielded a micro-F1 of .5265, a decrease of 4.2% over the baseline. One possible explanation for this poor performance is the high degree of ambiguity in the acronyms. For example, ISS refers to "Integrated Security System" or "International Space Station". In this case we put both expansions in the document.

Another possible use of named entities is to exploit the accuracy information from table 2. We have built a sentence filter that rejects a sentence if enough negative indicators are found. For indicators with a 100% accuracy, one instance is enough to reject a sentence. For others, we give a weight to each entity equals to its accuracy minus 75.7% (i.e. the accuracy of the always-negative classifier). We sum up the weights, and reject the sentence if it is above a threshold (which we have set to .40 in this experiment). The results of this filtering, under label "indicators", yields a micro-F1 of 0.5640, or +2.6% of the baseline.

We have tried combining bigrams and named entities in the following way. Each instance was replaced with a generic token, as above, and the bigrams

Table 3. FBO classification with named entities

method	macro-F1	micro-F1
tokens	.3246 (-1.5%)	.5514 ($\approx$)
acronym	.3222 (-2.3%)	.5265 (-4.2%)
indicators	.3325 ($\approx$)	.5640 (+2.6%)
trained	.3507 (+6.4%)	.5935 (+8%)
window-bigram	.3703 (+12.3%)	.6077 (+10.5%)

were computed with those tokens. The aim was to find more generic patterns inside the bigrams. For example, the bigrams now included patterns such as 'exceed-[money]' (as in "business size should not exceed \$10.4M"). Such a pattern could not be picked up before because money amounts, as other numbers, would be rejected by the tokeniser. Furthermore, using an entity tag increases the frequency of the bigram and therefore its chance to be included in the filter list. Unfortunately, as shown in table 3 under labels "trained" and "window-bigram", this combination does not significantly increase over the sentence and window filtering of the preceding section: the trained method goes from .5918 to .5935, and the window-bigram from .6101 to .6077.

6   Results on 4-Universities

We have tried these techniques on the 4-Universities collection, which can be obtained from CMU World Wide Knowledge Base project at URL `http://www-2.cs.cmu.edu/afs/cs.cmu.edu/project/theo-20/www/data/`. It contains 8282 Web pages collected mainly from four American universities, and manually classified in seven categories: student pages, faculty, staff, department, course, project or other.

The baseline is again a Naive Bayes classifier, this time using InfoGain with 2000 features, as suggested by the authors. We have also used their script to replace some numbers with generic tokens. We have not however implemented their cross-tests, i.e. train on three, and test on one university.

Table 4 shows some results. One can see some differences with our FBO collection. Contrary to FBO, the use of bigrams and named entity tokens (tokens) had a positive impact on the unfiltered collection, with an increase of 8.6 and

Table 4. Classification results on 4 Universities

method	macro-F1	micro-F1
unfiltered	.5918	.6492
unfiltered-bigram	.6205 (+4.8%)	.7055 (+8.6%)
window-bigram	.5346 (-9.7%)	.6723 (+3.6%)
tokens	.5864 ($\approx$)	.6664 (+2.6%)

2.6%, respectively. We did not test the "indicators" filtering, since we did not have information about the accuracy of the entities.

We tested the window-bigram method with the 1500 top bigrams according to the InfoGain measure, and obtained a micro-F1 value of 0.6723, an increase of 3.6% over the baseline. However, the macro-F1 has suffered a hefty drop (-9.7%). We have not yet studied the reasons for this.

7   Conclusion

We have investigated the use of bigrams and named entities to perform content filtering. Our domain of application was the classification of call for tenders. Our findings are that filtering a windows of terms around most frequent bigrams works well for this kind of collection: we could obtain an increase of 11% of micro-F1. We also get a moderate improvement of 2.6% by filtering sentences based on named entities; however this method relies on an accuracy estimate, which is not always practical to get in reality. We have tried combining the two approaches but so far our results are rather inconclusive.

We have tried this approach on the 4-Universities dataset and also found an increase of the micro-F1 using the window-bigram method. This is, we hope, an indication that this method is well-suited for Web collections. We plan to do more tests in the future to verify that claim.

When filtering with bigrams, we did not include simple terms in the list; similarly for trigrams we did not include bigrams. This might explain the lower results for trigrams, because they are too restrictive, and fail to capture common two-terms relationships. An obvious extension, as in [6], is to combine them.

Another idea worth pursuing is taking advantage of the sequence of relevant and non-relevant sentences in the document. This idea is similar to the HMM proposed in [9].

Acknowledgments

This project was financed jointly by Nstein Technologies and NSERC.

References

1. Paradis, F., Nie, J.Y.: Étude sur l'impact du sous-langage dans la classification automatique d'appels d'offres. In: CORIA, Grenoble, France. (2005)
2. Lehrberger, J. In: Automatic translation and the concept of sublanguage, in R. Kittredge et J. Lehrberger (eds.), Sublanguage: Studies of Language in Restricted Semantic Domains. (1982)
3. Biber, D.: Using register-diversified corpora for general language studies. Computational linguistics **19** (1993)
4. Yiming Yang, J.O.P.: A comparative study on feature selection in text categorization. In: Proceedings of ICML-97, 14th International Conference on Machine Learning. (1997)

5. Lewis, D.: An evaluation of phrasal and clustered representations on a text categorization task. In: 15th ACM International Conference on Research and Development in Information Retrieval (SIGIR). (1992) 37–50
6. Tan, C.M., Wang, Y.F., Lee, C.D.: The use of bigrams to enhance text categorizatio. Information Processing and Management: an International Journal **38** (2002) 529 – 546
7. Zhang, L., Yao, T.: Filtering junk mail with a maximum entropy model. In: Proceeding of 20th International Conference on Computer Processing of Oriental Languages (ICCPOL03). (2003) 446–453
8. Cavnar, W.: N-gram-based text filtering for trec-2. In: Second Text REtrieval Conference (TREC). (1993)
9. Denoyer, L., Zaragoza, H., Gallinari, P.: Hmm-based passage models for document classification and ranking. (2001)
10. Orasan, C., Pekar, V., L., L.H.: A comparison of summarisation methods based on term specificity estimation. In: Proceedings of the Fourth International Conference on Language Resources and Evaluation (LREC-04). (2004) 1037–1041
11. Nobata, C., Sekine, S., Murata, M., Uchimoto, K., Utiyama, M., Isahara, H.: Sentence extraction system assembling multiple evidence. (2001)
12. M., J.: Named entity extraction with conditional markov models and classifiers. In: The 6th Conference on Natural Language Learning. (2002)
13. Paradis, F., Ma, Q., Nie, J.Y., Vaucher, S., Garneau, J.F., Gérin-Lajoie, R., Tajarobi, A.: Mboi: Un outil pour la veille d'opportunités sur l'internet. In: Colloque sur la Veille Stratégique Scientifique et Technologique, Toulouse, France. (2004)
14. Jason D. M. Rennie, Lawrence Shih, J.T., Karger, D.R.: Tackling the poor assumptions of naive bayes text classifiers. In: Proceedings of the Twentieth International Conference on Machine Learning. (2003)
15. Yang, Y.: An evaluation of statistical approaches to text categorization. Journal of Information Retrieval **1** (1999) 67–88 An excellent reference paper for comparisons of classification algorithms on the Reuters collection.
16. Yang, Y.: A study on thresholding strategies for text categorization. In: Proceedings of SIGIR-01, 24th ACM International Conference on Research and Development in Information Retrieval. (2001)
17. McCallum, A.K.: Bow: A toolkit for statistical language modeling, text retrieval, classification and clustering. http://www.cs.cmu.edu/~mccallum/bow (1996)

The Spatial Indexing Method for Supporting a Circular Location Property of Object

Hwi-Joon Seon[1] and Hong-Ki Kim[2]

[1] Department of Computer Information Communication, Seonam University,
720 GwangchiDong, NamWon, JeollabukDo, Korea
hjseon@seonam.ac.kr
[2] Department of Computer Science, Dongshin University,
DaehoDong, Naju, JeollanamDo, Korea
hkkim@dongshinu.ac.kr

Abstract. To increase the retrieval performance in spatial and multimedia database systems, it is required to develop spatial indexing methods considering the spatial locality. The spatial locality is related to the location property of objects. Most spatial indexing methods, however, were not considered the circular location property of objects. In this paper, we propose a dynamic spatial index structure, called CR^*-tree. It is a new spatial index structure to support the circular location property of objects in which a search space is organized with the circular and linear domains. We include the performance test results that verify this advantage of the CR^*-tree and show that the CR^*-tree outperforms the R^*-tree.

1 Introduction

Spatial database systems are required to have high memory space and processing time for managing spatial objects. It is possible to process spatial queries efficiently by applying a suitable index structure and a query processing technique[1,2,5,6].

Most of the spatial indexing methods are assuming a domain in the search space, where the domain consists of a linear order range between minimum and maximum value that object attributes will be taken[4,8]. But, objects that are handled in many applications, such as Geographic Information Systems, CAD and VLSI design can have the circular location property. To reflect this circular location property of object efficiently, it is required that a search space consists of domains with the circular qualities.

The example of region and nearest neighbor queries occurring in the circular environment is as follows:

(1) find all objects at which X is from 315 to 20 degrees and Y is from 15 to 40 degrees, where the domain is between 0 and 360 degrees.
(2) find all objects that is occurred in the nearest time at 23:40, where the domain is between 0 and 24 o'clock.

The region query 1) is the example which is composed of a query range containing the circular and noncircular qualities, and 2) is a case that an object closest to a query

G.G. Lee et al. (Eds.): AIRS 2005, LNCS 3689, pp. 147–159, 2005.

point should be considered at the circular environment. In circular environments, the previous spatial indexing methods store spatially adjacent objects in different buckets. It cannot search efficiently for such a query type as in the example. Therefore, for efficient query processing it is important that objects are well clustered into buckets, i.e., that objects which are close to each other are likely to be stored in the same bucket.

In this paper, we present the circular R^*-tree, called CR^*-tree, which has been designed explicitly to cluster spatial objects considering the circular location property of objects in a search space with circular domains. We include the performance test results to verify this advantage of the CR^*-tree, and show that the CR^*-tree clearly outperforms the R^*-tree in the number of disk accesses, the storage requirement and the bucket utilization.

2 Circular Domain and Circular Region Queries

All previous spatial indexing methods have in common that any domain, D_i $(i = 0, 1, \cdots, N - 1)$ constructing N-dimensional search spaces is organized in a linear order range with m different values between minimum and maximum value, where i th attribute of objects will have these values in the corresponding search space. Any domain D_i is represented by $(d_0, d_1, \cdots, d_{m-1})$, where $d_i < d_{i+1}$, $i = 0, 1, \cdots, m - 2$.

To efficiently handle objects with the circular location property in spatial indexing methods, it is required that a search space consists of domains with a circular order range. And also the query range covered by a region query can get the circular range in N-dimensional search spaces.

Before proceeding, we need some definitions. Let *next* and *prev* be the functions returning a location attribute value of next or previous for any location attribute value. These functions have a location value as parameters.

We distinguish a domain into a circular domain and a linear domain by definition 1 and definition 2.

Definition 1: (Circular Domain)
The domain D_i is a circular domain, iff

1) $next(d_k) = d_{k+1}$ $(0 \le k < m-1)$ and $next(d_{m-1}) = d_0$

2) $prev(d_k) = d_{k-1}$ $(0 < k \le m-1)$ and $prev(d_0) = d_{m-1}$ □

Definition 2: (Linear Domain)
The domain D_i is a linear domain, iff

1) a location attribute value returning by $next(d_{m-1})$ and $prev(d_0)$ is not existing

2) $next(d_k) = d_{k+1}$ $(0 \le k < m-1)$ and $prev(d_k) = d_{k-1}$ $(0 < k \le m-1)$ □

A region query Q is represented by the Cartesian product of query ranges in N-dimensional search space: let $I_i = [s_i, e_i]$ be a query range occurring in domain D_i

where s_i and e_i is starting and ending value of a query range $(0 \le i \le N-1)$. Thus, Q is represented by $I_0 \times I_1 \times \cdots \times I_{N-1}$.

In this paper, Region queries are distinguished into circular region queries and linear region queries as noted in the following definitions.

Definition 3: (Circular Region Query)
A region query Q is called the circular region query, iff more than one query range I_i organizing a region query Q is occurring in a circular domain D_i and $d_0, d_{m-1} \in I_i$, $s_i > e_i$. $\square$

Definition 4: (Linear Region Query)
A region query Q is called the linear region query, iff all of query range I_i organizing a region query Q is occurring in a circular domain or a linear domain D_i and $s_i < e_i$. $\square$

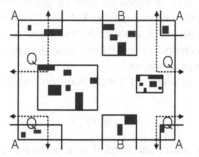

(a) Search spaces with circular domains

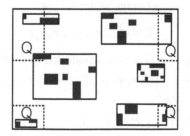

(b) Search spaces with linear domains

Fig. 1. Object clustering and circular region query

If the multi-dimensional search space with circular domains exists, object clustering considered a circular environment is able to increase a bucket utilization and a spatial locality, so that the total number of buckets accessing in response to region queries can be minimized.

Fig. 1 shows an example of object clustering that is considered the location attribute of objects in two-dimensional search spaces: (a) a search space with circular domains and (b) a search space with linear domains. In fig. 1(a), A and B are subsearch spaces of a bucket which is generated by a spatial indexing method clustering objects circularly. As shown fig. 1(b), object clustering by the R-tree family required more buckets than that of fig. 1(a) for good spatial locality.

When the circular region query Q is given as in fig. 1(a), the number of buckets accessing for Q is 2 in (a). But (b) must be handled in a way so that the circular region query Q is transformed to the 4 linear region queries. Therefore, the required number of access to buckets is 5.

3   CR*-Tree

3.1   Index Structure

The structure of the CR*-tree is based on that of the R*-tree[1]. The CR*-tree is a height-balanced tree which consists of buckets and nodes. N-dimensional search spaces in the CR*-tree consist of S circular domains and $N - S$ linear domains where $0 \le S \le N$. If S is 0, search spaces consist of linear domains that the previous spatial indexing methods have been assuming.

A bucket contains a header and more than one object. Each object has the following form,

$$(R, O_{id})$$

where O_{id} is an object identifier and is used as a pointer to a data object. The region value R is allocated to each object for searching. The R is the N-dimensional minimum bounding rectangle which is a minimal approximation for the region covered by a corresponding object in the search space.

$$R = (R_0, R_1, \cdots, R_{N-1})$$

Where R_i ($i = 0, 1, \cdots, N - 1$) is a closed bounded interval describing the extent of an object along dimension i. The region of subsearch space covering an object is represented as Cartesian products :

$$[RI_S, RI_E]_0 \times [RI_S, RI_E]_1 \times \cdots \times [RI_S, RI_E]_{N-1}$$

where RI_S is the starting value and RI_E is the ending value.

A node contains a header and 1-dimensional array structure, and each of them has the form,

$$(R, flag, P_{child})$$

where R is a N-dimensional subsearch space, $flag$ represents whether a subsearch space has the circular qualities or not, and P_{child} is a pointer to a successor node in the next level of the CR*-tree or an address-pointer of bucket.

If the entry is a leaf in the CR*-tree, R represents a subsearch space which is covered by one bucket and P_{child} is an address pointer of the corresponding bucket. Otherwise, R is a subsearch space which is containing all objects in a child node.

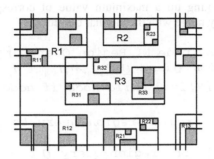

Fig. 2. Search spaces of the CR*-tree

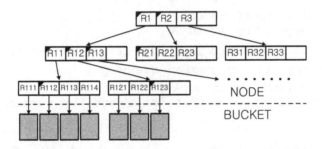

Fig. 3. The CR*-tree structure

In a search space with two circular domains, fig. 2 shows an example of the nested hierarchy of buckets and subsearch spaces and fig. 3 the corresponding CR*-tree(assuming a branching factor of 4). In the fig. 2, $R1$ and $R2$ are subsearch spaces with the circular qualities.

3.2   Algorithms

In all algorithms of the CR*-tree, subsearch spaces with a circular domain are handled by transforming into logical subsearch spaces. If any closed bounded interval organizing a subsearch space has $RI_S > RI_E$, then a corresponding subsearch space is transformed into a logical subsearch space which is summing up a maximum value of domain containing a closed bounded interval to RI_E.

The algorithms of the CR*-tree are based on that of the R*-tree. In this section, we only mention the difference between the algorithm of the CR*-tree and that of the R*-tree. Evidently, the CR*-tree is different from the R*-tree in handling subsearch spaces.

The search algorithm starts with a root and examines each branch that intersects the query region recursively following these branches. At the leaf level it reports all entries that intersect the query region as qualified objects.

The circular region query in the search algorithm is performed with the logical region query by summing up a maximum value of corresponding domain to the ending value of a query range with the circular qualities.

Algorithm SEARCH (node N, Region Query Q)
/* Perform Region Query Q $(I_0, I_1, \cdots, I_{N-1})$, I_i denotes a range $[s_i, e_i]$ of D_i, $N_i.child$ is a child node if node N_i. */
{
S1. [Convert a circular region query to a logical region query]
    For all I in the region query Q
        If s_i is more than e_i then e_i plus the maximum value of domain D_i equals e_i.
S2. [Search nonleaf nodes]
    For every entry N_i in N
        Invoke **SEARCH**($N_i.child$, Q) for every entry whose MBR intersects the region query Q.
S3. [Search objects in bucket]
    Output all objects that intersect the region query Q.
}

The strategy for object insertion is very important in the view of spatial locality. The insertion algorithm in the CR^*-tree is supporting a circular clustering of objects to the insertion strategy of the R^*-tree. Therefore, the CR^*-tree can ensure the highly spatial locality among objects contained in subsearch spaces and buckets.

Algorithm INSERT(node N, object o)
/* Insert object o into a tree rooted at N */
{
I1. [Find the bucket for new object o]
    Use **ChooseBucket**(o , ptr) to choose a bucket B in which to place o.
I2. [Add object o to bucket B]
    Insert o into B.
    If B is first overflow,
        then invoke ReInsert(o)
        else invoke SplitBucket(B , o), which will return new bucket if split was inevitable.
I3. [Propagate changes upward]
    Form a set S that contain B, its adjacent siblings, and the new bucket(if any).
    Invoke AdjustTree(S).

I4. [*Grow tree taller*]
    If node split propagation caused the root to split,
    create a new root whose children are the two
    resulting nodes.
}

To insert a new object in the insertion algorithm of the CR*-tree, we traverse the tree, choosing the node at each level whose subsearch space needs the least area enlargement to include the new object by considering the location attribute value circularly. Once we reach the leaf node, we insert the new object into the corresponding bucket whose subsearch space needs the least overlap enlargement to include the new object by considering the location attribute value circularly.

Algorithm ChooseBucket(object o, pointer p)

/* Return the bucket in which to place a new
   object o */
{
C1. [*Initialize*] Set N to be the root node.
C2. [*Leaf check*] If N is a leaf, return N.
C3. [*Choose subtree*]
        If the child pointer in N is a leaf, then
            considering the location attribute value of all
            entries in N circularly and non-circularly,
            choose the entry(o, p) with the least overlap
            enlargement to include the new object o; on
            tie, choose the entry with the least area
            enlargement
        If the child pointer in N is not a leaf, then
            considering the location attribute value of all
            entries in N circularly and Non-circularly,
            choose the entry(o, p) with the least area
            enlargement to include the new object o; on
            tie, choose the entry with the smallest area.
C4. [*Descend until a leaf is reached*]
        Set N to the node pointed by p and repeat from C2.
    }

When a node or a bucket is full, the CR*-tree reinserts a portion of its entries rather than splits it unless reinsertion has been made at the same node or bucket. Otherwise, the split algorithm has two phases. In the first phase, the split dimension is determined as follows. For each dimension, the objects are sorted according to their lower bound and according to their upper bound, and the area of the minimum bounding rectangles of all partitions is summed up and the least sum determines the split dimension. In the second phase, the split index is determined, minimizing overlap value between the subsearch space and the least coverage of dead space. After the insertion/split/re-insert, we update the node entries and information of the affected nodes along paths.

4 Performance Evaluations

4.1 Environment for Experiment

To show the practical impacts of our method, we performed an extensive experiment evaluation of the CR^*-tree and compared it to the R^*-tree.

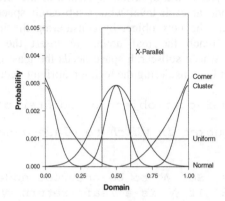

Fig. 4. Object distributions

The test data used for the experiments are 20,000 objects in 2-dimensional data space organized with 2 circular domains. And the region of object is square in size which is 0.1% of the whole search space. This is to demonstrate the performance of the CR^*-tree and the R^*-tree in case that most objects inserting into an index will usually overlap to a some extent.

To evaluate the performance of the CR^*-tree and the R^*-tree, we selected five object distribution. Because the object distribution in [7] is considered to be realistic, we decided to take these object distributions for performance comparison. Fig. 4 is the object distribution used in the experiments.

In fig. 4, the object is representing the probability that 1000 objects is occurring in the domain range [0,1), and the probability sum in each of the distributions is 1. By all experimental results for the five groups of object distribution, the characteristic of CR^*-tree is distinct especially in the uniform and the corner distribution. Therefore, we only describe the experiment results based on the uniform and the corner distribution. The uniform distribution was used to test the property of indexing method in which the object distribution is the ideal state. The corner distribution was used to compare the performance of the CR^*-tree and the R^*-tree in the distribution where the maximum of distribution density occurs in the part of search space and the circular quality is much reflected.

We constructed indices for these data sets and measured the number of disk accesses, storage space requirement, and bucket utilization.

To evaluate the performance for queries processing, we generated seven groups of circular region queries and linear region queries: The regions of the seven groups of 1000 queries are squares varying in size which are 0.01%, 0.1%, 0.5% and 1% of the whole search space, and their centers are uniformly distributed in the search space.

And the rate of each circular region query varies from 0%, 5%, 10%, 15%, 20%, 25% to 30% relatively to the number of queries.

In order to keep the performance comparison manageable, we have chosen the buffer size for buckets and nodes to be 1K, 2K, 4K and 8Kbytes. To evaluate the bucket utilization, the buffer size in this experiment is from 1K to 32Kbytes.

4.2 Experimental Results

When the size of region query is large and the buffer size is small, the number of disk accessed becomes maximal. In this paper, we have described the correlation between the rate of circular region query and the number of disk accesses in experimental environment where the number of disk accessed is maximal.

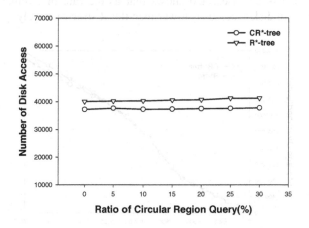

(a) Uniform distribution

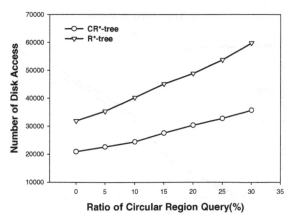

(b) Corner distribution

Fig. 5. The accumulated number of disk accesses

In the first experiment, we investigated the number of disk accesses over the rate of circular region query. Fig. 5 shows the accumulated number of disk accesses as the rate of circular region queries increased when the size of region query is 1% and the buffer size is 2Kbyte. As show in fig. 5, all of the CR*-tree and the R*-tree indicated for the corner distribution that as the rate of circular region queries grew, the number of disk accesses increased. And the uniform distribution shows consistently the number of disk accesses. They clearly depict that the CR*-tree outperforms the R*-tree for the both data distributions. This is due to the fact that the more the circular property is applied in the distribution, the more the objects exist at the corner of search space.

Therefore, the number of buckets accessing to the circular region query becomes large. From the experiment results, the CR*-tree consistently outperforms the R*-tree in the number of disk accesses, and shows that as the rate of circular region query grew, the increase in disk accesses is lower than the R*-tree relatively.

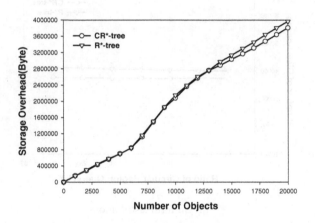

(a) Uniform distribution

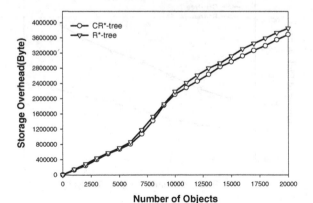

(b) Corner distribution

Fig. 6. Storage space requirements

In the second experiment, we measured the storage space requirement needed to insert the objects. Fig. 6 shows the storage space requirement over the number of inserted objects when the buffer size is 4Kbyte. By extensive experiment results, the increase in the storage space requirement of CR*-tree is almost identical with that of R*-tree regardless of the buffer size. But, the CR*-tree shows lower the storage space requirement than the R*-tree in distributions such that the concentration of objects in search space occurred and the circular clustering is possible or when the buffer size is large.

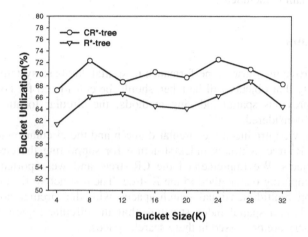

(a) Uniform distribution

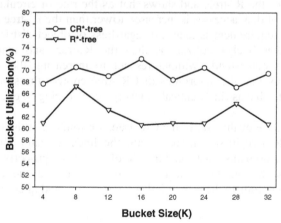

(b) Corner distribution

Fig. 7. Bucket utilization

In the third experiment, we examined the correlation between the increase in bucket capacity and the bucket utilization. To this end, we inserted all 20,000 objects in random order into the initially CR*-tree, varying the bucket capacity from 1K to

32Kbyte in steps of 4Kbyte. And we measured the bucket utilization for all data distributions. Fig. 7 shows the results of the CR*-tree for the uniform and the corner distribution respectively. As shown in fig. 7, the CR*-tree maintains higher bucket utilization than the R*-tree. For the uniform and the corner distribution, the CR*-tree shows 67~73% and 68~72% bucket utilizations consistently without respect to increasing the bucket size. The reason for the phenomenon is that the CR*-tree can reduce the number of buckets by storing spatially adjacent objects in identical buckets, considering the circular location property of objects in a search space where the circular domain is included.

5   Conclusions

In order to improve the retrieval performance in spatial database systems, the circular location property that objects will be taken should be considered for constructing the index. In the previous spatial indexing methods, the circular location property of objects was not considered.

In this paper, we introduced the circular domain and the circular region query, and proposed the CR*-tree as a new index structure for supporting the circular location property of objects. We implemented the CR*-tree, and we reported performance evaluations, comparing our method to the R*-tree. The distinctive feature of the CR*-tree is assuming multidimensional search spaces with the circular domain and the linear domain. It is a spatial index structure that the circular region query and the linear region query are processed in these search spaces.

According to the experiment results, the number of disk accesses of the CR*-tree is smaller than that of the R*-tree, and shows that as the rate of circular region queries grew, the number of disk accesses is increased lower than the R*-tree relatively. Also, the storage space requirement is identical regardless of object distributions. And the CR*-tree has higher bucket utilizations than the R*-tree, and maintains 67~73% bucket utilizations consistently without respect to increasing the bucket capacity. These results imply that the algorithms of CR*-tree contain the strategy for storing spatially adjacent objects in identical buckets, considering the circular location property of objects.

In our performance evaluation of the CR*-tree, we found that the CR*-tree slightly outperforms the R*-tree in search space with the linear domain. But, if the search space with circular domains exists, and the circular location property is much applied in the object distribution, the object clustering considered the circular location property is able to minimize the cost of index construction and query processing.

References

1. Beckmann.N., Kriegel.H., Schneider.R. and Seeger.B, "The R*-tree: an Efficient and Robust Access Method for Points and Rectangles," Proc. ACM SIGMOD Int. Conf. on Management of Data, . (1990) 322-331.
2. Brinkhoff.T., Kriegel.H.P, "The Impact of Global Clustering on Spatial Database Systems," Proc of the 20th VLDB Conf. (1994) 168-179.

3. Henrich. A, Six.H.W, "How to Split Buckets in Spatial Data Structures," Geographic DB Management Systems, Capri(Italy), (1991) 212- 244.
4. Joune.L.K., Robert.L, "The Spatial Locality and a Spatial Indexing Method by Dynamic Clustering in Hypermap System," Proc. of the 2nd Sym. on Large Spatial Databases, (1991) 207-223.
5. Katayama.N., Satoh.S., "The SR-tree :An Index Structure for High-Dimensional Nearest Neighbor Queries," Proc. ACM SIGMOD Int. Conf. on Management of Data, (1997) 369-380.
6. Kim.H.K, "A Spatial Index Structure for Dynamic Object Clustering in Spatial Database Systems," Ph.D. Thesis, University of Chonnam, (1996).
7. Jagadish.H.V., "Linear Clustering of Objects with Multiple Attributes," Proc. ACM SIGMOD Int. Conf. on Management of Data, (1990) 332-342.
8. Lu.H, Ooi.B.C., "Spatial Indexing: Past and Future," IEEE Data Engineering Bulletin, Vol.16, No.3, (1993) 16-21.
9. Theodoridis.Y.,Timos.K., "A Model for Prediction of R-tree Performance," Proc. of 15th ACM SIGACT-SIGMOD-SIGART Sym. on Principles of Database Systems, (1996) 161-171.
10. Yufel.T, Dimitris.P., "Spatial Queries in Dynamic Environments," ACM Transactions on Database Systems, Vol.28, No.2, (2004) 101-139.

Supervised Categorization of JavaScript™ Using Program Analysis Features

Wei Lu and Min-Yen Kan

Department of Computer Science, School of Computing,
National University of Singapore, Singapore, 117543
{luwei, kanmy}@comp.nus.edu.sg

Abstract. Web pages often embed scripts for a variety of purposes, including advertising and dynamic interaction. Understanding embedded scripts and their purpose can often help to interpret or provide crucial information about the web page. We have developed a functionality-based categorization of JavaScript, the most widely used web page scripting language. We then view understanding embedded scripts as a text categorization problem. We show how traditional information retrieval methods can be augmented with the features distilled from the domain knowledge of JavaScript and software analysis to improve classification performance. We perform experiments on the standard WT10G web page corpus, and show that our techniques eliminate over 50% of errors over a standard text classification baseline.

1 Introduction

Current generation web pages are no longer simple static texts. As the web has progressed to encompass more interactivity, form processing, uploading, scripting, applets and plug-ins have allowed the web page to become a dynamic application. While a boon to the human user, the dynamic aspects of web page scripting and applets impede the machine parsing and understanding of web pages. Pages with JavaScript, Macromedia Flash and other plug-ins are largely ignored by web crawlers and indexers. When functionality is embedded in such web page extensions, key metadata about the page is often lost. This trend is growing as more web content is provided using content management systems which use embedded scripting to create a more interactive experience for the human user. If automated indexers are to keep providing accurate and up-to-date information, methods are needed to glean information about the dynamic aspects of web pages.

To address this problem, we consider a technique to automatically categorize uses of JavaScript, a popular web scripting language. In many web pages, JavaScript realizes many of the dynamic features of web page interactivity. Although understanding embedded applets and plug-ins are also important, we chose to focus on JavaScript as 1) its code is inlined within an HTML page and 2) embedded JavaScript often interacts with other static web page components (unlike applets and plug-ins).

An automatic categorization of JavaScript assists an indexer to more accurately model web pages' functionality and requirements. Pop-up blocking, which has been

G.G. Lee et al. (Eds.): AIRS 2005, LNCS 3689, pp. 160–173, 2005.

extensively researched, is just one of the myriad uses of JavaScript that would be useful to categorize. Such software can assist automated web indexers to report useful information to search engines and allow browsers to block annoying script-driven features of web pages from end users.

To perform this task, we introduce a machine learning framework that draws on features from text categorization, program comprehension and code metrics. We start by developing a baseline system that employs traditional text categorization techniques. We then show how the incorporation of features that leverage knowledge of the JavaScript language together with program analysis, can improve categorization accuracy. We conduct evaluation of our methods on the widely-used WT10G corpus [4], used in TREC research, to validate our claims and show that the performance of our system eliminates over 50% of errors over the baseline.

In next section, we examine the background in text categorization and discuss how features of the JavaScript language and techniques in program analysis can assist in categorization. We then present our methods that distills features for categorization from the principles of program analysis. We describe our experimental setup and analysis and conclude by discussing future directions of our work.

2   Background

A survey of previous work shows that the problem of automated computer software categorization is relatively new. We believe that this is due to two reasons. First, programming languages are generally designed to be open-ended and largely task-agnostic. Languages such as FORTRAN, Java and C are suitable for a very wide range of tasks, and attempting to define a fixed categorization scheme for programs is largely subjective, and likely to be ill-defined. Second, the research fields of textual information retrieval (IR) and program analysis have largely developed independently of each other. We feel that these two fields have a natural overlap which can be exploited.

Unlike natural language texts, program source code is unambiguous to the compiler and has exact syntactic structures. This means that syntax plays an important role that needs to be captured, which has been largely ignored by text categorization research.

Ugurel et al.'s [11] work is perhaps the first work that uses IR methods to attack this problem. They employ support vector machines for source code classification in a two-phase process consisting of programming language classification followed by topic classification. In the second, topic classification task, they largely relied on each software projects' README file and comments. From the source code itself, only included header file names were used as features. We believe a more advanced treatment of the source code itself can assist such topic classification. These features, including syntactic information and some language-specific semantic information, could be important and useful for classification. Other recent work in categorizing web pages [14] has revived interest in the structural aspect of text. One hypothesis of this work is that informing these structural features with knowledge about the syntax of the programming language can improve source code classification.

Program analysis has developed into many subfields, in which formal methods are favored over approximation. The subfield of program comprehension develops models to explain how human software developers learn and comprehend existing code [9]. These models show that developers use both top-down and bottom-up models in their learning process [12]. Top-down models imply that developers may use a model of program execution to understand a program. Formal analysis via code execution [2] may yield useful evidence for categorization.

Comprehension also employs code metrics, which measure the complexity and performance of programs. Of particular interest to our problem scenario are code reuse metrics, such as [3,5,7], as JavaScript instances are often copied and modified from standard examples. In our experiments, we assess the predictive strength of these metrics on program categories.

We believe that a standard text categorization approach to this problem can be improved by adopting features distilled from program analysis. Prior work shows that the use of IR techniques, such as latent semantic analysis can aid program comprehension [8]. The key contribution of our work shows that the converse is also true: program analysis assists in text categorization.

3   JavaScript Categorization

The problem of JavaScript program categorization is a good proving ground to explore how these two fields can interact and inform each other. JavaScript is mostly confined to web pages and performs a limited number of tasks. We believe this is due to the restrictions of HTML and HTTP, and because web plug-ins are more conducive an environment for applications that require true interactivity and fine-grained control. This property makes the text categorization approach well-defined, in contrast to categorization of programs in other programming languages. Secondly, JavaScript has an intimate relationship with the HTML elements in the web page. Form controls, divisions and other web page objects are controlled and manipulated in JavaScript. As such, we can analyze how the web page's text and its HTML tags, in the form of a document object model (DOM), affect categorization performance.

Ugurel *et al.* [11] proposed 11 topic categories for source code topic classification task, including *circuits*, *database*, and *development*. They have assessed their work on different types of languages, such as Java, C, and Perl. Their work are based on large software systems and therefore these categories are designed for topical classification of general software systems and does not fit our domain well.

We examined an existing JavaScript categorization from a well-known tutorial site, *www.js-examples.com*. This site has over 1,000 JavaScript examples collected worldwide. To allow developers to locate appropriate scripts quickly, the web site categorizes these examples into 54 categories, including *ad*, *encryption*, *mouse*, *music* and *variable*.

While a good starting point, the *js-examples* categorization has two weaknesses that made it unusable for our purposes. First, the classification is intended for the developer, rather than the consumer. Examples that have similar effects are often categorized differently as the implementation uses different techniques. In contrast, we intend to categorize JavaScript functionality with respect to the end user. Second, the classification is used for example scripts, which are usually truncated and for illustrative purposes. We believe that their classification would not reflect actual JavaScript embedded on web sites.

Table 1. JavaScript functional categories, sorted by frequency. Number of instances indicated in parenthesis in the description field.

Category	Description (# units in corpus)
Dynamic-Text Banner	Displays a banner that changes content with time (264)
Initialization	Initialize/modifies variables for later use (123)
Form Processing	Passing values between fields, or computing values from form fields (119)
Calculator	Displays and manipulates a calculator (88)
Image Pre-load	Pre-load images for future use (87)
Pop-up	Pops up a new window (80)
Changing Image	Change the source of an image (79)
HTML	Generate HTML components, such as forms (68)
Web Application	Web applications such as games & e-commerce (62)
Background Color	Change or initialize the background color (50)
Form Validation	Validate a forms data fields (50)
Page	Load a new page to the browser window (49)
Plain Text	Print some text to the page (46)
Multimedia	Load multimedia (43)
Static-Text Banner	Displays a banner which does not change with time (42)
Static Time Information	Display static system time (41)
Loading Image	Load and display images (39)
Form Restore	Restore form fields to default values (37)
Server Information	Display page information from the server (36)
Dynamic Clock	Display a clock that changes with system time (35)
Navigation	Site navigator (32)
Browser Information	Check browser information (32)
Cookie	Store or retrieve data on server about client (26)
Trivial	Perform a simple one-liner task (24)
Interaction	User interaction with the page (24)
Warning Message	A static warning message (16)
Timer	Display a timer which is running (10)
Greeting	Display a greeting to the user (10)
CSS	Change the Cascading Style Sheet of the page (7)
Client-Time based Counter	Display interval between current time and another time relevant to page (7)
Visiting Browser History	Visit a page from the browser's history (6)
Calendar	Display a calendar (5)
Others	Multiple functionality or too few instances (133)

To deal with these shortcomings, we decided to modify the *js-examples* scheme based on a study of JavaScript instances in actual web documents. We use the WT10G corpus, commonly used in web IR experiments, as the basis for our work. In the WT10G corpus, we see that JavaScript that natively occurs in actual web pages are different and more difficult to handle. Actual web pages often embed multiple JavaScript instances to achieve different functionality. Also, scripts can be invoked at load time or by triggering events that deal with interaction with the browser. For example, a page could have a set of scripts that performs browser detection (that runs at load time) and another separate set that validates form information (that runs only when the text input is filled out). In addition, some scripts are only invoked as subprocedures of others.

As such, we perform categorization on individual JavaScript functional units, rather than all of the scripts on a single page. A *functional unit*, or simply *unit*, is defined as a JavaScript instance, combined with all of (potentially) called subprocedures. Any HTML involved in the triggering of the unit is also included. Figure 1 shows an example.

We base our categorization of JavaScript on these automatically extracted units. Based on our corpus study, we created a classification of JavaScript into 33 discrete

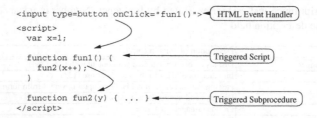

Fig. 1. A JavaScript unit, the basic element used for our classification

categories, shown in table 1. These categories are based on functionality rather than by their implementation technique. A single *other* category is used for scripts whose purpose is unclear or which contains more than one basic functionality.

We have made our dataset, annotations and categories freely available for research use and encourage others to make use of this resource. Details of these resources will be presented at the conclusion of the paper.

4   Methods

Given such a categorization, a standard text categorization approach would tokenize pre-classified input units and use the resulting tokens as features to build a model. New, unseen test units are then tokenized and the resulting features are compared to the models of each category. The category most similar to the test unit would be inferred as its category.

A simple approach to categorization uses a compiler's own tokenization, treating the resulting tokens as separate dimensions for categorization. An n dimensional feature vector results, where n is the total number of unique tokens that occur in all training unit instances.

We improve on this text categorization baseline in three ways. We first show how tokenization can be improved by exploiting the properties of the language. Second, we show that certain code metrics can help. Third, features distilled from program comprehension in the form of static analysis and dynamic execution allow us to analyze how objects interact with each other, which in turn influence an unit's classification.

4.1   Using Language Features for Improved Tokenization

A syntactic analysis of a programming language is instructive as it helps to type the program's tokens. After basic compiler-based tokenization, we distinguish the tokens of each unit as to whether they are numeric constants, string constants, operators, variable and method names, or language-specific reserved keywords, or part of comments. As JavaScript draws from Java and web constructs, we further distinguish regular expression operators, URLs, file extensions images and multimedia, HTML tags and color values. Tokens of these types are tagged as such and their aggregate type counts are used as features for categorization.

Variable and method names are special as they often convey the semantics of the program. However, for convenience, programmers frequently use abbreviations or short forms for these names. For example, in the JavaScript statement `var currMon = mydate.getMonth()`, `currMon`, `mydate` and `getMonth` are short forms for "current month", "my date" and "get month" respectively.

To a machine learner, the tokens `currMon` and `curMonth` are unrelated. To connect these forms together, we need to normalize these non-standard words (NSW) to resolve this feature mismatch problem [10]. We normalize such words by identifying likely splitting points and then expanding them to full word forms. Splitting is achieved by identifying case changes and punctuation use. Tokens longer than six letter in length are also split into smaller parts using entropy reduction, previously used to split natural languages without delimiters (*e.g.* Chinese). A following expansion phase is carried out, in which commonly abbreviated shortenings are mapped to the word equivalents (*e.g.* "curr" and "cur" $\rightarrow$ "current") using a small (around 20 entries) hand-compiled dictionary .

Table 2. Examples of Name token normalization

Example	Transition Pattern	Result (with expansion)
curMsg	single lowercase $\rightleftharpoons$ single uppercase	current message
IPAddress	consecutive uppercase $\rightarrow$ lowercase	ip address
thisweek	no transition and length ≥ 6	this week

4.2 Code Metrics

Complexity metrics measure the complexity of a program with respect to data flow, control flow or a hybrid of the two. Recent work in metrics [3,5] has been applied to specific software families and most metrics are targeted to much larger software projects (thousands of lines of code) than a typical JavaScript unit (averaging around 28 lines). As such, we start with simple, classic complexity metrics to assess their impact on categorization. Examples of them are:

Cyclomatic Complexity (CC) Cyclomatic complexity is a widely used control flow complexity metric. The cyclomatic complexity of a graph G is defined as $E-N+2$, where E is the number of edges in the control flow graph and N is the number of nodes in the same graph. In practice, it is the number of test conditions in a program.

Number of Attributes (NOA) is a data flow metric that counts the number of fields declared in the class or interface. In JavaScript, it counts the number of declared variables and newly created objects in the source code.

Informational fan-in (IFIN) is an information flow metric, defined as $IFIN = P + R + G$, where P is the number of procedures called, R is the number of parameters read, G is the number of global variables read. This metric is traditionally defined for class and interfaces, constructors and methods.

We also developed several metrics based on our observation of JavaScript instances in our corpus. These metrics count language structures that we found were prevalent in the corpus and may be indicative of certain program functionality.

Similar Statements (SS) counts the number of statements with similar structure.
Built-in Object References (BOR) counts the number of built-in objects (*e.g.* date, window) referenced by the unit.

In these metrics, similarity is determined by using a simple tree edit distance model based on the syntax of the language, discussed next.

4.2.1 Code Reuse Using Edit Distance

Aside from complexity metrics, we can also measure code reuse (also referred to as clone or plagiarism detection). This is particularly useful as many developers copy (and occasionally modify) scripts from existing web pages. Thus similarity detection may assist in classification. Dynamic programming can be employed to calculate a minimum edit distance between two inputs using strings, tokens, or trees as elements for computation.

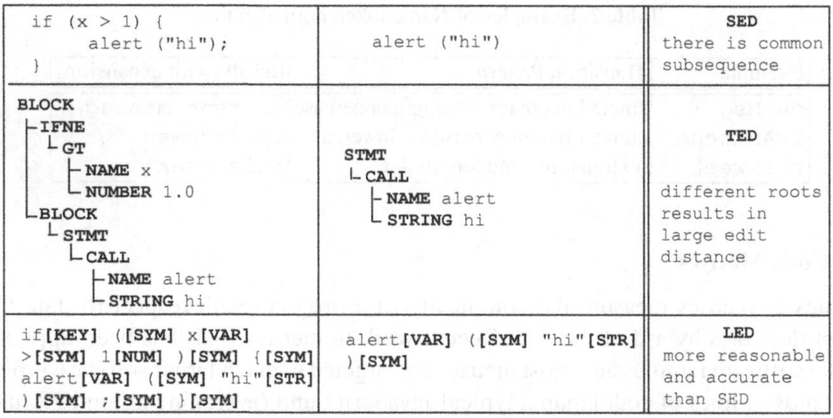

```if (x > 1) {` ` alert ("hi");` `}```	`alert ("hi")`	**SED** there is common subsequence
```BLOCK` `├IFNE` `└GT` ` ├NAME x` ` └NUMBER 1.0` `└BLOCK` ` └STMT` ` └CALL` ` ├NAME alert` ` └STRING hi```	```STMT` `└CALL` ` ├NAME alert` ` └STRING hi```	**TED** different roots results in large edit distance
```if[KEY] ([SYM] x[VAR]` `>[SYM] 1[NUM])[SYM] {[SYM]` `alert[VAR] ([SYM] "hi"[STR]` `)[SYM] ;[SYM] }[SYM]```	```alert[VAR] ([SYM] "hi"[STR]` `)[SYM]```	**LED** more reasonable and accurate than SED

Fig. 2. String based edit distance (SED), tree based edit distance (TED) and lexical-token based edit distance (LED)

We employ a standard string edit distance (SED) algorithm to calculate similarity between two script instances. We use the class of the minimal distance training unit as a separate feature for classification. However, this measure does not model the semantic differences that are introduced when edits result in structural differences as opposed to variable renaming. A minimal string edit distance may introduce drastic semantic changes, such as an addition of a parameter or deletion of a conditional statement.

In program analysis, abstract syntax trees (ASTs) [1] are often used to model source code and correct for these discrepancies. An AST is a parse tree representation of the source code that model the control flow of the unit and stores data types of its variables. Therefore we can use the AST model to define a tree-based edit distance (TED) measure between two JavaScript units. TED algorithms are employed in syntactic similarity detection [15]. However, as is shown in Figure 2, the given two code fragments are of the same functionality, but have different syntactic structures. Hence, syntactic difference does not imply functionality similarity, and vice versa. In this manner, a standard TED algorithm used in syntactic similarity detection is not likely to outperform a simple SED algorithm for our task. Aside from the tree-based edit distance measure, we can also measure similarity from a lexical-token approach (lexical-token based edit distance, LED) [6], in which source codes are parsed into a stream of lexical-tokens, and these tokens become the elements for computation. Edit costs are assigned appropriately depending on token types and values. We have implemented all three models and have assessed each approach's effectiveness.

4.3 Program Comprehension Using the Document Object Model

So far we have considered JavaScript units as independent of their enclosing web pages. In practice, since JavaScript units may be triggered by HTML objects and may manipulate these HTML objects in turn, a JavaScript unit has an intimate relation with its page and is often meaningful only in context. These objects are represented by a document object model (DOM)[1]. In fact, a unit which does not interact with a DOM object cannot interact with the user and is considered uninteresting. Many variables used in JavaScript are DOM objects whose data type can only be inferred by examining the enclosing HTML document. Table 3 illustrates two examples where the script references DOM objects.

Table 3. Units that reference their HTML context

`window.document.`
`getElementById(`
`''seminar'').`
`choice[2].value;`
	Accesses the value of the second radio button in a form "`seminar`"

`top.`
`newWin.document.`
`all.airplane.`
`img2.src;`
	Accesses the source of an image "img2" in the form "airplane", embedded in a window "newWin".

We classify references to DOM objects into three categories: *gets*, *sets*, and *calls*. These are illustrated in the JavaScript unit in Figure 3: on line 1 `DoIt()` gets a reference to a form object, on line 4 the input object represented by `frm.txt` is set to a value "`ok`", and on line 3 the object `document` calls its `write` method. The count of each of these DOM object references is added as an integer feature for categorization.

4.3.1 Static Analysis
Certain aspects of the communication between the DOM objects and the target JavaScript can be done by a straightforward analysis of the code. We extract two types

---

[1] Although the browser object model (BOM) is distinct from the DOM, we collectively refer to the two models as DOM for readability.

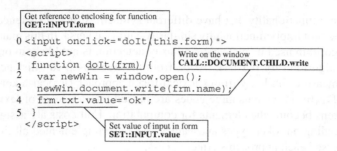

Fig. 3. Types of DOM object references

of information based on this static analysis: triggering information and variable data type information.

Certain classes of JavaScript are triggered by the user's interaction with an object (*e.g.* a form input field) and others occur when a page is loaded, without user interaction. This triggering type (interactive, non-interactive) is extracted for each unit by an inspection of the HTML. For units triggered by interaction, we further extract the responsible DOM object and event handler. We also extract the lexical tokens from the enclosing web page elements for interactive units. For example, an input button with a text value "restore" is likely to trigger a unit whose class is *form restore*; likewise, button inputs with text labels such as "0","1", and "9" are indicative of the class *calculator*.

DOM object settings and values may flow from one procedure to another. We recover the data type of objects by tracing the flow as variables are instantiated and assigned. This is done with the assistance of the abstract syntax tree described in 4.2.1. A variable and its data type form a single unified token (*e.g.* newWin↦WINDOW) used for categorization. In addition, all the JavaScript unit's interaction with DOM objects are then traced statically and recorded (*e.g.* GET::INPUT.value) as static analysis features for categorization.

4.3.2 Dynamic Analysis
Static analysis is not able to recover certain information that occurs at run time. Dynamic analysis (*i.e.*, execution of code) can extract helpful features along the single, default path of execution. Although dynamic analysis is incomplete (in the sense that it only examines a single execution path), such analyses can determine exact values of variables and may help by discarding unimportant paths.

We illustrate how dynamic analysis can yield additional features for categorization in Figure 4. This sample JavaScript unit, taken from the WT10G corpus, creates a dynamic text banner that scrolls in window's status bar. The function `window.setTime- out()` displays the string represented by `''banner''+index+'')''` after 100 milliseconds, which makes the banner text in the window change over time. Without dynamic analysis, we cannot recover what value `msg.substring(0,index)` refers to. More importantly, dynamic analysis allows us to extract the value of the expression `''banner(''+index+'')''`.

```
1 var msg = "Welcome to this page";
2 banner(0);
3 function banner (index) {
4   window.status =
      msg.substring(0, index);
5   seed = seed++;
6   if (index >= msg.length)
      index = 0;
7   window.setTimeout("banner("+index+
    ")", 100);
  }
```

Static Analysis Features

SET::WINDOW.status
CALL::WINDOW.setTimeout

Dynamic Analysis Features

SET::WINDOW.status{}
SET::WINDOW.status{W}
SET::WINDOW.status{We}
... ...

CHANGES::WINDOW.status

Fig. 4. Sample JavaScript unit (l), along with features extracted by static and dynamic analysis (r)

In this example, dynamic analysis also recovers the fact that the variable's value is changing, hence a new feature is added to the feature set (*i.e.* CHANGES::WINDOW.status).

5 Evaluation

We tested the above methods on the WT10G corpus, containing approximately 1.7 M web pages from over 11K distinct servers. After pre-processing and cleaning of the WT10G corpus, over 18 K pages contained processable JavaScript scripts units. String identical duplicates and structurally-identical script units were then removed. This resulted in a final corpus of 1,637 units, which are unique in textual form and structure. The high ratio of the number of script instances to unique scripts validates our claim that many scripts are simply clones.

We perform supervised text categorization using a support vector machine approach (SVM). SVMs were chosen as the machine learning framework as they handle high-dimensional datasets efficiently. This is extremely important as feature vectors contain anywhere from 3,000 to 8,000 features, depending on which feature sets are used in the model configuration. Specifically, we used the generic SVM algorithm (SMO) provided with WEKA [13]. We use a randomized, ten-fold cross validation of the final corpus of 1,637 script units, which excludes the *other* category. Instance accuracy is reported in the results. Due to space limitations, we report instance accuracy which has been used in previous work [11] and have omitted other IR metrics such as precision and recall.

Our experiments aim to measure the performance difference using different sets of machine learning features. In all of the experiments, the baseline model tokenizes units and passes the tokens as individual features to the learner.

Table 4 shows the component evaluation in which we selected certain combination of features as input to the SVM classifier. Here, we can see the majority class categorizer performs poorly, as this dataset consists of many classes without a dominating class. However, a simple text categorization baseline, in which strings are delimited by whitespaces performs very well, accurate on 87% of the test instances. When informed lexical tokenization is done and combined with features from software metrics, static and dynamic analysis, we are able to improve categorization accuracy to around 94%. Perhaps unsurprisingly, using only software metrics and program comprehension fea-

Table 4. Component Evaluation Results. Error reduction (ER) is measured against the text categorization baseline. (*) indicates the improvement over the approach using previous feature set is statistically significant at 0.05 level under T-test, (**) indicates statistically significant at 0.01 level.

Features used	Accuracy	ER
Most frequent class baseline	16.12%	–
Text categorization baseline	87.47%	–
L. All lexical analysis	89.61%(**)	17%
L_c. Language token counting	88.57%	8%
L_n. Function/variable normalization	87.66%	1%
M. All software metrics	77.76%	–
M_s. Standard classic metrics	20.46%	–
M_j. w/ new metrics (M_s+SS+BOR)	25.60%	–
M_e. String-based edit distance	73.85%	–
M_a. AST-based edit distance	72.69%	–
M_t. Token-based edit distance	74.89%	–
P. All program comprehension	87.29%	–
P_s. Static analysis	79.78%	–
P_d. Dynamic analysis	71.22%	–
L+M	90.04%(*)	21%
L+P	92.36%(**)	39%
L+M+P	93.95%(**)	52%

tures fail to contribute good classifiers. However, when coupled with a strong lexical feature component, we show improvement.

The performance improvement may seem marginal, but in fact they are statistically significant, as demonstrated by the use of a one-tailed t-test. We believe significance is achieved due to the large scale of the evaluation set's degrees of freedom present in the classification problem.

A good baseline performance may seem discouraging for research, but many important problems exist which exhibit the same property (*e.g.* spam detection, part of speech tagging). These problems are important and small gains in performance do not make advances in these problems less relevant. As such we also calculate the error reduction that is achieved by our methods over the text categorization baseline. By this metric, almost half of the classification errors are corrected by the introduction of our techniques.

Lexical Analysis. We hypothesized that token features and variable and function name normalization would enhance performance. The results show that simple typing of tokens as keywords, strings, URLs and HTML tags is effective at removing 8% of the categorization errors. Less effective is when variable and function names are normalization through splitting and expansion. When both techniques are used together, their synergy improves performance, removing 17% of errors. This validates our earlier hypothesis that program language features do positively impact program categorization.

Metrics. We also break down our composite metric feature set into its components to assess their predictive strength. Our results also show that edit distance alone is not sufficient to build a good categorizer. Such a code reuse metric is not as accurate as our simple text categorization baseline. A finding of our work is that applying published software metrics "as-is" may not boost categorization performance much, rather these metrics need to be adapted to the classes and language at hand. Only when collectively used with lexical analysis is performance increased.

Program Comprehension. Static and dynamic features alone perform do not perform well, but their combination greatly reduces individual mistakes (29% and 51% for the static and dynamic analyses, respectively). The combined feature set also does not beat the simple lexical approach, but serves to augment its performance.

A Note on Efficiency. The experiments in this paper were conducted on a single, modern desktop machine with two gigabytes of main memory. In general, feature creation is fast, for all 1.6K script instances in our corpus took approximately 3 minutes, and a 10-fold cross validation of the SMO classifier takes about 10 minutes. The exception to the feature creation is when edit distance-based code reuse metrics were computed. These features are computed in a brute-force, pairwise manner and took up to ten hours to generate. We are currently looking into faster approaches that may lower the complexity of the approach.

6   Shortcomings

Our results are promising, but we would like to call attention to some of the shortcomings of our work that we are currently addressing:

Annotator Agreement. Our corpus is annotated by one of the paper authors. While this provides for consistency, the annotator notes that some instances of problematic, even for a language whose applications are largely distinct. We feel this a source of some errors and are working on further annotation and finding inter-annotator agreement. A reasonable upper bound of performance may be less than 100%, meaning that our performance gains may be more signficant than discussed in this paper.

Dynamic Analysis Incompleteness. Many tasks are executed conditionally depending on the browser's type. In our dynamic analysis, we assume scripts are only executed under as MSIE 4.0, which causes certain analyses to fail to extract data. As browser checking is ubiquitous in JavaScripts, we may relax this constraint and follow all execution pathways that are conditional on the browser.

7   Conclusion and Future Work

We present a novel approach to the problem of program categorization. In specific, we target JavaScript categorization, as its use is largely confined to a small set of purposes and is closely tied to its enclosing web page. A key contribution of our work is to create a functional categorization of JavaScript instances, based on a corpus study of over 18,000 web pages with scripts. To encourage our researchers to use our dataset as a standard reference collection, we have made our dataset, annotations and resulting system freely available[2].

Although previous work [11] has examined the use of text classification approaches to classify source code, our method is the first method that employs the source code in a non-trivial way. Different from previous work which classified code into topic categories, our work attempts to achieve a more fine-grained functional categories with less data. In this work, rather than treating the problem merely as a straightforward text categorization problem, we incorporate and adapted metrics and features that originate in program analysis. Our corpus study confirms that many such scripts are indeed copies or simple modifications. While our baseline does well, performance is greatly improved by utilizing program analysis. By careful lexical analysis, 10% of errors are eliminated. Further improvements using static analysis and execution results in a 52% overall reduction of categorization error. We believe they provide evidence that program categorization can benefit from adapting work from program analysis.

We currently deploy our system as part of a smart JavaScript filtering system, that filters out specific JavaScript units that have functionality irrelevant to the web page (*e.g.* banner, pop-up). We plan to extend this work to other scripting languages and decompiled plug-ins appearing on web pages. The aim of such work is to assist end users to filter irrelevant material and to summarize such information for users to make more informed web browsing a wider variety of classification (including subject-based classification) on a wider range of computer languages in future work.

References

1. Baxter, I. D.; Yahin, A.; Moura, L. M. D.; SantAnna, M.; and Bier, L. 1998. Clone detection using abstract syntax trees. In ICSM, 368–377.
2. Blazy, S., and Facon, P. 1998. Partial evaluation for program comprehension. ACM Computing Surveys 30(3).
3. Cory Kapser and Michael W. Godfrey. Aiding Comprehension of Cloning Through Categorization. Proc. of 2004 International Workshop on Software Evolution (IWPSE-04), Kyoto, Japan, 2004.
4. D. Hawking. Web Research Collection. http://es.csiro.au/TRECWeb/, June 2004.
5. I. Krsul and E. H. Spafford. Authorship Analysis: Identifying the Author of a Program. Proc. 18th NIST-NCSC National Information Systems Security Conference, 514–524, 1995.
6. Kamiya, T., Kusumoto, S., Inoue, K. (2002). Ccfinder: a multilinguistic token-based code clone detection system for large scale source code. IEEE Trans. Softw. Eng., 28(7), 2002, 654–670.
7. Kontogiannis, K. 1997. Evaluation experiments on the detection of programming patterns using software metrics. In Proceedings of the Fourth Working Conference on Reverse Engineering (WCRE 97), 44–54. Washington, DC, USA: IEEE Computer Society.
8. Maletic, J. I., and Marcus, A. 2000. Using latent semantic analysis to identify similarities in source code to support program understanding. In Proceedings of the 12th IEEE International Conference on Tools with Artificial In- telligence (ICTAI00), 46.

---

[2] http://wing.comp.nus.edu.sg/~luwei/SMART/

9. Mathias, K. S.; II, J. H. C.; Hendrix, T. D.; and Barowski, L. A. 1999. The role of software measures and metrics in studies of program comprehension. In ACM Southeast Regional Conference.

10. Rowe, N., and Laitinen, K. 1995. Semiautomatic disabbreviation of technical text. Information Processing and Management 31(6):851–857.

11. S.Ugurel, B.Krovetz,C.L.Giles,D.Pennock,E.Glover,H.Zha. What is the code? Automatic Classification of Source Code Archives. Eighth ACM International Conference on Knowledge and Data Discovery (KDD 2002), 623–638 (poster), 2002.

12. von Mayrhauser, A., and Vans, A.M. 1994. Dynamic code cognition behaviors for large scale code. In Proceedings of the 3rd Workshop on Program Comprehension, 74–81.

13. Witten, I. H., and Frank, E. 2000. Data Mining: Practical machine learning tools with Java implementations. San Francisco: Morgan Kaufmann.

14. Wong,W.-C., and Fu, A.W.-C. 2000. Finding structures of web documents. In ACM SIGMOD Workshop on Research Issues in DataMining and Knowledge Discovery (DMKD).

15. Yang, W. (1991). Identifying syntactic differences between two programs. Software - Practice and Experience, 21(7), 1991, 739–755.

Effective and Scalable Authorship Attribution Using Function Words

Ying Zhao and Justin Zobel

School of Computer Science and Information Technology,
RMIT University GPO Box 2476V, Melbourne, Australia
{yizhao, jz}@cs.rmit.edu.au

Abstract. Techniques for identifying the author of an unattributed document can be applied to problems in information analysis and in academic scholarship. A range of methods have been proposed in the research literature, using a variety of features and machine learning approaches, but the methods have been tested on very different data and the results cannot be compared. It is not even clear whether the differences in performance are due to feature selection or other variables. In this paper we examine the use of a large publicly available collection of newswire articles as a benchmark for comparing authorship attribution methods. To demonstrate the value of having a benchmark, we experimentally compare several recent feature-based techniques for authorship attribution, and test how well these methods perform as the volume of data is increased. We show that the benchmark is able to clearly distinguish between different approaches, and that the scalability of the best methods based on using function words features is acceptable, with only moderate decline as the difficulty of the problem is increased.

1 Introduction

Authorship attribution is the task of deciding who wrote a document. In a typical scenario, a set of documents with known authorship are used for training; the problem is then to identify which of these authors wrote unattributed documents. Such attribution can be used in a broad range of applications. In plagiarism detection, it can be used to establish whether claimed authorship is valid. Academics use attribution to analyse anonymous or disputed documents such as the plays of Shakespeare[1] or the Federalist Papers [12,20]. Authorship attribution can also be used for forensic investigations. For example, it could be applied to verify the authorship of e-mails and newsgroup messages, or to identify the source of a piece of intelligence.

A variety of methods for attribution have been proposed. There are three main approaches: lexical methods [2,10,16,18], syntactic or grammatic methods [3,25,26], and language-model methods [19,22], including methods based on compression [5,20]. These approaches vary in evidence or features extracted from documents, and in classification methods applied to the evidence.

---

[1] See for example shakespeareauthorship.com.

G.G. Lee et al. (Eds.): AIRS 2005, LNCS 3689, pp. 174–189, 2005.

However, use of different data sets and measures — and lack of comparison to common baselines — means that these results cannot be compared. In most of the papers cited above, the attribution methods appear to succeed on the terms set by the authors, but there is no way of identifying which is the most successful. Inconsistencies in the underlying choices also lead to confusion; for example, no two papers use the same sets of extracted features. Nor is there any indication of how well the methods scale. Most of the data sets used are small, and change in performance as documents are added is not examined.

Our aim in this research is to investigate whether a standard benchmark can be used to evaluate the relative performance of different attribution methods. We develop a benchmark by using part of a newswire collection provided in the TREC data [14]. Many of the newswire articles have the author identified in their metadata; although the formatting of the authorship is inconsistent, it can readily be standardized [11]. Such data might be regarded as relatively challenging for the task of attribution, as articles with different authors may be edited towards a corporate standard and an author may use different styles for different kinds of article; for example, some authors write both features and reviews. However, our experiments show that all the methods we consider are at least moderately successful when applied to small volumes of data, and that the use of a benchmark allows differences in performance to be clearly identified.

To establish which attribution method is in practice the most effective — and to further demonstrate the value of a benchmark — we examine how well each of the methods scales. Scaling has many aspects: increase in the volume of positive training data, in the number of authors, and in the volume of negative training data. This last two cases are of particular interest in a domain such as newswire, where the number of documents and authors is large.

Many of the approaches to authorship attribution described in recent research literature are lexical, based on measures of distributions of word usage [2,8,10,16,18]. While other approaches are also of interest, the similarities in the principles of the lexical methods makes it interesting to discover which is most effective. We examine several attribution methods in our experiments, all based on standard approaches to text classification: naïve Bayesian, Bayesian networks, nearest-neighbour, and decision trees. The two Bayesian approaches are based on probabilities. The nearest-neighbour methods use vector differences. Decision trees are based on classifying training data by their distinguishing features. All of these techniques have been successfully used for classification in areas such as speech recognition, content-based text categorization, and language processing.

As features, we use occurrence counts of function words such as "the" and "once". Using sets of documents with varying number of authors (from two to five) and varying quantities of positive and negative training data, we find clear differences between the methods. In most of the experiments, the Bayesian networks were clearly the most effective, while the nearest-neighbour methods were best when given limited positive examples and attempting to distinguish the work of an author from a heterogeneous collection of other articles. The best methods proved to be reasonably scalable as the number of documents was increased, with for example an accuracy of around 50% when only 2% of the training documents were positive examples.

2   Background

The fundamental assumption of authorship attribution is that each author has habits in wording that make their writing unique. It is well known in the humanities, for example, that certain writers can be quickly identified by their writing style. The basis of a successful automatic attribution technique is, therefore, that it is possible to extract features from text that distinguish one author from another; and that some statistical or machine learning technique, given training data showing examples and counterexamples of an author's work, should be able to use these features for reliable attribution.

Authorship attribution problems can be divided into three categories: binary, multi-class, and one-class classification. Binary classification is when each of the documents being considered is known to have been written by one of two authors [7,12,16]. In multi-class classification, documents by more than two authors are provided. In one-class classification, some of the documents are by a particular author while the authorship of the other documents is unspecified, and the task is to determine whether given documents are by the single known author. In this paper, we study all three categories of classification.

Choice of feature is a key issue. In a problem domain such as information retrieval, documents are identified by their content [4], and the features used are usually the words of the document. Likewise, authorship attribution is distinctly different to document classification [24], where the task is to group documents by content. In attribution, words can be misleading, as two authors writing on the same topic or about the same event may share many words and phrases. Although the principles are superficially similar — features are extracted and then used to assign documents to a class — style markers are much harder to define than are content markers. This difficulty is evident at the reader level: a human can easily identify the topic of a document, but identifying the author is much harder. There is no guarantee that a classification method that is successful on features that mark content will be successful on features that mark style.

If words are to be used as features, it is therefore interesting to restrict attention to *function words*. These are words such as prepositions, conjunctions, or articles, or elements such as words describing quantities, that have little semantic content of their own and usually indicate a grammatical relationship or generic property. The appeal of function words is that they are a marker of writing style. Some less common function words — such as "whilst" or "notwithstanding" — are not widely used, and thus may be an indicator of authorship. Even common function words can be used to distinguish between authors. Table 1 gives an example of how usage of function words can vary. In this example from the AP data (discussed later), both authors use "and" and "of" with similar frequency,

Table 1. Usage statistics for common function words for two authors. Each number is, for that author, the percentage of function word occurrences that is the particular function word. Counts are averaged across a large set of documents by each author.

	a	and	for	in	is	of	that	the
Barry Schweid	6.28	9.22	4.94	6.50	1.62	14.66	1.89	29.13
Don Kendall	9.75	7.08	2.36	7.98	3.05	13.16	5.73	41.29

but Schweid's usage of "that" is a third of Kendalls's, and even the usage of "the" is very different.

The first research on attribution using function words was that of Burrows [8]. Function words are an appealing choice of feature because their incidence is often due to authorial style rather than the topic of a specific document. As presented by Baayen et al. [2], occurrence counts of 42 common function words and eight punctuation symbols were used to represent the authorial structures. Using principle component analysis and linear discriminant analysis, accuracy was 81.5%. The data was a collection of 72 student essays on three topics. On the same data, an accuracy of 87% is reported by Juola and Baayen [18]. They selected 164 function words of the highest frequencies and used cross-entropy.

Holmes et al. [16] used 50 common function words to discriminate between two authors on disputed texts. These 17 texts were journal articles. They claim that the pattern of function word usage successfully discriminates between authors. Binongo [7] used the 50 most common function words to examine the authorship of the fifteenth book of Oz.

Diederich et al. [10] obtained an accuracy of 60%–80% by employing all words and support vector machines, on German text by seven authors. The positive results imply that word usage can be used to address authorial issues, but the presence of content words means that these results are not reliable.

However, these studies left many questions unresolved. First, the corpuses used are totally different from each other. They were in different languages, including Dutch [2,18], English [7,9,16], and German [10]. (we use English texts only in our experiments.) Baayen et al. [2] use a proprietary data collection comprised of 72 articles by eight students, with nine articles from each student on three topics. Holmes et al. [16] chose seventeen journal articles for differentiating two authors on disputed texts. Diederich et al. [10] used the "Berliner Zeitung", a daily Berlin newspaper; seven authors are considered and approximately 100 texts are examined for each author.

In addition, none of this research is based on a large number of documents. The largest single-author collection is reported by Diederich [10], in which the number of documents per author is in the range 82–118. Nor are there any comparisons between methods.

A wide range of other surface aspects of text could be used as features, such as word length or sentence length. Richer features are available through natural-language processing or more sophisticated statistical modelling. Some are based on natural language processing (NLP). Baayen et al. [3] argued that syntactic annotation is at least as effective as lexical-based measures. They used two NLP tools to syntactically annotate a corpus. Then a set of rewrite rules are generated, which are considered as evidence for attribution. Using two novels each in ten segments they achieve perfect attribution Stamatatos et al. [25,26] used an NLP tool to identify 22 style markers. On Greek news articles by 10 authors they achieve 81% accuracy, and improve to 87% by including 50 common words. These papers show that NLP is a plausible source of alternative features for attribution, to which a classification method must, as for other features, be applied. However, while these features are potentially more informative than the simple features we explore, they are also more error prone.

Benedetto et al. [5] used a standard LZ77 compression program to measure the similarity among pieces of texts, reporting overall accuracy of 93%. In their approach, each unknown text is attached to every other known text and the compression program is applied to each composite file as well as to the original text. The author of the file with the least increase in size due to the unknown text is assumed to be the match. However, Goodman [13] failed to reproduce the accuracy of 93%, instead achieving only 53%. Moreover, the approach has other obvious flaws. Compression is based on modelling of character sequences, so there is a bias introduced by the subject of the text. Also, the method is not well designed. First, compression programs embody a range of ad hoc decisions and assumptions, and the simple bitcount due to additional text is likely to be much less informative than the models on which the program's output is based. Second, the quadratic complexity of the approach means that it cannot be scaled to significant quantities of text.

In this paper, we investigate the use of classification with function words as features, using consistent document collections and varying numbers of documents. We now review the classification methods we examine.

3   Classification

We use five classification techniques in our experiments, all of which have been reported as effective at attribution in recent literature.

The first two are Bayesian classifiers, based on Bayes theorem [17,21]. There are several variations of Bayesian classifiers. Among them, naïve Bayesian and Bayesian network classifiers are reported as successful algorithms and have been successfully applied to document classification [24]. The next two, nearest-neighbour and k-nearest-neighbour, are distance-based methods, which compute the distance from a new item to existing items that have been classified. The last technique is a decision tree.

In detail, these classifiers are as follows.

Naïve Bayesian. This method is based on the assumption that the occurrences of the features are mutually independent. Under this assumption, given the set of features $\{a_1, \ldots, a_n\}$ extracted from a document and an author v, we wish to compute

$$P\left(v|a_1, \ldots, a_n\right) = \frac{P(v) \cdot P\left(a_1, \ldots, a_n|v\right)}{P\left(a_1, \ldots, a_n\right)}$$

where $P\left(a_1, \ldots, a_n\right)$ is assumed to be uniform and n is fixed. Thus we can attribute the document to be classified by computing

$$P\left(a_1, \ldots, a_n|v\right) = \Pi_i \, P\left(a_i|v\right)$$

Using Bayes theorem, then, a naïve Bayesian classifier can be written as:

$$v = \mathrm{argmax}_{v \in V} \, P\left(v\right) \Pi_i \, P\left(a_i|v\right)$$

where $P\left(v\right)$ can be estimated by measuring the frequency with which author v occurs in the training data.

In our experiments, the frequencies of function words are used as the a_i values, after normalizing by document length. However, it is difficult to estimate the probabilities $P\left(a_i|v\right)$ from a limited data collection, as many of the function words are rare and have insufficient occurrences in the training data. We used a common assumption to address this issue, that the value of attributes are Gaussian distributed. We calculate the mean μ_i and standard distribution σ_i of the a_i values across the training data, giving the Gaussian estimate:

$$P(a_i|v) = g(a_i, \mu_i, \sigma_i) \quad \text{where}$$
$$g(a, \mu, \sigma) = \frac{1}{\sqrt{2\pi}\sigma} \, e^{\frac{(a-\mu)^2}{2\sigma^2}}$$

Note that the naïve Bayesian approach assumes that the likelihood of a new document being by a given author is conditioned by the distribution of authorship of existing documents. It is not clear that this is an appropriate assumption.

Bayesian networks. These are another method based on Bayes theorem. A Bayesian network structure [15] is an acyclic directed graph for estimating probabilistic relationships based on conditional probabilities. There is one node in the graph for each attribute and each node has a table of transition probabilities.

There are two learning steps in Bayesian networks, learning of the network structure and learning the probability tables. The structure is determined by identifying which attributes have the strongest dependencies between them. The nodes, links, and probability distributions are the structure of the network, which describe the conditional dependencies. Every node a_i has a posterior probability distribution derived from its parents. Attribution involves computation of the joint probability of attributes $a_1, \ldots, a_n$ taking dependencies into account:

$$P(a_1, \ldots, a_n) = \Pi_i P\left(a_i|\mathrm{Parents}\left(a_i\right)\right)$$

A Bayesian network is able to handle training data with missing attributes, for which a prediction value is given by the network structure and probabilities.

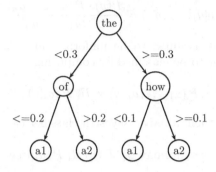

Fig. 1. A decision tree example showing classification using three function words

Nearest-neighbour methods. These measure the distance between a new pattern and existing patterns. The class of the new pattern is determined by a majority vote of its metrically nearest neighbours. For example, if Jones is the author of 75% of the closest patterns then the new pattern is classified to be by Jones.

The number of nearest neighbours is a parameter. The minimum, 1, gives a standard nearest-neighbour method, while use of k neighbours gives the k-nearest-neighbour method. In our experiments, we used $k = 3$. As discussed by Aha and Kibler [1], this kind of method makes no assumption about the probability distribution of the features, and so is suitable for data with complex boundaries between classes.

In our experiments with attribution, the normalized occurrence rate of function words are used as features. The standard Euclidean distance is used as a measure distance, as derived from the p-norm distance:

$$D_{x,y} = \sqrt[p]{\sum_i (|y_i - x_i|)^p}$$

Here x_i and y_i are the values of the ith attribute in documents x and y. The p-norm distance is appropriate due to its low computational cost and reported good effectiveness.

Decision Trees. These are a simple but successful inductive learning method. A binary tree is constructed to describe a set of attributes of a sample and return a "decision", the authorial information in our case. A simple decision tree structure for a mark ranking system is shown in Figure 1. The leaf nodes are labelled as classes, while other nodes are specified by the attribute values.

In the example, three attributes — "the", "of", and "how"— and six conditions are provided in the tree. Given an unattributed document, with corresponding attribute values of 0.2, 0.25, and 0 respectively, by either a_1 or a_2, we assign this document to author a_2 by traversing the tree from root to leaf.

We selected the C4.5 decision tree algorithm [23] for our experiment. It is based on information theory. Following Shannon, the information content can be measured by:

$$I\left(P\left(v_1\right)\cdots P\left(v_n\right)\right) = \sum_{i=1}^{n} -P\left(v_i\right)\log_2 P\left(v_i\right)$$

The information gain I measures the difference between the original information content and new information. Based on such a measurement, the feature with the largest information gain is selected as the root of the tree. The same process is applied recursively to generate the branches of the tree. When a new pattern is supplied, it is used to traverse the tree until a leaf is reached. The label of the leaf node is then the author of the given document [23]. As each attribute has only one node, paths are kept relatively short but only a limited subset of attributes is considered during attribution of a given document.

Other methods. As discussed above, success has also been reported with support vector machines, principal component analysis, and linear discriminant analysis. We believe that these methods are indeed worth exploring. However, in this paper our primary focus is on finding ways to compare attribution methods; due to time constraints we chose to limit the number of methods we examine.

4 Experiments

We use experiments to examine which of the classification methods described above is the most effective in practice. As data, we use collections of data extracted from the TREC corpus [14]. The documents are newswire articles from the AP (Associated Press) subcollection.

We believe that AP is a suitable benchmark data collection for attribution for several reasons. First, it is large, with many more documents and authors than the corpora in the literature noted above; it has over 200,000 documents by over 2380 distinct authors, as well as over 10 thousand anonymous documents. Second, the articles are on a wide range of topics, with some authors contributing diverse material while others are specialised. Third, the documents have been edited for publication, meaning that they are largely free of errors that might confound a categorizer. Fourth, many of the authors are regular contributors; seven authors contributed over 800 documents each. We used the documents by these seven authors in all the experiments described below, as well as, in our one-class experiments, documents randomly selected from the remaining authors.

In contrast, the largest number of documents by a particular author in collections used for attribution experiments in previous work is approximately 100 [10]. Thus the AP collection provides enough documents and enough authors for the investigation of the effects of scale.

A drawback of the AP collection is that it is often the case that it contains multiple versions of the same document (because the same article may be published in slightly different forms in different places). Such repetition can distort the statistics used to test for attribution, and can inflate the results; for example a nearest-neighbour approach will be all too successful if the test document is also present in the training data. However, detection of such near-duplicates is not straightforward. To remove these documents, we use the SPEX method of Bernstein and Zobel [6] to get rid of the near-duplicates. This process eliminated redundant 3179 documents.

To prepare the data, we grouped the documents by author, after standardizing names (the original format is not consistent from document to document). The 10,918 anonymous documents are collected into one group that can be used for one-class classification. Except where indicated, 365 function words are used as features. The magnitude of each feature is calculated from the normalized frequency of the word in that document. Therefore, we in most experiments we use a vector with 365 dimensions to represent each document.

We then use the classification methods in a variety of ways, to examine their robustness and their behaviour with scaling. Many previous papers use attribution methods for *two-class classification*, that is, to discriminate between two known authors. In this context, all the documents used for training and test are written by these two candidates. There is a natural generalization to n-class categorization for any $n \geq 2$. *One-class categorization* is used to determine whether the given text was written by a particular author. In contrast to n-class problem, the negative examples do not have to be by particular authors; they are anonymous or by any other author. We can refer to these negative documents as *noise*. One-class classification is generally more challenging than two-class classification. *Cross validation* is used when the amount of data is limited. The main idea of cross validation, or hold-out, is to swap the roles of training data and testing data to observe the overall results of prediction. In our experiments using cross validation, the data is split into a fixed number of *folds* of similar size. Each fold in turn is classified while the remaining fold are used for training. We used ten folds in our experiments.

Holding the number of folds to a fixed number means that results are obtained in a consistent way, but also means that results at different scales may not be comparable, as both the test and training data has changed. For this reason, in other experiments we reserved small sets of documents as test data, while varying the number of positive and negative documents used for training. Accuracy results are then directly comparable.

In all of our experiments we have used the public domain WEKA classifier available at www.cs.waikato.ac.nz/ml/weka [27].

5   Results

Two-Class Experiments

In the first experiment, we compared the five classification methods using cross-validation and two-class classification. We varied the size of the total document pool to see how the methods behaved at different scales. Results are shown in Table 2, where outcomes are averaged across all 21 pairs of authors. Several trends can be observed. The first, and perhaps the most important, is that function words can indeed be reliably used for authorship attribution.

Table 2. Effectiveness (percentage of test documents correctly attributed) of each method for attribution, using 10-fold cross-validation on two-class classification

Docs per author	Naïve Bayes	Bayes net	NN	3-NN	Decision tree
20	80.24	80.00	80.24	80.24	69.52
50	85.14	85.99	85.52	84.57	77.05
100	85.91	89.67	83.43	82.88	80.29
200	85.83	89.29	84.29	84.05	82.86
400	85.57	90.11	85.30	85.60	84.77
600	85.53	90.46	85.77	85.53	84.53

Table 3. Effectiveness (percentage of test documents correctly attributed) of each method for attribution, using the same 100 test queries per author on two-class classification. Results are averaged across eleven pairs of authors.

Training docs per author	Naïve Bayes	Bayes net	NN	3-NN	Decision tree
50	78.90	82.00	75.70	77.91	73.55
100	81.55	85.73	76.27	78.27	79.00
200	84.18	88.18	80.00	81.46	82.55
400	84.82	90.64	80.00	80.91	86.18
600	84.46	90.64	80.73	81.46	86.73
800	84.18	90.18	83.36	83.64	86.73

All the methods become more effective as further documents are included, but only up to a point; only for the decision tree does effectiveness significantly improve for classes of more than 100 documents. For larger sets of documents, little separates four of the methods, but the fifth, Bayesian networks, is markedly superior.

In our second experiment, we randomly chose eleven pairs of authors, ran the experiment on each pair; reported results are an average across these runs. These results are shown in Table 3. The methods are more clearly separated in these results than was the case above; the nearest-neighbour methods are poor, while Bayesian networks are effective at all scales, with slightly increasing accuracy as more training documents are included.

We observed significant inconsistency from one pair of authors to another, throwing considerable doubt over the results reported in many of the previous papers on this topic, most of which used only two authors.

In the next experiment, we increased the number of authors, examining the effectiveness as the number was increased from two to five. Results are averages across different sets of authors: we used 21 combinations of two and of five authors, and 35 combinations of three and of four authors. Results, shown in Table 4, are for cross-validation. The top half is with 50 documents per author, with 300 per author in the bottom half. (The use of different combinations of

Table 4. Effectiveness (percentage of test documents correctly attributed) of each method for attribution, using 10-fold cross-validation on two- to five-class classification

Number of authors	Naïve Bayes	Bayes net	NN	3-NN	Decision tree
50 documents per author					
2	85.91	89.67	83.43	82.88	80.29
3	77.50	79.49	75.96	74.57	70.48
4	69.90	75.83	71.57	70.62	63.10
5	66.44	71.72	69.51	66.21	58.90
300 documents per author					
2	85.53	90.46	85.77	85.53	84.53
3	76.53	85.22	78.71	78.98	74.96
4	70.51	80.63	73.66	74.03	67.22
5	65.97	76.33	70.54	69.98	62.15

authors is why these results are not for two-class classification are not the same as in Table 2.) Again, Bayesian networks are consistently superior, while the decision tree has been the poorest method.

These results are graphed in Figure 2, illustrating that the performance of the weaker methods declines sharply. We contend that these results demonstrate that multi-class classification is a much better test of effectiveness than is two-class classification: methods that are more or less indistinguishable for distinguishing between two authors are well separated for the task of identifying one author from amongst many. However, most prior work has focused on two-class classification.

Note, however, that the worst case differs depending on the number of authors. For two-class classification, a random assignment gives 50% accuracy, while for five-class random assignment gives 20%. Thus, while effectiveness does degrade as the number of authors is increased, it is also the case that the problem is becoming innately more difficult.

As an illustration of the limitations of some previous work on attribution, we ran experiments with the 65 Federalist papers of known authorship. This corpus has limitations, in addition to the small size; in particular that 50 of the papers are by one author and 15 by another, so that the worst case result — random assignment — is about 64%. However, this is the kind of corpus has been used in much of the previous work in the area.

Using cross-fold validation, results ranged from 77% for nearest-neighbour to 95% for the decision tree. Whether the differences are statistically significant is unclear. When the problem was reduced to 15 by each author, all methods but nearest-neighbour (which was inferior) did excellently, with only one or two errors each. However, while this accuracy is at first sight a success, we believe that it is a consequence of the inadequacy of the test data. Slight differences in assignment lead to large numerical differences in accuracy that are probably not statistically significant; in contrast, we expect to observe statistical significance

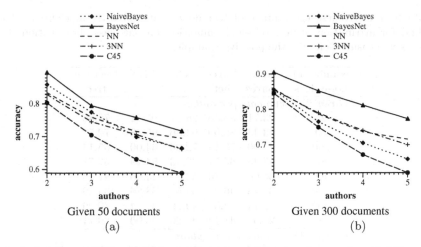

Fig. 2. Scalability of N-class attribution in the number of authors, using 10-fold cross-validation

for even small numerical differences in the previous experiments, due to the large number of documents involved. Although similar sets of test data have been widely used in previous work, we believe the observed results cannot be reliable.

One-Class Experiments

We then examined the effectiveness of each method for one-class classification, using cross-fold validation. Results, shown in Table 5 and Figure 3, are averaged across all seven authors. In each block of the table we had a fixed number of documents per author and varied the number of noise documents. This problem is inherently harder than the problems considered above, as the noise documents are not by a limited set of authors, and thus do not share style.

As the results show, accuracy declines significantly as the number of noise documents is increased. The best methods — nearest neighbour for a small set of positive examples and Bayesian networks and both nearest-neighbour methods for a larger set of positive examples — are markedly better than the alternatives. This experiment is in our view the most representative of attribution on a large collection, and has moreover shown the most power to distinguish between methods. We contend therefore that one-class classification is the best test of an attribution method.

These experiments have also shown that attribution is indeed reasonably effective. In even the most difficult case, where where only around 1 in 50 documents is a positive example, accuracy of the best method is nearly 50%.

As a final experiment, we timed each of the packages we used, to obtain an indication of the cost required for each classification method. These times are shown in Table 6, separated into training time and per-document attribution time. While they cannot be taken as conclusive, they do provide an indication of how well each approach scales. We can observe that the times do not strongly

Table 5. Effectiveness (percentage of test documents correctly attributed) of each method for attribution, using cross-fold validation on one-class classification. Effectiveness is measured on only the positive examples.

Number of noise docs	Naïve Bayes	Bayes net	NN	3-NN	Decision tree
Given 25 documents per author					
25	93.71	86.86	96.57	97.71	78.86
50	83.43	80.00	94.86	95.43	72.57
100	64.00	73.14	72.00	64.00	65.14
200	47.43	65.71	63.43	54.29	53.71
400	36.00	50.86	58.29	44.00	47.43
600	31.43	46.29	52.57	38.86	34.29
800	29.14	44.57	49.29	37.14	30.29
1200	27.91	41.14	46.29	36.00	29.71
Given 300 documents per author					
25	96.67	98.43	99.81	100.00	97.05
50	94.19	96.86	99.62	100.00	94.05
100	87.05	93.95	96.43	98.81	90.43
200	83.91	90.19	92.24	94.72	84.43
400	80.52	86.72	87.29	87.62	78.76
600	78.05	83.17	83.10	83.14	74.72
800	73.91	81.05	82.24	82.62	70.62
1000	73.38	80.24	81.24	80.86	67.67
1200	72.81	79.33	81.00	79.33	65.67
1600	72.76	78.91	78.52	76.91	61.33

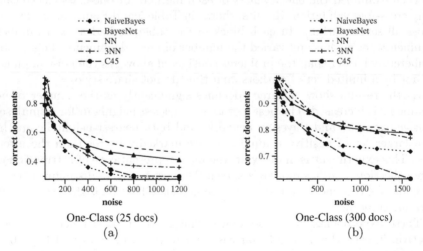

One-Class (25 docs)
(a)

One-Class (300 docs)
(b)

Fig. 3. Scalability of one-class classification, as the number of noise documents is increased

depend on whether the examples are positive or negative. Bayesian networks have by far the greatest training time, and the cost of training grows superlinearly. Training time for the other methods is small.

Table 6. Times (milliseconds) for each of the methods. Results in each column are total training time on the left and per-document classification time on the right, in a one-class experiment. Times are averaged over 70 runs.

Examples		Classifier				
Positive	Negative	Naïve Bayes	Bayes net	NN	3-NN	Decision tree
25	25	141/53	4513/12	20/86	20/100	310/2
25	400	490/38	16211/8	60/764	50/797	1517/1
300	25	301/28	16657/7	40/442	30/492	1060/1
300	400	581/25	76392/8	60/930	60/1033	3696/1

However, the per-document classification times are less consistent. Bayesian networks and decision trees are fast, while for the larger collections the nearest-neighbour methods are over a hundred times slower. Given the relatively poor effectiveness of the naïve Bayesian classifier and the decision tree — the only methods that are fast for both training and classification — choice of method in practice will depend on the application.

6 Conclusions

We have undertaken the first comparison of authorship attribution methods proposed in previous literature. These experiments have shown that Bayesian networks are the most effective of the methods we considered, while decision trees are particularly poor. We have also found that — given an appropriate classification method — function words are a sufficient style marker for distinguishing between authors, although it seems likely that further style markers could improve effectiveness. The best methods can scale to over a thousand documents, but effectiveness does decline significantly, particularly when the number of positive examples is limited.

We have shown that use of a consistent test corpus can be used to distinguish between different approaches to attribution. However, it is also important to design experiments appropriately. Results need to be averaged across multiple experiments, as some authors are easier to attribute than others. We have also found that one-class attribution provides the greatest discrimination between methods.

There are many alternative methods that have been proposed for authorship attribution, including other approaches to classification such as support vector machines, and methods based on compression and natural language processing. The effectiveness of such techniques is currently unknown, as they have not been evaluated on consistent data. Evaluation approaches such as ours need to be used to measure these methods.

Acknowledgements

We thank Yaniv Bernstein. This work was supported by the Australian Research Council.

References

1. D. Aha and D. Kibler. Instance-based learning algorithms. *Machine Learning*, 6:37–66, 1991.
2. H. Baayen, H. V. Halteren, A. Neijt, and F. Tweedie. An experiment in authorship attribution. *6th JADT*, 2002.
3. H. Baayen, H. V. Halteren, and F. Tweedie. Outside the cave of shadows: using syntactic annotation to enhance authorship attribution. *Literary and Linguistic Computing*, 11(3):121–132, 1996.
4. R. Baeza-Yates and B. Ribeiro-Neto. *Modern Information Retrieval*. Addison-Wesley Longman, May 1999.
5. D. Benedetto, E. Caglioti, and V. Loreto. Language trees and zipping. *The American Physical Society*, 88(4), 2002.
6. Y. Bernstein and J. Zobel. A scalable system for identifying co-derivative documents. In A. Apostolico and M. Melucci, editors, *Proceedings of the String Processing and Information Retrieval Symposium (SPIRE)*, pages 55–67, Padova, Italy, sep 2004. Springer. Published as LNCS 3246.
7. J. N. G. Binongo. Who wrote the 15th book of oz? an application of multivariate statistics to authorship attribution. *Computational Linguistics*, 16(2):9–17, 2003.
8. J. Burrows. Word patterns and story shapes: the statistical analysis of narrative style. *Literary and linguistic Computing*, 2:61–70, 1987.
9. J. Burrows. Delta: a measure of stylistic difference and a guide to likely authorship. *Literary and Linguistic Computing*, 17:267–287, 2002.
10. J. Diederich, J. Kindermann, E. Leopold, and G. Paass. Authorship attribution with support vector machines. *Applied Intelligence*, 19(1-2):109–123, 2003.
11. D. D'Souza, J. Thom, and J. Zobel. Collection selection for managed distributed document databases. *Information Processing & Management*, 40:527–546, 2004.
12. G. Fung. The disputed federalist papers: Svm feature selection via concave minimization. In *Proceedings of the 2003 conference on Diversity in computing*, pages 42–46. ACM Press, 2003.
13. J. Goodman. Extended comment on language trees and zipping.
14. D. Harman. Overview of the second text retrieval conference (TREC-2). *Information Processing & Management*, 31(3):271–289, 1995.
15. D. Heckerman, D. Geiger, and D. Chickering. Learning Bayesian networks: the combination of knowledge and statistical data. *Machine Learning*, 20:197–243, 1995.
16. D. I. Holmes, M. Robertson, and R. paez. Stephen crane and the new-york tribune: A case study in traditional and non-traditional authorship attribution. *Computers and the Humanities*, 35(3):315–331, 2001.
17. G. H. John and P. Langley. Estimating continuous distributions in Bayesian classifiers. In *Eleventh Conference on Uncertainty in Artificial Intelligence*, pages 338–345. Morgan Kaufmann Publisher, 1995.
18. P. Juola and H. Baayen. A controlled-corpus experiment in authorship identification by cross-entropy. *Literary and Linguistic Computing*, 2003.
19. V. Keselj, F. Peng, N. Cercone, and C. Thomas. N-gram-based author profiles for authorship attribution. In *Pasific Association for Computational Linguistics*, pages 256–264, 2003.
20. D. V. Khmelev and F. J. Tweedie. Using markov chains for identification of writers. *Literary and Linguistic Computing*, 16(4):229–307, 2002.

21. P. Langley and S. Sage. Tractable average-case analysis of naive Bayesian classifiers. In *Eleventh Conference on Uncertainty in Artificial Intelligence*, pages 220–228. Morgan Kaufmann Publisher, 1999.
22. F. Peng, D. Schuurmans, V. Keselj, and S. Wang. Language independent authorship attribution using character level language models. In *10th Conference of the European Chapter of the Association for Computational Linguistics, EACL*, 2003.
23. R. Quinlan. *C4.5: Programs for Machine Learning*. San Mateo, CA: Morgan Kaufmann, 1993.
24. F. Sebastiani. Machine learning in automated text categorization. *ACM Comput. Surv.*, 34(1):1–47, 2002.
25. E. Stamatatos, N. Fakotakis, and G. Kokkinakis. Automatic authorship attribution. In *Proceedings of the 9th Conference of the European Chapter of the Association for Computational Linguistics*, pages 158–164, 1999.
26. E. Stamatatos, N. Fakotakis, and G. Kokkinakis. Computer-based authorship attribution without lexical measures. *Computers and the Humanities*, 35(2):193–214, 2001.
27. I. H. Witten and E. Frank. *Data Mining: Practical machine learning tools with Java implementations*. Morgan Kaufmann, San Francisco, 2000.

Learning to Integrate Web Taxonomies with Fine-Grained Relations: A Case Study Using Maximum Entropy Model

Chia-Wei Wu[1], Tzong-Han Tsai[1,2], and Wen-Lian Hsu[1,3]

[1] Institute of Information Science, Academia Sinica, Nankang, Taipai, 115, Taiwan
[2] Department of Computer Science and Information Engineering, National Taiwan, University, Taipai, 640, Taiwan
[3] Department of Computer Science, National Tsing Hua University, Hsingchu, 300, Taiwan
{cwwu, thtsai, hsu }@iis.sinica.edu.tw

Abstract. As web taxonomy integration is an emerging issue on the Internet, many research topics, such as personalization, web searches, and electronic markets, would benefit from further development of taxonomy integration techniques. The integration task is to transfer documents from a source web taxonomy to a target web taxonomy. In most current techniques, integration performance is enhanced by referring to the relations between corresponding categories in the source and target taxonomies. However, the techniques may not be effective, since the concepts of the corresponding categories may overlap partially. In this paper we present an effective approach for integrating taxonomies and alleviating the partial overlap problem by considering fine-grained relations using a Maximum Entropy Model. The experiment results show that the proposed approach improves the classification accuracy of taxonomies over previous approaches.

1 Introduction

A web taxonomy, or directory, is a hierarchical collection of categories and documents [2]. In the last decade, thousands of such taxonomies have been developed for various services, such as electronic auction markets, online book stores, electronic libraries, and search engines. Yahoo! and Google Directories are two good examples. The benefits of taxonomies include encouraging the serendipitous discovery of information, improving navigation among related topics, and enhancing full-text searching. In a web taxonomy, a category's concept is its parent's sub-concept [9].

Many of these taxonomies cover similar topics and knowledge. In recent years, integrating these taxonomies, which enables the reuse of information more efficiently and correctly, has become increasingly popular. For instance, Google News [1] collects news articles from various news web sites and categorizes them into its taxonomy, which is a typical example of assigning data from an existing taxonomy to another taxonomy. In B2B systems, millions of items need to be exchanged among thousands of taxonomies [8].

Given the enormous scale of the Web, manually integrating taxonomies is labor-intensive and time consuming. In recent years, various machine learning approaches,

G.G. Lee et al. (Eds.): AIRS 2005, LNCS 3689, pp. 190–205, 2005.
© Springer-Verlag Berlin Heidelberg 2005

such as enhanced Naïve Bayes [3], Co-Bootstrapping [18], and SVM-based approaches [19] have been proposed. It is straightforward to formulate taxonomy integration as a classification task [3]. Suppose we want to integrate the BBC News web site with the Google News web site. The simplest way would be to assign news articles from BBC news to Google news based on the information contained in those articles. However, the relations between the categories in these two web sites could provide valuable information for assigning the articles. For example, if an article belongs to the *Sports* category of BBC news, it is likely that the article also belongs to the *Sports* category of Google news. Unfortunately, the relations between two categories in different taxonomies are inevitably fuzzy and noisy [19], since there are no standards for constructing taxonomies. In addition, taxonomies often overlap partially, as in *Software* and *Open source_software*, which could undermine the accuracy of taxonomy integration.

Our taxonomy integration approach exploits the relations between a category in the source taxonomy and a category in the target taxonomy to improve the classification performance. We also consider the issue of partial concept overlap.

The remainder of this paper is organized as follows: In Section 2, we define the taxonomy integration task. In Section 3, state-of-the-art taxonomy technologies are briefly introduced. The features used in our taxonomy integration approach are presented in Section 4. In Section 5, we describe our experiments, including the dataset, settings, and results. Finally, we close the paper with some concluding remarks and also indicate possible future research directions in Section 6.

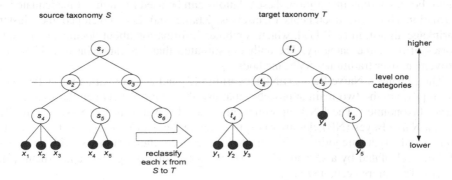

Fig. 1. The taxonomy integration task is to reclassify documents from a source taxonomy into a target taxonomy. The classification targets are the level-one categories in *T*.

2 Task Statement

The web taxonomy integration task in Fig.1 was originally defined by Agrawal and Srikant [3]. It can be formulated as the assignment of documents in a source taxonomy to a target taxonomy. The terms used in this task include:

– The source taxonomy, **S,** with a set of categories, $s_1, s_2, ..., s_i, ..., s_n$, each of which contains a set of documents.

- The target taxonomy, T, with a set of categories, $t_1, t_2, ..., t_i, ..., t_m$, each of which contains a set of documents.

For each document x in S, our task is to assign x to the target categories in T. In this paper, we follow the settings of Agrawal and Srikant [3] and Zhang and Lee [19] [18], which simply consider level-one categories in T as the target categories.

3 Related Works

Taxonomy integration is similar to text classification in that it also assigns a document to one or more target categories. However, in taxonomy integration, we have the additional information: the document's source categories in S. In addition, the relations between S and T can be used to enhance the accuracy of integration. For example, suppose most documents in category s_i are also in category t_j, we can then infer that these two categories are similar. Thus, any document x in s_i is likely to be categorized into t_j. From this example, we know that the relations between the source and target categories can be measured by estimating the degree of overlap between them. However, we have to resolve the following problems: (1) how to estimate the degree of overlap, and (2) how to use this information.

We now briefly introduce some state-of-the-art approaches that use the information about S, or the relations between S and T. The source taxonomy provides information about the relations between corresponding categories, including the documents in them. For taxonomy integration, these relations can be used to augment inadequate information about the documents themselves. Zhang and Lee developed the cluster shrinkage algorithm (CS) [19], which combines information about documents in categories of the same category. The authors estimated that CS can achieve a 15% improvement over traditional SVM methods.

The Enhanced Naïve Bayes (ENB) algorithm [3] and Co-Bootstrapping (CB) algorithm [18] are the two main approaches that use the relations between the source and target taxonomies. The ENB algorithm, proposed by Agrawal and Srikant, initially used a Naïve Bayes (NB) classifier [13] to estimate the degree of overlap between the source and target categories. The estimated scores were then combined with the probabilities calculated by a second NB classifier. According to Agrawal and Srikant [3], ENB is 15% more accurate than NB.

Similarly, Co-Bootstrapping (CB) [18] exploits inter-taxonomy relationships by providing category indicator functions as additional features of documents. According to Zhang and Lee [18], CB achieves close to a 15% improvement over NB. We discuss the above approaches in more detail in Section 4.2.

4 Learning to Integrate Taxonomies

We also use the relations between corresponding categories in S and T to enhance the integration process; however, unlike previous approaches, we do not consider a flattened taxonomy only, i.e., a taxonomy reduced to a single level [3].The relations between the level-one categories in S and T could be noisier than the relations between lower-levels, since the concept space of higher-level categories in taxonomies is more general. Therefore, we employ some features used in machine learning models to extract finer relations between lower-level categories in S and T.

In this section, we introduce five features used in our taxonomy integration approach. One feature is commonly used in text classification, two are derived from other taxonomy integration systems, and the remaining two are our own. We then introduce the Maximum Entropy (ME) model, a well-known classifier used in many applications. The section concludes with a discussion of ME's advantages and the process of our approach.

4.1 Features

Feature selection is critical to the success of machine learning approaches. In this section, we describe the features used in our system and discuss the effectiveness of each feature.

Word-TargetCat Features (WT)
When classifying a document, the collection of words it contains is important. More specifically, a distinct feature is initiated for each word-category combination. In addition, if a word occurs often in one class, we would expect the weight for that word-category pair to be higher than if the word were paired with other categories. In text classification, features accounted for the number of times a word appears should improve classification. For example, Naïve Bayes implementations that use word counts outperform implementations that do not [14]. Since taxonomy integration is an extension of text classification, we adopt these features in our approach. For each word, w, and category, t', in the target taxonomy, T, we formally define the Word-TargetCat feature as:

$$f_{w,t'}(x,t) = \begin{cases} \dfrac{N(x,w)}{N(x)} & \text{if } t = t' \\ 0 & \text{Otherwise} \end{cases} \tag{1}$$

where $N(x, w)$ is the number of times a word, w, appears in a document x, and $N(x)$ is the number of words in x.

Normalized Word-TargetCat Features (NWT)
In practice, the number of words contained in a document varies, and is relatively small compared to its vocabulary size in the document. According to the definition in Equation 1, most Word-TargetCat features will be zero. Therefore, it would be difficult to classify a web document by referring to a few words only. In text classification, solving this problem is difficult, since no more information can be used. In taxonomy classification, however, information about a document's category in both the source taxonomy and the target taxonomy is available. For each word, w, we can add the weight of w's total count of the documents in the same category to w's original count. We regard this step as a kind of normalization, after which many zero Word-TargetCat features become non-zero values. Zhang and Lee [19] developed the cluster shrinkage (CS) algorithm to perform this normalization, which conceptually moves each document to the center of its level-one parent category. Zhang and Lee showed

that this normalization significantly boosts the accuracy of taxonomy integration. Here, NWT is calculated by a modified version of CS. For each word w and category t' in the target taxonomy, T, we define the NWT feature as:

$$
f_{w,t'}(x,t,c_T) = \begin{cases} \eta \dfrac{N(x,w)}{N(x)} + (1-\eta)\dfrac{N(c_T,w)}{N(c_T)} & \text{if } t = t' \\ 0 & \text{Otherwise} \end{cases} \tag{2}
$$

where $N(x, w)$ is the number of times word w appears in a document x: $N(x)$ is the number of words in x; $N(c_T, w)$ is the number of times word w appears in x's level-one category c_T; $N(c_T)$ is the number of words in c_T: and η is the weight to control the strength of normalization effect.

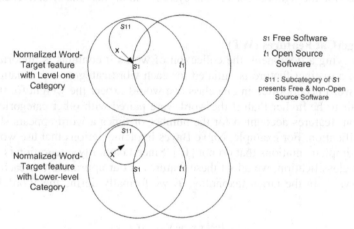

Fig. 2. With different level categories, the feature, NWTS, has different effects

Normalized Fine-Grained Word-TargetCat Features (NFWT)

As described in the last section, CS effectively helps Word-TargetCat features become non-zero values. That is, after applying CS, each document moves closer to its level-one parent category's center. In some cases, this can augment the correct information for classifying documents. However, the level-one parent category usually contains words that are too general or belong to cross-domains. Therefore, the accuracy improvement of taxonomy integration achieved by CS is reduced. In our approach, we consider the hierarchy's structure and regard the lowest-level parent category of the document as its category. Compared to the level-one parent category, the lowest-parent category contains more coherent information. As shown in Fig. 3, x is a document in the category s_{11}, and s_{11} is a subcategory of s_1. If we use CS as our normalization algorithm and s_1 is x's category, then x will be closer to s_1 after applying the normalization step, This could cause x to be misclassified into t_1, but taking the lowest-level as the document's category would avoid this potential error of Word-TargetCat features.

For each word w and category t in the target taxonomy, T, we define NFWT as:

$$f_{w,t'}(x,t,c_B) = \begin{cases} \eta \dfrac{N(x,w)}{N(x)} + (1-\eta) \dfrac{N(c_B,w)}{N(c_B)} & \text{if } t = t' \\ 0 & \text{Otherwise} \end{cases} \tag{3}$$

where $N(x, w)$ is the number of times word w appears in a document x; $N(x)$ is the number of words in x; $N(c_B, w)$ is the number of times word w appears in x's lowest parent category c_B; $N(c_B)$ is the number of words in c; and η is the weight to control the strength of normalization effect..

Normalized TargetCat-SourceCat Features (NTS)
For taxonomy integration, there is another type of information that can be used to decide a document's target category, namely, the relations between corresponding source categories and the target categories. Zhang and Lee [18] initiated a distinct feature for each target-source category combination. In the training phase, documents in S are used to train a multi-class classifier. Then, for each document y in T, we use the classifier to decide y's category in S, denoted as s'. The feature corresponding to the combination of t' and s' is enabled. In the test phase, when calculating t''s probability or score for each document x in S, the feature corresponding to the combination of t' and x's level-one parent category is enabled. Zhang and Lee [18] showed that using this feature boosts the classification accuracy. We implement such features as Normalized TargetCat-SourceCat features (NTS). For each category t' in the target taxonomy T, and each category s' in the target taxonomy S, we define the NTS features as:

$$f_{t',s'}(t,s) = \begin{cases} 1 & \text{if } t = t' \text{ and } s = s' \\ 0 & \text{Otherwise} \end{cases} \tag{4}$$

Normalized Word-TargetCat-SourceCatSourceCat Features (NWTS)
Although NTS improves the integration accuracy by relating each source and target category pair, the level-one category is so general that the relation between t' and s' is not precise enough to achieve a significant improvement. Since different words can have different impacts on a target-source category pair, we believe that these target-source combinations should be further divided by each distinct word. For each word w and category t' in the target taxonomy T, and category s' in the source taxonomy S, we define the normalized word count feature as:

$$f_{w,t',s'}(x,t,c,s) = \begin{cases} \eta \dfrac{N(x,w)}{N(x)} + (1-\eta) \dfrac{N(c,w)}{N(c)} & \text{if } t = t' \text{ and } s = s' \\ 0 & \text{Otherwise} \end{cases} \tag{5}$$

where $N(x, w)$ is the number of times word w appears in a document x; $N(x)$ is the number of words in x; $N(c, w)$ is the number of times word w appears in the source category c; $N(c)$ is the number of words in c; and η is the weight to control the strength of normalization effect.

We illustrate the use of the Word-TargetCat-SourceCat feature by the following example. As shown in Fig.2, to estimate the relation between t_1 and s_1, we assign documents in t_1 to s_1. From the classification result, we know that t_1 and s_1 overlap partially in the conceptual space. However, we still do not know which documents of s_1 should be classified into t_1. In fact, the instances of s_{11} should not be classified into t_1. We need other information to know the relations between the lower-level categories. Therefore, we add the word dimension to the original NTS, to combine the dimensions of the target and source categories.

4.2 Using Features in Maximum Entropy

We select the Maximum Entropy (ME) model [4] to implement our approach. ME is a statistical modeling technique used for estimating the conditional probability of a target label by the given information. ME computes the probability, $p(o|h)$, where o denotes all possible outcomes from the space, and h denoted all possible histories from the space. A history is all the conditioning data that enables one to assign probabilities to the space of outcomes. In the taxonomy integration task, the history can be viewed as all information derivable from the documents of the taxonomy relative to the current document, and the outcome can be viewed as the target category label. The computation of $p(o|h)$ in ME depends on a set of features, which is helpful for making predictions about the outcome.

Given a set of features and a training set, the ME estimation process produces a model where every feature f_i has a weight λ_i. From Berger [4], we can compute the conditional probability as:

$$p(o \mid h) = \frac{1}{z(h)} \exp\left(\sum_i \lambda_i f_i(h,o) \right) \qquad (6)$$

$$Z(h) = \sum_o \exp\left(\sum_i \lambda_i f_i(h,o) \right), \qquad (7)$$

The probability is derived by multiplying the weights of the active features (i.e., those $f_i(h,o) = 1$). The weight, λ_i, is estimated by a procedure called *improved iterative scaling* (IIS) [7], which improves the estimation of weights iteratively. The ME estimation technique guarantees that for every f_i, the expected value of λ_i will equal the empirical expectation of λ_i in the training corpus. The feature sets we use were introduced in Section 4.1. The process of our approach is shown in Fig. 3.

Advantages of Maximum Entropy

We use ME to build the classifier for taxonomy integration because it has a proven competitive performance in various tasks, including part-of- speech tagging [15], named entity recognition [5], English parser [6], prepositional phrase attachment [16], and text classification [14].

As noted in [5], ME allows users to focus on finding features that characterize the problem, while leaving feature weight assignment to the ME estimation routine. When new features are discovered, users do not need to reformulate the model as in other machine-based approaches, because the ME estimation routine automatically calculates new weight assignments.

Although using the ME model is a good choice, other machine learning algorithms, such as Support Vector Machine [10], Conditional Random Field [11], or Boosting [17], could also be adopted in our approach to improve taxonomy integration.

4.3 The Algorithm of Our Approach: NFWT+NWTS

Our proposed approach consists of NFWT and NWTS, which were introduced in Section 4.1. The procedure of NFWT+NWTS is shown in Fig.3.

```
T: target taxonomy   S: source taxonomy
Taxonomy_Integration_Main (T, S)
1: Use labeled documents in S to induce a ME-based
classifier with NFWT features for transferring the
document from T to S and then use these results to
measure the similarity between those corresponding
categories in S and T.
2: Use labeled documents in T to induce a ME-based
classifier with NWTS and NFWT features for transfer-
ring the document in S to T.
3: Return classification result;
```

Fig. 3. Our approach includes NFWT and NWTS features

There are two steps in NFWT+NWTS. The first step uses labeled documents in **S** as a training corpus to train a classifier of **S** with NFWT features. The classifier is used to generate feature values representing the source-target relations, which are necessary information of NWTS features. In the second step, we induce a classifier to transfer documents from **S** to **T** with both NWTS and NFWT features. Therefore, the final classifier will include NFWT, which uses lowest-level categories in the cluster shrinkage algorithm as well as NWTS, which considers word dimensions.

5 Experiments and Results

5.1 Datasets

We collected five datasets from the Google and Yahoo! Directories to evaluate our approach. Each dataset included a category in Google Directory, the corresponding category with a similar topic in Yahoo! Directory, and vice versa. Hyperlinks and web pages within these two categories were also stored in the dataset. Table 1 shows the five dataset names and their paths in the directories.

In the Google and Yahoo! Directories, each link/document includes the web page's title, URL, and description. For example:

```
Title: BBC News
URL : http://news.bbc.co.uk/
Description: offers U.K., world, business, science, and
entertainment news.
```

In the experiment, we used the information from the title, description, and content of the web page as the information for training and testing. All documents were pre-processed by removing the stop words, and stemming.

Table 1. Datasets

	Google Directory	Yahoo! Directory
Disease	Top/Health/ Conditions_and_Diseases	Health/ Diseases_and_Conditions/
Book	Top/Shopping/Publications /Books/	Business_and_economy/ shopping_and_services/ books/
Movies	Top/Arts/Movies/Genres/	Entertainment/ movies_and_film/genres/
Garden	Top/Shopping/ Home_and_Garden/	Business_and_economy/ shopping_and_services/ home_and_garden/
Outdoor	Top/Recreation/Outdoors/	Recreation/Outdoors/

In Table 2, each row shows the dataset name, the number of links within each directory, and the number of shared links between the two directories. In each dataset, the shared links, identified by their URLs, are used as the testing data, while the rest of the links are used as the training data. Only a small proportion of links are shared by the two web taxonomies, which shows the benefit of integrating them.

The number of categories is shown in Table 3. As mentioned earlier, we use the level-one categories as the target classes in our classification task.

Table 2. Number of links in each dataset

	Google	Yahoo!	Shared links
Disease	24,522	11,231	5,300
Book	58,46	8,168	567
Movies	30,438	19,223	2,560
Garden	13,058	4288	617
Outdoor	12,346	7,439	817
Total #	**80364**	**50349**	**9861**

Table 3. Number of categories

	Google	Yahoo!
	# of target categories	**# of target categories**
Disease	602	692
Book	44	43
Movies	23	23
Garden	37	18
Outdoor	37	65
Total #	**743**	**841**

5.2 Experimental Design

Our task is to classify documents from a source taxonomy into a target taxonomy. The experiment of each dataset consists of classifying a document from Google to Yahoo and vice versa. We use the documents of Yahoo (excluding the shared links) for training and classifying documents from Google into Yahoo. Similarly, we use documents from Google (excluding the shared documents) for training and classifying documents from Yahoo into Google. The shared documents are used as testing data.

To measure the correctness of all approaches, we defined the following classification accuracy:

$$\frac{\text{Number of instances in } S \text{ are classified correctly}}{\text{Number of instances in } S}\text{, where } S \text{ is the source taxonomy.}$$

5.3 Settings

In the NB and ENB experiments, we implement the NB and ENB modules. The parameter w of ENB is selected from a series of numbers: $\{0, 1, 3, 10, 30, 100, 300,$ and $1,000\}$ that have the best performance. The smoothing parameter [3] of the NB and ENB classifier is set to 0.1.

We use Maximum Entropy Toolkit [12] to implement the ME-based approaches. To compare our approach with normal text classification methods, we implement the ME-based text classification algorithm proposed by Kamal Nigam, John Lafferty, and Andrew McCallum [14]. We denote it as MEtext, which simply uses the Word-TargetCat features (WT).

We compare the features of our approach with the features used in previous approaches (NTS for [18] and NWT for [19] as discussed in Section 4). Although in previous works [18, 19], the features were implemented with other machine learning models, they can also be easily implemented with ME. The parameter η used in NWT, NFWT, and NWTS is set to 0.5.

5.4 Experimental Results

In Table 4, we denote the ME-based text classification that only uses the WT feature as MEtext, and our proposed approach as NFWT+NWTS. To make a distinction between our approach and the others, we use boldface and italic style for *NFWT* and *NWTS*. One can see that *NFWT+NWTS* performs significantly better than normal text classification approaches [14] in all five topics. These results suggest that our approach can effectively exploit the relations between corresponding categories in the target and source taxonomies to enhance the classification accuracy.

Next, we compare our approach (*NFWT+NWTS*) with NB and ENB. In Table 5, one can see that, as previous works showed, ENB performs slightly better than NB. However, our proposed approach, *NFWT+NWTS*, outperforms NB and ENB by 17% and 11%, respectively. These results show that referring to the relationships between taxonomies and replacing NB with ME can improve the accuracy of taxonomy integration. The former is due to the high degree of relevance between the two taxonomies. The latter is because ME can catch more dependencies among different features that commonly exist in text categorization and taxonomy integration problems.

Table 4. Experimental results of ME-based text classification approach and our approach

		MEtext	*NFWT+NWTS*	Improvement
G to Y	**Disease**	34.4%	46.3%	11.9%
	Book	48.8%	65.0%	16.2%
	Movies	56.8%	73.8%	17.0%
	Garden	75.2%	82.1%	6.9%
	Outdoor	59.6%	72.6%	13.0%
	Average	**55.0%**	**68.0%**	**13.1%**
Y to G	**Disease**	25.8%	47.0%	21.2%
	Book	39.7%	63.7%	24.0%
	Movies	44.7%	66.0%	21.3%
	Garden	59.4%	69.3%	9.9%
	Outdoor	62.7%	71.9%	9.2%
	Average	**46.5%**	**63.6%**	**17.1%**

Table 5. Experimental results of NB, ENB and our approach

		NB	ENB	*NFWT +NWTS*	Improvement over NB	Improvement over ENB
G to Y	**Disease**	25.2%	25.6%	46.3%	21.1%	20.7%
	Book	44.7%	51.4%	65.0%	20.3%	13.6%
	Movies	54.5%	68.0%	73.8%	19.3%	5.8%
	Garden	75.1%	79.4%	82.1%	7.0%	2.7%
	Outdoor	54.0%	60.3%	72.6%	18.6%	12.3%
	Average	**50.7%**	**56.9%**	**68.0%**	**17.3%**	**11.0%**
Y to G	**Disease**	25.8%	29.1%	47.0%	21.2%	17.9%
	Book	38.3%	44.0%	63.7%	25.4%	19.7%
	Movies	47.7%	54.9%	66.0%	18.3%	11.1%
	Garden	65.4%	66.1%	69.3%	3.9%	3.2%
	Outdoor	61.4%	67.9%	71.9%	10.5%	4.0%
	Average	**47.7%**	**52.4%**	**63.6%**	**15.7%**	**11.2%**

Unlike other approaches, our approach retains the hierarchical structure of taxonomies, and estimates the relationship between lower-level categories. Since the number of words on a web page may be significantly fewer than in a normal news article, the results of web page classification are more likely to be affected by the sparseness of words. The information in the source and target taxonomies can provide a great deal of help in smoothing the word frequency vectors of web pages, or measuring the similarity between source and target categories.

One may further ask: How can information in the source and target taxonomies be used to achieve better performance? Next, we will compare our approach and previous approaches on taxonomy integration.

Table 6. Experimental results of NWT and *NFWT*

		NWT	NFWT
G to Y	Disease	34.0%	38.0%
	Book	54.7%	58.6%
	Movies	61.5%	67.0%
	Garden	81.3%	82.3%
	Outdoor	65.8%	62.5%
	Average	**59.5%**	**61.6%**
Y to G	Disease	30.5%	38.2%
	Book	45.4%	48.1%
	Movies	49.1%	56.0%
	Garden	60.9%	69.4%
	Outdoor	67.6%	70.3%
	Average	**50.7%**	**56.4%**

In Table 6, the major difference between NWT and *NFWT* is that NWT uses level-one categories in the cluster shrinkage algorithm, while *NFWT* uses the lowest-level categories. The experimental results suggest that using lower-level categories yields a better performance than level-one categories. This supports our observation that level-one categories usually contain words that are too general or belong to cross-domains, which could undermine the performance. Even though the NWT is not as efficient as *NFWT*, its performance is still better than MEtext, as shown in Table 4.

Table 7. Four different configurations of feature combinations

	Use level-one category in the cluster shrinkage algorithm	Use lowest-level category in the cluster shrinkage algorithm
Considering document dimension	NWT +NTS	*NFWT*+NTS
Considering word dimension	NWT +*NWTS*	*NFWT* +*NWTS*

Now, we compare the effects of two factors: (1) using level-one or lowest-level categories in the cluster shrinkage algorithm, and (2) using document or word dimensions to represent the source-target relations. Table 7 shows all combinations of these two factors: NWT+NTS, NWT+*NWTS*, *NFWT*+NTS, and *NFWT*+*NWTS*. The configuration name is composed of the features it uses. For example, NWT +NTS means it uses level-one categories in cluster shrinkage algorithm as NWT and uses NTS to measure the source-target relations. In Table 8, we can see that *NFWT*+NTS outperforms NWT+NTS, and *NFWT*+*NWTS* outperforms NWT+*NWTS*. These results establish that lowest-level categories contain more precise information for categorization than level-one. Therefore, configurations using lowest-level categories in the cluster shrinkage algorithm (*NFWT*) outperform those using level-one categories (NWT). In addition, we can see that NWT+*NWTS* outperforms NWT+NTS, and *NFWT*+*NWTS* outperforms *NFWT*+NTS. These results demonstrate that using word-dimensions (*NWTS*) rather than document dimensions (NTS) to represent source-target relations could further alleviate the partial overlap problem.

Table 8. Experimental results of all combinations of features

		NWT+NTS	NWT+*NWTS*	*NFWT*+NTS	*NFWT*+*NWTS*
G to Y	Disease	38.7%	42.4%	44.0%	46.3%
	Book	59.0%	58.6%	64.2%	65.0%
	Movies	63.4%	68.4%	69.7%	73.8%
	Garden	78.2%	77.5%	81.8%	82.1%
	Outdoor	60.1%	68.2%	72.8%	72.6%
	Average	**59.9%**	**63.0%**	**66.5%**	**68.0%**
Y to G	Disease	39.8%	41.3%	46.9%	47.0%
	Book	52.2%	60.1%	59.5%	63.7%
	Movies	54.9%	59.4%	58.9%	66.0%
	Garden	60.5%	59.8%	71.1%	69.3%
	Outdoor	65.4%	68.2%	72.2%	71.9%
	Average	**54.5%**	**57.8%**	**61.7%**	**63.6%**

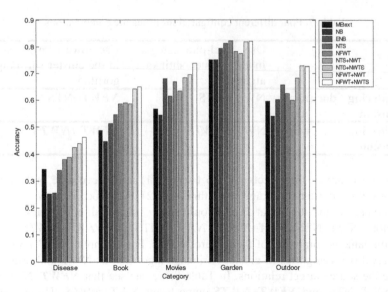

Fig. 4. Comparison of the experimental results of all taxonomy integration approaches and features (Google to Yahoo)

Generally speaking, using information of source category improves the categorization accuracy. We can see that NWT+NTS and NWT+*NWTS* outperform NWT, and *NFWT*+NTS and *NFWT*+*NWTS* outperform *NFWT*. Among these four configurations, the performance of NWT+NTS is the worst, such as in the Garden category. We believe this is because the classification criteria of Google's Garden directory is much different with that of Yahoo!'s Garden directory. As a result, the partial overlap problem becomes very serious in Garden category. To further justify this argument, we compare the name of level-one categories of Garden in Yahoo! and Google. It is found that there is no common name between those categories in Google and Yahoo!'s Garden directory. From this observation, we conclude that, NWT+NTS, which uses level-one categories in the cluster shrinkage algorithm and considers only document dimension in measuring the source-target relations, is influenced most deeply by the different classification criteria between the source and target taxonomy.

The experimental results of each taxonomy integration approach are shown in Fig. 4 and Fig. 5 respectively.

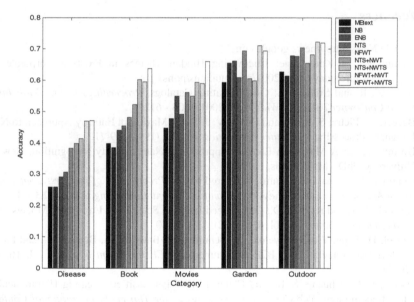

Fig. 5. Comparison of the experimental results of all taxonomy integration approaches and features (Yahoo to Google)

6   Conclusions

In this paper, we have proposed an approach that effectively uses the relations between corresponding categories in source and target taxonomies to improve taxonomy integration. Unlike previous works that use a flattened hierarchy as the information source, we utilize hierarchical information to extract fine-grained relations, which alleviates the partial concept overlap problem in taxonomy integration.

The proposed approach was tested using real Internet directories. Its performance was better than normal text classification approaches and other features in previous works. The experimental results also support the assumption that using a flattened hierarchy could cause the loss of valuable information about relations between corresponding categories.

In the future, more information, such as web resources, a third taxonomy, or existing knowledge ontology could be incorporated into our approach. It would also be interesting to see how our approach can be applied to other applications.

Acknowledgement

We are grateful for the support of National Science Council under grant NSC94-2752-E-001-001, and the support of the thematic program of Academia Sinica under grant AS91IIS1PP and 94B003.

References

1. Google News: http://news.google.com/
2. Taxonomies of Knowledge: Uncovering Hidden Themes in Existing Corporate Data: http://www.infotoday.com/it2001/presentations/pohs1.ppt
3. Agrawal, R. and Srikant, R.: On Integrating Catalogs. *Proceedings of the Tenth International Conference on World Wide Web* (2001), 603 - 612.
4. Berger, A., Pietra, S. A. D., and Pietra, V. J. D.: A Maximum Entropy Approach to Natural Language Processing. *Computer Linguistics*, vol. 22, (1996), 39-71.
5. Borthwick, A.: A Maximum Entropy Approach to Named Entity Recognition. New York University, PhD Thesis Thesis, (1999).
6. Charniak, E.: A maximum-entropy-inspired parser. *Proceedings of the First Conference on North American chapter of the Association for Computational Linguistics* (2000), 132 - 139.
7. Darroch, J. N. and Ratcliff, D.: Generalized Iterative Scaling for Log-linear Models. *Annals of Mathematical Statistics*, vol. 43, (1972), 1470-1480.
8. Fensel, D., Ding, Y., Omelayenko, B., Schulten, E., Botquin, G., Brown, M., and Flett, A.: Product Data Integration in B2B E-Commerce. *IEEE Intelligent Systems*, vol. 16, no. 4, (2001).
9. Huang, C.-C., Chuang, S.-L., and Chien, L.-F.: Liveclassifier: Creating Hierarchical Text Classifiers through Web Corpora. *Proceedings of the Thirteenth International Conference on World Wide Web*, (2004), 184-192.
10. Joachims, T.: Text Categorization with Support Vector Machines: Learning with Many Relevant Features. *Tenth European Conference on Machine Learning* (1998), 137-142.
11. Lafferty, J., McCallum, A., and Pereira, F.: Conditional Random Fields: Probabilistic Models for Segmenting and Labeling Sequence Data. *Proceedings of the Eighteenth International Conference on Machine Learning*, (2001), 282-289.
12. Maximum Entropy Toolkit: http://maxent.sourceforge.net
13. Mitchell, T.: Machine Learning, Singapore, McGraw Hill, (1997).
14. Nigam, K., Lafferty, J., and McCallum, A.: Using Maximum Entropy for Text Classification. *In IJCAI-99 Workshop on Machine Learning for Information Filtering*, (1999), 61-67.
15. Ratnaparkhi, A.: A Maximum Entropy Model for Part-Of-Speech Tagging. *Proceedings of the Conference on Empirical Methods in Natural Language Processing* (1996), 133-142.

16. Ratnaparkhi, A.: Statistical models for unsupervised prepositional phrase attachment. *Proceedings of the Thirty-Sixth conference on Association for Computational Linguistics*, vol. 2, (1998), 1079 - 1085.

17. Schapire, R. E. and Singer, Y.: BoosTexter: A Boosting-based System for Text Categorization. Machine Learning, vol. 39, (2000), 135-168.

18. Zhang, D. and Lee, W. S.: Web taxonomy integration through co-bootstrapping. *Proceedings of the Twenty-Seventh Annual International Conference on Research and Development in Information Retrieval* (2004), 410 - 417.

19. Zhang, D. and Lee, W. S.: Web taxonomy integration using support vector machines. *Proceedings of the Thirteenth International Conference on World Wide Web* (2004), 472 - 481.

WIDIT: Fusion-Based Approach to Web Search Optimization

Kiduk Yang and Ning Yu

School of Library and Information Science, Indiana University,
Bloomington, Indiana 47405, U.S.A
{kiyang, nyu}@indiana.edu

1 Introduction

To facilitate both the understanding and the discovery of information, we need to utilize multiple sources of evidence, integrate a variety of methodologies, and combine human capabilities with those of the machine. The Web Information Discovery Integrated Tool (WIDIT) Laboratory at the School of Library and Information Science, Indiana University-Bloomington, houses several projects that employ this idea of multi-level fusion in the areas of information retrieval and knowledge discovery. This paper describes a Web search optimization study by the TREC research group of WIDIT, who explores a fusion-based approach to enhancing retrieval performance on the Web. In the study, we employed both static and dynamic tuning methods to optimize the fusion formula that combines multiple sources of evidence. By static tuning, we refer to the typical stepwise tuning of system parameters based on training data. "Dynamic tuning", the key idea of which is to combine the human intelligence, especially pattern recognition ability, with the computational power of the machine, involves an interactive system tuning process that facilitates fine-tuning of the system parameters based on the cognitive analysis of immediate system feedback. The rest of the paper is organized as follows. The next section discusses related work in Web information retrieval (IR). Section 3 details the WIDIT approach to Web IR, followed by the description of our experiment using the TREC .gov data in section 4 and the discussion of results in section 5.

2 Research in Web IR

Information discovery on the Web is challenging. The complexity and richness of the Web search environment call for approaches that extend conventional IR methods to leverage rich sources of information on the Web. Text Retrieval Conference (TREC) has been a fertile ground for cutting-edge Web information retrieval (IR) research in a standardized environment. The Web IR experiment of TREC, otherwise known as the Web track, investigated in its initial stages the strategies for the same ad-hoc retrieval task as was done previously with plain text documents. Although many TREC participants explored methods of leveraging non-textual sources of information such as hyperlinks and document structure, the general consensus among the early Web track participants was that link analysis and other non-textual methods did not perform as well as the content-based retrieval methods fine-tuned over the years

G.G. Lee et al. (Eds.): AIRS 2005, LNCS 3689, pp. 206–220, 2005.
© Springer-Verlag Berlin Heidelberg 2005

(Hawking et al., 1999; Hawking et al., 2000; Gurrin & Smeaton, 2001; Savoy & Rasolofo, 2001).

There have been many speculations as to why link analysis, which showed much promise in previous research and has been so readily embraced by commercial Web search engines, did not prove useful in Web track experiments. Most such speculations point to potential problems with Web track's earlier test collections, from the inadequate link structure of truncated Web data (Savoy & Picard, 1998; Singhal & Kazkiel, 2001), and relevance judgments that penalize the link analysis by not counting the hub pages as relevant (Voorhees & Harman, 2000) and reward the content analysis by counting multiple relevant pages from the same site as relevant (Singhal & Kazkiel, 2001), to unrealistic queries that are too detailed and specific to be representative of real world Web searches (Singhal & Kaszkiel, 2001).

In an effort to address the criticism and problems associated with the early Web track experiments, TREC abandoned the ad-hoc Web retrieval task in 2002 in favor of topic distillation and named page finding task and replaced its earlier Web test collection of randomly selected Web pages with a larger and potentially higher quality domain-specific collection[1]. The topic distillation task in TREC-2002 is described as finding a short, comprehensive list of pages that are good information resources, and the named page finding tasks is described as finding a specific page whose name is described by the query (Hawking & Craswell, 2002; Craswell & Hawking, 2003). Adjustment of the Web track environment brought forth renewed interest in retrieval approaches that leverage Web-specific sources of evidences such as link structure and document structure.

For the home page finding task, where the objective is to find the entry page of a specific site described by the query, Web page's URL characteristics, such as its type and length, as well as the anchor text of Web page's inlinks proved to be useful sources of information to be leveraged (Hawking & Craswell, 2002). In the named page finding task, which is similar to home page finding task except that the target page described by the query is not necessarily the entry point of a Web site but any specific page on the Web, the use of anchor text still proved to be an effective strategy but the use of URL characteristics did not work well as it did in the home page finding task (Craswell & Hawking, 2003). In the topic distillation task, anchor text still seemed to be a useful resource, especially as a mean to boost the performance of content-based methods via fusion (i.e. result merging), although the level of its usefulness fell much below that achieved in named page finding tasks (Hawking & Craswell, 2002; Craswell & Hawking, 2003). Various site compression strategies, which attempt to select the "best" pages of a given site, was another common theme in the topic distillation task, once again demonstrating the importance of fine-tuning the retrieval system according to the task at hand (Amitay et al., 2003; Zhang et al., 2003). It is interesting to note that link analysis (e.g. PageRank, HITS variations) has not yet proven itself to be an effective strategy and the content-based method seems to be still the most dominant factor in the Web track. In fact, the two best results in

---

[1] TREC .GOV collection consists of 1.25 million Web pages (19 gigabytes) from .gov domain, which is larger, less diverse and likely to be of higher quality than the previous WT10g collection, which is a 10 gigabyte subset of the Web crawl from Internet Archive.

TREC-2002 topic distillation task were achieved by the baseline systems that used only the content-based methods (MacFarlane, 2003; Zhang et al., 2003).

In our earlier studies (Yang, 2002a; Yang, 2002b), where we investigated various fusion approaches for ad-hoc retrieval using the WT10g collection, we found that simplistic approach combining the results of content- and link-based retrieval results did not enhance retrieval performance in general. TREC participants in recent Web track environment, however, found that use of non-textual information such as hyperlinks, document structure, and URL could be beneficial for specific tasks such as topic distillation and named/home page finding tasks. We believe that this is not only due to the change in the retrieval environment (i.e. test collection, retrieval task) but also the result of more dynamic approach to combining multiple sources of evidence than straightforward result merging.

3 WIDIT Approach to Web IR

Based on the assumption that the key to effective Web IR lies in exploiting the richness of Web search environment by combining multiple sources of evidence, we focused our efforts on extending and optimizing the fusion methods. First, we combined multiple sets of retrieval results generated from multiple sources of evidence (e.g. body text, anchor text, header text) and multiple query formulations using a weighted sum fusion formula, whose parameters were tuned via a static tuning process using training data. The ranking of the fusion result was then "optimized" via a dynamic tuning process that involved iterative refining of fusion formula that combines the contributions of diverse Web-based evidence (e.g. hyperlinks, URL, document structure). The dynamic tuning process is implemented as a Web application; where interactive system parameter tuning by the user produces in real time the display of system performance changes as well as the new search results annotated with metadata of fusion parameter values (e.g. link counts, URL type, etc.). The key idea of dynamic tuning, which is to combine the human intelligence, especially pattern recognition ability, with the computational power of the machine, is implemented in this Web application that allows human to examine not only the immediate effect of his/her system tuning but also the possible explanation of the tuning effect in the form of data patterns.

3.1 WIDIT Web IR System Architecture

WIDIT Web IR system consists of five main modules: indexing, retrieval, fusion (i.e. result merging), query classification, and reranking modules. The indexing module processes various sources of evidence to generate multiple indexes. The retrieval module produces multiple result sets from using different query formulations against multiple indexes. The fusion module, which is optimized via the static tuning process, combines result sets using weighted sum formula. The query classification module uses a combination of statistical and linguistic classification methods to determine query types. The reranking module uses query type-specific reranking formulas optimized via dynamic tuning process to rerank the merged results. Figure 1 shows an overview of WIDIT Web IR system architecture.

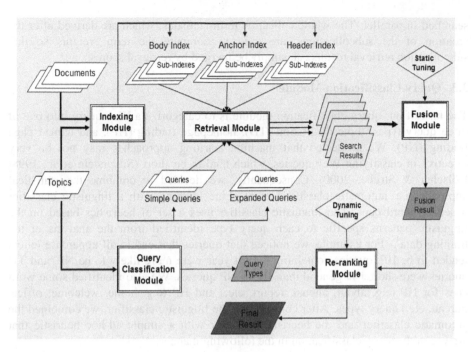

Fig. 1. WIDIT Web IR System Architecture

3.2 Indexing Module

WIDIT preprocesses documents by removing HTML tags and stopwords and applying the simple plural remover (Frakes & Baeza-Yates, 1992)[2]. The stopwords consist of non-meaningful words such as words in a standard stopword list, non-alphabetical words, words consisting of more than 25 or less than 3 characters, and words that contain 3 or more repeated characters. Hyphenated words are split into parts before applying the stopword exclusion, and acronyms and abbreviations are kept as index terms[3].

In addition to extracting body text terms (i.e. terms between <body> and </body> tags), WIDIT extracts terms from document title, meta keywords and descriptions, and "emphasized" text (e.g. text with <b>, <em>, <font>, <u>, <h1> tags) as well as extracting terms from the anchor texts of incoming links. Thus, WIDIT creates three sets of term indexes: first based on document content (i.e. body index), second based on document structure (header index), and third based on link structure (anchor index).

In order to enable incremental indexing as well as to scale up to larger collections, each of the indexes consists of smaller subcolllections, which are created and

---

[2] The simple plural remover is chosen to speed up indexing time and to minimize the overstemming effect of more aggressive stemmers.

[3] Acronym and abbreviation identification was based on simple pattern matching of punctuations and capitalizations.

searched in parallel. The whole collection term statistics, which are derived after the creation of the subcollections, are used to compute the term weights so that subcollection retrieval results can simply be merged by retrieval scores.

3.3 Query Classification Module

The task of our query classification module is to categorize a Web query into one of three query types: topic distillation (TD), homepage finding (HP), and named page finding (NP). We suspected that machine learning approaches may not be very effective in classifying Web queries, which tend to be short (Silverstein et al., 1998; Hölscher & Strube, 2000). Consequently, we decided to combine the statistical approach (i.e. automatic classifier) of machine learning with a linguistic classifier based on word cues. The linguistic classifier uses a set of heuristics based on the linguistic patterns specific to each query type identified from the analysis of the training data[4]. For example, we noticed that queries that end in all uppercase letters tended to be HP, queries containing 4-digit year were more likely to be NP, and TD queries were shorter in general than HP or NP queries. We also identified some word cues for NP (e.g. about, annual, report, etc.) and HP (e.g. home, welcome, office, bureau, etc.) query types. After constructing the linguistic classifier, we combined the automatic classifier and the heuristic classifier with a simple ad-hoc heuristic that arrived at the query classification in the following manner:

> *if single word, assign TD.*
> *else if strong word cue, assign linguistic classification.*
> *else assign statistical classification.*

3.4 Retrieval Module

The retrieval component of WIDIT implements both Vector Space Model (VSM) using the SMART length-normalized term weights and the probabilistic model using the Okapi BM25 formula. Documents are ranked in decreasing order of the inner product of document and query vectors,

$$\mathbf{q}^\mathrm{T}\mathbf{d}_i = \sum_{k=1}^{t} q_k d_{ik} \tag{1}$$

where q_k is the weight of term k in the query, d_{ik} is the weight of term k in document i, and t is the number of terms in the index.

For the VSM implementation, SMART *Lnu* weights with the slope of 0.3 are used for document terms (Buckley et al., 1997), and SMART *ltc* weights (Buckley et al., 1995) are used for query terms. *Lnu* weights attempt to match the probability of retrieval given a document length with the probability of relevance given that length (Singhal et al., 1996).

---

[4] TREC Web track queries were used as training data.

$$d_{ik} = \frac{\log(f_{ik}) + 1}{\sqrt{\sum_{j=1}^{t}(\log(f_{ij})+1)^2}} \qquad q_k = \frac{(\log(f_k)+1)*idf_k}{\sqrt{\sum_{j=1}^{t}[(\log(f_j)+1)*idf_j]^2}} \qquad (2)$$

Equation (2) describes the SMART formula, where d_{ik} is the document term weight (*Lnu*), q_k is the query term weight (*ltc*), f_{ik} is the number of times term k appears in document i, f_k is the number of times term k appears in the query, idf_k is the inverse document frequency of term k, and t is the number of terms in document or query.

The simplified version of the Okapi BM25 relevance scoring formula (Robertson & Walker, 1994), which is used to implement the probabilistic model, is described in equation (3), where N is the number of documents in the collection, df is the document frequency, dl is the document length, $avdl$ is the average document length, and k1, b, k3 are parameters (1.2, 0.75, 7 to 1000, respectively).

$$d_{ik} = \log\left(\frac{N-df_k+0.5}{df_k+0.5}\right)\frac{f_{ik}}{k_1((1-b)+b\cdot(\frac{dl}{avdl}))+f_{ik}} \quad , \quad q_k = \frac{(k_3+1)f_k}{k_3+f_k} \qquad (3)$$

Multiple sets of queries, resulting from various query formulation methods (e.g. noun extraction, phrase identification, synonym expansion) are applied against the three sets of document indexes[5] to produce multiple sets of retrieval results to be merged by the fusion module[6].

3.5 Fusion Module

The fusion module combines the multiple sets of search results after retrieval time. In addition to two of the most common fusion formulas, *Similarity Merge* (Fox & Shaw, 1995; Lee, 1997) and *Weighted Sum* (Bartell et al., 1994; Thompson, 1990), WIDIT employs variations of the weighted sum formula. The similarity merge formula multiplies the sum of fusion component scores for a document by the number of fusion components that retrieved the document (i.e. overlap), based on the assumption that documents with higher overlap are more likely to be relevant. Instead of relying on overlap, the weighted sum formula sums fusion component scores weighted with the relative contributions of the fusion components that retrieved them, which is typically estimated based on training data. Both formulas compute the fusion score of a document by a linear combination of fusion component scores.

In our earlier study (Yang, 2002b), similarity merge approach proved ineffective when combining content- and link-based results, so we devised three variations of the

---

[5] Body text index consists of title and body text terms. Anchor text index consists of title and inlink anchor text terms. Header text index consists of title, meta keywords and descriptions, and emphasized text terms.

[6] In practice, retrieval for each document index consists of parallel searches of multiple subcollections using the whole collection term weights, whose results are merged and sorted by document score.

weighted sum fusion formula, which were shown to be more effective in combining fusion components that are dissimilar (Yang, 2002a). Equation (4) describes the simple *Weight Sum* (WS) formula, which sums the normalized system scores multiplied by system contribution weights. Equation (5) describes the *Overlap Weight Sum* (OWS) formula, which multiplies the WS score by overlap. Equation (6) describes the *Weighted Overlap Weighted Sum* (WOWS) formula, which multiplies the WS score by overlap weighted by system contributions:

$$FS_{WS} = (w_i * NS_i), \tag{4}$$

$$FS_{OWS} = (w_i * NS_i * olp), \tag{5}$$

$$FS_{WOWS} = (w_i * NS_i * w_i * olp), \tag{6}$$

where: FS = fusion score of a document,

w_i = weight of system i,
NS_i = normalized score of a document by system i,
    = $(S_i - S_{min}) / (S_{max} - S_{min})$
olp = number of systems that retrieved a given document.

The normalized document score, NS_i, is computed by Lee's min-max formula (1997), where S_i is the retrieval score of a given document and S_{max} and S_{min} are the maximum and minimum document scores by method i.

One of the main challenges in using the weighted fusion formula lies in determination of the optimum weights for each system (w_i). In order to optimize the fusion weights, WIDIT engages in a static tuning process, where various weight combinations (e.g. 0.9 for body text, 0.08 for header text, 0.02 for anchor text) are evaluated with the training data of past Web track results in a stepwise fashion.

3.6   Reranking Module

In order to optimize retrieval performance in top ranks, fusion results are reranked based on the content- and link-based evidences (e.g. hyperlinks, URL, document structure). The reranking heuristic consists of a set of ranking and document score boosting rules arrived at by dynamic tuning process involving interactive retrieval and manual system tuning in real time. The dynamic tuning process is applied to the best single and best fusion systems to "tune" the ranking heuristic.

The dynamic tuning component of WIDIT produces retrieval results that display individual scores for each source of evidence such as inter/intrasite in/outdegree, phrase/proximity match counts in body/header/anchor texts, and query term matches in URL as well as ranking and retrieval scores before/after the adjustment of reranking parameters by dynamic tuning.

3.6.1   Reranking Factors
TREC participants found various sources of evidence such as anchor text (Craswell, Hawking & Robertson, 2001; Hawking & Craswell, 2002; Craswell & Hawking,

2003) and URL characteristics (Kraajj et al., 2002; Tomlinson, 2003, Zhang et al., 2003) to be useful in the Web track tasks. Based on those findings as well as the analysis of our previous Web IR studies, we decided to focus on four categories of the reranking factors. The first category is the field-specific match, where we score each document by counting the occurrences of query words (keyword, acronym, phrase) in URL, title, header, and anchor texts. The second category of reranking factors we use is the exact match, where we look for exact match of query text in title, header, and anchor texts (exact), or in the body text (exact2) of documents. The third category is link-based, where we count documents' inlinks (indegree) and outlinks (outdegree). The last category is the document type, which is derived based on its URL (Tomlinson, 2003; Kraajj et al., 2002), or derived using a linguistic heuristic similar to the one used in query classification.

3.6.2 Dynamic Tuning

The dynamic tuning interface is implemented as a Web application (Figure 2); where interactive system parameter tuning by the user produces in real time the display of system performance changes as well as the new search results annotated with metadata of fusion parameter values (e.g. link counts, URL type, etc.).

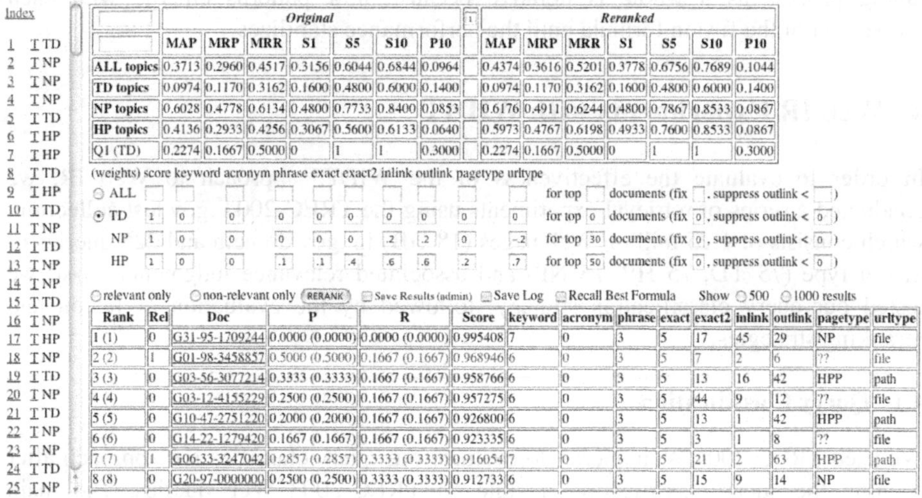

Index (1–25):
1 I TD, 2 I NP, 3 I NP, 4 I NP, 5 I TD, 6 I HP, 7 I HP, 8 I TD, 9 I HP, 10 I TD, 11 I NP, 12 I TD, 13 I NP, 14 I NP, 15 I TD, 16 I NP, 17 I HP, 18 I NP, 19 I TD, 20 I NP, 21 I TD, 22 I NP, 23 I NP, 24 I TD, 25 I NP

	Original							Reranked						
	MAP	MRP	MRR	S5	S5	S10	P10	MAP	MRP	MRR	S1	S5	S10	P10
ALL topics	0.3713	0.2960	0.4517	0.3156	0.6044	0.6844	0.0964	0.4374	0.3616	0.5201	0.3778	0.6756	0.7689	0.1044
TD topics	0.0974	0.1170	0.3162	0.1600	0.4800	0.6000	0.1400	0.0974	0.1170	0.3162	0.1600	0.4800	0.6000	0.1400
NP topics	0.6028	0.4778	0.6134	0.4800	0.7733	0.8400	0.0853	0.6176	0.4911	0.6244	0.4800	0.7867	0.8533	0.0867
HP topics	0.4136	0.2933	0.4256	0.3067	0.5600	0.6133	0.0640	0.5973	0.4767	0.6198	0.4933	0.7600	0.8533	0.0867
Q1 (TD)	0.2274	0.1667	0.5000	0	1	1	0.3000	0.2274	0.1667	0.5000	0	1	1	0.3000

(weights) score keyword acronym phrase exact exact2 inlink outlink pagetype urltype

○ ALL ... for top □ documents (fix □, suppress outlink < □)
⊙ TD 1 0 0 0 0 0 0 0 0 0 for top 0 documents (fix 0, suppress outlink < 0)
NP 1 0 0 0 0 0 .2 .2 0 -2 for top 30 documents (fix 0, suppress outlink < 0)
HP 1 0 0 .1 .1 .4 .6 .6 .2 .7 for top 50 documents (fix 0, suppress outlink < 0)

○ relevant only   ○ non-relevant only (RERANK) ☐ Save Results (admin) ☐ Save Log ☐ Recall Best Formula   Show ○ 500 ○ 1000 results

Rank	Rel	Doc	P	R	Score	keyword	acronym	phrase	exact	exact2	inlink	outlink	pagetype	urltype
1 (1)	0	G31-95-1709244	0.0000 (0.0000)	0.0000 (0.0000)	0.995408	7	0	3	5	17	45	29	NP	file
2 (2)	1	G01-98-3458857	0.5000 (0.5000)	0.1667 (0.1667)	0.968946	6	0	3	5	7	2	6	??	file
3 (3)	0	G03-56-3077214	0.3333 (0.3333)	0.1667 (0.1667)	0.958766	6	0	3	5	13	16	42	HPP	path
4 (4)	0	G03-12-4155229	0.2500 (0.2500)	0.1667 (0.1667)	0.957275	6	0	3	5	44	9	12	??	file
5 (5)	0	G10-47-2751220	0.2000 (0.2000)	0.1667 (0.1667)	0.926800	6	0	3	5	13	1	42	HPP	path
6 (6)	0	G14-22-1279420	0.1667 (0.1667)	0.1667 (0.1667)	0.923335	6	0	3	5	3	1	8	??	file
7 (7)	1	G06-33-3247042	0.2857 (0.2857)	0.3333 (0.3333)	0.916054	7	0	3	5	21	2	63	HPP	path
8 (8)	0	G20-97-0000000	0.2500 (0.2500)	0.3333 (0.3333)	0.912733	6	0	3	5	15	9	14	NP	file

Fig. 2. Dynamic Tuning Interface

The key idea of dynamic tuning, which is to combine the human intelligence, especially pattern recognition ability, with the computational power of the machine, is implemented in this Web application that allows human to examine not only the immediate effect of his/her system tuning but also the possible explanation of the tuning effect in the form of data patterns. By engaging in iterative dynamic tuning process that successively fine-tune the fusion parameters based on the cognitive analysis of immediate system feedback, WIDIT can increase system performance without resorting to an exhaustive evaluation of parameter combinations, which can not only be prohibitively resource intensive with numerous parameters but also fail to produce the optimal outcome due to its linear approach to fusion components combination.

The dynamic tuning interface, as can be seen in Figure 1, has a navigation pane on the left with query numbers[7], a click of which will populate the main display pane on the right. The main display pane has three horizontal components: side-by-side performance scores for original and reranked retrieval results at the top, weight specification form for fusion components (i.e. reranking factors) in the middle, and the ranked list of retrieved documents with individual fusion component scores at the bottom. The main idea is to discover patterns in fusion component scores across ranks that can be leveraged into improving retrieval performance by fine-tuning the fusion formula in the middle (i.e. reranking function). The translation of discerned pattern into an effective weighting function is a trial-and-error process guided by a real-time display of performance gain or loss affected by the tuning. Sometimes the cognitive analysis of identified patter+ns suggests reranking heuristic that goes beyond a simple linear combination of reranking factors (e.g. rerank only top n results, with top m ranked fixed). In such cases, one must update the fusion formula component of the main display pane to accommodate the devised reranking heuristic. The dynamic tuning process as a whole is iterative because new patterns emerge with each refinement of the fusion formula until the performance stabilizes.

4 Web IR Experiments with WIDIT

In order to evaluate the effectiveness of the WIDIT approach to Web IR, we conducted a series of retrieval experiments using the TREC-2004 .gov test collection, which consists of 1.25 million Web pages (18 GB) in .gov domain and 225 queries of mixed type (75 TD, 75 HP, 75 NP) and associated relevance judgments. First, we tested our query classification strategy, followed by the evaluation of fusion and reranking strategies.

4.1 Query Classification

We used TREC-2004 Web queries to evaluate our query classification approach after training the query classification module on TREC-2003 Web queries. The main challenge of the query classification task stemmed from the short length of the queries, which contained only three words on the average (Table 1). We suspected that machine learning approaches may not be very effective in classifying texts with only a few words. Furthermore, the quality and the quantity of the training data available from previous years also seemed suboptimal for machine learning. There were 100 TD training queries compared to 300 HP and 295 NP queries, which were also short in length (Table 2) and appeared to be often ambiguous upon manual examination.

---

[7] Clicking the letter 'T' next to a query number will display a pop up window with the XML formatted TREC topic associated with the query number.

Table 1. 2004 Web track queries

Query Length (# of words)	1	2	3	4	5	6	7	Avg.
TD queries	12	41	16	6	0	0	0	2.2
NP queries	2	11	28	20	9	4	1	3.5
HP queries	3	9	38	15	8	2	0	3.3
All queries	17	61	82	41	17	6	1	3.0

Table 2. Training queries from 2001-2003 Web tracks

	Query Counts			Avg. Length (# of words)
	2001	2002	2003	
TD queries		50	50	2.8
NP queries		150	150	4.0
HP queries	145		150	3.6
All queries	145	200	350	3.7

To supplement the training data for automatic classifiers, which had three times as many HP and NP than TD queries, we created a lexicon of US government topics by manually selecting keywords from the crawl of the Yahoo!'s U.S. Government category. We tested Naïve Bayes and SVM classifiers with the Yahoo-enriched training data, which showed little difference in performance. The classifier comparisons (i.e. statistical vs. linguistic vs. combination) showed the best performance by the combination classifier.

4.2 Static and Dynamic Tuning for Fusion

Having engaged in the query classification, our approach to handling the mixed query types was based on optimizing retrieval strategy for each of the query types. To leverage the multiple sources of evidence, we created separate document indexes for body text, anchor text of incoming links, and header text that consists of meta field text and emphasized portion of body text. The merging of the retrieval results were optimized via a static tuning process, where search results were combined using weighted sum with various weights without regards to query types.

After the fusion optimization by static tuning, we employed a post-retrieval rank-boosting strategy to rerank the merged results for each query type using the dynamic tuning process. In order to assess the effectiveness of dynamic tuning, we devised a static reranking approach based on previous TREC research. Our static approach to query type-specific reranking was as follows: boost the rank of potential homepages if the query is topic-distillation or homepage finding type; boost the rank of pages with keyword matches if the query is hompage or named page finding type. More specifically, our rank boosting heuristic kept top 5 ranks static, while boosting the ranks of potential homepages (identified by URL type determination) as well as pages with keyword matches in document titles and URLs.

We performed a series of dynamic tuning sessions using TREC-2003 training data, which involved repeated cycles of retrieval and tuning the reranking heuristic based on real time evaluation of retrieval results. In contrast to static tuning, dynamic tuning process allows tuning of systems with numerous parameters by leveraging human intelligence. The main components of reranking heuristic we used were inter/intrasite in/outdegree (e.g. boost score if large outdegree for topic distillation, boost score if large indegree for home/named page finding), phrase/proximity match (e.g. boost ranking if phrase match in title or anchor text), and query term match in URL (e.g. boost to top 10 rank if acronym match in URL). The reranking heuristics for home/named page finding task also involved the query classification component, which assigned different emphasis on evidence sources according to the query type.

The effective reranking factors observed from the iterations of dynamic reranking were: indegree, outdegree, exact match, and URL/Pagetype with the minimum number of outdegree of 1 for HP queries; indegree, outdegree, and URLtype for NP queries (1/3 impact of HP factors); acronym, outdegree, and URLtype with the minimum number of outdegree of 10 for TD queries. In addition to harnessing both the human intelligence and machine processing power to facilitate the process of system tuning with many parameters, dynamic tuning turned out to be a good tool for failure analysis. We examined severe search failure instances by WIDIT using the dynamic tuning interface and observed the following:

- Acronym Effect
  - WIDIT expanded acronyms and ranked documents about the acronym higher than the specific topic.
  - e.g. CDC documents ranked higher than Rabies documents for topic 89 ("CDC Rabies homepage")
- Duplicate Documents
  - WIDIT eliminated documents with the same URLs and ranked mirrored documents higher.
  - e.g. Relevant documents with the same URL (G00-74-1477693 and G00-05-3317821 for topic 215) were not indexed by WIDIT.
  - e.g. G32-10-1245341 is a mirror document of G00-48-1227124 (relevant for topic 188) but not counted as relevant by TREC official judgments.
- Link Noise Effect
  - Non-relevant documents with irrelevant links are ranked high by WIDIT
  - e.g. The relevant document for topic 197 ("Vietnam War") is Johnson Administration's "Foreign Relations" volumes with 4 links to Vietnam volumes, but WIDIT retrieved pages about Vietnam with many irrelevant (e.g. navigational) links at top ranks.

- Topic Drift
  - Topically related documents with high frequency of query terms were ranked high by WIDIT.
  - e.g. Documents about drunk driving victims, MADD, etc. were ranked higher than the impaired driving program of NHTSA page for topic 192 ("Drunk driving").

5 Results

Table 3 shows the retrieval results using the TREC-2004 mixed Web queries. The best fusion run (F3) combined the best individual result, which used anchor text index and Okapi weights, and the top two fusion runs, which merged the results of body, anchor, and header index results. The fusion improved the baseline performance by 31% for TD, 13% for NP, and 42% for HP queries. The static reranking run (SR_o) shows only a slight improvement over the fusion run, but the dynamic reranking run shows improvements of 39% for TD, 7% for NP, and 47% for NP over the fusion result. It is clear from the table that both static tuning for fusion and dynamic tuning for post-retrieval reranking are effective system performance optimization methods for leveraging diverse sources of evidence in Web IR.

Table 3. Mixed Query Task Results (MAP = mean average precision, MRR = mean reciprocal rank)

	MAP (TD)	MRR (NP)	MRR (HP)
B1	0.0744	0.5440	0.3006
F3	0.0974	0.6134	0.4256
SR_o	0.0986	0.6258	0.4341
DR_o	0.1349	0.6545	0.6265
TREC Median	0.1010	0.5888	0.5838

B1: Best individual run
F3: Best fusion run
SR_o: Static reranking run using the official query type
DR_o: Dynamic reranking run using the official query type

In order to assess the effect of query classification error, we generated random assignment of query types (DR_r) and worst possible assignment of query types (DR_b). Table 4.1 compares the classification error of WIDIT query classification algorithm with random and worst classification. Because TD task is biased towards homepages, HP-TD error is the least severe type of error. Since HP and NP tasks are both known-item search task, HP-NP error is less severe than NP-TD, which is the least similar. In table 4.2, which shows the results of dynamic reranking using each query classification, we can see that random or poor query classification will adversely affect the retrieval performance. Table 4.2 also shows the random query type results to be comparable with TREC median performance for TD and HP queries.

Table 4. Query classification error by error type

	Error Type		
	HP-TD	HP-NP	NP-TD
DR_g	26	49	17
DR_r	54	48	44
DR_b		75	150

Table 5. Query classification error by error type

	MAP (TD)	MRR (NP)	MRR (HP)
DR_o	0.1349	0.6545	0.6265
DR_g	0.1274	0.5418	0.6371
DR_r	0.1235	0.4450	0.5285
DR_b	0.0922	0.2995	0.3105
TREC Median	0.1010	0.5888	0.5838

DR_o: Dynamic reranking run using the official query type
DR_g: Dynamic reranking run using the guessed query type
DR_r: Dynamic reranking run using the random query type
DR_b: Dynamic reranking run using the bad query type

6   Concluding Remarks

We believe fusion is a promising area of investigation for Web IR. Our results show that exploiting the richness of Web search environment by combining multiple sources of evidence is an effective strategy. We extended the conventional fusion approach by introducing the "dynamic tuning" process with which to optimize the fusion formula that combines the contributions of diverse sources of evidence on the Web. By engaging in iterative dynamic tuning process, where we successively fine-tuned the fusion parameters based on the cognitive analysis of immediate system feedback, we were able to significantly increase the retrieval performance.

References

Amitay, E., Carmel, D., Darlow, A., Lempel, R., & Soffer, A. (2003). Topic Distillation with Knowledge Agents. *Proceedings of the11th Text Retrieval Conference (TREC 2002)*, 263-272.
Bartell, B. T., Cottrell, G. W., & Belew, R. K. (1994). Automatic combination of multiple ranked retrieval systems. *Proceedings of the ACM SIGIR Conference on Research and Development in Information Retrieval*.

Buckley, C., Salton, G., & Allan, J., & Singhal, A. (1995). Automatic query expansion using SMART: TREC 3. *Proceeding of the 3rd Text Rerieval Conference (TREC-3)*, 1-19.

Buckley, C., Singhal, A., & Mitra, M. (1997). Using query zoning and correlation within SMART: TREC 5. *Proceeding of the 5th Text REtrieval Conference (TREC-5)*, 105-118.

Craswell,N., & Hawking, D. (2003). Overview of the TREC-2002 Web track. *Proceedings of the 11th Text Retrieval Conference (TREC 2002)*, 86-95.

Craswell, N., Hawking, D., & Robertson, S. (2001). Effective site finding using link anchor information. *Proceedings of the 24th ACM SIGIR Conference on Research and Development in Information Retrieval*, 250-257.

Fox, E. A., & Shaw, J. A. (1995). Combination of multiple searches. *Proceeding of the3rd Text Rerieval Conference (TREC-3)*, 105-108.

Frakes, W. B., & Baeza-Yates, R. (Eds.). (1992). *Information retrieval: Data structures & algorithms*. Englewood Cliffs, NJ: Prentice Hall.

Gurrin, C., & Smeaton, A.F. (2001). Dublin City University experiments in connectivity analysis for TREC-9. *Proceedings of the 9th Text Retrieval Conference (TREC-9)*, 179-188.

Hawking, D., & Craswell, N. (2002). Overview of the TREC-2001 Web track. *Proceedings of the 10th Text Retrieval Conference (TREC 2001)*, 25-31

Hawking, D., & Craswell, N., Thistlewaite, P., & Harman, D. (1999). Results and challenges in web search evaluation. *Proceedings of the 8th WWW Conference*, 243-252.

Hawking, D, Voorhees, E, Craswell, N., & Bailey, P. (2000). Overview of the TREC-8 web track. *Proceedings of the 8th Text Retrieval Conference (TREC-8)*, 131-148.

Hölscher, C., & Strube, G. (2000). Web search behavior of internet experts and newbies. *Proceedings of the 9th International WWW Conference*.

Kraaij, W., Westerveld, T., & Hiemstra, D. (2002). The importance of prior probabilities for entry page search. *Proceedings of the 25th ACM SIGIR Conference on Research and Development in Information Retrieval*, 27-34.

Lee, J. H. (1997). Analyses of multiple evidence combination. *Proceedings of the ACM SIGIR Conference on Research and Development in Information Retrieval*, 267-276.

MacFarlane, A. (2003). Pliers at TREC 2002. *Proceedings of the 11th Text Retrieval Conference (TREC 2002)*, 152-155.

Robertson, S. E. & Walker, S. (1994). Some simple approximations to the 2-Poisson model for probabilistic weighted retrieval. *Proceedings of the 17th ACM SIGIR Conference on Research and Development in Information Retrieval*, 232-241

Savoy, J., & Picard, J. (1998). Report on the TREC-8 Experiment: Searching on the Web and in Distributed Collections. *Proceedings of the 8th Text Retrieval Conference (TREC-8)*, 229-240.

Savoy, J., & Rasolofo, Y. (2001). Report on the TREC-9 experiment: Link-based retrieval and distributed collections. *Proceedings of the 9th Text Retrieval Conference (TREC-9)*, 579-516.

Silverstein, C., Henzinger, M., Marais, H., & Moricz, M. (1998). Analysis of a very large AltaVista query log. *Technical Report 1998-014*, COMPAQ System Research Center.

Singhal, A., Buckley, C., & Mitra, M. (1996). Pivoted document length normalization. *Proceedings of the ACM SIGIR Conference on Research and Development in Information Retrieval*, 21-29.

Singhal, A., & Kaszkiel, M. (2001). A case study in Web search using TREC algorithms. *Proceedings of the 11th International WWW Conference*, 708-716.

Tomlinson, S. (2003). Robust, Web and Genomic retrieval with Hummingbird SearchServer at TREC 2003. *Proceedings of the 12th Text Retrieval Conference (TREC2003)*, 254-267.

Thompson. P. (1990). A combination of expert opinion approach to probabilistic information retrieval, part 1: The conceptual model. *Information Processing & Management*, 26(3), 371-382.

Voorhees, E., & Harman, D. (2000). Overview of the Eighth Text Retrieval Conference. *Proceedings of the 8th Text Retrieval Conference (TREC-8)*, 1-24.

Yang, K. (2002a). Combining Text-, Link-, and Classification-based Retrieval Methods to Enhance Information Discovery on the Web. (*Doctoral Dissertation*. University of North Carolina).

Yang, K. (2002b). Combining Text- and Link-based Retrieval Methods for Web IR. *Proceedings of the 10th Text Rerieval Conference (TREC2001)*, 609-618.

Zhang, M., Song, R., Lin, C., Ma, S., Jiang, Z., Jin, Y., Liu, Y., & Zhao, L. (2003). THU TREC 2002: Web Track Experiments. *Proceedings of the 11th Text Retrieval Conference (TREC 2002)*, 591-594.

Transactional Query Identification in Web Search

In-Ho Kang

Computing LAB,
Samsung Advanced Institute of Technology
inho97.kang@samsung.com

Abstract. User queries on the Web can be classified into three types according to user's intention: informational query, navigational query and transactional query. In this paper, a query type classification method and Service Link information for transactional queries are proposed. Web mediated activity is usually implemented by hyperlinks. Hyperlinks can be good indicators in classifying queries and retrieving good answer pages for transactional queries. A hyperlink related to an anchor text has an anticipated action with a linked object. Possible actions are reading, visiting and downloading a linked object. We can assign a possible action to each anchor text. These tagged anchor texts can be used as training data for query type classification. We can collect a large-scale and dynamic train query set automatically. To see the accuracy of the proposing classification method, various experiments were conducted. From experiments, I could achieve 91% of possible improvement for transactional queries with our classification method.

1 Introduction

The Web is rich with various sources of information. Therefore, the need behind a user's query is often not informational. Classic IR that focuses on content information cannot satisfy various needs [3]. Fusion IR studies have repeatedly shown that combining multiple types of evidence such as link information and url information can improve retrieval performance [10]. However, it is not easy to make a general purpose method that shows good performance for all kinds of need. There are studies that try classifying users' needs and solving each category with a different method [5]. [2] showed that users' queries can be classified into three categories according to the intention of a user.

- Informational Query
- Navigational Query
- Transactional Query

Users are interested in finding as much information as possible with informational queries. For example, *"What is a prime factor?"* or *'prime factor'* is an informational query. Its goal is finding the meaning of *'prime factor'*. Contrary to Informational queries, users are interested in navigating a certain site

G.G. Lee et al. (Eds.): AIRS 2005, LNCS 3689, pp. 221–232, 2005.
© Springer-Verlag Berlin Heidelberg 2005

with navigational queries. For example, *"Where is the site of Johns Hopkins Medical Institutions?"* or *'Johns Hopkins Medical Institutions'* is a navigational query. The goal of this query is finding the entry page of *'Johns Hopkins Medical Institutions'*. Users are interested in finding a document that offers the service described in a transactional query. For example, *"Where can I find Beatles' lyrics?"* or *'beatles lyrics'* is a transactional query. Users do not desire to learn about lyrics of Beatles' songs, but simply a desire to view the lyrics themselves [9].

Previous studies for query analysis employed handcrafted rules and used a natural language query to infer the expected type of an answer [6]. These rules were built by considering the first word of a query as well as large patterns of words identified in a query. For example, query *"Where was Babe Ruth born?"* might be characterized as requiring a reply of type *LOCATION*. While previous studies focused on informational queries, nowadays we should consider not only informational queries but also navigational queries and transactional queries for Web search. Previous methods need large-scale training data to extract rules and patterns for analyzing query [6]. However, there is a case in Web search when we cannot analyze a query with extracted rules and patterns. For example, two queries, *"Where is Papua New Guinea?"* and *"Where is Google?"* have the same sentence patterns. However, *'Google'* has special meaning on the Web. User wants to visit *'Google'* site on the Web. The intention of the latter query is not informational but navigational. To make matters worse, the properties of words are changed. For example, Korean query *'EOLJJANG'*[1] cannot be analyzed without the usage information on the Web. *'EOLJJANG'* was formerly an informational query. As an informational query, a possible answer document may contain a definition such as *"EOLJJANG means a good looking person."* Nowadays, *'EOLJJANG'* is a transactional query. What a user wants is finding and downloading pictures of *'EOLJJANG'*'s. We may use a dictionary to find the property of *'EOLJJANG'*, like previous query analysis methods. However it is not feasible to contain all new words and maintain their changes of properties.

[5] automatically classified queries into informational queries and navigational queries. They also proposed dynamic combination of content information, link information and URL information according to a query type. In this paper, I extend their classification and combining method to include transactional queries. Each hyperlink related to an anchor text has an anticipated action with a linked object. Possible actions include reading, visiting and downloading a linked object. These tagged anchor texts can be used training data for a query classification module. We can collect a large-scale and dynamic training data automatically.

The structure of this paper is as follows. In section 2, previous classification methods are briefly explained. In section 3, a query type classification method for classifying queries into informational, navigational and transactional is presented. In section 4, Service Link information is presented for transactional queries. Various experiments are conducted to show the performance of

---

[1] The Romanization of Korean word.

the proposing classification and combining method, in section 5. Conclusion is followed in section 6.

2   Related Work

2.1   Query Taxonomy

[2] and [9] randomly selected queries from a commercial search engine's query logs. They manually classified queries and showed the percentages of each query type. Although their hierarchies are not the same, top-level hierarchies are the same. From their results, over 40% of queries were non-informational. They all insisted the importance of processing transactional queries. [9] showed that navigational queries appear to be much less prevalent than generally believed. This implies that search engines should consider transactional queries to cover more queries.

Table 1. Percentage of Query Type

Query Type	Informational	Navigational	Transactional
Broder (user survey)	39%	24.5%	36%
Broder (log analysis)	48%	20%	30%
Rose (test set1)	60.9%	14.7%	24.3%
Rose (test set2)	61.3%	11.7%	27%
Rose (test set3)	61.5%	13.5%	25%

2.2   Automatic Query Type Classification

An entry page of a site usually does not have many words. It is not an explanatory document for some topic or concept, but a brief explanation of a site. We can assume that site entry pages have the different usage of words. If we find distinctive features for site entry pages, then we can classify a query type using keywords of a query. [5] proposed a method for classifying queries into informational queries and navigational queries. They divided a document collection into two sets whether the URL type of a document is 'root' type or not. The URL of a 'root' type document ends with a domain name like 'http://trec.nist.gov'. A document collection that includes only 'root' type documents represents navigational queries and other documents represent informational queries. If a given query's some measures in two collections show large difference, then we can assume the type of a query. Four classifiers were used to determine the type of a query. Four classifiers were as follows.

- Distribution of terms in a query
- Mutual Information of each term in a query
- Usage rate of query term as anchor texts
- POS information

[5] also showed the effects of each information and retrieval algorithm in Web search according to a type of a user's query. For navigational queries, combining link information like PageRank and URL information like the depth of directory improved the retrieval performance of a search engine [7]. However, for informational queries, it degraded the retrieval performance. In addition, retrieval algorithms such as TFIDF and OKAPI also show different effect in Web search. In this paper, I extend this classification in order to include transactional queries. In addition, I propose useful information for transactional queries.

3   Classifying Query Types

3.1   Preparation for Classification Model

Some expression can be used to tell the type of a query. For example, *'winamp download'* is a transactional query and *'the site of SONY'* is a navigational query. We can assume the types of two queries with cue expressions (e.g. *'download'* and *'the site of'*).

Query Q is defined as the sequence of words. Punctuation symbols are removed from the query. For example, *"What is a two electrode vacuum tube?"* is expressed as follows.

$$Q = (what, \ is, \ a, \ two, \ electorde, \ vacuum, \ tube) \tag{1}$$

[5] used only keywords of input queries by removing stop words. However, I use all words with the position in a query. I assume that the sequence and the position of word are important in classifying transactional queries. We can say [5] is a keyword-based classifier and my method is an expression-based classifier.

3.2   Extracting Cue Expressions

To extract cue expressions, anchor text and the title of a document are used. The definition or the explanation of a linked object can be extracted from a title and an anchor text. For example, a ticket reservation page has a title related to ticket reservation and a download button has an anchor text that explains a linked object. We can classify linked objects according to possible user's activities with them. Possible activities include reading, visiting and downloading. If a linked object is a binary file that is not readable, then its possible activity is downloading. However, in some cases, there is a linked object whose activity is ambiguous. For example, if a linked object is an html file, then assuming the action of the hyperlink is not easy. So, we clustered hyperlinks according to the extension of a linked object instead of using three categories: informational, navigational and transactional. If an expression occurs more frequently in a specific link type, then we can assume that it is a cue expression for a certain link type. For example, *'download file'* and *'reserve ticket'* can be key evidence that the type of a given query is a transactional query.

Table 2. Hyperlink Type

Type	Description	Example
Site	URL ends with a domain name, a directory name, and 'index.html'	http://cs.kaist.ac.kr/index.html
Subsite	URL ends with a directory name, with an arbitrary depth	http://trec.nist.gov/pubs/
Music	URL ends with a music file (mp3, wav, midi, etc.)	http://real.demandstremas.com/ragmen/mp3/corinth14.mp3
Picture	URL ends with a picture file (jpg, bmp, gif, etc.)	http://lylpan.com.ne.kr/pds/9.jpg
Text	URL ends with a text file (doc, ps, pdf, etc.)	http://www.loc.gov/legislation/dmca.pdf
Application	URL ends with an executable file (exe, zip, gz, etc.)	http://download.nullsoft.com/winamp/client/winamp3_0-full.exe
Service	URL ends with a cgi program (asp, pl, php, cgi, etc.)	http://www.google.com/search?q=IR
Html	URL ends with an html file	http://www.kaist.ac.kr/naat/interdept.html
File	other hyperlinked documents	http://ods.fnal.gov/ods/root-eval/out.log

To cluster titles and anchor texts, I classified hyperlinks according to a linked object (Table 2). In the Table 2 *Site* and *Subsite* are usually for navigational queries. For example, anchor texts *'Fan Club'* and *'Homepage'* can be extracted as *Site* and *Subsite* types.

Both titles and anchor texts are used to extract cue expressions for each tagged hyperlink. The first two words and the last two words are used to extract cue expressions. There are 5 templates for extracting candidates of cue expression.

Table 3. Template for Extracting Cue Expression

Type	Extracted Expression
ALL	Q
F_1	w_1
F_2	$w_1\ w_2$
L_1	w_l
L_2	$w_{l-1}\ w_l$

In the Table 3, l implies the number of words in query Q. For example, anchor text *'winamp full version download'* has 5 cue expression candidates (Table 4).

The WT10g collection is used to collect the frequency of each candidate expression [1]. The frequency of each candidate is normalized with the total number of expression in each link type.

Table 4. Example Cue Expression

Type	Expression
ALL	*winamp full version download*
F_1	*winamp*
F_2	*winamp full*
F_3	*download*
F_4	*version downoad*

$$freq(link\ type) = \sum_i freq(exp_i \cap link\ type) \tag{2}$$

$$score(exp_i \cap link\ type) = \frac{freq(exp_i \cap link\ type)}{freq(link\ type)} \tag{3}$$

To use cue expressions, we use all input queries without removing stop words. With a given query, we can calculate a link score for each link type by adding score of each candidate expression. For example, the link score of a site type is calculated as follows.

$$LinkScore_{site} = score(ALL \cap site) + score(F_1 \cap site) + \tag{4}$$
$$score(F_2 \cap site) + score(L_1 \cap site) + score(L_2 \cap site)$$

To use *LinkScore*, we need flags that indicate the type of a linked object and whether an index term is from an anchor text or not.

3.3   Combining Classifiers

To detect a transactional query, I extend the method of [5]. I used TiMBL [4], a Memory-Based Learning software package, to combine multiple classifiers. A Memroy-Based Learning is a classification-based supervised learning approach. It constructs a classifier for a task by storing a set of examples. Each example associates a feature vector (the problem description) with one of a finite number of classes (the solution). Given a new feature vector, the classifier extrapolates its class from those of the most similar feature vectors in memory. The metric defining similarity can be automatically adapted to the task at hand.

A vector for classification consists of following types of information.

- $IN(Q)$: whether a given query is an informational query or a navigational query?
- $isFileName?$: whether a given query is a file name or not? (e.g. '*stand by me.mp3*')
- w_1: the first word of a query
- w_l: the last word of a query

– $LinkScoreVec$: $LinkScore_{site}$, $LinkScore_{subsite}$, $LinkScore_{music}$,
$LinkScore_{picture}$, $LinkScore_{text}$, $LinkScore_{application}$,
$LinkScore_{service}$, $LinkScore_{html}$, $LinkScore_{file}$

where '$IN(Q)$' is the result of the Kang's method. The result of '$IN(Q)$' is Informational or Navigational. w_1 and w_l provide a special action verb such as '*download*' and an interrogative such as '*where*'. A query can be the name of the file that a user wants to achieve. '*isFileName?*' indicates whether a given query is a file name or not. Simple regular expression is used to decide the value of *isFileName*. $LinkScoreVec$ is a vector that consists of all kinds of link score.

For example, with query "*Do beavers live in salt water?*", '*beavers live salt water*' are extracted as keywords by excluding stop words. We assigned a Part-of-Speech Tag to each word. With tagged keywords, '$IN(Q)$' is calculated. Then calculate LinkScores for each link type. The result vector looks like as follows.

Table 5. Example Vectors with *"Do beavers live in salt water?"*

Type	Value
$IN(Q)$	*Informational*
w_1	*do*
w_l	*water*
$isFileName$	*No*
$LinkScore_{site}$	0.00001888148
$LinkScore_{subsite}$	0.00007382660
$LinkScore_{music}$	0.00000028322
$LinkScore_{picture}$	0.00000066085
$LinkScore_{text}$	0.00000000000
$LinkScore_{application}$	0.00000018881
$LinkScore_{service}$	0.00000037763
$LinkScore_{html}$	0.00006051515
$LinkScore_{file}$	0.00003068241

Since $LinkScore_{subsite}$ and $LinkScore_{html}$ are high among $LinkScores$, we can assume that this query does not have special cue expressions for transactional queries.

4   Service Link Information for Transactional Queries

In this section, useful information for a transactional query is proposed. A good result document for a transactional query should provide good service. To provide service, the further action of a user is needed. A user wants to buy some products, do some game, download a music file and a picture file, and so on. For example, query '*winamp download*' has the intention that a user wants to download a '*winamp*' program file by clicking or saving a linked file. Retrieved

Web documents should have a download button or a linked file. For a transactional query, designated service is implemented by some mechanisms. These mechanisms contain a CGI program, a linked file (except an html file), and so on. These mechanisms usually implemented by a hyperlink. If a Web document has useful hyperlinks, then we can assume it is a kind of a document that provides some types of transaction. I propose a formula that accounts for the existence of hyperlinks. We call this '*Service Link information*'.

$$Service\ Link\ Information(d) = \frac{\#service\ links}{\#service\ links + \gamma_1 + \gamma_2 \times \frac{link\ count(d)}{avg.\ link\ count}} \quad (5)$$

where, '*service links*' means the union of music, picture, text, application, service, and file links. *#service links* is normalized with the number of links. *link count* means the number of all hyperlinks in a document and *avg. link count* means the average number of all hyperlinks. In this paper, I set the value of γ_1 to 0.5 and γ_2 to 1.5.

$$link\ count(d) = \#site\ links + \#subsite\ links + \#music\ links + \quad (6)$$
$$\#picture\ links + \#text\ links + \#application\ links +$$
$$\#service\ links + \#html\ links + \#file\ links$$

Service Link information is normalized by the number of *link count(d)*. *Service Link information* is added to content information as follows to reorder result documents [5].

$$rel_{new}(d) = \alpha \times rel_{old}(d) + \beta \times Service\ Link\ Information(d) \quad (7)$$

5   Experiments

In this section, we conduct various experiments to see the usefulness of our classification method. In addition, experiments to see the usefulness of Service Link information for transactional queries are also conducted.

5.1   Test Set

Six query sets are used for experiments. For informational queries, queries of the TREC-2000 topic relevance task (topics 451-500) and queries of the TREC-2001 topic relevance task (topics 501-550) are used. We call them $QUERY_{I-TRAIN}$ and $QUERY_{I-TEST}$. For navigational queries, queries for randomly selected 100 homepages[2] and 145 queries of the TREC-2001 homepage finding task are used. We call them $QUERY_{N-TRAIN}$ and $QUERY_{N-TEST}$, respectively. For transactional queries, 100 service queries extracted from a Lycos log file are

---

[2] Available at http://www.ted.cmis.csiro.au/TRECWeb/Qrels/

Table 6. Example of Transactional Queries

airline tickets
acdsee.zip
free native American clip art
superbowl tickets
Trident blade 3d driver
download video card driver

used for training and testing. I divided 100 queries into $QUERY_{T-TRAIN}$ and $QUERY_{T-TEST}$. Table 6 shows selected examples of transactional queries. The WT10g collection is used for making a classification model. Training queries are used to calculate the value of constants such as α and β in the Eq. 7.

5.2 Distinguishing Query Types

To measure the performance of our classification model, precision and recall are calculated with the following equations.

$$Precision = \frac{\#correct\ classification}{\#total\ trials} \tag{8}$$

$$Recall = \frac{\#correct\ classification}{\#queries} \tag{9}$$

For the value of '$IN(Q)$', I used navigational queries as a default result [5]. Every query has at least one query type. Therefore the precision and the recall of classification are the same. Table 7 shows the results of classifying query types.

Table 7. Performance of Query Type Classification

	$QUERY_{I-TEST}$		$QUERY_{N-TEST}$		$QUERY_{T-TEST}$		$QUERY\text{-}TEST$	
	Precision	Recall	Precision	Recall	Precision	Recall	Precision	Recall
$IN(Q)$	58.0%	58.0%	97.9%	97.9%	0%	0%	69.8%	69.8%
w_1	34.0%	34.0%	97.9%	97.9%	14.0%	14.0%	67.8%	67.8%
w_l	2.0%	2.0%	99.3%	99.3%	34.0%	34.0%	66.1%	66.1%
$isFileName?$	0%	0%	100%	100%	2.0%	2.0%	59.6%	59.6%
$LinkScore$	62.0%	62.0%	73.8%	73.8%	74.0%	74.0%	71.4%	71.4%
ALL	74.0%	74.0%	79.3%	79.3%	78.0%	78.0%	78.0%	78.0%

ALL in the table means that all classifiers are combined for classification. The last column $QUERY\text{-}TEST$ means queries from all test sets were used. By combining each classifier, we could increase precision and recall. From the table, '$IN(Q)$' is good for distinguishing informational queries and navigational queries. '$LinkScore$' shows good performance in detecting transactional queries.

5.3   Service Link Information for Transactional Queries

For the evaluation, binary judgment was used to measure the retrieval performance of transactional queries. The version of a program and the media type
should be matched with a description in a query. The result document that needs
further navigation to listen or download an object is not correct. Since we do
not know all relevant results, precision at 1, 5, and 10 documents are used.

Table 8 shows a retrieval performance of Google search engine[3] with transactional queries. Top 100 documents were retrieved with Google, and then I
combined Service Link information to get new top 10 documents. Since we did
not know the similarity score of each result document, estimated score according
to a rank was used. 0.9 was calculated from a training phase with training data.

$$rel(d) = \frac{1}{e^{r(d)}} + 0.9 \times Service\ Link\ Info(d) \tag{10}$$

where, $r(d)$ is the rank of document d. I used an estimated score instead of a
real similarity score. Thus, the improvement of retrieval performance was low.
However, we can conclude that *Service Link Information* is good for transactional
queries.

Table 8. Retrieval Performance of Google over Transactional Queries

Model	$QUERY_{T-TRAIN}$			$QUERY_{T-TEST}$		
	P1	P5	P10	P1	P5	P10
Google	0.28	0.25	0.34	0.38	0.31	0.35
Google+Serv.	0.38	0.33	0.39	0.48	0.34	0.38

5.4   Retrieval Performance with Classification

Three ranking algorithms were used according to a query type. OKAPI algorithm
was used for informational queries. For navigational queries, PageRank and URL
information were combined with OKAPI score. For transactional queries, Service Link Information was combined with OKAPI score [5]. Table 9 shows the
retrieval performance with the best and worst possible performance that we
could achieve. Average Precision was used for measuring the retrieval performance of informational queries, MRR for navigational queries and precision at
10 documents for transactional queries. '*BEST*' is obtained when we have all
correct answers and '*WORST*' is obtained when we have all wrong answers in
classifying query types.

With our proposed query type classifier, 57% of possible improvement in informational queries, 90% in navigational queries and 91% in transactional queries
could be achieved.

---

[3] http://www.google.com

Table 9. Retrieval Performance with Classification

	$QUERY_{I-TEST}$	$QUERY_{N-TEST}$	$QUERY_{T-TEST}$
BEST	0.182	0.691	0.14
WORST	0.154	0.278	0.04
OURS	0.170	0.648	0.13

I also tested dynamic weighting of each type of information. Based on the probability of a query type, the proper weight of each type of information is decided, and then combined. The following equation was used to weight each type of information.

$$rel(d) = OKAPIscore + \lambda_1 \times URLInfo. + \lambda_2 \times PageRank + \quad (11)$$
$$\lambda_3 \times ServiceInfo.$$

where, the values of λ_1, λ_2, and λ_3 are determined based on the probability of query type. Table 10 shows the retrieval performance of dynamic weighting.

Table 10. Retrieval Performance with Dynamic Weighting

	$QUERY_{I-TEST}$	$QUERY_{N-TEST}$	$QUERY_{T-TEST}$
BEST	0.182	0.691	0.14
WORST	0.154	0.278	0.04
OURS	0.171	0.664	0.16

Dynamic weighting method showed a slightly better performance than the method that uses special engines for transactional queries. When a query type is ambiguous, proper weighting of both types showed a better performance.

6   Conclusion

We have various forms of resources in the Web and consequently purposes of users' queries are diverse. Classic IR that focuses on content information cannot satisfy the various needs of a user. Search engines need different strategies to meet the purpose of a query. In this paper, we presented a method for classifying queries into informational, navigational and transactional queries. To classify a query type, link type that exploits anchor texts is used. I tagged each anchor text according to a possible action with a linked object. 9 link types were used to tag an anchor text. These tagged anchor texts can be used as large-scale training data. Cue expressions of each type are automatically extracted from tagged anchor texts. After we classified the type of a query, different types of information for a search engine are used. To retrieve better results for a transactional query, we add Service Link information. In addition, I proposed dynamic weighting method that combines each type of information according to the probability of each query category. Dynamic weighting showed a slightly better performance than the method that uses special engines for transactional queries. When a query type is ambiguous, proper weighting of both types showed a better performance.

For a future work, the fine-grained categories have to be considered. In this paper, we use 9 link types for three categories: informational, navigational and transactional. However, we can pinpoint target categories with 9 clusters. Categories for explaining the need of user should be extended. In addition, research on indexing model for our classification method is needed.

References

1. Bailey, P., Craswell, N., Hawking, D. : Engineering a Multi-Purpose test Collection for Web Retrieval Experiments. Information Processing and Management 39(6), pages 853-871, (2003)
2. Broder, A. : A Taxonomy of Web Search. SIGIR Forum, pages 3-10, 36(2), (2002).
3. Croft, W. B. : Combining Approaches to Information Retrieval. In: W. B. Croft (Ed.) Advances in Information Retrieval: Recent Research from the center for intelligent information retrieval, pages 1-36, Kluwer Academic Publishers, (2000)
4. Daelemans, W., Zavrel, J., Sloot, K. van der, Bosch, A. van den. : TiMBL: Tilburg Memory Based Learner, version 3.0, reference guide (Tech. Rep.). ILK Technical Report 00-01, Available from http://ilk.kub.nl/~ilk/papers/ ilk0001.ps.gz, (2000)
5. Kang, I.-H., Kim, G.: Query Type Classification for Web Document Retrieval. In Proceedings of the 26th Annual International ACM SIGIR conference on Research and Development in Information Retrieval. pages 64-71, Toronto, Canada, (2003)
6. Moldovan, D., Harabagiu, S., Pasca, M., Mihalcea, R., Girju, R., Goodrum, R., Rus, V.: The Structure and Performance of an open-domain Question Answering System. In: Proceedings of the Conference of the Association for Computational Linguistics. pages 563-570, Hong Kong, (2000)
7. Page, L., Brin, S., Motwani, R., Winograd, T.: The PageRank citation ranking: Brining order to the Web. (Tech. Rep.), Stanford Digital Library Technologies Project, (1998)
8. Ratnaparkhi, A.:   A Maximum Entropy Part-of-Speech Tagger.   In: E. Brill & K. Church (Eds.), Proceedings of the Conference on Empirical Methods in Natural Language Processing, pages 133-142, Somerset, New Jersey: Association for Computational Linguistics, Available from http://www.cis.upenn.edu/~adwait/statnlp.html, (1996)
9. Rose, Daniel E. & Levinson, Danny: Understanding User Goals in Web Search. In: Proceedings of the 13th international conference on World Wide Web, pages 13-19, New York, New York, (2004)
10. Westerveld, T., Kraaij, W., and Hiemstra, D. :   Retrieving Web Pages using Content, Links, Urls and Anchors, In Proceedings of Text REtrieval Conference (TREC-10), pages 663-672, (2001)

Improving FAQ Retrieval Using Query Log Clustering in Latent Semantic Space

Harksoo Kim[1], Hyunjung Lee[2], and Jungyun Seo[3]

[1] CIIR in UMass, Amherst
LGRC A341, Computer Science Department, 140 Governors Driver, University of Massachusetts, Amherst, MA, 01003, USA
hskim@cs.umass.edu
[2] Department of Computer Science,
Sogang University, Sinsu-dong 1, Seoul, 121-742, Korea
juvenile@nlpzodiac.sogang.ac.kr
[3] Department of Computer Science and Program of Integrated Biotechnology,
Sogang University, Sinsu-dong 1, Seoul, 121-742, Korea
seojy@ccs.sogang.ac.kr

Abstract. Lexical disagreement problems often occur in FAQ retrieval because FAQs unlike general documents consist of just one or two sentences. To resolve lexical disagreement problems, we propose a high-performance FAQ retrieval system using query log clustering. During indexing time, using latent semantic analysis techniques, the proposed system classifies and groups the logs of users' queries into predefined FAQ categories. During retrieval time, the proposed system uses the query log clusters as a form of FAQ smoothing. In our experiment, we found that the proposed system could resolve some lexical disagreement problems between queries and FAQs.

1 Introduction

Databased-FAQs (frequently asked questions) are important knowledge sources to many B2C (business-to-customer) companies because the FAQs help customers efficiently access various products of the companies. With the emergence of e-commerce systems [11], successful information access on e-commerce websites that accommodates both customer needs and business requirements becomes essential. As a useful tool for information access, most commercial sites provide customers with a keyword search. However, sometimes the keyword search does not perform well in sentence retrieval domains like FAQ retrieval, as shown in Fig. 1.

In Fig. 1, the query "How can I remove my login ID" and the FAQ "A method to secede from the membership" have a very similar meaning, but there is no overlap between the words in the two sentences. This fact often makes keyword search systems misdirect users to irrelevant FAQs.

The representative FAQ retrieval systems are FAQ Finder [2], Auto-FAQ [20], and Sneiders' system [16]. FAQ Finder was designed to improve navigation through aleady existing external FAQ collections. To match users' queries to the FAQ collec-

G.G. Lee et al. (Eds.): AIRS 2005, LNCS 3689, pp. 233–245, 2005.
© Springer-Verlag Berlin Heidelberg 2005

tions, FAQ Finder uses a syntactic parser to identify verb and noun phrases. Then, FAQ Finder performs concept matching using semantic knowledge like WordNet [11]. Auto-FAQ matches users' queries to predefined FAQs using a keyword comparison method based on shallow NLP (natural language processing) techniques. Sneiders' system classifies keywords into three types: required keywords, optional keywords and irrelevant keywords. Sneiders' system retrieves and ranks relevant FAQs according to the three types. Although the representative systems perform well, we think that it is not easy to expand them into other domains because they require high-level knowledge bases or handcrafted rules.

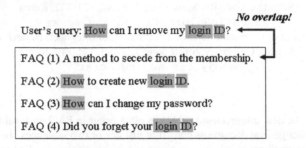

Fig. 1. Motivational example

There have been numerous studies on how clustering can be employed to improve retrieval results [8]. The cluster-based retrieval can be divided into two types: static clustering methods [4], [13] and query specific clustering methods [3], [17]. The static clustering methods group entire collections in advance, independent of the user's query, and clusters are retrieved based on how well their centroids match the user's query. The query specific clustering methods group the set of documents retrieved by an IR system for a query. The main goal of the query specific clustering methods is to improve the rankings of relevant documents on searching time. Some studies have shown that cluster-based retrieval did not outperform document-based retrieval, except with the small size of collection [1], [17], [18], [21].

In this paper, we propose a cluster-based FAQ retrieval system called FRACT (Faq Retrieval And Clustering Technique). FRACT consists of two sub-systems: FRACT/LSC and FRACT/IR. FRACT/LSC periodically collects and refines users' query logs that are recorded in files or databases. Then, FRACT/LSC considers each FAQ as an independent category containing a sentence. Unlike ordinary text classifiers, FRACT/LSC groups the query logs by predefined FAQ categories only based on sentence-by-sentence similarities between FAQs and query logs without any training processes. Based on this reason, we can consider FRACT/LSC as a kind of unsupervised sentence classifier. When a user inputs his/her query, FRACT/IR calculates the similarities between the query and the FAQs smoothed by the query log clusters. According to the similarities, FRACT/IR ranks and returns a list of relevant FAQs. In spite of the skepticism with cluster-based retrieval, FRACT use clusters as a form of document smoothing [8] in order to resolve lexical disagreement problems. We expect that FRACT will outperform traditional document-based retrieval systems because the size of FAQ collections is probably much smaller than the size of ordinary document collections, as mentioned in [18], [21]. In addition, we expect that FRACT will be less sensitive to application domains than the previous FAQ retrieval systems because FRACT uses only statistical methods without additional knowledge sources. The current version of FRACT operates in Korean, but we believe that language conversion will not be a difficult task because FRACT uses only language-independent statistical knowledge.

This paper is organized as follows. In Section 2, we propose a method of clustering query logs and a cluster-based FAQ retrieval method. In Section 3, we explain experimental results. Finally, we conclude in Section 4.

2 High-Performance FAQ Retrieval System

2.1 Term-Document Matrix Construction

In IR (information retrieval), sentences are generally represented as a set of unigrams, but the unigrams do not provide contextual information between co-occurring words. A possible solution to this problem is to supplement the flaws of unigrams with dependency bigrams (i.e. modifier-modified words) in order to provide further control over phrase formation. Unfortunately, automatic syntactic parser of a free-style text is still not very efficient, and the number of dependency bigrams extracted by parsing is not enough to measure similarity between sentences if we do not have a large corpus. Therefore, FRACT uses simple co-occurrence information extracted with a sliding window. A sliding window technique [9] consists of sliding a window over the text and storing pairs of words involving the head of the window if it is a content word and any of the other content words of the window. The window slides word by word from the first word of the sentence to the last, the size of the window decreasing at the end of the sentence so as not to cross boundaries between sentences. The window size being smaller than a constant, the number of extracted bigrams is linear to the number of unigrams in the sentence. In our experiment, we set the window size to three. Fig. 2 illustrates the process of term extraction with examples.

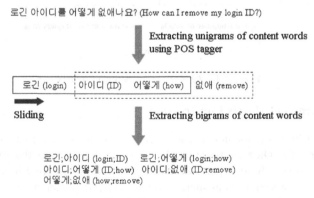

Fig. 2. Term extraction

After extracting indexing terms, FRACT assigns weight scores to each term according to the weighting scheme of the 2-poisson model [14], as shown in Equation (1).

$$w_{ij} = \frac{tf_j}{k_1 \cdot \left((1-b)+b \cdot \dfrac{dl_i}{avdl}\right)+tf_j} \cdot \log\left(\frac{n-df_j+0.5}{df_j+0.5}\right)$$ (1)

In Equation (1), w_{ij} is the weight score of the jth term in the ith document, and tf_j is the frequency of the jth term in the document. In this paper, we consider FAQs or query logs as short documents. dl_i is the length of the ith document, and $avdl$ is the average length of documents. N is the total number of documents, and df_j is the number of documents including the jth term. k_1 and b are constant values for performance tuning. In the experiments, we set k_1 and b to 1.2 and 0.75 respectively according to Okapi BM-25 [14]. When sets of weighted terms have been constructed, it is very straightforward to construct an $m \times n$ term-document matrix $X_{m \times n}$, where m is the number of terms, n is the number of documents, and an element w_{ij} indicates the degree of association between the ith term and the jth document. Fig. 3 shows the $m \times n$ term-document matrix that consists of q FAQ vectors and n-q query log vectors in m-dimensional space.

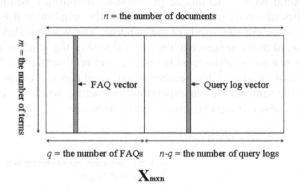

Fig. 3. The $m \times n$ term-document matrix

2.2 Latent Centroid Matrix Construction

The similarities between documents can be calculated by popular methods such as the cosine measure, the Dice coefficients, Jaccard coefficients and the overlap coefficients [12]. However, these popular measures may not be effective in calculating the similarities between sentences as there is often very little overlap between the words in the sentences. LSA (latent semantic analysis) is a method of extracting and representing the contextual-usage meaning of words by statistical computations [5]. Some researchers have shown that LSA can bridge some lexical gaps between two words by mapping all terms in the texts to a representation in so-called latent semantic space.

Based on this fact, we apply the LSA techniques to FRACT/LSC in order to increase the performance of unsupervised sentence classification.

To classify query logs into FAQ categories, FRACT/LSC first applies SVD (singular vector decomposition) to the term-document matrix $X_{m \times n}$, as shown in Equation (2).

$$X_{m \times n} = U_{m \times m} \cdot S_{m \times n} \cdot V_{n \times n}^T,$$ (2)

where $U_{m \times m}$ is an $m \times m$ orthonormal matrix, and $V_{n \times n}$ is an $n \times n$ orthonormal matrix. $S_{m \times n}$ is an $m \times n$ positive matrix whose nonzero values are $s_{11}, \cdots s_{rr}$, where r is the rank of X, and they are arranged in descending order $s_{11} \geq s_{22} \geq \cdots \geq s_{rr} > 0$. Fig. 4 shows the results of SVD.

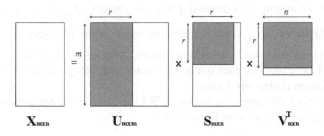

$$X_{m \times n} \qquad U_{m \times m} \qquad S_{m \times n} \qquad V_{n \times n}^T$$

Fig. 4. Singular value decomposition

In Fig. 4, the shaded portions of the matrices are what FRACT/LSC uses as the basis for its term and document vector representations. As shown in Fig. 4, FRACT/LSC selects the top r elements among diagonal elements in $S_{m \times n}$ to reduce the representation dimension. Therefore, the actual representations of the term and document vectors are $U_{m \times r}$ and $V_{n \times r}$ scaled by elements in $S_{r \times r}$. After reducing the representation dimension, FRACT/LSC transposes the term-document matrix $\hat{X}_{m \times n}$ that is reconstructed on r-dimensions, as shown in Equation (3).

$$\hat{X}_{m \times n}^T = V_{n \times r} \cdot S_{r \times r} \cdot U_{m \times r}^T$$ (3)

Then, FRACT/LSC multiplies both sides on the right by $U_{m \times r}$, as shown in Equation (4).

$$\hat{X}_{m \times n}^T \cdot U_{m \times r} = V_{n \times r} \cdot S_{r \times r}$$ (4)

Finally, FRACT/LSC obtains a pseudo-document matrix, $V_{n \times r} \cdot S_{r \times r}$, in r-dimensional space called latent semantic space.

After constructing the pseudo-document matrix, FRACT/LSC compares FAQ vectors to query log vectors in the latent semantic space by using cosine similarity measure, as shown in Equation (5) [15]. In this step, we expect FRACT/LSC to calculate degrees of semantic associations that cannot be found in the original term-document space.

$$\cos(f_i, ql_j) = \frac{\sum_{k=1}^{r} f_{ik} \cdot ql_{jk}}{\sqrt{\sum_{k=1}^{r} (f_{ik})^2 \cdot \sum_{k=1}^{r} (ql_{jk})^2}} \tag{5}$$

In Equation (5), when n documents consist of q FAQs and n-q query logs, f_i is the ith one among the q FAQ vectors in the pseudo-document matrix $V_{n \times r} \cdot S_{r \times r}$, and ql_j is the jth one among the other n-q query log vectors. f_{ik} is the kth element value of the ith FAQ vector, ql_{jk} is the kth element value of the jth query log vector, and r is the dimension of the pseudo-document matrix. After calculating the cosine similarities, FRACT/LSC classifies each query log vector into categories of the FAQ vectors with the maximum cosine similarities.

After classifying the query log vectors, FRACT/LSC generates centroid vectors of each FAQ category, as shown in Equation (6).

$$c_i = \frac{f_i + \sum_{ql_j \in cat_i} ql_j}{qln_i + 1}, \quad if \ \cos(f_i, ql_j) > \theta \tag{6}$$

In Equation (6), cat_i is the category of the ith FAQ vector f_i, and c_i is the centroid vector of the category cat_i. qln_i is the number of query logs belonging to cat_i, and θ is a threshold value. If the cosine similarity between a FAQ vector and a query log vector is smaller than the predefined threshold value θ, FRACT/LSC considers the query log vector an uninformative vector and discards the query log vector. Otherwise, FRACT/LSC sums up all query log vectors belonging to cat_i and generates an average vector between the ith FAQ vector and the summed query log vector. As shown in Equation (6), the average vector c_i is not a real centroid vector. We expect that this summation method will prevent the cluster centroids from leaning excessively toward query logs that may be misclassified. Then, FRACT/LSC constructs the centroid matrix $C_{q \times r}$, where q is the number of FAQ categories and r is the reduced dimension, by gathering the centroid vectors. Next, FRACT/LSC restores the representation dimension to original m dimension by multiplying $C_{q \times r}$ and $U_{m \times r}^T$ together, as shown in Equation (7).

$$\hat{C}_{q \times m} = C_{q \times r} \cdot U_{m \times r}^T \tag{7}$$

Finally, FRACT/LSC sets the element values smaller than zero to zero in $\hat{C}_{q \times m}$ because term weights should be generally bigger than zero. We call each element value in $\hat{C}_{q \times m}$ latent term weights because the element values represent potential weight scores that are not directly calculated according to the actual occurrence of terms. We also call the adjusted matrix $\hat{C}_{q \times m}$ a latent centroid matrix and call each column vectors in $\hat{C}_{q \times m}$ latent centroid vectors.

2.3 Cluster-Based Retrieval Using the Vector Space Model

The vector space model has been widely used in the traditional IR field. Many search engines also use similarity measures based on this model to rank documents. The model creates a space in which both documents and queries are represented by vectors. Then, the model computes the closeness between a document and a query by using a vector similarity function.

In the vector space model, given a query and FAQs, we can calculate the cosine similarity between the the ith FAQ vector f_i and the query vector q in m-dimensional space, as shown in Equation (8).

$$\cos(f_i, q) = \frac{\sum_{k=1}^{m} f_{ik} \cdot q_k}{\sqrt{\sum_{k=1}^{m} (f_{ik})^2 \cdot \sum_{k=1}^{m} (q_k)^2}} \qquad (8)$$

In Equation (8), f_{ik} is the kth term weight of the ith FAQ vector f_i, and q_k is the kth term weight of the query q. To smooth individual FAQs using the latent term weights, we modify Equation (8), as shown in Equation (9).

$$\cos(f_i, q) = \frac{\sum_{k=1}^{m} f_{ik} \cdot q_k}{\sqrt{\sum_{k=1}^{m} (cf_{ik})^2 \cdot \sum_{k=1}^{m} (q_k)^2}} \qquad (9)$$

In Equation (9), cf_{ik} is the estimated term weight of the kth term in the ith FAQ vector. We calculate cf_{ik} according to Equation (10).

$$cf_{ik} = \lambda \cdot f_{ik} + (1 - \lambda) \cdot c_{ik} \qquad (10)$$

In Equation (10), c_{ik} is the kth term weight in the latent centroid vector associated with the ith FAQ vector f_i. λ is a constant value for smoothing.

FRACT/IR calculates the similarities between a query and FAQs using Equation (10), and then ranks relevant FAQs according to the similarities. We believe that

FRACT/IR can reduce lexical disagreement problems, as FRACT/IR utilizes term weights smoothed by query log clusters including various terms. For example, if FRACT/IR has the latent centroid vector *[goods:0.5, merchandise:0.1, method:0.1, return:0.5, send:0.1]* associated with the FAQ "How to return goods", FRACT/IR may highly rank the FAQ "How to return goods" when a user inputs the query "A method to send back merchandise" because there are three common elements between the query vector and the latent centroid vector although there is no common element between the query vector and the FAQ vector.

3   Empirical Evaluation

3.1   Data Sets and Experimental Settings

We collected 406 Korean FAQs from three domains; LGeShop (www.lgeshop.com, 91 FAQs), Hyundai Securities (www.youfirst.co.kr, 81 FAQs) and KTF (www.ktf.com, 234 FAQs). LGeShop is an internet shopping mall, Hyundai Securities is a security corporation, and KTF is a mobile communication company. For two months, we also collected a large amount of query logs that were created by previous search engines. After eliminating additional information except users' queries, we automatically selected 5,845 unique query logs (1,549 query logs from LGeShop, 744 query logs from Hyundai Securities, and 3,552 query logs from KTF) that consisted of two or more content words. Then, we manually classified query logs into the 406 FAQ categories and annotated each query log with the identification numbers of the FAQ categories. Finally, we constructed a test collection called KFAQTEC (Korean test collection for evaluation of FAQ retrieval systems). KFAQTEC consists of 6,251 sentences (406 FAQs and 5,845 query logs). The number of content words per query is 5.337, and the number of FAQ categories per content word is 0.342. Table 1 shows a sample of KFAQTEC.

Table 1. A sample of KFAQTEC

Domain	Type	ID	Sentence
KTF	FAQ	8	멤버쉽 탈퇴 방법 (A method to secede from the membership)
KTF	LOG	8	로긴 아이디 삭제 (The removal of login ID)
KTF	LOG	8	멤버쉽 탈퇴는 어떻게 (How to secede from the membership)
LGeShop	FAQ	4	사이버 머니 사용법 (How to use e-money)
LGeShop	LOG	4	사이버 머니로 물건 살 수 있나? (Can I buy goods using e-money?)

The manual annotation was done by graduate students majoring in language analysis and was post-processed for consistency. In KFAQTEC, we found 150 query logs that did not overlap with original FAQs at all. This fact reveals that these lexical disagreement problems can often occur in short document retrieval.

To experiment with FRACT, we divided KFAQTEC into a seed data (FAQs), 10 training data (nine tenth of query logs per training data), and 10 testing data (a tenth of query logs per testing data). Then, we performed 10-fold cross validation in each domain. In detail, the seed data is used as both retrieval target sentences for

FRACT/IR and category data for FRACT/LSC. The training data is used as both categorization-target sentences for FRACT/LSC and parameter-tuning data for FRACT/IR. As the result of parameter tuning only using the training data, we set the reduced dimension r in Equation (3) to 200, the threshold value θ in Equation (6) to 0.3, and the smoothing rate λ in Equation (10) to 0.7 since FRACT/IR showed the highest performance in that point. The test data is a set of sentences completely disjoint from both the seed data and the training data. In other words, the test data is a set of open sentences that was not used to develop FRACT.

3.2 Evaluation Methods

To evaluate the performances of FRACT/LSC, we computed the precisions, the recall rates, and F-measures of query log classification. To evaluate the performances of FRACT/IR, we computed the MRRs (Mean Reciprocal Rank) and the miss rates. The MRR represents the average value of the reciprocal ranks of the first relevant FAQs given by each query, as shown in Equation (11) [19].

$$MRR = \frac{\sum_{i=1}^{qn} \dfrac{1}{rank_i}}{qn} \tag{11}$$

In Equation (11), $rank_i$ is the rank of the first relevant FAQ given by the ith query, and qn is the number of queries. The miss rate means the ratio of the cases that FRACT/IR fails to return relevant FAQs, as shown in Equation (12).

$$MissRate = \frac{the\ number\ of\ failure\ queries}{the\ number\ of\ queries} \tag{12}$$

3.3 Performance Evaluation

To evaluate FRACT/LSC, we calculated the average precisions and average recall rates of two query log classifiers, as shown in Table 2.

Table 2. The comparison of precisions and recall rates

Domain	FRACT/LSC			FRACT/COS		
	Precision	Recall	F-measure	Precision	Recall	F-measure
LGeShop	0.52903	0.35734	0.426557	0.72745	0.11460	0.198007
Hyundai	0.77658	0.53693	0.634893	0.86476	0.31592	0.462776
KTF	0.43515	0.38530	0.408711	0.73493	0.19485	0.308032
Total	0.48209	0.37132	0.419516	0.73119	0.15473	0.255411
Domain	FRACT/LSC+IR			FRACT/COS+IR		
	MRR	Miss rate		MRR	Miss rate	
LGeShop	0.53554	0.04011		0.50172	0.22221	
Hyundai	0.72244	0.04200		0.68082	0.17425	
KTF	0.50181	0.01779		0.48769	0.16575	
Total	0.58660	0.03330		0.49470	0.19398	

In Table 2, FRACT/COS is a query log classifier of the same framework as FRACT/LSC except the representation dimension. In other words, FRACT/COS classifies query logs into FAQ categories using the cosine similarity in the original term-document space. As shown in Table 2, FRACT/LSC highly outperforms FRACT/COS in the average recall rates. Based on the high recall rates, we can indirectly estimate that FRACT/LSC partially bridges the lexical chasms between sentences. In addition, FRACT/IR based on FRACT/LSC showed an increase in average MRR of 0.0919 and a high decrease in average miss rate of 0.16068 on FRACT/IR based on FRACT/COS. This fact reveals that the proposed latent term weights hold more effective information although the average precisions of FRACT/LSC are much lower than FRACT/COS.

To evaluate FRACT/IR, it was unfair to directly compare the performances of FRACT/IR with those of the previous FAQ systems like FAQ Finder [2] and Auto-FAQ [20] because the performances of the previous FAQ systems were easily affected by high-level knowledge and handcrafted rules. Instead, we compared the average performances of FRACT/IR with those of conventional IR systems because both FRACT/IR and the IR systems were fully automatic systems only using statistical knowledge, as shown in Table 3.

Table 3. The performances on each IR systems

System	LGeShop		Hyundai	
	MRR	Miss rate	MRR	Miss rate
FRACT/IR	0.53554	0.04011	0.72244	0.04200
IDEAL-FRACT	0.58860	0.01874	0.76193	0.03367
TFIDF	0.46923	0.24999	0.63116	0.20152
OKAPI	0.49898	0.24999	0.67775	0.20152
KL	0.50462	0.24999	0.67616	0.20152
System	KTF		Total	
	MRR	Miss rate	MRR	Miss rate
FRACT/IR	0.50181	0.01779	0.58660	0.03330
IDEAL-FRACT	0.55830	0.01043	0.63628	0.02095
TFIDF	0.41272	0.23543	0.50437	0.22898
OKAPI	0.47053	0.23543	0.54909	0.22898
KL	0.46778	0.23543	0.54952	0.22898

In Table 3, IDEAL-FRACT means FRACT/IR with ideal FRACRT/LSC of which both the precision and the recall rate are 1.0. TFIDF is the simple vector space model based on TFIDF weights [15]. OKAPI is the Okapi BM25 retrieval model [14], and KL is the KL-divergence language model using JM smoothing [22]. TFIDF, OKAPI, and KL did not use query logs as extra information because they did not have any mechanism to introduce extra queries. We implemented these IR systems using Le-Mur Toolkit version 3.0 [7]. As shown in Table 3, FRACT/IR outperforms all comparison systems except IDEAL-FRACT in both the average MRR and the average miss rate. Specifically, FRACT/IR highly reduced the average miss rate by 0.19568. Based on this experimental result, we conclude that the conventional IR systems only using FAQ sentences have critical lexical disagreement problems and the proposed method using query logs is a good solution to the lexical disagreement problems in

FAQ retrieval. The difference between the performance of FRACT/IR and the performance of IDEAL-FRACT was 0.04968 MRR (0.01235 miss rate). This fact reveals that the more we can increase the performance of FRACT/LSC, the more we can increase the performance of FRACT/IR.

Table 4 shows the changes of ranks on the basis of top-10 in comparison with OKAPI.

Table 4. The changes of ranks in comparison with OKAPI

Domain	# of relevant FAQs upgraded into top-10	# of relevant FAQs degraded out of top-10	# of relevant FAQs newly found in top-10
LGeShop	45	28	136
Hyundai	1	4	57
KTF	135	73	195
Avg.	60.3	35.0	129.3

As shown in Table 4, FRACT/IR made about 60.3 relevant FAQs ranked into top-10. Moreover, FRACT/IR ranked about 129.3 relevant FAQs in top-10 that OKAPI could not find at all. This fact reveals that FRACT/IR highly ranks relevant FAQs more than OKAPI.

We analyzed the cases where FRACT failed to highly rank relevant FAQs. We found some reasons why the relevant FAQs were low ranked or missed. First, there were still the lexical disagreement problems between users' queries and FAQs. FRACT could resolve some lexical disagreement problems because it used query log clusters in order to smooth the FAQs. However, we found many cases where there was very little overlap between the words in queries and the words in query log clusters. To solve this problem at a basic level, we need to study new methods that match users' queries with FAQs on the semantic levels. Second, there were some cases where only one query was associated with several FAQs. In these cases, we could not select the FAQs that were entirely relevant to those queries. To solve this problem, information suppliers should accurately construct initial FAQs and should constantly update the FAQs. Finally, there were some cases where several relevant FAQs were much lower ranked, as compared with OKAPI. To solve this problem, we need to study new methods that effectively combine latent term weights with original term weights.

4 Conclusion

We present a cluster-based FAQ retrieval system using LSA techniques. The FAQ retrieval system is divided into two sub-systems: a query log clustering system and a cluster-based retrieval system. During the indexing time, the query log clustering system gathers user's query logs and classifies the query logs into relevant FAQ categories in the latent semantic space. Then, based on the results of the classification, the query log clustering system groups the query logs and generates centroids representing each cluster. During the searching time, the cluster-based retrieval system uses the centroids as smoothing factors in order to bridge the lexical chasms between users' queries and FAQs. In our experiment, the proposed system outperformed traditional

IR systems in FAQ retrieval and resolved some of lexical disagreement problems. For further studies, we will study methods to apply query log information to the other IR models like statistical models and language models.

Acknowledgement

This research was performed for the Intelligent Robotics Development Program, one of the 21st Century Frontier R&D Programs funded by the Ministry of Commerce, Industry and Energy of Korea.

References

1. El-Hamdouchi, A., Willet, P.: Comparison of Hierarchic Agglomerative Clustering Methods for Document Retrieval. The Computer Journal, Vol. 32(3). (1989) 220–227
2. Hammond, K., Burke, R., Martin, C., Lytinen, S.: FAQ Finder: a Case-Based Approach to Knowledge Navigation. Proceedings of the 11th Conference on Artificial Intelligence for Applications. (1995) 80–86
3. Hearst, M. A., Pedersen, J. O.: Re-examining the Cluster Hypothesis: Scatter/Gather on Retrieval Results. Proceedings of SIGIR 1996. (1996) 76–84
4. Jardine, N., van Rijsbergen, C. J.: The Use of Hierarchical Clustering in Information Retrieval. Information Storage and Retrieval, Vol. 7. (1971) 217–240
5. Landauer, T. K., Foltz, P. W., and Laham, D.: Introduction to Latent Semantic Analysis. Discourse Processes, Vol. 25. (1998) 259–284.
6. Lee, S.: A Korean Part-of-Speech Tagging System with Handling Unknown Words, (in Korean) MS thesis, KAIST, Korea. (1992)
7. Lemur-3.0. The Lemur Toolkit for Language Modeling and Information Retrieval (Version 3.0). Copyright (c) 2000–2004 Carnegie Mellon University
8. Liu, X., and Croft, W. B.: Cluster-Based Retrieval Using Language Models. Proceedings of SIGIR 2004. (2004) 25–29
9. Maarek, Y. S., Berry, D. M., and Kaiser, G. E.: An Information Retrieval Approach for Automatically Construction Software Libraries, IEEE Transaction on Software Engineering, Vol. 17(8). (1991) 800–813
10. Miller, G.: WordNet: An On-Line Lexical Database. International Journal of Lexicography, Vol. 3(4). (1990) 1–12
11. Muller, J., Pischel, M.: Doing Business in the Information Marketplace. Proceedings of 1999 International Conference on Autonomous Agents. (1999) 139–146
12. van Rijsbergen, C. J.: Information Retrieval (2nd ed.). London: Butterworths. (1979)
13. van Rijsbergen, C. J., Croft, W. B.: Document Clustering: An Evaluation of Some Experiments with the Cranfield 1400 Collection. Information Processing and Management, Vol. 11. (1975) 171–182
14. Robertson, S. E., Walker, S., Jones, S., Beaulieu, M. M., Gatford, M.: Okapi at TREC–3. Proceedings of TREC–3. (1994) 109–126
15. Salton, G., McGill, M. J.: Introduction to Modern Information Retrieval (Computer Series), New York:McGraw-Hill. (1983)
16. Sneiders, E.: Automated FAQ Answering: Continued Experience with Shallow Language Understanding. Papers from the 1999 AAAI Fall Symposium. (1999) 97–107

17. Tombros, A., Villa, R., van Rijsbergen, C. J.: The Effectiveness of Query-specific Hierarchic Clustering in Information Retrieval. Information Processing and Management, Vol. 38. (2002) 559–582
18. Voorhees, E.: The Cluster Hypothesis Revisited. Proceedings of SIGIR 1985. (1985) 188–196
19. Voorhees, E., Tice, D. M.: The TREC-8 Question Answering Track Evaluation. Proceedings of TREC-8. (1999) 83–105
20. Whitehead, S. D.: Auto-FAQ: an Experiment in Cyberspace Leveraging. Computer Networks and ISDN Systems, Vol. 28(1-2). (1995) 137–146
21. Willet, P.: Recent Trends in Hierarchical Document Clustering: A Critical Review. Information Processing and Management, Vol. 24(5). (1988) 577–597
22. Zhai, C., Lafferty, J.: A Study of Smoothing Methods for Language Models Applied to Ad hoc Information Retrieval. Proceedings of SIGIR 2001. (2001) 334–342

Phrase-Based Definitional Question Answering Using Definition Terminology

Kyoung-Soo Han, Young-In Song, Sang-Bum Kim, and Hae-Chang Rim

Dept. of Computer Science and Engineering, Korea University
1, 5-ga, Anam-dong, Seongbuk-gu, Seoul 136-701, Korea
{kshan, song, sbkim, rim}@nlp.korea.ac.kr

Abstract. We propose a definitional question answering method using linguistic information and definition terminology-based ranking. We introduce syntactic definition patterns which are easily constructed and reduce the coverage problem. Phrases are extracted using the syntactic patterns, and the redundancy is eliminated based on lexical overlap and semantic matching. In order to rank the phrases, we used several evidences including external definitions and definition terminology. Although external definitions are useful, it is obvious that they cannot cover all the possible targets. The definition terminology score, reflecting how the phrase is definition-like, is devised to assist the incomplete external definitions. Experimental results support our method is effective.

1 Introduction

Definitional question answering is a task of answering definition questions, such as *What are fractals?* and *Who is Andrew Carnegie?*, initiated by TREC Question Answering Track[1]. Most of the definitional question answering systems consist of the following three components: question analysis, passage retrieval, and answer extraction. Contrary to factoid or list questions, having a narrow question focus, definition questions do not have expected answer type but contain only the question target in the question, so relatively simple works are done in question analysis phase. In the question analysis phase, a question target is extracted from the question sentence. For example a question target *ETA* or *ETA in Spain* should be extracted from the question *What is the ETA in Spain?*. Most efforts to the retrieval phase are concentrated on expanding the question, characterized by the insufficient information and vague question focus. Most systems regard all sentences in the retrieved passages as answer candidates, and rank the candidates using several evidences.

Definition patterns and external definitions, definitions from external resources such as online dictionaries, are known to be so useful for ranking answer candidates[2]. Most researches use the manually constructed lexical patterns, and the construction task is labor-intensive. Although the lexical patterns can be automatically trained and collected[3], they suffer from little coverage. Moreover, external resources may not contain any information about the question target, although the external definitions, if exist, provide relevant information

G.G. Lee et al. (Eds.): AIRS 2005, LNCS 3689, pp. 246–259, 2005.

so much. Therefore, we propose ranking methods using syntactic patterns and the characteristics of the definition itself, which can be applied to the question targets for which there is no lexical pattern matching and external definition entry.

Although various NLP techniques seem to be used in definitional question answering, many systems participating in the past TREC QA Track definitional question answering only used lexical and POS information. The main reason is that further syntactic or semantic analysis using NLP techniques requires a lot of resources as well as usually shows the disappointing result in terms of accuracy or precision. However, even naive syntactic or semantic analysis can significantly help some process. For instance, phrase detection using a syntactic parser could be very useful to reduce the length of the answer by just taking exact noun phrase describing the definition of the target, and semantic matching using the thesaurus such as WordNet could be helpful for eliminating redundant information between phrases or sentences.

The idea of using more fine-grained text unit than raw sentence as answer candidate was adopted by a few researchers[4][5][6]. [5] extracted linguistic constructs called linguistic features using information extraction tools. The linguistic features, including relations and propositions, are more fine-grained than our phrases. [6] also uses the predicate set defined by semantic categories such as genus, species, cause, and effect. However, we are to show that using a little linguistic information could increase system performance although so many resources and tools are not applied.

In this paper, we suggest a phrase-based definitional question answering method mainly characterized as follows:

- Anaphora resolution technique is used to expand the retrieved passages where we find the answer candidates.
- Syntactic patterns are used to find the boundary of short and exact answer candidates, and POS-based boundary modification is also proposed to alleviate the problem caused by parsing errors.
- WordNet is used to check the redundancy of the answer candidates.
- Term statistics peculiar to the general definitions, not the target-specific definitions, are used to rank answer candidates.

These contributions are explained in detail in section 2, and experimental results and analyses are given in section 3. We conclude our work in section 4.

2   Phrase-Based Definitional Question Answering

2.1   Question Analysis

In the question analysis phase, the question sentence is parsed to extract the head word of the target. Then, the type of the target is identified using named entity tagger. We classified the target into one of the three types: persons, organizations, and other things. We use the target type for calculating the weights of the words in definitional phrases in later stage.

2.2 Passage Retrieval

Two-Phase Retrieval. As the target tends to be used with different expression in documents from that in the question, a lot of relevant information could not be retrieved or lots of irrelevant information would be retrieved by one phase passage retrieval. For example, for a target *Bill Clinton*, it would be expressed in a text by *Clinton, president Clinton, he*, etc. A strict phrase query *bill_clinton* would suffer from low recall because of differently-represented phrases in documents, while a relaxed query *clinton* would be overloaded by a plenty of irrelevant information such as *George Clinton*.

Therefore, we firstly retrieve only relevant documents to the target by relatively strict query, and then extract relevant sentences by using more relaxed one. The query for the document retrieval consists of the words and phrases of the target filtered with a stop word list. If there is a sequence of two words starting with a capital letter, a phrase query is generated with the two words. The remaining words are also used as single query words. For example, for a target *Berkman Center for Internet and Society*, the query would include a phrase *berkman_center* and two words *internet* and *society*.

Once the documents are retrieved, we generate proper passages consisting of one or more sentences containing head word of the target, initially set to one sentence. Then, we check whether the passage can be expanded to the multiple-sentence passage using anaphora resolution technique described in the next subsection.

Passage Expansion Using Target-Focused Anaphora Resolution. In many cases, the definition of the given target does not occur with the target word or phrase, but with its anaphora. For example, it is easy to observe that an anaphora refers to the target if the anaphora is used as a subject and the target is also used as a subject in the previous sentence like:

(a) Former president **Bill Clinton** was born in Hope, Arkansas.
(b) **He** was named William Jefferson Blythe IV after his father, William Jefferson Blythe III.

As shown in the above example, if the sentence (b) is next to the sentence (a) in a document, the anaphora *he* in (b) refers to *Bill Clinton* in (a).

For this reason, sentences in which the head word is represented as an anaphora are also extracted by using simple rules. When the head word is used as a subject in a sentence, the following anaphora resolution rules are applied to the next *aw* sentences according to the target type. The *aw* is the anaphora resolution window size.

Persons. If a first word of the sentence is *he* or *she*, then it is replaced with the question target.
Organizations or things. If a first word of the sentence is *it* or *they*, then it is replaced with the question target.

Without the full anaphora resolution for all anaphors in the documents, we can extract efficiently the informative sentences related to the question target by using the target-focused anaphora resolution.

2.3 Candidates Extraction Using Syntactic Patterns

We suggest an answer candidate extraction method based on syntactic patterns, easily constructed manually and freer from the coverage problem than lexical patterns. Another advantage of syntactic patterns is that the answer candidates extracted using the syntactic patterns can reduce answer granularity. A shorter text unit than a sentence is necessary for generating a more fine-grained answer because the sentences in news articles are generally so long that the answer length limit is used up quickly by sentences.

We extract answer candidates from the retrieved passages using the syntactic patterns shown in Table 1. In this study, we use the syntactic information generated by a dependency parser, Conexor FDG parser[1] [7].

From the above example, the following phrases would be extracted by applying the syntactic patterns:

(1) Former president
(2) born in Hope, Arkansas
(3) named William Jefferson Blythe IV after his father, William Jefferson Blythe III

Third candidate clearly shows the advantage of using syntactic patterns rather than lexical patterns. While the lexical patterns capable of extracting the verb phrases such as the candidate can be hardly constructed, our syntactic patterns are useful for extracting such verb phrases, specifically distant one from the target, although the patterns sometimes might extract unimportant phrases.

The syntactic information induced from the syntactic parser sometimes generates erroneous results or there are sentences from which the information is not obtained. In order to alleviate the problem, we complement the syntactic information with POS information.

- If any word between the first word and the last of a phrase in the sentence is not extracted, it is also extracted to the phrase.
- If the last word of extracted phrase is labeled with noun-dependent POSs such as adjective, determiner and preposition, the immediate noun phrase is put together into the extracted phrase.
- If the extracted phrase is incomplete one, that is, ended with one of the POSs such as conjunction or relative pronoun, the last word is removed from the extracted phrase.

The phrases which contain more than two content words and at least one noun or number is considered to be valid.

---

[1] For newspaper articles, the parser can attach heads with 95.3% precision and 87.9% recall.

Table 1. Syntactic patterns for extracting answer candidates

Pattern	Descripton	Example
Noun phrases modifying the question target	Noun phrases that have a direct syntactic relation to the question target	**Former world and Olympic champion** Alberto Tomba missed out on the chance of his 50th World Cup win when he straddled a gate in the first run.
Relative pronoun phrases	Verb phrases where a nominative or possessive relative pronoun modifies directly the question target	Copland, who was **born in Brooklyn**, would have turned 100 on Nov. 14, 2000.
Participle phrases	Present or past participles, without its subject, modifying directly the question target or the main verb directly related to the question target.	Tomba, **known as "La Bomba,"** (the bomb) **for his explosive skiing style**, had hinted at retirement for years, but always burst back on the scene to stun his rivals and savor another victory.
Copulas	Noun phrases used as a complement of the verb *be*.	TB is **a bacterial disease caused by the Tuberculosis mycobacterium and transmitted through the air.**
General verb phrases	Verb phrases modified directly by the question target which is the subject of the sentence. If the head word of a phrase is among stop verbs, the phrase is not extracted. The stop verbs indicate the functional verbs, which is not informative one such as *be*, *say*, *talk*, and *tell*.	Iqra will **initially broadcast eight hours a day of children's programs, game shows, soap operas, economic programs and religious talk shows.**

2.4   Redundancy Elimination Using WordNet

In order to eliminate the redundancy among answer candidates, at least two decisions have to be made: which candidates are redundant one another, and which candidates has to be eliminated from them. The word overlap ratio of content words is calculated in each candidate. If any word overlap ratio between two candidates is greater than high threshold T_{high}, the two candidates are determined redundant. The candidates of which no word overlap ratio amount to low threshold T_{low} are regarded not redundant. If any word overlap is between the two threshold value, T_{high} and T_{low}, the redundancy decision is not made based only the overlap. Instead, the semantic class of the head word is checked in WordNet, and two candidates are considered redundant if the two head words from each candidate belong to same synset in WordNet. Once the redundancy is detected, the highly overlapped candidate is eliminated.

Although the redundancy is a problem to making a short novel definition, the redundant information are likely to be important, which is also used as an effective ranking measure in factoid question answering system[8]. Therefore, the redundant count of the eliminated candidates is inherited by the survived one, used in the candidate ranking phase.

2.5   Answer Selection

The decision which candidates are definition or not is so difficult that ranking the candidates according to the definition likelihood can be an alternative. Our system used several evidences to rank answer candidates: head redundancy, term statistics in the relevant passages, external definitions, and definition terminology.

Head Redundancy. The important facts or events are usually mentioned repeatedly, and the head word is the core of each answer candidate. Mentioned in the previous section, a pair of candidates is redundant when one of them is heavily overlapped by lexical or the semantic classes of each head word are identical. Therefore, we consider the redundancy of answer candidate C by using following formula.

$$Rdd(C) = \exp\left(\frac{r}{n}\right) - 1 \tag{1}$$

where r represents the redundant count of answer candidate C in the candidate set, and n is the total number of answer candidates. For most terms, the fraction r/n is so smaller than 1 that the $Rdd(C)$ is hardly over 1.

Local Term Statistics. In addition to the head word, the frequent words in the retrieved passages are important. The $Loc(C)$ presents a local score based on the term statistics in the retrieved sentences, local sentences, and is calculated as follows:

$$Loc(C) = \frac{\sum_{t_i \in C} \frac{sf_i}{maxsf}}{|C|} \tag{2}$$

where sf_i is the number of sentences in which the term t_i is occurred, $maxsf$ is the maximum value of sf among all terms, and $|C|$ is the number of all content words in the answer candidate C.

External Definitions. We tried to use external definitions from various online resources by designing a scoring formula based on the probability model. If we introduce binary random variable A which is true when the candidate C is a real answer, the probability that answer candidate C is an answer to the question target is as follows:

$$P(A = 1|C) = \frac{P(C|A = 1)P(A = 1)}{P(C)}$$

As the prior probability $P(A = 1)$ is independent of ranking the candidates, the score of C by external definition is defined by:

$$Ext(C) = \log(\frac{P(C|A = 1)}{P(C)} + 1) \tag{3}$$

where $P(C)$ is a priori probability of the candidate.

Given that the external definitions are also the real answer, we can estimate the probability $P(C|A = 1)$ using following external definition model:

$$P(C|A = 1) = \prod_{t_i \in C} (\frac{freq_{E_i}}{|E|})^{\frac{1}{|C|}}$$

$$P(C) = \prod_{t_i \in C} (\frac{freq_{B_i}}{|B|})^{\frac{1}{|C|}} \tag{4}$$

where $freq_{E_i}$ is the number of occurrence of term t_i in the external definitions E in which there are the total $|E|$ term occurrences. $freq_{B_i}$ and $|B|$ are those of in the background collection. $|C|$ is the number of content word in the answer candidate C, used for normalizing the probabilities.

Definition Terminology. Although external definitions are useful for ranking candidates, it is obvious that they cannot cover all the possible targets. For the targets of which definition do not exist in external resources, we device another score called *definition terminology score*, reflecting how the candidate phrase is definition-like. The definition terminologies depend on the type of question target. For example, *born* or *died* is widely used to describe essential information about persons, while *found* or *locate* is used to describe information about organizations.

While [9] used similar approaches for ranking answer candidates, the difference is that we identify the target type and build definition terminology according to the type. In order to get the definition terminology, we collected external definitions according to the three target types: persons, organizations, and other things. These external definitions must be a good training data for learning about the definition generation. We compare the term statistics in the definitions to those in the general text, believing the difference of the term statistics to be a measure for the definition terminology.

Since the probability ratio is not bounded, we rescaled the value by taking the logarithm for combining with other scores described in the above sections appropriately.

$$Pratio(t) = \log(\frac{P_D(t)}{P(t)} + 1)$$

where $P_D(t)$ is the probability of term t in the definitions, and $P(t)$ is that of in the general text. The probability $P(t)$ is estimated as the equation 4, except the length normalization factor. The terms having a high value of $Pratio(t)$ is considered to be important for generating definitions.

The ratio is used as a definition terminology score for ranking candidates as follows:

$$Tmn(C) = \frac{\sum_{t_i \in C} Pratio(t_i)}{|C|} \qquad (5)$$

The score $Tmn(C)$ measures the average probability ratio of content terms in the answer candidate C.

The evidence mentioned so far is linearly combined into a score.

3   Experimental Results

3.1   Experiments Setup

We experimented with 50 TREC 2003 topics and the AQUAINT corpus used in TREC Question Answering Track evaluation. As the manual evaluation such as TREC evaluation requires a lot of cost, we evaluated our system automatically. The evaluation of definition answer is very similar to that of summaries, so we used a package for automatic evaluation of summaries called ROUGE[10]. ROUGE has been used for automatic evaluation of summary in Document Understanding Conference (DUC), and was successfully applied for evaluation of definitional question answering[5]. We used ROUGE-L among several measures because it is known to be highly correlated with human judgement.

$$R_{lcs} = \frac{LCS(A,S)}{|A|} \qquad P_{lcs} = \frac{LCS(A,S)}{|S|} \qquad (6)$$

$$F_{lcs} = \frac{(1 + \beta^2) R_{lcs} P_{lcs}}{R_{lcs} + \beta^2 P_{lcs}} \qquad (7)$$

where $LCS(A, S)$ is the length of the longest common subsequence of the reference answer A and the system result S, and $|A|$ and $|S|$ are the length of them respectively. The LCS-based F-measure F_{lcs} is called ROUGE-L, and β controls the relative importance of recall and precision. We evaluated the systems with stop words excluded.

We used external definitions from various online sites: Biography.com, Columbia Encyclopedia, Wikipedia, FOLDOC, The American Heritage Dictionary of the English Language, Online Medical Dictionary, and Web pages returned by Google search engine. The Google search results are used for supplying wider coverage of the external definitions. The external definitions are collected in query time by throwing a query consisting of the head words of the question target into the site. If the Google search results are not considered, 14% (7 out of 50) topics are not covered by the external definitions.

In order to extract definition terminology, we also collected definitions according to the target type. We collected 1,174 person entries from the above sites using the person name list gathered from Identifinder resources and Columbia

Encyclopedia, 545 organizations, and 696 things entries. The AQUAINT collection is used for general text.

We used our document retrieval engine based on BM25 of OKAPI, and processed top 200 documents retrieved in all experiments.

3.2 Target-Focused Anaphora Resolution

Table 2 shows the effect of target-focused anaphora resolution, when the system outputs the definition up to 500 non-white-space characters. In this experiment, we did not extract the phrases, but rank the retrieved sentences. The system 500B.Exp0, 500B.Exp1, and 500B.Exp2 are the systems in which the anaphora resolution size aw is 0, 1, and 2, respectively. The +S column shows the number of sentences added to the answer candidates using the anaphora resolution.

Table 2. Effect of target-focused anaphora resolution

System	+S	R	P	$F(\beta = 1)$	$F(\beta = 3)$
500B.Exp0	-	0.2184	0.1169	0.1429	0.1903
500B.Exp1	179	0.2195	0.1182	0.1441	0.1914
500B.Exp2	16	0.2195	0.1182	0.1441	0.1914

The system 500B.Exp1 expanded 179 sentences, and the ROUGE values show that the added sentences are useful one for definition generation. For only 20 questions, the anaphora resolution condition is satisfied and the anaphora is resolved. The resolution added on the average 8.95 sentences per the applied question. Although the resolution is not frequently applied and few sentences are added, the performance increased a bit. It says that the added sentences are related to the question target, and the target-focused anaphora resolution is useful for definitional question answering. When we resolve the anaphora, distant more than one sentence from the target, the expansion did not affect the performance, though few sentences are added. It is necessary to increase the application ratio of the resolution method.

3.3 Candidate and Answer Text Unit

Table 3 displays the system performance according to the answer length measured by the number of non-white-space characters, and Figure 1 shows the performance change according to the answer length. The system name suffix S.S, S.P, P.S, and P.P denote the text unit for answer candidate and final answer. S and P mean the sentences and phrases, respectively. The 500B.S.P represents the system where sentences are used as the candidates and phrases are used as the final answer limited up to 500 non-white-space characters.

As shown in Figure 1, our phrase-based system P.P outperforms the sentence-based system S.S. As the answer length limit gets longer, the performance difference becomes smaller, because, as shown in Table 3, the recall of S.S increases

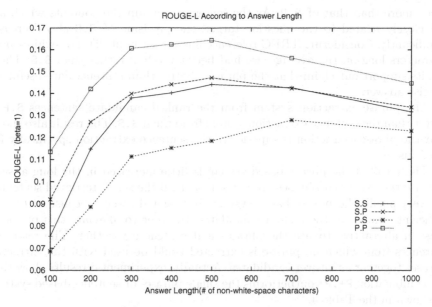

Fig. 1. Performance changes according to answer length

Table 3. System performance according to answer length and text unit: sentences vs. phrases

System	R	P	$F(\beta = 1)$	$F(\beta = 3)$
100B.S.S	0.0513	0.1667	0.0754	0.0546
100B.S.P	0.0643	0.2041	0.0920	0.0682
100B.P.S	0.0470	0.1407	0.0686	0.0501
100B.P.P	0.0801	0.2365	0.1135	0.0849
200B.S.S	0.1022	0.1470	0.1147	0.1037
200B.S.P	0.1143	0.1868	0.1270	0.1155
200B.P.S	0.0798	0.1144	0.0886	0.0807
200B.P.P	0.1270	0.2058	0.1420	0.1287
300B.S.S	0.1596	0.1382	0.1379	0.1511
300B.S.P	0.1591	0.1748	0.1398	0.1497
300B.P.S	0.1214	0.1135	0.1113	0.1177
300B.P.P	0.1764	0.1977	0.1606	0.1686
500B.S.S	0.2195	0.1182	0.1441	0.1914
500B.S.P	0.2051	0.1624	0.1472	0.1820
500B.P.S	0.1693	0.0985	0.1184	0.1524
500B.P.P	0.2260	0.1789	0.1644	0.2017
1000B.S.S	0.3149	0.0873	0.1315	0.2355
1000B.S.P	0.2420	0.1408	0.1336	0.1959
1000B.P.S	0.2649	0.0872	0.1228	0.2034
1000B.P.P	0.2573	0.1496	0.1446	0.2108

much more than that of P.P. As the sentences contain the contents which are not closely related to the question target, the precision of S.S also decreases significantly. Considering TREC reference answer is about 250 non-white-space characters long on the average, we had better use P.P rather than S.S. These results support our claim that the phrases shorter than sentences are useful for concise answer.

The phrase extraction system from the ranked candidate sentences S.P is better than the sentence extraction system from them S.S. The result also shows that the phrase extraction is superior to the sentence extraction specifically for brief answer.

The recall of the phrase-based system is little increased in the long answer because the extracted phrases are not sufficient. If the set of retrieved sentences are very small, the phrase-based system could not do well, because of the insufficient number of the answer candidates. In order to alleviate this problem, it is an alternative to use the phrases and sentences together. The retrieved sentences from which no phrase is extracted could be used with the extracted phrases together as answer candidates. Actually, experimental results show that the combination P+.P+ outperforms the single phrase- or sentence-based system, as shown in the Table 4.

Table 4. Combination of phrases and sentences

System	R	P	$F(\beta = 1)$	$F(\beta = 3)$
100B.P+.P+	0.0816	0.2230	0.1140	0.0862
200B.P+.P+	0.1371	0.1877	0.1503	0.1384
300B.P+.P+	0.1797	0.1650	0.1627	0.1736
500B.P+.P+	0.2610	0.1387	0.1702	0.2270
1000B.P+.P+	0.3461	0.0971	0.1457	0.2593

3.4 Redundancy Elimination

The effect of the redundancy elimination is shown in Table 5 where NORE, LRE, and SRE denote no redundancy elimination, lexical overlap-based method, and semantic-based method, respectively. The length limit is set to 500 non-white-space characters, and the threshold values T_{high} and T_{low} are set to 0.7 and 0.5, respectively.

The lexial- and semantic-based redundancy elimination improve the performance very slightly. As reported in [5], the redundancy elimination seems not to have great effect on the performance.

Table 5. Redundancy elimination effect

System	R	P	$F(\beta = 1)$	$F(\beta = 3)$
NORE	0.2202	0.1653	0.1524	0.1933
LRE	0.2245	0.1745	0.1612	0.1997
SRE	0.2248	0.1783	0.1637	0.2008

3.5   Answer Ranking Measures

Table 6 shows the system performance according to the ranking score combinations. The length limit is set to 500 non-white-space characters, and T_{high} and T_{low} is set to 0.8 and 0.5, respectively. The system ALL uses all the equally-combined scores, and -Rdd, -Loc, -Ext, and -Tmn is the system which each score is excluded from the ALL score, respectively. The system Rdd, Loc, Ext, and Tmn is one used the own score only, respectively.

Table 6. System performance according to the ranking score combinations

System	R	P	F($\beta = 1$)	F($\beta = 3$)
500B.ALL	0.2267	0.1799	0.1656	0.2028
500B.-Rdd	0.2266	0.1795	0.1654	0.2027
500B.-Loc	0.2250	0.1798	0.1650	0.2014
500B.-Ext	0.1926	0.1605	0.1429	0.1728
500B.-Tmn	0.1977	0.1637	0.1461	0.1772
500B.Rdd	0.1919	0.1586	0.1405	0.1712
500B.Loc	0.1924	0.1617	0.1436	0.1729
500B.Ext	0.1919	0.1586	0.1405	0.1712
500B.Tmn	0.1711	0.1463	0.1257	0.1522
500B.Ext+Tmn	0.2245	0.1785	0.1640	0.2008

The table shows that local statistics, head redundancy, and external definitions are useful as a single scoring measure, and the external definitions and definition terminology have a great influence on the combined score. Although the definition terminology is not so good measure used alone, it shows true value when used with other ranking measures. The significant performance degradation without the definition terminology shows it has useful information for ranking candidates, which cannot be replaced with other measures. From this point of view, the external definitions are the best measures of them, but the incomplete coverage has to be complemented. The combination of the external definitions and the definitional terminology Ext+Tmn shows that the definition terminology is adequate for the role.

3.6   TREC 2004 Evaluation Results

We participated in TREC 2004 Question Answering Track with a preliminary system[11]. Our TREC 2004 system used the definition terminology only for persons based on an encyclopedia, not using the external definition score for answer ranking. The evaluation results of our system was 0.246 based on the $F(\beta = 3)$ measure, compared to 0.184 of the median performance of all participation systems. Ours was among top 10 systems.

4   Conclusions

We proposed a definitional question answering system using linguistic information, and tried various ranking measures, specifically definition terminology. Our interesting findings in this study can be summarized as follows:

- Target-focused anaphora resolution can be applied to expand the retrieved passages without any performance degradation. The added sentences by the anaphora resolution are useful for definition generation.
- Phrases are likely to be a good processing unit rather than sentences for the definitional question answering. The phrases are effectively extracted by syntactic patterns.
- Redundancy elimination seems not to have great effect on the performance, though improves a bit.
- External definitions and definition terminology are efficient and harmonic measures for ranking candidates.

We designed our method to use effectively with error-prone linguistic tools, so the conditions in which the method can be applied are very strict. Our future work is that the constraint will be gradually relaxed without performance degradation.

References

1. Voorhees, E.M.: Overview of the TREC 2003 question answering track. In: Proceedings of the 12th Text Retrieval Conference (TREC-2003). (2003) 54–68
2. Hang Cui, Min-Yen Kan, T.S.C., Xiao, J.: A comparative study on sentence retrieval for definitional question answering. In: SIGIR Workshop on Information Retrieval for Question Answering (IR4QA). (2004)
3. Cui, H., Kan, M.Y., Chua, T.S.: Unsupervised learning of soft patterns for generating definitions from online news. In: Proceedings of the 13th international conference on World Wide Web (WWW-2004). (2004) 90–99
4. Harabagiu, S., Moldovan, D., Clark, C., Bowden, M., Williams, J., Bensley, J.: Answer mining by combining extraction techniques with abductive reasoning. In: Proceedings of the 12th Text Retrieval Conference (TREC-2003). (2003) 375–382
5. Jinxi Xu, Ralph Weischedel, Ana Licuanan: Evaluation of an extraction-based approach to answering definitional questions. In: Proceedings of the 27th Annual International ACM SIGIR Conference on Research and Development in Information Retrieval (SIGIR-2004). (2004) 418–424
6. Blair-Goldensohn, S., McKeown, K.R., Schlaikjer, A.H.: A hybrid approach for qa track definitional questions. In: Proceedings of the 12th Text Retrieval Conference (TREC-2003). (2003) 185–192
7. Tapanainen, P., Jarvinen, T.: A non-projective dependency parser. In: Proceedings of the 5th Conference on Applied Natural Language Processing. (1997) 64–71
8. Dumais, S., Banko, M., Brill, E., Lin, J., Ng, A.: Web question answering: Is more always better? In: Proceedings of the 25th Annual International ACM SIGIR Conference on Research and Development in Information Retrieval (SIGIR-2002). (2002) 291–298

9. Echihabi, A., Hermjakob, U., Hovy, E., Marcu, D., Melz, E., Ravichandran, D.: Multiple-engine question answering in textmap. In: Proceedings of the 12th Text Retrieval Conference (TREC-2003). (2003) 772–781
10. Lin, C.Y.: Rouge: A package for automatic evaluation of summaries. In: Proceedings of Workshop on Text Summariation Branches Out, Post-Conference Workshop of ACL 2004. (2004)
11. Han, K.S., Chung, H., Kim, S.B., Song, Y.I., Lee, J.Y., Rim, H.C.: Korea university question answering system at TREC 2004. In: Proceedings of the 13th Text Retrieval Conference (TREC-2004). (2004)

Enhanced Question Answering with Combination of Pre-acquired Answers

Hyo-Jung Oh, Chung-Hee Lee, Hyeon-Jin Kim, and Myung-Gil Jang

ETRI(Electronics and Telecommunications Research Institute),
161 Gajeong-dong, Yuseong-gu, Daejeon, 305-700, Korea
{ohj, forever, jini, mgjang}@etri.re.kr
http://km.etri.re.kr/index.php

Abstract. Recently there is a need for QA system to answer various types of user questions. Among these questions, we focus on record questions and descriptive questions. For these questions, pre-acquired answers should be prepared, while traditional QA finds appropriate answers in real-time. In this paper, we propose enhanced QA model by combining various pre-acquired answers in encyclopedia. We defined pre-acquired answer types, 55 Record Type(RT)s and 10 Descriptive Answer Type(DAT)s, in advance. To construct answer units, we built 183 Record Answer Indexing Templates and 3,254 descriptive patterns. We discussed how our proposed model was applied to the record and descriptive questions with some experiments.

1 Introduction

Recently in QA, we need to deal with various types of user questions. With view of answers, some questions are looking for the 'short answers' in sense of traditional QA. Among these questions, some are focused on 'record information' like World Record or Olympic Record. These questions are defined as factoid questions, which answer questions for which the correct response is a single word or short phrase from the answer sentence. However, most of user's frequently asked questions are not only factoid questions but also definitional questions. There are many questions, named descriptive questions, which are better answer with a longer description or explanation in logs of web search engines[1]. With view of finding answers, pre acquired answers should be prepared for some questions, while traditional QA finds appropriate answer in real-time[2, 3, 4].

On the other side, we have various sources in which we can use to find answers, such as web documents, electronic newspaper, and encyclopedia[5, 6]. Especially, there is a lot of record information in encyclopedia like Guinness Book. Contrary to web documents which contain indefinite information in terms of uncertainty of web, encyclopedia contains the facts which were already approved or occurred in the past. It is true that encyclopedia provides much descriptive information and it appears in particular forms.

In this paper, we propose enhanced QA model by combining various pre-acquire answers. We define pre-acquired answer types as answer types which can be extracted in advance as candidate answers of question types that are frequently asked. Our talk

G.G. Lee et al. (Eds.): AIRS 2005, LNCS 3689, pp. 260–273, 2005.

will be developed with two directions: both *record information questions* and *descriptive questions*. We also present the result of a system which we have built to answer these questions.

Firstly, we focus on record information questions, such as "Which is the highest mountain?" The answer for these questions can be extracted in the World record or Guinness record, e.g. "Mt. Everest is the highest mountain in the world." We define sentences which reveal the record information as *'record sentence'*. Record information questions have some characteristics. Its length is short, so it has few queries. And it consists of general words. It has effects on decreasing the performance of QA retrieval step.

As it was mentioned early, QA system to process record question can be classified into two types. One is to search document or passage using the record information question as query then extract answer[7]. Another system is to use knowledge about record information generated by manual[8]. AnswerBus^{tm}[7] does real-time search, so response time is quite long. It also perform low accuracy because it dose not consider that record information has particular context. In Encarta^{tm} QA system[8], they built record information knowledge manually, so it obtains both high precision and short response time. But it has difficulties which are long term of update and lack of flexibility. To solve problem in prior, we define template that can express particular context in record sentence.

Second point of views is descriptive question. Descriptive question are questions such as "What is tsunami?" or "Why is blood red?" which need answer that contain the definitional information about the search term, explain some special phenomenon.(i.e. chemical reaction) or describe some particular events. At the recent works[4, 5, 6, 8], definitional QA, namely questions of the form *"What is X?"*, is a developing research area related with a subclass of descriptive questions. Especially in TREC-12 conference[1], they had produced 50 definitional questions in QA track for the competition. The systems in TREC-12[8, 10] applied complicated technique which was integrated manually constructed definition patterns with statistical ranking component.

Some experiments[5, 6, 11] tried to use external resources such as WordNet and Web Dictionary associated with a syntactic pattern. Further recent work tried to use online knowledge bases on web[4]. Domain-specific definitional QA systems in the same context of our works have been developed. [12] applied on biographical summaries for people with data-driven method and [13] proposed mining topic-specific definition for scientific subjects. In contrast to former research, we focus on the other descriptive question, such as 'why', 'how', and 'what kind of'.

2 Pre-acquired Answer

Sentences including record information generally have specific words which indicate that the sentence is record sentence. We defined specific words as *'center vocabulary'* to identify record information and determined Record Type(RT) by it. We defined sentences which contain the center vocabulary as *'record sentence'*.

Exam1**:** Fish House of the Britain is the first aquarium in the world

Exam1 is a record sentence and *'the first'* is center vocabulary. By means of encyclopedia sample contents, we defined 55 center vocabularies. Table 1 shows examples of record sentences and center vocabularies.

Table 1. Example of Center Vocabulary and Record Sentence

Center Vocabulary	Record Sentence
the biggest	Jupiter is the biggest planet from solar system.
for the first time	Wig was used for the first time in ancient Egypt about BC 30th century.
the best	YANGGUIBI known as the best beauty of the Orient was killed by the soldiers.
first	GAESEONG developed to first business city in whole country.
…	…

Our QA system is a domain specific system for encyclopedia. One of the characteristics of encyclopedia is that it has many descriptive sentences. Because encyclopedia contains facts about many different subjects or about one particular subject explained for reference, there are many sentences which present definition such as "*X is Y.*" On the other hand, some sentences describe the process of some special event(i.e. the 1st World War) so that it forms particular sentence structures(5W1H) like news article.

We defined Descriptive Answer Type (DAT) as answer types for descriptive questions with two points of view: *what kind of descriptive questions are in the use's frequently asked questions?* and *what kind of descriptive answers can be patternized in the our corpus?* The result of analyzing the logs of our web site shows that there are many questions about not only 'why' and "how' but also definition. Descriptive answer sentences in corpus show particular syntactic patterns such as appositive clauses, parallel clauses, and adverb clauses of cause and effect. In this paper, we defined 10 types of DAT to reflect these features of sentences in encyclopedia.

Table 2. Descriptive Answer Type

DAT	Example/Pattern
DEFINITION	*A tsunami* is a large wave, often caused by an earthquake. [X is Y]
FUCTION	*Air bladder* is an air-filled structure in many fishes that functions to maintain buoyancy or to aid in respiration. [X that function to Y]
KIND	*The coins* in States are 1 cent, 5 cents, 25 cents, and 100cents. [X are Y_1, Y_2,.. and Y_n]
METHOD	The method that *prevents a cold* is washing often your hand. [The method that/of X is Y]
CHARCTER	*Sea horse*, characteristically swimming in an upright position and having a prehensile tail. [X is characteristically Y]
OBJECTIVE	*An automobile* used for land transports. [X used for Y]
REASON	*A tsunami* is a large wave, often caused by an earthquake. [X is caused by Y]
COMPONENT	*An automobile* usually is composed of 4 wheels, an engine, and a steering wheel. [X is composed of Y_1, Y_2,.. and Y_n]
PRINCIPLE	*Osmosis* is the principle, transfer of a liquid solvent through a semipermeable membrane that does not allow dissolved solids to pass. [X is the principle, Y]
ORIGIN	*The Achilles tendon* is the name from the mythical Greek hero Achilles. [X is the name from Y]

Table 2 shows example sentences with pattern for each DAT. For instance, "A tsunami is a large wave, often caused by an earthquake." is an example for 'Definition' DAT with pattern of [X is Y]. It also can be an example for 'Reason' DAT because of matching pattern of [X is caused by Y].

3   Construction of Pre-acquired Answer

The step of construction of pre-acquired answer corresponds to the indexing step in traditional QA. Building process of pre-answer passes through the next two steps: 1) defining templates or patterns which express context and 2) extracting Answer Unit(AU) and storing storage.

3.1   Record Answer Indexing

3.1.1   Defining RAIT
All record sentences which contain center vocabulary are not useful. For example, a sentence, "This song was made on the most sensitive season." has '*the most*' as center vocabulary. But the sentence does not contain record information. We extract valid record information only when the sentence satisfies context restriction on structure and term. For example, Exam1 has structure of "*B of A is the first D in C*" and restriction which is A: AT_COUNTRY|GEN[1], B: TAG_NN|SUBJ[2], C: MORP_WORLD[3] and D: TAG_NN+CP[4].

We define Record Answer Indexing Template (RAIT) that can represent contextual information of the record sentence. We acquired record answer from a sentence that matches with the context. RAIT consists of two pieces of information: *context restriction* and *RIU*. RIU (Record Indexing Unit) is what is worthy to be extracted for record QA.

Context Information: We put restrictions on Eojeol[5] as following by all 5. It is possible that two more restrictions simultaneously exist in one Eojeol.

- Distance restriction: Eojeol distance information from center vocabulary Eojeol (must required)
- Morpheme restriction: Morpheme information that appear to Eojeol
- POS(Part of Speech)[6] restriction: POS information that appear to Eojeol
- AT (Answer Type) restriction: AT information that appear to Eojeol
- Case restriction: Case information about Eojeol.

RIU: RIU consists of 6 units

- Answer: main subject of a record (must required)
- Verb: verb related to an answer

---

[1] AT_COUNTRY|GEN: AT of the target has to be country, and the target has to be genitive.
[2] TAG_NN|SUB: The target has to be subject, and its POS has to be noun.
[3] MORP_WORDL: Word of the target has to be 'world'.
[4] TAG_NN+CP: the target word has to consist of *be* verb and noun.
[5] Eojeol is language unit separated by blank in Korean.
[6] Our morphological analyzer uses 26 tag set. As important tag, there are NN (noun), JO (postposition word), VV (verb), CP (be verb) and so forth.

- Location: location or field which a record occurs (must required)
- AK: kind of answer
- Subject: the second subject of verb
- Object: object of verb

3.1.2 Extracting RIU

This is the step that extracts RIU using RAIT. Fig.1 shows RIU indexing process. The template 101 in Fig. 1 is the example when center vocabulary is '*the first*' and the structure has "*A is the first C in B*".The following is explanation of context restriction for each Eojeol.

- **A:** It is the left second Eojeol from center vocabulary, POS of Eojeol has to consist of noun and postposition word, and it has to be subject.
- **B:** It is the left first Eojeol from center vocabulary, and its morpheme has to be 'world'.
- **C:** It is the right first Eojeol from center vocabulary and its morpheme has to consist of be verb and noun.

From indexing information, we know that A, B, and C have Answer, Location, and AK, respectively. The result sentence, "*ENIAC is the first computer in the world*," satisfies the context restriction of template 101, so the system extracts [Location=world], [AK=computer], and [Answer=ENIAC] as RIU.

3.2 Descriptive Answer Indexing

3.2.1 Descriptive Pattern Extraction

Descriptive answer sentences generally have a particular syntactic structure. For instance, definitional sentences has patterns such as "*X is Y*", "*X is called Y*", and "*X means Y*". In case of sentence which classifies something into sub-kinds, i.e. "Our coin are 50 won, 100 won and 500 won.", it forms parallel structure like "*X are Y_1, Y_2,.. and Y_n.*"

To extract descriptive answers using a pattern matching technique, we must construct descriptive patterns from pre-tagged corpus using DAT workbench. The DAT workbench was built to help DAT tagging and descriptive pattern extraction by manual. Extraction of descriptive patterns processes in a number of steps. First, we manually construct initial surface patterns using training corpus with 10 DAT tags. Second, we extend patterns using linguistic analysis. And finally, we generalize the achieved patterns to adapt to variation of terms.

For building initial patterns, we constructed pre-tagged corpus with 10 DAT tags, then performed alignment of the surface tag boundary. The tagged sentences are then processed through POS tagging in the first step. In this stage, we can get descriptive clue terms and structures, such as "*X is caused by Y*" for 'Reason', "*X was made for Y*" for 'Function', and so on. We review the initial patterns using our workbench.

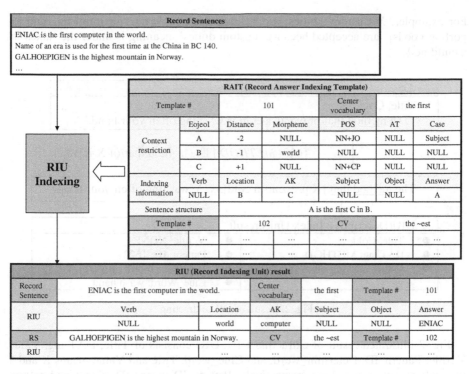

Fig. 1. RIU indexing process and result

In the second step, we used linguistic analysis including chunking and parsing to extend initial patterns automatically. Initial patterns are too rigid because we look up only surface of sentences in the first step. If some clue terms appear with long distance in a sentence, it can fail to be recognized as a pattern. To solve this problem, we added sentence structure patterns on each DAT patterns, such as appositive clause patterns for 'Definition', parallel clause patterns for 'Kind', and so on.

Finally, we generalized patterns to conduct flexible pattern matching. We need to group patterns to adapt to various variations of terms which appear in un-training sentences. Several similar patterns under the same DAT tag integrated regular-expression union which is to be formulated Finite State Automata(FSA). For example, 'Definition' patterns are represented by [X<NP> be called/named/known as Y<NP>].

3.2.2 Extracting DIU

We defined DIU as indexing unit for descriptive answer candidate. In DIU indexing stage performed pattern matching, extracting DIU, and storing our storage. We built a pattern matching system based on automata. After pattern matching, we need to filtering over-generated candidates because descriptive patterns are naive in a sense. In case of 'Definition', "X is Y" is matched so many times, that we restrict the pattern when 'X' and 'Y' under the same meaning on our ETRI-LCN for Noun[7] ontology.

---

[7] LCN: Lexical Concept Network. ETRI-LCN for Noun consists of 120,000 nouns and 224,000 named entities.

For example, "X[Customs duties] are Y[taxes that people pay for importing and exporting goods]" are accepted because 'custom duties' meaning is under the 'taxes' as a child node.

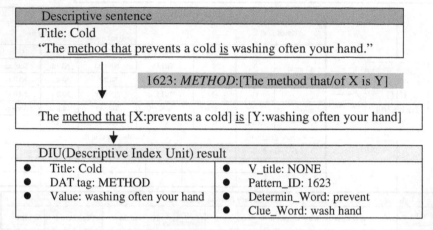

Fig. 2. Result of DIU extracting

Fig. 2 illustrated result of extracting DIU. DIU consists of Title, DAT tag, Value, V_title, Pattern_ID, Determin_word, and Clue_word. Title and Value means X and Y in result of pattern matching, respectively. Pattern_ID means ID of matched pattern. Determin_word and Clue_word are used to restrict X and Y in the retrieval stage, respectively. V_title is distinguished from Title by whether X is an entry in the encyclopedia or not. Some sentences in encyclopedia do not explain their subject explicitly. In example of "It is the war fought between 1994 and 1918 in Europe" in the 'the 1st World War' entry, 'It' means title, 'the 1st World War'.

4   Use of Acquired Answer for QA

Our system combines pre-acquired answers for finding answer. It is against the fact that general QA retrieves answers in real-time when a user question entered. To find appropriate answers in our pre-built knowledge, we perform query processing to identify what kinds of question user wants, especially looking for RIU or DIU.

4.1   Record Answer Retrieval

In the same meaning of record sentence in corpus, question which ask record information also have particular context. We define Record Question Indexing Template (RQIT) that can express contextual information of record question, like RAIT. RQIT have same restriction with RAIT and Question RIU (QRIU) of RQIT consists of 5 units (Verb, Location, AK, Subject, and Object) except target answer. Fig. 3 shows process that give answer to record question.

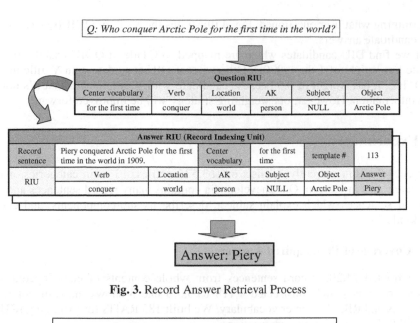

Fig. 3. Record Answer Retrieval Process

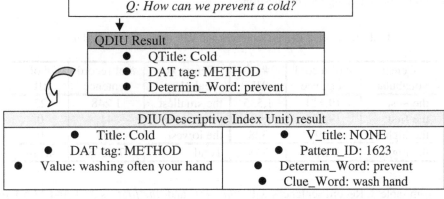

Fig. 4. Descriptive Answer Retrieval Process

4.2 Descriptive Answer Retrieval

Descriptive answer retrieval performs finding DIU candidates which are appropriate to user questions through query processing. The important role of query processing is to catch out <QTitle, DAT> pair in the user question. QTitle means the key search word in a question. We used LSP[8] patterns for question analysis. Another function of query processing is to extract Determin_word or Clue_Terms in question in terms of

---

[8] LSP pattern: Lexico-Syntactic Pattern. We built 774 LSP patterns.

determining what user questioned. Fig. 4 illustrates the result of QDIU(Question DIU) and candidate answers.

If we find DIU candidates which are mapped to QTitle of QDIU exactly, the candidate has weight of 1 through 0.7. Otherwise, if DIU candidate with V_title mapped to QTitle, it has weight of 0.5 because candidate with V_title means that it's not certain information. However, our weighting strategy will be improved forward.

5 Experiments

Our encyclopedia currently consists of 163,535 entries, 13 main categories, and 41 sub categories in Korean. Our encyclopedia contains many record sentences and definitional sentences which explain subject, describe its sub-components, and classify sub kinds.

5.1 Coverage of Pre-acquired Answer

We extracted 74,203 record sentences from whole contents of encyclopedia using center vocabulary and constructed 4,118 RIUs. Table 3 shows the result of record sentences and RIUs by center vocabulary. We built 183 RAITs for extracting RIU and 63 RQITs for analyzing record question.

Table 3. Result of Record sentences and RIU using Center vocabulary

Center vocabulary	# of record sentence	# of RIU	Center vocabulary	# of record sentence	# of RIU
the ~est	19,414	1,535	the smallest	1,248	22
the first	19,698	1,485	the greatest	41	0
the highest	6,196	328	the lowest	633	0
the biggest	5,219	738	Total	74,203	4,118

From table 3, Record sentences with 'the ~est' and 'the first' is 37% and 37.6% respectively, and RIU also is 37.4% and 36.1%. 'the ~est' is center vocabulary for several adjectives. So we know that useful record sentences with 'the first' occupy a major portion in encyclopedia. In the result of RIU indexing, 'the greatest' and 'the lowest' are not extracted. The reason is that most record sentences with that center vocabulary do not have useful information. So we do not notice that sentences when making RAIT.

To extract descriptive patterns, we built 1,853 pre-tagged sentences within 2,000 entries. About 40%(760 sentences) of all are tagged with 'Definition, while only 9 sentences were assigned to 'Principle'. Table 4 shows the result of extracted descriptive patterns using tagged corpus. 408 patterns are generated for 'Definition' from 760 tagged sentences, while 938 patterns for 'Function' from 352 examples. That means the sentences of describing something's function formed very diverse expressions. We integrated patterns to 279 regular-expression unions which are to be formulated as automata.

Table 4. Result of Descriptive Pattern Extraction

DAT	# of Patterns	DAT	# of Patterns
DEFINITION	408(22)	OBJECTIVE	166(22)
FUCTION	938(26)	REASON	38(15)
KIND	617(71)	COMPONENT	122(19)
METHOD	104(29)	PRINCIPLE	3(3)
CHARCTER	367(20)	ORIGIN	491(52)
		Total	3,254(279)

* The count in ( ) means # of groups of patterns.

Table 5. Result of DIU Indexing

DAT	# of DIUs	DAT	# of DIUs
DEFINITION	164,327	OBJECTIVE	9,381
FUCTION	25,105	REASON	17,647
KIND	45,801	COMPONENT	12,123
METHOD	4,903	PRINCIPLE	64
CHARCTER	10,397	ORIGIN	10,504
		Total	300,252

Table 5 shows the result of DIU indexing. We extracted 300,252 DIUs from the whole encyclopedia using our Descriptive Answer Indexing process. Most DIUs(about 50%, 164,327 DIUs) are 'Definition' and 14%(45,802 DIUs) are 'Kind'. We assumed that the entries belonging to the 'History' category had many sentences about 'Reason' because history usually describes some events. However, we obtained only 25,110 DIUs of 'Reason'. The reason for the small fragment is because patterns of 'Reason' have lack of expressing syntactic structure of adverb clauses of cause and effect. 'Principle' also has same problem of lack of patterns.

5.2 Evaluation of Use of Acquired Answer in QA

To evaluate effects of pre-acquired answers, we built test collection, named ETRI QA Test Set[2] judged by 4 assessors. ETRI QA Test Set 2.0 consists of 1,047 <question, answer> pairs including both factoid and descriptive questions for all categories in encyclopedia. For performance comparisons, we used Top 1 and Top 5 precision, recall and F-score. Top 5 precision is a measure to consider whether there is a correct answer in top 5 ranking or not. Top 1 measured only one best ranked answer.

For our experimental evaluations we constructed an operational system in the Web, named "AnyQuestion 2.0." To demonstrate how effectively our model works, we compared to traditional QA engine for record answer and to a sentence retrieval system for descriptive answer. While we built a question answering system for short answers, we did not compare our descriptive model with short answer engine because descriptive questions need long answers like sentences.

5.2.1 Effect of Record Answer

For testing our record QA system, we used 510 questions of ETRI QA test Set 2.0 and left 537 questions for other test. In the 510 questions, there are 61 record questions.

We expected that QA precision about record questions would be lower than general questions. So we compared QA performance for record questions with general questions in traditional QA system. Table 6 shows the result with Top 5 measure.

Table 6. Traditional QA performance: General question vs. Record question

Q type	# of Q	Retrieved	Corrected	Precision	Recall
General	449	449	336	0.748	0.748
Record	61	61	37	0.607	0.607

As the second test, we compared our proposal record system with traditional QA system. As shown in Table 7, the precision of proposal system improved by 34.8%. In general, precision is more important than recall at QA. Hence, we can say that template based record QA is very effective.

Table 7. Record QA performance: Proposed system vs. Traditional QA system

System	# of Q	Retrieved	Corrected	Precision	Recall	F-score
Our Record QA	61	22	21	**0.955** (+34.8%)	0.344	0.650
Traditional QA	61	61	37	0.607	0.607	0.607

5.2.2 Effect of Descriptive Answer

To evaluate our descriptive question answering method, we used all 152 descriptive questions from ETRI QA Test Set 2.0. Table 8 shows that the scores using our proposed method are higher than that of traditional sentence retrieval system. As expected, we obtained better result(0.625) than sentence retrieval system(0.508). We gain 85.5%(0.290 to 0.538) increase on Top1 than sentence retrieval and 23.0%(0.508 to 0.625) on Top5. It is remarkable that the accuracy on Top1 has dramatically increased, in sense that question answering wants exactly only one relevant answer.

Table 8. Descriptive QA Performance: Sentence Retrieval vs. Proposed Model

	Sentence Retrieval		Our Descriptive QA	
	Top 1	Top 5	Top 1	Top 5
Retrieved	151	151	101	101
Corrected	44	77	68	79
Precision	0.291	0.510	0.673	0.782
Recall	0.289	0.507	0.447	0.520
F-score	0.290.	0.508	**0.538** (+85.5%)	0.625 (+23.0%)

Whereas the difference between the recall of sentence retrieval system(0.507) and descriptive QA result(0.520) on Top5 is small, the F-score(0.508) is quite lower than that(0.625). It comes from the fact that sentence retrieval system tends to produce more number of candidates retrieved. While sentence retrieval system retrieved 151 candidates on Top5, our descriptive QA method retrieved 101 DIUs under the same condition that the number of corrected answers of sentence retrieval is 77 and ours is 79. That is the reason why our descriptive QA model obtained better precisions both on Top1 and Top5.

We further realize that our system has a few week points. Our system is poor for the inverted retrieval which should answer to the quiz style questions, such as "What is a large wave, often caused by an earthquake?" Moreover, our system depends on initial patterns. For the details, 'Principle' has few initial patterns, so that it has few descriptive patterns. This problem has influence on retrieval results, too.

5.2.3 Effect of Combining Pre-acquired Answers

As the last analysis, our proposed model combined pre-acquired answers, record answer and descriptive answer. We evaluated the final performance of our model with 137 questions which consisted of 61 record questions and 76 descriptive questions. The comparison with the left 373 questions in 510 questions is needless because these questions are general questions which can be processed with traditional QA at the same mechanism. Our traditional QA[2] focus on factoid questions and answer with 'short answer' like previous works. That QA also used language analysis component which include AT tagging, chunking and parsing. The result on Top 5 showed in Table 9.

As we expected, F-score(0.608) of our combining model is higher than traditional QA(0.389). We can see the same results in Precision and Recall, too. Although the F-score(0.608) of our combining model is a little lower than sentence retrieval result(0.614), we nevertheless emphasis the fact that the precision(0.825) of ours is even higher than that(0.630). That means our proposed model showed enhanced performance in QA.

Table 9. Overall comparison Performance on Top5

System	Retrieved	Corrected	Precision	Recall	F-score
Our proposed QA	80	66	**0.825**	0.482	0.608
Traditional QA	53	37	0.698	0.270	0.389
Sentence Retrieval	130	82	0.630	0.598	0.614

6 Conclusion

We have proposed enhanced QA model with combination of various pre-acquired answers for record and descriptive questions. We also presented the result of a system which we had built to answer these questions. To reflect characteristics of record and descriptive sentences in encyclopedia, we defined 55 RTs by center vocabulary and 10 DATs as answer types. We explained how our system constructed descriptive patterns and record templates and how these patterns and templates work on our indexing process. We had shown that our proposed models outperformed the traditional QA system with some experiments. We evaluated the coverage of indexing unit candidates(DIU and RIU) which archived using pre-defined patterns and the effect of pre-acquired answer in QA. For record questions, we compared with traditional QA system. The result showed that precision of proposal record QA model is higher than traditional model by about 35% on Top5. And in descriptive QA, we obtained F-score of 0.520 on Top1 and 0.680 on Top5. It showed better results when compared with sentence retrieval system on both Top1 and Top5. From the overall comparison, we prove that our proposed model which combined pre-acquired answers has enhanced.

In record QA, our model has problem that it can not extract RIU from complex sentences. The recall of our system becomes low due to limitation of target sentences. As the future work, we plan to expand restriction information and use sophisticated linguistic processing for improving recall. In descriptive QA, our further works will concentrate on reducing human efforts for building descriptive patterns. To achieve automatic pattern generation, we will try to apply machine learning technique like the boosting algorithm. We also try to improve performance of our system by analyzing results of individual DATs, to figure out which DATs shows poor accuracy. More urgently, we have to build an inverted retrieval method. Finally, we will compare with other systems which participated in TREC by translating definitional questions of TREC in Korean.

References

1. Ellen M, Voorhees: Overview of TREC 2003 Question Answering Track. The Proceedings of the twelfth Text REtreival Conference(TREC-12), November 2003.
2. H. J. Kim, H. J. Oh, C. H. Lee., et al.: The 3-step Answer Processing Method for Encyclopedia Question-Answering System: AnyQuestion 1.0. The Proceedings of Asia Information Retrieval Symposium (AIRS) (2004) 309-312
3. Vlado Keselj, Anthony Cox: DalTREC 2004: Question Answering using Regular Expression Rewriting. The Proceedings of the thirteenth Text REtreival Conference(TREC-13), November 2004
4. Lide Wu, Xuangjing Huang, Lan You, Zhushuo Zhang, Xin Li, Yaqian Zhou: FDUQA on TREC2004 QA Track. The Proceedings of the thirteenth Text REtreival Conference(TREC-13), November 2004
5. B. Katz, M. Bilotti, S. Felshin, et. al.: Answering Multiple Questions on a Topic from Heterogeneous Resources. Proceedings of the thirteenth Text REtreival Conference(TREC-13), November 2004.
6. W. Hilderbrandt, B. Katz, and J. Lin: Answering Definition Question using Multiple Knowledge Sources. The Proceedings of HLT/NAACL 2004, pp. 49-56, May 2004.
7. AnswerBus[tm] QA system: www.answerbus.com
8. Encarta[tm] QA system: www.msn.com
9. S. Blair-Goldensohn, K. R. Mcheown, and A, H, Schlaikjer: A Hybrid Approach for QA Track Definitional Questions. The Proceedings of the twelfth Text REtreival Conference(TREC-12), pp. 336-342, November 2003.
10. J. Xu, A. Licuanan, and R. Weischedel: TREC 2003 QA at BBN: Answering Definitional Questions. The Proceedings of the twelfth Text REtreival Conference(TREC-12), November 2003.

11. H. Cui, M-Y. Kan, T-S. Chua, and J. Xian: A Comparative Study on Sentence Retrieval for Definitional Question Answering. The Proceedings of SIGIR 2004 workshop on Information Retrieval 4 Question Answering(IR4QA), (2004)
12. B. Shiffman, I. Mani, and K.Concepcion: Producing Biographical Summaries: Combining Linguistic Resources and Corpus Statistics. The Proceedings of the European Association for Computational Linguistics (ACL-EACL 01), (2001)
13. B. Liu, C-W. Chin, and H-T. Ng: Mining Topic Specific Concepts and Definitions on the Web. The Proceedings of International Conference on World Wide Web(WWW 2003), 251-260

An Empirical Study of Query Expansion and Cluster-Based Retrieval in Language Modeling Approach

Seung-Hoon Na, In-Su Kang, Ji-Eun Roh, and Jong-Hyeok Lee

Division of Electrical and Computer Engineering,
POSTECH, AITrc, Republic of Korea
{nsh1979, dbaisk, jeroh, jhlee}@postech.ac.kr

Abstract. In information retrieval, the word mismatch problem is a critical issue. To resolve the problem, several techniques have been developed, such as query expansion, cluster-based retrieval, and dimensionality reduction. Of these techniques, this paper performs an empirical study on query expansion and cluster-based retrieval. We examine the effect of using parsimony in query expansion and the effect of clustering algorithms in cluster-based retrieval. In addition, query expansion and cluster-based retrieval are compared, and their combinations are evaluated in terms of retrieval performance. By performing experimentation on seven test collections of NTCIR and TREC, we conclude that 1) query expansion using parsimony is well performed, 2) cluster-based retrieval by agglomerative clustering is better than that by partitioning clustering, and 3) query expansion is generally more effective than cluster-based retrieval in resolving the word-mismatch problem, and finally 4) their combinations are effective when each method significantly improves baseline performance.

1 Introduction

Recently, language modeling approach has become a popular IR model based on its sound theoretical basis and good empirical success [2], [3], [4], [5], [9], [10], [11], [12], [14], [15], [16], [17], [19], [20], [21]. In contrast to the probabilistic model [18], the language modeling does not explicitly infer the relevance information, estimating individual document models that use unique probability distribution of words. The main difference between the language modeling and the probabilistic model is what relevance measure of documents is. In the language modeling, relevance of document is calculated by query likelihood generated from document language models. On the other hand, the probabilistic model infers a hidden relevance set from the user's query, estimates naïve Bayesian relevance probabilistic model, and ranks documents by posterior probability of the model, called the probability ranking principle.

From the perspective of information retrieval, the language modeling approach provides a very flexible framework which enables deal with complex relationship among terms. For example, adjacent two terms in a query has a dependency in bi-term language model [19], whereas a term in a query can have a syntactic dependency with any terms within query in dependency language model [2]. Language modeling approach also can be incorporated with some advanced techniques to resolve word mismatch problem, such as query expansion and cluster-based retrieval. Lafferty and

G.G. Lee et al. (Eds.): AIRS 2005, LNCS 3689, pp. 274–287, 2005.
© Springer-Verlag Berlin Heidelberg 2005

Zhai [9] introduced the concept of query model within language modeling approach, and regarded retrieval as ranking by KL divergence between query model and document language model. Cluster-based retrieval within language modeling approach was explored by two methods, interpolation [8] and cluster-based smoothing [12].

Until now, there was no empirical or theoretical comparison between query expansion and cluster-based retrieval in resolving word mismatch problem. It is meaningful to investigate a theoretical difference between two approaches in that it enables to easily identify how to approximate from one method to another method, and how to induce optimal parameters in one method from those of another method. This paper focuses on empirical experiments for query expansion and cluster-based retrieval on various issues, and thus provides reasonable direction to develop theoretical argument between two approaches and is used as empirical justification for a new theory. The following summarizes several issues of this paper.

1) What is the effect of using parsimony in query expansion?
Parsimonious language models reduce the number of terms with non-zero probabilities by eliminating common terms in document [5]. It enables to decrease storage size in indexing database. Previous studies showed that parsimonious language models are effective not only in initial retrieval and local feedback [5] but also in query expansion [15]. Especially, it is mandatory to use parsimony in query expansion because term co-occurrence statistics requires large time complexity. However, retrieval performance by using parsimony has not been investigated so far, even though it was proved that it drastically reduces time- and space-complexity. In this regard, this paper performs several kinds of experiments to investigate an effectiveness of parsimony in terms of retrieval performance.

2) What is difference in retrieval performance by each query expansion and cluster-based retrieval?
Query expansion and cluster-based retrieval have some differences when applying it in retrieval model. Consider another technique, *document expansion* which determines score of a document according to similarities of retrieved documents. In contrast to query expansion that deals with the word mismatch problem in word level, document expansion do in document level. Cluster-based retrieval can be viewed as approximation of document expansion that similarities among documents is indirectly considered through clusters. Are these two approaches almost same? Or, is one approach approximation of another one? To answer these theoretical questions is not easy. This paper does not try to find *theoretical* relation. Instead, we perform comparison of retrieval performances of two approaches in several collections. This result can be starting point to discover meaningful differences of two approaches in the future.

3) What is the effect of clustering algorithm in cluster-based retrieval?
Intuitively, cluster-based retrieval's performance depends on clustering algorithms. Then, what is the degree of performance difference in clustering algorithms? Which clustering algorithm is more effective? What is common feature of effective clustering algorithm? To draw potential answers for these questions, we compare two traditional clustering approaches: *Agglomerative clustering* and *partitional clustering*. Agglomerative clustering fully utilizes structure of documents by explicitly using document-to-document similarities, while partitioning clustering has a limit to utilize

the structure because document-to-document similarities are indirectly calculated via cluster. Comparison results provide conclusion for whether fully utilizing document structures is essential or not.

4) Is there a novel method to combine query expansion and cluster-based retrieval?
In this paper, two methods are proposed to combine query expansion and cluster-based retrieval: a) *Cluster-based Retrieval after Query Expansion* (Q&C) and b) *Cluster-dependent Query Expansion* (C&Q). In Q&C query terms are first expanded and then cluster-based retrieval is performed using the expanded query terms. In C&Q cluster-based retrieval is first performed and expanded query terms are weighted according to their cluster membership. Evaluation of combining methods will help clarify discussion for second question. For example, if combined method is effective, two approaches may play a different role for resolving word mismatch problem.

This paper is organized as follows. In Section 2, we briefly review the language modeling approach and methods for query expansion and cluster-based retrieval. In Section 3, experimental results for the above issues are presented and discussed. Finally, a conclusion will be given in Section 4.

2   Query Expansion and Cluster-Based Retrieval in Language Modeling Approach

2.1 Kullback-Leiber Divergence Framework

Basically, original language modeling approach ranks documents in collection with the query-likelihood that a given query **q** would be observed during repeated random sampling from each document model. To allow relevance feedback and query expansion, Lafferty and Zhai [9] proposed the Kullback-Leiber(KL) divergence framework by introducing a query language model, the probabilistic model for user's information need. In the framework, the query likelihood of original language modeling approach is generalized to negative KL divergence between the query model and document language models as follows.

$$-KL\left(\theta_Q \mid \theta_D\right) \propto \sum_w p\left(w \mid \theta_Q\right) log\ p\left(w \mid \theta_D\right) \tag{1}$$

Let us note that $p(w|\theta_Q)$ is a query model for user's query Q, and D is a document and $p(w|\theta_D)$ is a document language model for D.

2.2 Methods for Query Expansion

In this section, we introduce two methods of query expansion, Markov Chain Translation Model and Parsimonious Translation Model.

Markov Chain Translation Model (MCTM). Estimation of the query model is performed by term co-occurrence statistics, based on MCTM between words and documents [9]. For given term q, translation model (word transition probabilities) induced from the Markov chain is calculated in random walk as follows [9].

$$t(w \mid q) = \sum_D p(w \mid \theta_D) p(\theta_D \mid q).$$

(2)

Translation model $t(w|q)$ means the probability to generate w from document which topically related to q.

Formula (2) is rewritten as follows by applying the Bayesian theorem on $p(\theta_D|q)$.

$$t(w \mid q) = \frac{1}{p(q)} \sum_D p(w \mid \theta_D) p(q \mid \theta_D) p(\theta_D).$$

(3)

where the summation part $\sum_D p(w|\theta_D) p(q|\theta_D) p(\theta_D)$ is related to the document co-occurrence information. It implies that the translation model is used as another measurement of co-occurrence statistics.

Given query Q, we can estimate an expanded query model from the translation model as follows, similar to [9].

$$p(w \mid \theta_Q) = \sum_{q \in Q} t(w \mid q) p(q \mid \hat{\theta}_Q)$$

(4)

where θ_Q is the directly inferred query model from the translation model and $\hat{\theta}_Q$ is a query model of MLE for given Q.

The final query model $\theta_{Q'}$ is obtained by mixing the expanded query model and the MLE of the query model using parameter α.

$$p(w \mid \theta_{Q'}) = \alpha \, p(w \mid \theta_Q) + (1-\alpha) p(w \mid \hat{\theta}_Q)$$

(5)

Parsimonious Translation Model (PTM). The parsimonious translation model first estimates parsimonious language models for available documents and calculate word translation probabilities by pairs of topical terms selected from documents [15]. There are two possible techniques to select topical terms. The one is *select_top(k)*, where terms are sorted by $p(w|\theta_D)$, and only top k ranked terms are selected. The other one is *select_ratio(P)*, where terms are selected as long as summation of probabilities of the selected terms is below the probability P. This paper adopts the *select_ratio(P)* method for this experimentation due to its generality.

To derive parsimonious document language model, document specific topic model to maximize the document likelihood is first constructed. It is assumed that document is generated from mixture model of unknown document specific topic model θ_D and global collection model θ_C.

$$P(D) = \prod_{w \in D} (\lambda \, p(w \mid \theta_D) + (1-\lambda) \, p(w \mid \theta_C))$$

(6)

where λ is smoothing parameter. The document specific topic model θ_{D*} is θ_D to maximize the document likelihood D. θ_{D*} is calculated by applying the EM algorithm [4].

Let us define the *parsimonious document language model* θ_D^s consisting of topical terms selected by *select_ratio(P)*. Let D_s be a set of topical terms of the document D selected by *select_ratio(P)*. D_s is a maximal subset of words of document D that satisfies the constraint $\sum_{w \in D_s} p(w|\theta_{D*}) < P$.

$$p\left(w\mid\theta_D^s\right)=\begin{cases}\alpha_D\,p\left(w\mid\theta_{D*}\right) & \text{if } w\in D_s \\ 0 & \text{otherwise}\end{cases} \tag{7}$$

where α_D is a normalization factor with value $1/\sum_{w\in Ds}p(w|\theta_{D*})$.

The parsimonious translation model is derived by substituting the document language model in formula (3) into the parsimonious document language model of formula (7) as follows.

$$t^s\left(w\mid q\right)=\frac{1}{p(q)}\sum_D p\left(w\mid\theta_D^s\right)p\left(q\mid\theta_D^s\right)p\left(\theta_D^s\right) \tag{8}$$

2.3 Methods for Cluster-Based Retrieval

Interpolation Method. The main intuition of cluster-based retrieval is to rank documents which belong to high relevant clusters more highly. In the interpolation method, scoring schemes of document for given query reflect the score of cluster that the document belongs to, with interpolation format.

To derive the interpolation method, let us first introduce the aspect-x method. For a given query Q, a scoring function for aspect-x [6] is motivated by appealing to the probabilistic derivation of the aspect model as follows [8].

$$-KL\left(\theta_Q\mid\theta_D\right)\propto p\left(Q\mid\theta_D\right)=\sum_C p(Q\mid C,D)p(C\mid D) \tag{9}$$

where C is one of the clusters and $p(C|D)$ indicates of the degree that document D belongs to cluster C. $p(Q|C,D)$ can be shrinken into $p(Q|C)$ by assuming the generating words from the cluster is independent to a document. Then formula (9) is rewritten by

$$p(Q\mid\theta_D)=\sum_c p(Q\mid C)p(C\mid D) \tag{10}$$

Cluster-based retrieval induced from this formula (10) is called the aspect-x method. Formula (11) shows the interpolation method which is derived by substituting $p(Q|C,D)$ into $\beta p(Q|D)+(1-\beta)p(Q|C)$, where β indicates the degree of emphasis on individual-document information [8].

$$p(Q\mid D)=\beta p(Q\mid D)+(1-\beta)\sum_C p(Q\mid C)p(C\mid D) \tag{11}$$

In this paper, the interpolation method for cluster-based retrieval is fixed by empirical experiments. From the fact that the multiplication mixture is well performed than the linear mixture in our experiments, the following ranking formula is derived

$$p(Q\mid D)\propto p(Q\mid D)^\beta\left(\sum_c p(Q\mid C)p(C\mid D)\right)^{(1-\beta)} \tag{12}$$

$$\propto \beta\log p(Q\mid D)+(1-\beta)\log\left(\sum_C p(Q\mid C)p(C\mid D)\right)$$

If we use not a soft cluster but a hard cluster where each document D belongs to single cluster c_D, formula (12) can be simplified as follows, since $p(c_D|D) = 1$ and $p(C|D) = 0$ for $C \neq c_D$.

$$p(Q \mid D) \propto \beta \log p(Q \mid D) + (1-\beta) \log p(Q \mid c_D) \tag{13}$$

where c_D indicates a cluster to which document D belongs.

2.4 Combining Methods for Cluster-Based Retrieval and Query Expansion

Although both query expansion and cluster-based retrieval aim to resolve the word mismatch problem in IR, each method differs each other in terms of effectiveness. It is valuable to explore how to the combine methods of cluster-based retrieval and query expansion to identify difference.

As mentioned in the Section 1, this paper examines two combining methods-, cluster-based retrieval from query expansion and cluster-dependent query expansion.

Cluster-Based Retrieval after Query Expansion (Q&C). This performs cluster-based retrieval from query model estimated after query expansion. Q&C is used as baseline method in our experiments in combining cluster-based retrieval and query expansion because its simplicity. If cluster-based retrieval and query expansion does not conflict with retrieval performance and not share all their effectiveness, the combining methods will improve performance over that of each method alone.

Cluster-Dependent Query Expansion (C&Q). In the language modeling approach, C&Q is formulated with the *cluster-dependent translation model* to generalize the translation model.

The cluster-dependent translation model $t(w|q, C)$ means the probability to generate w from a document that contains q, with the additional restriction that the document belongs to cluster C. The model is given by adding cluster conditional term.

$$t(w \mid q, C) = \sum_D p(w \mid \theta_D) p(\theta_D \mid q, C) \tag{14}$$

By applying the Bayesian rule for $p(\theta_D|q, C)$ in formula (5), we can further derive it as follows.

$$
\begin{aligned}
t(w \mid q, C) &= \sum_D p(w \mid \theta_D) p(\theta_D \mid q, C) \\
&= \sum_D \frac{p(w \mid \theta_D) p(q \mid \theta_D, C) p(\theta_D \mid C)}{p(q \mid C)} \\
&= \sum_D \frac{p(w \mid \theta_D) p(q \mid \theta_D) p(\theta_D \mid C)}{p(q \mid C)}
\end{aligned} \tag{15}
$$

Now, for a given query Q, the *query-context dependent translation model* is derived by using the cluster-dependent translation model as follows.

$$t(w \mid q, Q) = \sum_C t(w \mid q, C) p(C \mid Q) \tag{16}$$

where C is cluster and $p(C|Q)$ is the posteriori probability of cluster for the given query. $t(w|q,C)$ is the cluster-dependent translation model. The posteriori probability $P(C|Q)$ of cluster C for given query Q is rewritten by.

$$p(C \mid Q) \propto p(Q \mid C)p(C) \tag{17}$$

3 Experimental Results

This Section shows experimental results for four issues in noted in Section 1 in order.

3.1 Experimental Setup

Our experimental database consists of two collections in Korean, and five TREC4 data collections in English. Table 1 summarizes the information of the seven data collections. The "# Doc" is the total number of documents, "# D.T." indicates the average number of unique terms of documents, "# Q" is the number of topics and "# R" is the number of relevant documents in each test set.

In Korean documents, it is well known that bi-character (n-Gram) indexing units are highly reliable [13]. Thus the bi-character indexing unit is used in this experimentation. For indexing English documents, the typical preprocessing step is performed, where stop words are removed and then Poster stemming is applied.

Table 1. Collection summaries

Collection	# Doc	# D.T.	# Q	# Term	# R
KT 1.0	1,000	125.9	30	15,772	424
NTCIR3-K	66,147	176.3	30	180,294	3,868
TREC4-AP	158,240	156.6	49	26,8411	3,055
TREC4-SJM	90,257	142	48	259,434	1,297
TREC4-WSJ	74,250	171.6	45	193,398	1,183
TREC4-ZIFF	217,940	90.6	32	578,607	512
TREC4-FR	19,860	124.1	27	98,567	416

3.2 Effects of Parsimony on Query Expansion

Figure 1 shows the average precision for three query models in seven different test collections by changing the parsimony level from 0.1 to 1.0. (Results of combining methods will be discussed in Section 3.4). The three query models is like that: the baseline language model using the MLE of the query sample, the query model estimated from the original translation model (formula (3)), and the query model estimated from the parsimonious translation model (formula (8)). Interpolation parameter α is fixed at 0.1, which was performed well in all test collections.

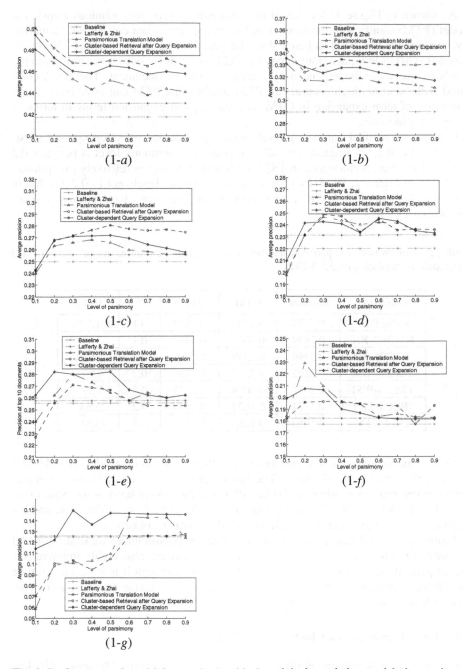

Fig. 1. Performance of combining methods with the original translation model, the parsimonious translation model and the baseline language model in six different collections. KTSET 1.0 : (1-a), NTCIR3-K: (1-b), TREC4 AP: (1-c), TREC4-SJM: (1-d),TREC4-WSJ: (1-e), TREC4-ZIFF: (1-f), TREC4-FR: (1-g). The number of clusters used in combining methods is same to optimal number for CR in Table 3.

As shown in Figure 1, for almost all parsimony levels, parsimonious translation model (PTM) significantly improves baseline in the seven data collections. Remarkably, performance of PTM is better than the performance of the original translation model (OTM) at low parsimony level. In OTM, some noise occurs because common words of query can be expanded by common terms of document. Therefore, compared with baseline, high accuracy of PTM implies that PTM can effectively eliminate noise of term expansion in OTM, and select good expansion terms in terms of retrieval performance.

Concerning optimal parsimony level, while for Korean collection optimal parsimony level is 0.1, for English test collection optimal parsimony level is between 0.2 and 0.4. However, performance in TREC4-FR test collection is relatively exceptional. As shown in Figure 1, PTM does not good in parsimony levels not in 0.2~0.4 but in 0.6 ~0.8. It seems that in TREC4-FR good expansion terms have relatively small probabilities value.

Table 2. Comparison of performance between original translation model (OTM) and parsimonious translation model (PTM)

Collection	Baseline	OTM	PTM*	P*	%chg
KTSET 1.0	0.4174	0.4302	0.4809	0.1	11.79%
NTCIR3-KK	0.2899	0.3076	0.3315	0.1	7.7%
TREC4-AP	0.2499	0.2558	0.2685	0.4	4.96%
TREC4-SJM	0.2202	0.2313	0.2468	0.3	6.70%
TREC4-WSJ	0.2031	0.2054	0.2175	0.3	5.89%
TREC4-ZIFF	0.1774	0.1824	0.2290	0.2	25.55%
TREC4-FR	0.1250	0.1260	0.1434	0.6	13.81%

Table 2 summarizes the best performance of the parsimonious models (PTM*) and OTM in the seven test collections. The last column with symbol "%chg" indicates improvement ratio of PTM* over OTM. P* is the parsimony level at the best. From this table, we know that PTM highly outperforms baseline from 5% to 25%, and especially 25.55% improvement is achieved at TREC4-ZIFF collection.

From these experiments, we can conclude that the parsimonious translation model not only drastically reduces time- and space-complexity but also highly improves retrieval performance at the optimal parsimony levels. Although it is necessary to tune for different collections for an optimal parsimony level, it seems that an optimal parsimony level is almost same for the same language.

3.3 Query Expansion vs. Cluster-Based Retrieval

For document clustering, the K-means clustering algorithm is used because of its low time complexity. Similarity measure for K-means clustering between a document and a cluster is regarded as negative KL divergence between a parsimonious document language model (set P be 1.0 with *select_ratio(P)*) and cluster language model.

$$-KL(D \mid C) \propto \sum_w p(w \mid \theta_D^s) \log p(w \mid C) \qquad (18)$$

For the cluster language model, JM(Jerlinek Mercer) smoothing with smoothing parameter 0.25 is used. We randomly select K documents and use them as initial cluster centroids. To perform Cluster-based Retrieval (CR), formula (13) is utilized where β is set to be 0.8 which is known to be relatively good in preliminary experimentation.

To calculate the query likelihood of clusters $p(q|c_D)$, cluster language models are smoothed with collection language models by using an parameter γ. In the experimentation, interpolating parameter γ is set to 0.8.

Table 3. The performance of cluster-based retrieval

Collection	OTM	K=100	K=200	K=500	K=1000
NTCIR3-KK	0.3076	0.3077	0.3142	**0.3151**	0.3111
TREC4-AP	0.2558	0.2653	0.2623	**0.2735**	0.2722
TREC4-SJM	0.2313	0.2387	0.2360	**0.2395**	0.2164
TREC4-WSJ	0.2054	0.2056	0.2054	**0.2096**	0.2060
TREC4-ZIFF	0.1824	0.1570	**0.1784**	0.1742	0.1559
TREC4-FR	0.1260	0.1248	0.1267	**0.1289**	0.1261

The number of clusters in CR is an important parameter in clustering. Instead of analytic determination of the number of clusters, we perform cluster-based retrieval for each different parameter (i.e. 100, 200, and 500 and 1000) and select the best one. The results are described in Table 3 with the original translation model (OTM) in the six data collections. The result in KTSET 1.0 will be discussed in next Section. Bold faces express best performance in each collection. In five test sets except for TREC4-ZIFF, the best performances are achieved at $K = 500$.

Overall, the effect of CR differs in each test set. In NTCIR3-KK and TREC4-AP CR is highly effective, improving the baseline with a difference between 2% and 3%, obtaining better performances over OTM. However, in other test sets, performance improvements are not significant over the baseline. The possible reason is that initial centroids randomly selected are not good for those test sets. Due to local convergence characteristics of K-Means, final clustering result is very sensitive to initial condition, so with a bad initial condition it is likely that the resulting clusters obtained from the local maximum result are not adequate for CR. We believe that the result can be improved more, if better clustering algorithms with global maximum characteristics or good criterion are used.

Let's compare the performance by PTM in Table 2 and CR in Table 3. In five test collections except for TREC-AP, the best performance by CR is generally lower than performance by PTM. In these five test sets, the best performances are achieved at $K = 500$, and at $K = 200$ in TREC4-ZIFF. They are not as good as the best performances of the parsimonious translation models. There is one exceptional case, in TREC4-AP, where cluster-based retrieval is better than the optimal parsimonious translation model at $K = 500$.

3.4   Effects of Clustering Algorithms in Cluster-Based retrieval

For analysis of the effects of clustering algorithms for cluster-based retrieval, we consider two clustering algorithms: the Agglomerative and Partitional. The agglomerative clustering methods group the documents into a hierarchical tree structure using bottom-up approaches. For constructing K clusters in agglomerative clustering, clusters are merged until total K clusters are obtained. In other words, the top K disjoint cluster trees in hierarchical clusters are extracted. We use group average criterion for merging clusters [7].

The partitioning methods decompose the document set into a given number of disjoint clusters, and are generally used given some predefined criterion functions. K-Means clustering belongs to partitional clustering approach. Because the size of KTSET 1.0 is small, we could successfully perform agglomerative clustering at computationally feasible time.

Figure 2 shows the results of CR in KTSET 1.0 varying the number of clusters from 10 to 100 increasing by 10. β is the same as the value in Section 3.3. K-Means clustering is unstable according to the number of clusters and sometimes is worse than baseline. On the other hand, agglomerative clustering outperforms baseline in all parameters showing a maximum difference of about 6%. In addition, it is always better than K-Means regardless of the number of clusters and more stable than K-Means.

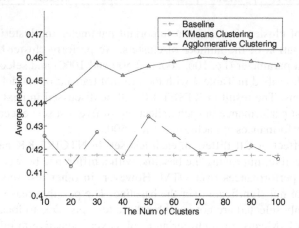

Fig. 2. Comparison of K-Means clustering and agglomerative clustering

3.5   Combining Methods of Query Expansion and Cluster-Based Retrieval

Again, let us look at Figure 1. Figure 1 compares performance of baseline, PTM*, and two kinds of combination methods of query expansion (QE) and CR (Q&C and C&Q). In this experiments, the interpolation parameters α and β of QE and CR are same to those in individual method.

Concerning Q&C and C&Q, in Korean collection, two methods are successful, showing that they outperform the baseline and individual methods of QE and CR. Especially, Q&C is better than C&Q. However, two combining methods are not successful in the English test collection. Only in the AP collection combining methods are successful having with a similar tendency to the result in Korean, while they do not improve individual methods or sometimes are worse in other four collections. One possible reason is that the performance of CR is not good in those collections. In KTSET 1.0, NTCIR3-K, and TREC4-AP, the best performance of CR is higher than baseline (about 3%) and QTM (about 1.5%). On the other hand, in the other four collections, the performance of CR is higher than baseline and QTM at most 1% or rather is worse than them. To sum up, combination of QE and CR is meaningful, only if performance of each method is higher than baseline. In addition, in such a case, the Q&C is slightly better than the C&Q.

Let's consider relationship between performance by Q&C and C&Q and performance by CR. From our additional experiments (we do not give a detail information about this experiment due to limits of this paper) we found a tendency that performance of Q&C was highly dependent on the performance by CR. It is reasonable because Q&C is basically cluster-based retrieval. From this, we can expect that Q&C can be more improved if clustering algorithm is more refined. However, performance of C&Q is relatively less dependent on performance of CR and is highly depends on the number of clusters. It is understandable because C&Q has almost the same effect with local feedback (pseudo relevance feedback) if one distinct cluster is formed for each document, resulting in total N clusters given N documents.

Table 4 presents performance of PTM* (best performance by PTM in each collection), Q&C*, and C&Q* (best performance by Q&C and C&Q in each collection) Compared with performance by PTM*, performance by Q&C is higher about 2% in only three collections (KTSET 1.0, NTCIR3-KK, and TREC4-AP).

Table 4. Comparison of PTM*, C&Q*, and C&Q*. K is the number of clusters, and P is parsimony level at the best.

Collection	Baseline	PTM*	Q&C*	C&Q*
KTSET 1.0	0.4174	0.4809	**0.5013**	0.4944
($K = 30$)		($P = 0.1$)	($P = 0.1$)	($P = 0.1$)
NTCIR3-KK	0.2899	0.3315	**0.3438**	0.3358
($K = 500$)		($P = 0.1$)	($P = 0.1$)	($P = 0.1$)
TREC4-AP	0.2499	0.2685	**0.2808**	0.2723
($K = 500$)		($P = 0.4$)	($P = 0.5$)	($P = 0.5$)
TREC4-SJM	0.2202	0.2468	**0.2489**	0.2455
($K = 500$)		($P = 0.3$)	($P = 0.3$)	($P = 0.6$)
TREC4-WSJ	0.2031	0.2175	0.2118	**0.2202**
($K = 500$)		($P = 0.3$)	($P = 0.9$)	($P = 0.3$)
TREC4-ZIFF	0.1774	**0.2290**	0.1966	0.2074
($K = 200$)		($P = 0.2$)	($P = 0.4$)	($P = 0.2$)
TREC4-FR	0.1250	0.1434	0.1179	**0.1497**
($K = 500$)		($P = 0.6$)	($P = 1.0$)	($P= 0.3$)

4 Conclusion

This paper performs an empirical study of query expansion and cluster-based retrieval in order to resolve the word mismatch problem in a language modeling framework. From this work, several conclusions are derived as follows.

- *The parsimonious translation model not only remarkably reduces time- and space-complexity but also highly improves retrieval performance at the optimal parsimony levels.*
- *Cluster-based retrievals depend on clustering algorithm and the number of clusters. Cluster-based retrieval outperforms the baseline language modeling in almost all cases, but, generally it is worse than the parsimonious translation model.*
- *Combination of cluster-based retrieval and query expansion is effective in the case that each query expansion and cluster-based retrieval outperforms baseline language modeling. In such case, cluster-based retrieval after query expansion is slightly better than cluster-dependent query expansion.*

And, the following potential conclusions are also derived.

- *For cluster-based retrieval, agglomerative clustering directly using document-to-document similarities are more effective than partitioning clustering such as K-Means based on centroid-to-document similarities*

Cluster-based retrieval in our work considers only two traditional approaches, but, many clustering algorithms such as spectral clustering, information bottleneck method and subspace methods, etc. exist. Thus, we have a plan to investigate cluster-based retrieval according to various clustering algorithms in detail. In addition, we will investigate a theoretical relationship between cluster-based retrieval and query expansion based on our experimental results. Finally, more elegant method to combine cluster-based retrieval and query expansion is remained as a challenging research issue

Acknowledgements

This work was supported by the KOSEF through the Advanced Information Technology Research Center(AITrc) and by the BK21 Project.

References

1. A. Berger and J. Lafferty. Information Retrieval as Statistical Translation. In *Proceedings of 22nd Annual International ACM SIGIR Conference on Research and Development in Information Retrieval*, pages 222-229, 1999
2. J. Gao, J. Nie and G. Wu and G. Cao. Dependence Language Model for Information Retrieval. In *Proceedings of 27nd Annual International ACM SIGIR Conference on Research and Development in Information Retrieval*, pages 170-177, 2004
3. D. Hiemstra, S. Robertson, and H. Zaragoza. Parsimonious Language Models for Information Retrieval. In *Proceedings of 27th Annual International ACM SIGIR Conference on Research and Development in Information Retrieval*, pages 178-185, 2004

4. D. Hiemstra. Term Specific Smoothing for Language Modeling Approach to Information Retrieval: The Importance of a Query Term. In *Proceedings of 25th Annual International ACM SIGIR Conference on Research and Development in Information Retrieval*, pages 35-41, 2002

5. D. Hiemstra. Using Language Models for Information Retrieval. In *PhD Thesis, University of Twente*, 2001

6. T. Hoffman. Unsupervised Learning by Probabilistic Latent Semantic Analysis. *Machine Learning*, 42(1-2), pages 177-196, 2001

7. S. Kamvar, D. Klein, and C. Manning. Interpreting and Extending Classical Agglomerative Clustering Algorithms using a Model-based Approach. In *Proceedings of 19th International Conference on Machine Learning*, pages 283-290, 2002

8. O. Kurland and L. Lee. Corpus Structure, Language Models, and Ad hoc Information Retrieval. In *Proceedings of 27th Annual International ACM SIGIR Conference on Research and Development in Information Retrieval*, pages 194-201, 2004

9. J. Lafferty and C. Zhai. Document Language Models, Query Models, and Risk Minimization for Information Retrieval. In *Proceedings of 24th Annual International ACM SIGIR Conference on Research and Development in Information Retrieval*, pages 111-119, 2001

10. V. Lavrenko, M. Choquette and W. Croft. Cross-Lingual Relevance Model. In *Proceedings of 25th Annual International ACM SIGIR Conference on Research and Development in Information Retrieval*, pages 175-182, 2002

11. V. Lavrenko and B. Croft. Relevance-based Language Models. In *Proceedings of 24th Annual International ACM SIGIR Conference on Research and Development in Information Retrieval*, pages 120-127, 2001

12. X. Liu. Cluster-Based Retrieval Using Language Models. In *Proceedings of 27th Annual International ACM SIGIR Conference on Research and Development in Information Retrieval*, pages 186-193, 2004

13. J. Lee, H. Cho, H. Park. n-Gram-based Indexing for Korean Text Retrieval. *Information Processing & Management*, vol 35(4), pages 427-441, 1999

14. D. Miller and T. Leek and R. Schwartz. A Hidden Markov Model Information Retrieval System. In *Proceedings of 22nd Annual International ACM SIGIR Conference on Research and Development in Information Retrieval*, pages 214-221, 1999

15. S, Na, I. Kang, and S. Kang and J. Lee. Estimation of Query Model from Parsimonious Translation Model. In *Asia Information Retrieval Symposium (AIRS) 2004*, pages 239-250, 2004

16. A. Ponte and J. Croft. A Language Modeling Approach to Information Retrieval. In *Proceedings of 21st Annual International ACM SIGIR Conference on Research and Development in Information Retrieval*, pages 275-281, 1998

17. A. Ponte. A Language Modeling Approach to Information Retrieval. In *PhD thesis, University of Massachusetts*, 1998

18. S. Robertson, and K. Sparck Jones. Relevance Weighting of Search Terms. *Journal of the American Society for Information Science*, 27(3), pages 143-160, 1979

19. F. Song and W. Croft. A General Language Model for Information Retrieval. In *Proceedings of 22nd Annual International ACM SIGIR Conference on Research and Development in Information Retrieval*, pages 279-280, 1999

20. C. Zhai and J. Lafferty. Model-based Feedback in the Language Modeling Approach to Information Retrieval. In *Proceedings of the 10th International Conference on Information and Knowledge Management*, pages 430-410, 2002

21. C. Zhai and J. Lafferty. A Study of Smoothing Methods for Language Models Applied to Ad Hoc Information Retrieval. In *Proceedings of 24th Annual International ACM SIGIR Conference on Research and Development in Information Retrieval*, pages 334-342, 2001

Effective Query Model Estimation Using Parsimonious Translation Model in Language Modeling Approach

Seung-Hoon Na, In-Su Kang, Ji-Eun Roh, and Jong-Hyeok Lee

Division of Electrical and Computer Engineering,
POSTECH, AITrc, Republic of Korea
{nsh1979, dbaisk, jeroh, jhlee}@postech.ac.kr

Abstract. The KL divergence framework, the extended language modeling approach has a critical problem with estimation of query model, which is the probabilistic model that encodes user's information need. At initial retrieval, estimation of query model by *translation model* had been proposed that involves term co-occurrence statistics. However, the translation model has a difficulty to applying, because term co-occurrence statistics must be constructed in offline. Especially in large collection, constructing such large matrix of term co-occurrences statistics prohibitively increases time and space complexity. More seriously, because translation model comprises noisy non-topical terms in documents, reliable retrieval performance cannot be guaranteed. This paper proposes an effective method to construct co-occurrence statistics and eliminate noisy terms by employing *parsimonious translation model*. Parsimonious translation model is a compact version of *translation model* and enables to drastically reduce number of terms that includes non-zero probabilities by eliminating non-topical terms in documents. From experimentations, we show that query model estimated from parsimonious translation model significantly outperforms not only baseline language modeling but also non-parsimonious model.

1 Introduction

In the recent past, the language modeling approach has become popular IR model based on its sound theoretical basis and good empirical success [3], [4], [5], [8], [9], [10], [11], [14], [15], [16], [17], [19], [20], [21], [22], [23]. However, the original language modeling had a trouble with incorporation of the relevance feedback or query expansion. Relevance feedback (or pseudo relevance feedback) is the well-known technique that improves significantly initial retrieval results. In probabilistic model, relevance feedback can be well explained in its framework, while language modeling approach can not. The main reason of this limit is that language modeling does not explicitly assume a relevance document set [15].

Risk minimization framework and query model concept, suggested by Lafferty and Zhai [8], extend the language modeling approach to incorporate relevance feedback or query expansion. In risk minimization framework, language modeling is re-designed by KL(Kullback-Leiber) divergence between query model and document model. Query model is probabilistic version of user's query sample, which encodes knowledge about a user's information need.

G.G. Lee et al. (Eds.): AIRS 2005, LNCS 3689, pp. 288–298, 2005.

Obtaining high initial retrieval performance is very important problem, since post processing such as pseudo relevance feedback is highly dependent on initial retrieval performance. To improve an initial retrieval performance, query expansion based on word co-occurrence can be one of good strategies. In language modeling approach, word co-occurrence was formulated by translation model [1], [8]. First translation model, suggested by Berger and Lafferty, is document-query translation model [1]. And, this model was expanded with Markov Chain Translation Model (MCTM) [8]. Both translation models as expanded language modeling approaches, showed improvements over baseline performance. However, MCTM yields high time complexity. Especially in offline construction, its time complexity is $O(NK)$, where N is number of documents and K is average number of terms in document. More seriously, non-topical terms are left in the model and their selection as expansion terms causes unstable retrieval results, so retrieval performance cannot be guaranteed.

To resolve these problems, we propose to use *Parsimonious Translation Model (PTM)*. It conceptually corresponds to MCTM, but there is a difference in using document language model. In general Markov chain translation model (called original translation model, OTM), document language model is regarded as a mixture model of MLE document model and global collection language model. On the other hand, in PTM, document language model is regarded as is a mixture model of *document specific topic model* and global collection language model. Document specific topic model is obtained by eliminating global common portions and using document topic portions from MLE document model.

The paper is organized as follows. In Section 2 we briefly review KL divergence framework of the language modeling approaches and query model estimation problem. In Section 3 we examine our query model estimation method, including construction method of parsimonious translation model, in more detail. A series of experiments to evaluate our method is presented in Section 4 and Section 5. Finally, Section 6 concludes and points out possible directions for future work.

2 Kullback-Leiber Divergence Framework and Query Model Estimation

2.1 Kullback-Leiber Divergence Framework

Basically, the language modeling approach ranks documents in the collection with the query-likelihood (formula 1) that a given query Q would be observed during repeated random sampling from each document model [3], [4], [13], [19], [23]. [1]

$$p(Q \mid \theta_D) = \prod_w p(w \mid \theta_D)^{c(w;Q)}. \tag{1}$$

where $c(w;Q)$ is the number of term w in a given query, D is a document and $p(w \mid \theta_D)$ is document language model for D.

---

[1] There is some difference between authors about interpretation of a query. [15] treats a query as a set, while [3], [4], [13], [19], [20] interpreted a query as a sequence of words. We adopt the sequence interpretation.

Laffery and Zhai [8], proposed Kullback-Leiber divergence framework for language modeling so that allows modeling of both queries and documents and incorporates relevance feedback or query expansion. The risk between documents and query is defined as follows.

$$Risk(D;Q) \propto -\sum_w p(w \mid \theta_Q) log\ p(w \mid \theta_D). \qquad (2)$$

where $p(w|\theta_Q)$ is query model, and documents are ranked in inverse proportion to its risk.

2.2 Query Model Estimation Problem

Laffery and Zhai [8] suggested Markov chain word translation model, where word translation events occur by random work processes on Markov chain [8], so that training and application costs are significantly reduced without harming performance. In translation model based on this Markov chain, model construction has high time complexity. For given term q, translation model on Markov chain (using one step) is calculated as follows.

$$t(w \mid q) = \sum_D p(w \mid \theta_D) p(\theta_D \mid q). \qquad (3)$$

Translation model $t(w|q)$ means the probability to generate w from document topically related to q. Translation model is mixture model of document models which is weighted by posterior probabilities of documents for given term q. Similar concepts are suggested in relevance model of Lavrenko and Croft [10].

We can rewrite formula (3).

$$t(w \mid q) = \frac{1}{p(q)} \sum_D p(w \mid \theta_D) p(q \mid \theta_D) p(\theta_D). \qquad (4)$$

where $p(w|\theta_D)p(q|\theta_D)$ corresponds to co-occurrence probability in document between two terms q and w.

2.3 Problems of Translation Model

To obtain single translation probability, co- occurrence probabilities must be summed across whole documents. And time complexity for summation is $O(N)$ for given pair w and q, where N is the number of documents. This translation model has two problems. The first problem is its complexity. At retrieval time, it is not practical to calculate translation probability of entire vocabulary for each query term. To make this calculation quickly, a well known strategy is to restrict extraction of term pairs within *local context*: small windows such as few words or phrase level or sentence level [7], [18], [19], [20]. However, *topical context* and local context play different roles in almost all NLP applications, such as word sense disambiguation [7]. Therefore co-occurrence from only local context cannot completely substitute co-occurrence from global context. Essentially, in query expansion problem, 'topically' related terms are more desirable than locally related terms, because topically related terms can encode more correctly user's information need.

The second problem is in retrieval performance. Retrieval performance by the translation model is not guaranteed reliably, because non-topical terms of documents can be extracted for query expansion and react as noise. Once non-topical terms are selected, their negative effects on retrieval performance may be serious. Therefore, a methodology is needed to prevent it from expanding non-topical terms.

In these regards, we propose query expansion by *Parsimonious Translation Model* (PTM). In the model, highly topical terms are first selected in each document and co-occurrence statistics are constructed by only these terms among whole documents, ignoring non-topical terms. New probabilities of highly topical terms in document are modeled by *document specific topic model*, which is a kind of parsimonious language model [3]. In the document specific topic model, there are only few terms having non-zero probabilities. Parsimonious translation model is derived by applying Markov chain process among parsimonious document models.

3 Estimating Query Model from Parsimonious Translation Model

In this section, we describe our method to construct PTM and to estimate query model from it. As mentioned in Section 2, document specific topic model is constructed at first. Next, PTM is acquired from these document specific topic models. Pseudo query model is calculated from this translation model. It is more elaborated by applying refinement process. In addition, we also argue that PTM can be effectively used in constructing two-dimensional features such as bi-gram and tri-gram.

3.1 Estimating Document Specific Topic Model

As noted in Section 2, document language models are constructed by mixing MLE document language model and global collection language model. MLE for document is far from document specific model because it contains global common words. To construct document specific topic model, we assume that documents are generated from mixture model with document specific model and global collection model. For given document D, the likelihood of document is as follows.

$$P(D)=\prod_{w\in D}(\lambda\, p(w\,|\,\theta_D)+(1-\lambda)\, p(w\,|\,\theta_C))$$ (5)

where is $p(w|\theta_D)$ document specific topic model for estimation.

To maximize the document likelihood, we apply EM algorithm [2].

E-step:

$$p[w\in D]=\frac{\lambda\, p(w\,|\,\theta_D)^{(i)}}{\lambda\, p(w\,|\,\theta_D)^{(i)}+(1-\lambda)\, p(w\,|\,\theta_C)}.$$ (6)

M-step:

$$p(w\,|\,\theta_D)^{(i+1)}=\frac{c(w;D)p[w\in D]}{\sum_w c(w;D)p[w\in D]}.$$ (7)

where $p[w \in D]$ is the probability such that given w is document specific term and i indicates the number of EM iterations. As iterations increase, global collection model is not changed and only document specific topic models are iteratively updated. For simplicity, let us denote θ_{D*} to convergent document specific topic model.

Next, selection process is performed, where only highly topical terms are selected, and non-topical terms are discarded. For non-topical terms w, it probability $p(w|\theta_D^s)$ becomes 0. Discarded probability is re-distributed to topical-terms, uniformly. There are two possible techniques to select topical terms. One method is *select_top(k)*, where terms are sorted by $p(w|\theta_D)$, and only top k ranked terms are selected (k is about between 50 and 100). Another method is *select_ratio(P)*, where top terms are selected as much as summation of probabilities of selected terms is below limit probability P (P is about between 0.6 and 0.9). After now, we will further explain with *select_ratio(P)*.

Let us define *parsimonious document language model* θ_D^s consisting of topical terms selected by *select_ratio(P)*. Let D_s be a set of topical terms of the document D selected by *select_ratio(P)*. D_s is a maximal subset of words of document D that satisfies the constraint $\sum_{w \in Ds} p(w|\theta_{D*}) < P$.

$$p\left(w \mid \theta_D^s\right) = \begin{cases} \alpha_D p\left(w \mid \theta_{D*}\right) & \text{if } w \in D_s \\ 0 & \text{otherwise} \end{cases} \tag{8}$$

where α_D is a normalization factor with value $1/\sum_{w \in Ds} p(w|\theta_{D*})$.

3.2 Parsimonious Translation Model

As mentioned in Section 2, translation probability $t(w|q)$ is the probability generating w in the document that includes given term q. Since word translation model is mixture model of different document models, it is one of document language model. As substituting document language model of formula (4) into summation of document specific model and global collection model, we further derive translation model.

$$t(w \mid q) = \frac{1}{p(q)} \left(\begin{matrix} \eta^2 \sum_D p(w \mid \theta_D^s) p(q \mid \theta_D^s) p(\theta_D) + \eta(1-\eta) \sum_D p(w \mid \theta_D^s) p(q \mid \theta_C) p(\theta_D) + \\ \eta(1-\eta) \sum_D p(w \mid \theta_C) p(q \mid \theta_D^s) p(\theta_D) + (1-\eta)^2 \sum_D p(w \mid \theta_C) p(q \mid \theta_C) p(\theta_D) \end{matrix} \right) \tag{9}$$

where η is a smoothing parameter for mixing document specific model, and collection language model. Conceptually, although η corresponds to the smoothing parameter λ for initial retrieval, we treat η differently to λ.

Translation model consists of three summation parts: Document specific co-occurrence model $\sum p(w|\theta_D^s) p(q|\theta_D^s) p(\theta_D)$, global co-occurrence model $p(w|\theta_C) p(q|\theta_C)$, and term topicality $\sum p(w|\theta_D^s) p(\theta_D)$. PTM $t^s(w|q)$ is defined as model which divides document specific co-occurrence model by global likelihood $p(q)$.

$$t^s(w \mid q) = \frac{1}{p(q)} \sum_D p(w \mid \theta_D^s) p(q \mid \theta_D^s) p(\theta_D). \tag{10}$$

At offline indexing stage, of these quantities, we need to pre-calculate only document specific co-occurrence model $\Sigma p(w|\theta_D^s)p(q|\theta_D^s)p(\theta_D)$. Other quantities can be calculated easily from information of basic language modeling.

When using *select_ratio(P)* method for document specific model, time complexity for constructing co-occurrence information is about $O(P^2N)$. Compared with K, the average number of unique terms in document, P is very small. When P is 0.1, P^2 is 0.01. In this case, reduction ratio of time complexity is about 100 times.

3.3 Estimation of Query Model

Given query terms Q, we can infer query model from translation model as following, similar to [8].

$$p(w|\theta_Q) = \sum_{q \in Q} t(w|q)p(q|\hat{\theta}_Q)$$ (11)

where θ_Q is inferred query model directly from translation model.

Final query model $\theta_{Q'}$ is acquired by mixing MLE query model and above inferred relevance document model using parameter α.

$$p(w|\theta_{Q'}) = \alpha\, p(w|\theta_Q) + (1-\alpha)p(w|\hat{\theta}_Q)$$ (12)

4 Experimentation Setup

Our experimental database consists of two collections for Korean, and five TREC4 data collections for English. Table 1 summarizes the information of total seven data collections. The "# Doc" is the total number of documents, "# D.T." indicates the average number of unique terms of documents and "# Q" is the number of topics and "# R" is the number of relevant documents in each test set.

In Korean documents, it is well known that bi-character (n-Gram) indexing units are highly reliable [12]. Thus the bi-character indexing unit is used in this experimentation. For indexing English documents, the typical preprocessing step is performed, where stop words are removed and then Poster stemming is applied.

Table 1. Collection summaries

Collection	# Doc	# D.T.	# Q	# Term	# R
KT 1.0	1,000	125.9	30	15,772	424
NTCIR3-K	66,147	176.3	30	180,294	3,868
TREC4-AP	158,240	156.6	49	26,8411	3,055
TREC4-SJM	90,257	142	48	259,434	1,297
TREC4-WSJ	74,250	171.6	45	193,398	1,183
TREC4-ZIFF	217,940	90.6	32	578,607	512
TREC4-FR	19,860	124.1	27	98,567	416

For baseline language modeling approach, we use Jelinek smoothing, setting the smoothing parameter λ into 0.25. This smoothing parameter value is acquired empirically, by performing several experimentations across different parameters.

5 Evaluation Results

5.1 Retrieval Effectiveness of Parsimonious Translation Model

Figure 1 shows an average precision for three query models in seven different test collections by changing parsimony level from 0.1 to 1.0. (Results of combining methods will be discussed in Section 3.4). Three query models is like that: baseline language model using MLE of query sample, query model estimated from OTM (formula (3)), and query model estimated from PTM (formula (8)). Interpolation parameter α is fixed at 0.1 which was well performed in all test collections. And smoothing parameter η is fixed at 1.0 because of full parsimony.

As shown in Figure 1, in almost all parsimony levels, PTM significantly improves baseline in six data collections. Remarkably, performance of PTM is better than performance of OTM at low parsimony level. In OTM, some noise can occur because common words of query can be expanded by common terms of document. Therefore, compared with baseline, high accuracy of PTM implies that PTM can effectively eliminate noise of term expansion in OTM, and select good expansion terms in terms of retrieval performance.

Concerning optimal parsimony level, while for Korean collection optimal parsimony level is 0.1, for English test collection optimal parsimony level is between 0.2 and 0.4. However, performance in TREC4-FR test collection is relatively exceptional. As shown in Figure 1, PTM does not good in parsimony levels not in 0.2~0.4 but in 0.6 ~0.8. It seems that in TREC4-FR good expansion terms have relatively small probabilities value. In Section 5.2, the reason will be discussed in detail.

Table 2 summarizes the best performance of parsimonious models (PTM*) and OTM in seven different test collections. The last column with symbol "%chg" indicates improvement ratio of PTM* over OTM. P* is the parsimony level at the best. From this table, we know that PTM highly improves baseline from 5% to 25%, and especially 25.55% improvement is achieved at TREC4-ZIFF test collection.

From these experiments, we can conclude that PTM highly improves retrieval performance at the optimal parsimony levels.

5.2 Storage Size of Parsimonious Translation Model

Table 3 shows the storage size of PTM across various parsimony levels (0.1 ~ 0.6 and 1.0) and the reduction ratio of the size to OTM. Here, there are two numbers in one cell; numbers in top are storage size, and numbers of in bottom is the ratio of the size to OTM. Bold numbers express the best performance in each collection. In Korean test sets, reduction ratio of size at optimal parsimony level is lower than 1%. In English test sets, reduction ratios of size at optimal parsimony level vary from 0.75% at TREC4-ZIFF to 13.14% at TREC4-AP. At this time, exceptional phenomenon of optimal parsimony level in TREC4-FR can be interpreted in terms of the size reduction, since degree of size reduction is slowly increased according to parsimony level. It requires parsimony level of 0.6 to achieve size reduction of about 10%.

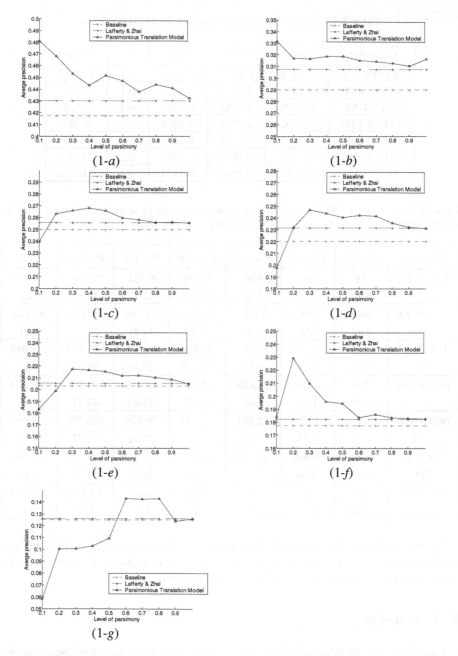

Fig. 1. Performance of OTM, PTM and baseline language model in seven test collections. KTSET 1.0 : (1-a), NTCIR3-K: (1-b), TREC4 AP: (1-c), TREC4-SJM: (1-d),TREC4-WSJ: (1-e), TREC4-ZIFF: (1-f), TREC4-FR: (1-g)

Table 2. Comparison of performance between OTM and PTM

Collection	Baseline	OTM	PTM*	P*	%chg
KTSET 1.0	0.4174	0.4302	0.4809	0.1	11.79%
NTCIR3-KK	0.2899	0.3076	0.3315	0.1	7.7%
TREC4-AP	0.2499	0.2558	0.2685	0.4	4.96%
TREC4-SJM	0.2202	0.2313	0.2468	0.3	6.70%
TREC4-WSJ	0.2031	0.2054	0.2175	0.3	5.89%
TREC4-ZIFF	0.1774	0.1824	0.2290	0.2	25.55%
TREC4-FR	0.1250	0.1260	0.1434	0.6	13.81%

Table 3. Storage size of PTM across various parsimony levels in seven collections (Unit: KB) and the reduction ratio of the size to OTM (Unit: %)

Collection	$P = 0.1$	$P = 0.2$	$P = 0.3$	$P = 0.4$	$P = 0.5$	$P = 0.6$	$P = 1.0$
KTSET 1.0	**48**	360	896	1,676	8,324	9,956	12,176
	0.39	2.95	7.36	13.76	24.47	40.30	100
NTCIR3-KK	600	2,880	7,692	16,756	33,236	50,416	95,348
	0.63	3.02	8.07	17.57	34.86	52.88	100
TREC4-AP	1,000	5,732	16,680	**35,724**	74,668	125,684	271,940
	0.37	2.11	6.13	**13.14**	27.46	46.22	100
TREC4-SJM	796	4,688	**13,680**	31,056	65,296	107,376	252,804
	0.31	1.85	**5.41**	12.28	25.83	42.47	100
TREC4-WSJ	800	4,352	**12,392**	27,792	56,876	102,396	248,096
	0.32	1.75	**5.00**	11.20	22.92	41.27	100
TREC4-ZIFF	616	**3,660**	10,528	24,676	52,932	103,208	182,544
	0.12	**0.76**	2.18	5.11	10.97	21.39	100
TREC4-FR	120	740	1,848	3,720	6,644	**11,180**	140,464
	0.085	0.53	1.32	2.65	4.73	**7.96**	100

From Table 3, we can see that PTM remarkably reduce space complexity. This also implies that PTM reduces time complexity, because in constructing co-occurrence statistics time complexity is proportional to space complexity

6 Conclusion

Summing up, we propose effective construction method for co-occurrence statistics using parsimonious translation model. Parsimonious translation model involves an elegant method for selecting highly topical terms in documents, by document specific topic model. Basically, our idea is to use the several states of art methods in language modeling approach for information retrieval. From our experimentation on two different collections, Parsimonious translation model not only drastically reduces time- and space-complexity but also highly improves retrieval performance at the optimal parsimony levels.

Acknowledgements

This work was supported by the KOSEF through the Advanced Information Technology Research Center(AITrc) and by the BK21 Project.

References

1. Berger, A. and Lafferty, J. Information Retrieval as Statistical Translation. In *Proceedings of 22nd Annual International ACM SIGIR Conference on Research and Development in Information Retrieval*, pages 222-229, 1999
2. Dempster, A. Maximum Likelihood from Incomplete Data via the EM algorithm. In *Journal of Royal Statistical Society*, vol. 39, no. 1, pages 1-39, 1977
3. Hiemstra, D. Robertson, S. and Zaragoza, H. Parsimonious Language Models for Information Retrieval. In *Proceedings of 27th Annual International ACM SIGIR Conference on Research and Development in Information Retrieval*, pages 178-185, 2004
4. Hiemstra, D. Term Specific Smoothing for Language Modeling Approach to Information Retrieval: The Importance of a Query Term. In *Proceedings of 25th Annual International ACM SIGIR Conference on Research and Development in Information Retrieval*, pages 35-41, 2002
5. Hiemstra, D. Using Language Models for Information Retrieval. In *PhD Thesis, University of Twente*, 2001
6. Hofmann, T. Unsupervised Learning by Probabilistic Latent Semantic Analysis. *Machine Learning*, vol 42(1-2), pages 177-196, 2001
7. Ide, N. and Veronis, J. Introduction to the Special Issue on Word Sense Disambiguation: The State of the Art. *Computational Linguistics*, vol 24(1), pages 1-40, 1998
8. Lafferty, J. and Zhai, C. Document Language Models, Query Models, and Risk Minimization for Information Retrieval. In *Proceedings of 24th Annual International ACM SIGIR Conference on Research and Development in Information Retrieval*, pages 111-119, 2001
9. Lavrenko, V., Choquette, M. and Croft, W. Cross-Lingual Relevance Model. In *Proceedings of 25th Annual International ACM SIGIR Conference on Research and Development in Information Retrieval*, pages 175-182, 2002
10. Lavrenko, V. and Croft, B. Relevance-based Language Models. In *Proceedings of 24th Annual International ACM SIGIR Conference on Research and Development in Information Retrieval*, pages 120-127, 2001
11. Liu, X. Cluster-Based Retrieval Using Language Models. In *Proceedings of 27th Annual International ACM SIGIR Conference on Research and Development in Information Retrieval*, pages 186-193, 2004
12. Lee, J., Cho, H., and Park, H. n-Gram-based Indexing for Korean Text Retrieval. *Information Processing & Management*, vol 35(4), pages 427-441, 1999
13. Miller, D., Leek T. and Schwartz, R. A Hidden Markov Model Information Retrieval System. In *Proceedings of 22nd Annual International ACM SIGIR Conference on Research and Development in Information Retrieval*, pages 214-221, 1999

14. Nallapati, R. and Allen, J. Capturing Term Dependencies using a Language Model based on Sentence Trees. In *Proceedings of the 10th International Conference on Information and Knowledge Management*, pages 383-390, 2002
15. Ponte, A. and Croft, J. A Language Modeling Approach to Information Retrieval. In *Proceedings of 21st Annual International ACM SIGIR Conference on Research and Development in Information Retrieval*, pages 275-281, 1998
16. Ponte, A. A Language Modeling Approach to Information Retrieval. In *PhD thesis, University of Massachusetts*, 1998
17. Robertson, S. and Hiemstra, D. Language Models and Probability of Relevance. In *Proceedings of the Workshop on Language Modeling and Information Retrieval*, 2001
18. Sperer, R. and Oard, D. Structured Translation for Cross-Language Information Retrieval. In *Proceedings of 23rd Annual International ACM SIGIR Conference on Research and Development in Information Retrieval*, pages 120-127, 2000
19. Song, F. and Croft, W. A General Language Model for Information Retrieval. In *Proceedings of 22nd Annual International ACM SIGIR Conference on Research and Development in Information Retrieval*, pages 279-280, 1999
20. Srikanth, M. and Srihari, R. Biterm Language Models for Document Retrieval. In *Proceedings of 25th Annual International ACM SIGIR Conference on Research and Development in Information Retrieval*, pages 425-426, 2002
21. Zaragoza, H. and Hiemstra, D. Bayesian Extension to the Language Model for Ad Hoc Information Retrieval", In *Proceedings of 26th Annual International ACM SIGIR Conference on Research and Development in Information Retrieval*, pages 4-9, 2003
22. Zhai, C. and Lafferty, J. Model-based Feedback in the Language Modeling Approach to Information Retrieval. In *Proceedings of the 10th International Conference on Information and Knowledge Management*, pages 430-410, 2002
23. Zhai, C. and Lafferty, J. A Study of Smoothing Methods for Language Models Applied to Ad Hoc Information Retrieval. In *Proceedings of 24th Annual International ACM SIGIR Conference on Research and Development in Information Retrieval*, pages 334-342, 2001

Chinese Document Re-ranking Based on
Term Distribution and Maximal Marginal Relevance

Lingpeng Yang, Donghong Ji, and Munkew Leong

Institute for Infocomm Research,
21 Heng Mui Keng Terrace, Singapore 119613
{lpyang, dhji, mkleong}@i2r.a-star.edu.sg

Abstract. In this paper, we propose a document re-ranking method for Chinese information retrieval where a query is a short natural language description. The method bases on term distribution where each term is weighted by its local and global distribution, including document frequency, document position and term length. The weight scheme lifts off the worry that very fewer relevant documents appear in top retrieved documents, and allows randomly setting a larger portion of the retrieved documents as relevance feedback. It also helps to improve the performance of MMR model in document re-ranking. The experiments show our method can get significant improvement against standard baselines, and outperforms relevant methods consistently.

1 Introduction

How to further improve the rankings of the relevant documents after an initial search has been extensively studied in information retrieval. Such studies include two main streams: automatic query expansion and automatic document re-ranking. While the assumption behind automatic query expansion is that the high ranked documents are likely to be relevant so that the terms in these documents can be used to augment the original query to a more accurate one, document re-ranking is a method to improve the rankings by re-ordering the position of initial retrieved documents without doing a second search. After document re-ranking, it's expected that more relevant documents appear in higher rankings, from which automatic query expansion can benefit.

Many methods have been proposed to re-rank retrieved documents. Lee et al. proposes a document re-ranking method based on document clusters [6]. They build a hierarchical cluster structure for the whole document set, and use the structure to re-rank the documents. Balinski J. et al. proposes a document re-ranking method that uses the distances between documents for modifying initial relevance weights [1]. Luk et al. uses the title information of documents to re-rank documents [7], while Crouch et al. uses the un-stemmed words in queries to re-order documents [3]. Xu et al. makes use of global and local information to do local context analysis and then use the information acquired to re-rank documents [12, 13]. Qu et al. uses manually built thesaurus to re-rank retrieved documents [10], and each term in a query topic is expanded with a group of terms in the thesaurus. Bear et al. uses manually crafted grammars for topics to re-order documents by matching grammar rules in some segment in articles [2]. Kamps proposes a re-ranking method based on assigned

G.G. Lee et al. (Eds.): AIRS 2005, LNCS 3689, pp. 299–311, 2005.
© Springer-Verlag Berlin Heidelberg 2005

controlled vocabularies [4]. Yang et al. [14, 15] use query terms which occur in both query and top N ($N<=30$) retrieved documents to re-rank documents.

One problem in automatic document re-ranking (also for query expansion) is how many top documents are regarded as relevance feedback in the first retrieval results, which is also faced by most methods mentioned above [3, 4, 6, 7, 14, 15]. Usually, a pre-defined smaller number of the documents (say top 10 to 30) are considered. However, in the cases that very few relevant documents fall within the range, the method will fail. On the other hand, if a larger scope (say 500, 1000) is considered, many irrelevant documents will come inside, and the noisy terms will dominate.

Another problem is that most methods mentioned above don't consider correlation between query terms. Mitra et al. [8] uses Maximal Marginal Relevance (MMR) to adjust the contribution of relevant terms. They argue that usually a document covering more aspects of a query should get higher score, which can be captured somehow by word correlation. The new score for a document is computed by summing the *idf* (inverse document frequency) of each query word where each word is normalized by correlation probability based on a large number of retrieved documents (say top 1000 documents). It's reported that their method achieves better result in re-ranking top 50 to 100 documents. But we find that within top initially retrieved documents, some really relevant terms do appear in larger portion of the documents, which will be unexpectedly assigned lower scores by *idf* scheme.

In this paper, we propose a new term weighting scheme to deal with the two problems mentioned above. First, we consider document rankings, i.e., document positions in the ranking list, in the weighting scheme of the terms. Intuitively, a term gets a lower document frequency when occurring in a lower-ranking document, and a higher document frequency when occurring in a higher-ranking document (in contrast, the usual way for document frequency is that a document gets 1 count no matter where the document is located in the list). In this way, we can randomly choose a larger number of the documents as relevance feedback, without any worry about the irrelevant documents inside. Furthermore, we don't need to worry about the cases that top documents only contain very few relevant documents, since we can randomly set a larger scope as relevance feedback.

Second, the weighting scheme incorporates both local (feedback) and global distribution of the terms, and we use it to replace the *idf* scheme in MMR. If a term occurs in feedback documents more frequently than in the whole collection, it tends to have more contribution to document re-ranking; otherwise, it will be a noise.

Our method doesn't use word but uses the key terms extracted from queries and top retrieved documents. One motivation of this choice is that terms (including multi-word units) usually contain more complete information than individual words, and have more potential for improving the performance of information retrieval. Another motivation of this method is specifically for Chinese language information retrieval, where a word segmentation module is usually needed, which, however, generally requires some manual resources and suffers from the problem of portability. An automatic term extraction module could be a good alternative.

The rest of this paper is organized as the following. In section 2, we describe key term extraction from documents. In section 3, we talk about term weighting. In section 4, we specify how to re-rank the documents based on the key terms and their weighting together with MMR based on term correlation. In section 5, we evaluate the method on NTCIR3 CLIR dataset and give some analysis. In section 6, we present the conclusion and future work.

2 Term Extraction

Term extraction concerns the problem of what is a term. Intuitively, key terms in a document are some word strings which are conceptually prominent in the document and play main roles in discriminating the document from other documents.

We use a seeding-and-expansion mechanism to extract key terms from documents. The procedure of term extraction consists of two phases, seed positioning and term determination. Intuitively, a seed for a candidate term is an individual word (or a Chinese character in the case of Chinese language, henceafter, we focus on Chinese language), seed positioning is to locate the rough position of a term in the text, while term determination is to figure out which string covering the seed in the position forms a term.

To determine a seed needs to weigh individual Chinese characters to reflect their significance in the text. We make use of a very large corpus r (LDC's Mandarin Chinese News Text) as a reference corpus. Suppose d is a document, c is an individual Chinese Character in the text, let $P_r(c)$ and $P_d(c)$ be the probability of c occurring in r and d respectively, we adopt relative probability or salience of c in d with respect to r [11], as the criteria for evaluation of seeds.

$$P_d(c) / P_r(c) \qquad (1)$$

We call c a *seed* if $P_d(c) / P_r(c) \geq \delta$ (δ=1). That is, its probability occurring in document must be equal with or higher than its average probability in the reference corpus.

Although it is difficult to give out the definition of terms, we have the following definition about a key term in a document.

   i. A term contains at least one seed.
   ii. A term occurs at least L (L>1) times in the document.
  iii. A maximal word string meeting i) and ii) is a term.
  iv. For a term, a real maximal substring meeting i) and ii) without considering their occurrence in all those terms containing the sub-string is also a term.

Here a maximal word string meeting i) and ii) refers to a word string meeting i) and ii) while no other longer word strings containing it meet i) and ii). A real maximal substring meeting i) and ii) refer to a real substring meeting i) and ii) while no other longer real substrings containing it meet i) and ii).

The above assumptions tell us a term is an independent maximal string which must contain a seed and occur at least 2 times in a document. For example, given a document d, suppose a Chinese character 博 (bo3) is a seed in d, 故宫博物院 (National Palace Museum) occurs 3 times in d, 博物院 (Museum) occurs 5 times in d, if we set the parameter L as 2, then both string 故宫博物院 (National Palace Museum) and 博物院 (Museum) are terms in d; but if we set the parameter L as 3, then 故宫博物院 (National Palace Museum) is term in d, but 博物院 (Museum) is not a term in *d* because its independent occurrence is 2 (excluding 3 occurrences as a sub-string in 故宫博物院 (National Palace Museum)).

3 Query Term Weighting Based on Term Distribution

To re-rank retrieved documents, we use the key terms in the documents, and suppose that these key terms will contribute to the re-rankings. Here, we only focus on the terms which also occur in the queries, which means that we don't use any query expansion. So, the terms can also be referred to as query terms. To weigh a query term, we consider the following three factors.

i) Relative distribution: the ratio of document frequency of a term in the top *K* retrieved document against the document frequency of the term in the whole document collection.

Intuitively, the more frequently a term occurs in the *K* documents relative with the whole collection, the more important the term tends to be.

ii) Term length: the number of Chinese characters a term contains.

Intuitively, the longer a term is, the more contribution to the precision the term may have.

iii) Document ranking position: the serial number of a document in top *K* documents.

Intuitively, the higher ranking a document is, the more important the terms in it tend to be.

Given top *K* retrieved documents and query term *t*, the weight assigned to *t* is given by the following formula.

$$\sqrt{\frac{(\sum_{i=1}^{K} df\ (t,d_i) \times f\ (i))/K}{DF\ (t,C)/R}} \times \sqrt{|\ t\ |} \tag{2}$$

$$df\ (t,d_i) = \begin{cases} 1 & t \in d_i \\ 0 & t \notin d_i \end{cases} \tag{3}$$

where d_i is the *i-th* (*i=1, ..., K*) document, *R* is the total number of documents in the whole collection *C*, *DF(t,C)* is the number of documents which contain *t* in *C*, |*t*| is the length of term *t*, *f(i)* is the document frequency weighting given to d_i. Table 1 lists 6 document frequency weighting schemes used in our experiments.

Table 1. Document Frequency Weighting

Scheme Name	Scheme Definition	Scheme Name	Scheme Definition
W4	f(i) = 1/sqrt(i)	W7	f(i) = 1
W5	f(i) = 1+1/sqrt(i)	W8	f(i)= 1/i
W6	f(i) = 1/(1+log(i))	W9	f(i) = 1+1/i

4 Document Re-ranking

In the re-ranking phase, we consider queries with multiple aspects or concepts. To prevent from query drift, we prefer a document that matches the query on multiple independently concepts. In other words, we need to distinguish multiple query-document matches: matches on query terms related to the same aspect, or matches on query terms from different aspects of the query. Thus, a match on two independent query concepts should be considered more useful than a match on two strongly related query terms.

We use term correlation to measure the relatedness or independence of query terms and use MMR criteria to reduce redundancy of query terms while maintaining query relevance in re-ranking retrieved documents.

To estimate the relatedness or independence of query terms, we study their co-occurrence patterns in top K initially retrieved documents. If two query terms are correlated, then they are expected to occur together in many of these documents. Given the presence of one of the query terms in a document, the chance of the other occurring within the same document is likely to be relatively high. On the other hand, if two query terms deal with independent concepts, the occurrences of the query terms should not be strongly correlated. Given query term t_j, top K retrieved documents as document set S, we define the correlation in S between query term t_i and t_j regarding t_j as $P(t_i \mid t_j)$:

$$P(t_i \mid t_j) = \frac{\text{number of documents in S containing query term } t_i \text{ and } t_j}{\text{number of documents in S containing query term } t_j} \qquad (4)$$

To re-rank each document d in top M ($M <= K$) retrieved documents, we first find out the query terms which occur in d, then we consider the matching query terms in decreasing order of query term weight. The first matching query term contributes its full weigh to $Weight_{new}$. The contribution of any subsequent match is deprecated on how strongly this match was predicted by a previous match – if a matching query term is highly correlated to a previous match, the contribution of the new match is proportionally down-weighted. Finally, we use $Weight_{new}$ and the initial similarity between d and query q to calculate a new ranking score and then use the new ranking score to re-order the M documents. More precisely, if $\{t_1, ..., t_m\}$ is the set of query terms presented in document d (ordered by decreasing query term weight), then $Weight_{new}$ and $Score_{new}$ are given by:

$$Weight_{new} = w(t_1) + \sum_{i=2}^{m} w(t_i) \times \min_{j=1}^{i-1} (1 - P(t_i \mid t_j)) \qquad (5)$$

$$Score_{new} = (1 + Weight_{new}) \times Sim_{old} \qquad (6)$$

where Sim_{old} is the original similarity value between document d and query q in initial retrieval, $w(t_i)$ is the weight of query term t_i.

The top M retrieved documents are re-ordered by their new ranking score $Score_{new}$. Figure 1 gives out the pseudo code of the procedure of document re-ordering for query q and top M retrieved documents.

Given q is a query, K is the number of top initial retrieved documents from which to collect term correlation and query term weighting, and M ($M<=K$) is the number of retrieved documents to be re-ordered in initial retrieval.

Step 1: Acquiring query terms in q and their weights;

    1.1. Extract terms from each document d in top K retrieved documents; in practice, term extraction from each document is done only once and this process can be considered as a part of indexing.

    1.2. Collect terms that occur in q and calculate their weights by formula (2) and (3);

Step 2: Acquiring query term correlation from top K retrieved documents;

    Calculate query term correlation by equation (4);

Step 3: Re-order top M documents;

    3.1 For each document d_i in the M documents, calculate its new ranking value $Score_i$ by (5) and (6);

    3.2 Re-order top M retrieved documents by $\{Score_1, ..., Score_M\}$.

Fig. 1. The Procedure of Document Re-Ranking

5   Experiments and Evaluation

We use NTCIR3 CLIR dataset as our test dataset to re-rank top 1000 retrieved documents. The dataset contains Chinese document set CIRB011 (132,173 documents) and CIRB20 (249,508 documents). We use the officially released 42 Chinese-Chinese D-run query topics in NTCIR3 CLIR as query topics where each query is a short description of a topic by Chinese language.

Chinese sentence is a contiguous Chinese character sequence without space between Chinese words. Chinese Character, bi-gram, n-gram (n>2) and word are the most widely used indexing units in Chinese information retrieval. The comparison between the three kinds of indexing units (single Characters, bi-grams and short-words) is given in [5]. It shows that single character indexing is good but not sufficiently competitive, while bi-gram indexing works surprisingly well and it's as good as short-word indexing in precision. [9] suggests that word indexing and bi-gram indexing can achieve comparable performance but if we consider the time and space factors, it is preferable to use words (and characters) as indexes.

In our experiments, for initial retrieval, we use bi-gram as index unit. We use vector space model as retrieval model. The initial retrieval result is used as baseline.

We use NTCIR3's relax relevance judgment and rigid relevance judgment to measure the precision of retrieved documents. Relax relevance judgment considers highly relevant, relevant and partially relevant documents, while rigid relevance judgment only considers highly relevant and relevant documents. We use PreAt10 and PreAt100 to represent the precision of top 10 retrieved documents and top 100 retrieved documents respectively, and use (relax) and (rigid) to represent relax and rigid relevance judgment respectively.

In the vector space model, each document or query is represented as a vector in vector space where each dimension of the vector is a bi-gram. The weight of bi-gram b in document d is given by the following tf•idf weighting scheme:

$$w(b, d) = \log(T(b, d)+1) * \log(R/D(b)+1) \tag{7}$$

where, $w(b, d)$ is the weight given to b in d, $T(b, d)$ is the frequency of b in d, R is the number of documents in document set, $D(b)$ is the number of documents in document set which contain b.

The weight of bi-gram b in query q, $w(b, q)$, is given by the following weight scheme:

$$w(b, q) = T(b, q) \tag{8}$$

where $T(b, q)$ is the frequency of b in q.

We'll do two kinds of experiments. The first focuses on the performance with various parameter settings for term extraction and various document frequency weighting schemes. The second focuses on the comparison between the performance of our method and that of other methods.

5.1 Comparison on Different Parameter Setting

Regarding term quality, there are two parameters (δ and L) in our term extraction method, and the following is the parameter setting in our experiments:

$$\delta = 1, 10; \quad L = 2, 3, 4.$$

For document frequency weighting scheme, we test the six weighting schemes listed at Table 1.

The comparison of precisions at different parameters settings is given at Table 2-4. In Table 2-4, [PreAt10(relax)] and [PreAt10(rigid)] represent the average precision of 42 topics on PreAt10 relax and rigid relevance judgment respectively. [PreAt100(relax)] and [PreAt100(rigid)] represent the average precision of 42 topics on PreAt100 relax and rigid relevance judgment respectively. Each item in table represents the precision and its improvement over the baseline [INI] with the conditions expressed by [Column] and [Row].

Table 2. Statistics on (δ=1 or 10, L=2)

	PreAt10(relax)		PreAt10(rigid)		PreAt100(relax)		PreAt100(rigid)	
	δ=1	δ=10	δ=1	δ=10	δ=1	δ=10	δ=1	δ=10
INI	0.3619	0.3619	0.2595	0.2595	0.1886	0.1886	0.1279	0.1279
W4	0.4381	0.4405	0.3214	0.3167	0.2152	0.216	0.1469	0.1469
	+21.1%	+21.7%	+23.9%	+22%	+14.1%	+14.5%	+14.9%	+14.9%
W5	0.4524	0.4571	0.3286	0.3310	0.2136	0.2174	0.1448	0.1469
	+25%	+26.3%	+26.6%	+27.5%	+13.3%	+15.3%	+13.2%	+14.9%
W6	0.4476	0.4595	0.3262	0.3333	0.2148	0.2169	0.146	0.1474
	+23.7%	+27%	+25.7%	+28.4%	+13.9%	+15%	+14.2%	+15.3%
W7	0.4571	0.4595	0.3310	0.3333	0.2129	0.2174	0.1443	0.1471
	+26.3%	+27%	+27.5%	+28.4%	+12.9%	+15.3%	+12.8%	+15%
W8	0.4310	0.4286	0.3167	0.3119	0.2155	0.2155	0.1474	0.1481
	+19.1%	+18.4%	+22%	+20.2%	+14.3%	+14.3%	+15.3%	+15.8%
W9	0.4548	0.4571	0.3286	0.3310	0.2129	0.2169	0.1443	0.1469
	+25.7%	+26.3%	+26.6%	+27.5%	+12.9%	+15%	+12.8%	+14.9%

Table 3. Statistics on (δ=1 or 10, L=3)

	PreAt10(relax)		PreAt10(rigid)		PreAt100(relax)		PreAt100(rigid)	
	δ=1	δ=10	δ=1	δ=10	δ=1	δ=10	δ=1	δ=10
INI	0.3619	0.3619	0.2595	0.2595	0.1886	0.1886	0.1279	0.1279
W4	0.4595	0.4548	0.3310	0.3262	0.2224	0.2233	0.1514	0.1521
	+27%	+25.7%	+27.5%	+25.7%	+17.9%	+18.4%	+18.4%	+19%
W5	0.4690	0.4667	0.3429	0.3357	0.22	0.2221	0.1507	0.1514
	+29.6%	+28.9%	+32.1%	+29.4%	+16.7%	+17.8%	+17.9%	+18.4%
W6	0.4667	0.4595	0.3381	0.3262	0.2202	0.2214	0.1507	0.1510
	+28.9%	+27%	+30.3%	+25.7%	+16.8%	+17.4%	+17.9%	+18.1%
W7	0.4595	0.4643	0.3357	0.3333	0.2193	0.2219	0.1502	0.1514
	+27%	+28.3%	+29.4%	+28.4%	+16.3%	+17.7%	+17.5%	+18.4%
W8	0.4476	0.4429	0.3262	0.3214	0.2176	0.2193	0.1488	0.1493
	+23.7%	+22.4%	+25.7%	+23.9%	+15.4%	+16.3%	+16.4%	+16.8%
W9	0.4667	0.4643	0.3429	0.3333	0.2195	0.2221	0.1502	0.1514
	+28.9%	+28.3%	+32.1%	+28.4%	+16.4%	+17.8%	+17.5%	+18.4%

Table 4. Statistics on (δ=1 or 10, L=4)

	PreAt10(relax)		PreAt10(rigid)		PreAt100(relax)		PreAt100(rigid)	
	δ=1	δ=10	δ=1	δ=10	δ=1	δ=10	δ=1	δ=10
INI	0.3619	0.3619	0.2595	0.2595	0.1886	0.1886	0.1279	0.1279
W4	0.4548	0.4595	0.3333	0.3357	0.2252	0.2293	0.1536	0.1555
	+25.7%	+27%	+28.4%	+29.4%	+19.4%	+21.6%	+20.1%	+21.6%
W5	0.4619	0.4595	0.3381	0.3333	0.2226	0.2298	0.1536	0.1557
	+27.6%	+27%	+30.3%	+28.4%	+18.1%	+21.8%	+20.1%	+21.8%
W6	0.4524	0.4571	0.3310	0.3310	0.2238	0.2283	0.1531	0.1548
	+25%	+26.3%	+27.5%	+27.5%	+18.7%	+21.1%	+19.7%	+21%
W7	0.4595	0.4619	0.3333	0.3357	0.2217	0.2298	0.1536	0.1557
	+27%	+27.6%	+28.4%	+29.4%	+17.6%	+21.8%	+20.1%	+21.8%
W8	0.4405	0.4405	0.3190	0.3190	0.225	0.2255	0.1536	0.1536
	+21.7%	+21.7%	+22.9%	+22.9%	+19.3%	+19.6%	+20.1%	+20.1%
W9	0.4619	0.4595	0.3357	0.3333	0.2224	0.2295	0.1538	0.156
	+27.6%	+27%	+29.4%	+28.4%	+17.9%	+21.7%	+20.3%	+22%

From Table 2-4, we see that the method achieves significant improvement against [INI] in every parameter setting.

If only considering the effectiveness of term frequency to document re-ranking, (L=3) or (L=4) produce better results. If only considering the effectiveness of document frequency weighting schemes to document re-ranking, W5, W7 and W9 produce better results.

If considering both term frequency and document frequency weighting, the parameter setting (L=3 or L=4, W5, W7 or W9) produces better results. Under such parameter settings, our method achieves 27%-28.9% improvement for PreAt10(relax), 28.4%-32.1% improvement for PreAt10(rigid), 15.9%-18.8% improvement for PreAt100(relax) and 16.3%-21.8% improvement for PreAt100(rigid).

To explore the co-effects of the two parameters (L, δ) on the precision, we fix one parameter and see how the precision changes with the other.

One setting is that we fix L as 2, 3 or 4 and with δ changing from 1 to 10. One finding is that the precision improves or keeps the same in most cases, while decreases in fewer cases. The reason is that the terms with lower salience seeds tend to be noises, and removing the noises leads to improvement of the precision. However, not all relevant terms do hold higher salience seeds, in addition, some documents, although containing good terms, but they are not relevant (due to different focus). However, this chance is rare, so in fewer cases, we can see that the precision decreases. Another finding is that for both PreAt100(relax) and PreAt100(rigid), most precision improves with δ changing from 1 to 10, while for PreAt10(relax) and PreAt10(rigid), less improves. The reason may be that for top 10 documents, the terms with higher salience seeds may take decisive shares in deciding on the ranking positions of the documents, so with δ increasing, the precision doesn't improve obviously, although some noisy terms are removed.

Another setting is that we fix δ as 1 or 10 and with L changing from 2 to 3. It demonstrates that whether δ=1 or 10, all the precision improves when L increases to 3 from 2. This means that when L=2, there may be too many noisy terms, and when L=3, some noisy terms can be removed. That's why all the precision improves.

Another setting is that we fix δ as 1 or 10 and with L changing from 3 to 4. It demonstrates that for top 100 documents, the precision improves universally, while for top 10 documents, it doesn't. The reason may be that for top 10 documents, some terms with L=3 have contribution to the document ranking, with L changing from 3 to 4, they are removed. While for top 100 documents, the terms with L=4 may have decisive shares in deciding on the document ranking positions, as L increases from 3 to 4, some terms (L=3) are removed, and some relevant documents with those terms recede behind the top 100 documents, but more documents containing terms with (L=4) will move forward.

Regarding the effect of document ranking positions, it is noticed that with scheme W5, W7 or W9, it tends to get higher performance, while with scheme W8, it tends to get lower performance. The reason is that not all documents with top ranking are relevant in most cases. In particular, for the first retrieval, among the top 10 documents, there are only 3.6 relevant documents in average, while among the top 100 documents, there are 18.9 relevant documents in average. This means that many relevant documents are located outside the top 10, but within the top 100 in the first retrieval. With W5, W9 and W7, the terms in these documents get higher weights, and then the documents tend to move forward during the re-ranking process. On the contrary, with W8, the weights of the terms decrease dramatically as the rank goes down, and the terms in lower ranking documents get very lower weights. So the relevant documents containing the terms cannot move forward during the re-ranking.

5.2   Comparison with Other Document Re-ranking Methods

We first compare our method with Mitra et al. [8]'s method. Mitra et al. [8] uses term correlation to re-order retrieved documents. If $\{w_1, ..., w_m\}$ is the set of query words presented in document d (ordered by decreasing idf), then the new ranking score between q and d is calculated by following formula:

$$Sim_{new} = idf(w_1) + \sum_{i=2}^{m} idf(w_i) \times \min_{j=1}^{i-1}(1 - P(w_i \mid w_j)) \tag{9}$$

where $idf(w_i)$ is the inverse document frequency of word w_i in retrieved documents to be re-ranked, $P(w_i \mid w_j)$ is the word correlation between w_i and w_j in top K retrieved documents calculated by the same formula (4).

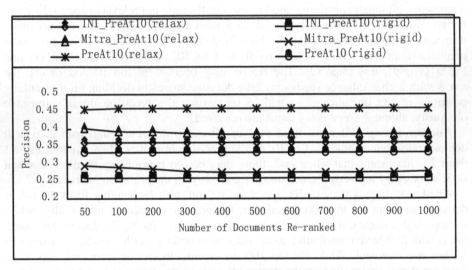

Fig. 2. Comparison at PreAt10

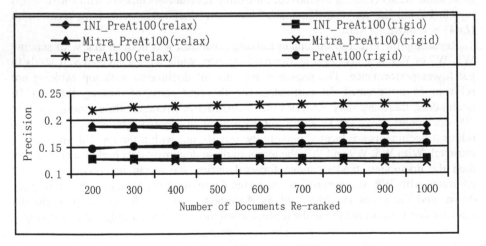

Fig. 3. Comparison at PreAt100

Figure 2 and Figure 3 list the comparison of performance of Mitra's document re-ranking method and our method at parameter setting (δ=10, L=4 and f(i)=w5) at PreAt10 and PreAt100. In our experiments, we set K as 1000 and re-rank top 50, 100, 200, 300, 400, 500, 600,700, 800, 900 and top 1000 documents. For Mitra's method, each query and each document is segmented into Chinese words, and Chinese words are used to re-rank documents.

In Figure 2 and Figure 3, PreAt10 and PreAt100 represent the performance of our method, INI_PreAt10 and INI_PreAt100 refer the initial results, and Mitra_PreAt10 and Mitra_PreAt100 represents the performance of Mitra's method.

From Figure 2 and Figure 3, we can see that our method achieves better result than that of Mitra's method for both PreAt 10 and PreAt 100 consistently at every document number setting. For example, when reordering top 50, 100 or 1000 documents, Mitra_PreAt10(relax) is 0.4024, 0.3929 and 0.3860 respectively, while our PreAt10(relax) is 0.4571, 0.4595 and 0.4595 respectively.

On the other hand, for our method, the improvement keeps or increases in a stable way as the number of documents to be re-ranked increases, while for Mitra's method, the improvement generally decreases as the document number increases. For example, Mitra_PreAt10(rigid) decreases from 0.2952 to 0.2905 and 0.2786 as document number increase from 50 to 100 and 1000, while our PreAt10(rigid) keeps as 0.3333 all the way.

Another finding is that Mitra's method is really applicable to top (50 to 100) ranking documents, as is claimed in Mitra's paper, while our method is more robust and applicable to a larger scope of documents.

The reason for these findings is that our weighting scheme makes it possible to make use of the information of a larger scope of the retrieved documents, while resisting the impact of noisy documents by assigning lower weights for terms in lower ranking documents. In contrast, the *idf*-based weighting in Mitra's method assigns lower scores to some really relevant terms, and subjects to the noisy terms within a larger range of the documents.

We also compare our method with Yang et al. [15] where a smaller top N (20, 25 or 30) documents are considered as relevance feedback. The comparison of precisions at different document number is given at Table 5. In Table 5, Row [Our] represents our proposed document re-ranking method at K=1000, L=4 and δ=10.

Table 5. Comparison: Re-rank Top 1000 Documents with L=4 and δ=10

	PreAt10(relax)	PreAt10(rigid)	PreAt100(relax)	PreAt100(rigid)
INI	0.3619	0.2595	0.1886	0.1279
Yang(N=20)	0.4405 +21.7%	0.3262 +25.7%	0.2129 +12.9%	0.141 +10.2%
Yang(N=25)	0.4405 +21.7%	0.3238 +24.8%	0.2112 +12%	0.1402 +9.6%
Yang(N=30)	0.4381 +21.1%	0.3238 +24.8%	0.21 +11.3%	0.139 +8.7%
Our	**0.4595 +27%**	**0.3333 +28.4%**	**0.2298 +21.8%**	**0.1557 +21.8%**

From Table 5, we see that our method achieves better result. Especially in PreAt100 level, our method achieves more 10% improvement against Yang's method. One possibility is that Yang's method only uses information in top 20-30 documents while we use information in top 1000 documents. When there are fewer relevant documents falling in top 20-30 documents, their method cannot capture enough information for re-ranking.

5.3 Experiments on Okapi BM25 Model

We also do experiments on OKAPI BM25 model and we use the default parameter setting of OKAPI BM25. The comparison of precisions at different parameters settings (δ=1 or 10, L=4) is given at Table 6. From Table 6, we see that the method achieves 9.5%-13.5% improvements against [INI] in every parameter setting at PreAt10 and achieves 12.5%-15.3% improvements against [INI] in every parameter setting at PreAt100.

Table 6. Statistics on (δ=1 or 10, L=4)

	PreAt10(relax)		PreAt10(rigid)		PreAt100(relax)		PreAt100(rigid)	
	δ=1	δ=10	δ=1	δ=10	δ=1	δ=10	δ=1	δ=10
INI	0.4190	0.4190	0.3	0.3	0.1907	0.1907	0.1293	0.1293
W4	**0.4655**	0.4638	0.3357	0.3357	0.2162	0.2174	0.1476	**0.1488**
	+11.1%	+10.7%	+11.9%	+11.9%	+13.4%	+14%	+14.2%	**+15.1%**
W5	0.4613	0.4613	0.3381	0.3381	**0.2183**	**0.2181**	0.1488	0.1486
	+10.1%	+10.1%	+12.7	+12.7%	**+14.5%**	**+14.4%**	+15.1%	+14.9%
W6	0.4651	0.4588	0.3381	0.3286	0.2152	0.2171	0.1469	**0.1488**
	+11%	+9.5%	+12.7	+9.5%	+12.9%	+13.9%	+13.6%	**+15.1%**
W7	0.4638	0.4638	**0.3405**	**0.3405**	0.2181	0.2176	**0.149**	0.1486
	+10.7%	+10.7%	**+13.5%**	**+13.5%**	+14.4%	+14.1%	**+15.3%**	+14.9%
W8	0.4651	**0.4684**	0.3286	0.3310	0.2145	0.2155	0.1471	**0.1488**
	+11%	**+11.8%**	+9.5%	+10.3%	+12.5%	+13%	+13.8%	**+15.1%**
W9	0.4588	0.4588	0.3357	0.3357	0.2176	0.2174	0.1486	0.1483
	+9.5%	+9.5%	+11.9%	+11.9%	+14.1%	+14%	+14.9%	+14.7%

7 Conclusions and Future Work

In this paper, we propose a new term weighting scheme and use it in document re-ranking. The weighting scheme for terms is based on their local and global distribution in top retrieved documents and the whole document set respectively, which combines the information regarding relative document frequency, document ranking positions as well as term length. The scheme allows randomly setting a larger portion of documents as relevance feedback, and helps to improve the performance of MMR model in document re-ranking.

Our experiments based on NTCIR3 CLIR task show that our proposed approach achieves significant improvement against the baseline by 18.4%-32.1% at top 10 documents and 12.8%-22% at top 100 documents in their respective precision. Compared with other two document re-ranking methods, our method also gets higher performance on NTCIR3 CLIR dataset. Furthermore, the performance of the approach generally improves or keeps as the number of the re-ranking documents increases, which shows that it is robust against the noisy documents included.

The experimental results support our assumptions: key terms in top K retrieved documents can be used to improve precision; long key term may contain more precise information and can be used to improve precision; document frequency distribution of query term in top K retrieved documents against the whole retrieved document set implies the importance of query term.

As the basis of this method, the term extraction module is very simple, which is a purely statistical method. In future, we will also consider more effective approaches for term extraction.

Our experiments are all based on Chinese information retrieval. In fact, our method is language independent. In the future, we'll do further tests on other languages.

References

[1] Balinski, J., Danilowicz, C.: Re-ranking Method Based on Inter-document Distance. Information Processing and Management 41(2005) 759-775.

[2] Bear J., Israel, D., Petit J., Martin D.: Using Information Extraction to Improve Document Retrieval. Proceedings of the Sixth Text Retrieval Conference, 1997.

[3] Crouch, C., Crouch, D., Chen, Q. and Holtz, S.: Improving the Retrieval Effectiveness of Very Short Queries, Information Processing and Management, 38(2002).

[4] Kamps, J.: Improving Retrieval Effectiveness by Reranking Documents Based on Controlled Vocabulary. The 21th European Conference on Information Retrieval, 2004.

[5] Kwok K.L.: Comparing Representation in Chinese Information Retrieval. In Proceedings of the ACM SIGIR-97, pp. 34-41.1997

[6] Lee K., Park Y., Choi, K.S.: Document Re-ranking Model Using Clusters. Information Processing and Management. V. 37 n.1, p1-14, 2001.

[7] Luk, R. W. P., Wong, K. F.: Pseudo-Relevance Feedback and Title Re-Ranking for Chinese IR, In Proceedings of NTCIR Workshop 4.

[8] M. Mitra., A. Singhal. and C. Buckley: Improving Automatic Query Expansion. In Proc. ACM SIGIR'98, Aug. 1998.

[9] Nie J.Y., Gao J., Zhang J., Zhou M.: On the Use of Words and N-grams for Chinese Information Retrieval. In Proceedings of the Fifth International Workshop on Information Retrieval with Asian Languages, IRAL-2000, pp. 141-148, 2000

[10] Qu, Y.L., Xu, G.W.,Wang J.: Rerank Method Based on Individual Thesaurus. Proceedings of NTCIR2 Workshop. 2000.

[11] Schutze, H.: The Hypertext Concordance: A Better Back-of-the-Book Index. Proceedings of First Workshop on Computational Terminology. 101-104, 1998.

[12] Xu J., Croft, W.B.: Query Expansion Using Local and Global Document Analysis. In Proc. ACM SIGIR'96, 1996.

[13] Xu J., Croft, W.B.: Improving the Effectiveness of Information Retrieval with Local Context Analysis. ACM Transactions on Information Systems, 18(1):79--112, 2000.

[14] Yang L.P., Ji D.H., Tang L.: Document Re-ranking Based on Automatically Acquired Key Terms in Chinese Information Retrieval. Proceedings of 20th International Conference on Computational Linguistics (COLING). 2004.

[15] Yang L.P., Ji D.H., Zhou G.D. and Nie Y. Improving Retrieval Effectiveness by Using Key Terms in Top Retrieved Documents. Proceedings of 27th European Conference on Information Retrieval. 2005.

On Effectiveness Measures and Relevance Functions in Ranking INEX Systems

Huyen-Trang Vu and Patrick Gallinari

Laboratory of Computer Science (LIP6),
University Pierre and Marie Curie,
8, rue du capitaine Scott - 75015 Paris, France
{vu, gallinari}@poleia.lip6.fr

Abstract. This paper investigates the effect of performance measures and relevance functions in comparing retrieval systems in INEX, an evaluation forum dedicated to XML retrieval. We focus on two interdependent challenges which arise when evaluating XML retrieval systems, namely weak ordering issue of retrieved lists and multivalued relevance scales. Our analysis provides empirical evidence about the reasonableness of popular assumptions in information retrieval (IR) evaluation which state that ties can be ignored and binary relevance is sufficient. We also shed light on the impact of a parameter in Q-measure [18] on the sensitivity of the metric.

1 Introduction

IR is one of scientific disciplines where theoretical and empirical researches are closely intertwined. A pure theoretical retrieval model might probably fail in operational environment and appropriate parameter tuning for such theoretical model is impossible without extensive experiments on benchmarks. To set up benchmarks, evaluation criteria have to be first of all determined. Such criteria must not only express the functionality of a system, which is its principal aim, but also be feasible in ways to obtain test collections (document collection, information needs and relevance judgment of each topic). Relevance and measurement definitions are therefore the essential components of an evaluation criterion.

Evaluation measures used in most IR evaluation forums (such as TREC, NTCIR, CLEF) share two common issues: they omit ties and use a binary relevance. Despite a lot of criticisms against their simplicity, these assumptions are employed in popular performance metrics such as MAP, R-Precision or precision at n documents retrieved (Prec@n). We formulate three reasons for that paradox. First, there is no more complicated evaluation proposal which has not only a theoretically sounded metric and for which relevance assessments can be easily collected. It has been reported that it is impossible to ask a person to identify more than 11 relevance levels and all the aforementioned forums find 3 or 4 levels feasible in practice [18]. Second, even if there are new metrics, there is no standard way to verify their outstanding features in practice. How to quantify the reliability and stability of an evaluation metric is still an open question in IR evaluation. In physical experiment, the fact that measurement values vary across tests is mainly due to natural factors such as instrument, temperature or experimenter

G.G. Lee et al. (Eds.): AIRS 2005, LNCS 3689, pp. 312–327, 2005.

health. Sources of uncertainty in IR evaluation, are contrarily due to the suitability of metric assumptions and the fact of too small sample size (of topics for instance) in the particular case. Third, despite theoretical modeling for ties, they do not happen so frequently with automatic retrieval systems and even if they do, a simple solution such as sorting according to submission order is sufficient enough.

XML content-based retrieval is a recent and emerging retrieval task, partly justified by the increasing availability of documents in XML format available in Internet. This discipline is still in its infancy and XML search engine performance is still far below that of flat text retrieval. To promote research, INEX[1] aims at providing infrastructure to evaluate and compare retrieval systems dedicated to XML retrieval task. INEX states that when scaling down retrievable units from entire documents to arbitrary XML elements, two interdependent challenges caused by the appearance of XML elements with parent-child relationship in retrieved lists arise while evaluating. Firstly, there are so many ties in retrieved lists which cannot be neglected. Secondly, it is necessary to use a multivalued[2] bidimensional relevance scale to express better different relevance levels rather than binary values. inex_eval is the current official criterion used by INEX to rank systems [11] and tries to handle the two challenges in a unified framework. However, from the practical viewpoint of a comparative evaluation of many systems, after averaging evaluation scores over a sufficient amount of topics, some questions arise about the necessity and the reliability of such measure:

1. whether ties happen frequently in retrieved lists, and if this depends on system or on topic characteristic.
2. whether inex_eval handles ties better than other measures which neglect this issue.
3. whether a graded scale is necessary: if a graded scale offers more information about system performance than its corresponding binary one does.

Like TREC, INEX objective is not to identify a winner but to verify in practice "what works and what does not in XML content-based retrieval". This question will never be answered until an appropriate evaluation protocol is set up. As we mentioned above, since there is no standard way to verify the reliability of an evaluation measure in IR, our proposal in this paper might therefore not only be helpful specially for INEX or even for XML retrieval but also contribute novel and empirical ways to evaluate the reliability of an evaluation setting in IR.

In this paper, we will investigate the three above points in a practical perspective. Effectiveness performance will be analysed based on the averaged measure currently employed to rank systems and not on individual topics or on theoretical aspects. We examine not only pairwise effects as used in previous work such as [18,2,12] (Kendall's τ, scatterplot, swap of systems in lists ordered by average values over the topic set) but also go into detail of pointwise by quantifying characteristics of each evaluation setting independent to others: interval aspect and discrimination power. The main studied object in our analysis is the inex_eval measure which was chosen as the official measure in INEX. Contrary to inex_eval, we choose MAP (mean of average precision over relevant documents) and Q-measure [18] which both omit ties issue in retrieved lists and handle

---

[1] http://inex.is.informatik.uni-duisburg.de/
[2] From now on, for simplicity, "graded" will be used instead of "multivalued".

graded relevance. These measures are quite compatible with inex_eval: they are system-oriented evaluations, single value measures, rank-based (vs set-based of R-Precision, F-measure, etc) evaluations by making use of both precision and recall facets. More-over, previous researches have shown that MAP with a binary relevance scale gives the most reliable and stable evaluation in comparison with others such as R-Precision and Prec@n, especially with a limited size of the topic set [1] or with a very large document collection [7]. Kekäläinen & Jarvelin [12] has extended MAP to the graded case. The Q-measure proposed by Sakai [18] is dedicated to NTCIR system comparison, either in *ad hoc* retrieval task or in Question-Answering task with 4-point relevance judgment. This measure corrects undernormalization weakness of a previous measure (AWP) also proposed in NTCIR for graded evaluation with an additional parameter β which has to be set up manually.

The paper is organized as follows. We first introduce effectiveness measures and rel-evance functions used in our analysis (Section 2). Our experiment concerns two main issues about particularities of XML element retrieval evaluation: ties handling (Sec-tion 3) and graded relevance scale adaptation (Section 4). We present also results about confidence interval of systems (Section 5) and discrimination power of an evaluation setting (a combination of a relevance function and a measure) in Section 6. We review briefly some related work in Section 7 before concluding and sketching our future work (Section 8).

2 Background

2.1 Effectiveness Measures

Let $g(d)$ be gain value of document d. In popular binary scale, $g(.)$ has either a value of 0 or 1 depending on the relevance of d. With a graded scale, $g(d) \in [0, 1]$. Let $isrel(d)$ be a boolean value about the relevance status of document d, $isrel(d)$ will be set up if d is relevant, otherwise 0. Assuming an ordered set of documents, $count(r)$ will denote the number of relevant documents ($g(d) > 0$) among the first r retrieved documents ($count(r) \leq r$); $cg(r)$ is the cumulated gain of this subset of r documents and $cig(.)$ for an ideal list where documents are sorted by non increasing order of their gain values. R is the number of relevant documents for the considered topic. Given these notations, we can formally describe MAP, Q-measure and inex_eval measures as follows. For the sake of simplicity, the outer averaging operator over all topics is omitted in the formulas.

MAP is defined as follows:

$$\text{MAP} \triangleq \frac{1}{R} \sum_{r=1}^{L} isrel(r).\frac{count(r)}{r}$$

To extend MAP to graded relevance, we follow [12] in replacing $count(r)$ by $cg(r)$. Note that if replacing also the denominator r by $cig(r)$, one will return to AWP[3] with the drawback of freezing evaluation on relevant documents found after rank R. Without

---

[3] See [18] about this measure and its drawback.

ambiguity, in this paper, we will use the same notation MAP for both binary and graded scales.

$$[\text{g}]\text{MAP} \triangleq \frac{1}{R} \sum_{r=1}^{L} isrel(r).\frac{cg(r)}{r} \tag{1}$$

Q-measure is an integration of both MAP and AWP:

$$\text{Q-measure} \triangleq \frac{1}{R} \sum_{r=1}^{L} isrel(r).\frac{\beta.cg(r) + count(r)}{\beta.cig(r) + r} \tag{2}$$

β is a positive coefficient to control the favor of MAP aspect $\frac{count(r)}{r}$ or of AWP aspect $\frac{cg(r)}{cig(r)}$. The magnitude of β will be manually fixed.

It is easy to show that in binary case, MAP is always at most equal to Q-measure. The latter is proportional to the magnitude of β. However, the offset magnitude is not the same across topics and across runs, the output system rankings will possibly be different.

Details about inex_eval are in [11]. We summarize here the main features which are related to our discussion. The inex_eval metric uses *precall* [16] which computes the probability $P(rel|retr)$ that an element viewed by the user is relevant knowing that (s)he wants to see a specified amount of relevant material:

$$P(rel|retr)(x) \triangleq \frac{x.R}{x.R + \text{ESL}_{x.R}} \tag{3}$$

where $\text{ESL}_{x.R}$ denotes the Expected Search Length [3], i.e. the expected number of non-relevant elements retrieved until an arbitrary recall point x is reached. The inex_eval value reported in this paper has been averaged over 100 recall points: 0.01, ..., 1.00. Being adapted from the measure *precall*, inex_eval is expected to be an intuitive method for interpolation and to handle weakly ordered ranks correctly. Theoretically, thank to $\text{ESL}_{x.R}$ component, it is straighforward to extend *precall* (originally dedicated to binary scales) to graded quantisation functions. In practice, there are however a lot of technical problems, for instance, because of submission length limit, the number of elements of the last rank must be approximated. Moreover, in graded scales both MAP (equation 1) and inex_eval are *under* normalized: the metric value of the ideal lists is less than 1, each topic has therefore different "upper bound" values. This raises a worry about zooming bias towards easy topics when averaging over different topics, systems with capacity to perform well on difficult topics will hardly be recompensed.

2.2 Experimental Setting

We performed experiments on the INEX document collection. According to INEX, XML retrieval amounts at retrieving document elements (e.g. paragraphs, sections, etc) relevant to a query need. The relevance criterion is therefore defined at the XML element level, with two interdependent axes: exhaustivity e (describing the extent to which the element discusses the topic of request) and specificity s (describing the extent to which the element *focuses* on the topic of request). Each dimension contains four values of $\{0, 1, 2, 3\}$ corresponding to non-relevant, marginally, fairly and highly relevant levels. Since a non-relevant element in terms of exhaustivity (specificity resp.) must be non-relevant in the other axis, there are finally ten valid combinations rather than sixteen.

INEX separates two retrieval scenarios: content-only (simple queries by keywords, aka CO) and content-and-structure (complex queries with constraints of both content and XML structure of the target, aka CAS). While the task definition of the former is well set up, this is not the case for the latter. Our discussion concentrates therefore on the CO task. Moreover, due to limit of space, all results presented in this paper are on the data set of the second round of INEX (INEX'03 for short). This data set involves 54 retrieved lists[4] and 32 judged topics (the last version 2.5).

In our experiment, all INEX graded relevance functions, namely gen[eralized] (5-point $\{0.0, 0.25, 0.5, 0.75, 1.0\}$) and sog "specificity-oriented generalized" (7-point $\{0.0, 0.1, 0.25, 0.5, 0.75, 0.9, 1.0\}$), and two INEX binary relevance functions: strict $(g(e = 3, s = 3) = 1$, otherwise 0), s_3e_{321} $(g(e > 0, s = 3) = 1$, otherwise 0) are examined. These binary functions are considered to express user preference in retrieving *specificity*-oriented XML element. Note that although we include "strict" in the discussion, the question about intuitiveness and the effect of too small sample size, of very few relevant answers (as shown in table 1) of such relevance function remains unknown, any conclusion based on that function should be viewed with caution. Detail about INEX relevance functions can be consulted in [5]. We include also the most liberal relevance definition, called "trec" in this paper, where all elements with positive values of specificity and exhaustivity are considered equally relevant. This relevance function results in the same number of relevant elements R as in "gen" and "sog". Note that "trec" has not been included in INEX official forum. From theoretical viewpoint, it seems meaningless to equally reward a highly relevant answer with a marginal one. However, we show later how existing metrics can identify such difference. These relevance functions result in not only different user preferences but also in the number of right answers per topic as shown in table 1.

In graded cases of MAP and Q-measure, we adopt directly two INEX relevance functions, gen and sog. Three values of β for Q-measure are taken into consideration: 0.1 (favoring MAP aspect), 1 (default) and 10 (favoring AWP aspect).

Table 1. Statistics about number of relevant elements per topic of INEX'03 collection. There are 32 topics with relevance assessment but 5 without *strict* judgment.

statistics	trec/gen/sog	s_3e_{321}	strict
min.	8	3	3
max.	3499	1104	175
mean	815.78	271.63	55.07
median	556	221	34

---

[4] Two too poor runs due to their format errors are taken out from the original data set

Since both MAP and Q-measure do not cope with ties in retrieved lists, like TREC we respect submitted order of answers rather than try to simulate random distribution of answers at the same rank.

In pairwise comparison, we follow previous IR evaluation research by examining the similarity of system rankings produced by two different settings. Kendall's τ rank correlation is used to quantify the magnitude of that relationship. We adopt also 0.9 as practical threshold to suggest that two rankings highly agree in order of sorted items.

3   Ties Handling

First of all, let us show how often ties happen in INEX collections. Table 2 gives some statistics about ties phenomenon in INEX'03 test collection. We define the averaged rank size for each topic as $\frac{\text{list size}}{\#\text{ranks}}$, then average it over all topics. Since INEX limits submission length of 1500 elements per topic, when a system lacks answer list for a topic, its rank size will be set to 1500. In our opinion, such averaged rank size is more intuitive than its reciprocal which is named "resolving power" in [13–ch. 4]. A thorough view on these systems reveals that ties phenomenon is system-dependent (even participant-dependent) rather than topic-dependent (table 3). This consolidates thus the validation of traditional assumption that ties issue is controllable. Remind that such assumption has been used in popular evaluation measures such as MAP, R-Precision, Prec@n. Moreover, examining relationship between rank size and evaluation score, we cannot draw any pattern for each category of ties: runs of very weak ordering might be at top ranks, runs at the other side can be inversely ties free.

Table 2. Statistics about weakly ordering phenomenon in INEX'03 test collection

	avg. rank size		
	= 1	< 2.10	> 43.80
#runs (/54)	22	16	16
#participants (/22)	11	6	7

Now let us show how well inex_eval handles weak ordering in terms of system ranking. From table 4 and figure 1 which concern binary relevance, one can observe that inex_eval behaves quite similarly to MAP. With the same relevance function, there is no clear difference in system ranking produced by inex_eval and that by MAP, especially with ten runs at two ends. This suggests that ties handling of inex_eval might have an impact on ranking systems but this impact seems not quite clear. In other words, in this circumstance, ties handling capacity of inex_eval is not outstanding as proved theoretically.

4   Graded Scales

To examine how different measures handle graded relevance scales, we rely on the similarities of system rankings produced by a measure under difference relevance scales (table 5 and figure 2) or by different measures (table 4). As we remarked previously, there

Table 3. Two-way ANOVA of rank size according to topic and run factors on INEX'03 data set. Although both factors affect rank size with significance $\ll 0.001$, run effect dominates topic one. XX give a more complete legend - maybe remove the table and leave only the text "we performed ANOVA [...]. That shows that..."

variation factors	Df	Sum Sq	Mean Sq	F value	Pr$(> F)$
topic	31	3602350	116205	2.5875	4.574e-06
runs	53	111588370	2105441	46.8818	< 2.2e-16
Residuals	1643	73786469	44910		

Table 4. Kendall's τ coefficient of system rankings produced by each pair of measures. At each row, <u>Underline</u> for the maximal of that row, **bold** for the maximal of the four first columns (concerning inex_eval). *Italic* for values inferior to 0.9.

quant.	inex_eval	inex vs Q-measure			MAP vs Q-measure		
	vs MAP	$\beta = 0.1$	$\beta = 1$	$\beta = 10$	$\beta = 0.1$	$\beta = 1$	$\beta = 10$
trec	0.980	**0.982**	0.981	0.974	<u>0.999</u>	0.990	0.974
s$_3$e$_{321}$	**0.983**	**0.983**	0.970	0.945	<u>0.997</u>	0.984	0.953
strict	0.964	**0.965**	0.930	*0.832*	<u>0.992</u>	0.928	*0.824*
gen	**0.956**	0.932	0.940	0.933	0.958	<u>0.960</u>	0.949
sog	**0.936**	*0.873*	*0.892*	0.906	0.912	0.931	<u>0.938</u>

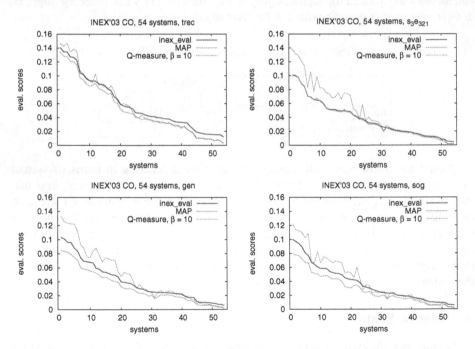

Fig. 1. Agreement of measures on a per-system basis. Systems are sorted by decreasing order of their *inex_eval* scores.

are some topics without strict relevance judgment: conclusions about strict relevance function will be drawn with caution. Moreover, from the previous section, we know that Q-measure with $\beta = 1$ provides no particular information given the two extremes $\beta = 0.1$ and $\beta = 10$. We therefore do not present graphics for "strict" and $\beta = 1$. We also neglect in table 4 some relevance pairs whose Kendall's τ is inferior to 0.9 in all metrics. The low correlation of these pairs should be examined in a separate report by taking into consideration how the number of right answers affect system comparison.

Table 5. Kendall's τ coefficient of system rankings produced by a measure under two relevance functions. <u>Underline</u> for the maximal of the two first columns, **boldface** for the maximal of all five columns. *Italic* for values inferior to 0.9.

rel. pairs	inex_eval	MAP	Q-measure		
			$\beta = 0.1$	$\beta = 1$	$\beta = 10$
gen - trec	0.931	<u>0.955</u>	**0.998**	0.992	0.982
sog - trec	*0.869*	<u>0.910</u>	**0.999**	0.976	0.944
gen - sog	0.915	0.932	0.999	0.975	0.949
gen - s_3e_{321}	<u>*0.856*</u>	*0.843*	*0.829*	*0.829*	*0.845*
sog - s_3e_{321}	**0.942**	0.910	*0.829*	*0.846*	*0.880*
trec - s_3e_{321}	*0.816*	<u>*0.829*</u>	*0.826*	*0.824*	***0.838***

Our remarks from tables 4, 5 and figure 2 are as follows:

– gen, sog, trec have a high agreement on low evaluations for all measures. These agreements look less clear among top runs. This suggests that tuning relevance values seems to affect mainly the order of top runs, nearly no influence on runs at the other end.
– gen has higher correlation to trec than sog has. It suggests an approximation of gen function by trec function without loss of information.
– These measures do not agree about the similarity of sog to trec and to s_3e_{321} respectively: inex_eval favors s_3e_{321} while Q-measure favors trec, and MAP seems neutral in Kendall's τ values. However, from plots, it seems that MAP agrees to inex_eval.
– In table 4, there is a clear separate of binary and graded groups: given a metric pair, their association in *binary* relevance scales is always higher than that in graded scale (except for *strict* with $\beta = 1$ and $\beta = 10$). This consolidates the theoretical argument that in binary circumstances, these metrics work in the similar manner. However, graded function makes system ranking of inex_eval closer to that of MAP than to that produced by Q-measure($\beta = 0.1$). This difference must be argued for undernormalization issue of inex_eval and MAP in graded cases.

Now let us concentrate on MAP and Q-measure:

– Both MAP and Q-measure discourage too short runs. A representative example is the 31st run in gen and s_3e_{321} (the 32nd in sog). This run adopted a quite different protocol by submitting only 100 answers rather than up to 1500 as guided by INEX.

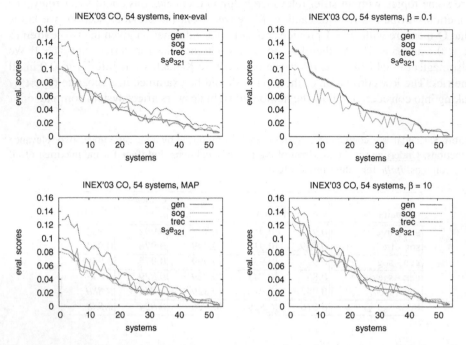

Fig. 2. Agreement of relevance functions on a per-system basis. Systems are sorted by decreasing order of their *gen* scores.

- On Q-measure figures, curves of s_3e_{321} are fairly different to those of gen/sog/trec, this suggests that Q-measure has a stronger dependence on the number of relevant elements (which relevance value is positive) than the other measures.
- In comparison with inex_eval and MAP, Q-measure enlarges the distance between the top and the bottom runs, even in binary cases. Moreover, offset magnitude seems large in top runs and then decreasing in runs at the other end.
- In binary cases, correlation of MAP and Q-measure decreases when increasing β magnitude. This illustrates our previous remark on Q-measure formulae (equation 2). However, this order does not hold in graded cases. This suggests that in graded cases, either MAP is not reliable due to its undernormalization issue or β plays an important role which is not simple to control.

5   Interval Performance

Our discussions have focused so far on *point* estimators. We present now *interval* estimators which provides more insight on the statistical analysis of the results.

Given the small topic set size, we adopted a non-parametric estimation technique, the bootstrap [4], to estimate confidence interval (c.i.) of the sample mean of a run over the topic set. We got 5000 bootstrap samples and used the percentile interval technique for obtaining confidence intervals at a 95% confidence level[5].

For illustration purposes, confidence intervals of two relevance functions, gen and trec are presented in figure 3. From the figure, one can observe that (i) despite differences in absolute values, confidence interval lengths of a system are highly similar under a performance measure and that (ii) confidence intervals of top runs are longer than those of low runs. The first issue means that although inex_eval and MAP are undernormalized in graded scales, this does affect only point estimator but not distort interval estimator at all. The second however seems not intuitive from standpoint of system behavior: a poor performing system is equally bad for all topics, which is not the case for a better one.

6 Discrimination Power Analysis

Voorhees & Buckley [26] proposed to measure the sensitivity of a test collection through its capacity to distinguish retrieval systems. However, their method must be conducted on at least 50 topics for achieving stable results. Such requirement is infeasible in the INEX case. We follow therefore the definition of discrimination power of a performance measure proposed by Tague-Sutcliffe & Blustein [23], namely its capacity to distinguish different systems from the top run (the so-called size of group A in multiple comparison test grouping). We used the tools provided in their IR-STAT-PAK programme[6]. ANOVA prerequisite of homogeneity of variances is still violated in our case even after arcsine ($\arcsin \sqrt{x}$) and rank transformations. Tukey grouping results should therefore be interpreted with caution before more complicated power simulation such as that in [8] is carried out. Since sizes of group A after arcsine and rank transformation are quite close in each evaluation setting, only the former is presented in table 6.

Another simple technique which can give a rough estimation of the discrimination power is the following: from c.i. results in the previous section, runs whose confidence intervals overlap with the one of the top run are supposed to be in group A (this is a naive form of unpaired test). The corresponding figures are visualized in table 7.

Despite differences in absolute magnitude, these tables 6 and 7 both agree that three measures work in very similar manner in each binary relevance case, the difference in their discrimination power if happens is so small that one can think of by chance. In graded case, both tables agree that Q-measure($\beta = 10$) is less discriminating than both lower β's, inex_eval and MAP. In conjunction with figures in table 4, we can suggest that the high weight of AWP factor affects not only to system ranking but also to capacity to distinguish systems of Q-measure. This is totally different to Sakai's argument about the role of β in [18].

---

[5] The bootstrap package is available in R (http://cran.r-project.org/src/contrib/Descriptions/boot.html)

[6] http://www.csd.uwo.ca/~jamie/IRSP-overview.html

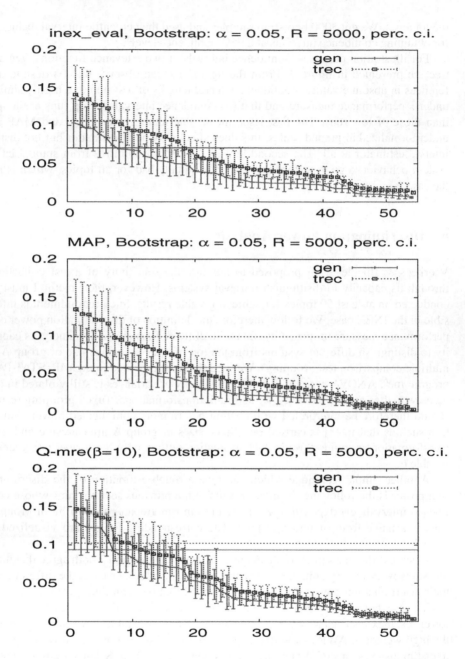

Fig. 3. Confidence interval (Bootstrap with 5000 iterations, 95% confidence level, percentile interval) of sample mean scores. Systems are sorted by decreasing order of their *sample mean* values.

Table 6. Number of runs of group A (which are not statistically different to the top run, this run included) on *arcsine* transformed scores. On each relevance function: the highest and the smallest values are marked by bold font and followed by an asteric respectively.

quant	inex_eval	MAP	Q-measure		
			$\beta = 0.1$	$\beta = 1$	$\beta = 10$
trec	13	13	13	13	13
s_3e_{321}	14	**15**	**15**	**15**	**15**
strict	**17**	**17**	**17**	16	15*
gen	12*	13	12*	12*	**14**
sog	15	**16**	13	13	**16**

Table 7. Similar to table 6 but calculated by overlap of c.i. with respect to the top run

quant	inex_eval	MAP	Q-measure		
			$\beta = 0.1$	$\beta = 1$	$\beta = 10$
trec	16*	16*	17	17	**18**
s_3e_{321}	**21**	18*	21	20	20
strict	15	**16**	15	15	13*
gen	16*	17	16*	17	**18**
sog	17	18	16*	17	**19**

7   Related Work

In this section, we briefly review work on three issues: ties handling, metric for graded relevance scales and techniques to evaluate robustness of an effectiveness measure.

About evaluation metrics which handle weak ordering, we are only aware of *pre-call* [16] which is based on Expected Search Length [3]. With the same objective to investigate ties, Kraaij described occurrence of ties in a retrieved list via "resolving power" in [13–ch. 4].

Despite plenty of metric proposal for graded relevance scales in IR evaluation ([12] provides a relatively thorough review), in our awareness, this is the first time three performance measures dedicated to graded relevance, namely inex_eval, MAP and Q-measure, are together taken into consideration. Note that we do not include ADM [14] in the discussion. In our opinion, such measure, even if being shown reliable (which is still an open question), will go better in the future rather than with current human assessment protocol. It has been reported that it is very difficult for human to distinguish more than 11 relevance levels [12]. So there is no reason to encourage retrieval systems to identify strictly continuous relevance values.

In the spirit of graded measures, Sakai proposed Q-measure and checked it in NT-CIR context, for *ad hoc* retrieval task [18] and Question-Answering application [17]. However, it surprises us when he states that MAP can not be extended to graded scales without reference to work of Kekäläinen & Jarvelin [12]. That is why his experiment concerns therefore only binary MAP and the other proposal of the two aforementioned authors, the so-called Cumulated Gain. We share with [18] and [13] that Cumulated

Gain family, since estimating performance at document cutoff, is more suitable for visual purpose from user standpoint rather than as a reliable single value measure. In the latter, the metric score must be averaged in an unbiased manner over different topics, how to determine an appropriate document cutoff when the number of relevant answers varies largely across topics (which often happens in IR test collections) is not simple at all. This is also the first time the role of β in Q-measure is brought to light. Relying on experiment of NTCIR systems, Sakai [18] argued that this parameter, like gain (relevance) values, has secondary impact on stability and meaning of Q-measure. We have shown that it is not the case in INEX context.

Note that graded relevance functions in INEX are much more difficult to define than in existing IR evaluation forums such as TREC Web and NTCIR. With two relevance dimensions (exhaustivity and specificity), not only the number of possible relevance values increases but the standard relevance axis becomes a relevance circle; relevance thresholds (to separate relevance and non relevance parts) are therefore not quite explicit. Sakai suggested in [17] ways to create graded relevance judgment for Question-Answering by equivalence class of answers. We argue that such solution is not suitable for INEX case due to complicate nesting issue of XML elements and the goal of best matching, relevance assessment is therefore done in elements themselves rather than as concept judgment in Question-Answering.

Furthermore, other retrieval scenarios and performance measures have been proposed in INEX, such as XCG [9] with empirical results available in [10] or T2I [6]. The former, inspired from the aforementioned Cumulated Gain family, aims at a unified solution which employs graded relevance scale and handles physical overlap of XML element in both assessment set and retrieved lists. The latter is dedicated to a new user model which is tolerant to the physical overlap issue. Since both of these measures aim at weakening another traditional assumption of IR about independence among retrieved items, they are therefore out of scope of this paper. Moreover, to become a robust metric in practice, they also encounter the bottleneck of empirical validation which we discuss in the next paragraph.

Despite different proposals, how to evaluate and compare effectiveness measures is still an open question. Besides simple index of Kendall's τ used in most of papers about IR evaluation, there are other examples such as discrimination power [23] which we adopted in this paper, "error rate" estimator proposed by Voorhees & Buckley [1,26,2,20]. Let us cite van Rijsbergen's remark in 1979 which is unfortunately still valid "there are no known statistical tests applicable to IR" [24–p. 136]. The difficulty is due to various particularities of IR evaluation in comparison with standard statistical framework for instance the fact of very small sample size, the violation of some prerequisites such as equality of variances in ANOVA. We have presented simple ways to empirically compare effect of different evaluation setting by existing statistical tools. Up to our knowledge, this is the first time confidence intervals have been taken into account in estimating discrimination power. Tague-Sutcliffe and Blustein [23], Hull et al. [8] used standard multicomparison tests that simply make use of *point* estimators. Savoy [21] used Bootstrap to compare each *pair* of runs which does not extend yet to multicomparison tests. We have gone further by using Bootstrap to estimate c.i. which reveals more detail about INEX system behavior, such as the high variance of top runs.

8 Conclusions and Discussion

We have taken a close view on INEX evaluation, concentrating on two stated challenges in evaluating XML element retrieval, weak ordering and graded relevance scales. Let us now summarize drawn conclusions:

- Existing retrieval models are able to distinguish fine relevance status of XML elements. Ties issue is not so serious as being supposed and quite controllable in practice. The validation of traditional assumption of independence relevance between documents still holds in XML element scope.
- Even assuming that it is possible to obtain graded relevance assessments (continuous scale included), there is always a real challenge in distinguishing graded relevance scales, for both retrieval systems and evaluation measure.
- From practical standpoint, as long as human relevance assessment procedure is employed, it is not simple to define suitable graded relevance function for current INEX system evaluation.
- Q-measure is not clearly more reliable than MAP. It remains a question about reasonable setting of β value in Q-measure.
- Advantage of interval confidence with respect to popular point estimator in comparing retrieval systems has been illustrated. Orders of systems sorted by their mean values are not quite the same by different measures, yet results in terms of confidence interval seem highly similar.

It sounds disappointing that empirical experiments do not encourage development of new evaluation measures which are expected to better describe characteristics of retrieval systems. However, we interpret this in three different ways. First, like in research of retrieval techniques, a pure theoretical evaluation measure must be checked in large scale testbeds before concluding about its power. Second, until new methods to collect test collections, especially to simplify the bottleneck of relevance judgment become feasible, it is not urgent to either tune graded relevance values or to propose effectiveness measures for graded relevance scale. Such scale makes assessment procedure more difficult, even infeasible, thus less reliable while existing measures cannot benefit later. Finally, from retrieval model viewpoint, the fact that graded relevance scale is not clearly necessary in IR evaluation seems to take a good news: even in the simple binary relevance case, how to design retrieval systems which optimize adaptively its performance towards some popular evaluation measures such as MAP or Prec@10 is still an open question, let alone for graded (ordinal but not continuous) relevance scale.

Our future work concerns different issues around evaluating suitability of evaluation measures in XML element retrieval context. First of all, we intend to open the box of "mystery" about confidence interval length of top runs by per topic analysis. To better understand effect of normalization per topic in measure stability, we will employ other statistics to sort systems, such as sample median [21] or geometric mean [25]. These statistics are expected to appropriately describe systems, especially for small topic set size and for heterogeneous environment. Regardings discrimination power estimation, we tend to adopt also techniques to get "error rate" estimator proposed by Buckley & Voorhees to circumstances of very small sample size such as INEX by replacing the random checking [26] by statistical significance test and the query version [1] by bootstrap samples.

Note that all techniques presented in this paper are totally task independent, they operate on retrieved lists delivered by systems but not on details of retrieval step. It is therefore straighforward to apply these techniques to compare systems in other retrieval scenarios. We are replicating the aforementioned tests on XML *document* retrieval, which seems more realistic than current INEX task of retrieving arbitrary XML elements[7]. This is not a newly born task at all but has been simply considered as a secondary to XML *element* retrieval [15]. In our understanding, such scenario is similar to topic distillation task in TREC Web Track. While the latter raises practical challenge for existing evaluation metrics in discrimination power aspect [22], we fear that this is also the case of INEX. If this is confirmed in practice, more well-designed evaluation procedure might be necessary to have reliable conclusions about INEX system performance. A recently proposed measure by [2], the so-called *bpref*, which is dedicated to incomplete and imperfect judgment with assumption of binary relevance and ties free in retrieved results, will also be examined in this retrieval scenario.

Acknowledgements

The authors are thankful to both INEX participants for creating test collections and INEX organizers for letting these data be accessible. We are grateful to T. Sakai for the official version of [17], D. Hull for the unpublished report [8] and J. Blustein for providing IR-STAT-PAK programme. We are especially in debt of anonymous reviewers whose thoughtful comments make this paper much better than the initial version.

References

1. C. Buckley and E. M. Voorhees. Evaluating evaluation measure stability. In *ACM SIGIR'00*, pages 33 – 40, Athens, Greece, 2000. ACM Press.
2. C. Buckley and E. M. Voorhees. Retrieval evaluation with incomplete information. In Sanderson et al. [19], pages 25–32.
3. W. S. Cooper. Expected Search Length: A Single Measure of Retrieval Effectiveness Based on the Weak Ordering Action of Retrieval Systems. *American Documentation*, 19(1):30–41, 1968.
4. A. C. Davison and D. V. Hinkley. *Bootstrap Methods and Their Application*. Cambridge University Press, 1997.
5. A. P. de Vries, G. Kazai, and M. Lalmas. Evaluation metrics 2004. In *INEX 2004 Workshop Pre-Proceedings*, pages 249–250, 2004. Available at http://inex.is.informatik. .uni-duisburg.de:2004/pdf/INEX2004PreProceedings.pdf.
6. A. P. de Vries, G. Kazai, and M. Lalmas. Tolerance to Irrelevance: A User-effort Oriented Evaluation of Retrieval Systems without Predefined Retrieval Unit. In *RIAO 2004*, pages 463–473, Avignon, France, Apr. 2004.
7. D. Hawking and S. Robertson. On collection size and retrieval effectiveness. *Information Retrieval*, 6(1):99–105, 2003.

---

[7] It is clear that current INEX protocol encourages overlap in retrieved lists, which is against user preference.

8. D. A. Hull, P. Kantor, and K. Ng. Advanced approaches to the statistical analysis of TREC information retrieval experiments. Technical report, 1997. Unpublished, contact the first author for a copy: hull@clairvoyancecorp.com.

9. G. Kazai, M. Lalmas, and A. P. de Vries. The overlap problem in content-oriented XML retrieval evaluation. In Sanderson et al. [19], pages 72–79.

10. G. Kazai, M. Lalmas, and A. P. de Vries. Reliability Tests for the XCG and inex-2002 Metric. In N. Fuhr, M. Lalmas, S. Malik, and Z. Szlávik, editors, *Advances in XML Information Retrieval. Third Workshop of the INitiative for the Evaluation of XML Retrieval INEX 2004, LNCS 3493*, pages 60–72, 2004.

11. G. Kazai, M. Lalmas, N. Fuhr, and N. Gövert. A report on the first year of the INitiative for the evaluation of XML retrieval (INEX'02). *Journal of the American Society for Information Science and Technology (JASIST)*, 55(6):551–556, 2004.

12. J. Kekäläinen and K. Järvelin. Using graded relevance assessments in IR evaluation. *Journal of the American Society for Information Science and Technology (JASIST)*, 53(13):1120–1129, 2002.

13. W. Kraaij. *Variations on Language Modeling for Information Retrieval*. PhD thesis, University of Twente, 2004.

14. V. D. Mea and S. Mizzaro. Measuring retrieval effectiveness: a new proposal and a first experimental validation. *Journal of the American Society for Information Science and Technology (JASIST)*, 55(6):530–543, 2004.

15. S. H. Myaeng, D.-H. Jang, M.-S. Kim, and Z.-C. Zhoo. A Flexible Model for Retrieval of SGML documents. In *SIGIR'98*, pages 138–140, Melbourne, Australia, Aug. 1998.

16. V. V. Raghavan, G. S. Jung, and P. Bollmann. A critical investigation of recall and precision as measures of retrieval system performance. *ACM Transactions on Information Systems*, 7(3):205–229, 1989.

17. T. Sakai. New Performance metrics based on Multigrade Relevance: Their Application to Question Answering. In *NTCIR-4 Proceedings*, 2004.

18. T. Sakai. Ranking the NTCIR Systems Based on Multigrade Relevance. In S. H. Myaeng, M. Zhou, K.-F. Wong, and H.-J. Zhang, editors, *Information Retrieval Technology, Asia Information Retrieval Symposium, AIRS 2004, Revised Selected Papers*, pages 251–262, 2004.

19. M. Sanderson, K. Järvelin, J. Allan, and P. Bruza, editors. *SIGIR 2004: Proc. of the 27th Annual Int. ACM SIGIR Conf. on Research and Development in Information Retrieval, Sheffield, UK, July 25-29, 2004*, 2004.

20. M. Sanderson and J. Zobel. Information retrieval system evaluation: Effort, sensitivity, and reliability. In *ACM SIGIR'05*, 2005. To appear.

21. J. Savoy. Statistical inference in retrieval effectiveness evaluation. *Info. Process. Management*, 33(4):495–512, 1997.

22. I. Soboroff. On evaluating web search with very few relevant documents. In Sanderson et al. [19], pages 530–531.

23. J. Tague-Sutcliffe and J. Blustein. A statistical analysis of the TREC-3 data. In *Proceedings of TREC-3, NIST Special Publication 500-225*, pages 385–398, Apr. 1995.

24. C. J. Van Rijsbergen. *Information Retrieval*. Butterworths, 1979.

25. E. M. Voorhees. The TREC robust retrieval track. *SIGIR Forum*, 39(1):11–20, 2005.

26. E. M. Voorhees and C. Buckley. The effect of topic set size on retrieval experiment error. In *ACM SIGIR'02*, pages 316–323. ACM Press, Aug. 2002.

Home Photo Categorization Based on Photographic Region Templates

Sang-Kyun Kim[1], Seungji Yang[2], Kyong Sok Seo[2], Yong Man Ro[2],
Ji-Yeon Kim[1], and Yang Suk Seo[1]

[1] Computing Lab., Digital Research Center, Samsung Advanced Institute of Technology,
(SAIT), San 14-1, Giheung, Yongin, Kyunggi, South Korea
skkim@sait.samsung.co.kr
[2] Image and Video Systems Lab., Information and Communications University (ICU),
Munji 119, Yuseong, Daejeon, South Korea
yro@icu.ac.kr

Abstract. In this paper, we propose new photo categorization which is suitable for a home photo album. To enhance the categorization, both local and global concepts of the photos are modeled and their combined concept learning method for the photo categorization is proposed. The local and global concepts are trained by individual support vector machines. Region templates for the local concepts of generic home photos are proposed. Further, local concepts are merged with confidence to lead to the global concept to achieve reliable categorization. Experiment results show that the proposed method is useful to detect multi-category concepts for the home photo album.

1 Introduction

Recently, digital camera is getting popular as a convenient means for users to easily take a lot of photos anytime. At home, it is gradually replacing traditional film camera, so the volume of digital photos is continually increasing. The digitization of photo makes easier for the users to share memory and experience with their friends or family. Usually, people would not frequently move their photos from digital cameras to their personal storages in PC or PMP (portable multimedia player) since 'moving' photos would often mean extra works such as sorting, selecting, and annotating pictures manually. Unless ones have not only enough time to do that but also strong wills to take care of the photos for each event, they would rather leave the photos in the memory stick of digital camera.

The problem in the traditional digital photo albums is that the users have been forced to do those manual works. The users often feel that it is nuisance and hard to browse their photos in some meaningful orders when they arrange their photos to the digital photo album. This manual cataloguing is quite time-consuming, tedious, erroneous, and inconsistent, so that it has been a big hurdle for users to use digital cameras. Thus the categorizing lot of photos in some automatic manner is strongly needed, in which general users would get some easy ways to browse groups of photos that are semantically linked together.

G.G. Lee et al. (Eds.): AIRS 2005, LNCS 3689, pp. 328–338, 2005.
© Springer-Verlag Berlin Heidelberg 2005

Under the circumstances, classifying photos into several meaningful categories like landscape, architecture, people, indoor, etc. is an essential one. The category classification also improves capabilities for effectively searching and filtering the desired photos by reducing search ranges [1]. Image retrieval and categorization have been recently advanced by content-based analysis. Many related researches have been proposed in [1 - 5]. In the content-based retrieval and categorization, an important issue is reducing the gap between the low-level features and the high-level semantic description, which is close to human visual perception. In previous works, multiple features description has been used in [3 - 5], where color, shape, and texture features are combined to describe images and to measure inter-image similarity. Further, more reliable performance has been achieved by weighted feature selection [4, 5].

In general, an image may contain multiple semantic concepts, and thus it is natural to obtain multiple concepts (i.e., categories) from the categorization process. In order to detect multi-concepts, concept learning with segmented region has been reported in recent works [6, 7].

In this paper, we propose a new photo categorization method in the home photo album using concept learning. In the proposed concept learning method, two kinds of concept detectors are used: local concept and global concept detectors. Photographic region template set suitable for generic home photos is proposed in detecting local concept. Using these templates, entire image region is divided into sub-region which could show local semantics. The proposed image localization is faster and easier than elaborate region segmentation, and effective enough to catch local concept on image. Each local/global concept is trained by support vector machine (SVM) [8 - 10]. Multiple low-level features are input to local concept detector. Then, the output of every local concept detector constructs a confidence vector of local concepts, which is input to global concept detector. In this paper, how to select the most confident local concepts on overlapped regions is also proposed to reduce classification error due to image localization.

2 Method

This section covers the details regarding the proposed photo categorization method. It starts from summarizing the overall procedure of the proposed method. Then the algorithms in detail are described.

2.1 Overview

The overall procedure of the proposed photo categorization is shown in Fig. 1. An entire image region is divided by 10 sub-regions in terms of the photographic region template set, which consists of 1 center, 4 edges, 2 horizontal, 2 vertical, and a whole image regions. Multiple low-level features of the local region are used in learning and detecting local concepts. Once the local concept detectors have been built, confidence values for each sub-region are measured for all the local concepts. In order to find out the most confident local concepts on the overlapped regions, a local concept merging is carried out. This aims to reduce classification error due to image localization with a fixed block size.

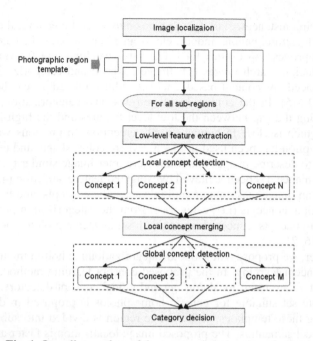

Fig. 1. Overall procedure of the proposed photo categorization

A global concept can be a composite of one or more local concepts, meaning that it represents higher-level of semantics than the local concepts. In this paper, the global concept detectors are trained with the confidence vectors of the local concepts. The confidence vectors represent how a region is related with the local concepts. With the confidence vectors, the global concept detectors measure how much the region is related with the global concepts.

2.2 Photographic Region Templates

In order to detect local semantics of image, an entire image region is divided into several sub-regions. The most popular methods used to localize image regions are object-based region segmentation and block-based one [6].

An object can be a fundamental unit to represent a semantic concept. The union of several objects often contains multiple semantic concepts. Even though elaborated object segmentation is the best representation of object semantics, it is quite time-consuming and complex to achieve reliable performance in automated ways. On the other hand, the block-based region segmentation is simpler as well as faster than the object-based one. In the block-based method, a whole image region is tessellated with a fixed or variable block size. There is no need for complex algorithm to detect objects. But the problem is how to decide the block size since there is a trade-off in the block size decision, i.e., too small block size could lead to be time-consuming due to many local blocks while too large block size is difficult to detect small object semantics.

In this paper, in order to overcome the aforementioned problems, we propose image localization with photographic region template set suitable for home photographs.

Simply, a photo can be composed of two region templates; foreground and background. There may be some objects in foreground and scenery in background. Without any help of object detection, the location and contour of foreground objects are unpredictable. Thus, we assume that foreground objects could be located in any subregion of image. In other words, semantic objects or scenes in home photo could be located in center, edge, horizontal, vertical or a whole region.

To find meaningful region templates, three important requirements are considered; one is that the region template should be large enough to detect local image semantic, another is that the region template should be small enough not to be time-consuming in practice, and the other is that the template should be scalable to support multi-resolution.

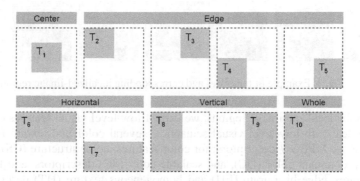

Fig. 2. Photographic region template set

Fig. 2 shows the proposed photographic region template. The region template set is composed of 10 sub-regions; they are 1 center region (T_1 in Fig.2), 4 edge regions (T_2, T_3, T_4, and T_5 in Fig.2), 2 horizontal regions (T_6 and T_7 in Fig.2), 2 vertical regions (T_8 and T_9 in Fig.2), and a whole region (T_{10} in Fig.2). The 4 edge regions are totally parts of the vertical, horizontal, and whole regions. The center region is partially overlapped with the edge, vertical, and horizontal regions, and totally with the whole image regions. The proposed photographic region template set **T** can be written as,

$$\mathbf{T} = \left\{ T_j \middle| T_j = \left(x_{tx}, y_{ty}, x_{bx}, y_{by} \right), j = 1, \cdots, 10 \right\} \tag{1}$$

where x_{tx} and y_{ty} are x-position and y-position of top-left of rectangle image region, respectively, and x_{bx} and y_{by} are x-position and y-position of bottom-right of rectangle image region, respectively. The 10 region templates can be written as,

$$T_1 = \left(\frac{w}{4}, \frac{h}{4}, \frac{3w}{4}, \frac{3h}{4} \right), \ T_2 = \left(0, 0, \frac{w}{2}, \frac{h}{2} \right), \ T_3 = \left(\frac{w}{2}, 0, w, \frac{h}{2} \right), \ T_4 = \left(0, \frac{h}{2}, \frac{w}{2}, h \right),$$

$$T_5 = \left(\frac{w}{2}, \frac{h}{2}, w, h \right), \ T_6 = \left(0, 0, w, \frac{h}{2} \right), \ T_7 = \left(0, \frac{h}{2}, w, h \right), \ T_8 = \left(0, 0, \frac{w}{2}, h \right), \tag{2}$$

$$T_9 = \left(\frac{w}{2}, 0, w, h \right), \text{ and } T_{10} = (0, 0, w, h),$$

where w is image width and h is image height. Fig. 3 shows some examples about the images with different photographic composition can be localized well by the region templates. In the first example, the image can be represented well using three region templates; they are top-vertical region showing sky, left-bottom-edge region showing lake, and right-bottom edge region showing field, where the sky, lake, and field can be regarded as local semantic concepts of the first example image.

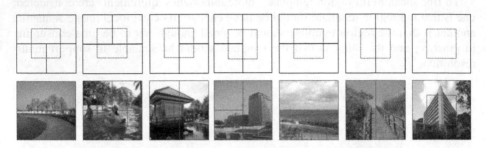

Fig. 3. Example of templates and corresponding localized-image region

Given the localized image regions, we extract low-level visual features on those. In order to deal with low-level visual semantics, several color and texture features are used. We use MPEG-7 descriptors; for color features, color structure (CS), color layout (CL), dominant color (DC), and scalable color (SC) descriptors, and for the texture features, edge histogram (EH) and homogeneous texture (HT) descriptors. The CS and CL features are known to be good to represent local color characteristics while the DC and SC features are good to represent global color characteristics. Note that even gray-scaled photo can be described by the texture features. The low-level feature vector ($\mathbf{X}|_T$) in the given local region ($T \in \mathbf{T}$) can be written as,

$$\mathbf{X}|_T = \left\{ \mathbf{x}_{cs}, \mathbf{x}_{cl}, \mathbf{x}_{dc}, \mathbf{x}_{sc}, \mathbf{x}_{eh}, \mathbf{x}_{ht} \right\}, \tag{3}$$

where $\mathbf{x}_{cs}$, $\mathbf{x}_{cl}$, $\mathbf{x}_{dc}$, $\mathbf{x}_{sc}$, $\mathbf{x}_{eh}$, and $\mathbf{x}_{ht}$ are CS, CL, DC, SC, EH, and HT feature vectors, respectively.

2.3 Local Concept Learning

For local concept learning, local concept lexicon is defined first. Let us denote the local concept lexicon as L_k, where k = 1, 2, 3,..., N_k and N_k is the number of local concepts. The local concept should have relatively lower level of semantics than global (category) concept.

In this paper, the local semantic concepts are trained with low-level visual feature vectors extracted from the local regions of image. A SVM is employed as a concept detector. The SVM is a binary classifier [8, 9] used to find the decision function of optimal linear hyperplane given a labeled data that is linearly separable in the feature space $\mathbf{H}$. In the SVM, the input feature in the space $\mathbf{X}$ is mapped to a feature space $\mathbf{H}$ via a nonlinear mapping $\phi(\cdot) : \mathbf{X} \rightarrow \mathbf{H}$ that allows ones to perform nonlinear analysis of the input data using a linear method. In general SVM, a kernel is designed to map the input data space $\mathbf{X}$ to the feature space $\mathbf{H}$. With the 'kernel trick' property [8, 9], the kernel can be considered as measures of similarity between two feature vectors without explicit computation of the map $\phi(\cdot)$. In this paper, we have not focused on selecting kernel type of the SVM. Rather, the kernel $(\mathbf{K})$ is considered as a simple dot product similarity measure between two feature vectors as follows:

$$K(\mathbf{X}_a, \mathbf{X}_b) = \langle \phi(\mathbf{X}_a), \phi(\mathbf{X}_b) \rangle = \phi(\mathbf{X}_a) \cdot \phi(\mathbf{X}_b) = \frac{\sum_{x_b \in \mathbf{X}_b, x_a \in \mathbf{X}_a}(x_a \cdot x_b)}{|\mathbf{X}_a||\mathbf{X}_b|} \tag{4}$$

where $\phi(\cdot)$ maps nonlinear input feature vector $\mathbf{X}$ into linear feature space $\mathbf{H}$.

Given the kernel, the SVM for each concept is trained with low-level features $\mathbf{X}$ of training data. To solve the SVM, an optimal hyperplane is found to correctly classify the training data, i.e., it satisfies $\phi^T(\mathbf{X}_i) \cdot \mathbf{w} + b > 0$ for every training sample $\mathbf{X}_i$ with positive class label $y_i = 1$ and $\phi^T(\mathbf{X}_i) \cdot \mathbf{w} + b < 0$ for every training sample $\mathbf{X}_i$ with negative class label $y_i = -1$. The optimization problem to find the optimal hyperplane is a quadratic problem that can be solved by converting it into the Wolfe dual problem [8, 9]. The optimization problem can be written as,

$$\min_{\mathbf{w},b} \frac{\|\mathbf{w}\|^2}{2} \text{ subject to } y_i \{\phi^T(\mathbf{X}_i) \cdot \mathbf{w} + b\} \geq 1 \tag{5}$$

By solving the optimization problem, the optimal hyperplane f_k to predict the L_k concept of unseen data $\mathbf{X}$ is formed as follows:

$$f_k(\mathbf{X}) = \sum_{i=1}^{n} a_i y_i K(\mathbf{X}_i, \mathbf{X}) + b \tag{6}$$

where a_i is support vector that is always positive.

The hyperplane f_k constructs the L_k concept detector D_k. Given an input of feature vector $\mathbf{X}$ to the D_k, the D_k outputs a confidence value which is considered as distance of the input feature vector from the trained hyperplane f_k. A series of the confidence values for every concept detector forms a confidence vector $\mathbf{C}$ as follows:

$$\mathbf{C}_{local} = \left\{ c_k \middle| c_k = D_k(f_k(\mathbf{X})) = D_k\left(\sum_{i=1}^{n} a_i y_i K(\mathbf{X}_i, \mathbf{X}) + b\right), k = 1,2,3,,N_k \right\}, \tag{7}$$

where c_k is confidence value of the L_k concept detector D_k. Note the N_k confidence values construct a confidence vector $\mathbf{C}_{local}$.

2.4 Local Concept Merging

Before proceeding to the global concept learning, local concepts on sub-regions are merged with its confidence value. For the concept merging, the local concept of the 5 basic regions is determined. The 5 basic regions are the region T_1, T_2, T_3, T_4, and T_5, which has an overlapped region with other region templates. With 5 basic regions, 10 templates are grouped into 5 groups by gathering overlapped regions. Figure 4 shows the overlapped region set. The region T_1 is overlapped with the region T_{10}. The region

T_2 is overlapped with the region T_6, T_8, and T_{10}. The region T_3 is overlapped with the region T_6, T_9, and T_{10}. The region T_4 is overlapped with the region T_7, T_8, and T_{10}. The region T_5 is overlapped with the region T_7, T_9, and T_{10}.

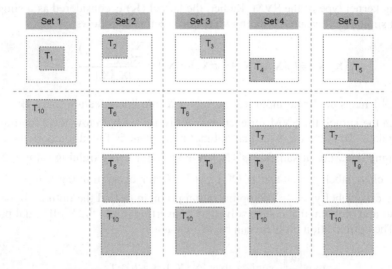

Fig. 4. Overlapped region set for local concept merging

The goal of the concept merging is to predict the most reliable local concept on the 5 local region bases. The local concepts of the 10 sub-regions are merged into the local concepts of the 5 basic regions as holding higher confidence of the local concept on the local regions while ignoring lower confidence. Thus, the local concept of the 5 regions is measured as follows:

$$\mathbf{Y}_{local} = \{\mathbf{y}_1, \mathbf{y}_2, \mathbf{y}_3, \mathbf{y}_4, \mathbf{y}_5\},$$
$$\text{where } \mathbf{y}_1 = \left\{ y_k = \max\left(c_k\big|_{T \in (T_1, T_{10})}\right) \middle| k = 1,2,3,\cdots, N_k \right\}$$
$$\mathbf{y}_2 = \left\{ y_k = \max\left(c_k\big|_{T \in (T_2, T_6, T_8, T_{10})}\right) \middle| k = 1,2,3,\cdots, N_k \right\},$$
$$\mathbf{y}_3 = \left\{ y_k = \max\left(c_k\big|_{T \in (T_3, T_6, T_9, T_{10})}\right) \middle| k = 1,2,3,\cdots, N_k \right\}, \quad (8)$$
$$\mathbf{y}_4 = \left\{ y_k = \max\left(c_k\big|_{T \in (T_4, T_7, T_8, T_{10})}\right) \middle| k = 1,2,3,\cdots, N_k \right\},$$
$$\text{and } \quad \mathbf{y}_5 = \left\{ y_k = \max\left(c_k\big|_{T \in (T_5, T_7, T_9, T_{10})}\right) \middle| k = 1,2,3,\cdots, N_k \right\},$$

where $\mathbf{Y}_{local}$ is a confidence vector of the local concept on the 5 basic regions. $\mathbf{y}_j$ is the set of confidence values of the N_k local concepts for the T_j region.

2.5   Global Concept Learning

Figure 5 shows an example of the relations between local concept and global concepts. There are 8 local concepts of sky, tree-wood, flower, rock, bridge, windows, streets and building, and 2 global concepts of terrain and architecture. In general, the 'terrain' is strongly linked with the 'sky', 'tree-wood', 'flower' and 'rock', and it is loosely linked with the 'bridge', 'windows', 'street', and 'building'. On the contrary, the 'architecture' is strongly linked with the 'bridge', 'windows', 'street', and 'building', and it is loosely linked with the 'sky, 'tree-wood', 'flower' and 'rock.

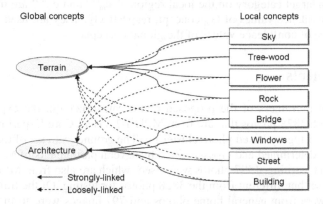

Fig. 5. Semantic relation between local concepts and global concepts

In this paper, the global concepts are trained based on the confidence vectors of the local SVMs. It also characterizes global concept detectors like local concept detectors. As mentioned above, the global concepts should have relatively higher level of semantics than the local concepts.

Similar to local concept learning, the N_m global concept lexicons are defined as G_m, where m = 1, 2, 3,..., N_m ($N_m < N_k$). The kernel for the global SVM is the same as that for the local SVM. By solving the optimization problem similar to local concept learning, the optimal hyperplane f_m to predict the global concept G_m of unseen data Y is formed as follows:

$$f_m(Y) = \sum_{i=1}^{n} a_i y_i K(Y_i, Y) + b \qquad (9)$$

The hyperplane f_m constructs the G_m concept detector D_m. Given an input of feature vector Y to the D_m, the D_m outputs a confidence value which is considered as distance of the input feature vector from the trained hyperplane f_m. A series of the confidence values for every concept detector forms a confidence vector C as follows:

$$C_{global} = \left\{ c_m \middle| c_m = D_m(f_m(Y)) = D_m\left(\sum_{i=1}^{n} a_i y_i K(Y_i, Y) + b\right), m = 1,2,3,,N_m \right\}, \qquad (10)$$

where c_m is confidence value of the G_m concept detector D_m. Note the N_m confidence values construct a confidence vector C_{global}.

2.6 Category Decision

Given the confidence vectors of the global concepts, we detect the target category set $G_{category}$ of input image. Given a local region T, the target categories can be a set of global concept with highest confidence value.

$$\mathbf{G}_{category} = \left\{ G_T \middle| G_T = \underset{G_m \in \mathbf{G}, m=1,2,\cdots,N_m}{\arg\max} \left\{ \frac{\left(c_m - c_m^{min}\right)}{\left(c_m^{max} - c_m^{min}\right)} \right\}, T \in \mathbf{T} \right\} \tag{11}$$

where G_T is a target category on the local region T. c_m^{min} and c_m^{max} are minimum and maximum confidence values of G_m concept, respectively. They are used to normalize different range of confidence values of the global concepts.

3 Experiments

To verify the usefulness of the proposed photo categorization, the experiment was performed with 3828 photos that are from MPEG-7 Visual Core Experiment 2 (VCE-2) data set for category-based photo clustering. The ground truth set of the test images was officially determined and cross-verified by several participants of MPEG-7.

For concept learning, 1597 photos were used, which are also from MPEG-7 VCE-2 training data set but different from the 3828 photos for testing. Of the training images, 800 images were from general home photos and 797 images were from Corel Image Collection.

In the experiment, we first defined 20 local concepts for local concept learning. For the SVM learning, we utilized verified software, called SVM^{light} developed in [10]. The training data set was localized to sub-images and then positive samples for each concept were selected from the sub-images by human visual perception. The negative samples were randomly selected from the positive samples of other concepts.

Table 1 shows the description of local concepts and corresponding sample data for each local concept. We preliminarily defined 7 global concepts that are the most popular categories in web photo collection. The global concepts consists of 'architecture', 'terrain', 'indoor', 'waterside', 'night-scene', 'snowscape', and 'sunset'. Then we found local concept set that can belong to the global concepts in human visual perception.

In human visual perception, the architecture is strongly linked with the building, bridge, skyscraper, street, and window local concepts. The terrain is strongly linked with the flowers, mountain-field, rock, sky, and wood local concepts. The indoor is strongly linked with the interior local concept. The waterside is strongly linked with beach, lake-river, pool, waterfall, and wave local concepts. The night-scene is strongly linked with the night-scene local concepts. The snowscape is strongly linked with the snow-covered-mountain local concept. The sunset is strongly linked with the sunset local concept. Of the global concepts, the indoor, night-scene, snowscape, and sunset concepts are composed of a single local concept since they have no other local concepts.

The global concepts were used for category concept learning. Each global concept was also trained by SVM. Table 2 shows the global concepts defined in the experiment and the number of positive and negative samples for each global concept.

Table 3 shows experiment results with the 3828 query photos. As shown in Table 3, the overall average performance of categorization is around 73% recall and 57% precision. The average performance is normalized by the number of ground truth images for each concept as follows,

Table 1. Training data for local concept learning

Local concepts	# of positive samples	# of negative samples	Local concepts	# of positive samples	# of negative samples
Beach	423	410	Rock	182	181
Bridge	58	73	Sky	688	690
Building	908	683	Skyscraper	173	139
Flowers	73	81	Snow-covered-mountain	869	584
Interior	993	878	Street	125	120
Lake-river	81	131	Sunset	325	307
Mountain-field	843	705	Waterfall	132	135
Night-scene	717	664	Wave	73	92
People	583	540	Windows	168	135
Pool	41	48	Wood	576	364

Table 2. Training data for global concept learning

Local concepts	# of positive samples	# of negative samples
Architecture	1429	1223
Indoor	993	878
Terrain	1641	1331
Night-scene	717	664
Snowscape	865	584
Waterside	325	307

Table 3. Experiment results

Category (# of ground truth)	Performance (%)	
	Recall	Precision
Architecture (1625)	0.836308	0.640434
Interior (904)	0.715708	0.378806
Terrain (1707)	0.762156	0.746414
Night-scene (456)	0.824561	0.506057
Snowscape (227)	0.660793	0.147059
Sunset (117)	0.982906	0.108291
Waterside (745)	0.366443	0.500000
Weighted average performance	**0.730157**	**0.571773**

$$p' = \frac{\sum_m \{n(m) \cdot p_m\}}{\sum_m n(m)} \text{ and } r' = \frac{\sum_m \{n(m) \cdot r_m\}}{\sum_m n(m)}, \tag{12}$$

where p' is weighted precision and r' is weighted precision. p_m is precision of the mth global concept and r_m is precision of the mth global concept. $n(m)$ is the number of ground truth images of the mth global concept

In results, the architecture and terrain categories outperformed others. The problem might be caused by a semantically-biased local concept structure, i.e., currently, most of the local concepts are strongly linked with a few global concepts. For example, as shown in Table 1, the terrain seems to be strongly linked with woods, mountain-field, flowers, rock, beach, lake-river, etc, so that the terrain category might be better trained with more local concepts than the other categories like snowscape or sunset.

4 Conclusions

In this paper, we propose a photo categorization method for digital home photos. The proposed method combines local concept and global concept learning together. The local concept detector is trained separately from global concept detector. In order to localize image into small region, a photographic region template set is proposed, which is built for generic home photos. All the local and global concepts are trained by SVM. To achieve more reliable performance, the local concepts are merged with confidence. Experiment results showed that the proposed method would be useful to detect multi-category concepts for home photo albuming. However, some category concepts might not be trained sufficiently. Thus, in the future, it is much needed for constructing a systematic ontology that should be semantically-unbiased. Further, the categorization performance should be also compared when using other types of kernel of SVM.

References

1. Newsam S., Sumengen B., and Manjunath B. S.: Category-based Image Retrieval. IEEE ICIP. Vol.2. (2003) 596-599
2. Djeraba C.: Content-based Multimedia Indexing and Retrieval. IEEE Trans. On Multimedia., Vol.9. (2002) 18-22
3. Smith J., Naphade M., and Natsev A.: Multimedia Semantic Indexing using Model Vectors IEEE ICME. Vol.2. (2002) 445-448
4. Loui A.C. and Savakis A.: Automated Event Clustering and Quality Screening of Consumer Pictures for Digital Albuming. Multimedia, IEEE Trans. On, Vol.5. No.3. (2003) 390-402
5. Lim J.H., Tian Q., and Mulhem P.: Home Photo Content Modeling for Personalized Event-Based Retrieval. Multimedia. IEEE Trans. On, Vol.10. No.4. (2003) 24-37
6. Carson C. et al.: Blobworld: Image Segmentation Using Expectation-Maximization and Its Application to Image Querying. Pattern Analysis and Machine Intelligence. IEEE Trans. On. Vol.24. (2002) 1026-1038
7. Fuh C., Cho S., and Essig, K.; Hierarchical Color Image Region Segmentation for Content-Based Image Retrieval System. Image Processing. IEEE Transs On, Vol.9. (2000) 156-162
8. Schölkopf B. and Smola A.: Learning with Kernels. The MIT Press, London (2002)
9. Muller K et al.: An Introduction to Kernel-Based Learning Algorithms. Neural Networks, IEEE Trans. On. Vol.12. No.2. (2001)
10. Joachims T.: Making large-Scale SVM Learning Practical. Advances in Kernel Methods - Support Vector Learning, B. Schölkopf and C. Burges and A. Smola (ed.). The MIT-Press. (1999)

MPEG-7 Visual-Temporal Clustering for Digital Image Collections

Robert O'Callaghan and Mirosław Bober

Mitsubishi Electric ITE, Visual Information Laboratory,
The Surrey Research Park, Guildford GU2 7YD, UK
{rob.ocallaghan, miroslaw.bober}@vil.ite.mee.com

Abstract. We present a novel, yet simple algorithm for clustering large collections of digital images. The method is applicable to consumer digital photo libraries, where it can be used to organise a photo-album, enhancing the search/browse capability and simplifying the interface in the process. The method is based on standard MPEG-7 visual content descriptors, which, when combined with date and time metadata, provide powerful cues to the semantic structure of the photo collection. Experiments are presented showing how the proposed method closely matches consensus human judgements of cluster structure.

1 Introduction

Semantic access to visual content is becoming a key goal in the development of a wide variety of consumer electronics products. The digital revolution has unleashed a tide of content, which is being created, transmitted and stored in a plethora of ways. Although a great deal of research effort has addressed the problems associated with intelligent management of this multimedia data, to date there has been comparatively little impact on the marketplace. This is due to change. This year is likely to see the first examples of actual products with automated content-indexing functionality. Soon, gadgets employing technology like automatic video summarization, face-recognition and still image search will start to take the wave of digital content in hand, give it structure and unlock its true value.

Consumer digital photography is one example of the type of application where existing (visual) content-based techniques have not yet fulfilled their potential. There is an established, growing market and a clear need to manage the image-data created. Crucially, these photos lack any alternative source of semantic desctription—unless the photographer manually annotates each one, there is no audio-track or text description that can be used to index and organise them. The meta-data that is stored (*e.g.*, in EXIF format), relates mainly to the technical parameters of capture. This increases the importance and usefulness of visual content-based analysis.

In this paper, using MPEG-7 standardised descriptors [1] as a starting point, we will describe a simple but powerful technique that can enable practical,

G.G. Lee et al. (Eds.): AIRS 2005, LNCS 3689, pp. 339–350, 2005.

content-enhanced functionality for real consumer digital-imaging applications. The experiments presented will demonstrate that the"low-level" features in the standard can support content processing that is semantically accurate.

2   Consumer Digital Photography

Digital camera users can easily and rapidly generate sizeable private collections of digital images. However, they cannot fully enjoy their photographs unless they are also able to efficiently navigate through all this content. The traditional "shoebox" approach to photographic prints does not scale well to large digital collections—a keen photographer might take hundreds of shots in the space of a few days and assembling the images into albums is time consuming. The net effect is that searching for specific images or even just browsing for interesting ones will be very troublesome.

The ability to organise the collection to improve access is therefore highly desirable, especially if it can be done with minimal manual effort. Unfortunately, most current software offers only the most rudimentary, tedious ways to index these images—tools like free-text annotation or labelling, for instance. However, this ignores the fact that there are simple content cues that could easily be used to assist the user and relieve the boredom of such tasks.

In a simple application of MPEG-7 technology, we can create a content-based description of each image and use this to group together "similar" pictures. One simple but very effective structure is to group images by the occasion or situation in which they were taken. This is natural for the user since they will often remember the circumstances much better than a date, time or explicit label attached to the picture. It is possible to automatically cluster images into such "situations" by using MPEG-7 visual features, together with the time stamp of the image. Based on the assumption that each situation is contiguous in time, the organisational structure is defined by the time-sequence of images, together with an indication of the boundaries between clusters (*cf.* Fig. 3). This provides the user with a simple, intuitive and effective means to browse through their collection, without placing any additional burden on them to spend time organising it.

There are many ways to visualise the cluster structure, but they all share the potential to reduce redundancy and improve the user's navigation experience. The enhanced access to the content could be realised in several ways:

- Browsing
  - Display a cluster of images per page, or...
  - Display a single thumbnail or icon for each cluster
- Annotation
  - Users can easily assign a single label to all the images in a cluster
- Sharing
  - Users can select images by cluster and...
  - Print

- Copy
- Upload to website

To automatically generate the clustering calls for a number of tools. Firstly, we need the actual content-description and associated methods for extracting it and comparing multiple images. Secondly, there is the analysis algorithm, which will use these comparisons to decide which images to group together and which to separate into distinct clusters.

The next section will give a brief overview of the MPEG-7 standard and, in particular, the visual descriptors used by the current clustering algorithm. Section 4 will then describe how the descriptive information is assembled to determine the actual clusters. Finally, Sect. 5 details the results of quantitative experiments performed, as well as showing some visual examples of how the clustering compares to human judgements of the "correct" organization.

3   Overview of MPEG-7

In October 1996, realising the increasing ubiquity of audiovisual media, MPEG started a new work item, called "Multimedia Content Description Interface", with the objective of providing standardised technologies for describing audiovisual content in multimedia environments. The resulting international standard now consists of ten parts, the first of which were published in 2002. Since then, several amendments have added further tools, including the extension of Part 3 (Visual) in 2004 [2]. For a good overview of the context, scope and structure of the standard, the interested reader is referred to [3] or [4]. Briefly, the main elements of MPEG-7 are:

Description Tools: *Descriptors* (D), that define the syntax and the semantics of each feature (metadata element) and *Description Schemes* (DS), that specify the structure and semantics of the relationships between their components. These components may be both Descriptors and Description Schemes. Several descriptors are discussed in the following section, but these are just a sample of the full array. The descriptors are the individual tools, which can be selected, as desired, for particular qualities. The Description Scheme is like a toolbox—carrying a range of tools that are likely to be of use for a given problem.

Description Definition Language: (DDL), based on XML Schema language, to define the syntax of the MPEG-7 Description Tools. It also allows the creation of new Description Schemes and, possibly, Descriptors as well as allowing the extension and modification of existing Description Schemes. The DDL is the language used to stock the toolbox with tools—it allows the author to define the toolset and how it is assembled in the toolbox. Since these instructions can be understood and implemented by any application that speaks the same language, it achieves the twin goals of interoperability and flexibility.

System Tools: to support binary coded representation, transmission mechanisms, multiplexing of descriptions, synchronization with actual content, *etc.*

Following the same analogy, the system tools solve the logistical problems—how to carry the toolbox with minimal effort and make sure nothing gets lost in transit.

3.1   Visual Descriptors

Of the visual descriptors we will focus only on the six used by the current method. More details on the implementation of each of these can be found in [3] or, of course, the relevant part of the international standard [1].

Dominant Colour: The Dominant Colour Descriptor is a compact summary of colour distribution. This descriptor is most suitable in situations where a small number of colours are enough to characterize the colour information in the image or region of interest. Vector quantization is used to extract a small number of representative colours in each region/image. The variance and percentage of each quantized colour in the region is calculated correspondingly. This means that the dominant color descriptor effectively characterizes the colour distribution as a mixture of Gaussians. A spatial coherency on the entire descriptor is also defined, and is used in similarity retrieval.

Scalable Colour: The Scalable Colour Descriptor is a colour histogram in HSV colour space, which is encoded by a Haar transform. Its binary representation is scalable in terms of bin numbers and bit accuracy, over a broad range of data rates. The scalable colour descriptor is useful for image-to-image matching and retrieval based on colour features. Retrieval accuracy increases with the number of bits used in the representation. Similarity matching does not require inversion of the Haar transform, increasing the efficiency of this tool further.

Colour Layout: The Colour Layout Descriptor effectively represents the spatial layout of colour images in a very compact form. It is based on generating a tiny (8x8) thumbnail of the image, which is encoded via Discrete Cosine Transform (DCT) and quantized. Further compression is achieved by discarding high-frequency detail. This allows visual matching with high retrieval efficiency at a very low computational cost. It offers both image-to-image matching as well and high-speed sequence-to-sequence matching, which requires many repeated similarity calculations. Furthermore, it offers a quick way to visualize the appearance of an image, by reconstructing an approximation of the thumbnail, using the inverse DCT.

Colour Structure: The Colour Structure Descriptor captures both colour content (just like a colour histogram) and information about the spatial structure of the colours. Its main function is image-to-image matching and its intended use is for still-image retrieval, where an image may consist of either a single rectangular frame or arbitrarily shaped, possibly disconnected, regions. The extraction method embeds structure information into the descriptor by taking into account all colours in a structuring element of 8x8 pixels that slides over the image, instead of considering each pixel separately. As a result, unlike the colour histogram, this descriptor can distinguish between two images in which a given colour is present in identical amounts but where the structure of the groups of pixels having that colour is different in the two images.

Edge Histogram: The edge histogram descriptor represents the spatial distribution of five types of edges, namely four directional edges and one non-directional edge. Since edges play an important role in visual perception, it can retrieve images with similar semantic meaning. Thus, it primarily targets image-to-image matching (by example or by sketch), especially for natural images with non-uniform edge distributions.

Homogeneous Texture: The Homogeneous Texture descriptor is designed to characterise the properties of texture in an image (or region), based on the assumption that the texture is homogeneous—*i.e.*, the visual properties of the texture are relatively constant over the region. To extract the descriptor, the image is filtered with a bank of orientation- and scale-tuned Gabor filters. The first and the second moments of the energy in the frequency domain in the corresponding sub-bands are then used as the components of the texture descriptor. The number of filters used is 5 (scales) x 6 (orientations) = 30. However, an efficient implementation using projections and 1-D filtering operations exists for feature extraction.

4   Situation-Clustering Algorithm

MPEG-7 standardises the syntax and semantics of descriptors. Their actual usage is left open to the implementer. Here, we adhere to the recommended matching methods from Part 8 of the standard. These have been suggested as the most appropriate ways to exploit the features' potential. Here "matching" means comparing the descriptors extracted from two images, to give a single numerical measure of similarity (or, conversely, difference). To proceed, we use the matching information from the six descriptors to drive the clustering algorithm.

Choosing that the clusters should lie along the time axis constrains the problem significantly. We imagine laying the images out in sequence, just like a roll of film. Clustering this sequence is like deciding where to cut the roll—we need only decide if each image belongs with the next. The boundaries define the clusters, which are contiguous groups of images. Intuitively, the information about whether to break at a given point in the chain or not lies in the few photographs before and after in the sequence. Therefore, by making some measurements in the vicinity, we can determine if a cut is appropriate. This neighbourhood and the pair-wise comparisons used are illustrated in Fig. 1.

Another advantage of temporal consistency is that the date and time of capture can be used as additional input to the clustering engine. This information is already routinely stored in the EXIF [5] metadata by digital still cameras and

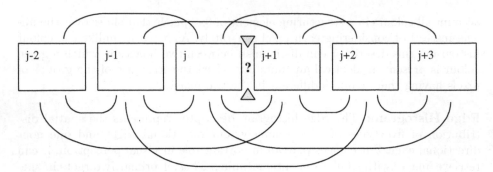

Fig. 1. Neighbourhood comparisons evaluated to determine if a boundary is present

can also be included in the MPEG-7 description of the image. Jointly characterising the temporal and visual homogeneity of the clusters means that they should better correspond to human understanding of scenes, situations and views. The time difference is measured on a logarithmic scale, to compress the range of values and allow meaningful comparisons. Time distance is therefore defined as:

$$D_T(i, i+1) = \ln\left(10^{-5} + (T_{i+1} - T_i)\right) \qquad (1)$$

The unit of time used for T_i is days. The logarithm is applied to normalise the range of time distances, since time differences will vary over several orders of magnitude. After this transformation, the variation of the time distance is comparable to the remaining features. Meanwhile, the constant, 10^{-5}, chooses the minimum scale of the distance—just under one second, in this case.

The input to the clustering engine includes the first-, second- and third-order distances in a short time interval around the boundary to be tested. Here "first-order" refers to the difference, for any given feature, between two images that are adjacent in the sequence—*i.e.*, $D_F(i, i+1)$. A second-order distance is the difference between two images that are separated by one other image— *i.e.*, $D_F(i, i+2)$. Similarly, a third-order distance is the difference between two images that are separated by two other images—*i.e.*, $D_F(i, i+3)$. The total measurement of difference between images j and $j+1$ is now:

$$D(j, j+1) = \sum_F \left\{ \sum_{i=-2}^{2} \alpha_{Fi} D_F(j+i, j+i+1) \right. \qquad (2)$$

$$+ \sum_{i=-2}^{1} \beta_{Fi} D_F(j+i, j+i+2)$$

$$\left. + \sum_{i=-2}^{0} \gamma_{Fi} D_F(j+i, j+i+3) \right\}$$

This is a summation over a set of 12 distance measurements for each of 6 visual features (the outer summation being over the set of features, F). For time difference, only the first order distances are used, since higher order time difference measurements intuitively add no additional information. Time therefore adds just five more distance measurements. The total set of 77 numbers is linearly combined using 77 weights α, β and γ, which correspond to first, second and third order measurements, respectively.

The real number, $D(j, j + 1)$, provides an indicator of the confidence or likelihood that there is a boundary at this point in the sequence. A threshold is then applied to give the final binary-valued answer. Alternatively, the vector of D values can be sorted, to provide an ordering by the most likely boundary positions. Users could then choose to keep a fixed proportion of boundaries (*i.e.*, a fixed average cluster-size), to best suit their own preferences and photo library.

The key strengths of the proposed method are its simplicity and the integrated treatment of time and visual appearance. Previous work has considered temporal event clustering, but where visual similarity was also introduced it has been in an ad-hoc fashion. The method of [6], for example, combines the visual and temporal similarity using a fixed heuristic rule at the first stage of the algorithm. This means that the time-distances in the neighbourhood cannot be weighted independently of the visual. One of the insights of the current method is that the comparison of two images cannot be distilled into a single number at such an early stage of processing.

5   Results

Obviously there is a trade-off between finding as many useful boundaries as possible while eliminating the spurious ones. Measuring this forms the basis for the experimental evaluation.

As mentioned above, the purpose of the clustering is to generate semantically meaningful groups in the sequence of images. This should offer a significant improvement the conventional approach of dividing the images by fixed time periods (*e.g.*, filing in different folders by month, day or hour). The weights in (2) were therefore chosen to obtain groupings by "situation" or "view"[1]. For example, on a sight-seeing trip, a camera user may visit several different sites, generating clusters of visually similar photos that correspond to the different scenes. Alternatively, at an event like a dinner party, there may be pictures of the food, closely interspersed with pictures of the guests—so although the visual similarity is low, the user would still choose to group the images from this event together. In this case we expect the algorithm to use the time-span cue to correctly merge the images with different compositions. This is possible because the temporal and visual information is considered jointly.

The behaviour of the clustering algorithm has been investigated using two independent datasets of images. These were collected and contributed by a number of participants in MPEG-7 visual activities, therefore they respresent diverse

---

[1] This can be achieved either heuristically, or using standard numerical optimization methods. The best way to choose the weights is an open problem and is outside the current scope.

Table 1. Experimental Data

Dataset	Size	Boundaries	%
1st	2344	495	21.1
2nd	2063	342	16.6
$1^{st}+2^{nd}$	4408	841	19.1

content, styles and camera usage habits. A Ground Truth (GT) of manual boundaries among these images was created, against which automated algorithms could be compared. The statistics of the data and GT are shown in Table 1. The weight values used in the experiments are given in Table 2.

Table 2. Weights used in the experiments

	DC	SC	CL	CS	HT	EH	T
α_0	0.0583	0.2598	0.4546	0.2661	-0.0718	0.4890	2.8952
α_1	0.1976	-0.0077	-0.0986	-0.3279	-0.1370	-0.3108	-0.2911
α_2	-0.0425	0.1117	0.0543	0.0594	-0.0089	-0.1642	-0.0035
α_{-1}	0.2718	-0.1835	-0.0640	-0.1153	0.0102	-0.3534	-0.3748
α_{-2}	0.0085	-0.0259	-0.0539	-0.1419	-0.0725	0.0951	-0.0786
β_{-1}	-0.0249	-0.0107	0.4662	0.3828	0.0567	-0.2351	
β_0	0.1718	-0.0788	-0.0086	0.2190	0.2653	0.2186	
β_{-2}	0.0958	-0.2618	-0.0520	-0.0652	-0.0496	0.1157	
β_1	0.2785	0.0072	-0.3648	-0.1872	-0.0611	0.1439	
γ_{-1}	-0.1955	0.1203	-0.0767	-0.0567	0.0148	0.1178	
γ_{-2}	0.0324	0.1808	-0.2327	0.2665	0.0167	0.2029	
γ_0	-0.1199	0.0196	0.0477	0.1841	0.0288	0.1436	

Clearly, there is no single "correct" cluster configuration in this situation. Nonetheless it was possible to reach a consensus in the majority of cases, with the more subjective choices being left to the original photographer's discretion. Note that, because the contributions from different sources were merged, these subjective judgements are considered "noise" in the GT, rather than the process to be modelled.

Results are presented in terms of Precision and Recall (P, R), defined as:

$$P = \frac{\text{No. of detections}}{\text{No.of boundaries labelled}} \tag{3}$$

$$R = \frac{\text{No. of detections}}{\text{No. of target boundaries}} \tag{4}$$

Figure 2 shows the performance of the algorithm over the two independent collections and also their combination. A more intuitive illustration is offered by Fig. 3—this shows a typical screen-capture from a software implementation, displaying part of the clustering output. The groupings are visually coherent, so

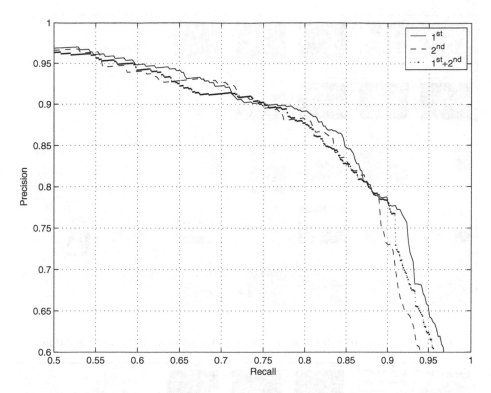

Fig. 2. Performance of the clustering algorithm with respect to human-generated judgements

that browsing can be enhanced by "collapsing" each cluster into a single thumbnail (however, for display here, all the clusters have been expanded). Figure 4 shows the associated manual GT judgements. The correspondence between the two is clear. The algorithm has, in this case, produced some spurious boundaries, but these still occur at points in the sequence where either temporal or visual similarities (or both) are low. Therefore, the user will probably form the impression that the granularity of the segmentation is too fine, rather than thinking that the algorithm is making inexplicable mistakes.

Next, we consider the effect of reducing the amount of information

available to the algorithm. By setting some weights to zero (and adjusting the remaining non-zero ones), we can model a simplified version of the method, where a smaller set of measurments (< 77) is available to the algorithm. The graph in Fig. 5 measures the performance as the value of "Precision=Recall"—in other words, the point at which the (P,R) curve crosses the diagonal. As Fig. 5 shows, the performance degrades very gracefully, with 80% precision and recall still possible using just 7 measurements. These depend on the Scalable Colour, Colour Structure, Edge Histogram and Time features only.

It is perhaps surprising that such a simple algorithm can match human perception convincingly. Nonetheless, the correlation with human judgement of "sit-

Fig. 3. Examples of automatic clustering judgements made by the algorithm

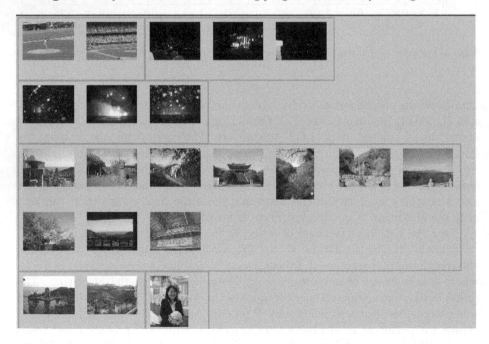

Fig. 4. Human GT judgements corresponding to Fig. 3

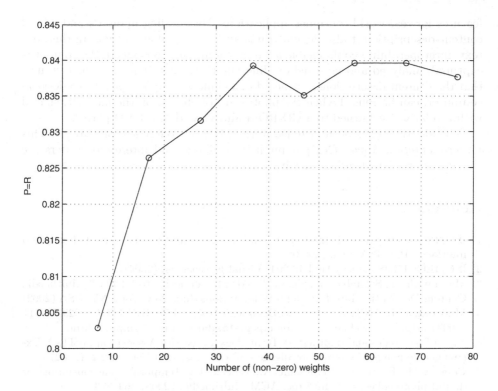

Fig. 5. Variation of clustering performance with a reduced set of distance measurements

uation" clusters has been shown experimentally. Tuning the weights on a set of reasonably consistent examples, the algorithm gives over 80% accuracy (precision) while finding 80% of the cluster-boundaries (recall). Even more impressive is the observation that three quarters of the boundaries can be found with accuracy greater than 90%. As mentioned above, human subjectivity comes into play here, but the point is not to try to model this—rather to automate the obvious and remove some of the tedium, while freeing the user to concentrate on the difficult, subjective or ambiguous cases.

6 Conclusions

We have presented a simple algorithm for clustering images in a digital photo collection. As experiments have shown, it neatly captures the bursty nature of consumer digital photography and allows greater flexibility in how pictures are organised. By performing much of the tedious labour for the user it can increase satisfaction as well as improve the overall experience.

Obviously this is not the only way to organize an image collection. It is merely intended to showcase the possibilities offered by low-level content-based features for real-world consumer applications. By building upon a standardised content-descpription it also demonstrates an interoperable solution. In this context, interoperability could enable a variety of applications where the content is captured, analysed and accessed on different platforms. It means, for instance, that the content descriptions, extracted in a camera or upon upload to a desktop computer, can be reused when the photos are published on the internet, shared with a relative, or burned to a CD-ROM and viewed in a DVD player.

The algorithm has been included in the MPEG-7 reference software [7]. This *eXperimentation Model* (XM) is publicly available and interested readers are encouraged to download and use it.

References

1. ISO/IEC: 15938-3:2002, Information technology—Multimedia content description interface—Part 3: Visual. (2002)
2. ISO/IEC: 15938-3:2002/Amd 1:2004, Visual Extensions. (2004)
3. Manjunath, B., Salembier, P., Sikora, T., eds.: Introduction to MPEG-7: Multimedia Content Description Interface. John Wiley & Sons, Inc., New York, NY, USA (2002)
4. Martínez, J.M.: MPEG-7 overview. Document N5525, ISO/IEC JTC1/SC29/WG11 (2003) http://www.chiariglione.org/mpeg/standards/mpeg-7/mpeg-7.htm.
5. Japan Electronics and Information Technology Industries Association (JEITA): Exchangeable image file format for digital still cameras: Exif Version 2.2. (2002)
6. Cooper, M., Foote, J., Girgensohn, A., Wilcox, L.: Temporal event clustering for digital photo collections. In: Proc. ACM Multimedia. (2003) 364–373
7. Yamada, A., Kim, S.: MPEG-7 visual XM document version 23.0. Document N6904, ISO/IEC JTC1/SC29/WG11 (2005)

A Structured Learning Approach to Semantic Photo Indexing and Query

Joo-Hwee Lim[1], Jesse S. Jin[2], and Suhuai Luo[2]

[1] Institute for Infocomm Research,
21 Heng Mui Keng Terrace, Singapore 119613
joohwee@i2r.a-star.edu.sg
[2] University of Newcastle,
Callaghan NSW 2308, Australia
{jesse.jin, Suhuai.Luo}@newcastle.edu.au

Abstract. Consumer photos exhibit highly varied contents, diverse resolutions and inconsistent quality. The objects are usually ill-posed, occluded, and cluttered with poor lighting, focus, and exposure. Existing image retrieval approaches face many obstacles such as robust object segmentation, small sampling problem during relevance feedback, semantic gap between low-level features and high-level semantics, etc.

We propose a structured learning approach to design domain-relevant visual semantics, known as semantic support regions, to support semantic indexing and visual query for consumer photos. Semantic support regions are segmentation-free image regions that exhibit semantic meanings and that can be learned statistically to span a new indexing space. They are detected from image content, reconciled across multiple resolutions, and aggregated spatially to form local semantic histograms.

Query by Spatial Icons (QBSI) is a unique visual query language to specify semantic icons and spatial extents in a Boolean expression. Based on 2400 heterogeneous consumer photos and 26 semantic support regions learned from a small training set, we demonstrate the usefulness of the visual query language with 15 QBSI queries that have attained high precision values at top retrieved images.

1 Introduction

Low-level features can be easily extracted from images. However, they are not completely descriptive for meaningful retrieval. High-level semantic information is useful and effective in retrieval. But it depends heavily on semantic regions, which are difficult to obtain themselves. Between low-level features and high-level semantic information, there is an unsolved "semantic gap" [19]. The semantic gap is due to two inherent problems. One problem is that the extraction of complete semantics from image data is extremely hard as it demands robust object recognition and scene understanding. This is the *semantic extraction problem*. The other problem is the complexity, ambiguity and subjectivity in user interpretation i.e. the *semantic interpretation problem*.

G.G. Lee et al. (Eds.): AIRS 2005, LNCS 3689, pp. 351–365, 2005.

In fact, relevance feedback is regarded as a promising technique to bridge the semantic gap in image retrieval [3,18]. However the correctness of user's feedback may not be statistically reflected due to the small sampling problem.

Image classification is another approach to bridge the semantic gap and has received more attention lately [26]. However, image classification or class-based retrieval approaches are adequate for query by predefined image class. In general, the set of relevant images may not correspond to any predefined class.

Consumer photos exhibit highly varied contents and imperfect image quality due to spontaneous and casual nature of image capturing. The objects in consumer images are usually ill-posed, occluded, and cluttered with poor lighting, focus, and exposure. Robust object segmentation for such noisy images is still an unsolved problem [19].

To alleviate the *semantic extraction problem*, we propose a structured learning framework to facilitate systematic design and extraction of domain-relevant visual semantics, known as *Semantic Support Regions* (SSRs) in building content-based image retrieval systems. SSRs are segmentation-free image regions that exhibit semantic meanings and are learned statistically to span a new indexing space. They are detected in image content, reconciled across multiple resolutions, and aggregated spatially to form local semantic histograms.

To address the *semantic interpretation problem* during query formulation, a unique visual query language, Query by Spatial Icons (QBSI), allows a user to specify his or her query as a Boolean expression of semantic icons and spatial extents. Based on 2400 heterogeneous consumer photos and 26 SSRs learned from a small training set, we demonstrate the usefulness of QBSI with 15 queries that have attained high precision values at top retrieved images.

2   Related Work

2.1   Semantic Extraction and Indexing

Town and Sinclair [25] described a semantic labeling approach to image retrieval. An image is segmented into non-overlapping regions. Each region is then classified into one of the 11 predefined visual categories (for outdoor scenes) by artificial neural networks. Both similarity-based and region-based matching are supported. The evaluation was carried out on over 1000 Corel images and about 500 home photos, with better classification and retrieval results obtained for the professional Corel images even that the home photo set is smaller than the Corel image set.

A generative approach to segment and label regions was given in [11]. While generative models offer modular framework for learning the semantic classes, it may not work well when the classes have close multimodal distributions and the data near the discriminative boundary will not be emphasized.

The major problem in the semantic labeling approach is image segmentation. Highly accurate segmentation of objects is a major bottleneck except for selected narrow domains when few dominant objects are recorded against a clear background [19].

The recent monotonic tree approach [22] provides a unique framework to analyze scenery images. Based on a new concept of *monotonic line*, image data are progressively represented as hierarchies of structural elements, which are classified and clustered into semantic regions of sky, building, tree, waves, placid water, lawn, snow, and others with qualifying scores. The qualifying scores for different element categories are computed based on different assumptions about the color, location, harshness, and shape of scenery features. The scenery features were tested on 6776 Corel and 1444 PhotoDisc images with very good retrieval results.

From the perspective of using local semantics to bridge the semantic gap, our SSR approach can be viewed as an extended effort upon the monotonic tree approach in several aspects. The SSR approach deals with more heterogeneous consumer images using statistical learning method to automatically map the relationships between second-order statistical local color and texture features and a larger local visual vocabulary (8 versus 26).

Motivated as an analogy of "keywords" of an image, the theory of Keyblocks [27] and Visual Keywords [13,14] also build image index from multi-resolution image blocks without segmentation. However, the generation of Keyblocks or Visual Keywords are based on either clustering [27,13] or manual selection [27,14]. While the semantics obtained from unsupervised learning is not strong, the manual selection approach requires intensive human expert labor. Although automatic selection was proposed as an alternative for Keyblock generation [27], the codebook-based process is primarily cluster-based and may not be discriminative enough for semantic detection.

2.2   Semantic Query Specification

Query By Example (QBE) (e.g. QBIC [7], Photobook [16]) requires a relevant image to be visible or available as a query example to start with the search. For example, the ImageRover [24] and Webseek [21] systems deploy text-based queries to obtain an initial set of images, and the PicToSeek [8] approach allows the user to supply a query image. Query By Canvas (QBC) (e.g. QBIC [7], Virage [2]) let user compose a visual query using geometrical shapes, colors and textures. Inherently this approach tends to specify things/stuff of interest in an indirect way using primitive features. Moreover the similarity matching between query and images relies on effective pre-segmentation of regions in the images which is complex and difficult in general [5,20].

Query by Keywords (QBK) allows information need to be described in high-level meaningful terms. But they cannot be generated automatically by the current content-based image indexing systems. However, manual annotation is usually incomplete, inconsistent, and context sensitive. Moreover there are situations when image semantics cannot be captured by labeling alone [1]. Query By Sketches (QBS) (e.g. [6]) let user draw the shape of an object as query. But it may not be easy to articulate a shape precisely or draw some ill-defined shapes (e.g. tree, sitting person, mountain). Automatic object shape extraction from cluttered scene images is also an open problem. Hence QBS applications have been limited to images of dominant objects on uniform background [6].

3 Structured Learning for Image Indexing

Semantic support regions (SSRs) are salient image patches that exhibit semantic meanings to us. A cropped face region, a typical grass patch, and a patch of swimming pool water etc can all be treated as SSR instances. In this paper, the SSRs are learned a priori and detected during image indexing from multi-scale block-based image regions without a region segmentation step. The key in image indexing here is not to record the primitive feature vectors themselves but to project them into a classification space spanned by semantic labels and uses the soft classification decisions as the local indexes for futher aggregation.

3.1 SSR Learning

To compute the SSRs from training instances, we use Support Vector Machines (SVMs) [9]. We extract suitable features such as color and textures for a local image patch and denote this feature vector as z. A support vector classifier $\mathcal{S}_i$ devoted to a class i of SSR is treated as a function on z, $\mathcal{S}_i(z) \in (-\infty, +\infty)$. Then elements in the classification vector T for region z can be normalized within $[0, 1]$ using the softmax function [4] as

$$T_i(z) = \frac{\exp^{\mathcal{S}_i(z)}}{\sum_j \exp^{\mathcal{S}_j(z)}}. \tag{1}$$

For the experiments described in this paper, since we are dealing with heterogeneous consumer photos, we adopt color and texture features to characterize SSRs. Hence a feature vector z has two parts, namely, a color feature vector z^c and a texture feature vector z^t. For the color feature, as the image patch for training and detection is relatively small, the mean and standard deviation of each color channel are deemed sufficient (i.e. z^c has 6 dimensions). In our experiments, we used the YIQ color space over other color spaces (e.g. RGB, HSV, LUV) as it performed better in our experiments. For the texture feature, we adopted the Gabor coefficients which have been shown to provide excellent pattern retrieval results [15]. Similarly, the means and standard deviations of the Gabor coefficients (5 scales and 6 orientations) in an image block are computed as z^t which has 60 dimensions. To normalize both the color and texture features, we use the Gaussian (i.e. zero-mean) normalization.

The distance or similarity measure depends on the kernel adopted for the support vector machines. For the experimental results reported in this paper, we have adopted the polynomial kernels. In order to balance the contributions of the color and texture features, we have modified the similarity measure $sim(y, z)$ between feature vector y and z as,

$$sim(y, z) = \frac{1}{2}\left(\frac{y^c \cdot z^c}{|y^c||z^c|} + \frac{y^t \cdot z^t}{|y^t||z^t|}\right) \tag{2}$$

where $y \cdot z$ denotes dot product operation.

Fig. 1. Examples of semantic support regions (top-down, left-to-right): People (Face, Figure, Crowd, Skin), Sky (Clear, Cloudy, Blue), Ground (Floor, Sand, Grass), Water (Pool, Pond, River), Foliage (Green, Floral, Branch), Mountain (Far, Rocky), Building (Old, City, Far), Interior (Wall, Wooden, China, Fabric, Light)

For the data set and experiments reported in this paper, we have designed 26 classes of SSRs (i.e. $S_i, i = 1, 2, \cdots, 26$ in Equation (1)). They are organized into 8 superclasses, namely `People`, `Sky`, `Ground`, `Water`, `Foliage`, `Mountain`, `Building`, and `Interior`. Fig. 1 shows single examples of these 26 classes of SSRs. This visual vocabulary is decided by 3 human subjects in consensus after studying the test collection. That is, visual entities that are relatively common in the test collection are selected as axes to span a new pattern space for representing the image semantics.

We cropped 554 image regions from 138 images and used 375 (i.e. two-third) of them (from 105 images) as training data for support vector machines to compute the support vectors of the SSRs and the remaining one-third as test data for generalization performance. In other words, both the training and test data for SSRs only utilize a small percentage (5.8%) of the 2400 collection. We experimented with the polynomial and radial basis function kernels with different parameter values. Among all the kernels evaluated, those with better generalization result on the test data were used for the indexing and retrieval tasks. A polynomial kernel with degree 2 and constant 1 ($C = 100$) [9] produced the best result on precision and recall. Hence it was adopted in the rest of our experiments.

Table 1 lists the training statistics of the 26 SSR classes. The columns show, left to right, the minimum, maximum, and average of the number of positive training examples (from a total of 375), the number of support vectors computed from the training examples, the number of positive test examples (from a total of 179), the number of misclassified examples on the 179 test set, and the percentage

Table 1. Training statistics of the 26 SSR classes

	min.	max.	avg.
num. pos. trg.	5	26	14.4
num. sup. vec.	9	66	33.3
num. pos. test	3	13	6.9
num. errors	0	14	5.7
error (%)	0	7.8	3.2

of error on test set. The negative training (test) examples for a SSR class are the union of positive training (test) examples of the other 25 classes.

3.2 Multi-scale SSR Detection and Reconciliation

To detect SSRs with translation and scale invariance in an image to be indexed, the image is scanned with windows of different scales. More precisely, given an image I with resolution $M \times N$, the middle layer (Fig. 2), Reconciled Detection Map (RDM), has a lower resolution of $P \times Q, P \leq M, Q \leq N$. Each pixel (p, q) in RDM corresponds to a two-dimensional region of size $r_x \times r_y$ in I. We further allow tessellation displacements $d_x, d_y > 0$ in X, Y directions respectively such that adjacent pixels in RDM along X direction (along Y direction) have receptive fields in I which are displaced by d_x pixels along X direction (d_y pixels along Y direction) in I. At the end of scanning an image, each pixel (p, q) that covers a region z in the pixel-feature layer will consolidate the SSR classification vector $T_i(z)$ (Equation (1)).

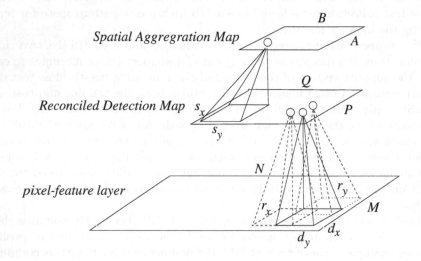

Fig. 2. A 3-layer architecture for image indexing

In our experiments, we progressively increase the window size $r_x \times r_y$ from 20×20 to 60×60 at a displacement (d_x, d_y) of $(10, 10)$ pixels, on a 240×360 size-normalized image. That is, after the detection step, we have 5 maps of detection of dimensions 23×35 to 19×31, which are reconciled into a common RDM as explained below.

To reconcile the detection maps across different resolutions onto a common basis, we adopt the following principle: if the most confident classification of a region at resolution r is less than that of a larger region (at resolution $r + 1$) that subsumes the region, then the classification output of the region should be replaced by those of the larger region at resolution $r + 1$. For instance, if the detection of a face is more confident than that of a building at the nose region (assuming nose is not in the SSR vocabulary), then the entire region covered by the face, which subsumes the nose region, should be labeled as face.

Using this principle, we compare detection maps of two consecutive resolutions at a time, in descending window sizes (i.e. from windows of 60×60 and 50×50 to windows of 30×30 and 20×20). After 4 cycles of reconciliation, the detection map that is based on the smallest scan window (20×20) would have consolidated the detection decisions obtained at other resolutions for further spatial aggregation.

3.3 Spatial Aggregation

The purpose of spatial aggregation is to summarize the reconciled detection outcome in a larger spatial region. Suppose a region Z comprises of n small equal regions with feature vectors $z_1, z_2, \cdots, z_n$ respectively. To account for the relative proportion of detected SSRs in the spatial area Z, the SSR detection vectors of the RDM is aggregated as

$$T_i(Z) = \frac{1}{n} \sum_k T_i(z_k). \tag{3}$$

This is illustrated in Fig. 2 where a Spatial Aggregation Map (SAM) further tessellates over RDM with $A \times B, A \leq P, B \leq Q$ pixels. The SAM has similar representation scheme as local color histograms, except that the bins refer to proportions of SSRs instead of proportions of colors. They are invariant to translation and rotation about the viewing axis and change only slowly under change of angle of view, change of scale, and occlusion [23]. The effect of averaging in Equation (3) will not dilute $T_i(Z)$ into a flat histogram. As an illustration, we list the SSRs (shown in Fig. 1) with $T_i(Z) \geq 0.1$ in Table 2, and show corresponding 3 tessellated blocks (outlined in red) in Fig. 3. We observe that the

Fig. 3. An example to illustrate image index

Table 2. Key SSRs recorded as index for image shown in Fig. 3

Image Block	Key SSR Aggregated	$T_i(Z)$
top	Foliage:Green	0.78
top	Foliage:Branch	0.11
center	People:Crowd	0.52
center	Foliage:Green	0.20
right	People:Crowd	0.36
right	Building:Old	0.32

dominant $T_i(Z)$ shown captures the content essence in each block with small values distributed in other bins.

4 Query by Spatial Icons (QBSI)

A QBSI query is composed as a spatial arrangement of visual semantics. A Visual Query Term (VQT) q specifies a region R where a SSR i should appear and a query formulus chains these terms up via logical operators. The truth value $\lambda(q, x)$ of a VQT q for any image x is simply defined as

$$\lambda(q, x) = T_i(R) \tag{4}$$

where $T_i(R)$ is defined in Equation (3).

In our current implementation, we support a two-level Is-A hierarchy of SSRs (Fig. 1) though it can be extended to deeper or other form of hierarchies (e.g. Part-Whole hierarchy). A VQT can involve a specific visual semantics (e.g. swimming pool water, denoted as Water:Pool) or a more abstract semantics (e.g. water, denoted as Water). On the other hand, the spatial constraint R defines the location and size of the specified visual semantics as drawn on a canvas.

As the visual semantics is learned based on the specific SSR i, the truth value of a VQT that specifies a more abstract visual semantics j (People, Sky, Ground, Water, Foliage, Mountain, Building, and Interior) is computed as

$$T_j(R) = max_{i \in V_j} T_i(R) \tag{5}$$

where V_j denotes the set of classes i that belongs to superclass j.

A QBSI query Q can be specified as a disjunctive normal form of VQT (with or without negation),

$$Q = (q_{11} \wedge q_{12} \wedge \cdots) \vee \cdots \vee (q_{c1} \wedge q_{c2} \wedge \cdots) \tag{6}$$

Then the query processing of query Q for any image x is to compute the truth value $\lambda(Q, x)$ using appropriate logical operators. As uncertainty values are involved in SSR detection and indexing, we adopt fuzzy operations [10] as follows:

$$\lambda(\bar{q}, x) = 1 - \lambda(q, x), \tag{7}$$

$$\lambda(q_i \wedge q_j, x) = min(\lambda(q_i, x), \lambda(q_j, x)), \tag{8}$$

$$\lambda(q_i \vee q_j, x) = max(\lambda(q_i, x), \lambda(q_j, x)). \tag{9}$$

In our existing web-based prototype, an intuitive graphical interface is provided for a user to specify a QBSI query. To specify a VQT, the user first selects a SSR (specific or abstract) from a palette of icons associated with the SSR. Then a spatial image region based on the selected icon can be drawn by clicking and dragging a rectangular box in a canvas. If the user wishes to apply a negation operator, he or she can click on the "NOT" button followed by the drawn region. A yellow cross will be superimposed on the selected region. The user can continue to specify more VQT in a conjunct by repeating the above steps. The user can also start a new conjunct in the disjunctive normal form (Equation (6)) by clicking on the "OR" button to bring up a new window with canvas and icons. A reset button is provided to clear all the icons drawn for a conjunct in a given window. A typical screen shot is given in Fig. 4 (note that only a subset of the visual icons are displayed in this prototype).

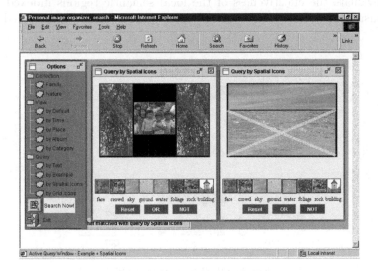

Fig. 4. A screen shot for QBSI interface: a disjunct of two conjuncts, one with 3 visual query terms (left) and the other with 2 visual query terms (right), one of which is a negation on water

As the region specified by a VQT is arbitrary, the precise computation of $T_i(R)$ using Equation (3) on reconciled small regions z_k is not cost effective in terms of speed and storage. Hence as a trade-off in our implementation, we pre-indexed the images using a uniform 3×3 spatial tessellation with the 26 SSR defined in Fig. 1 based on Equations (1) and (3). The truth value of a VQT q with region R and SSR i is approximated as,

$$\lambda(q, x) = \frac{\sum_{Z_j \in Z} T_i(Z_j)}{|Z|} \tag{10}$$

where Z consists of any of the 3×3 blocks that has more than half of its area covered by region R.

5   Experimental Results

In this paper, we evaluate our proposed approach on 2400 heterogeneous consumer photos from a single family. These genuine consumer photos are taken over 5 years in several countries with both indoor and outdoor settings. The images are those of the smallest resolution (i.e. 256×384) from Kodak PhotoCDs, in both portrait and landscape layouts. After removing possibly noisy marginal pixels, the images are of size 240×360. The indexing process automatically detects the layout and applies the corresponding tessellation template. On one hand, the small size of images allows for more efficient processing. On the other hand, they pose greater challenge for feature extraction and SSR detection. Photos of bad quality (e.g. faded, over-exposed, blurred, dark etc) are retained to reflect the complexity of the original data.

To evaluate the effectiveness of the local semantic regions indexed for the 2400 consumer photos, we have designed 15 QBSI queries as illustrated in Fig. 5 to 9.

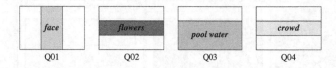

Fig. 5. QBSI queries 01 to 04

Fig. 6. QBSI queries 05 to 07

Fig. 7. QBSI queries 08 to 10

While queries 01 to 04 focus on single VQT, queries 05 to 15 demonstrate multiple VQTs. In particular, query 06 is composed to look for indoor images with close-up of people. Query 07 specifies faces in 3 different regions to enforce "small group of people". Query 10 intends to retrieve images related to wedding events whereby auspicious fabric can be seen. Query 14 shows the use of the

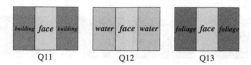

Fig. 8. QBSI queries 11 and 13

Fig. 9. QBSI queries 14 and 15

negation operator. Last but not least, query 15 illustrates the usefulness of disjunct operator. All the queries except 05 and 08 involve specific SSRs. Queries 05 and 08 are based on superclass of SSRs. Queries 11 to 13 illustrate the flexibility of mixing SSR (face) and the superclasses (building, water, and foliage). Our SSR indexing framework supports query with different levels of visual semantics and their mixture.

The indexes are computed based on Equations (1) and (3) with face detection enhancement [17].

Table 3 lists the number of relevant images among the top 20 and 30 retrieved images as well as the size of the ground truth (G.T.) for each of the queries tested. As shown in the table, the average precisions for the top 20 and 30 retrieved

Table 3. Precisions at top retrieved images for QBSI experiment

Query	Top 20	Top 30	G.T.
Q01	14	24	590
Q02	18	23	26
Q03	14	16	44
Q04	16	19	78
Q05	19	26	281
Q06	14	20	302
Q07	20	20	380
Q08	18	25	83
Q09	12	16	19
Q10	14	17	112
Q11	16	25	523
Q12	11	16	61
Q13	18	25	259
Q14	18	25	107
Q15	15	20	234
Avg	15.8	21.1	

Fig. 10. Top 18 retrieved images for QBSI query 02

Fig. 11. Top 18 retrieved images for QBSI query 05

images are 0.79 (i.e. $\frac{15.8}{20}$) and 0.70 (i.e. $\frac{21.1}{30}$) respectively, which we consider effective for practical applications. Interestingly, queries 02 and 09 demand small number of specific images (i.e. around 1%) to be found among 2400 images. The recall among top 30 retrieved images is high with recall values 0.88 (i.e. $\frac{23}{26}$) and 0.84 (i.e. $\frac{16}{19}$) respectively.

Next we show the top retrieved images for 3 of the 15 queries, namely queries 02, 05, and 07, in Fig. 10, 11, and 12 respectively. In the figures, the top 18 images retrieved are shown in top-down, left-to-right order of decreasing relevance.

For query 02 (Fig. 5), the intention was to look for images with flowers (c.f. Foliage:Floral in Fig. 1) at the center. Among the top 18 images shown in Fig. 10, only image 15 is irrelevant as the flower regions is considered too small.

With query 05 (in Fig. 6), we look for images with a spatial layout of sky, building, and ground (c.f. Fig. 1). Only the last image in Fig. 11 is a false positive where the greyish water was incorrectly detected as ground.

Fig. 12. Top 18 retrieved images for QBSI query 07

In the case of query 07 (in Fig. 6) that looks for small group of people appearing at the center of an image (c.f. `People:Face` in Fig. 1), the top 18 images shown in Fig. 12 are all found in the ground truth list for the query.

Compared to existing query formulation methods, our QBSI approach allows explicit specification of visual semantics as illustrated by the 15 queries in Fig. 5 to 9. Consider the case of Query By Canvas (QBC). How would a user express visual concepts such as flowers, faces, and buildings using color and texture or their combination? Query by Sketches (QBS) is not very useful either as the shapes of flowers, faces, sky, water etc are ill-defined. Compared to the ImageScape system [12] that also allows placement of visual icons as query, our QBSI approach has richer expressive power as we support spatial constraints (Q01 to Q15), negation (Q14), disjunction (Q15), and concept hierarchy (Q05, Q08, Q11-13). Hence it is not appropriate to compare the performance with existing query methods that are unnatural, if not impossible, to formulate the queries presented above.

6   Conclusion and Future Work

In this paper, we have presented an adaptive view-based detection approach to index and query images based on semantic regions. More specifically, our contributions can be listed as follows.

- The proposed SSR approach provides a systematic framework to index image contents based on local semantics learned from domain examples. The modular framework also allows new and better view-based object detectors to be embedded easily to enhance retrieval performance as illustrated by the face detector in our experiments.
- A novel indexing algorithm detects, reconciles, and aggregates SSRs in an image to form semantic histograms without the need of robust region segmentation.

– A unique visual query language and its corresponding query processing formalism have been shown to support intuitive and semantic query formulation, that is not available in existing systems, using 15 QBSI queries on 2400 consumer photos.

Currently, we also apply the framework to other content domains such as medical images and integrate with other semantic sources such as text. We also explore means to reduce the extent of supervision in learning while retaining high degree of semantic interpretation.

Acknowledgments

The authors wish to thank J.L. Lebrun for lending his family photos, CMU for their face detector, and T. Joachims for his great SVM^{light} software.

References

1. L. Armitage and P. Enser. Analysis of user need in image archives. *J. Information Science*, 23(4): 287-299. 1997.
2. J.R. Bach et al. Virage image search engine: an open framework for image management. In *Storage and Retrieval for Image and Video Databases IV*, Proc. SPIE 2670, pp. 76-87, 1996.
3. I. Cox et al. The Bayesian image retrieval system, PicHunter: theory, implementation and psychophysical experiments. *IEEE Trans. on Image Processing*, 9: 20-37, 2000.
4. C.M. Bishop. *Neural Networks for Pattern Recognition*. Clarendon Press, Oxford, 1995.
5. C. Carson et al. Blobworld: image segmentation using expectation-maximization and its application to image querying. *IEEE Trans. on PAMI*, 24(8): 1026-1038, 2002.
6. M. Daoudi and S. Matusiak. Visual image retrieval by multiscale description of user sketches. *J. of Visual Languages & Computing*, 11: 287-301, 2000.
7. M. Flickner et al. Query by image and video content: the QBIC system. *IEEE Computer*, 28(9): 23-30, 1995.
8. T. Gevers and A. Smeulders. PicToSeek: a content-based image search system for the world wide web. In *Proc. Visual 97*, pp. 93-100, 1997.
9. T. Joachims. Making large-scale SVM learning practical. *Advances in Kernel Methods - Support Vector Learning*. B. Scholkopf, C. Burges, and A. Smola (ed.). MIT-Press, 1999.
10. G.J. Klir and T.A. Folger. *Fuzzy Sets, Uncertainty, and Information*. Prentice Hall, 1992.
11. S. Kumar, A.C. Loui and M. Hebert. Probabilistic classification of image regions using an observation-constrained generative approach. *First Intl. Workshop on Generative-Model-Based Vision, June 2002*.
12. M. Lew. Next-generation web searches for visual content. *IEEE Computer*, 33(11): 46-52, 2000.
13. J.H. Lim. Visual keywords: From text IR to multimedia IR. In F.Crestani & G.Pasi (ed.), *Soft Computing in Information Retrieval: Techniques and Applications*, Physica-Verlag, Springer Verlag, Germany, pp. 77-101, 2000.

14. J.H. Lim. Building visual vocabulary for image indexation and query formulation. *Pattern Analysis and Applications* (Special Issue on Image Indexation), 4(2/3): 125-139, 2001.

15. B.S. Manjunath and W.Y. Ma. Texture features for browsing and retrieval of image data. *IEEE Trans. on PAMI*, 18(8): 837-842, 1996.

16. A. Pentland, R.W. Picard, and S. Sclaroff. Photobook: content-based manipulation of image databases. *Int. Journal of Computer Vision*, 18(3): 233-254, 1995.

17. H.A. Rowley, S. Baluja, and T. Kanade. Neural network-based face detection. *IEEE Trans. on PAMI*, 20(1): 23-38, 1998.

18. Y. Rui, T.S. Huang, and S. Mehrotra. Content-based image retrieval with relevance feedback in MARS. In *Proc. IEEE Int. Conf. on Image Proc.*, pp. 815-818, 1997.

19. A.W.M. Smeulders et al. Content-based image retrieval at the end of the early years. *IEEE Trans. on PAMI*, 22(12): 1349-1380. 2000.

20. J.R. Smith & S.-F. Chang. VisualSEEk: a fully automated content-based image query system. In *Proc. ACM Multimedia 96*, Boston, MA, Nov. 20, 1996.

21. J.R. Smith & S.-F. Chang. Visually searching the web for content. *IEEE Multimedia*, July-Sept., pp. 23-32, 1997.

22. Y. Song and A. Zhang. Analyzing scenery images by monotonic tree. *Multimedia Systems*, 8(6): 495-511, 2003.

23. M.J. Swain and D.N. Ballard. Color indexing. *Intl. J. Computer Vision*, 7(1): 11-32, 1991.

24. L. Taycher, M. Cascia, and S. Sclaroff. Image digestion and relevance feedback in the ImageRover WWW search engine. In *Proc. Visual 97*, pp. 85-91, 1997.

25. C. Town and D. Sinclair. Content-based image retrieval using semantic visual categories. *Technical Report 2000.14*. AT&T Research Cambridge. 2000.

26. A. Vailaya et al. Bayesian framework for hierarchical semantic classification of vacation images. *IEEE Trans. on Image Processing*, 10(1): 117-130, 2001.

27. L. Zhu, A.B. Rao, and A.D. Zhang. Theory of keyblock-based image retrieval. *ACM Trans. on Information Systems*, 20: 224-257, 2002.

Image Retrieval Using Sub-image Matching in Photos Using MPEG-7 Descriptors

Min-Sung Ryu, Soo-Jun Park, and Chee Sun Won*

Dept. of Electronic Eng., Seoul, 100-715, South Korea
ETRI, 161 Kajeong-dong, Yuseong-gu, Daejeon, 305-350, Korea
cswon@dongguk.edu

Abstract. Regions of interest in photos are important clues for the content-based image retrieval. However, segmenting semantically meaningful objects in the photo automatically for the query and similarity matching is known to be an unsolved problem. As an alternative, in this paper, we propose a scheme to form a query region in the image space in terms of 4×4 sub-images. The set of query sub-images, which include the region of interest in the image space, is used for the basic unit for the similarity matching. Specifically, the edge histogram descriptor and the color layout descriptor in MPEG-7 are used to extract image features in the chosen sub-images and are compared to those extracted from the test images in the database. Experimental results show that the proposed method can retrieve images with similar regions in the images, even if the background regions look quite different from each other.

1 Introduction

Digital camera becomes increasingly popular. People now can take digital photos by the digital camera embedded in the mobile phone as well as the conventional digital cameras. As opposed to the conventional film-based photo shots, it is almost free of cost to take a digital shot, since we can easily delete the digital photos any time without consuming any memory space. This makes people to take less serious consideration in making every shot, leaving many multiple and redundant ones. This also makes it tedious to browse the entire shots in the flash memory. One way to alleviate this difficulty is to retrieve similar looking images from the stored image database and discard those that are duplicates. Since people tend to take pictures with an identical background but different persons or with a group of similar persons but different background, it should be able to retrieve images in terms of partial region similarity in the image space. This is also achieved by the region-of-interest (ROI) queries [3].

As opposed to the query-by-example (QBE), which tries to find a similarity matching for the whole image space, the ROI query method is to seek images with similar objects in the image. Once the ROIs are similar each other, then the ROI query does not care about the remaining regions in the image space. Of

---

* Corresponding author.

G.G. Lee et al. (Eds.): AIRS 2005, LNCS 3689, pp. 366–373, 2005.

course, to make this ROI query possible, image segmentation extracting ROIs should be done beforehand. However, it is well known that an automatic object segmentation with semantic meaning is an unsolved problem. Instead, each meaningful object in the image can be automatically divided into multiple homogeneous regions. In region-based image matching, visual features such as color, texture, shape, and size of the homogeneous regions are compared to measure the similarity [1]. Again, the performance of this method is sensitive to the segmentation result.

Another approach to achieve the ROI-based query is to allow the user to delineate the ROI in the image space. With this user interaction, the ROI is extracted from the image and is compared to those regions in the image database. In [3], 16 × 16-pixel blocks are sampled and are used to select ROIs in the image space. Although this sample matching method can take the arbitrary shape information into the similarity matching, the selecting 16 × 16-pixel blocks for the identification of ROI requires user's careful attention. In this paper, to solve this problem, we divide the image space into larger 4 × 4 sub-images and then, on this 4 × 4 image grid, the sub-images covering the ROI are selected for the query regions. In the selected sub-images, we extract visual features for the similarity matching. Visual features extracted from each sub-image for the similarity matching includes edge histogram descriptor (EHD) and color layout descriptor (CLD) of MPEG-7. Thus, our image retrieval method is compliant to the MPEG-7 standard.

2   Characteristics of EHD and CLD

2.1   EHD

The EHD (Edge Histogram Descriptor) of MPEG-7 visual descriptors [2] represents the distribution of 5 edge types, namely vertical, horizontal, 45-degree diagonal, 135-degree diagonal, and non-edge types. We generate 16 edge histograms, each one represents the edge distribution for each of 16 sub-images (see Figure 1 for the definition of sub-image). That is, an image is divided into non-overlapping 4x4 sub-images. Then, each sub-image serves a basic region to generate an edge histogram, which consists of 5 bins with vertical, horizontal, 45-degree diagonal, 135-degree diagonal, and non-directional edge types. Since it is required to extract the non-directional edge as well as the four directional ones, a small image block rather than a pixel is needed to extract an edge type [4]. To this end, we further divide the sub-image into non-overlapping image blocks with a small size. Note that the image block may or may not have an edge in it. If there is an edge in the block, we increase the counter of the corresponding edge type by one. Otherwise, the image block has monotonous gray levels and no histogram bin is increased. After examining all image blocks in the sub-image, the 5-bin values are normalized by the *total number of blocks* in the sub-image. Thus the sum of the normalized 5 bins is not necessarily 1. Finally, the normalized bin values are quantized for the binary representation. Since there are 16 (4 × 4) sub-images, each image yields an edge histogram with a total of 80

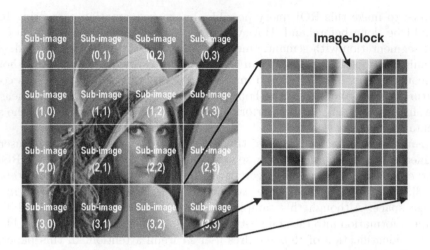

Fig. 1. Sub-images and image-blocks of the EHD

(16×5) bins. These normalized and quantized 80 bins constitute the EHD of the MPEG-7. That is, arranging edge histograms for the sub-images in the raster scan order (i.e., $(0,0), \cdots, (0,3), (1,0), \cdots, (3,3)$), 16 local histograms are concatenated to have an integrated histogram with $16 \times 5 = 80$ bins. Let us denote $E_{ij}(k)$ as a normalized and quantized bin value for a sub-image at $(i,j) \in \Omega$, where $\Omega = \{(i,j); 0 \leq i \leq 3, \ 0 \leq j \leq 3\}$ is a set of indices for sub-images and $k \in \{1, \cdots, 5\}$ indicates one of 5 edge types.

2.2 CLD

The Color Layout Descriptor (CLD) of MPEG-7 visual descriptors [2] is designed to represent spatial distribution of color features in the image. To satisfy this requirement, the CLD is obtained by applying DCT (Discrete Cosine Transform) on a 2-D image space. Specifically, as shown in Figure 2, the image space is first divided into 8×8 non-overlapping blocks and a representative color for each block is determined. Adopting Y-Cb-Cr color space, three 8×8 representative color components are applied to obtain three 8×8 DCT components of Y-Cb-Cr. Then, some of low frequency DCT components for each Y-Cb-Cr planes are selected and quantized for the CLD. Now, the indexed CLD can be used for the similarity matching. Note that, considering the 4×4 grid structure for the EHD, we further take the 8×8 IDCT (Inverse DCT) to the CLD to obtain the localized 8×8 color values. Then, these 8×8 IDCT vaues, instead of the quantized 8×8 DCT coefficients of CLD, can be spatially grouped together such that one sub-image of the EHD overlay 2×2 of the 8×8 IDCT values (see Figure 3). Then, in each sub-image, we can extract the color information as well as the edge histogram. Now, let us denote Y_{ij}, Cb_{ij}, and Cr_{ij} as the IDCT values (i.e.,

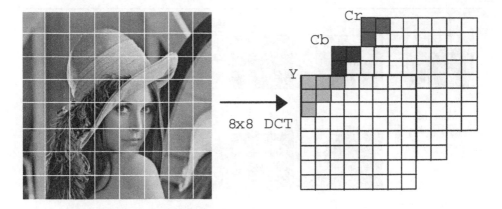

Fig. 2. The CLD; (a) 8×8 subdivision of the image, (b) 8×8 DCT for Y, Cb, and Cr planes

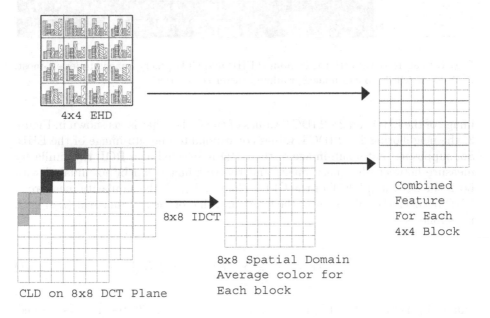

Fig. 3. Combining the EHD and the IDCT values of the CLD

the recovered spatial image data) for Y, Cb, and Cr components at the block (i, j), respectively, where, $0 \leq i \leq 7$, $0 \leq j \leq 7$.

3   Similarity Matching by Combining EHD and CLD

Since the EHD and the IDCT coefficients of the CLD are based on 4×4 and 8×8 grids, respectively, there exists a locational correspondence between the sub-

Fig. 4. Imageretrieval with the combined EHD and CLD (query image: upperleft-most, ROI: lower left 3 × 3 sub-images, ranking: raster scan order).

image of the EHD and 2×2 IDCT values of the CLD. That is, as shown in Figure 3, the neighboring 2 × 2 IDCT values correspond to one sub-image of the EHD. So, supposing that a sub-image of the EHD is selected as a ROI, the similarity measure between the query image and the test image can be formulated with both the EHD and IDCT of the CLD. That is, S_{ij}^{EHD}, the similarity measure of EHD between the sub-image of the query and that of the test image at $(i, j) \in \Omega$, is as follows

$$S_{ij}^{EHD}(l) = \frac{1}{S_{max}^{EHD}} \sum_{k=1}^{5} |E^Q(k) - E_{ij}^{T_l}(k)|, \tag{1}$$

where superscripts Q and T_l represent the query and the lth test images, respectively. Also, S_{max}^{EHD} is a normalizing constant such that

$$S_{max}^{EHD} = \max_{\substack{l=1,\cdots,L \\ 0 \le i \le 3, \ 0 \le j \le 3}} S_{ij}^{EHD}(l), \tag{2}$$

where L is the total number of test images. This implies that $S_{ij}^{EHD}(l)$ is normalized such that $0 \le S_{ij}^{EHD}(l) \le 1$. Similarly, we have the similarity of CLD as follows

$$S_{ij}^{CLD}(l) = \frac{1}{3S_{max}^{CLD}} \left(|Y^Q - Y_{ij}^{T_l}| + |Cb^Q - Cb_{ij}^{T_l}| + |Cr^Q - Cr_{ij}^{T_l}| \right). \tag{3}$$

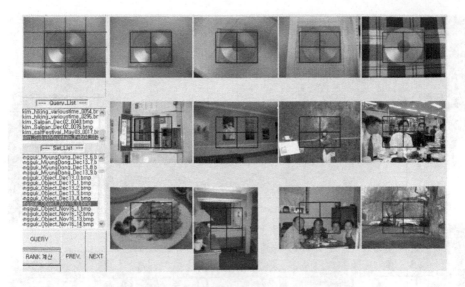

Fig. 5. Image retrieval with the combined EHD and CLD (query image: upper left-most, ROI: central 2×2 sub-images, ranking: raster scan order).

Finally, combining equations (1) and (3), we have a combined similarity as follows

$$S_{ij}(l) = \frac{S_{ij}^{EHD}(l) + S_{ij}^{CLD}(l)}{2}. \tag{4}$$

Now, smaller $S_{ij}(l)$ value means higher similarity between the two regions. Calculating (4) for all test images and for all sub-images Ω in the test image, we can find the best matching regions in test images.

4 Experiments

Suppose that there are photos with three people standing with different background. In this case, as shown in Figure 4, we may want to retrieve all photos with those three men. To achieve this goal, we may choose 3×3 bottom-left sub-images as shown in the upper and left-most photo. Thus, this upper and left-most photo is the query image and the 3×3 bottom-left sub-images are the ROI. Applying the similarity measure of (4) for all selected sub-images and for all test images, we can retrieve photos with the best matching regions and display them from top-left to bottom-right with the decreasing order of the similarity. As shown in the figure, photos with three same men but different background are ranked for the top-four photos. Another retrieval result is shown in Figure 5. In this figure, the ROI is the central 2×2 sub-images and the highest ranked 4 images have the same ROIs but different background.

We have tested our algorithm with 2440 images. Among them 20 query images are selected. Figure 6 shows the selected query images and their query

Fig. 6. Selected 20 query images and their query sub-images

regions. For each query image region, a number of ground truth images with similar ROIs are also manually determined. Then, the performance of the proposed algorithm is evaluated in terms of ANMRR [2]. The proposed algorithm yields ANMRR=0.1255 for the 20 query images.

5   Summary

A region-based image retrieval method has been proposed. A subset of 4×4 sub-images covering the ROI is selected as a region for the similarity matching.

Then, the EHD and the IDCT values of the CLD in the selected sub-images are used as the features for the similarity matching. Thus, the proposed region-based retrieval method is MPEG-7 compliant. Experimental results show that the proposed method can retrieve the same foreground but different background or vice versa quite well.

Acknowledgements

This work was partially supported by the Korea Science Engineering Foundation (KOSEF) under the ERC program through the MINT research center at Dongguk University, Seoul, Korea.

References

1. Carson, C., et al.: Blobworld: A system for region-based image indexing and retrieval, Proc. of Third Int'l Conf. Visual Information Systems, (1999) 509–516
2. Manjunath, B.S., Salembier, P., Sikora, T.: Introduction to MPEG-7, Wiley (2002)
3. Vu, K, A. Hua, and W. Tavanapong: Image retrieval based on regions of interest. IEEE Tr. on Knowledge and Data Engineering, Vol. 15, No. 4, (2003) 1045–1049
4. Won, C.S., Park, D.K., Park, S.-J.: Efficient use of MPEG-7 edge histogram descriptor, ETRI Journal, vol. 24, No. 1, (2002) 23–30

An Incremental Document Clustering for the Large Document Database

Kil Hong Joo[1] and Won Suk Lee[2]

[1] Dept. of Computer Education, Gyeongin National University of Education,
Gyodae Street 45, Gyeyang-gu, Incheon, Korea 407-753
khjoo@ginue.ac.kr
[2] Dept. of Computer Science, Yonsei University, 134 Shinchondong Seodaemoongu,
Seoul, Korea 120-749
lee@amadeus.yonsei.ac.kr

Abstract. With the development of the internet and computer, the amount of information through the internet is increasing rapidly and it is managed in document form. For this reason, the research into the method to manage for a large amount of document in an effective way is necessary. The document clustering is integrated documents to subject by classifying a set of documents through their similarity among them. Accordingly, the document clustering can be used in exploring and searching a document and it can increase accuracy of search. This paper proposes an efficient incremental clustering algorithm for a set of documents increase gradually. The incremental document clustering algorithm assigns a set of new documents to the legacy clusters which have been identified in advance. In addition, to improve the correctness of the clustering, removing the stop words can be proposed and the weight of the word can be calculated by the proposed TF×NIDF function. In this paper, the performance of the proposed method is analyzed by a series of experiments to identify their various characteristics.

1 Introduction

Various methods and techniques for processing unstructured data such as textual data are introduced in the field of information retrieval (IR). Basically, the main purpose of these techniques is to construct a large set of well-categorized documents automatically for effective searching and browsing [1]. For this purpose, *document clustering* and *classification* are actively studied [2] since they can play an important role in helping an information retrieval system with a huge number of documents. Given a predefined set of document classes, document classification is identifying the appropriate class of a particular document [3]. Traditionally, the document classification is carried out manually. In order to assign a document to an appropriate class manually, a user should analyze the contents of the document. Therefore, a large amount of human effort would be required. There has been some research work on automatic document classification. One approach is learning appropriate text classifiers by machine learning techniques [4, 5] based on a training data set containing positive and negative examples. The accuracy of a resulting classifier is

G.G. Lee et al. (Eds.): AIRS 2005, LNCS 3689, pp. 374–387, 2005.
© Springer-Verlag Berlin Heidelberg 2005

highly dependent on the fitness of the training data set. However, there are lots of terms and various classes of documents. In addition, many new terms and concepts are introduced everyday. Consequently, it is quite impossible to learn a classifier for each document class in such a manner.

In order to group a set of related documents automatically, clustering techniques [6, 7, 8] have been widely employed. The attractiveness of these cluster techniques is that they can find a set of similar data objects as a cluster directly from a given data set without relying on any predefined information such as training examples provided by domain experts [6, 7]. In most cases of such an application, a set of new documents is incrementally added to the data set.

This paper proposes an incremental document clustering method. The characteristics of a document are represented by a set of keywords that are extracted by evaluating the term weight of each word in the document. The term weight of each keyword for a document indicates the relative importance of the keyword in the document. Given a finite data set of documents, most document clustering algorithms use a TF*IDF function [17] to find the term weight of a word in a document. The term frequency (TF) of a word in a document is the number of occurrences of the word in the document. The inverse document frequency (IDF) of a word is the number of documents containing the word and it indicates how commonly the word is used in the documents of the data set. When the IDF of a word is high, the usage of the word is localized to a small number of documents in the data set. However, the TF*IDF function is not suitable for an incremental document clustering algorithm due to the following reasons: (1) A word with a relatively low document frequency tends to have a high term weight, so that a large number of document clusters can be generated potentially. (2) As the number of documents in a data set becomes larger, the effect of the IDF of a word on the term weight of the word in each document is increased specially when most of the documents contain a small number of words as in web documents. This is because the TF of a word in a document becomes small relative to its IDF. Furthermore, if document clustering should be performed in an incremental way, this effect is amplified since the value of IDF is increased continuously. For these reasons, a normalized inversed document frequency (NIDF) is used instead in this paper.

Given an initial set of documents, the initial clusters of similar documents are found by a seed document clustering method called SCUP (Seed Clustering Using Participation and cohesion) in this paper. The SCUP algorithm is a kind of an average link method of hierarchical agglomerative clustering [9, 10]. In a hierarchical agglomerative clustering algorithm, two clusters of the highest similarity are merged in each step. However, there may be a more similar cluster in the future when a set of new documents is incrementally added. Accordingly, the accuracy of a cluster can be degraded in the future. To resolve this problem of a hierarchical agglomerative clustering algorithm, this paper proposes two similarity measures: a cluster cohesion rate and a cluster participation rate. The cluster participation rate is examined to merge a new document with current set of clusters. By using the cluster participation rate, the accuracy of end cluster can be guaranteed at any time. In addition, the hierarchical agglomerative clustering algorithm generally requires a great amount of memory space since it is proportional to the square of the number of documents in a data set [11]. In order to minimize the usage of memory space, the SCUP algorithm produces dendrogram. The resulting dendrogram of the SCUP algorithm is used by an incremental document clustering algorithm (IDC) proposed in this paper in order to construct the category tree of identified clusters. Consequently, as a new document is incrementally added to the data set, the most appropriate cluster for the document can be found in the IDC algorithm based on the category tree efficiently.

Figure 1 illustrates the overall procedure of the proposed seed clustering SCUP algorithm. The SCUP algorithm is composed of the following steps. First, the keywords of each document in the initial set of documents are selected by the TF*NIDF method. Second, the proposed SCUP algorithm is performed to generate a set of initial clusters. Finally, a category tree for the resulting clusters is generated to be used by the incremental document clustering (IDC) algorithm for a new document.

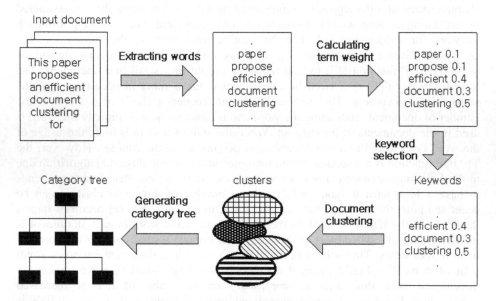

Fig. 1. Procedure of the SCUP algorithm

This paper is organized as follows. Section 2 describes related works. Section 3 introduces how the term weight of a word for a document in a dataset of documents is calculated to choose the keywords of the document. In Section 4, the proposed SCUP algorithm is presented in detail. Furthermore, the structure of a category tree for identified clusters is described. In Section 5, an incremental document clustering (IDC) algorithm is proposed. Section 6, several experiment results are comparatively analyzed to illustrate the various characteristics of the proposed algorithms. Finally, Section 7 draws overall conclusions.

2 Related Work

Current document clustering techniques can be broadly classified into two categories: partitional and hierarchical methods. The popular K-Means [12] and K-Medoid [13] methods are partitional methods which maintain k cluster representatives and assign each document to the cluster with its representative closest to the document. The strong point of the K-Means algorithm is that it is relatively scalable and efficient because it has low time complexity. However, a noise document can substantially influence the generation of a cluster, so it may be difficult to produce a correct result in some cases. The K-Medoid algorithm selects the centers of k clusters initially, and repeatedly replaces one of the selected centers until it finds the best set of k centers. The hierarchical method such as BIRCH [14] confined hierarchy of the clusters in a data set to a tree-like structure. In BIRCH, a CF (Clustering Feature) tree which is used to summarize cluster representations is generated dynamically. After the CF tree is built, any clustering algorithm such as a typical partitioning algorithm is then used. The memory requirement problem of K-Means is resolved and thus the method is suitable for a large data set. However, these algorithms[12, 13, 14] are not suitable to solve the document clustering problem since the number of clusters in a set of documents is usually unknown to user [2].

Scatter/Gather [15] is a document browsing system based on the clusters of similar documents. It proposes two clustering techniques: buckshot algorithm and fractionation algorithm. The buckshot algorithm selects sample documents to find a set of clusters and assigns remaining documents to the identified clusters. The fractionation algorithm distributes documents into a fixed number of buckets.

For the hierarchical method, there are two main approaches: divisive clustering and agglomerative clustering. The divisive clustering approach regards all documents in a data set as a single cluster. It splits a cluster into two clusters step by step until each single document is a cluster. The agglomerative clustering approach performs in reverse order. In [9, 10], document clustering algorithms based on the hierarchical agglomerative clustering approach are proposed. Each document itself is regarded as a cluster initially and the similarity between two clusters is examined for every pair of clusters. Subsequently, the most similar pair of two clusters is repeatedly merged until a predefined number of clusters are left. There are three different schemes in a hierarchical agglomerative clustering algorithm, namely a single link, a complete link and an average link [12]. A single link method measures the similarity of two clusters based on the largest document similarity among the similarity of two documents contained in each cluster. On the contrary, a complete link method uses the smallest document similarity between two documents in distinct clusters. Accordingly, unless most documents of two clusters are similar, two clusters are not merged. In the average link method, the similarity of two clusters is determined by the average document similarity instead. Among the three methods, clusters generated by the average link method are most accurate since every document of one cluster is examined to each document of the other cluster. However, researchers have found an agglomerative clustering algorithm is not suitable for maintaining clusters of an incrementally growing set of documents [16].

3   Extraction of Keywords by Normalized Term Weight

For each word used in a document of an initial data set, its term weight is calculated to choose the keywords of the document. For this purpose, the TF*IDF (Term Frequency Inversed Document Frequency) [17] is used widely to reflect the importance of a specific word in a document. According to the TF*IDF method, the weight $tfidf_{ij}$ of a word w_j in a document d_i is defined as follows:

$$tfidf_{ij} = tf_{ij} \times \ln \frac{N}{df_j} \qquad (1)$$

where N is the total number documents in a data set and the term frequency tf_{ij} denotes the frequency of a word w_j occurred in a document d_i. In addition, the document frequency df_j denotes the number of documents that the word w_j appears in the data set. Equation (1) means that the possibility of a specific word representing the key concept of a particular document is proportional to the frequency of the word in the document. As the same time, it is also inversely proportional to the number of documents that contain the word. In other words, a word can be one of keywords for a document if it appears frequently in a small number of documents in a data set.

However, as the total number of documents N becomes larger, the effect of the inversed document frequency on a term weight is increased. This is because the term frequency of a word in a document is usually in a certain range specially for a short document. On the other hand, the IDF has the range of [0, lnN], and hence the value of the IDF is greatly influenced by the total number of documents in a data set. Furthermore, when new documents are incrementally added to a data set continuously, the number of documents N is continuously increased. In order to avoid this, the value of the IDF should be confined within a certain range regardless of N. This paper introduces a TF*NIDF (Term Frequency Normalized Inversed Document Frequency) function in which the maximum value of the IDF is normalized within a range [0, μ] for a fixed value of μ. The IDF idf_j of a word w_j is represented as follows

$$idf_j = \ln \frac{N}{df_j} = \ln N - \ln df_j$$

the target range of its normalized inversed document frequency (NIDF) $nidf_j$ is $[0, \mu]$, so that $nidf_j$ can be represented like idf_j as follows:

$$nidf_j = \mu - \ln y$$

where y is a certain linear function of df_j. Given the range of df_j $[1, N]$, the following function makes the value of $\ln y$ be the range $[0, \mu]$.

$$y = \frac{e^\mu - 1}{N - 1}(df_j - 1) + 1$$

Based on the above function y, the term weight $tfnidf_{ij}$ of a word w_j in a document d_i is defined by Equation (2).

$$tfnidf_{ij} = tf_{ij} \times \left\{ \mu - \ln\left(\left(\frac{e^\mu - 1}{N - 1} \right) \times (df_j - 1) + 1 \right) \right\} \qquad (2)$$

A word in a document is chosen as a keyword of the document if the term weight TF*NIDF of the word is larger than the average term weight of words in the document. Since the number of words in each document can be different, the range of the term frequency TF of a word in each document is not the same. In other words, when a word appears frequently in a long document, the TF of the word becomes large. As a result, its term weight can become large even though its NIDF is relatively small. To prevent this, the length of a document should also be normalized.

To normalize the number of words in a document, the maximum frequency normalization [18] can be considered. In this method, it uses the ratio of the frequency of each word in a document over the most frequently used word in the document. However, this can cause a problem when the frequency of a specific word is exceptionally large. This paper uses a cosine normalization which has been widely used in a vector space model. In the cosine normalization, given a vector $V = \{v_1, v_2, ..., v_n\}$, each element of the vector is divided by a cosine normalization element $\sqrt{v_1^2 + v_2^2 + ... + v_n^2}$. This cosine normalization makes it possible to normalize the length of a document based on the frequencies of all words in a document together. In this paper, the normalized term weight of a keyword k_j in a document d_i containing n distinct words represented by the cosine normalization is denoted by $t(d_i, k_j)$ as follows:

$$t(d_i, k_j) = \frac{tfnidf_{ij}}{\sqrt{\sum_{k=1}^{n} tfnidf_{ik}^2}} \tag{3}$$

4 Seed Clustering Using a Participation and Cohesion Method

Given an initial data set of documents, the SCUP algorithm finds the initial clusters of the data set. Although the SCUP algorithm can be solely used as a clustering method for a set of documents, it can also provide an initial set of document clusters for an incrementally growing data set of documents. It is basically the same as the hierarchical agglomerative clustering algorithm [10] but uses different similarity measures defined in Definition 1 and Definition 2.

Definition 1. Document Similarity
Given two documents d_i and d_j with their keyword sets K_i and K_j respectively, their document similarity measure $s(d_i, d_j)$ is defined as follows:

$$s(d_i, d_j) = \frac{1}{2} \left(\frac{\sum_{w \in K_i \cap K_j} t(d_i, w)}{\sum_{w \in K_i} t(d_i, w)} + \frac{\sum_{w \in K_i \cap K_j} t(d_j, w)}{\sum_{w \in K_i} t(d_j, w)} \right) \tag{4}$$

∎

The above document similarity measure can provide the rate of similarity between only two documents. As a similarity measure for all the documents of a cluster, a *cluster cohesion* measure is defined in Definition 2. A cluster cohesion measure indicates how tightly the documents of a cluster are related in terms of their keywords. It is the average of the document similarities of all pairs of documents in a cluster.

Definition 2. Cluster Cohesion

Given a cluster C, let $|C|$ denotes the number of documents in C and $s(d_i, d_j)$ denotes the document similarity of two documents d_i and d_j in the cluster C. The cluster cohesion rate $h(C)$ of the cluster C is defined as follows:

$$h(C) = \frac{\sum\limits_{d_i \in C} \sum\limits_{d_j \in C - \{d_i\}} s(d_i, d_j)}{|C|C_2} \tag{5}$$

∎

In the conventional agglomerative approach, a cluster is forced to be merged with another cluster until a predefined number of clusters are left. However, the SCUP algorithm is intended to be used in an incrementally growing set of documents. Consequently, clusters should be carefully merged. In other words, a cluster should not be merged with another cluster unless the documents of the two clusters are similar enough to be merged. If a cluster can not find another cluster that is eligible to be merged in the current set of clusters, it should not be merged. This is because there may be a more similar cluster in the clusters of incrementally added documents in the future. For this purpose, a cluster participation measure between two clusters of documents is defined in Definition 3. The union of the document keyword sets of all documents in a same cluster is named as the *cluster keyword set* of the cluster.

Definition 3. Cluster Participation

Given two clusters C_m and C_n of documents with cluster keyword sets CK_m and CK_n, a cluster participation rate $CP(C_m | C_n)$ of the cluster C_n to the cluster C_m is defined as follows:

$$CP(C_m | C_n) = \frac{\sum\limits_{d_i \in C_m} \sum\limits_{w \in CK_m \cap CK_n} t(d_i, w)}{\sum\limits_{d_i \in C_n} \sum\limits_{w \in CK_n} t(d_i, w)} \tag{6}$$

∎

Given a minimum cluster participation rate *MinClPar* and a minimum cluster cohesion rate *MinClCoh*, two clusters C_m and C_n are eligible to be merged into one cluster C_{mn} which contains all the documents of the two clusters if the following conditions are satisfied.

(i) $CP(C_m | C_n) \geq MinClPar$ and $CP(C_n | C_m) \geq MinClPar$ and

(ii) $h(C_{mn}) \geq MinClCoh$

Among the pairs (C_m, C_n) of clusters that satisfy the above two conditions, the one with the highest cluster cohesion rate $h(C_{mn})$ merged into one cluster. The dendrogram [9] of the SCUP algorithm is used as a category tree. It is widely used to represent the hierarchical cluster structure of a data set. It is generated by keeping merging two similar clusters repeatedly until all documents of the data set are grouped into one cluster. A node of a category tree represents a category. It contains its *category keywords* which are the union of the cluster keyword sets of all the clusters of its sub-tree. A category tree can be used as an index in searching and browsing a specific cluster.

5 Incremental Document Clustering (IDC)

Most conventional document clustering algorithms [10, 19] are not intended to be used in an incrementally growing set of documents. Therefore, whenever a set of new documents is added incrementally, all documents in the enlarged data set should be reclustered from scratch. To avoid this, this section presents an incremental document clustering algorithm (IDC) based on the result of the SCUP algorithm presented in Section 4. When a new document is added to a data set of documents, among the current clusters, the most appropriate cluster is identified by traversing the category tree of the clusters starting from the root node of the category tree. The node participation rate of a new document d_l for a node N in the category tree defined in Definition 4 is used to traverse the tree.

Definition 4. Node Participation in the Category Tree
Given a new document d_m with its keyword set K_m and a node N of a category tree, let NK denote the set of category keywords in the node N. The node participation rate $NP(d_m \mid N)$ of the document d_m for the node N is defined as follows:

$$NP(d_m \mid N) = \frac{\sum_{d_i \in N} \sum_{w \in NK \cap K_m} t(d_i, w)}{\sum_{d_i \in N} \sum_{w \in NK} t(d_i, w)} \tag{7}$$

■

For a newly added document d, starting from the root node of a category tree, a document d recursively searches down to its corresponding leaf node based on the node participation rate of each node in its path from the root node. Figure 2 illustrates how a newly added document is incrementally clustered.

Whenever visiting a node of the category tree for a new document d, among the children of the node N, the one with the highest node participation rate for the document is identified. If the highest node participation rate is greater than or equal to a predefined minimum node participation rate, the corresponding child node is visited. Otherwise, the document is regarded as a noise document temporarily. This traversal is performed repeatedly until a document d visits a leaf node. When a leaf node is visited successfully, the document d is inserted to the cluster of the leaf node if the

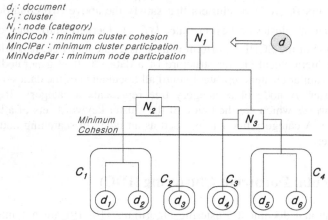

(a) Search an eligible cluster in a category tree

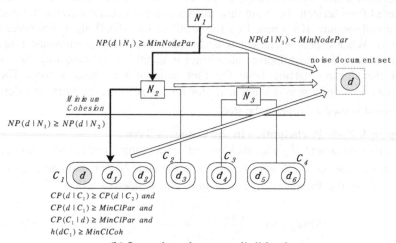

(b) Insert into the most eligible cluster

Fig. 2. Example of an incremental document clustering

document d is greater than or equal to a predefined minimum cluster cohesion rate. If the above condition is not satisfied, the document is regarded as a noise document too. When a considerable number of noise documents are collected, the SCUP method is performed to generate a set of new clusters from the set of noise documents and the category tree is modified accordingly. Figure 3 shows how to insert a set of new documents incrementally.

On the other hand, when a document in a cluster is deleted, if the updated cluster cohesion rate of the cluster becomes less than a minimum cluster cohesion rate, the documents of the cluster are reclustered by the SCUP algorithm to partition the documents into groups of more similar documents.

d : new document
i : node level
N : the node of a category tree
MinNodePar : Minimum node participation

PROCEDURE *insert(N, d, i)*
BEGIN
    IF NP(d|N) < MinNodePar THEN
        set *d* as noise document;
    ELSE
        IF *i* is a leaf node THEN
            find_clusters(N, d, i);
            Insert *d* into a selected cluster;
        ELSE
            Select a node of the highest *NP(d|N)*
            insert(N, d, i+1);
        END IF
    END IF
END

Fig. 3. Document insertion algorithm

6 Experiments and Analysis of Result

To illustrate the performance of the proposed method, several experiment results are presented in this section. Among news categories provided in 'Yahoo', documents in 10 different domains such as business, science, politics and society are extracted as a data set of documents to be used in these experiments. For each domain, the average number of documents is 1026 and the average number of words in a document is 800.

In Figure 4, the clustering result of the SCUP algorithm is compared with that of the hierarchical agglomerative clustering algorithm (HAC). To show the relative effectiveness of the proposed clustering algorithm the same similarity measures as described in Section 4 is used for the hierarchical agglomerative clustering algorithm. The resulting number of clusters generated by each algorithm is compared in Figure 4-(a). The average number of documents in a cluster is compared in Figure 4-(b). In addition, the average cluster cohesion rate is compared in Figure 4-(c). The number of clusters generated by the proposed SCUP algorithm is much smaller than that by the hierarchical agglomerative clustering algorithm. However, their order is reversed in terms of the average number of documents in a cluster. However, the average cluster cohesions of two algorithms are almost the same.

About 10000 documents in the business domain of Yahoo are used to illustrate the performance of the proposed IDC algorithm. The proposed IDC algorithm requires a minimum cluster participation rate additionally. When the value of a minimum cluster participation rate is set to 0.2, the IDC algorithm shows the best result. When the value of a minimum cluster participation rate is set 0.2, in Figure 5, the result of

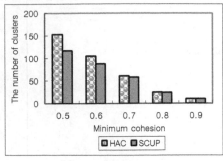

(a) The number of clusters

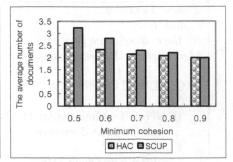

(b) The average number of documents in a cluster

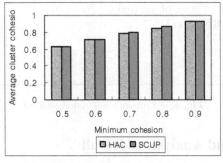

(c) Average cohesion of clusters

Fig. 4. Performance of the SCUP algorithm

the IDC algorithm is composed with the HAC algorithm. Since the HAC clustering is not an incremental algorithm, all documents of the data set are clustered together at the same time in terms of the number of generated clusters and the average number of documents in a cluster by varying the value of a minimum cluster cohesion rate.

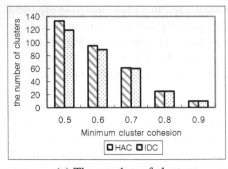

(a) The number of clusters

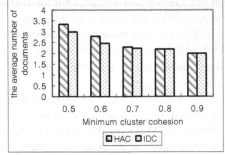

(b) The average number of documents in a cluster

Fig. 5. Performance of the IDC algorithm

Given a set of document clusters $HC = \{p_1, p_2, ..., p_m\}$ generated by the HAC algorithm and a set of document clusters $IC = \{q_1, q_2, ..., q_n\}$ generated by the IDC algorithm, let $sim(q_i, HC)$ denote the ratio of the number of common documents of a cluster q_i ($1 \leq i \leq n$) in the IC and a cluster p_j ($1 \leq j \leq m$) in the HC over the number of documents in the cluster q_i. The cluster p_j includes most documents belonging to a cluster q_i among clusters in HC. Accordingly, $sim(q_i \mid IC, HC)$ is defined by Equation (8).

$$sim(q_i, HC) = \max\left(\frac{|q_i \cap p_j|}{|q_i|}\right) \quad (\forall p_j \in HC \ (1 \leq i \leq m)) \tag{8}$$

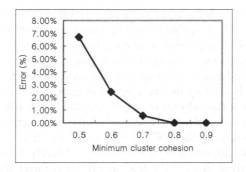

Fig. 6. Difference ratio between *HAC* and *IDC*

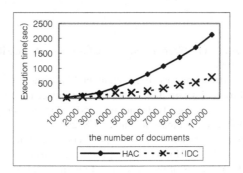

Fig. 7. Processing times between *HAC* and *IDC*

Based on this, the similarity $sim(IDC, HAC)$ between the result of the *HAC* algorithm and that of the *IDC* algorithm is defined by Equation (9).

$$sim(IDC, HAC) = \frac{1}{n}\sum_{i=1}^{n} sim(q_i, HC) \tag{9}$$

Hence, the difference δ between the result of the *HAC* algorithm and that of the *IDC* algorithm is defined by Equation (10).

$$\delta = 1 - sim(IDC, HAC) \tag{10}$$

In Figure 6, the difference is illustrated when the values of a minimum cluster participation rate and a minimum cluster cohesion rate are varied from 0.5 to 0.9. As the value of a minimum cluster cohesion rate becomes higher, the results of the two algorithms become more similar. By varying the number of documents, the processing times of the *HAC* algorithm and the IDC algorithm are compared in Figure 7. As the number of documents is increased, the processing time of the *HAC* algorithm is increased more rapidly since the HAC algorithm is not incremental.

7 Conclusion

A TF*NIDF function is introduced to overcome the weak points of the TF*IDF function since the SCUP algorithm should be performed in an incremental way. This paper proposes the SCUP algorithm to find the initial clusters of similar documents in a set of document based on a cluster cohesion rate as well as a cluster participation rate. This paper introduces a category tree for incremental hierarchical document clustering, so that it is used by the incremental document clustering (IDC) algorithm to find the most appropriate cluster if any efficiently. In the IDC algorithm, a newly added document is examined to be clustered to the most appropriate cluster in the category tree. By comparing the IDC algorithm with the HAC algorithm, the cluster accuracy of the IDC algorithm is more similar relatively to the HAC algorithm. However, the processing time of the IDC algorithm is faster than that of the HAC algorithm when the number of document is increased.

References

1. Zamir, O. and Etzioni, O. "Web Document Clustering: A Feasibility Demonstration", SIGIR, pp. 46-54, 1998
2. Wai-cjiu Wong and Ads Wai-chee Fu, Incremental Document Clustering for Web Page Classification, In Proceedings of 2000 International Conference on Information Society in the 21st Century: Emerging Technologies and New Challenges (IS2000), Aizu-Wakamatsu City, Fukushima, Japan November 5-8, 2000
3. C. J. Van Rijsvergen, "Information Retrieval", Butterworth, London, 2nd edition, 1979
4. Wai Lam and Chao Yang Ho. Using a generalized instance set for automatic text categorization. In Proceedings of the 21th annual international ACM SIGIR conference on Research and development in information retrieval, p.81-89, Melbourne, Australia, August 1998.
5. Sean Slattery and Mark Craven, Combining statistical and relation methods for learning in hypertext domains. In proceedings of the 8th International Conference on Inductive Logic Programming, Madison, Wisconsin, USA, July 1998.
6. David D. Lewis, Robert E. Schapire, James P.Callan, Ron Papka, "Training Algorithms for Linear Text Classifiers", *Proceedings of 19th ACM International Conference on Research and Development in Information Retrieval*, 1996
7. Eui-Hong (Sam) Han, George Karypis, and Vipin Kumar, "Text Categorization Using Weight Adjusted k-Nearest Neighbor Classification", *5th Pacific Asia Conference on Knowledge Discovery And Data Mining*, 2001

8. Yiming Yang, "Expert Network: Effective and efficient learning from human decisions in text categorization and retrieval", *17th ACM SIGIR Conference on Research and Development in Information Retrieval*, 13-22, 1994

9. B. W. Frakes and R. Baeza-Yates, "Information Retrieval: Data Structures & Algorithms", Prentice Hall, 1992

10. Jain, A. K. and Dubes, R. C., "Algorithms for Clustering Data", Prentice Hall, 1988

11. Arnard Ribert, Abdel Ennaji, Yves Lecourtier, An Incremental Hierarchical Clustering, Vision Interface '99. Trois-Rivieres, Canada, 19-21 May, p.586-591.

12. R. O. Duda and P. E. Hart. Pattern Classification and Scene Analysis. Wiley, 1972.

13. L. Kaufman and P.J. Rousseeuw. Finding Groups in Data. An Introduction to Cluster Analysis. Wiley, New York, 1990.

14. Tian Zhang, Raghu Ramakrishnan, and Miron Livny, BIRCH : An efficient data clustering method for very large databases. In Proceedings of the ACM SIGMOD Conference on Management of Data, p.103-144, Montreal, Canada, June 1996.

15. Douglass R. Cutting, David R. Karger, Jao O. Pedersen., and John W. Tukey, "Scatter/Gather: A Cluster-based Approach to Browsing Large Document Collections", *15th International ACM SIGIR Conference on Research and Development in Information Retrieval*, pp.318-329, 1992

16. Moses Charikar, Chandra Chekuri, Tomas Feder, and Rajeev Motwani. Incremental clustering and dynamic information retrieval. In Proceedings of 29th Annual ACM Symposium on the Theory of Computing, p.626-635, El Paso, Texas, USA, May 1997.

17. G. Salton, C. Buckley, "Term-weighting approaches in automatic text retrieval", *Information Processing and Management*, Vol. 24 No. 5 pp. 513-523, 1988

18. Amit Singhal, Chris Buckley, and Mandar Mitra, "Pivoted Document Length Normalization", *Proceedings of 19th ACM International Conference on Research and Development in Information Retrieval*, 1996

19. Drug fisher, Iterative Optimization and Simplification of Hierarchical Clusterings, Journal of Artificial Intelligence Research, 1995

Subsite Retrieval: A Novel Concept for Topic Distillation

Tao Qin[1,2,*], Tie-Yan Liu[2], Xu-Dong Zhang[1], Guang Feng[1,2,*],
and Wei-Ying Ma[2]

[1] MSP Laboratory, Dept. Electronic Engineering, Tsinghua University,
Beijing, 100084, P.R. China (8610)62789944
{qinshitao99, fengg03}@mails.tsinghua.edu.cn
zhangxd@tsinghua.edu.cn
[2] Microsoft Research Asia, No. 49, Zhichun Road, Haidian District,
Beijing, 100080, P. R. China (8610)62617711
{t-tyliu, wyma}@microsoft.com

Abstract. Topic distillation is one of the main information needs when users search the Web. In previous approaches to topic distillation, the single page was treated as the basic searching unit. This strategy is inherited from general information retrieval, which has not fully utilized the structure information of the Web. In this paper, we propose a novel concept for topic distillation, named subsite retrieval, in which the basic searching unit is the subsite instead of the single page. As indicated by the name, the subsite is a subset of website, consisting of a structural collection of pages. The key of subsite retrieval is to extract effective features to represent a subsite by utilizing both the content in each page and the structural information in the subsite. Specifically, we propose a so-called PI algorithm for this purpose, which is based on the modeling of website growth. Testing on the topic distillation task of TREC 2003 and TREC 2004, subsite retrieval gets significant improvement of retrieval performance over the previous single page based methods.

1 Introduction

While the Web grows exponentially along with time, the amount of information that the users can digest remains roughly constant. With such background, search engines came out as the widely-recognized tools in helping users to retrieve information. Among all the information needs of web users, topic distillation is one of the most common and important forms. User surveys have shown that about 39% [4] web search queries belong to topic distillation, while query log analysis has given an even higher proportion of 48% [4]. Because of the popularity of topic distillation, the TREC conference has included it in the Web track since the year of 1999.

So far in existing approaches for topic distillation, the single page was treated as the basic searching unit. It has been a common strategy in the literature to use TF-IDF [2] of the query term in the page content to compute a relevance score (such as BM2500 [16]) and use hyperlinks to get an importance score (such as PageRank 2)14

---

* This work was performed when the first and the fourth authors were interns at Microsoft Research Asia.

G.G. Lee et al. (Eds.): AIRS 2005, LNCS 3689, pp. 388–400, 2005.
© Springer-Verlag Berlin Heidelberg 2005

and HITS [13]), then combine them to rank the retrieved web pages. However, this strategy has not successfully served the queries for topic distillation. According to the report of TREC 2003 [8], the best result based on such approaches only has marginal retrieval accuracy: precision at 10 (P@10) of 12.8% and mean average prevision (MAP) of 15.43%. That is, there is still a long way to go if one wants to get a satisfactory search result for topic distillation.

As indicated by the ground truth provided by the TREC committee, the labeled answer for topic distillation is often the entry point of a collection of pages devoted to the query topic. That is, for topic distillation, whether a page is an appropriate answer to a query is not only determined by itself, but also by all the other pages for which it serves as the entry point. In this regard, topic distillation is very different from the traditional information retrieval. Actually, its aim is not to find a single page but a group of pages, although only the entry point of the page group is delivered to the users. Therefore, we should make use of this characteristic of topic distillation to improve the retrieval performance.

The organizational structure of the website is usually represented by a tree, and the parent-child relationship can be easily got between any two pages through site map construction [5]. Through the entry point, we can access many descendant pages, which are usually quite relevant to the query. In many cases, some descendant pages are even more relevant than the labeled page in terms of TF-IDF [2]. It is just because the labeled page is usually a navigation center with only a few words while concrete contents are placed in its descendant pages. This truth leads to the major difficulty in topic distillation. Take Table 1 as an example, there are totally seven pages coming from the same site (http://cio.doe.gov/) in the top 1000 retrieval results produced by BM2500 model [16] for the fourth query "wireless communication" of the topic distillation task in TREC 2003 Web track.

Table 1. Retrieval results for the query "wireless communication"

Rank	Document ID	Relevance	URL
70	G35-97-1056561	9.858	cio.doe.gov/wireless/3g/3g_index.htm
470	G07-38-3990160	9.508	cio.doe.gov/spectrum/groups.htm
477	G35-75-1119753	9.481	cio.doe.gov/spectrum/philo.htm
518	G36-35-1278614	9.320	cio.doe.gov/wireless/background.htm
571	G07-10-2999356	9.093	cio.doe.gov/spectrum/background.htm
648	G35-01-1537522	8.817	cio.doe.gov/wireless/wwg/wwg_index.htm
649	**G07-78-3824915**	**8.815**	**cio.doe.gov/wireless/**
...	...	...	...

As we can see, the relevance score of the labeled page (which document ID is G07-78-3824915, and labeled in bold) is much smaller than its child pages G35-97-1056561, G36-35-1278614 and G35-01-1537522. If using single page based feature extraction, it will be very difficult to guarantee that the labeled pages are retrieved with a higher rank. One possible way to succeed in this case is to involve the structural information of the site. This is just the motivation of our paper.

A subsite is a sub tree of the website, which contains an entry page and all the descendent pages of it. We denote such a subsite rooted by p as $S(p)$. With such a definition, it is easy to understand that each page in the Web could correspond to a subsite. See the website shown in Figure 1. Here we use p_j to denote the web pages in this website, and use $l(p_j)$ to denote the level of a page in the website (for example, $l(p_1)=1$, $l(p_2)=2$ and $l(p_{10})=3$). Then, the pages in the solid circle compose a subsite $S(p_1)=\{p_1, p_2, \dots p_{13}\}$, while the pages in the dashed and the dot circles compose subsites $S(p_4)=\{p_4, p_8, p_9, p_{10}\}$ and $S(p_{10})=\{ p_{10}\}$ respectively. Furthermore, if we use $h(S(p))$ to denote the number of levels in subsite $S(p)$, we will have $h(S(p_1))=3$, $h(S(p_4))=2$, and $h(S(p_{10}))=1$. Besides, we denote the first-generation child pages of p as $R(p)$. For example, $R(p_1)=\{p_2, p_3, p_4\}$, $R(p_4)=\{p_8, p_9, p_{10}\}$. Note that $R(p_1)\neq\{p_2, p_3, p_4, p_5, \dots p_{13}\}$.

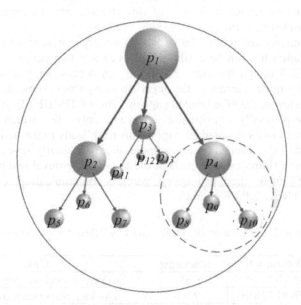

Fig. 1. Illustration for the subsite

Based on the above definition of subsite, we further propose a novel search strategy, called subsite retrieval, for topic distillation. In this strategy, we no longer use single page but subsite as the basic searching unit in the retrieval process. In other words, a page can get the support from its child pages and thus may get a higher rank than before. In the experiments on both TREC 2003 and 2004, the subsite retrieval gives out a much better performance on topic distillation.

The rest of the paper is organized as follows. In Section 2, we briefly introduce the task of topic distillation, and review some related works. In Section 3, we give an expansion model to describe website growth process, and the PI algorithm for subsite feature extraction is proposed based on this expansion model. We conduct a set of experiments to evaluate the effectiveness of subsite retrieval in Section 4. And last, we give the concluding remarks and future research directions in Section 5.

2 Related Works

Topic distillation is a general concept: given a broad topic, distill a small number of high-quality web pages that are most representatives of the topic. The task aims at finding the key entry pages of some related websites. Here key entry pages must obey the following rules:

(i) They should be principally devoted to the topic.

(ii) They should not be part of larger sites which are also principally devoted to the same topic.

For example, for the topic of "science", the following pages might be considered as key entry points in .gov domain:

http://www.nsf.gov/ (National Science Fondation)

http://science.nasa.gov/ (NASA Science)

http://www.science.gov/ (Government Science Portal)

http://www.house.gov/science/welcome.htm (House Committee on Science)

However, the page http://www.house.gov/ will not be regard as key entry point because it disobeys the first rule while the page http://www.nsf.gov/home/bio/ fails in passing the second rule.

In addition, key entry pages often provide many access points to their child pages so that users can easily find further information about the topics contained in those pages. In other words, a key entry page is also a good starting point for users to navigate the corresponding (sub) site because it contains rich organizational structure information.

From the above analysis, we can see that the task of topic distillation is quite different from traditional retrieval. Therefore, treating each page as the basic searching unit might not work effectively for topic distillation although it has been already working quite well for other search tasks. In this regard, we will propose a novel concept: subsite retrieval, in which the basic searching unit becomes subsite. The basic idea of subsite retrieval is to improve search accuracy for topic distillation with the help of site structure information. As a reference, we will first give a brief literature review on how previous works utilize the structure information of the Web.

There are many works which try to use web structure to assist topic distillation, such as [1,3,4,6,7,18]. Here we will introduce the relevance propagation model [18] in details, because the motivation of [18] is similar to our idea.

Shakery, et al [18] considers how to use Web structure to further improve relevance weighting. They propagate the relevance score of a page to another page through hyperlink between them. They define the so-called hyper relevance score of each page as a function of three variables: its content similarity to the query (self relevance), a weighted sum of the hyper relevance scores of all the pages that point to it, and a weighted sum of the hyper relevance scores of all the pages it points to. According to these definitions, their relevance propagation model can be written as:

$$h(q) = f\left(S(q), \sum_{q_i \to q} h(q_i)\omega_I(q_i,q), \sum_{q \to q_j} h(q_j)\omega_O(q,q_j) \right) \tag{1}$$

where $h(q)$ is the hyper relevance score of page q, $S(q)$ is the content similarity between the page q and the query, and ω_I and ω_O are weighting functions for in-link and out-link pages. For implementation, they give three special case of the relevance propagation model: weighted in-link case, weighted out-link case, and uniform out-link case[1].

Their experimental results show that relevance propagation generally performs better than using only content information. However, the amount of improvement is sensitive to the document collection and the tuning of parameters [18].

In this paper, we make use the subsite structure to boost the topic distillation in the Web. The subsite structure becomes the key component of the retrieval framework.

3 Subsite Retrieval

In this section, we will exhibit the details of subsite retrieval. As referred in the introduction, we will treat the subsite as the basic searching unit to improve the retrieval performance for topic distillation. Different from the traditional texts, the information in the website is well structured. The author would like to design an appropriate expression structure to help users well catch and understand what he wants to show. By exploring the expression structure of the website, we find the topics usually organized in a hierarchical structure so that it is very natural to use the subsite as basic searching unit for topic distillation.

Specifically, we propose a generative model to simulate the growing process of websites. That is, how a subsite is formed starting from its original idea. Then, we discuss how to recover that original idea based on an existing website reversely. Actually, this reverse engineering could just be regarded as a feature extraction algorithm. After that, we can compute a relevance score for the subsite using a certain relevance weighting function, just like what people have done for single page based retrieval

3.1 Expansion Model

The Web is not a restricted space. The content and the structure of each website are either not restricted. People can add almost anything into their website and organize it in any manner. So, it is difficult to design a generative model to cover the growing processes of all the websites rigorously. Here, we give a very representative and simple model to describe the general growing process of websites in statistical sense. We call it expansion model, illustrated as follows.

When an author starts to build a website, he only has some original idea in mind about what this website should talk about. According to this idea, he can first build a homepage with some related materials. See in Figure 2(a), the homepage is denoted by a circle. Obviously, the author will not be satisfied with only one page in his website. He will gradually enrich the website later. Suppose the original idea can separated into four sub ideas, distinguished by white, green, cyan and magenta in Figure 2(a). The author determines that three of them should be expatiated in new pages respectively. Then, he will collect materials and resources to realize three new pages to illustrate each part, seen in Figure 2(b). The region with horizontal bars in the child

---

[1] For details, we refer to [18].

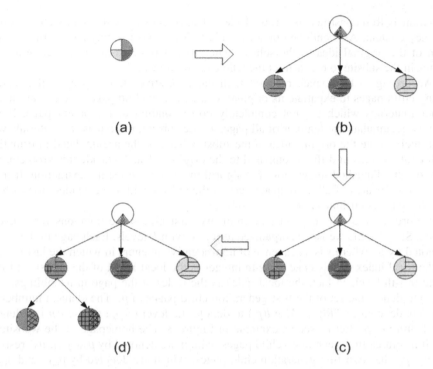

Fig. 2. Illustration for divide-expand model

page denotes the new collected materials and the other region is inherited from its parent page. Notice that the new collected materials are not completely consistent. Meanwhile, in the homepage, the original region for each separated topics is reduced. There are only a few sentences, even a few hyperlinks, left in the homepage for each sub idea. If we extract the feature of each sub topic from the homepage at this time, we only can get a very little value on the separated three because the main words for them are scatted in the child pages although they are indeed the major part of the site. Then for the next steps, some of these sub topics will also be enriched in similar manners and some grandchild pages are formed, seen in Figure 2(c). The green one can be considered to include three sub topics and two of them are separated away and expand to two child pages of the green one, also the grandchild pages of the homepage. This is a divide-expand process, which recursively build a content-rich website starting from only some original ideas. Through this process, the original idea of each subsite is scattered in a hierarchical organized structure. Besides, much more materials and resources are brought into the subsite to support each sub topics. We believe that the above model can describe its heart and sole although the real-world website authoring process might be much more complex.

3.2 Subsite Feature Extraction

Subsite feature extraction is just the reverse process of the website authoring as described in the expansion model. Actually, this time, we already have a website. What we want is to reconstruct the original idea of each subsite, which can well represent the key content. As mentioned in above subsection, a page is only part of the realization of the original idea of the subsite. Therefore it is necessary to integrate all the pages in the subsite to reconstruct the whole original idea.

According to the expansion model, in each iterative step, a page will generate many child pages to expatiate its original idea and each child page may contain many other materials which are not completely corresponding to the parent page. If we simply accumulate the features of all pages in the subsite, these mass of materials will extremely dilute the original idea of the subsite. That is, the accumulated information will contain concept drift as compared to the original idea. To tackle this problem, we propose the Punished Integration (PI) algorithm for subsite feature extraction. It integrates the features of all individual pages in the subsite with the consideration of how much a page contributes to the whole subsite.

Before the illustration of PI algorithm, we first give some notations for convenience. Suppose the website is organized as a tree with L levels. Each page in the site is denoted by p_s, where s is a sequence of non-negative integers in which the last integer is the local index of this page and i-th integer is the local index of the ancestor of this page in i-th level. In fact, the local index is the order of the page in its siblings. Use $R(p_s)$ to denote the set of the first-generation child pages of p_s. The element number of $R(p_s)$ is denoted by $\|R(p_s)\|$. Use $l(p_s)$ to denote the level of p_s and use $f(p_s)$ to denote the feature of p_s. Let us see an example in Figure 3. The homepage of the website is p_0. It has three first-generation child pages, which are denoted by $p_{0,0}, p_{0,1}, p_{0,2}$ respectively. $p_{0,1}$ has two first-generation child pages, which are denoted by $p_{0,1,0}$ and $p_{0,1,1}$. Furthermore, $\|R(p_0)\| = 3$ and $l(p_{0,2,0})=3$ and $R(p_0)=\{p_{0,0}, p_{0,1}, p_{0,2}\}$.

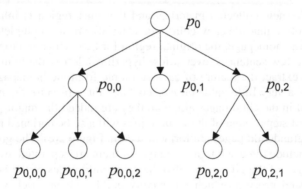

Fig. 3. A simple website

Denote the subsite with entry point p_s by $S(p_s)$,

$$S(p_s) = \left\{ p_{s,s_c} \in W \mid s_c \in \bigcup_{i=0}^{L-l(p_s)} Q(i) \right\} \tag{2}$$

where W is the page collection of the whole Web, and $Q(k)$ denotes the set of sequences of k non-negative number.

$$Q(k) = \left\{ i_1, i_2, \cdots i_k \mid i_k \in \overline{Z^-} \right\} \tag{3}$$

If $k = 0$, $Q(k) = \varnothing$.

Furthermore, we use $h(p_s)$ to denote the height of $S(p_s)$, i.e.

$$h(p_s) = L - l(p_s) \tag{4}$$

And use $F[S(p_s)]$ to denote the feature of $S(p_s)$. Our PI algorithm is just to extract a suitable $F[S(p_s)]$ which can better represent $S(p_s)$ than $f(p_s)$. As mentioned above, $F[S(p_s)]$ can not be the accumulation of all $f(p_s)$ in $S(p_s)$ because of the concept drift in the growth process of website expansion model. Thus, we had better punish the features of the child pages in the integration. In our model, there are two kinds of punishment.

1) *The feature of the page will be punished with a factor $\alpha(\Delta l)$, where Δl is the level difference with respect to the entry point.*

If a page is far from the entry point of the subsite, it will contain more post-imported materials. Thus, it should be sharply punished to weaken the concept drift. In particular $\alpha(\Delta l)$ is a monotonically decreasing function and its range is between 0 and 1. In our experiment, it has an exponential form.

$$\alpha(\Delta l) = \lambda^{\Delta l} \tag{5}$$

where λ is an adjustable variant. For the entry point, the punished factor always equals to one since $\Delta l = 0$.

2) *The feature of a page will be further punished by the number of its sibling pages.*

In the real website, some page may have many child pages. In this case, even with the punishment in 1), the concept drift is still very remarkable. Therefore, we must repress the magnitude of the concept drift derived from the amount of the sibling pages. In such a way, we can guarantee that the total of contributions of child pages to the subsite will not overwhelm the parent page.

By jointly considering 1) and 2), the feature of subsite $S(p_s)$ can be extracted by

$$F\left[S(p_s)\right] = \alpha(0) f(p_s) +$$

$$\frac{1}{\|R(p_s)\|} \sum_{u=1}^{h(p_s)-1} \left[\alpha(u) \sum_{p_{i_1} \in R(p_s)} \sum_{p_{i_2} \in R(p_{i_1})} \cdots \sum_{p_{i_u} \in R(p_{i_{u-1}})} \frac{f(p_{i_u})}{\prod_{k=1}^{u} \|R(p_{i_k})\|} \right] \tag{6}$$

From (6), we can see that the feature of a subsite consists of two parts. The first part is the feature of the entry point, of the subsite. The second part is the sum of the features of other pages in the subsite with appropriate punishments.

3.3 Other Routines

After feature extraction, we can use the relevant function to calculate the relevance score for each subsite. Here, we just use BM2500 because it is widely used in many kinds of retrieval works and always gives fairly good performances.

Although we use the subsite as the basic searching unit, we return not the whole subsite but the entry point to users in order to keep the style of results accordant to other methods. To evaluate the performance of subsite retrieval, we used two criterions: mean average precision (MAP) and precision at 10 (P@10) [2].

4 Experiments

In this section, several experiments were conducted to test the effectiveness of subsite retrieval for topic distillation. Firstly, we introduce the experimental settings and some implementation issues, then experimental results and discussions will be given.

4.1 Experiment Setup

We chose the topic distillation task in TREC 2003 and TREC 2004 Web track as the benchmark. The corresponding data set used is the ".GOV" collection, which was crawled in the year of 2002. It contains 1,247,753 documents. 1,053,111 of them are html files, which were used in our experiments. There are totally 50 topic distillation queries in TREC 2003 and 75 queries in TREC 2004.

As aforementioned, the main contribution of our paper is feature extraction for subsite representation. To show the effectives of the subsite features, we used the same relevance ranking function (BM2500 [16]) to get retrieval lists based on both subsite and single page based features.

To be noted, for simplicity, we did not parse the web pages into title, body, anchor and so on. Instead we use the query term frequency in free text of the whole html file as the feature for each web page. The baseline (single page based retrieval with BM2500) has MAP of 0.1237 and P@10 of 0.110 on TREC 2003, and MAP of 0.1324 and P@10 of 0.1693 on TREC 2004.

When testing subsite retrieval, we substituted the page-based features in the above formulas with the subsite based features extracted by our models. The corresponding retrieval results and the comparison with the single page based baseline will be given in the successive sub sections.

4.2 Performance of Subsite Retrieval

In this sub section, we tested the performance of our subsite retrieval comparing with single page based retrieval. As a comparison algorithm, we also implemented the three relevance propagation models in [18]. Our implementation is close to that in [18]. The difference is that they used language model for relevance weighting, but we adopted BM2500.

Figure 4 shows the performance of subsite retrieval on topic distillation task of TREC 2003.

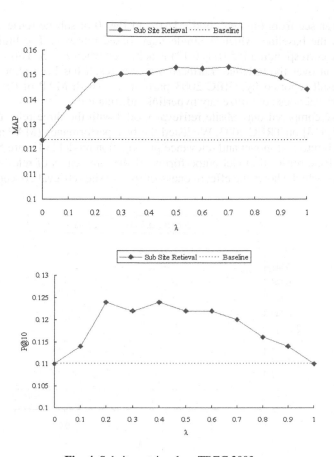

Fig. 4. Subsite retrieval on TREC 2003

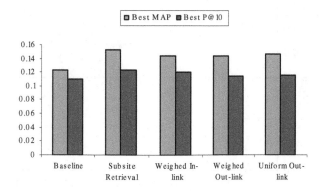

Fig. 5. Comparison of subsite retrieval model and relevance propagation model on TREC 2003

As we can see from Figure 4, both MAP and P@10 of subsite retrieval are always better than the baseline, which is single page based retrieval. The highest MAP of 0.1531 (the corresponding P@10 is 0.12) is achieved when λ=0.5. This equals to 20% improvement over the baseline. Furthermore, this result has been almost as good as the best result reported by TREC 2003 participants (with MAP of 0.1543), even if subsite retrieval does not utilize any hyperlink information.

Then, we compared our subsite retrieval model with the three relevance propagation models [18] on TREC 2003. We listed the best performance (MAP and P@10) of both the sub-retrieval model and relevance propagation model in Figure 5. We can see that our subsite retrieval model outperforms all the three cases of relevance propagation models, which shows the effectiveness of the subsite retrieval concept.

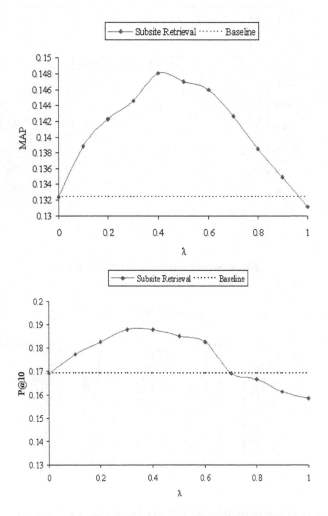

Fig. 6. Subsite retrieval on TREC 2004

Figure 6 shows the performance of subsite retrieval on topic distillation task of TREC 2004. From Figure 6, the MAP is almost always better than the baseline on TREC 2004. However, the P@10 overcomes the baseline only when $\lambda<=0.7$. Since λ is the level decrease factor, this means that features propagated from children to parent should not be too large.

We listed the best performance (MAP and P@10) for TREC 2004 of both the subretrieval model and relevance propagation model in Figure 7. Similar to Figure 6, our subsite retrieval model get the best performance of MAP. Although the subsite retrieval model do not overcome all the three cases of relevance propagation model, it is better than two of the three. Again, this approves the value of subsite retrieval.

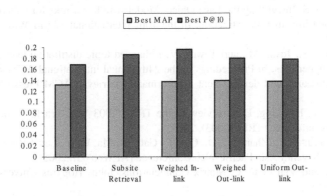

Fig. 7. Comparison of subsite retrieval model and relevance propagation model on TREC 2004

5 Conclusions and Future Work

In this paper, we proposed a novel concept, i.e. subsite retrieval, for topic distillation in the Web. We argued that subsite retrieval was a better and natural choice from the topic distillation because it was consistent with the growth manner of websites. Treating subsite as the based searching unit, we proposed an expansion model to describe the website growth process, and based on this expansion model we proposed the PI algorithm to extract the feature of the subsite instead of the single page. Then, with BM2500, we could get the relevance score of the subsite. Experiments on topic distillation task of TREC 2003 and 2004 Web track showed that subsite retrieval greatly boosted performance as compared to the single page based retrieval.

For our future work, there is still a large space to explore.

1) How to carefully design relevance computation algorithms for subsite retrieval? In this paper, we just adopt BM2500 for simplicity. However, BM2500 is designed for single pages based retrieval. It is more likely that there are some better algorithms than BM2500 to calculate the relevance score for subsites.
2) How to calculate importance score for subsite retrieval? In this paper, we focus on relevance weighting for subsite retrieval. However, the importance score is significant in web search. In our future work, we will develop the effective link analysis algorithms for subsite retrieval.

References

1. Amitay, E., Carmel, D., Darlow, A., Lempel, R., and Soffer, A. Topic Distillation with Knowledge Agents, in the eleventh Text Retrieval Conference (TREC 2002), 2002.
2. Baeza-Yates, R., Ribeiro-Neto, B. Modern Information Retrieval, Addison Wesley, 1999.
3. Bharat, K., and Henzinger, M. R. Improved algorithms for topic distillation in a hyperlinked environment. In Proceedings of the ACM-SIGIR, 1998.
4. Bharat, K., and Mihaila, G. A. When Experts Agree: Using Non-affiliated Experts to Rank Popular Topics. In Proceedings of the Tenth International World Wide Web Conference, 2001.
5. Broder, A. A Taxonomy of Web Search. SIGIR Forum 36(2), 2002.
6. Chakrabarti, S. Integrating the Page Object Model with hyperlinks for enhanced topic distillation and information extraction, In the 10th International World Wide Web Conference, 2001.
7. Chakrabarti, S., Joshi, M., and Tawde, V. Enhanced topic distillation using text, markup tags, and hyperlinks, In Proceedings of the 24th annual international ACM SIGIR conference on Research and development in information retrieval, ACM Press, 2001, pp. 208-216.
8. Craswell, N., Hawking, D. Overview of the TREC 2003 Web Track, in the twelfth Text Retrieval Conference (TREC 2003), 2003.
9. Feng, G., Liu, T. Y., Zhang, X. D., Qin. T., Gao, B., Ma, W. Y. Level-Based Link Analysis, in The Seventh Asia Pacific Web Conference (APWeb'05), 2005.
10. Golub G., and Van Loan, C. Matrix Computations. Johns Hopkins University Press, 3rd edition, 1996.
11. Hawking, D. Overview of the TREC-9 Web Track, in the ninth Text Retrieval Conference (TREC 9), 2000.
12. Ingongngam, P., and Rungsawang, A. Report on the TREC 2003 Experiments Using Web Topic-Centric Link Analysis, in the twelfth Text Retrieval Conference (TREC 2003), 2003.
13. Kleinberg, J. Authoritative sources in a hyperlinked environment, Journal of the ACM, Vol. 46, No. 5, pp. 604-622, 1999.
14. Kleinberg, J., and Lawrence, S. The Structure of the Web. Science 294(2001), pp. 1849.
15. Page, L., Brin, S., Motwani, R., and Winograd, T. The PageRank citation ranking: Bringing order to the web, Technical report, Stanford University, Stanford, CA, 1998.
16. Robertson, S. E. Overview of the okapi projects, Journal of Documentation, Vol. 53, No. 1, 1997, pp. 3-7.
17. Robertson, S. E., and Sparck Jones, K. Relevance weighting of search terms, Journal of the American Society of Information Science, Vol. 27, No. May-June, 1976, pp. 129-146.
18. Shakery, A., Zhai, C. X. Relevance Propagation for Topic Distillation UIUC TREC 2003 Web Track Experiments, in the twelfth Text Retrieval Conference (TREC 2003), 2003.
19. TREC-2004 Web Track Guidelines, http://es.csiro.au/TRECWeb/guidelines_2004.html.
20. Wen, J. R., Song, R., Cai, D., Zhu, K., Yu, S., Ye, S., and Ma, W. Y. Microsoft Research Asia at the web track of TREC 2003, in the twelfth Text Retrieval Conference (TREC 2003), 2003.

A Rough Set-Based Fuzzy Clustering

Zhao Yaqin[1], Zhou Xianzhong[2], and Tang Guizhong[3]

[1] Department of Automation, Nanjing University of Science & Technology,
210094 Nanjing, China
yaqinzhao@163.com
[2] School of Management and Engineering, Nanjing University, 210093 Nanjing, China
zhouxizh@public1.ptt.js.cn
[3] School of Automation, Nanjing University of Technology, 210009 Nanjing, China
tanggz128@163.com

Abstract. This paper presents a rough set-based fuzzy clustering algorithm in which the objects of fuzzy clustering are initial clusters obtained in terms of equivalence relations. Initial clustering is performed directly by judging whether equivalence relations are equal, not computing the intersection of equivalence classes as usual, and the correctness of the theory is proved using rough set theory. Excessive generation of some small classes is suppressed by secondary clustering on the basis of defining fuzzy similarity between two initial clusters. Consequently the dimension of fuzzy similarity matrix is reduced. The definition of integrated approximation precision is given as evaluation of clustering validity. The algorithm can dynamically adjust parameter to get the optimal result. Some experiments were performed to validate this method. The results showed that the algorithm could handle preferably the clustering problems of both numerical data and nominal data.

1 Introduction

Clustering analysis is one of important techniques in data mining. Application fields include statistics, mathematical evolutionary (such as location selecting, scheduling and assignment problems, etc.) and computer science (including pattern recognition, learning theory, image processing, and graphics, etc.)[1]. Nowadays, There exist many usual clustering approaches, such as hierarchical clustering [2], partitive clustering [3], density-based clustering [4], probabilistic model in clustering analysis [5], etc. However, most of them can deal with data only having numerical attributes, or has inferior performance in handling dataset of symbolical attributes. Recently, some researches tried to apply rough set theory [6] to clustering analysis [7] [8] [9] [10], and harvested some fruits.

This paper presents a rough set-based fuzzy clustering algorithm (RSFCL). In RSFCL algorithm, the initial equivalence relations [7] [11] among objects are first performed according to their relative dissimilarity. We propose a theorem that two objects are partitioned into the same initial cluster if and only if their equivalence relations are equal. We also prove correctness of the theorem using rough set theory. Therefore, initial clustering result can be obtained directly and simply by judging whether equivalence relations are equal, not computing the intersection of

G.G. Lee et al. (Eds.): AIRS 2005, LNCS 3689, pp. 401–409, 2005.

equivalence classes as [7] [11]. We adopt two different dissimilarity measures for two types of data: the Euclidean distance for numerical data and the matching measure for nominal data. Unfortunately, similar equivalence relations will cause to excessive generation of small classes. And the results have little capability of noise resistance. Accordingly, the fuzzy similarity between two initial clusters is defined as the basis of establishing fuzzy similar matrix so that fuzzy equivalence relations represents more simple knowledge that generates adequate number of categories. But our approach is different from usual fuzzy clustering algorithm [12] at the aspect of clustering objects. Namely the objects of fuzzy clustering are not original data in a dataset, but some initial clusters. Base on these, the dimension of fuzzy similarity matrix is reduced, and clustering performance is increased. The definition of integrated approximation precision is given as evaluation of the validity of different clustering results in order to yield the optimal result. Some experiments were made on the datasets in UCI (University of California, Irvine) machine learning repository. The experimental results showed that the algorithm had good performance for both numerical attributes and symbolic attributes.

The remainder of this paper is organized as follow. In section 2, we elaborate RSFCL algorithm. Section 3 presents our experimental results, and finally, in section 4, we present our conclusions.

2   RSFCL Algorithm

In RSFCL algorithm, initial clustering result is obtained directly by judging whether indistinguishable relations are equal, in which a category corresponds to a cluster. Afterwards, the fuzzy similarity between two initial clusters is calculated as a basis of fuzzy clustering. Detailed steps are given as follows.

2.1   Initial Clustering

Definition 1. *Equivalence Relation*

Equivalence relation of one object x_i is defined: $R_i = \{\{[x_i]_{R_i}\}, \{U - [x_i]_{R_i}\}\}$, where $\{[x_i]_{R_i}\} = \{x_j \mid d(x_i, x_j) \le \beta_1\}$, for all $j(1 \le j \le n)$, $d(x_i, x_j)$ denotes the dissimilarity between two objects x_i and x_j, and β_1 is a dissimilarity threshold. Obviously, "$\{[x_i]_{R_i}\} \cap \{U - [x_i]_{R_i}\} = \varnothing$ and $\{[x_i]_{R_i}\} \cup \{U - [x_i]_{R_i}\} = U$" hold [7].

The attributes of different datasets can be not identical. Hence computing methods of dissimilarity measure are also different. In RSFCL algorithm, for numerical data, each attribute value is first normalized, and then the dissimilarity between two objects is computed using Euclidean distance. For nominal data, the dissimilarity is defined as $d(x_i, x_j) = a / b$, where a denotes the number of the attributes that the attribute values of the two objects x_i and x_j are different, and b denotes the number of all the attributes.

Let $U = \{x_1, x_2, \ldots, x_n\}$, for one object x_i, we compute the dissimilarity $d(x_i, x_j)$. For given dissimilarity threshold β_1, equivalence class of the object x_i is

$\{[x_i]_{R_i}\}=\{x_j \mid d(x_i,x_j)\le \beta_1\}$,   so   its   equivalence   relation   is
$R_i = \{\{[x_i]_{R_i}\},\{U-[x_i]_{R_i}\}\}$. In this way, n objects form a set of equivalence

relations. Suppose we obtain a dissimilarity matrix $D=\begin{bmatrix} 0 \\ 0.84 & 0 \\ 0.25 & 0.93 & 0 \\ 0.77 & 0.11 & 0.86 & 0 \\ 0.67 & 0.92 & 0.50 & 0.92 & 0 \\ 0.33 & 0.93 & 0.33 & 0.87 & 0.56 & 0 \\ 0.14 & 0.92 & 0.14 & 0.85 & 0.62 & 0.25 & 0 \\ 0.25 & 0.93 & 0.25 & 0.86 & 0.67 & 0.12 & 0.14 & 0 \end{bmatrix}$.

If β_1 is set to 0.25, then we obtain $R_1= R_3=\{\{x_1,\ x_3,\ x_7,\ x_8\},\ \{x_2,\ x_4,\ x_5,\ x_6\}\}$,
$R_2= R_4=\{\{x_2,\ x_4\},\ \{x_1,\ x_3,\ x_5,\ x_6,\ x_7,\ x_8\}\}$, $R_5=\{\{x_5\},\ \{x_1,\ x_2,\ x_3,\ x_4,\ x_6,$
$x_7,\ x_8\}\}$, $R_6=\{\{x_6,\ x_7,\ x_8\},\ \{x_1,\ x_2,\ x_3,\ x_4,\ x_5\}\}$, $R_7= R_8=\{\{\ x_1,\ x_3,\ x_{6,},\ x_7$
$,\ x_8\},\ \{x_2,\ x_4,\ x_5\}\}$。

The initial partition of the dataset can be obtained by computing the intersection of equivalence class in terms of rough set theory, but it is unnecessary and time-consuming to take such calculating methods. In fact, the initial clusters may obtain directly and simply. The detailed discuss is given as follow.

Theorem 1. *Let R is a group of equivalence relations defined by Definition 1, and let $R_i, R_j \in R$, then the objects x_i and x_j are partitioned into the same cluster if and only if $R_i = R_j$.*

Proof: I. If $R_i = R_j$, and then it is certain that x_i and x_j are partitioned into the same cluster.

Let U is be the entire set of objects, for $\forall x_k \in U$, and then $x_k \in [x_i]_{R_i}$ or $x_k \in \{U-[x_i]_{R_i}\}$. Since the equivalence relations $R_i = R_j$, the equivalence classes $[x_i]_{R_i} = [x_j]_{R_j}$ holds.

(i) For $\forall x_k \in U$, for all $k(1\le k \le n)$, suppose $x_k \in [x_i]_{R_i}$, then $x_k \in [x_j]_{R_j}$ since $[x_i]_{R_i} = [x_j]_{R_j}$. According to Definition 1, $d(x_i,x_k)\le \beta_1$ and $d(x_j,x_k)\le \beta_1$, hence $x_i \in [x_k]_{R_k}$ and $x_j \in [x_k]_{R_k}$. Namely x_i and x_j are partitioned into the same equivalence class $[x_k]_{R_k}$, for all $k(1\le k \le n)$. Thus x_i and x_j are certain to be partitioned into the same cluster.

(ii) For $\forall x_k \in U$, for all $k(1\le k \le n)$, suppose $x_k \in \{U-[x_i]_{R_i}\}$. The equation $\{U-[x_i]_{R_i}\}=\{U-[x_j]_{R_j}\}$ holds since $[x_i]_{R_i} = [x_j]_{R_j}$. Thus $x_k \in \{U-[x_j]_{R_j}\}$. According to Definition 1, $d(x_i,x_k)> \beta_1$ and $d(x_j,x_k)> \beta_1$. So $x_i \in \{U-[x_k]_{R_k}\}$ and $x_j \in \{U-[x_k]_{R_k}\}$, for all $k(1\le k\le n)$. Namely x_i and x_j are certain to be partitioned into the same cluster.

From above proofs, we educe that x_i and x_j are certain to be partitioned into the same cluster if $R_i = R_j$.

II. If $R_i \neq R_j$, and then x_i and x_j are certain to be partitioned into two different clusters.

Since $R_i \neq R_j$, $[x_i]_{R_i} \neq [x_j]_{R_j}$ holds. Then there is at least one object $x_k \in [x_i]_{R_i}$ and $x_k \notin [x_j]_{R_j}$, or $x_k \notin [x_i]_{R_i}$ and $x_k \in [x_j]_{R_j}$ in U. Let us assume that $x_k \in [x_i]_{R_i}$ and $x_k \notin [x_j]_{R_j}$. According to Definition 1, $d(x_i, x_k) \leq \beta_1$ and $d(x_j, x_k) > \beta_1$. Hence $x_i \in [x_k]_{R_k}$ and $x_j \notin [x_k]_{R_k}$, namely x_i and x_j are certain to be partitioned into two different equivalence class by equivalence relation R_k. According to rough set theory, x_i and x_j are certain to be partitioned into two different clusters if $R_i \neq R_j$.

Integrating I and II, we can educe that x_i and x_j are partitioned into the same cluster iff $R_i = R_j$.

For above example, since equivalence relation $R_1 = R_3$; $R_2 = R_4$; $R_7 = R_8$, initial clustering result is $U/R = \{\{x_1, x_3\}, \{x_2, x_4\}, \{x_5\}, \{x_6\}, \{x_7, x_8\}\}$, which can be obtained directly and simply by judging whether two equivalence relations are equal, and almost have no use for any additional calculation.

2.2 Secondary Clustering

Analyze the equivalence relations $R = \{R_1, R_2, R_3, R_4, R_5, R_6, R_7, R_8\}$ in section 2.1, we find only the equivalence relation R_6 partitions the objects x_1, x_3, x_7, x_8 into two different equivalence classes, whereas the other equivalence relations partition the objects x_1, x_3, x_7, x_8 into the same equivalence classes. These similar objects are classified into different categories due to R_6 making slightly different classification to the others. In addition, if x_6 is a noise, it disturbs the validity of clustering result. Therefore we define fuzzy similarity between two initial clusters so as to avoid the error that similar objects are classified into different categories. Each initial cluster is regarded as a new big granule, such that fuzzy clustering is applied in a big granular world.

Definition 2. *Fuzzy Similarity Between Two Initial Clusters*
Let C_i and C_j are two initial equivalence clusters, for $\forall x_k \in C_i$ and $\forall x_l \in C_j$, and then the fuzzy similarity between the two initial clusters is defined by

$$r(C_i, C_j) = \frac{\sum_{s=1}^{n_k} \delta_s}{n_k + n_l - \sum_{s=1}^{n_k} \delta_s} \tag{1}$$

Where $\delta_s = \begin{cases} 1 & if \ x_s \in [x_l]_{R_l} \ for \ all \ x_s \in [x_k]_{R_k} \\ 0 & otherwise \end{cases}$, $n_k = \left| [x_k]_{R_k} \right|$ and $n_l = \left| [x_l]_{R_l} \right|$.

Theorem 2. *Let $U/R = \{C_1, C_2, \cdots, C_m\}$, if fuzzy similarity between the two initial clusters is computed using (1), and then there exists certainly an m-order fuzzy* `similar matrix corresponding with U/R, and the matrix can be transformed into an m-order fuzzy equivalence matrix $\tilde{R}$.

Proof: I.   For $\forall x_k, x_l \in C_i$,   according   to   Definition   2,   we

obtain $r_{ii} = r(C_i, C_i) = \dfrac{\sum_{s=1}^{n_k} \delta_s}{n_k + n_l - \sum_{s=1}^{n_k} \delta_s}$.   Since $[x_k]_{R_k} = [x_l]_{R_l}$,   two   equations

$n_k = n_l$ and $\sum_{s=1}^{n_k} \delta_s = n_k$ hold. Hence $r_{ii} = r(C_i, C_i) = 1$.

II.   For $\forall x_k \in C_i$ and $\forall x_l \in C_j$, if $x_k \in [x_l]_{R_l}$, such that it is obvious that

$x_k \in [x_k]_{R_k} \cap [x_l]_{R_l}$ holds, Hence $\sum_{s=1}^{n_k} \delta_s = \left| [x_k]_{R_k} \cap [x_l]_{R_l} \right|$. For the same reason,

we can educe that $\sum_{s=1}^{n_l} \delta_s = \left| [x_l]_{R_l} \cap [x_k]_{R_k} \right|$ holds. From Definition 2, we obtain

$$r_{ij} = r(C_i, C_j) = \frac{\sum_{s=1}^{n_k} \delta_s}{n_k + n_l - \sum_{s=1}^{n_k} \delta_s} = \frac{\sum_{s=1}^{n_l} \delta_s}{n_l + n_k - \sum_{s=1}^{n_l} \delta_s} = r(C_j, C_i) = r_{ji}.$$

Therefore the matrix $\tilde{R}$ satisfies that $r_{ii} = 1$ and $r_{ij} = r_{ji}$, according to the theory

of fuzzy set [13], we can educe that $\tilde{R}$ is an m-order fuzzy similar matrix, then there

exists certainly an m-order fuzzy similar matrix $\tilde{R}$ corresponding with U/R. By

computing transitive closure $t(\tilde{R})$ of $\tilde{R}$, the matrix can be certainly transformed into

an m-order fuzzy equivalence matrix $\tilde{R}$.

For above example, the fuzzy similarity matrix $\tilde{R} = \tilde{R}^{(0)} = \begin{bmatrix} 1 & 0 & 0 & 0.4 & 0.8 \\ 0 & 1 & 0 & 0 & 0 \\ 0 & 0 & 1 & 0 & 0 \\ 0.4 & 0 & 0 & 1 & 0.6 \\ 0.8 & 0 & 0 & 0.6 & 1 \end{bmatrix}$.

Since $\tilde{R}^{(1)} = \begin{bmatrix} 1 & 0 & 0 & 0.6 & 0.8 \\ 0 & 1 & 0 & 0 & 0 \\ 0 & 0 & 1 & 0 & 0 \\ 0.6 & 0 & 0 & 1 & 0.6 \\ 0.8 & 0 & 0 & 0.6 & 1 \end{bmatrix}$ and $\tilde{R}^{(0)} < \tilde{R}^{(1)} = \tilde{R}^{(2)}$, the matrix $\tilde{R}^{(1)}$ is a fuzzy

equivalence matrix. If the threshold β_2 is set as $0.6 < \beta_2 \le 0.8$, then we obtain the fuzzy

clustering result $U/\tilde{R} = \{\{C_1, C_5\}, \{C_2\}, \{C_3\}, \{C_4\}\}$. Hence clustering result is

$U/\tilde{R} = \{\{x_1, x_3, x_7, x_8\}, \{x_2, x_4\}, \{x_5\}, \{x_6\}\}$.

2.3 Evaluation of Validity

Depending on the choice of thresholds β_1 and β_2, a variety of partitions of a universe can be obtained in the preceding steps. We then evaluate validity of the clustering results based on the following criteria. A high validity is assigned to the equivalence clusters based on fuzzy clustering when it is obtained with less modification of initial clusters based on equivalence relations.

Definition 3. *Integrated Approximate Precision*
Let U denote the non-empty universe of objects, R denote an initial set of equivalence relations, and $\tilde{R}$ denote fuzzy equivalence matrix. Suppose that U is classified into r equivalence classes, namely, fuzzy clustering result is $C = \{C_1, C_2, \cdots, C_r\}$. Each cluster corresponds with an approximate precision $\alpha(C_k)$, and $\alpha(C_k)$ is defined by

$$\alpha(C_k) = \frac{|\underline{RC}_k|}{|\overline{RC}_k|}, \text{ where } \underline{RC}_k \text{ and } \overline{RC}_k \text{ denote respectively } R\text{-lower and } R\text{-upper}$$

approximations of C_k given below.

$$\underline{RC}_k = \{x_i \in C_k \mid [x_i]_{R_i} \subseteq C_k\} \tag{2}$$

$$\overline{RC}_k = \{x_i \in C_k \mid [x_i]_{R_i} \cap C_k \neq \varnothing\} \tag{3}$$

Therefore each cluster corresponds with an approximate precision, the integrated approximate precision $H(C)$ is defined by

$$H(C) = -\sum_{i=1}^{r} \alpha(C_k) \log_2(\alpha(C_k)) \tag{4}$$

Total validity of the clustering result is evaluated by the integrated approximate precision. Finally, the optimal clustering result is obtained by dynamically setting various values of the threshold β_2.

3 Experimental Results

Four datasets of symbolical attributes and three datasets of numerical attributes were considered for the purpose of conducting the experiments. These data sets come from UCI machine learning database [14]. For the first part of the experiments, we chose four datasets of symbolical attributes: balloon, soybean, voting-records and zoo. For the second part of the experiments, we chose three datasets of numerical attributes: Iris, thyroid-disease and glass. Table 1 shows brief introduction of seven datasets.

Shoji Hirano [7] presented a clustering method based on rough sets (Marked Algorithm A), in which initial classification was performed according to equivalence relations defined on the basis of similarity between objects, and excessive generation of small categories was suppressed by modifying similar equivalence relations into the same equivalence relations. Both formation of initial clusters and modification of equivalence classes require computing equivalence relation of each object and intersection of equivalence classes. Sun HQ [12] proposed a fuzzy cluster based on rough set (Marked Algorithm B) in which the objects of fuzzy clustering were original data objects in decision table of rough set. RSFCL algorithm is similar to other two clustering algorithms to a certain extent, but initial clusters are performed directly by comparing whether equivalence relations are equal, not computing intersection of equivalence classes as [7], and objects of fuzzy clustering are initial clusters, not original data objects in a dataset as [12]. In this section the performances of the three clustering algorithms were compared in terms of clustering average accuracy obtained for 50 different run times. RSFCL algorithm and Algorithm A were also compared in terms of response time with different datasets for 50 different run times.

Table 1. The testing datasets

Datasets	The number of objects	The number of attributes	The number of classes
Balloon	20	4	2
Soybean	47	35	4
Voting-records	435	16	2
Zoo	101	16	7
Iris	150	4	3
Thyroid-disease	215	5	3
Glass	214	9	7

3.1 Clustering Validity

The three algorithms all computed the dissimilarity using Euclidean distance for numerical data, and using $d(x_i, x_j) = a/b$ for nominal data. Table 2 shows clustering accuracy obtained by the three clustering algorithms.

As seen from Table 2, the performances of Algorithm A and RSFCL algorithm are superior over Algorithm B, and clustering validity of RSFCL algorithm is slightly inferior to that of Algorithm A.

Table 2. Comparison of experimental results

Data set	RSFCL algorithm	Algorithm A	Algorithm B
Balloon	78.13%	79.88%	70.42%
Soybean	80.56%	82.72%	73.43%
Voting-records	83.33%	83.41%	74.29%
Zoo	81.14%	82.05%	72.98%
Iris	92.31%	94.16%	88.00%
Thyroid-disease	82.74%	83.21%	75.53%
Glass	42.86%	48.13%	41.27%

3.2 Run Efficiency

Since Algorithm A and RSFCL algorithm both have favorable clustering validity, run efficiency of the two algorithms were compared. Fig.1 depicts the variation of response time for the above seven datasets, respectively for 50 different run times. Note that response time of RSFCL algorithm is shorter than that of Algorithm A for testing datasets, especially when the number of data objects is high in datasets.

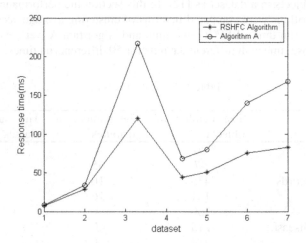

Fig. 1. Variation of response time with seven datasets

The computations of the dissimilarity between two objects and initial equivalence relation of each object are identical for RSFCL algorithm and Algorithm A. But computational requirements of the two algorithms for performing initial clusters are different. Clustering results of the former can be obtained directly by judging whether equivalence relations are equal, and hence results in $O(mn)$ computation, where $m(m < n)$ represents the number of initial clusters. The later requires computing the intersections of equivalence classes and thus results in $O(n^2)$ computation. For RSFCL algorithm, the secondary clustering requires computing square of fuzzy similarity matrix, hence is $O(m^2)$. For Algorithm A, the modification of equivalence classes still requires computing the intersection of n equivalence classes, hence is $O(n^2)$. Thus computing complexity of RSFCL algorithm is lower than Algorithm A. The experimental results were consistent with above analysis.

4 Conclusions

In the research on information retrieval, lots of clustering algorithms have been developed, and most of them had inferior performance in handling nominal data. However, the datasets with symbolical attributes are frequently met in clustering analysis. We introduced a rough set-based fuzzy clustering that consisted of two steps, initial clustering based on rough set and secondary clustering based on fuzzy equivalence relations. Four datasets of symbolical attributes and three datasets of numerical attributes were chose to perform experiments. The results showed that RSFCL algorithm had preferable clustering validity and high run efficiency in handling the clustering problems of both numerical data and nominal data.

Additionally, Exact equivalence relations become fuzzy due to fuzzy similarity between two initial clusters, which can avoid the disturbance of the noise to a certain extent. One should stress, however, that the thresholds could influence the clustering result.

References

1. Han JW, Kamber M.: Data Mining Concepts and Techniques. China Higher Education Press, Beijing (2001)
2. L Kaufman, PJ Rousseeuw: Finding Groups in Data: An Introduction to Clustering Analysis. John Wiley & Sons, New York (1990)
3. Mac Queen J.: Some Methods for Classification and Analysis of Multivariate Observations. In: 5th Berkeley Symposium on Mathmatics, Statistics and Probability, Berkeley, California, Vol. 1, (1967) 281-297
4. Ester M., Kriegel H., Sander J., Xu XW: A Density-Based Algorithm for Discovering Clusters in Large Spatial Databases with Noise. In: Simoudis E, Han JW, Fayyad UM. Eds. Proceeding of the 2nd International Conference on Knowledge Discovery and Data Mining, Portland, AAAI Press, (1996) 226-231
5. H.H. Bock: Probabilistic Models in Cluster Analysis. Computational Statistics & Data Analysis, Vol. 23, (1996) 5-28
6. Z. Pawlak: Rough Sets. International Journal of Information and Computer Sciences, Vol. 11, (1982) 145-172
7. Hirano S, Tsumoto S, Okuzaki T, Hata Y: A Clustering Method for Nominal and Numerical Data Based on Rough Set Theory. In: Bulletin of International Rough Set Society Proceeding of Rough Set Theory and Granular Computing, Matsue, Shimane, Japan, (2001) 211-216
8. P. Lingras, C. Davies: Application of Rough Genetic Algorithm. Computational Intelligence, Vol. 17, No. 3, (2001) 435-445
9. Liu SH, Hu F, Jia BY, Shi ZZ: A Rough Set-Based Hierarchical Clustering Algorithm. Vol. 41, No. 4, (2004) 553-556
10. P. Lingras, C. West: Interval Set Clustering of Web Users with Rough k-means. Technical Report No. 2002-002, Department of Mathematics and Computer Science, St. Mary's University, Halifax, Canada (2002)
11. An QS, Shen JY: The Study of Clustering Algorithm Based on Information Granular and Rough Set. Pattern Recognition & Artificial Intelligence, Vol. 16, No. 4, (2003) 412-416
12. Sun HQ, Xiong Z: Fuzzy Cluster Based on Rough Set and Result Evaluating. Journal of Fudan University (Nature Science), Vol. 43, No. 5, (2004) 819-822
13. Liu PY, Wu MD: Fuzzy Theory and its Application. National Defense University Press, Changsha (1998)
14. C.L. Blake, C.J. Merz: UCI Repository of Machine Learning Databases, http://www.ics.uci.edu/~mlearn/ MLRepository.html, (1998)

Effective Use of Place Information for Event Tracking[†]

Yun Jin[1], Sung Hyon Myaeng[2,*], Mann-Ho Lee[1], Hyo-Jung Oh[3],
and Myung-Gil Jang[3]

[1] Chungnam National University, Korea
{wkim, mhlee}@cnu.ac.kr
[2] Information and Communications University, Korea
myaeng@icu.ac.kr
[3] ETRI, Korea
{ohj, mgjang}@etri.re.kr

Abstract. The main purpose of topic detection and tracking (TDT) is to detect, group, and organize newspaper articles reporting on the same event. Since an event is a reported occurrence at a specific time and place, and the unavoidable consequences, it is conceivable that place information in a news article plays an important role in TDT. We analyzed news articles for their characteristics of place information and devised a new topic tracking method incorporating the analysis results. Experiments show that appropriate use of place information indeed helps identifying news articles reporting on the same events.

1 Introduction

It is a time consuming and laborious task for individuals to detect a new event and track news articles reporting on the particular event from a variety of resources [3, 11]. Topic detection and tracking (TDT) [1] attempts to automate the process and provide a topic that consists of a seminal event or activity, along with all directly related events or activities. Here an event is a reported occurrence at a specific time and place and the unavoidable consequences, whereas an activity is a connected set of actions that have a common focus or purpose [14]. Unlike traditional information retrieval or filtering, TDT focuses not just on topicality but on events or activities which often occur at a specific time and specific place [2, 11].

Time information has been used in TDT. Based on the observation that articles reporting on a particular event tend to appear within a time window of two weeks, for example, publication dates of new articles were used in topicality-based document clustering [9]. More recent approaches attempted to automatically extract time information embedded in news article text and use it in determining whether the event described in an article refers to the event being tracked [7,10].

While place information seems to be as important as time in identifying an event, it has neither been used nor tested extensively for TDT. Possible reasons are:

- Some time information such as publication dates is easily available from news articles, but place information needs to be extracted from news article text.

[†] This research was partially supported by ETRI QA project.
[*] Corresponding author.

G.G. Lee et al. (Eds.): AIRS 2005, LNCS 3689, pp. 410–422, 2005.
© Springer-Verlag Berlin Heidelberg 2005

- Time information is one-dimensional and thus relatively easy to represent and compare, but place information is at least two-dimensional and more complex to determine its relationship with others. If place information is represented in a hierarchical way, for example, we should consider not only a parent-child relationship (e.g. Korea-Seoul) but also a sibling relationship (Seoul-Incheon).
- Although time information extraction needs to deal with ambiguity to some extent, place names seem to be more difficult to detect because of the variety of expressions and ambiguities (e.g. Washington can be a person name or a state name.)

Despite the relative difficulty of extracting and normalizing place information, advances in related techniques such as named entity recognition make our research amenable. Since our current work focuses on the use of place information for TDT, not on the techniques for extracting place information, we use exiting techniques and resources for place name recognition. For instance, we made use of some portal sites [15,16] that provide services related to place name information, such as hierarchical information and/or location on a map for a given place name. This service is useful for determining the semantic relationship between two place names.

Assuming that place information can be extracted from news article text, we concentrate on the way we use the information for topic tracking in this paper. For effective use of place information, it is important to understand the characteristics observable in an event description. For instance, the place name as well as the time information tends to appear in the first sentence of a news article describing an event. By giving different weights for place names occurring in different parts of a new article, for example, we can increase the chance to associate a place name with an event. In this paper, we describe four different characteristics of place names, incorporate them in the proposed event tracking method, and evaluate their roles in a series of event tracking experiments.

In sum, the contributions made in the research are as follows:

- We analyzed news articles to find important characteristics of how place information is used.
- We developed a novel event tracking method using place information extracted automatically, which incorporates the characteristics explicitly.
- We demonstrated the value of place information in event tracking as predicted by observed characteristics.

2   Related Work

While it is not straightforward to use place information for TDT, research on place name recognition and extraction has been around for many years, especially with the need to fill a pre-defined template by extracting information from text and to answer questions involving place information. For example, research on distinguishing place and organization names as part of named entity recognition was reported in MUC(Message Understanding Conference)-6 [13]. With the goal of better utilizing place information, a work on classifying such place information into categories like "city", "country", "region", and "water" was reported [4,5,8]. Categorization of place names helps determining whether two names refer to the same location. For instance, tagging a place name "Geneva, New York" with [location] and [location], respectively, is less useful than tagging them with [city] and [state], since the latter can tell the relationship between "Geneva, New York" and "New York" with the aid of a place entity hierarchy. In other words, for example, "the accident in the state of New York" and "the accident in Geneva" may be considered the same event with a detailed place name tagging.

A few papers address the issue of using place information to improve effectiveness of TDT. Smith [12] used place information for tracking similar historical events in unstructured history documents, not news paper articles. Documents containing the same dates and places, which were identified by named entity recognition, were considered as describing the same historical event. Juha et al. [6] extracted person names, places, temporal expressions, and general terms to form four vectors, each representing one of the four types. The similarity between two documents was computed based on four vectors that were treated with the equal weights in computing similarities and clustering documents. For place information, all the place names were used as elements of the vector.

3 Characteristics of Place Information in News Paper

We investigated on some characteristics of place information in news paper articles reporting on events and activities, by analyzing Chosunilbo news articles in 2002. The purpose of this analysis was to improve on the straightforward way of treating place names as terms in event tracking. In other words, we felt that the unique characteristics of occurrences of place names in news articles should be taken into consideration when we develop a method for event tracking.

3.1 Concentration on a Short Time Window

News articles on a particular event begin to appear from the day it occurs and continue for a while, mostly within two weeks. As a result, a place name for an event also tends to be concentrated within the time window. While this tendency has been utilized in TDT when time information is used [2, 3, 6], we observe that place names tend to share the same pattern.

Fig. 1 shows the distribution of news articles related to twenty distinct events. It appears that a bunch of articles are published during the first five days. By the end of two weeks, the number of related articles becomes almost zero. Of course, the number of articles varies depending on the importance of the event.

This tendency can be reflected in the way we treat place names in news articles. Each occurrence of a place name can potentially serve as a piece of evidence for the event being tracked, if it is identical to the place name of the target event. As time goes by, however, the place name may refer to a different event that occurred in the same place at a different time.

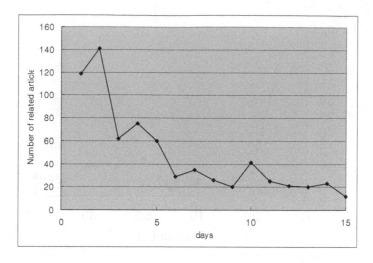

Fig. 1. Distribution of articles related to an event along the time line

3.2 Decreasing Levels of Detail

We observed that descriptions of place names tend to be maximally precise at the time of the event and become simpler often at a higher level of abstraction. For example, "fire on A Street, Albany, New York" is referred to as "fire on D street" (a simpler form) or "fire in Albany" (a simper form at a higher level of abstraction) at a later time.

Based on our analysis of news articles, we found that only 69% of the articles contain complete descriptions of place names; 23% use partial or simpler descriptions and 8% have no place name.

In order to take advantage of this tendency, we should be able to form an equivalence class of place names for a particular event. For example, "fire in Albany" can be an exact match with an event description like "fire on D Street, Albany, New York" if the place name hierarchy verifies that Albany is a city in the state of New York. However, a description like "fire on Elm Street, Albany" should be interpreted as referring to a different event because the street names conflict each other in the same city.

3.3 Locations of Place Names

It was observed that a majority of place names for the main event occur at the beginning of news articles. This tendency is similar to the fact that the first sentence of an article contains the key information and serves as a summary sentence in automatic summarization. It is natural that place information is included in the key sentences because it is a key element in describing the main thrust of the event being reported. Place names occur in later sentences, too, but they usually refer to other related events rather than the main event being described in the article.

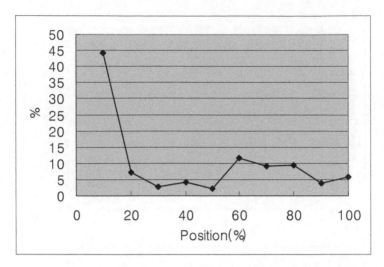

Fig. 2. Distribution of place names in different locations

Fig. 2 depicts the tendency described above. As shown in the graph, the majority of place names occur at the beginning of articles. This tendency becomes useful information when we develop an algorithm for handling multiple occurrences of place names in a single article. That is, the place names appearing at the beginning part of an article would be more likely to be related to the main event of the article.

3.4   The Number of Place Names in an Article

The number of place name occurrences in an article is an indication of whether the article describes an event; the more occurrence of place names in an article, the less chance it describes an event. That is, an event article tends to have only a small number of place names because it would mention a place name for the event without making references to other places.

4   Topic Tracking Using Place Names

This Section describes the core part of the proposed approach to event tracking. We first describe how place names were identified, extracted, and canonicalized, and then explain how place name-based similarity was computed between a target class and a news article. Finally we show how the total score was computed between a class and a news article.

4.1   Place Name Extraction from News Paper Text

Place names are not always extractable unambiguously because a word or phrase can be a place name, organization name, or a person name depending on the contexts. For example, "Washington" can refer to a person, a state, or a city. Since there is no concept of capital letters in Korean, it is not easy to distinguish proper nouns from general nouns. Moreover, some place names are identical to verb stems, making it even more difficult to recognize them. For example, 부여 (Booyuh), a city name, can be the stem of a verb, 부여하다 (Booyuh-Hada) although their meanings are not related at all.

We used the named entity recognizer (NER) [8] borrowed from ETRI to automatically extract place names from Korean news papers. This NER is a hybrid system combining both pattern rules and statistical techniques, with the following 13 place name tags: COUNTRY, PROVINCE, CITY, CAPITALCITY, COUNTY, CONTINENT, MOUNTAIN, OCEAN, RIVER, ISLAND, TOPOGRAPHY, CANYON, and BAY. The NER tagger accepts a news article and tags each place name with one of the 13 place names. The performance of the NER tagger was known to be 81.8 % in F measure.

4.2 Canonicalization and Place Hierarchy

Once place names have been recognized and tagged with the labels, at least two problems need to be handled before they are used for event tracking. Since the actual descriptions of a place name in news articles may change as time goes by, the extracted place names must be examined for their hierarchical relationships. In an article, for example, 개복동(Gabokdong) is used as the name of the specific area for an accident, but 군산시(Goonsan city), the name of the city that covers the specific place, may be used in a later article referring to the same accident. In this case, the hierarchical relationship between the two place names must be established so that they are treated as referring to the same region as far as the accident is concerned.

The second issue is related with abbreviated form of place names, which are used when a place name is mentioned multiple times or referred to in a later article for a known event. For example, a province name 전북(Chonbuk) is a short form for 전라북도(Cholabukdo), and their identity must be established by consulting a dictionary. We call this process as canonicalization.

As a way to handle these issues, we utilized resources available on the Web. Some Web sites [15,16] in Korea provide an information service for various regions and locations in Korea. They accept a place name as a query and return its canonicalized form (full name) and its super-region and sub-regions, together with other information about the place such as restaurants, motels, banks, etc. Fig. 3 shows the overall process where a place name extracted by the named entity recognizer is used as the query to the Web site [15] that provides regional information. The result is the canonical form of the place name and hierarchically related place names.

4.3 Similarity Calculation Using Place Names

Given canonicalized place names and hierarchically related names, the next step is to incorporate the place information into the event tracking process per se. A news article is compared with representations of various events and classified into the best matching category [7]. Consequently, similarity calculation between two articles is the key process for event tracking. In this sub-section, we describe four similarity measures that take into account the four characteristics of place names in news articles mentioned in Section 3.

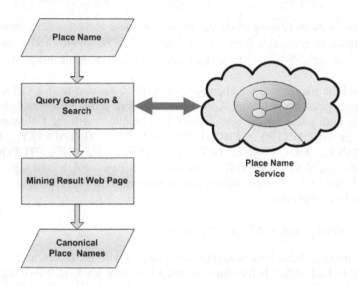

Fig. 3. Canocialization and determination of hierarchical relations

Similarity Based on a Place Name Hierarchy

Given a hierarchy of place names, news articles may use names at different levels of abstraction. Assuming that the target event description has the fullest and most specific expression for the place where the event occurred, we attempt to compute the degree to which a place name appearing in a news article matches the target place name. The computation specified below can be seen as measuring semantic distance between two nodes in a concept hierarchy although our hierarchy consists of place names only. Similarity between n_t, the target event place name, and n_d, a place name in a news article, is defined to be:

$$Sim_h(n_t, n_d) = \frac{|n_t \cap n_d|}{|n_t|} \qquad \textit{if there is no conflict}$$
$$= 0 \qquad \textit{otherwise} \qquad (1)$$

where |.| is the size of a place name, i.e. the number of name units. For example, if the target event place name is "D Street in Albany, New York," the similarity between this and the place name in a new article "Albany" becomes 1/3. While "Albany, New York" and "Albany" would be the same node in a place name hierarchy if the latter actually refers to the city in New York, the former has a higher similarity value of 2/3 according to the formula. We believe this reflects that "Albany" without the specific state name carries some uncertainty, resulting in a smaller similarity value. It should be noted that similarity becomes zero if the most specific description units of the target event and the place name in the article do not match. For example, "D Street in Albany, New York" does not match with "Elm Street, Albany, New York," resulting in a conflict.

Using the Position of Place Names

Based on the observation in Section 3, we consider the location of place names in news articles. This information is likely to determine whether the place name is actually associated with the main event being described in the article. We compute the degree of certainty that a place name refers to the main event in an article as follows:

$$Loc(n_d) = 1 - \frac{Pos(n_d)}{|d|} \qquad (2)$$

where d is the news article where the place name appears and $Pos(n_d)$ is the position of the sentence containing the place name, which starts from 0. If a place name appears in the first sentence, for example, $Pos(n_d)$ is 0 and $Loc(n_d)$ becomes the maximum value being 1.

Calculating Coherence of Place Names

Based on the observations mentioned in Section 3, we discriminate against a news article containing many place names that seem to suggest that it does not describe a specific event. We compute the degree of coherence of a place name with respect to an event as follows:

$$Coh(n_d) = \omega + \frac{\sum n_d}{\sum N_d} \qquad (3)$$

where $\sum n_d$ is the count of the place name being considered and $\sum N_d$ is the count of the all place names in the article. ω is a constant determined by experiments. For the work reported in this article, we used 0.5.

4.4 Combining Three Features

Given an event description and an article, evidence gathered from the hierarchical information, position feature, and coherence feature need to be combined to affect the final similarity value. Since the place name similarity with hierarchical information is the most crucial for matching, we use it as the basis and try to adjust it by considering the two feature values. Following is the heuristics we used:

If $Sim_h(n_t, n_d) = 1.0$ and
$Loc(n_d) < 0.5$ and $Coh(n_d) < 0.55$, Sim_{final} is reduced to 0.8.
If $0.5 < Sim_h(n_t, n_d) < 0.8$ and
$Loc(n_d)$, $Coh(n_d) > 0.7$, Sim_{final} is increased to 0.8.
Otherwise, $Sim_{final} = Sim_h(n_t, n_d)$.

The first case was based on our observation that even thought the matching between two place names is perfect, there is a chance that the one in a news article may not be the place for the event if the location and coherence feature values are very low. In such a case, the overall similarity value for place names should be lowered. The second case was developed to boost the final similarity based on place names when the location and coherence feature values are high enough.

4.5 Final Similarity

The final similarity value for a given event category and a news article can be obtained by combining the content similarity ($Sim_{content}$) and place-based similarity values as follows:

$$Sim_{total}(t,d) = \alpha \times Sim_{content}(t,d) + \beta \times Sim_{place}(t,d)$$

where $\alpha = 0.6$ and $\beta = 0.4$.

$Sim_{content}$ was computed using the Cosine similarity measure in the vector space model. The news articles were processed with the standard indexing method including stemming, removal of stop words, and TF-IDF to compute the weights of terms.

5 Experimental Evaluation

In order to test our initial hypothesis that place information would help improving the event tracking task and also to verify our schemes for using place information, we conducted a set of experiments using 110,000 news articles published in 2002 by Chosunilbo, which has the largest number of subscribers in Korea.

Among the seventy topics, we selected twenty that include place names and use them as events for which event tracking would be done. For each event, relevant articles were pre-selected by people and used for evaluation of system-generated output. The total number of "answer" articles is 990 for the twenty events. Relevance judgments for each documents were made by two people after reading the articles. Table 1 shows a sample of event topics and the number of "answer" documents.

Table 1. Event Topics

ID	Event Title	Articles
1	Fire in the amusement quarter of Gunsan-si	25
2	Protest against Kim Dong-Sung's disqualification at the Winter Olympics Game	81
...	...	...
20	Death of Sohn Kee-Chung – a marathon hero	18
Total		990

5.1 Evaluation of Place Name Features

Before we finalize our event tracking system with place information, we tested the efficacy of individual features of the place names as reflected in the formulas (1) through (3) in Section 4. This set of experiments would help us finalize our method of combining pieces of evidence coming from different aspects of place information and test our initial hypotheses based on the characteristics of place names in news articles.

We came up with four different cases beyond the baseline that is just based on content similarity. The first three are for the three different formulas and the fourth one is for a combination of the three. In addition, we implemented the method used in [6] to validate our approaches. Following are all the cases compared:

- Baseline: event tracking based on topical content only
- Case A: Baseline + use of hierarchical information of place names
- Case B: Baseline + position of place names
- Case C: Baseline + coherence of place names
- Case D: A + B + C
- Case E: the method in [6]

Table 2. Different Aspects of Place Information

Approaches		Precision	Recall	F-measure[1]
Baseline		68.77%	66.13%	67.42%
Location Feature base	Case A	73.0%	68.34%	70.59% (+4.70%)
	Case B	71.26%	67.16%	69.14% (+2.5%)
	Case C	70.57%	67.08%	68.77% (+2.0%)
	Case D	74.56%	70.22%	72.33% (+7.27%)
	Case E	72.16%	67.20%	69.59% (+3.21%)

As shown in Table 2, the results are promising in that each feature appears to make some contribution and the combination of the three features gave a 7.27% of improvement. Given that it is more difficult to extract place information, unlike time information that is immediately available with publication dates, the results seem to show some potential. Even the relatively low performance increases in Cases C and D attest to their values when combined with others. It should be noted that the previous approach in [6] gives performance increase almost identical to that of individual features as in the last row of the table. A conclusion we can draw from the experiments is that it is worthwhile using various features of place names based on their characteristics and take them into consideration when place information is used in combination with the content of articles.

5.2 Evaluation with Place and Time Information

We ran experiments to investigate on the complementary aspects of both place and time information. Since time information that has been used for TDT is publication dates and time information automatically extracted from text as in [7], we investigated three different cases:

---

[1] $F(r, p) = \dfrac{2\,rp}{r + p}.$

Case 1: Use of both place and time information (extracted from text)
Case 2: Use of publication dates (time information only)
Case 3: Use of both place information and publication dates
Case 4: Use of both extracted time and publication dates (time information only)
Case 5: Use all the three kinds of information

As in Table 3, the result shows that when combined with place information, publication dates were slightly more useful than the time information extracted from the news paper text. Comparing Case2 and Case 3, adding place information improved effectiveness by about 2 percent, whereas the improvement from Case 4 to Case 5 shows a slightly less improvement. We feel that the amounts of improvement over the use of time information is not as great as expected, perhaps due to the inaccuracies of place name recognition. Nonetheless, by using all the three types of information as in Case 5, we obtained the best performance. This implies that although the improvements we get from individual sources may be small, their combination can make a significant improvement.

Table 3. Evaluation Result with Location and Time

Approaches	Precision	Recall	F-measure
Baseline	68.77	66.13	67.42%
+ Extracted Time + Place	75.18%	69.54%	72.25% (+7.2%)
+ Pub. Date	76.18	69.54	72.71% (+7.8%)
+ Pub. Dates + Place	77.91%	70.66%	74.11% (+9.9%)
+ Extracted Time + Pub. Dates	79.17	72.59	75.74% (+12.3%)
+ Extracted Time + Pub. Dates + Place	80.59%	73.19%	76.71% (+13.8%)

5.3 Success and Failure Analyses

As an effort to understand individual contributions to and/or failures of the place name features in performance increases, we analyzed their roles in some events. Biggest improvements were possible when the place information in the target events was clearly described, particularly with hierarchical information. For instance, the improvement was more than 30% with the event containing "경상남도 김해시 지내동 동원아파트 뒤편 돗대산", which includes the province name, city name, town name, apartment name, and the name of the mountain behind the apartment, as the place name.

However, the event tracking task for some events was negatively influenced by our method as in Table 4.

Further analysis of the results revealed some issues to be addressed in the future. The first two below are the problems caused by place name ambiguities, and the third one is caused by the difficulty of even extracting place information..

Table 4. Events for successes and failures

	Success			Failure		
	T5	T3	T1	T2	T10	T15
Without Place Info.	56.71%	77.29%	87.63%	39.1%	67.7%	79.4%
With Place Info.	74.27%	91.6%	97.31%	31.4%	55.7%	77.7%
Improvement	30.96%	18.51%	11.05%	-24.5%	-21.5%	-2.1%

- Similar events occurred in the same place

When two distinct events occurred in the same place, two articles describing them respectively should be separated and fallen into two different event categories. However, the existence of the place name in both articles would make them look more similar, increasing the possibility that they are classified into the same event category. Place information also makes two separate specific incidents look similar if they are sub-events of a large event like Olympic Games, because the place where the games took place are the same. As a result, a variety of news articles on Olympic Games would be incorrectly classified into a very specific event when the place names are given too big a weight.

- The place name not specified or fixed

Although two articles mention the same event, the place name found in the text may be too generic like "북한군 서해 도발 사건" (North Korean Navy's attack in the *West Sea*). The place name *West Sea* is too general, and at the same time, the region could be referred to in other articles with different names like NIT or Northern Boundary.

- Not easy to extract a place name

When the place name is part of the event name, it is difficult to extract it, because the place name is concatenated with other words without any spacing. Unless such a complex noun is decomposed into simple nouns, the current named entity recognizer will never find the place name. For instance, the word "칸" (Cannes) in the event title "칸영화제 수상" (awards in Cannes Film Festival) is the place where the film festival was held, but since the first four syllables are considered a single word, it is not possible to extract the place name unless noun segmentation is done first.

6   Conclusion

We addressed the issues related to using place names that appear in news paper articles in the context of event tracking, a task in TDT. Instead of extracting all place names from news articles and treat them as elements of vectors, we attempted to use a kind of concept hierarchy specialized in place names for partial matching and characteristics of place name occurrences such their relative locations and coherence in a news article. In other words, the proposed method for using place information for event tracking was based on our initial investigation on their occurrence characteristics we also reported in this paper.

We ran experiments to evaluate the amount of contributions made by the individual features of place names and to test whether using place information in addition to the topical content and time information used in previous research for topic tracking. We also compared our approach against a recent work that used place information and concluded that more careful use of place names indeed improve effectiveness of event tracking. After failure analysis, we also identified problem areas that should be addressed in the future.

With the proposed method proven to be promising, we plan to apply the same method to English collections. Since place name recognition is likely to be easier and more accurate in English than in Korean, with the use of capital letters for proper nouns, we expect to see more dramatic improvements. We also intend to find a more principled way to apply various insights and heuristics in incorporating feature values and computing similarities.

References

1. Allan, J. et al. Topic Detection and Tracking pilot Study Final Report. In Proceedings of the DARPA Broadcast News Transcription and Understanding workshop. (1998)
2. Allan, J. (ed.): Topic Detection and Tracking: Event based Information Organization. Kluwer Academic Publishers, (2000)
3. Allan, J.: Introduction to Topic Detection and Tracking. In Topic Detection and Tracking: Event-based Information Organization, Kluwer Academic Publishers, (2002) 1-16
4. Chinchor, N.: MUC-7 Information Extraction Task Definition, Version 5.1, In Proceedings of the 7th Message Understanding Conference(MUC-7), (1998)
5. Chung, E.S., Lim, S.J., Hwang, Y.G., Jang, M.G.: Hybrid Named Entity Recognition for Question-Answering System. INTERSPEECH2004 ICSLP, (2004)
6. Juha M., Helena A.M., Marko M.K.: Simple Semantic in Topic Detection and Tracking. Information Retrieval, 7, 347-368, Kluwer Academic Publishers. (2004)
7. Kim, P., Myaeng, S.H.: Usefulness of Temporal Information Automatically Extracted from News Articles for Topic Tracking. The Journal of ACM Translations on Asian Language Information Processing(TALIP), Vol3, Issue 4. (2004).
8. Lee, S.W., Lee, G.B.: A bootstrapping Approach for Geographic Named Entity Annotation. Asia Information Retrieval Symposium, (AIRS2004). (2004)
9. Mani, I., Schiffman, B., and Zhang, J.: Inferring temporal ordering of events in news. Short paper. In Proceedings of the Human Language Technology Conference (HLT-NAACL'03) (2003)
10. Mani, I., and Wilson, G.: Robust temporal processing of news. In Proceedings of the 38th Annual Meeting of the Association for Computational Linguistics(ACL'2000). (2000) 67-76.
11. Nallapati, R., Feng, A., Peng, F., Allan, J.: Event threading within news topics. In Proceedings of the Thirteenth ACM Conference on Information and Knowledge Management (CIKM), 2004.
12. Smith, D.A.: Detecting Events with Date and Place Information in Unstructured Text. JCDL'02. Portland, Oregon, USA (2002)
13. Sundheim, B., Chinchor, N.: Named Entity Task Definition, Version 2.0. In Proceedings of the 6th Message Understanding Conference (MUC-6). (1995)
14. Yang, Y., Pierce T., and Carbonell, J.: A Study on Retrospective and On-Line Event Detection. In Proceedings of ACM SIGIR Conference on Research and development in information retrieval. (1998) 28-36
15. http://local.naver.com/
16. http://cube.paran.com/

A Classifier Design Based on Combining Multiple Components by Maximum Entropy Principle

Akinori Fujino, Naonori Ueda, and Kazumi Saito

NTT Communication Science Laboratories, NTT Corporation,
2-4, Hikaridai, Seika-cho, Soraku-gun, Kyoto, Japan 619-0237
{a.fujino, ueda, saito}@cslab.kecl.ntt.co.jp

Abstract. Designing high performance classifiers for structured data consisting of multiple components is an important and challenging research issue in the field of machine learning. Although the main component of structured data plays an important role when designing classifiers, additional components may contain beneficial information for classification. This paper focuses on a probabilistic classifier design for multiclass classification based on the combination of main and additional components. Our formulation separately considers component generative models and constructs the classifier by combining these trained models based on the maximum entropy principle. We use naive Bayes models as the component generative models for text and link components so that we can apply our classifier design to document and web page classification problems. Our experimental results for three test collections confirmed that the proposed method effectively combined the main and additional components to improve classification performance.

1 Introduction

Structured documents such as web pages or multimodal data usually consist of main and additional information. Namely, they have multiple components. Additional information includes citations in books and papers, hyperlinks and images on web pages, and text descriptions added to images and music. Although the main information plays an important role when designing a classifier, additional data may contain substantial information for classification. Recently, classifiers have been developed for dealing with multiple components such as text and hyperlinks on web pages [4,6,16,10], text and citations in papers [6,10], and text and music [2].

In this paper, we focus on probabilistic approaches to classifier design for dealing with arbitrary multiple components, rather than for special relations between components such as a pair consisting of Web text and its hyperlinks as studied in [4]. Here we categorize probabilistic approaches into generative, discriminative, and a hybrid of the two.

Generative classifiers learn the joint probability model, $P(\boldsymbol{x}, y)$, of input $\boldsymbol{x}$ and class label y, compute $P(y|\boldsymbol{x})$ by using the Bayes rule, and then take the most

G.G. Lee et al. (Eds.): AIRS 2005, LNCS 3689, pp. 423–438, 2005.

probable label y. However, such direct modeling is hard for arbitrary components consisting of completely different types of media. In [2], under the assumption of the class conditional independence of all components, the class conditional probability $P(\boldsymbol{x}_j|y)$ for each component is modeled separately, where $\boldsymbol{x}_j$ stands for the feature vector corresponding to the jth component. Hence, as described later, the joint probability is expressed by the simple product of $P(\boldsymbol{x}_j|y)$.

Discriminative classifiers directly model posterior probability $P(y|\boldsymbol{x})$ and learn mapping from $\boldsymbol{x}$ to y. Multinomial logistic regression [8] can be used for this purpose. However, we believe that any approach that ignores structural information has an intrinsic limitation in terms of achieving good classification performance. In [10], the class posterior probability $P(y|\boldsymbol{x}_j)$ for each component is modeled separately, and then the simple product of $P(y|\boldsymbol{x}_j)$ is used for predicting the class that $\boldsymbol{x}$ belongs to.

For real classification tasks, however, the simple product approaches described above might not always be sufficiently effective for designing high performance classifiers because the component models for noisy additional information may degrade the classification performance. The main and additional information differ in importance as regards classification. We consider the hybrid approach described below to be promising with a view to effectively combining such component classifiers.

Hybrid classifiers learn a separate class conditional probability model for each component, $P(\boldsymbol{x}_j|y)$, and directly model class posterior probability $P(y|\boldsymbol{x})$ by using trained component models. Namely, each component model is estimated on the basis of the generative approach, while the classifier is constructed on the basis of the discriminative approach. For *binary* classification problems, such a hybrid classifier has already been proposed and applied to the document classification of two components ("subject" and "body") [13]. It has been shown experimentally that the hybrid classifier achieves higher accuracy than either a pure generative or a pure discriminative classifier.

We present a new hybrid classifier formulation for *multiclass* classification. More specifically, we separately design component generative models $P(\boldsymbol{x}_j|y)$ for main and additional information, and estimate the models individually. Then, based on the *maximum entropy* (ME) principle [3], we design the class posterior probability $P(y|\boldsymbol{x})$ by using the estimated generative models. Unlike standard ME approaches to classification that deal directly with input vectors $\boldsymbol{x}$ [11], with our ME approach, the formulation deals with generative component models.

It might be thought that the binary hybrid classifiers proposed by [13] can be applied to multiclass classification problems by using the well-known one-against-all (OAA) or all-pairs (AP) schemes (cf. [1,14]). However, we consider there are problems in the application of the OAA and AP schemes to the binary hybrid classifiers. The OAA scheme designs a binary classifier for a single class against the other classes. Here, we need to assume a single generative model for samples belonging to the other classes by ignoring the individual characteristics of each class. However, this assumption is unlikely to make full use of the advantage of the generative model. The AP scheme designs an individual binary hybrid classifier for each pair of classes. Here, each classifier can only classify samples into one of a pair of classes. For multiclass classification, in some way, we need to combine the results obtained from these classifiers. However, the combination of the binary hybrid classifiers might not provide the accurate discriminative boundary needed to classify samples into the most probabilistically appropriate class.

On the other hand, with our formulation, we design an individual generative model for each class and construct a single hybrid classifier, which provides discriminative boundaries between all classes. Therefore, our hybrid approach to multiclass classification avoids the problems of the OAA and AP schemes.

We apply the proposed method to document and web page classification. Documents consist of text components. Web pages consist of text and link components. We use naive Bayes models as generative models for both text and link components. Using three test collections, we show experimentally that our hybrid classifier design method is more effective than the conventional approaches for multiclass classification problems.

2   Conventional Approaches

In multiclass (K classes) classification problems, a classifier categorizes a feature vector x into one of K classes $y \in \{1, \ldots, k, \ldots, K\}$. Each feature vector consists of J separate components as $x = \{x_1, \ldots, x_j, \ldots, x_J\}$. The classifier is trained on training sample set $D = \{x_n, y_n\}_{n=1}^{N}$. In the following, we derive basic formulas for the conventional approaches.

2.1   Generative Approach

Generative classifiers model a joint probability $P(x, y)$. However, as mentioned above, such direct modeling is hard for arbitrary components that consist of completely different types of media. Under the assumption of the class conditional independence of all components, the joint probability can be expressed as

$$P(x, y|\Theta) = P(y) \prod_{j=1}^{J} P(x_j|y, \Theta_j), \qquad (1)$$

where Θ_j is a model parameter for the jth component, and $\Theta = \{\Theta_j\}_{j=1}^{J}$. Note that the component generative model $P(x_j|k, \Theta_j)$ should be selected according to the features of the component: for example, a multinomial model for text information or a Gaussian model for continuous feature vectors.

Model parameter set Θ is computed by maximizing the posterior $P(\Theta|D)$ (MAP estimation). According to the Bayes rule, $P(\Theta|D) \propto P(D|\Theta)P(\Theta)$, the objective function of MAP estimation is given by

$$J(\Theta) = \sum_{n=1}^{N} \left\{ \log P(y_n) + \sum_{j=1}^{J} \log P(x_{nj}|y_n, \Theta_j) \right\} + \sum_{j=1}^{J} \log P(\Theta_j). \qquad (2)$$

Here, $P(\Theta_j)$ is a prior over parameter Θ_j. Clearly, component model parameter Θ_j can be optimized without considering the other parameters.

According to the Bayes rule, the class posterior probability $P(k|\boldsymbol{x}, \Theta)$ can be derived as

$$P(k|\boldsymbol{x}, \Theta) = \frac{P(k) \prod_{j=1}^{J} P(\boldsymbol{x}_j|k, \Theta_j)}{\sum_{k'=1}^{K} P(k') \prod_{j=1}^{J} P(\boldsymbol{x}_j|k', \Theta_j)}. \tag{3}$$

The class of $\boldsymbol{x}$ is determined as the k that maximizes $P(k|\boldsymbol{x}, \Theta)$. Note that since the denominator of Eq. (3) is same for all k, it can almost be predicted from the simple product of $P(\boldsymbol{x}_j|k, \Theta_j)$.

2.2 Discriminative Approach

Discriminative classifiers directly model posterior class probabilities $P(y|\boldsymbol{x})$ for all classes. With multinomial logistic regression [8], the posterior class probabilities are modeled as

$$P(k|\boldsymbol{x}, W) = \frac{\exp(\boldsymbol{w}_k \cdot \boldsymbol{x})}{\sum_{k'=1}^{K} \exp(\boldsymbol{w}_{k'} \cdot \boldsymbol{x})}, \ \forall k, \tag{4}$$

where $W = \{\boldsymbol{w}_1, \ldots, \boldsymbol{w}_K\}$ is a set of unknown model parameters. $\boldsymbol{w}_k \cdot \boldsymbol{x}$ represents the inner product of $\boldsymbol{w}_k$ and $\boldsymbol{x}$. W is estimated to maximize the following penalized conditional log-likelihood:

$$J(W) = \sum_{n=1}^{N} \log P(y_n|\boldsymbol{x}_n, W) + \log P(W). \tag{5}$$

Here $P(W)$ is a prior over parameter W.

In [10], the multinomial logistic regression model $P(k|\boldsymbol{x}_j, W_j)$ is designed separately for each component, and the estimate $\hat{W}_j$ of the model parameter is independently computed. The class of $\boldsymbol{x}$ is determined as the y that maximizes the product of the posterior probabilities estimated in the components as

$$y = \max_k \prod_{j=1}^{J} P(k|\boldsymbol{x}_j, \hat{W}_j), \tag{6}$$

2.3 Hybrid Approach for Binary Classification

Hybrid classifiers learn the class conditional probability model separately for each component, $P(\boldsymbol{x}_j|y)$, and directly model the class posterior probability $P(y|\boldsymbol{x})$ by using the trained component models. In [13], binary classifiers are derived as follows. The class posterior probability in Eq. (3) is equivalently transformed to

$$P(k=1|\boldsymbol{x}, \Theta) = \frac{1}{1 + \exp\left\{\sum_{j=1}^{J} \log \frac{P(\boldsymbol{x}_j|k=2, \Theta_j)}{P(\boldsymbol{x}_j|k=1, \Theta_j)} + \log \frac{P(k=2)}{P(k=1)}\right\}}. \tag{7}$$

Then by introducing the weight parameters b_j for the components and $b_0 = \frac{P(k=2)}{P(k=1)}$, the class posterior probability is extended as follows:

$$R(k = 1|\boldsymbol{x}, \Theta, B) \equiv \frac{1}{1 + \exp\left\{\sum_{j=1}^{J} b_j \log \frac{P(\boldsymbol{x}_j|k=2,\Theta_j)}{P(\boldsymbol{x}_j|k=1,\Theta_j)} + b_0\right\}}. \tag{8}$$

The weight parameter set $B = \{b_j\}_{j=0}^{J}$ is estimated as the parameter of logistic regression, according to the maximum class posterior likelihood as mentioned above.

3 Proposed Method

As mentioned earlier, we present a new hybrid classifier formulation extended for *multiclass* classification. In this section, we provide details of our formulation and our parameter estimation method.

3.1 Component Generative Models

In our formulation, we simply design each component generative model separately without strictly assuming class conditional independence as described in Section 2.1. Let $P(\boldsymbol{x}_j|k, \Theta_j)$ be the jth component generative model, where Θ_j denotes the model parameter. Θ_j is computed using MAP estimation. The Θ_j estimate is computed to maximize the objective function using training sample set D.

3.2 Discriminative Posterior Design

After computing the estimates $\{\hat{\Theta}_j\}_{j=1}^{J}$ of the component generative model parameters, we provide the posterior probability based on the weighted combination of the component generative models to improve the classification performance. More specifically, based on the maximum entropy (ME) principle [3], we design the class posterior probability using component generative models.

The ME principle is a framework for obtaining a probability distribution, which prefers the most uniform models that satisfy any given constraints. Let $R(k|\boldsymbol{x})$ be a target distribution that we wish to specify using the ME principle. A constraint is that the expected value of log-likelihood w.r.t. the target distribution $R(k|\boldsymbol{x})$ is equal to the expected value of log-likelihood w.r.t. the empirical distribution $\tilde{P}(\boldsymbol{x}, k) = \frac{1}{N}\sum_{n=1}^{N} \delta(\boldsymbol{x} - \boldsymbol{x}_n, k - y_n)$ of the training samples as

$$\sum_{\boldsymbol{x},k} \tilde{P}(\boldsymbol{x}, k) \log P(\boldsymbol{x}_j|k, \hat{\Theta}_j) = \sum_{\boldsymbol{x},k} \tilde{P}(\boldsymbol{x}) R(k|\boldsymbol{x}) \log P(\boldsymbol{x}_j|k, \hat{\Theta}_j), \forall j \tag{9}$$

where $\tilde{P}(\boldsymbol{x}) = \frac{1}{N}\sum_{n=1}^{N} \delta(\boldsymbol{x} - \boldsymbol{x}_n)$ is the empirical distribution of $\boldsymbol{x}$. We also restrict $R(k|\boldsymbol{x})$ so that it has the same expected value for the class indicator

---

Given training sets: $D = \{(\boldsymbol{x}_n, y_n)\}_{n=1}^{N}$
1. Compute $\hat{\Theta}$ and $\hat{\Theta}^{(-n)}$, $\forall n$ using Eq. (2).
2. Compute Λ using Eq. (12) under fixed $\hat{\Theta}^{(-n)}$.
3. Output a classifier $R(k|\boldsymbol{x}, \hat{\Theta}, \hat{\Lambda})$.

Fig. 1. Algorithm of learning model parameters

variable $z_{k'}$ as seen in the training data, where $z_{k'} = 1$ if $\boldsymbol{x}$ belongs to the k'-th class, otherwise $z_{k'} = 0$, such that

$$\sum_{\boldsymbol{x},k} \tilde{P}(\boldsymbol{x}, k) z_{k'} = \sum_{\boldsymbol{x},k} \tilde{P}(\boldsymbol{x}) R(k|\boldsymbol{x}) z_{k'}, \forall k'. \tag{10}$$

By maximizing the conditional entropy $H(R) = -\sum_{\boldsymbol{x},k} \tilde{P}(\boldsymbol{x}) R(k|\boldsymbol{x}) \log R(k|\boldsymbol{x})$ under these constraints, we can obtain the target distribution:

$$R(k|\boldsymbol{x}, \hat{\Theta}, \Lambda) = \frac{e^{\mu_k} \prod_{j=1}^{J} P(\boldsymbol{x}_j|k, \hat{\Theta}_j)^{\lambda_j}}{\sum_{k'=1}^{K} e^{\mu_{k'}} \prod_{j=1}^{J} P(\boldsymbol{x}_j|k', \hat{\Theta}_j)^{\lambda_j}}, \tag{11}$$

where $\Lambda = \{\{\lambda_j\}_{j=1}^{J}, \{\mu_k\}_{k=1}^{K}\}$ is a set of Lagrange multipliers. λ_j represents the combination weight of the jth component generative model, and μ_k is the bias parameter for the kth class. The distribution $R(k|\boldsymbol{x}, \hat{\Theta}, \Lambda)$ gives us the formulation of a discriminative classifier that consists of component generative models.

Parameter Λ is estimated by maximizing the conditional likelihood of training sample set D. However, since D is used for estimating Θ and Λ, a biased estimator may be obtained. Thus, when Λ is estimated, a leave-one-out cross-validation of the training samples is used [13]. Let $\hat{\Theta}^{(-n)}$ be a generative model parameter estimated by using all the training samples except $(\boldsymbol{x}_n, y_n)$. The objective function of Λ then becomes

$$J(\Lambda) = \sum_{n=1}^{N} \log R(y_n|\boldsymbol{x}_n, \hat{\Theta}^{(-n)}, \Lambda) + \log R(\Lambda), \tag{12}$$

where $R(\Lambda)$ is a prior over parameter Λ. We used the Gaussian prior [5] as $R(\Lambda) \propto \prod_j \exp(\frac{\lambda_j^2}{\sigma_j^2})$. We can compute the Λ estimate to maximize $J(\Lambda)$ by using the L-BFGS algorithm [9], which is a quasi-Newton method. We summarize the algorithm for estimating these model parameters in Fig. 1.

3.3 Discussion

We can regard the class posterior $R(k|\boldsymbol{x}, \hat{\Theta}, \Lambda)$ derived from the ME principle as a natural extension of the class posterior $P(k|\boldsymbol{x}, \Theta)$ shown in Eq. (3). Actually, if $\lambda_j = 1, \forall j$ and $P(k) = e^{\lambda_k}$, $R(k|\boldsymbol{x}, \hat{\Theta}, \Lambda)$ is reduced to $P(k|\boldsymbol{x}, \Theta)$.

We can also regard $R(k|\boldsymbol{x}, \hat{\Theta}, \Lambda)$ shown in Eq. (11) as a natural extension of $R(k|\boldsymbol{x}, \Theta, B)$ for the binary classifications shown in Eq. (8). If $K = 2$, $b_j = \lambda_j$, and $b_0 = \mu_2 - \mu_1$, $R(k|\boldsymbol{x}, \hat{\Theta}, \Lambda)$ is reduced to $R(k|\boldsymbol{x}, \Theta, B)$.

According to the ME principle, we can obtain the class posterior distribution based on a hybrid of the generative models and multinomial logistic regression as

$$R(k|\boldsymbol{x}, \hat{\Theta}, \Lambda) = \frac{\exp\left\{\sum_{j=1}^{J} \lambda_{jk} \log P(\boldsymbol{x}_j|k, \hat{\Theta}_j) + \mu_k\right\}}{\sum_{k'=1}^{K} \exp\left\{\sum_{j=1}^{J} \lambda_{jk'} \log P(\boldsymbol{x}_j|k', \hat{\Theta}_j) + \mu_{k'}\right\}}, \quad \forall k, \quad (13)$$

by using the constraint:

$$\sum_{\boldsymbol{x}} \tilde{P}(\boldsymbol{x}, k) \log P(\boldsymbol{x}_j|k, \hat{\Theta}_j) = \sum_{\boldsymbol{x}} \tilde{P}(\boldsymbol{x}) R(k|\boldsymbol{x}) \log P(\boldsymbol{x}_j|k, \hat{\Theta}_j), \forall j, \forall k, \quad (14)$$

instead of Eq. (9), following the feature setting in [11]. In the next section, we will omit the experimental results for the classifier obtained by using Eq. (13), because the classifier was overfitted into a small number of training samples in our experiments.

4   Experiments

4.1   Test Collections

Empirical evaluation was performed on three test collections: **20 newsgroups (20news)**, **NIPS**, and **WebKB** data sets. 20news and WebKB have often been used as benchmark tests of classifiers in text classification tasks [11], and NIPS[1] is the ASCII text collection of papers from NIPS conferences created by Yann using optical character recognition.

20news consists of 20 different UseNet discussion groups and contains 18828 articles. Each article belongs to one of the 20 groups. We extracted two components, **main (M)** and **title (T)**, from each article, where T is the text description following "Subject:" and M is the main information in each article except for the title. Each component contains words as features. We removed vocabulary words included either in the stoplist [15] or in only one article. There were 52313 and 5320 vocabulary words, respectively, in components M and T in the data set.

NIPS consists of 1740 papers from NIPS conferences 1-12. We used 1164 papers from NIPS conferences 5-12 in our experiments. Each paper is related to one of nine research topics, for example, neuroscience, theory, and applications. We extracted four components, **main (M)**, **title (T)**, **abstract (A)**, and **references (R)**, from each paper, where M is the main information in each paper excluding the title, abstract, and references. We removed vocabulary words in

---

[1] http://www.cs.toronto.edu/~roweis/data.html

the same way as for 20news. There were 20485, 904, 5021, and 8303 vocabulary words, respectively, in components M, T, A, and R in the data set.

WebKB contains web pages from universities. This data set consists of seven categories, and each page belongs to one of these categories. Following the setup in [11], only four categories **course, faculty, project**, and **student** were used. The categories contained a total of 4199 pages. We extracted six components, **main (M), title (T), in-links (IL), out-links (OL), file-links (FL)**, and **anchor-text (AT)**, from each page. Here, T is the text description between <TITLE> and </TITLE> tags, and M is the main information except for the title, tags, and links. The IL for a page is the set of links from the other pages to the page. AT is the set of anchor text for each page, which consists of text descriptions that express the link to the page found on other web pages. We collected IL and AT from the links within the data set. The OL for a page is the set of links to the other pages, and the FL is the set of links to files such as images. M, T, and AT contain words as features, and IL, OL, and FL contain URLs for web pages. We removed vocabulary words in the same way as for 20news and removed URLs included in only one page for each component. There were 18471, 995, and 496 vocabulary words, respectively, in components M, T, and AT in the data set. Components IL, OL, and FL contained 500, 4131, and 484 different URLs, respectively.

In Table 1, $|D_f|$ for each component shows the number of documents (articles or web pages) whose components are not empty. $|F_t|$ for each component shows the total number of features (words or URLs) contained over all the documents in the data sets. $|D_t|$ is the total number of documents in a data set. As shown in Table 1, $|D_f|/|D_t|$ for component M was close to 100 % in the three data sets. This shows that M is not empty in most of the documents. $|D_f|/|D_t|$ for the other components, especially AT, IL, OL, and FL with respect to hyperlinks on WebKB, were smaller than in component M. This shows that AT (IL/OL/FL) were empty in many documents. The average feature frequency $|F_t|/|D_t|$ in M was much larger than in the other components in all the data sets.

4.2   Experimental Settings

Generative Models for Proposed Method. For text information, we employed naive Bayes (NB) models [12] as component generative models $P(\boldsymbol{x}_j|k, \boldsymbol{\theta}_{jk})$ using an independent word-based representation, known as the Bag-of-Words (BOW) representation. Let $\boldsymbol{x}_j = (x_{j1}, \ldots, x_{ji}, \ldots, x_{jV_j})$ represent the word-frequency vector of the jth component (text information) of a data sample, where x_{ji} denotes the frequency of the ith word in the jth component and V_j denotes the total number of words in the vocabulary included in the jth component in a text data set. In an NB model, text information $\boldsymbol{x}_j$ in the kth class is assumed to be generated from a multinomial distribution

$$P(\boldsymbol{x}_j|k, \boldsymbol{\theta}_{jk}) \propto \prod_{i=1}^{V_j} (\theta_{jki})^{x_{ji}}. \tag{15}$$

Table 1. Number of documents containing features in each component and the total feature frequency for all the documents in each data set

(a) 20news ($|D_t| = 18828$)

	M	T
$|D_f|$	18782	18456
$|D_f|/|D_t|$	99.8 %	98.0 %
$|F_t|$	1960166	59261
$|F_t|/|D_t|$	104.1	3.1

(b) NIPS ($|D_t| = 1164$)

	M	T	A	R
$|D_f|$	1164	1160	1164	1164
$|D_f|/|D_t|$	100 %	99.7 %	100 %	100 %
$|F_t|$	1386484	5903	74385	161992
$|F_t|/|D_t|$	1191.1	5.1	63.9	139.2

(c) WebKB ($|D_t| = 4199$)

	M	T	AT	IL	OL	FL
$|D_f|$	4199	3851	1101	1242	3273	969
$|D_f|/|D_t|$	100 %	91.7 %	26.2 %	29.6 %	77.9 %	23.1 %
$|F_t|$	668192	10403	5882	2547	16535	3165
$|F_t|/|D_t|$	159.1	2.5	1.4	0.6	3.9	0.8

Here, $\theta_{jki} > 0$ and $\sum_{i=1}^{V_j} \theta_{jki} = 1$. θ_{jki} is the probability that the ith word appears in the jth component of a document belonging to the kth class.

We also used NB models as component models for link information. For IL, OL, and components, we used the Bag-of-URLs representation as well as BOW for text information. $\boldsymbol{x}_j$ for the link information represents the URL-frequency vector. x_{ji} for the IL component, for example, represents the frequency of the ith URL linked from the web page $\boldsymbol{x}$.

As the prior $P(\Theta_j)$ in Eq. (2), we used the following Dirichlet prior over Θ_j as $P(\Theta_j) \propto \prod_{k=1}^{K} \prod_{i=1}^{V_j} (\theta_{jki})^{\xi_{jk}-1}$. In the proposed method, we tuned hyper parameters ξ_{jk} by using the leave-one-out cross-validation of labeled samples to maximize the log likelihood of generative probabilities estimated for unseen samples with the help of the EM algorithm [7], because we confirmed the hyperparameter tuning was practically useful for classification. Since it is not an essential part of the method and because of space constraints, we will omit the details of the hyperparameter estimation procedure.

Applying the NB models normalized using $|\boldsymbol{x}_j| = \sum_{i=1}^{V_j} x_{ji}$ to the component generative models in Eq. (5), we obtain the class posterior distribution for the hybrid classifier:

$$R(k|\boldsymbol{x}, \Theta, \Lambda) = \frac{e^{\mu_k} \prod_{j=1}^{J} \left[\prod_{i=1}^{V_j} (\theta_{jki})^{x_{ji}} \right]^{\lambda_j/|\boldsymbol{x}_j|}}{\sum_{k'=1}^{K} e^{\mu_{k'}} \prod_{j=1}^{J} \left[\prod_{i=1}^{V_j} (\theta_{jk'i})^{x_{ji}} \right]^{\lambda_j/|\boldsymbol{x}_j|}}. \tag{16}$$

Comparison Method. The proposed method was compared with classifiers based on either the generative or discriminative approach. First, the proposed classifier was compared with naive Bayes (NB) and multinomial logistic regression (MLR) using only component M, in order to examine the effect of combining additional information on classification performance. Second, we compared the proposed classifier with the four classifiers that used additional information employed in the other methods. One method involves designing classifiers based on the *simple product* of the component models as presented in Section 2. We examined the performance of two *product*-based classifiers that used naive Bayes (PNB) or multinomial logistic regression (PMLR) models as component models. Another method involves designing a single model without considering the separate components. Although the model design might be inappropriate when the features are different from those of the other components, we used a *single* model for evaluating the proposed method. We examined the classification performance of *single* naive Bayes (SNB) and multinomial logistic regression (SMLR) classifiers.

In our experiments, we fixed the values of the hyperparameters in the Dirichlet prior for NB/PNB/SNB and in the Gaussian prior for MLR/PMLR/SMLR that provided high average classification accuracy for the test samples to observe the potential ability of the methods.

Evaluation Measure. We examined the classification accuracy with test samples to evaluate the proposed and conventional methods. In our experiments, we selected the training and test samples randomly from each data set. We made ten different evaluation sets for each data set by random selection. For 20news, 8000 articles were selected as test samples for each evaluation set. For NIPS and WebKB, 500 papers and 2000 web pages were selected as test samples, respectively. After extracting the test samples, training samples were selected from the remaining samples in each data set. The average classification accuracy over the ten evaluation sets was used to evaluate the methods with each of the three data sets.

4.3   Results and Discussion

Effect of Combining Additional Information. The proposed method was compared with NB and MLR classifiers using only component M. With the proposed method, we designed the classifier using all the components for 20news and NIPS. For WebKB, we designed two classifiers, one using two text components, M and T, the other using all the components of the text and link information. We examined the classification accuracy by changing the number of training samples. Figure 2 shows the average classification accuracies over the ten different evaluation sets for (a) 20news, (b) NIPS, and (c) WebKB.

With 20news and NIPS, the proposed method performed better than NB and MLR using only component M. That is, we confirmed that combining the additional information improved the classification performance.

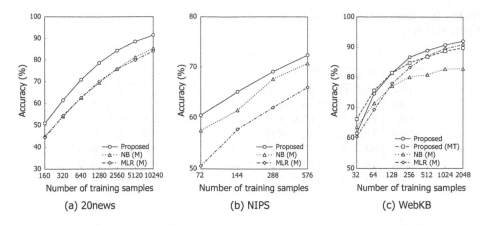

Fig. 2. Classification accuracies (%) with the proposed method, NB, and MLR

With WebKB, the classifier using all the components outperformed NB and MLR except when there were 32 training samples. The classifier using components M and T performed better than the classifier using all the components when the number of training samples was small. In Table 1, $|D_f|/|D_t|$ for AT, IL, OL, and FL is small. This indicates that there are few training samples whose components (AT/IL/OL/FL) are not empty. A classifier that uses all the components might be more overfitted into the training samples than a classifier that uses M and T, when the number of training samples is small.

Effect of Combination Weight of Component Models. We compared our proposed classifier with PNB/PMLR and SNB/SMLR classifiers. For this comparison, we designed these classifiers using all the components in the data sets. Table 2 shows the average accuracies over the ten different evaluation sets for (a) 20news, (b) NIPS, and (c) WebKB. Each number in parentheses in the table denotes the standard deviation of the ten evaluation sets. $|D|$ represents the number of training samples.

With 20news and NIPS, the proposed method provided the best performance of the five. We confirmed that the proposed method provided the combination weight of the component generative models thus improving the classification performance.

With WebKB, the proposed method performed better than the pure generative classifiers, PNB and SNB, except when $|D| = 32$. The performance of the proposed method was similar to or better than that of the pure discriminative classifiers, PMLR and SMLR.

The proposed method provided similar or better performance than the pure generative (discriminative) classifiers when the SMLR (SNB) performance was better than that of SNB (SMLR). When the performance of the pure generative and classifier classifiers was similar, the proposed method performed better than the classifiers.

Table 2. Classification accuracies (%) with the proposed method, PNB/PMLR, and SNB/SMLR

(a) 20news

$|D|$	Proposed	PNB	PMLR	SNB	SMLR
160	**50.9** (1.9)	47.3 (1.8)	47.4 (1.4)	47.5 (1.8)	46.3 (1.9)
320	**61.5** (1.4)	56.8 (1.3)	57.2 (1.6)	56.9 (1.3)	56.3 (1.5)
640	**70.9** (0.9)	65.8 (1.2)	66.3 (0.7)	66.0 (1.1)	64.7 (1.1)
1280	**78.6** (0.5)	72.9 (0.9)	74.6 (0.6)	73.3 (0.9)	72.2 (0.9)
2560	**84.3** (0.5)	79.3 (0.6)	80.5 (0.5)	79.8 (0.6)	78.7 (0.6)
5120	**88.5** (0.2)	84.3 (0.4)	85.5 (0.3)	85.0 (0.4)	83.0 (0.4)
10240	**91.5** (0.2)	88.0 (0.4)	89.3 (0.3)	88.9 (0.3)	87.0 (0.3)

(b) NIPS

$|D|$	Proposed	PNB	PMLR	SNB	SMLR
72	**60.5** (2.3)	57.2 (3.5)	50.4 (2.9)	57.8 (2.5)	51.1 (3.2)
144	**65.1** (1.7)	62.3 (2.7)	56.8 (2.6)	62.6 (2.2)	57.2 (2.4)
288	**69.1** (2.1)	67.6 (1.7)	61.9 (1.7)	68.6 (1.5)	62.7 (2.1)
576	**72.4** (1.8)	70.3 (1.7)	65.4 (1.3)	71.6 (1.6)	66.7 (1.7)

(c) WebKB

$|D|$	Proposed	PNB	PMLR	SNB	SMLR
32	61.5 (3.3)	**64.5** (4.6)	61.6 (6.3)	63.6 (4.6)	60.3 (5.7)
64	**74.6** (3.0)	72.5 (4.2)	70.6 (3.6)	71.8 (4.5)	69.7 (3.7)
128	**81.4** (1.1)	78.7 (2.4)	78.2 (1.5)	78.4 (2.6)	78.3 (2.3)
256	**86.7** (1.4)	82.0 (1.6)	82.8 (0.7)	82.0 (1.7)	83.8 (1.5)
512	**88.9** (0.7)	83.6 (2.7)	85.7 (0.8)	83.6 (2.7)	87.9 (0.8)
1024	**90.7** (0.7)	85.7 (1.6)	88.3 (0.8)	85.8 (1.5)	90.6 (0.4)
2048	92.0 (0.4)	86.6 (0.8)	88.9 (0.5)	86.5 (0.8)	**92.4** (0.6)

Analysis of Estimated Combination Weight. We examined the combination weight of the component generative models based on the ME principle. In Fig. 3, the circles represent the average estimated combination weight $\hat{\lambda}_j$ in the proposed method. In these experiments, we used 10240, 576, and 2048 training samples for 20news, NIPS, and WebKB, respectively. The bars in Fig. 3 represent the test average classification accuracies of naive Bayes classifiers designed using only one component. The test classification accuracy of the naive Bayes model for each component (component NB model) was examined using only test samples whose component was not empty. Figure 3 confirms that the proposed method provided a larger estimate of the combination weight for components that provided better classification performance.

In Fig. 3, the triangles represent $\alpha_j = \hat{\lambda}_M |F_t|_j / |F_t|_M$, where $|F_t|_M$ and $\hat{\lambda}_M$ represent $|F_t|$ and $\hat{\lambda}_j$ for component M. $|F_t|_j$ is equivalent to the average $|\boldsymbol{x}_j|$ of the data samples, where $|\boldsymbol{x}_j|$ denotes the total number of features (words or URLs) included in the jth component of data sample $\boldsymbol{x}$. If $|\boldsymbol{x}_j|$ is constant over all the data samples and $\lambda_j = \alpha_j$, $\lambda_j / |\boldsymbol{x}_j| = \hat{\lambda}_M / |F_t|_M$ for every component j.

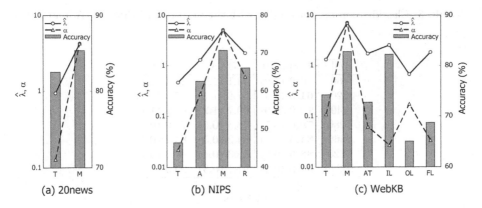

Fig. 3. Combination weight of component models and classification accuracies (%)

Then, the combination of component NB models in Eq. (16) is consistent with the simple product of those models as shown in Eq. (3). Although $|x_j|$ is not constant over real data samples, we can roughly examine the difference between the combination of component NB models in the proposed method and the simple product by comparing the estimate of λ_j with α_j. In Fig. 3, the estimate of λ_j for components other than M is larger than the α_j values. We confirmed that the proposed method adjusted the combination weight so that *minor* components ignored in the classifier based on the simple product were used effectively.

Our experimental results suggest that it is promising to combine components with weights induced from the classification performance of individual components. However, we can consider there to be various possible functional forms for combining components and various possible methods for inducing the combination weights. The proposed method provides one formulation for the weighted combination of components according to the ME principle and can compute the combination weights on the basis of a discriminative approach. We experimentally confirmed that the proposed method adequately combined components and thus improved classification performance.

Comparison with Straightforward Extensions of Binary Hybrid Classifiers to Multiclass Classification Problems. We can straightforwardly extend binary hybrid classifiers as shown in Eq. (8) to multiclass classification problems according to the well-known *one-against-all* (OAA) or *all-pairs* (AP) schemes (cf. [1,14]). In the OAA scheme, K different binary classifiers are trained. The kth binary classifier was designed to classify samples in the kth class from samples in the other classes. We estimated the kth class posterior probability using the kth trained binary classifier and determined the class of x as the k that maximized the probabilities. In the AP scheme, $K(K-1)/2$ different binary classifiers for all pairs of classes are trained. The class of x was determined as the k that won the most choices from these classifiers.

Table 3 shows the classification accuracies for (a) 20news, (b) NIPS, and (c) WebKB obtained with the proposed method, OAA, and AP. The performance

Table 3. Classification accuracies (%) with the proposed method, OAA, and AP

(a) 20news

$|D|$	Proposed	OAA	AP
160	**50.9** (1.9)	44.1 (2.9)	45.3 (2.1)
320	**61.5** (1.4)	57.6 (1.4)	57.3 (1.4)
640	**70.9** (0.9)	69.7 (1.2)	68.1 (1.1)
1280	**78.6** (0.5)	78.3 (0.5)	77.0 (0.5)
2560	**84.3** (0.5)	84.2 (0.5)	83.2 (0.4)
5120	**88.5** (0.2)	88.3 (0.4)	87.6 (0.4)
10240	**91.5** (0.2)	91.1 (0.3)	90.9 (0.3)

(b) NIPS

$|D|$	Proposed	OAA	AP
72	**60.5** (2.3)	56.8 (2.8)	56.9 (3.9)
144	**65.1** (1.7)	63.7 (2.2)	63.1 (1.4)
288	**69.1** (2.1)	68.4 (1.4)	68.3 (2.2)
576	**72.4** (1.8)	71.5 (1.4)	71.7 (1.6)

(c) WebKB

$|D|$	Proposed	OAA	AP
32	61.5 (3.3)	**62.0** (4.8)	59.6 (5.5)
64	**74.6** (3.0)	72.8 (3.3)	73.6 (3.3)
128	**81.4** (1.1)	80.6 (1.6)	80.6 (1.7)
256	**86.7** (1.4)	85.0 (1.4)	85.0 (1.2)
512	**88.9** (0.7)	87.3 (1.3)	87.5 (1.2)
1024	**90.7** (0.7)	89.2 (0.8)	89.9 (1.0)
2048	**92.0** (0.4)	90.3 (0.7)	91.1 (0.7)

of the proposed method was better than that of the OAA and AP schemes for all data sets except when there were 32 training samples in WebKB. This indicates that the problems in the application of the OAA and AP schemes to binary hybrid classifiers as mentioned in the introduction might prevent them from achieving a high level of performance.

5 Conclusion

We proposed a new classifier formulation that effectively uses both main and additional information for multiclass classification based on a hybrid of generative and discriminative approaches. The main idea is to design separate component generative models for the main and additional information and model the class posterior based on the combination of these models by employing the maximum entropy principle.

In our experiments using two text and one web page (text and links) data sets, we confirmed that the classification performance of the proposed method was generally better than that of classifiers based on the simple product of component models. The proposed method was especially useful when the classification performance levels of the pure generative and discriminative classifiers were comparable. We believe that the proposed method improved the classification performance by providing combination weights of component generative models. The combination weights estimated with the proposed method tended to be larger for the component generative model, which provided better classification performance. We also confirmed that the proposed method was effective in terms of classification performance when compared with straightforward extensions of binary hybrid classifiers to multiclass classification problems using the one-against-all or all-pairs schemes.

Future work will involve applying the proposed method to multimodal data in which different generative models are employed, to show the usefulness of the method for more general multi-component data.

References

1. Allwein, E. L., Schapire, R. E., and Singer, Y. (2000). Reducing multiclass to binary: A unifying approach for margin classifiers. *Journal of Machine Learning Research 1*, 113–141.
2. Brochu, E. and Freitas, N. (2003). "Name that song!": A probabilistic approach to querying on music and text. In *Advances in Neural Information Processing Systems 15* (pp. 1505–1512). Cambridge, MA: MIT Press.
3. Berger, A., Della Pietra, S., and Della Pietra, V. (1996). A maximum entropy approach to natural language processing. *Computational Linguistics*, **22(1)**, 39–71.
4. Chakrabarti, S., Dom, B., and Indyk, P. (1998). Enhanced hypertext categorization using hyperlinks. In *Proceedings of ACM International Conference on Management of Data (SIGMOD-98)*, 307–318.
5. Chen, S. F. and Rosenfeld, R. (1999). A Gaussian prior for smoothing maximum entropy models, Technical Report, Carnegie Mellon University.
6. Cohn, D. and Hofmann, T. (2001) The missing link - A probabilistic model of document content and hypertext connectivity. In *Advances in Neural Information Processing Systems 13* (pp. 430–436). Cambridge, MA: MIT Press.
7. Dempster, A. P., Laird, N. M., and Rubin, D. B. (1977). Maximum likelihood from incomplete data via the EM algorithm. *Journal of the Royal Statistical Society, Series B*, **39**, 1–38.
8. Hastie, T., Tibshirani, R., and Friedman, J. (2001). *The Elements of Statistical Learning: Data Mining, Inference, and Prediction*. Springer-Verlag New York Berlin Heidelberg.
9. Liu, D. C. and Nocedel, J. (1989). On the limited memory BFGS method for large scale optimization. *Math. Programming*, **45(3, (ser. B))**, 503–528.
10. Lu, Q. and Getoor, L. (2003). Link-based text classification. In *IJCAI Workshop on Text-Mining & Link-Analysis (TextLink 2003)*.
11. Nigam, K., Lafferty, J., and McCallum, A. (1999). Using maximum entropy for text classification. In *IJCAI-99 Workshop on Machine Learning for Information Filtering*, 61–67.

12. Nigam, K., McCallum, A., Thrun, S., and Mitchell T. (2000). Text classification from labeled and unlabeled documents using EM. *Machine Learning*, **39**, 103–134.
13. Raina, R., Shen, Y., Ng, A. Y., and McCallum, A. (2004). Classification with hybrid generative/discriminative models. In *Advances in Neural Information Processing Systems 16*. Cambridge, MA: MIT Press.
14. Rifkin, R. and Klautau, A. (2004). In defense of one-vs-all classification. *Journal of Machine Learning Research 5*, 101-141.
15. Salton, G. and McGill, M. J. (1983). *Introduction to Modern Information Retrieval*. New York: McGraw-Hill.
16. Sun, A., Lim, E. -P., and Ng, W. -K. (2002). Web classification using support vector machine. In *Proceedings of 4th Int. Workshop on Web Information and Data Management (WIDM 2002) held in conj. with CIKM 2002*, 96–99.

A Query-by-Singing Technique for Retrieving Polyphonic Objects of Popular Music

Hung-Ming Yu, Wei-Ho Tsai, and Hsin-Min Wang

Institute of Information Science, Academia Sinica, Taipei, Taiwan, Republic of China
{donny, wesley, whm}@iis.sinica.edu.tw

Abstract. This paper investigates the problem of retrieving popular music by singing. In contrast to the retrieval of MIDI music, which is easy to acquire the main melody by the selection of the symbolic tracks, retrieving polyphonic objects in CD or MP3 format requires to extract the main melody directly from the accompanied singing signals, which proves difficult to handle well simply using the conventional pitch estimation. To reduce the interference of background accompaniments during the main melody extraction, methods are proposed to estimate the underlying sung notes in a music recording by taking into account the characteristic structure of popular song. In addition, to accommodate users' unprofessional or personal singing styles, methods are proposed to handle the inaccuracies of tempo, pause, transposition, or off-key, etc., inevitably existing in queries. The proposed system has been evaluated on a music database consisting of 2613 phrases extracted manually from 100 Mandarin pop songs. The experimental results indicate the feasibility of retrieving pop songs by singing.

1 Introduction

Currently, the most prevalent way to music information retrieval is based on the so-called metadata search, which operates by manually annotating music data according to the title, lyrics, performer, composer, etc., so that users can retrieve their desired music in the same way as they retrieve the text information. However, since the concrete descriptions, such as title or lyrics, usually cannot reflect the abstract content of music directly, it is often the case that users know what the song they want sounds like, but just cannot recall or totally have no idea about its title or lyrics. As a result, formulating a text query explicitly sometimes could be a difficulty for users. To overcome this handicap, a new promising solution is the so-called query-by-humming or query-by-singing [1-9], which allows users to retrieve a song by simply humming or singing a fragment of that song. Since no textual input is needed, query-by-humming or query-by-singing could not only increase the usability of a music retrieval system, but also allow the access to the system with no keyboard supported, e.g., to retrieve music via mobile devices.

The format of digital music can be divided into two categories. One is the symbolic representation based on musical scores. It specifies some manner of instructions about what, when, and how long a note should be played with which instruments. Examples of this category include MIDI (Musical Instrument Digital

G.G. Lee et al. (Eds.): AIRS 2005, LNCS 3689, pp. 439–453, 2005.

Interface) and Humdrum. Since no real acoustic signal is included, a MIDI or Humdrum file would have different sounds when it is played by different devices. The second category of digital music is concerned with the data containing the acoustic signals recorded from real performances. The most widespread formats are CD (.wav) and MP3 (MPEG-I Layer 3). This type of music is often *polyphonic*, in which many notes may be played simultaneously, in contrast to *monophonic* music, in which at most one note is played at any give time. From the perspective of music retrieval, searching for a MIDI object from a database is much easier than searching for an MP3 object, because extracting score information is easy from a symbolic file, but is rather difficult from a polyphonic music. Due to this difficulty, research on query-by-humming or query-by-singing [1-6] has almost focused on MIDI music. However, methods, specifically designed to retrieve CD or MP3 music [7-9] are still very scarce and needed to be explored.

Previous work on query-by-humming primarily concentrates on the similarity comparison between the symbolic sequences. Ghias *et al.* [1] proposed an approximate pattern matching approach, which converts a query or each of the MIDI documents as a sequence of symbols 'U' (the note is higher than its preceding one), 'D' (the note is lower than its preceding one), and 'S' (the note is the same as its preceding one). The similarity between a query's sequence and each of the MIDI documents' sequences are then computed by string matching. Since most users are not professional singers, a query's sequence inevitably contains transposition errors (e.g., UUSDD → UDSDD), dropout errors (e.g., UUSDD → USDD), and duplication errors (e.g., UUSDD → UUUSDD). To tolerate the above errors, several methods have been further proposed, with the dynamic time warping (DTW) [4][5] being the most popular. Moreover, it is obvious that the three symbols 'U', 'D', and 'S' are not sufficient to represent all kinds of melody patterns precisely. Thus, more sophisticated representations, such as MIDI note number representation and broken-edge graph representation [4], have been studied subsequently. In addition, related work in [2][3] further considered the tone distribution in a song, tone transition between two adjacent notes, and the difference with respect to the first note.

In contrast to the retrieval of MIDI music, this study presents our first investigation on retrieving polyphonic objects of popular music. To permit the comparison between monophonic queries and polyphonic documents, methods of main melody extraction and error correction are proposed, with the statistical analysis of the compositional structure of pop songs being taken into account. In addition, to accommodate users' unprofessional or personal singing styles, methods are proposed to handle the inaccuracies of tempo, pause, transposition, or off-key, etc., inevitably existing in queries.

The rest of this paper is organized as follows. The general characteristics of popular music are discussed in Section 2. The configuration of our music retrieval system is introduced in Section 3. Our approaches for melody extraction and melody comparison are presented in Sections 4 and 5, respectively. Finally, the experimental results are discussed in Section 6 and conclusions are drawn in Section 7.

2 General Characteristics of Popular Music

Characteristic analysis of the data to be processed is an essential step in designing a reliable information retrieval system. It is known that popular music is simple by the melody that is easy to sing and memorize, but is, however, also complicated by the melody that is difficult to extract automatically. This section briefs some characteristics of popular music, which could be exploited to benefit the realization of a popular music retrieval system.

In general, the structure of a popular song can be divided into five sections:

1. *intro*, which is usually the first 10-20 seconds of a song, and simply an instrumental statement of the subsequent sections;
2. *verse*, which typically comprises the main content of story represented in a song's lyrics;
3. *chorus*, which is often the heart of a song where the most recognizable melody is present and repeated;
4. *bridge*, which comes roughly two-thirds into a song, where a key change, tempo change or new lyric is usually introduced to create a sensation of something new coming next;
5. *outro*, which is often a fading version of chorus or an instrumental restatement of some earlier sections to bring the song to a conclusion.

Except for intro and outro, each of the sections may repeat several times with varying lyrics, melodies, etc. The most common structure of a popular song consists of "intro-verse-chorus-verse-chorus-bridge-outro" or "intro-verse-verse-chorus-chorus-bridge-outro". In essence, verse and chorus contain the vocals sung by the lead singer, while intro, bridge, and outro are often largely accompaniments. This makes it natural that verse and chorus are the favorites that people go away humming when they hear a good song, and hence are often the query that a user may hum or sing to a music retrieval system.

Depending on the song, the notes produced by a singer may vary from F2 (87.3 Hz) to B5 (987.8Hz), corresponding to a varying range of 43 *semitones*[1]. However, it is observed that the sung notes within a music recording usually vary less than this range, and the varying range of the sung notes within a verse or chorus section can be even narrower. Fig. 1 shows an example of a segment of a song performed with MIDI[2]. It is clear that the range of notes within the verse can be distinguished from that of the chorus, because the sung notes within a section do not spread over all the possible notes, but only distribute in their own narrower range. An informal survey using 50 pop songs shows that the range of sung notes within a whole song and within a verse or chorus section are around 25 and 22 semitones, respectively. Fig. 2 details our statistic results. This information is useful for those attempting to transcribe the sung notes, by discarding the virtually impossible notes.

---

[1] A semitone is one twelfth part of the interval (called *octave*) between two sounds one of which has twice the frequency of the other.
[2] We convert the sung notes into MIDI note numbers for ease of illustration.

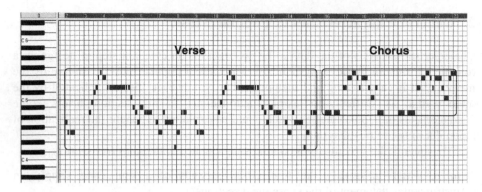

Fig. 1. A fragment of the pop song "Yesterday" by *The Beatles*, in which the singing is converted into a MIDI file and shown by software Cakewalk[TM] [11] for ease of illustration

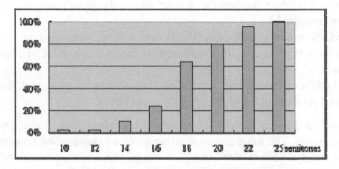

(a)   The range of sung notes within a pop song

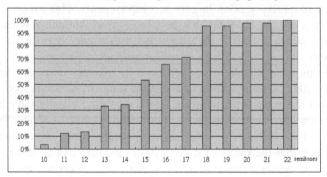

(b) The range of sung notes within a verse or chorus section

Fig. 2. Statistics of the range of sung notes in 50 pop songs

In addition to the singing, a vast majority of popular music contain background accompaniment during most or all vocal passages. Various signals from different sources are mixed together into a single track in a CD. Even in stereo, signals in each of the channels are the accompanied voice, rather than the solo voice or accompaniment only. This makes it more difficult to design a system for retrieving

CD music than to design a system for retrieving MIDI music, since the desired information, usually residing in the solo voice, is inextricably intertwined with the background signals. In addition, the background accompaniments often play notes several octaves above or below the singing, in order that the mix of music can sound harmonically. However, such harmonicity between singing voice and accompaniments further make the vocal melody notoriously difficult to extract. An example of song performed with MIDI is shown in Fig. 3. We can see from the notes indicated by arrows that a large proportion of sung notes are accompanied by the notes one or two octaves above them. Nevertheless, the harmonicity, viewed from another angle, may be exploited as a constraint in the determination of sung notes. A method based on this idea to improve the main melody extraction is discussed in a greater detail in Section 4.

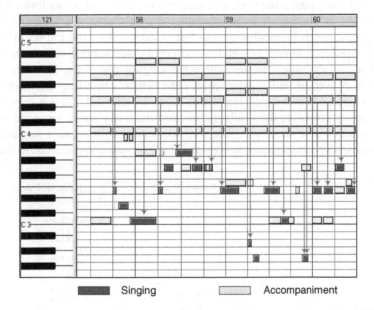

Fig. 3. A fragment of the pop song "Let It Be" by *The Beatles*, in which the tune is converted manually into a MIDI file

3 System Configuration

Our popular music retrieval system is designed with such an aim to take as input an audio query sung by a user, and to produce as output the song containing the most similar melody to the sung query. Fig. 4 shows a block diagram of the retrieval system. It operates in two phases: indexing and searching.

The indexing phase is concerned with the generation of melody description for each of the songs in the collection. It starts with the segmentation of each song into *phrases* which reflect the expected patterns of query that users would like to sing to the system. In view of the fact that the length of a popular song is normally several minutes, it is virtually impossible that a user sings a whole song as a query to the system. Further, a user's singing tends to begin with the initial of a sentence of lyrics. For instance, a user may query the system by singing a piece of *The Beatle's* "Yesterday" like this, "Suddenly, I'm not half to man I used to be. There's a shadow hanging over me." By contrast, a sung query like "I used to be. There's a shadow" or "half to man I used to be." is believed almost impossible. Therefore, segmenting a song into semantically-meaningful phrases could not only match users' queries better, but also improve the efficiency of the system in the searching phase. Next, the second step of the indexing proceeds with the main melody extraction for each of the phrases. It converts an audio signal from the waveform samples into a sequence of musical note symbols. Accordingly, the database is composed of note-based sequences of phrase, referred to as documents' note sequences hereafter. During the initial design stage of this system, the phrase segmentation is performed manually.

In the searching phase, the system determines the song that a user looks for based on what he/she is singing. It is assumed that a user's sung query can be either a complete phrase or an incomplete phrase but always starts from the beginning of a phrase. The system commences with the end-point detection that records the singing voice and marks the salient pauses within the singing waveform. Next, the singing waveform is converted into a sequence of note symbols by using the main melody extraction modular as in the indexing phase. Then, the retrieval task is narrowed down to a problem of comparing the similarity between the query's note sequence and each of the documents' note sequences. The song associated with the note sequence most similar to the query's note sequence is regarded as relevant and presented to the user.

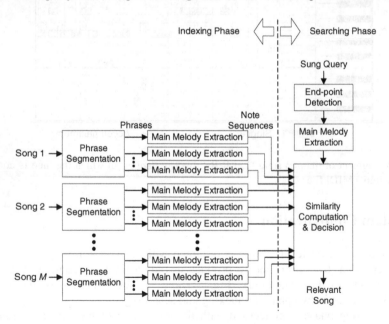

Fig. 4. The proposed popular song retrieval system

4 Main Melody Extraction

Given a music recording, the aim of main melody extraction is to find the sequence of musical notes produced by the singing part of the recording. Let $e_1, e_2, \ldots, e_N$ be the inventory of possible notes performed by a singer. The task, therefore, is to determine which among N possible notes is most likely sung at each instant. To do this, the music signal is first divided into frames by using a fixed-length sliding window. Every frame is then convolved with a Hamming window and undergoes a fast Fourier transform (FFT) with size J. Since musical notes differ from each other by the fundamental frequencies (F0s) they present, we may determine if a certain note is sung in each frame by analyzing the spectral intensity in the frequency region where the F0 of the note is located.

Let $x_{t,j}$ denote the signal's energy with respect to FFT index j in frame t, where $1 \le j \le J$. If we use the MIDI note number to represent $e_1, e_2, \ldots, e_N$, and map the FFT indices into MIDI note numbers according to the F0 of each note, the signal's energy on note e_n in frame t can be estimated by

$$y_{t,n} = \underset{\forall j, U(j)=e_n}{\arg\max} \; x_{t,j}, \tag{1}$$

and

$$U(j) = \left\lfloor 12 \cdot \log_2\left(\frac{F(j)}{440}\right) + 69.5 \right\rfloor, \tag{2}$$

where $\lfloor \; \rfloor$ is a floor operator, $F(j)$ is the corresponding frequency of FFT index j, and $U(\cdot)$ represents a conversion between the FFT indices and the MIDI note numbers.

Ideally, if note e_n is sung in frame t, the resulting energy, $y_{t,n}$, should be the maximum among $y_{t,1}, y_{t,2}, \ldots, y_{t,N}$. However, due to the existence of harmonics, the note numbers that are several octaves higher than the sung note can also receive a large proportion of the signal's energy. Sometimes the energy on a harmonic note number can be even larger than the energy on the true sung note number; hence, the note number receiving the largest energy is not necessarily what is sung. To determine the sung note more reliably, this study adapts Sub-Harmonic Summation (SHS) [10] to this problem.

The principle applied here is to compute a value for the "strength" of each possible note by summing up the signal's energy on a note and its harmonic note numbers. Specifically, the strength of note e_n in frame t is computed using

$$z_{t,n} = \sum_{c=0}^{C} h^c \, y_{t,n+12c}, \tag{3}$$

where C is the number of harmonics that are taken into account, and h is a positive value less than 1 to discount the contribution of higher harmonics. The result of this summation is that the note number corresponding to the signal's F0 will receive the largest amount of energy from its harmonic notes. Thus, the sung note in frame t could be determined by choosing the note number associated with the largest value of the strength, i.e.,

$$o_t = \underset{1 \le n \le N}{\arg\max} \; z_{t,n}. \tag{4}$$

However, since popular music usually contains background accompaniments during the vocal passages, the note number associated with the largest value of strength may not be produced by a singer, but the concurrent instruments instead. As a consequence, whenever the strength of the sung note is not the maximum, an error estimation of the sung note would happen. This problem may be alleviated by using the *tone chroma*, which maps all the notes into 12 tone classes (C, Db, D, Eb, E, F, Gb, G, Ab, A, Bb, and B) by ignoring the difference between octaves. As mentioned in Section 2, since the background accompaniments often play notes several octaves above or below the singing, a mis-estimated sung note could still map to a correct tone class. However, because of using 12 classes only, tone chroma cannot express a melody pattern with sufficient precision to distinguish from one another. Recognizing this, we focus on investigating the method to correct the error estimation of the sung notes, instead of using the tone chroma representation.

The method to correct the error estimation of the sung notes is based on a concept of rectification, which identifies the abnormal individuals in a note sequence and forces them back to the normal. The abnormality in a note sequence roughly arises from two types of errors: short-term error and long-term error. The short-term error is concerned with the rapid changes, e.g. jitters, between adjacent frames. This type of error could be amended by using the median filtering, which replaces each note of frame with the local median of its neighboring frames. One the other hand, the long-term error is concerned with a succession of the estimated notes not produced by a singer. These successive wrong notes are very likely several octaves above or below the true sung notes, which could result in the range of the estimated notes within a sequence being wider than that of the true sung note sequence. As mentioned in Section 2, the sung notes within a verse or chorus section usually vary no more than 22 semitones. Therefore, we may adjust the suspect notes by shifting them several octaves up or down, so that the range of the notes within an adjusted sequence can conform to the normal range. Specifically, let $\mathbf{o} = \{o_1, o_2,..., o_T\}$ denote a note sequence estimated using Eq. (4). An adjusted note sequence $\mathbf{o}' = \{o'_1, o'_2..., o'_T\}$ is obtained by

$$o'_t = \begin{cases} o_t & , \text{ if } |o_t - \overline{o}| \le (R/2) \\ o_t - 12 \times \left\lfloor \dfrac{o_t - \overline{o} + R/2}{12} \right\rfloor, & \text{ if } o_t - \overline{o} > (R/2) \ , \\ o_t - 12 \times \left\lfloor \dfrac{o_t - \overline{o} - R/2}{12} \right\rfloor, & \text{ if } o_t - \overline{o} < (-R/2) \end{cases} \tag{5}$$

where R is the normal varying range of the sung notes in a sequence, say 22, and $\overline{o}$ is the mean note computed by averaging all the notes in $\mathbf{o}$. In Eq. (5), a note o_t is considered as a wrong note and needs to be adjusted, if it is too far away from $\overline{o}$, i.e., $|o_t - \overline{o}| > R/2$. The adjustment is done by shifting the wrong note $\lfloor (o_t - \overline{o} + R/2)/12 \rfloor$ or $\lfloor (o_t - \overline{o} - R/2)/12 \rfloor$ octaves.

5 Melody Similarity Comparison

Given a user's query and a set of music documents, each of which is represented by a note sequence, our task here is to find a music document whose note sequence is most similar to the query's note sequence. Since users' singing may be significantly different from what they want to retrieve in terms of key, tempo, ornamentation, etc., it is impossible to find a document's sequence exactly match the query's sequence. Moreover, the main melody extraction is known to be frequently imperfect, which further introduces errors of substitution, deletion, and insertion into the note sequences. To perform a reliable melody similarity comparison, an approximate matching method tolerable to occasional note errors, is therefore needed.

Let $\mathbf{q} = \{q_1, q_2,..., q_T\}$, and $\mathbf{u} = \{u_1, u_2,..., u_L\}$ be the note sequences extracted from a user's query and a particular music document to be compared, respectively. The most apparent problem we face here is that the lengths of $\mathbf{q}$ and $\mathbf{u}$ are usually unequal. Thus, it is necessary to temporally align $\mathbf{q}$ and $\mathbf{u}$ before computing their similarity. For this reason, we apply Dynamic Time Warping (DTW) to find the mapping between each q_t and u_ℓ, $1 \le t \le T$, $1 \le \ell \le L$. DTW constructs a $T{\times}L$ distance matrix $\mathbf{D} = [D(t, \ell)]_{T \times L}$, where $D(t, \ell)$ is the distance between note sequences $\{q_1, q_2,...,q_t\}$ and $\{u_1, u_2,..., u_\ell\}$, computed using:

$$D(t,\ell) = \min \begin{cases} D(t-2,\ell-1)+2{\times}d(t,\ell) \\ D(t-1,\ell-1)+d(t,\ell)-\varepsilon \\ D(t-1,\ell-2)+d(t,\ell) \end{cases}, \quad (6)$$

and

$$d(t,\ell) = |\, q_t - u_\ell\,|, \quad (7)$$

where ε is a small constant that favors the mapping between note q_t and u_ℓ, given the distance between note sequences $\{q_1, q_2,...,q_{t-1}\}$ and $\{u_1, u_2,..., u_{\ell-1}\}$. The boundary conditions for the above recursion are defined by

$$\begin{cases} D(1,1) = d(1,1) \\ D(t,1) = \infty, 2 \le t \le T \\ D(1,\ell) = \infty, 2 \le \ell \le L \\ D(2,2) = d(1,1)+d(2,2)-\varepsilon \\ D(2,3) = d(1,1)+d(2,2) \\ D(3,2) = d(1,1)+2{\times}d(2,2) \\ D(t,2) = \infty, 4 \le t \le T \\ D(2,\ell) = \infty, 4 \le \ell \le L \end{cases}, \quad (8)$$

where we have assumed that a sung query always starts from the beginning of a document. After the distance matrix $\mathbf{D}$ is constructed, the similarity between $\mathbf{q}$ and $\mathbf{u}$ can be evaluated by

$$S(\mathbf{q},\mathbf{u}) = \begin{cases} \max_{T/2 \le \ell \le \min(2T,L)} [1/D(T,\ell)], & \text{if } L \ge T/2 \\ 0 & , \text{if } L < T/2 \end{cases}, \quad (9)$$

where we assume that the end of a query's sequence should be aligned to a certain frame between $T/2$ and $\min(2T,L)$ of the document's sequence, and assume that a document whose length of sequence less than $T/2$ would not be a relevant document to the query.

Since a query may be sung in a different key or register than the target music document, i.e., the so-called *transposition*, the resulting note sequences of the query and the document could be rather different. To deal with this problem, the dynamic range of a query's note sequence needs to be adjusted to that of the document to be compared. This could be done by shifting the query's note sequence up or down several semitones, so that the mean of the shifted query's note sequence is equal to that of the document to be compared. Briefly, a query's note sequence is adjusted by

$$q_t \leftarrow q_t + (\bar{u} - \bar{q}), \tag{10}$$

where $\bar{q}$ and $\bar{u}$ are the means of the query's note sequence and the document's note sequence, respectively. However, our experiments find that the above adjustment can not fully overcome the transposition problem, since the value of $(\bar{q} - \bar{u})$ can only reflect a global difference of key between a query and document, but cannot characterize the partial transposition or key change over the course of a query. To handle this problem better, we further modify the DTW similarity comparison by considering the key shifts of a query's note sequence. Specifically, a query sequence $\mathbf{q}$ is shifted with ± 1, ± 2,..., $\pm K$ semitones to span a set of note sequences $\{\mathbf{q}^{(1)}, \mathbf{q}^{(-1)}, \mathbf{q}^{(2)}, \mathbf{q}^{(-2)},..., \mathbf{q}^{(K)}, \mathbf{q}^{(-K)}\}$. For a document sequence $\mathbf{u}$, the similarity $S(\mathbf{q}, \mathbf{u})$ is then determined by choosing one among $\{\mathbf{q}^{(0)}, \mathbf{q}^{(1)}, \mathbf{q}^{(-1)}, \mathbf{q}^{(2)}, \mathbf{q}^{(-2)},..., \mathbf{q}^{(K)}, \mathbf{q}^{(-K)}\}$ that is most similar to $\mathbf{u}$, i.e.,

$$S(\mathbf{q},\mathbf{u}) = \max_{-K \leq k \leq K} S(\mathbf{q}^{(k)},\mathbf{u}), \tag{11}$$

where $\mathbf{q}^{(0)} = \mathbf{q}$.

In addition to the difference of key and tempo existing between queries and documents, another problem needed to be addressed is the existence of voiceless regions in a sung query. The voiceless regions, which may arise from the rest, pause, etc., result in some notes being tagged with "0" in a query's note sequence. However, the corresponding non-vocal regions in the document are usually not tagged with "0", because there are accompaniments in those regions. This discrepancy may severely discount the similarity $S(\mathbf{q}, \mathbf{u})$ for any $\mathbf{q}$ and $\mathbf{u}$ having the same tune. Fig. 5 shows an example illustrating this problem. The regions in Fig. 5(b) marked in gray are those do not contain singing voice. Although the voiceless regions in a sung query can be detected by simply using the energy information, the accurate detection of non-vocal regions in a music document remains a very difficult problem. Therefore, to sidestep this problem, we further modify the computation of $d(t,\ell)$ in Eq. (7) by

$$d(t,\ell) = \begin{cases} |q_t - u_\ell|, & q_t \neq 0 \\ \varphi, & q_t = 0 \end{cases}, \tag{12}$$

where φ is a small constant. Implicit in Eq. (12) is equivalent to bypassing the voiceless regions of a query.

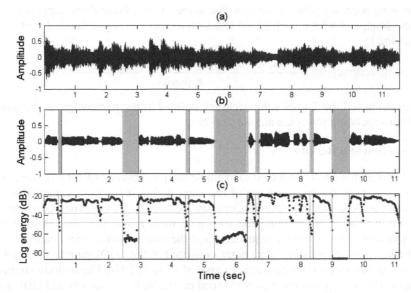

Fig. 5. (a) a phrase document, (b) a query sung according to this phrase, (c) the log-energy profile of this sung query

6 Experiments

6.1 Music Database

The music database used in this study consisted of 100 tracks[3] from Mandarin pop music CDs. Each of the tracks was segmented manually into several phrases, which gives a total of 2,613 phrase documents. The waveform signal of each phrase document was down-sampled from the CD sampling rate of 44.1 kHz to 22.05 kHz, to exclude the high frequency components that usually contain sparse vocal information. In addition, we collected 253 queries sung by 5 male and 2 female users. Each query is sung according to one of the 2,613 phrase documents, but can be an incomplete phrase.

Performance of the song retrieval was evaluated on the basis of phrase accuracy and song accuracy. The phrase accuracy is defined as the percentage of the queries that can receive their corresponding phrase documents, i.e.,

$$\text{Phrase accuracy}(\%) = \frac{\#\,\text{queries receiving the corresponding phrase documents}}{\#\,\text{queries}} \times 100\%.$$

In addition, considering a more user-friendly scenario that a list of phrase documents ranked according to the query-document similarity can be provided for users' choices, we also computed the Top-N phrase accuracy defined as the percentage of the querieswhose corresponding phrase documents are among Top-N.

---

[3] The database did not contain the 50 pop songs used for analyzing the range of sung notes, described in Section 2.

The song accuracy reflects the fact that some of the phrase documents belong to the same song, and what a user would like to retrieve is a song instead of a phrase. It is computed by

$$\text{Song accuracy}(\%) = \frac{\#\text{queries receiving the corresponding songs}}{\#\text{queries}} \times 100\%.$$

We also computed the Top-N song accuracy defined as the percentage of the queries whose corresponding songs are among Top-N.

6.2 Experimental Results

Our first experiment was conducted to evaluate the performance of song retrieval with respect to the potential enhancement of the main melody extraction. Specifically, we compared the three methods to main melody extraction, namely, the note sequence generation by Eq. (4) along with the six-frame median filtering, the conversion of note sequences to tone chroma sequences, and the note sequence rectification by Eq. (5). The inventory of possible sung notes consisted of the MIDI numbers from 41 to 83, which corresponds to the frequency range of 87 to 987 Hz. The melody similarity comparison in this experiment was performed on the basis of Eqs. (9) and (10). Table 1 shows the retrieval results. We can see from Table 1 that the retrieval performance obtained with the method of using Eq. (4) and median filtering was the worst among the three methods compared, mainly because this method determines the sung notes based on the largest values of strength, which is vulnerable to the interference of background accompaniments. It is also shown in Table 1 that a slightly better performance can be achieved by converting note sequences into tone chroma sequences, which avoids the risk of mis-estimating a sung note as its octaves. However, due to the limited precision in melody representation, the tone chroma method has its inherent limit in distinguishing among songs, and so in the retrieval performance. By contrast, the note sequence rectification by Eq. (5) keeps the fine precision of using note numbers in melody representation and tries to correct the errors in a note sequence. We can see from Table 1 that the note sequence rectification noticeably improves the retrieval performance, and proves superior to the tone chroma method.

Table 1. Performance of the song retrieval for different main melody extraction methods

Main melody extraction method		Phrase accuracy / Song accuracy (%)		
		Top 1	Top 3	Top 10
Note sequence generation by Eq. (4) and six-frame median filtering		32.0 / 37.9	41.1 / 49.8	50.6 / 62.9
Conversion of note sequences to tone chroma sequences		36.8 / 45.1	45.9 / 55.7	54.2 / 68.4
Note sequence rectification by Eq. (5)	$R = 16$	40.3 / 45.9	48.6 / 61.3	60.1 / 72.3
	$R = 18$	42.7 / 49.4	49.4 / 62.5	60.5 / 72.7
	$R = 20$	39.9 / 49.0	47.0 / 59.7	57.7 / 71.9
	$R = 22$	37.6 / 46.3	46.3 / 59.3	54.6 / 70.4

Next, we examined if the retrieval performance can be improved by further addressing the transposition problem. Specifically, we used the method of shifting a query's note sequence upward or downward several semitones together with Eq. (11) to perform the similarity comparison with each of the documents' sequences. Table 2 shows the experimental results. Here, $K = 0$ means that no shifting is performed, and its result corresponds to the best result (note sequence rectification with $R = 18$) shown in Table 1. We can see from Table 2 that the retrieval performance improves as the value of K increases, which indicates that the more the possible changes of key is taken into account, the greater the chance that a query's sequence matches the correct document's sequence. However, increasing the value of K heavily increases the computational cost, because the similarity comparison requires two extra DTW operations whenever the value of K is increased by one. An economic value of $K = 1$ was thus chosen in our subsequent experiments.

Table 2. Performance of the song retrieval obtained with and without upward/downward shifting a query's note sequence during the DTW similarity comparison

Value of K in Eq. (11)	Phrase accuracy / Song accuracy (%)		
	Top 1	Top 3	Top 10
0	42.7 / 49.4	49.4 / 62.5	60.5 / 72.7
1	47.0 / 56.1	59.3 / 70.0	66.8 / 77.9
2	48.6 / 58.1	60.5 / 71.5	68.4 / 78.7

Finally, we compared the retrieval performance obtained with and without explicitly considering the singing pause of a query, that is, Eq. (7) vs. Eq. (12). The experimental results are shown in Table 3. It is clear that the retrieval performance can benefit greatly by detecting and excluding the non-singing segments of a query during the DTW similarity comparison. This indicates that the proposed system is capable of handling the inadequate pause, key-shifting, or tempo of a sung query. In summary, our experimental results show that whenever a user sings a query to search for one of the one hundred songs, the probability that the desired song can be found in a Top-10 list is around 0.8, in a Top-3 list is around 0.7, and in a Top-1 list is around 0.6. Although there is much room to further improve, our system shows the feasibility of retrieving polyphonic pop songs in a query-by-singing framework.

Table 3. Performance of the song retrieval obtained with and without explicitly considering the singing pause of a query

	Phrase accuracy / Song accuracy (%)		
	Top 1	Top 3	Top 10
DTW with Eq. (7)	47.0 / 56.1	59.3 / 70.0	66.8 / 77.9
DTW with Eq. (12)	52.6 / 60.5	62.5 / 71.9	72.7 / 80.6

7 Conclusions

This study has presented a popular song retrieval system that allows users to search for their desired songs by singing. Since in most pop songs, the singing voices and various concurrent accompaniments are mixed together into a single track, the melody extraction process can be seriously interfered by the accompaniments, leading to the inevitable errors. Drawn from the observations that the varying range of the sung notes within a verse and chorus section is usually less than 22 semitones and a large proportion of sung notes are accompanied by the notes several octaves above or below them, we have developed a feasible approach to melody extraction and error correction. Meanwhile, we have also devised a similarity comparison method based on DTW to handle the discrepancy of tempo variation, pause, transposition between queries and documents.

With regard to practicability, more work is needed to extend our current system to handle a wider variety of queries and songs. Specifically, the current system assumes that a query can be either a complete phrase or an incomplete phrase of a song, and a query must start from the beginning of a phrase. It is necessary to further address the case when a query contains multiple phrases of a song or when a query does not start from the beginning of a phrase. In addition, methods for automatic segmentation of songs into phrases are needed in order to automate the whole indexing process. Furthermore, our future work will incorporate some sophisticated methods in the general document-retrieval field, such as relevance feedback, to improve the current system.

Acknowledgement

This work was supported in part by the Nation Science Council, Taiwan, under Grants NSC92-2422-H-001-093 and NSC93-2422-H-001-0004.

References

1. Ghias, A., H. Logan, D. Chamberlin, and B. C. Smith, "Query by Humming: Musical Information Retrieval in an Audio Database," *Proc. ACM International Conference on Multimedia*, pp. 231-236, 1995.
2. Kosugi, N., Y. Nishihara, T. Sakata, M. Yamamuro, and K. Kushima, "Music Retrieval by Humming," *Proc. IEEE Pacific Rim Conference on Communications, Computers and Signal Processing*, pp. 404-407, 1999.
3. Kosugi, N., Y. Nishihara, T. Sakata, M. Yamamuro, and K. Kushima, "A Practical Query-By-Huming System for a Large Music Database," *Proc. ACM International Conference on Multimedia*, 2000.
4. Mo, J. S., C. H. Han, and Y. S. Kim, "A Melody-Based Similarity Computation Algorithm for Musical Information," *Proc. Workshop on Knowledge and Data Engineering Exchange*, pp. 114-121, 1999.
5. Jang, J. S. Roger, and H. R. Lee, "Hierarchical Filtering Method for Content-based Music Retrieval via Acoustic Input," *Proc. ACM International Conference on Multimedia,* pp. 401-410, 2001.

6. Liu, C. C., A. J. L. Hsu, and A. L. P. Chen, "An Approximate String Matching Algorithm for Content-Based Music Data Retrieval," *Proc. IEEE International Conference on Multimedia Computing and Systems,* 1999.
7. Nishimura, T., H. Hashiguchi, J. Takita, J. X. Zhang, M. Goto, and R. Oka, "Music Signal Spotting Retrieval by a Humming Query Using Start Frame Feature Dependent Continuous Dynamic Programming," *Proc. International Symposium on Music Information Retrieval,* 2001.
8. Doraisamy, S., and S. M. Ruger, "An Approach Towards a Polyphonic Music Retrieval System," *Proc. International Symposium on Music Information Retrieval,* 2001.
9. Song, J., S. Y. Bae, K. Yoon, "Mid-Level Music Melody Representation of Polyphonic Audio for Query-by-Humming System," *Proc. International Conference on Music Information Retrieval,* 2002.
10. Piszczalski, M., and B. A. Galler, "Predicting musical pitch from component frequency ratios," *Journal of the Acoustical Society of America,* 66(3), pp. 710–720, 1979.
11. Cakewalk, Inc., http://www.cakewalk.com/

Integrating Textual and Visual Information
for Cross-Language Image Retrieval

Wen-Cheng Lin, Yih-Chen Chang, and Hsin-Hsi Chen

Department of Computer Science and Information Engineering,
National Taiwan University, Taipei, Taiwan
{denislin, ycchang}@nlg.csie.ntu.edu.tw
hhchen@csie.ntu.edu.tw

Abstract. This paper explores the integration of textual and visual information for cross-language image retrieval. An approach which automatically transforms textual queries into visual representations is proposed. The relationships between text and images are mined. We employ the mined relationships to construct visual queries from textual ones. The retrieval results of textual and visual queries are combined. We conduct English monolingual and Chinese-English cross-language retrieval experiments to evaluate the proposed approach. The selection of suitable textual query terms to construct visual queries is the major concern. Experimental results show that the proposed approach improves retrieval performance, and nouns are appropriate to generate visual queries.

1 Introduction

Multimedia data has an explosive growth nowadays. Internet, for example, contains millions of images, videos and music. Finding the requesting information from large amount of multimedia data is challenging. Two types of approaches, i.e., content-based and text-based approaches, are usually adopted in image retrieval [8]. Content-based image retrieval (CBIR) uses low-level visual features such as color, texture and shape to represent images. Users can employ example images as queries, or directly specify and weight low-level visual features to retrieve images. Images that are visually similar to an example image or contain the specified visual features are returned.

In text-based approaches, text is used to describe images and formulate queries. Because images and image representations are in different types of media, media transformation is required. The medium of data collection is transformed from image into text and a text retrieval system is used to index and retrieve images. Textual features can be derived from the text accompanying with an image such as caption or surrounding text. Text-based approach encounters the following problems.

(1) Image captions are usually short. The short annotation cannot represent the image content completely.
(2) Image captions are not always available. Manually assigning captions to images is time consuming and costly.

G.G. Lee et al. (Eds.): AIRS 2005, LNCS 3689, pp. 454–466, 2005.

(3) Some visual properties cannot be described in captions directly. For example, the styles of images, e.g., warm, cold, dark, sharp, or blurry, are usually not specified in captions.

(4) Users' queries may have different levels of semantics. Users may search for images at a higher semantic level or at a primitive level.

Since images are produced by people familiar with their own languages, they can be annotated in different languages. In this way, text-based image retrieval has multilingual nature. Besides, images are neutral to different language users. They can resolve the major argument in cross-language information retrieval, i.e., users that are not familiar with the target language still cannot afford to understand the retrieved documents. In such a situation, cross-language image retrieval has attracted researchers' attentions recently and is organized as one of evaluation tasks in Cross-Language Evaluation Forum (CLEF) [6]. In addition to media transformation, language translation is also necessary to unify the language usages in queries and documents in cross-language image retrieval.

Textual and low-level visual features have different semantic levels. Textual feature is highly semantic, while low-level visual feature is less semantic and is relative to human perception. These two types of features are complementary and provide different aspects of information about image. In this paper, we explore the integration of textual and visual information in cross-language image retrieval. An approach that automatically transforms textual queries into visual representations is proposed. The generated visual representation is treated as a visual query to retrieve images. The results using textual and visual queries are combined to generate the final result.

The rest of this paper is organized as follows. Section 2 introduces the proposed model. The integration of textual and visual information is illustrated. Section 3 models the relationships between text and images. How to generate visual representation of textual query is introduced. Section 4 shows the experiment designs. The selection of suitable textual query terms to construct visual queries is the major concern. Besides, three types of experiments, including monolingual image retrieval, cross-language image retrieval and ideal visual queries, are made. Finally, we conclude our work in Section 5.

2   Integrating Textual and Visual Information

Several hybrid approaches that integrate visual and textual information have been proposed. A simple approach is: conducting text- and content-based retrieval separately and merging the retrieval results of the two runs [1, 10, 12]. In contrast to the parallel approach, a pipeline approach employs textual or visual information to perform initial retrieval, and then uses the other features to filter out the irrelevant images [16]. In the above two approaches, users have to issue two types of queries, i.e., textual and visual queries. Sometimes it is not intuitive to find an example image or to specify low-level visual features.

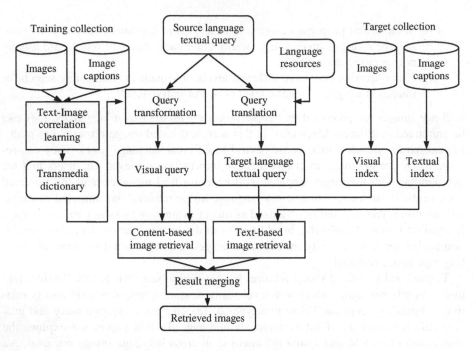

Fig. 1. Flow of cross-language image retrieval

Figure 1 shows the flow of a cross-language image retrieval system. This system automatically transforms textual queries into visual representations. The generated visual representation is treated as a visual query and is used to retrieve images. First, the relationships between text and images are mined from a set of images annotated with text descriptions. A transmedia dictionary which is similar to bilingual dictionary is set up. When a user issues a textual query, the system automatically transforms the textual query into a visual one using the transmedia dictionary. In this way, we have both textual and visual queries.

Given an image collection, two kinds of indices are generated for image retrieval. One is textual index of image descriptions, and the other one is visual index of images. A textual query is used to retrieve image descriptions using the textual index. Comparatively, a visual representation of the textual query retrieves images using the visual index. The retrieval results of textual and generated visual queries are merged together.

The proposed approach can be applied to monolingual and cross-language image retrieval. In cross-language information retrieval, translation ambiguity and target polysemy problems have to be tackled in the translation process. If a word is not translated correctly, we cannot capture the correct meaning of the word in its context. If the translation is polysemous, the undesired documents that contain the translation with other senses could be reported even if the translation is correct. Visual queries could be helpful to reduce these problems.

3   Visual Representation of Text

Given a set of images with text descriptions, we can learn the relationships between images and text. For an image, each word in its description may relate to a portion of this image. If we divide an image into several smaller parts, e.g., blocks or regions, we could link the words to the corresponding parts. This is analogous to word alignment in sentence aligned parallel corpus. If we treat the visual representation of the image as a language, the textual description and visual parts of an image is an aligned sentence. The correlations between the vocabularies of two languages can be learned from the aligned sentences. Given a picture of sunset, for example, we can link textual feature "sunset" to visual feature "red circle".

In automatic annotation task, several approaches have been proposed to model the correlations between text and visual representation, and generate text descriptions from images. Mori, Takahashi and Oka [14] divided images into grids, and then the grids of all images are clustered. Co-occurrence information is used to estimate the probability of each word for each cluster. Duygulu, *et al.* [7] used blobs to represent images. First, images are segmented into regions using a segmentation algorithm. All regions are clustered and each cluster is assigned a unique label (blob token). EM algorithm constructs a probability table that links blob tokens with word tokens. Jeon, Lavrenko, and Manmatha [9] proposed a cross-media relevance model (CMRM) to learn the joint distribution of blobs and words. They further proposed continuous-space relevance model (CRM) that learned the joint probability of words and regions, rather than blobs [11].

This paper considers blobs as a visual representation of images, and adopts Blobworld [3] to segment an image into regions. Blobworld groups pixels in an image into regions which are coherent in low-level properties such as color and texture, and which roughly correspond to objects or part of objects. For each region, a set of features such as color, texture, shape, position and size are extracted. The regions of all images are clustered into 2,000 clusters by the K-means clustering algorithm according the extracted features. Each cluster is assigned a unique number, i.e., blob token, and each image is represented by the blob tokens of clusters that its regions belong to. We treat blobs as a language in which each blob token is a word. In this way, we can use text retrieval system to index and retrieve images using blob language.

Given the textual descriptions and blob tokens of images, we mine the correlation between textual and visual information. Mutual Information (MI) is adopted to measure the strength of correlation between an image blob and a word. Let x be a word and y be an image blob. The Mutual Information of x and y is defined as follows.

$$MI(x, y) = p(x, y) \times \log \frac{p(x, y)}{p(x)p(y)} \qquad (1)$$

Where $p(x)$ is the occurrence probability of word x in text descriptions,

$p(y)$ is the occurrence probability of blob y in image blobs, and

$p(x,y)$ is the probability that x and y occur in the same image.

In Formula 1, the probabilities are estimated by maximum likelihood estimation. After the MIs between words and blobs are computed, we can generate related blobs for a given word w_i. The blobs whose MI values with w_i exceed a threshold are associated to w_i. The generated blobs can be regarded as the visual representation of w_i. In this way, a transmedia (word-blob) dictionary is established.

4   Experiments

4.1   Test Data and Indexing

St. Andrews image collection which was used in ImageCLEF 2004 ad hoc task [6] is adopted to evaluate our system. The image collection consists of 28,133 photographs from St. Andrews University Library's photographic collection, which is one of the largest and most important collections of historic photography in Scotland. The majority of images (82%) in the St. Andrews image collection are in black and white. Sample images are shown in Figure 2. All images are accompanied by a textual description written in English by librarians working at St. Andrews Library. Figure 3 shows an example of image and its caption in the St. Andrews image collection. The captions are semi-structured and consist of several fields including document number, headline, record id, description text, category, and file names of images. The test set contains 25 topics, and each topic has text description and an example image. The English version of the topics has two fields, i.e., title and narrative. The titles of each topic are translated into several languages. Figure 4 shows topic 2 as an example, which is in Chinese.

In the experiments, we adopt title field in topics to retrieve images. Okapi IR system [15] is used to build both the textual and visual indices. For the textual index, the caption text, <HEADLINE> and <CATEGORIES> fields of English captions are used for indexing. All words in these fields are stemmed and stopwords are removed. For visual index, the blob tokens of each image are indexed. The weighting function used is BM25.

4.2   Monolingual Image Retrieval

We evaluate our approach in monolingual image retrieval at first. The correlations between text and images are learned from St. Andrews image collection. The title field of a topic is used as a query to retrieve images. For each textual query, a visual query is generated from the query terms according to the mined relationships. The first issue to be considered is which query terms are adopted to generate the visual query. Intuitively, we can generate visual representation for each query term. However, not all query terms are relative to the visual content of images. Here, we employ part-of-speech (POS) to select suitable query terms to generate visual representations. Brill tagger [2] is used to tag English topics. Different types of POSes are explored to tell which types of query terms are useful. Nouns only (without named entities), nouns with named entities, verbs only, adjectives only, or nouns, verbs, and adjectives together are experimented.

For each selected query term, the top n blobs of MI values with it exceed a threshold t are regarded as its visual representation. The values of parameter n from 10 to 40 and t from 0.1 to 0.4 are experimented. The blobs corresponding to the selected query terms form a visual query. It is used to retrieve images using visual index. The results of textual and generated visual queries are merged into the final result. For each image, the similarity scores of textual and visual retrieval are normalized and linearly combined using weights 0.9 and 0.1 for the textual and visual runs, respectively. The top 1000 images of the highest combined scores are reported.

Fig. 2. An example of image in St. Andrews image collection

```
<DOC>
<DOCNO> stand03_1041/stand03_9914.txt </DOCNO>
<HEADLINE> Azay le Rideau. Bridge. </HEADLINE>
<TEXT>
<RECORD_ID> JEAS-.000032.-.000045 </RECORD_ID>
    Azay le Rideau.
    Round tower with conical roof attached to large three-
    storey building; low bridge spanning still water to right.
    1907 John Edward Aloysius Steggall
    Indre et Loire, France
    JEAS-32-45 pc/jf
<CATEGORIES>
    [towers - round], [towers - conical roofed], [France urban
    views], [France all views]
</CATEGORIES>
<SMALL_IMG>
    stand03_1041/stand03_9914.jpg
</SMALL_IMG>
<LARGE_IMG>
    stand03_1041/stand03_9914_big.jpg
</LARGE_IMG>
</TEXT>
</DOC>
```

Fig. 3. An example of image and description in St. Andrews image collection

```
<top>
<num> Number: 2 </num>
<title> Photos of Rome taken in April 1908 </title>
<narr>
    Any view of Rome including buildings and specific loca-
    tions (e.g. the coliseum) taken in April 1908 is relevant. Pic-
    tures by any photographer are relevant, but taken at any
    other time are not relevant.
</narr>
</top>

<top>
<num> Number: 2 </num>
<title>
    1908年 (nián) 四 (sì) 月 (yuè) 拍 (pāi) 攝 (shè) 的 (de)
    羅 (luó) 馬 (mǎ) 照 (zhào) 片 (piān)
</title>
</top>
```

Fig. 4. An example of a topic in Chinese

The performance of the proposed approach is shown in Figure 5. Mean average precision measures the retrieval performances. The approach of nouns only, higher threshold and more blobs has better performance than that of using verbs and adjectives. The performances of using verbs or adjectives only in different setting of n and t are similar. This is because there are only a few verbs and adjectives in the topic set, e.g., only 4 adjectives in 4 topics and 9 verbs in 8 topics, and the MI values of blobs with verbs and adjectives tend to be low. When using nouns, verbs and adjectives, the performance is slightly worse than using nouns only. The performance is dropped when name entities are added. It is even worse than using all words with stopword removal (ALL-SW).

The best performance is 0.6591 when using nouns only, $n>20$, and $t=0.4$. Comparing to using textual query only, the mean average precision is increased. The performances of textual query and generated visual query are shown in Table 1. The results show that the proposed approach increases retrieval performance. Although the generated visual queries are not so good enough, the integration of them is useful to improve retrieval performance. Several factors may affect the visual query construction. First, the image segmentation has a large effect. Because the majority of images in the St. Andrews image collection are in black and white, that makes image segmentation more difficult. Second, clustering affects the performance of the blobs-based approach. If image regions that are not similar enough are clustered together, the cluster (blob) may have several different meanings. That is analogous to the polysemy problem.

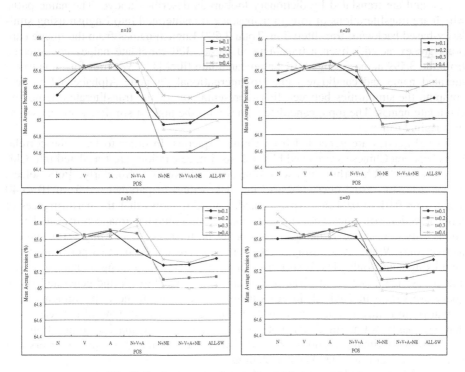

Fig. 5. Performances of monolingual image retrieval

Table 1. Performances of integrating textual and generated visual query in monolingual cases

Query Type	Average Precision
Textual Query	0.6304
Generated Visual Query (14 topics)	0.0036
Textual Query + Generated Visual Query (N, $n=20$, $t=0.4$)	0.6591

4.3 Cross-Language Image Retrieval

In the experiments of cross-language image retrieval, Chinese queries are used as source queries and translated into English to retrieve English captions of images. First, the Chinese queries are segmented by a word recognition system and tagged by a POS tagger. Named entities are identified by Chinese NER tools [4]. For each Chinese query term, we find its translation equivalents using a Chinese-English bilingual dictionary. If a query term has more than one translation, the first two translations with the highest frequency of occurrence in the English image captions are considered as the target language query terms.

For those named entities that are not included in the dictionary, a similarity-based backward transliteration scheme [13] is adopted. First, transformation rules [5] tell out the name and the keyword parts of a named entity. The keyword parts are general nouns, and are translated by dictionary lookup as described above. The name parts, which are transliterations of foreign names, are transliterated into English using similarity-based backward transliteration. Total 3,599 English names from the image captions are extracted. Given a transliterated name, 300 candidate names are selected from the 3,599 names using an IR-based candidate filter [12]. We transform the transliterated name and candidate names to International Phonetic Alphabet (IPA), and compute the similarities between IPA representations of the transliterated name and candidate names. The top 6 candidate names with the highest similarity are chosen as the original names.

Visual queries are generated from Chinese queries. In order to learn the correlations between Chinese words and blob tokens, image captions are translated into Chinese by SYSTRAN (http://www.systransoft.com/) system. Similarly, POS selects query terms for visual query construction. The values of parameter n from 10 to 40 and t from 0.01 to 0.04 are experimented. Figure 6 shows that the performances of term selection strategies are similar to that of monolingual image retrieval. Using nouns only to generate visual query has better performance than using verbs and adjectives only. When n>30, using nouns, verbs and adjectives together performs better than using nouns only. The best performance is 0.4441 when using nouns, verbs and adjectives, n>30, and t=0.02. The performances of textual query and generated visual query are shown in Table 2. In cross-language experiment, the improvement of retrieval performance is not as well as monolingual experiment. One of the reasons is that the quality of training data is not good. We use a famous machine translation system to translate image captions. However, there are still many translation errors that affect the correctness of learned correlations.

The performance of generated visual query is not so good enough. One of the reasons is that we use only a part of query terms to generate visual query, thus some in-

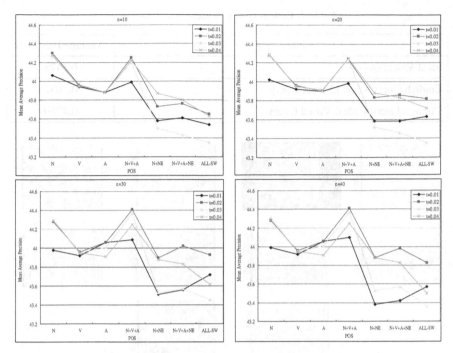

Fig. 6. Performances of cross-language image retrieval

formation is lost. In some topics, the retrieved images are not relevant to the topics, while they are relevant to the query terms that are used to generate visual query. Take Topic 13, i.e., 1939年聖安德魯斯高爾夫球公開賽 (The Open Championship golf tournament, St. Andrews 1939), as an example. "聖" (St), "高爾夫球" (golf) and "公開賽" (Open Championship) are tagged as nouns, thus are selected to generate visual query. In the top 10 images shown in Figure 7, 9 images are about the Open Championship golf tournament, but are not the one held in 1939. It shows that using visual information only is not enough, integrating textual information is needed.

Table 2. Performances of using textual and generated visual query in cross-language cases

Query Type	Average Precision
Textual Query	0.4395
Generated Visual Query (18 topics)	0.0110
Textual Query + Generated Visual Query (N+V+A, n=30, t=0.02)	0.4441

Table 3. Performances of ideal visual queries

Query Type	Average Precision
Ideal Visual Query	0.1478
English Query + Ideal Visual Query	0.7082
Chinese Query + Ideal Visual Query	0.4780

Fig. 7. Top 10 image of Topic 13 in generated visual query run

4.4 Ideal Visual Query

Since the performance of generated visual query depends on image segmentations, blob clustering, and so on, we create an ideal query from relevant images to test if a visual query can help increase the performance of image retrieval. A useful visual query will exist if the relevant images for a query share some image features. The common image features can help us retrieve the relevant images well. We use x^2 score to select blobs from relevant images. For each query we generate 10 blobs whose x^2 scores are larger than 7.88 ($v=1$, $p=0.005$). The selected blobs form a visual query to retrieve images. The retrieval result is combined with that of a textual query. The performances are shown in Table 3. The results show that a good visual query can improve performance of image retrieval.

5   Conclusion

This paper explores the uses of both textual information and visual features to cross-language image retrieval. We conduct English monolingual and Chinese-English cross-language retrieval experiments to evaluate our approach. Experimental results show that combining retrieval results of textual and generated visual query improves retrieval performance. The generated visual query has little impact in the cross-lingual experiments. One of the reasons is that using machine translation system to translate

English captions into Chinese introduces many translation errors that affect the correctness of learned correlations. We also construct an ideal visual query from relevant images. Using the ideal visual query increases retrieval performance about 12.3% and 8.8% in monolingual and cross-language image retrieval, respectively. The results show that a good visual query can improve performance of image retrieval.

We use POS to select query terms for constructing a visual query. Experiments show that nouns are appropriate to generate visual queries, while using named entities is helpless. Nouns usually indicate the objects in images, which is the kernel of an image, thus it is reasonable to link nouns to the image regions which correspond to objects. Named entities, such as person name, location name and date, do not have strong relations with image regions, and cannot be represented well by visual representations. In this way, the visual representations of named entities introduce noise and decrease the retrieval performance. Similarly, verbs that indicate actions are hardly represented by visual features. Thus, verbs are not feasible for visual query generation. Some adjectives that are relative to visual features could be used to generate visual queries. For example, red is relative to color, a low-level visual feature. In the experiments, we use syntactic information to select query terms. Semantic information which may provide more clues for term selection is not used. We will investigate query term selection on semantic level in the future.

Acknowledgement. Research of this paper was partially supported by National Science Council, Taiwan, under the contracts NSC93-2752-E-001-001-PAE and NSC94-2752-E-001-001-PAE.

References

1. Besançon, R., Hède, P., Moellic, P.A., and Fluhr, C.: LIC2M Experiments at ImageCLEF 2004. In: Working Notes for the CLEF 2004 Workshop. (2004) 555-560.
2. Brill, E.: Transformation-Based Error-Driven Learning and Natural Language Processing: A Case Study in Part of Speech Tagging. Computational Linguistics, 21(4). (1995) 543-565.
3. Carson, C., Belongie, S., Greenspan, H., and Malik, J.: Blobworld: Image Segmentation Using Expectation-Maximization and Its Application to Image Querying. IEEE Transactions on Pattern Analysis and Machine Intelligence, 24(8). (2002) 1026-1038.
4. Chen, H.H., Ding, Y.W., Tsai, S.C., and Bian, G.W.: Description of the NTU System Used for MET2. In: Proceedings of Seventh Message Understanding Conference. (1998).
5. Chen, H.H., Yang, C. and Lin, Y.: Learning Formulation and Transformation Rules for Multilingual Named Entities. In: Proceedings of ACL 2003 Workshop on Multilingual and Mixed-language Named Entity Recognition: Combining Statistical and Symbolic Models. Association for Computational Linguistics (2003) 1-8.
6. Clough, P., Sanderson, M. and Müller, H.: The CLEF Cross Language Image Retrieval Track (ImageCLEF) 2004. In: Working Notes for the CLEF 2004 Workshop. (2004) 459-473.
7. Duygulu, P., Barnard, K., Freitas, N., and Forsyth, D.: Object Recognition as Machine Translation: Learning a Lexicon for a Fixed Image Vocabulary. In: Proceedings of Seventh European Conference on Computer Vision, Vol. 4. (2002) 97-112.
8. Goodrum, A.A.: Image Information Retrieval: An Overview of Current Research. Information Science, 3(2). (2000) 63-66.

466   W.-C. Lin, Y.-C. Chang, and H.-H. Chen

9. Jeon, J., Lavrenko, V. and Manmatha, R.: Automatic Image Annotation and Retrieval using Cross-Media Relevance Models. In: Proceedings of the 26th Annual International ACM SIGIR Conference on Research and Development in Information Retrieval (SIGIR 2003). ACM Press (2003) 119-126.
10. Jones, G.J.F., Groves, D., Khasin, A., Lam-Adesina, A., Mellebeek, B., and Way, A.: Dublin City University at CLEF 2004: Experiments with the ImageCLEF St Andrew's Collection. In: Working Notes for the CLEF 2004 Workshop. (2004) 511-515.
11. Lavrenko, V., Manmatha, R. and Jeon, J.: A Model for Learning the Semantics of Pictures. In: Proceedings of the Seventeenth Annual Conference on Neural Information Processing Systems. (2003).
12. Lin, W.C., Chang, Y.C. and Chen, H.H.: From Text to Image: Generating Visual Query for Image Retrieval. In: Working Notes for the CLEF 2004 Workshop. (2004) 517-524.
13. Lin, W.H. and Chen, H.H.: Backward Machine Transliteration by Learning Phonetic Similarity. In: Proceedings of Sixth Conference on Natural Language Learning. Association for Computational Linguistics (2002) 139-145.
14. Mori, Y., Takahashi, H. and Oka, R.: Image-to-Word Transformation Based on Dividing and Vector Quantizing Images with Words. In: Proceedings of the First International Workshop on Multimedia Intelligent Storage and Retrieval Management. (1999).
15. Robertson, S.E., Walker, S. and Beaulieu, M.: Okapi at TREC-7: Automatic Ad Hoc, Filtering, VLC and Interactive. In: Proceedings of the Seventh Text Retrieval Conference (TREC-7). National Institute of Standards and Technology (1998) 253-264.
16. The Lowlands Team: Lazy Users and Automatic Video Retrieval Tools in (the) Lowlands. In: Proceedings of the Tenth Text Retrieval Conference (TREC 2001). National Institute of Standards and Technology (2002) 159-168.

Practical Application of Associative Classifier for Document Classification

Yongwook Yoon and Gary Geunbae Lee

Department of Computer Science & Engineering,
Pohang University of Science & Technology,
Pohang 790-784, South Korea
{ywyoon, gblee}@postech.ac.kr

Abstract. In practical text classification tasks, the ability to interpret the classification result is as important as the ability to classify exactly. The associative classifier has favorable characteristics, rapid training, good classification accuracy, and excellent interpretation. However, the associative classifier has some obstacles to overcome when it is applied in the area of text classification. First of all, the training process of the associative classifier produces a huge amount of classification rules, which makes the prediction for a new document ineffective. We resolve this by pruning the rules according to their contribution to correct classifications. In addition, since the target text collection generally has a high dimension, the training process might take a very long time. We propose mutual information between the word and class variables as a feature selection measure to reduce the space dimension. Experimental classification results using the 20-newsgroups dataset show many benefits of the associative classification in both training and predicting.

1 Introduction

An associative classifier is a classifier using classification rules that are produced through a frequent pattern mining process from a training data collection. This process is the same one used in traditional data mining for large log data of transactional database. Utilizing associative classifiers in the area of classification task [1,4,12] has a relatively short history compared to other classifiers such as Naïve Bayes, k-NN, or Support Vector Machine (SVM). It seems more difficult to find a study in which an associative classifier is applied in the text classification task.

When performing a text classification task in a real world situation, the ability to provide abundant interpretation on the classification result is often as important as the ability to classify new documents exactly. Classification by a concrete form of rules (*"Features→ Class"*) has many benefits including this easy interpretability. The associative classifier is one of the rule-based classifiers. In contrast, some classifiers such as SVM or Neural Network cannot provide this easy interpretation for the classification result, though they may achieve excellent classification accuracy.

G.G. Lee et al. (Eds.): AIRS 2005, LNCS 3689, pp. 467–478, 2005.

We can acquire several additional advantages from using rule-based classifier. One is that since the rules can be expressed in a very intuitive form, humans can easily understand them and can even edit them directly after the rules are produced by some inductive learning process. A human expert could delete the weak rules from the original rule set and add new rules that they carefully handcrafted. This can improve the classification accuracy remarkably with a little bit of added effort. Another is that the rules can be updated incrementally by other machine learning processes later.

Another benefit of the associative classifier is that it can exploit the combined information of more than one feature as well as a single feature, while SVM or k-NN classifiers consider only the effects of each single feature. This means that in document classification tasks it is possible to use phrase occurrence information as well as word occurrence information.

To apply an associative classifier to the text classification problem in the real world, however, we need to remove several obstacles encountered during the training and testing phase. One of those is a high dimensional feature space. Dataset in the area of text classification, in many cases, has a very large number of features that are distinct lexical words. For example, the 20-newsgroups test collection has more than one hundred thousand lexical word features. Most documents of the 20-newsgroups have more than one hundred words; they are sparsely distributed in their word feature space. In associative classification, however, we consider all subsets of those words. Therefore, the effective number of features grows exponentially, and we cannot take into account all of them due to computational intractability.

To overcome this problem we adopt some dimensionality reduction techniques at the same time maintaining necessary performance in classification. Many well-known methods of dimensionality reduction exist. We used the mutual information measure of the information theory. From the training dataset we calculated the mutual information between the word and the class variables. And we selected words that have high mutual information, and used only those in classifying and neglected the others.

Another obstacle in associative text classification is the large number of classification rules that are produced in the training phase. Since using all of them is both inefficient computationally and ineffective in classifying, we should select a part of those rules that have high quality. This process has been called *Pruning* in associative classification. Liu et al. [7] proposed pruning by database coverage, which is a kind of validation process using the training set for the purpose of choosing the best classification rules among others. Li et al. [6] refined the concept of the database coverage.

In addition, they proposed two other pruning methods. One is to prune low-ranked rules in the confidence and the support of the rules. The other is to prune the rules in which the correlation between the pattern and the class variables is weak. In this paper, we adopted the pruning methods of Li et al.'s and modified them to work for text classification.

Another issue of associative classification is the prediction of a new document using classification rules. With a large number of rules the prediction result of a test document often shows a split decision between different classes. A method is needed to select one correct class among many in an efficient and effective way. It is not a simple problem because if we extract a relatively small portion of rules to avoid having too many contradicting rules for a document, we might lose latent candidate classes that maybe the correct answer. To handle this problem, Li et al. [6] used the weighted chi-square method. We try to resolve this problem by simple voting on the different answer classes.

In Sect. 2 we introduce the general aspects of associative classification. In Sect. 3 we explain the overall architecture of our text classification system using association rules and addressing the issues such as rule pruning and prediction from multiple rules. Experimental results and analysis of text classification using a large dataset are presented in Sect. 4, and we conclude our works in Sect. 5.

2 Associative Classification

2.1 Association Rule Mining

Associative rules originate from the market basket analysis in which we seek some pattern of purchasing. The term *Mining* indicates that we should apply much effort to searching the log database to acquire valuable information.

An association rule is a kind of co-occurrence information on items. Consider a transaction log database of a large modern retailing market. We want to extract some pattern of co-purchasing of product items from this database. Let a set of product items be $I = \{I_1, ..., I_n\}$ and a transaction $t \subseteq I$. Then the set of transaction $T = \{t_1, ..., t_N\} \subseteq 2^I$. An association rule is composed of two item sets called an *antecedent* and a *consequent*. The consequent often is restricted to containing a single item [11]. The rules typically are displayed with an arrow leading from the antecedent to the consequent:

$$\{I_{i_1}, ..., I_{i_k}\} \rightarrow \{I_c\}, \tag{1}$$

for example, {plums, lettuce, tomatoes}→{celery}. For an item set A and B, *Support(A)* is defined as the number of t including A divided by N, and *Confidence(A→B)* as *Support(A→B) / Support(A)*. A user provides thresholds on the support and confidence of a rule denoted as *minsup* and *minconf* respectively.

Definition 1 (Association Rule). *Given an item set X and an item Y, let s be Support(X→Y) and c be Confidence(X→Y). Then, the expression $X \rightarrow Y/(s, c)$ is an association rule, if $s \geq minsup$ and $c \geq minconf$.*

The two constraints about the support and the confidence of a rule imply that we search some level of "frequent" patterns. In the training phase of associative classification, the main task is to extract association rules, in other words, *frequent pattern mining*. Unfortunately, as the number of items grows linearly, the number of the antecedents in the left-hand side of (1) grows exponentially. Though we can reduce the size of the subset of patterns by the two parameters, *minsup* and *minconf*, the search often becomes computationally intractable when we use naïve methods. Many efficient algorithms were proposed to search frequent patterns more efficiently [1,4]. We modified the algorithm by Han et al. [4], the *Frequent Pattern tree growth*, and applied it when we mined frequent patterns.

2.2   Associative Classifier

Consider the association rule in the view of a classification rule. Let $A = \{A_1, ..., A_n\}$ be a set of attribute domains, and a data object $obj = (a_1, ..., a_n)$ be a sequence of attribute values, i.e. $a_j \in A_j$, $1 \leq j \leq n$. Given a pattern $P = a_{i_1}...a_{i_k}$ where $a_{i_j} \in A_{i_j}$ for $1 \leq j \leq k$ and $i_j \neq i_{j'}$ for $j \neq j'$, a data object *obj* is said to *match* pattern P if and only if, for $1 \leq j \leq k$, *obj* has value a_{i_j} in attributeA_{i_j}.

Definition 2 (Associative Classifier). *Let $C = \{c_1, ..., c_m\}$ be a set of class labels. An associative classifier is the mapping R from the set of attribute values to a set of class labels*

$$R : (A_1, A_2, ..., A_n) \rightarrow C \ . \tag{2}$$

According to (2), given a test data $obj = (a_1, ..., a_n)$, the associative classifier returns class label $c \in C$.

Let a pattern variable be P and a class variable c. If we rewrite the rule in the form of $R : P \rightarrow c$ and have a training set $T = \{(P_i, c_i)\}$, then the learning process is to induce the rule set R for which the element has the *Suppot(P→c)*$\geq$ *minsup* and *Confidence(P→c)*$\geq$ *minconf*. The procedure of associative classification rule mining is not much different from that of general association rule mining. One difference is that in associative classification rule mining, the information of the distribution of word patterns matching each class is additionally maintained.

Now that we have a classification system, it requires a decision on which class to assign a new test document. First, we search for the rules of which the pattern matches the document. Next, from these rules, we perform a prediction based on some predefined decision criterion. The details are explained in Sect. 3.

3   Text Classification with Associative Classifier

3.1   Overall Architecture

The overall system architecture for associative classification is shown in Fig. 1. The left-hand side of the figure denotes the training process and the right-hand side the testing process.

First, raw data for training is processed to fit to an appropriate form for training. This is called *Pre-processing*. We index every word of training documents and test it for the quality of its contribution to classifying exactly the

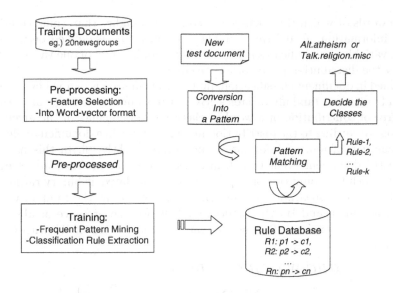

Fig. 1. Associative Classification – Training and Testing

given training documents. Each document is converted into a word-vector format and normalized to its length.

From the pre-processed database, we mine frequent patterns, i.e. classification rules. Because the initial number of rules is very large, we select a part of them and drop the remaining rules; this process is called *Pruning*. Finally, we construct a classification-rule database with these selected rules.

When a new document comes in to be classified, we convert it into a pattern of words and search the database for matching rules. With the rules matched, we decide which class the test document is assigned to.

3.2 Feature Selection

We cannot use all of the words that appear in the training documents due to the computational complexity. Our goal is to minimize the number of features and at the same time not to lose classification performance compared with that we may acquire when we classify without any reduction of original word features.

There are many ways to acquire a less number of good features from the original feature set. In the area of document classification, two types of dimensionality reduction exist [10]. One is *term selection* where we select a subset of words from the original word set. The other is *term extraction* where we derive new features combining several original features; the extracted set of features has a lower dimension than the original one. Considering the characteristic of pattern mining, we decided to adopt the term selection method.

Term selection-based methods utilize as selection criteria *Document Frequency* or *Mutual Information* function. Document frequency is the number of the documents in which the word of our concern appears. In general, we select the words of which the document frequency is higher than some threshold. Mutual information, an Information-Theoretic measure, is defined between two random variables and indicates a degree of information gain of one variable when we know the distribution of the other variable.

Applied in document classification, mutual information is defined between the class and the word random variables. By mutual information we can estimate the degree of contribution of a word in classifying documents of the given data collection. According to the distribution model of words in a document collection, the calculation of mutual information may differ slightly [9]. In this paper we adopted the document event model, in other words, the *multivariate Bernoulli model* in which the count of word appearance is calculated as binary rather than the real count of appearance in a document. Denote C as the random variable for the class label, and W_t the random variable for the presence or absence of a word w_t in a document. The average mutual information of W_t with C [3] is defined as:

$$MI(C; W_t) = H(C) - H(C|Wt)$$
$$= \sum_{c \in C} \sum_{f_t \in \{0,1\}} P(c, f_t) \log \frac{P(c, f_t)}{P(c)P(f_t)} \qquad (3)$$

where $H(C|W_t)$ is the entropy of C given W_t, and $f_t \in \{0,1\}$ is an indicator variable denoting the absence or presence of the word w_t. And $P(c, f_t)$ is the joint probability , which is calculated as the number of word occurrences of word w_t that also appear in documents with class label c, divided by the total number of word occurrences.

We selected M words with the highest average mutual information with the class variable among total N words. In general, we select the parameter $M << N$.

Finally, we convert original training documents into the documents of word-vector format that has M dimension. Moreover, since the length of each document has much variation, we should normalize the length of document in order to reduce some biases between the assigned classes as much as possible. In this paper, we introduced a parameter L indicating the maximum length of a document (by the length we mean the count of distinct words in it). We construct a transaction record with at most L words which are sorted in the order of descending average mutual information.

3.3   Pruning Rules

It is not always helpful to have a large number of rules when we classify a new test document. There is a greater chance of having more than one rule contradicting each other in the answer class. In addition, the rules may over fit the training document set. We want to have a small number of the most powerful rules. In this pruning process, duplicate rules are eliminated and rules that might produce wrong classification results are removed. We perform two types of rule pruning; the first is pruning by rule ranking and the other is by the Chi-square statistic.

Before we prune rules by rank, we must first assign a rank to each rule. The rule-ranking criterion is as follows: (i) The rule with a higher confidence has a higher rank than others. (ii) If the confidences are the same between two rules, then the one with a higher support has a higher rank than the other. (iii) If the supports of the two are the same as well, then the one with the fewer number of words in the left-hand side of the rule has a higher rank. In other words, we prefer "short" rules rather than long ones if other conditions are equal. The short length of the rules means general rules, while long rules are prone to over fit. Therefore, we can reduce the test errors by adopting more general rules.

Table 1. Classification Rules and the Ranks

Rule-id	Rule	Sup	Conf	Rank
1	$abc \rightarrow A$	20	95%	2
2	$abcf \rightarrow C$	16	81%	3
3	$rq \rightarrow B$	67	61%	8
4	$bdf \rightarrow A$	120	78%	6
5	$bdef \rightarrow C$	105	71%	7
6	$bcdf \rightarrow A$	58	80%	4
7	$cdefg \rightarrow D$	7	80%	5
8	$g \rightarrow D$	3	100%	1

Assume that the eight rules in Table 1 were found as a result of the frequent pattern mining process. The minsup and minconf of the rules were taken as 3 and 60% respectively. Rule-8 has the highest rank since its confidence is the best. Though rule-6 and rule-7 have the same confidence, rule-6 is ranked higher due to the higher support.

By the pruning criterion of the rule ranking, rule-5 will be pruned because rule-5 is more specific than rule-4 but has a lower confidence. However, rule-2 will not be pruned off because it has a higher confidence than the more general rule-1. We can see that the third ranking criterion reflects the generality.

Another type of pruning utilizes the Chi-square statistic, which provides correlation information between two random variables. We want to evaluate the quality of a rule by calculating the Chi-square statistic of the pattern and the class label that are the left-hand and the right-hand side of the rule respectively. We can easily calculate the Chi-square statistic of each rule during frequent pattern mining. We denote the word pattern of a rule as P and the class label as c. Then, we present the number of the documents of the four possible cases in a box in Table 2.

A denotes the number of all the documents. B denotes the number of the documents with the class label c. D denotes the number of the documents matching pattern P, and E denotes the number labeled with class c and matching pattern P. The values of all the other cells can be calculated using these four values. In addition, we need the expected values of the numbers of documents in the four cells located at the center of the table. We can easily calculate these values as

Table 2. Calculation of the Chi-square statistic of a rule

	Class C	$\sim$ Class C	Total
match P	E	D−E	D
$\sim$ match P	B−E	A−B−D+E	A−D
Total	B	A−B	A

well using the ratios of the values of the marginal column and row. Finally, the statistic is calculated as follows:

$$\chi^2 = \sum_{i \in four\ Center\ Cells} \frac{(observed_i - expected_i)^2}{expected_i} \tag{4}$$

where i denotes the index of four center cells in the table.

Now, we can perform a hypothesis test whether the rule is important by the Chi-square statistic. According to some significance level, we decide whether we select the rule or not.

3.4   Prediction with Multiple Classification Rules

After the training process is finished, we obtain a final set of classification rules. In general, when we predict the class of a test document, we seek the rules matching the document and the system produces more than one rule to classify. Sometimes, the number of the matching rules is large, which may lead to a difficult situation. If all of the rules have identical class labels, the problem is simple; we assign that class to the document. But if we have many different classes from the extracted rules, we need to decide on one rule as the correct one.

For example, assume that from Table 1 we acquired rule-2, rule-4, and rule-6 as matched rules of a test document. We have a split decision between class A and class C. According to the rule ranking criteria, we would select C as an answer class. However, inspecting more deeply, though the confidence of rule-2 is slightly better than the other two, the support values of the two are much higher than that of rule-2. Therefore, we know that we cannot always reliably select rule-2 as a correct answer.

Therefore, it is dangerous that we estimate a class label only by the rule ranking system. We adopt the majority-voting method in deciding on a correct class from multiple classification rules for a test document. Assume that we have K rules which are matched to a test document and of the form of $R_k : P_i \rightarrow c_j$ for $1 \leq k \leq K$ where c_j is an element of the set of the class labels of the k-th rule, $C_k = \{c_{k_1}, ..., c_{k_n}\}$, $k_n \leq K$. And let $|c_j|$ be the number of R_k's whose class label is c_j (also note that $\sum_{j=k_1}^{k_n} |c_j| = K$). Then, with the majority voting we select the class label $\hat{c}$ such that:

$$\hat{c} = \arg\max_{c_j \in C_k} |c_j| \tag{5}$$

4   Experiments and Analysis

We performed some experiments of associative classification using the 20 Newsgroups document collection [5]. This collection is slightly multi-labeled; 541 documents of the total 19,997 documents are posted to more than one newsgroup.

We pre-processed the raw texts into word vectors. For this purpose, we used
the BOW toolkit [8]. We removed general stop words, but did no stemming.
During the training process, we included only the body part and the *Subject*
line of the articles because other parts may contain the words that may indicate
the answer class directly. We reduced the dimension of word feature space of

Table 3. Words in the order of highest Mutual Information

Avg. Mu-Info	Word	Avg. Mu-Info	Word
0.10436	windows	0.07930	clipper
0.09510	god	0.07536	government
0.08341	christian	0.07086	team
0.08288	sale	0.07060	writes
0.08018	dod	0.06838	game

Table 4. Classification Accuracy of 20 Newsgroups

Class Label	# Rules	Accuracy (%)	Potential Top-3 Acc.
alt.atheism	8,455	76.0	91.2
comp.graphics	3,663	49.6	67.2
comp.os.ms-windows.misc	12,895	81.0	89.1
comp.sys.ibm.pc.hardware	11,629	60.4	80.4
comp.sys.mac.hardware	9,026	80.0	86.4
comp.window.x	6,746	72.7	85.5
misc.forsale	9,817	78.0	85.2
rec.autos	6,276	92.0	85.5
rec.motorcycles	6,858	81.6	95.2
rec.sport.baseball	12,222	96.0	89.2
rec.sport.hockey	26,218	95.6	97.2
sci.crypt	28,596	46.8	97.6
sci.electronics	3,148	75.6	67.6
sci.med	5,015	88.8	80.8
sci.space	10,155	86.6	92.4
soc.religion.misc	18,900	88.4	93.1
talk.politics.guns	14,769	91.2	98.0
talk.politics.mideast	25,870	58.8	92.8
talk.politics.misc	8,613	53.2	87.2
talk.religion.misc	5,383	76.5	87.2
Total	234,254	**76.5**	**87.4**

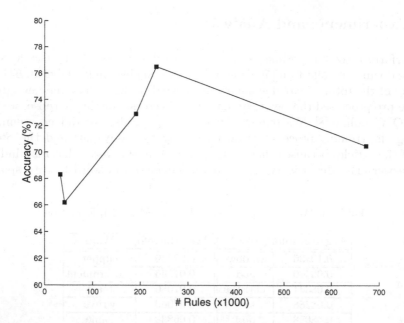

Fig. 2. Relation between # of Rules and Accuracy

the original 20 Newsgroups to three thousands, which was originally over one hundred thousand. In Table 3, we list the words with the highest average mutual information. We normalized the length of the training documents so that they cannot contain over a certain number of words.

We executed our code that implemented the associative classification system on a Linux machine with a 2.2 GHz CPU and 2 GBytes of memory. The best classification results are shown in Table 4.

The overall performance of the system is a little bit lower than that of the current state-of-the-art research [2,13]. However, some classes show equal to or higher accuracy than those of the state-of-the-art systems. At the last column of Table 4, we show the potential accuracy that we acquired by considering the second and the third majority classes as answers as well as the first one. This fact shows that there is a big room for some improvement in the future. In addition, since the rules are expressed in the intuitive form of word strings (refer to (2)), we can manually edit the rules and improve the classification accuracy with little effort. For example, we may add the words listed in Table 3 that could best represent the target class. This is important in a practical application of the classifier since the real performance can be varied with the characteristic of the domain and the test data.

Notice that the training time is very short; it never took more than 10 minutes. This is remarkable compared to the case of SVM or even Naïve-Bayesian classifiers. Let the maximum length of a document be L, the size of the selected word features M, and the number of the whole words in the training collection N. In general, we take these parameters as $L << M << N$. The time complex-

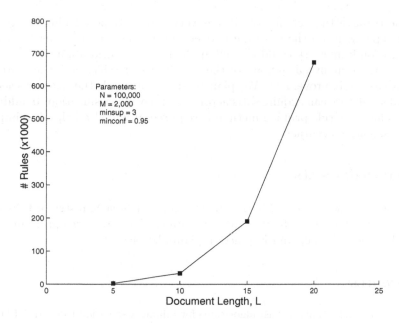

Fig. 3. Relation between Document Length and # of Rules

ity in the training using the whole words is $O(2^N)$. But our training time in this paper is $O(2^L)$, which becomes much shorter due to the reduced dimension. In the cases of SVM, the complexity is $O(N^2)$.

Figure 2 shows the relation between the number of classification rules and the overall accuracy. The more rules we have the higher accuracy we can achieve. However, as the number of rules increase, the classification time is increased as well. In addition, an effect of overfitting appears.

The increase in the number of rules, however, elongates the training time of the classifier as well as slows the prediction process due to the longer rule matching time. If the document length L gets larger, we have more rules to classify with. Figure 3 represents the number of rules in relation to the document length L.

We can see from these relations that the rule pruning is very important in associative classification. We should improve the classification performance while avoiding the increase in the number of features and hence the increase in the computational complexity.

5   Conclusion

Associative classification is a new method in the area of document classification. The expression of the rule is easy and human-readable. Therefore, it presents an excellent interpretation on the classification result as well as considerable effectiveness. In addition, the construction of the classification framework is simple, and the training time of the classifier is very short. By performing the classification experiment on the large data collection, we showed that this associative classification framework could be well applied to real world applications.

With these many advantages of the associative classification, there are still some areas for improvement. We plan to study in depth the feature selection method so that we can acquire satisfactory accuracy in classification. In addition, a more elaborate rule-pruning method is required. It will also helpful to improve the classification accuracy.

Acknowledgments

This research was supported by BK21 program of Korea Ministry of Education and the grant No. R01-2003-000-10181-0 from the basic research program of the KOSEF (Korea Science and Engineering Foundation).

References

1. Agrawal, R., Srikant, R. Fast algorithms for mining association rules. In VLDB'94, pp. 487-499, Santiago, Chile, Sept. 1994.
2. Bekkerman, R., El-Yaniv, R., Tishby, N., Winter, Y. On Feature Distributional Clustering for Text Categoriztion. *Proceedings of SIGIR 2001,* , pp.146-153, 2001.
3. Cover, T., Thomas, J. Elements of Information Theory. John Wiley, 1991.
4. Han, J., Pei, J., Yin, Y. Mining frequent patterns without candidate generation. In *SIGMOD'00*, pp. 1-12, Dallas, TX, May 2000.
5. Lang, K. NEWSWEEDER: learning to filter netnews. *Proceedings of ICML-95, 12th International Conference on Machine Learning* (pp.331–339), 1995.
6. Li, W., Pei, J., Han, J. CMAR: Accurate and Efficient Classification Based on Multiple Class-Association Rules. In *ICDM'01*, pp. 369-376, San Jose, CA, Nov., 2001.
7. Liu, B., Hsu, W., Ma, Y. Integrating classification and association rule mining. In KDD'98, pp. 80-86, New York, NY, Aug. 1998.
8. McCallum, A. "Bow: A toolkit for statistical language modeling, text retrieval, classification and clustering." http://www.cs.cmu.edu/~mccallum/bow. 1996.
9. McCallum, A. and Nigam, K. A comparison of event models for nave Bayes text classification. AAAI-98 Workshop on Learning for Text Categorization. AAAI Press, 1998.
10. Sebstiani, F. Machine Learning in Automated Text Categorization. *ACM Computing Surverys*, 34(1):1-47, 2002.
11. Webb, G. Association Rules. In: Ye, N.(ed.) The Handbook of Data Mining, Lawrence Erlbaum Associates, Inc. 2004
12. Yin, X., Han, J. CPAR: Classification based on Predictive Association Rules. In *SDM'03*, San Francisco, CA, May 2003.
13. Yoon, Y., Lee, C., Lee, G. Systematic Construction of Hierarchical Classifier in SVM-Based Text Categorization. In *IJCNLP 2004*: pp616-625, 2004.

A Method for Query Expansion Using a Hierarchy of Clusters[1]

Masaki Aono and Hironori Doi

Toyohashi University of Technology,
1-1 Hibarigaoka, Tempaku-cho, Toyohashi, Aichi-ken 441-8580, Japan
aono@ics.tut.ac.jp, doi@kde.ics.tut.ac.jp

Abstract. We will present a new algorithm for improving the retrieval performance using query expansion, based on a hierarchy of clusters. In order to create
this hierarchical data structure, a clustering algorithm is executed multiple times
with different initial conditions. With the aid of this hierarchical data structure,
we have achieved significant improvement in retrieval performance over previously known methods in terms of both recall and precision. In our experiments
with Japanese patent data, we have employed a co-clustering algorithm as a
clustering method.

1 Introduction

It has been pointed out that conceptual search technologies using vector space models,
unlike string-matching-type text retrieval, are quite effective for information retrieval
on patent and paper archive datasets. This is in part because there is a tendency that
patent and paper archive datasets have a structural property that each sentence is
longer and includes many keywords in a document. In vector space models, input
sentences are tokenized into a set of words ("bag-of-words"), followed by similarity
computation typically with cosine similarity measure.

Unlike Web document retrieval, "recall" is more important than "precision" in information retrieval on patent and paper archive data. Besides, the number of synonyms and the number of different ways of expressing the same entity (polysemy) are
much larger than those of a typical Web page.

A standard tool which has been often used in conceptual search using vector space
models is dimensionality reduction such as LSI (Latent Semantic Indexing) [4] and
PCA (Principal Component Analysis) [8], both of which are based on the theory of
linear algebra. It has been known that these technologies are useful for reducing the
dimension of words, and have sound feature that synonyms get closer in lower dimensional space if we wisely choose k, the number of dimension to reduce. However, the
selection of the most appropriate dimension k has been a controversial problem.

Assistance of information retrieval with clustering has been reported by many researchers since late 1990's. Examples on information retrieval using clustering include Cutting [3], Eguchi [7], and Chang [1].

---

[1] This research was partially supported by the Ministry of Education, Science, Sports and Culture, Grant-in-Aid for Scientific Research (C), 16500057, 2004, and by Telecommunication
Advancement Foundation (TAF), 2004.

G.G. Lee et al. (Eds.): AIRS 2005, LNCS 3689, pp. 479–484, 2005.

In this paper, we will describe a method for enhancing retrieval performance using query expansion with a novel data structure, which we call "cluster granularity hierarchy". This is a hierarchical data structure, where a hierarchy consists of a granularity defined by the number of clusters, and of links between two cluster nodes, where links are generated when the similarity between the two clusters in different granularity levels are higher than a predefined threshold.

In our experiment, we have used Japanese patent data, and the granularity of clusters has been set to the power of two (i.e.16, 32, 64, 128, 256, 512, ⋯). We adopted co-clustering as our clustering algorithm since it takes advantages of the co-occurrence of words and documents. We also conducted comparative experiments of our method with naïve vector space model and dimensionality reduction techniques such as LSI.

2   Clustering to Support Information Retrieval

Previous work using clustering to improve information retrieval has primarily limited to a single clustering (i.e. document clustering). We have observed that the co-occurrence of documents and words are higher in patent and paper archive dataset unlike ordinary Web documents. Co-clustering is a technology proposed by Dhillon et al [5,6], which generates both document and word clusters simultaneously. In co-clustering, we seek document and word clusters that minimize a Kullback Leibler distance (See [2] for more details).

Generally, clustering is expected to provide a useful piece of information for given data set. However, regardless of minute differences among a variety of clustering methods, they tend to suffer from the following problems:

(1) If the number of clusters to be generated is too large or too small, the resulting clusters may contain useless information or noise.
(2) The resulting cluster quality might be heavily affected by the choice of the initial seed of random variables.
(3) The naïve application of cluster information without removing noise may aggravate the performance of relevance feedback of information retrieval.

3   Cluster Hierarchy Generation

Salient features of co-clustering, including the ability of keeping locality of co-occurrence between documents and words, are expected to be effective for patent and paper archive dataset. For instance, every patent data has one or more IPCs (International Patent Classification codes) and technical terms specific to IPC subclasses. An example is an IPC subclass "D05B", where technical terms such as "sewing", "perforation", "needle work", and "sewing machine" are frequently used.

3.1   Our Solutions to Clustering Problems

To mitigate problem (1), we have run the clustering algorithm multiple times by changing the number of clusters to be generated by, say, the power of two (e.g., 16, 32, 64, 128, $\cdots$). This makes a variety of clusters inherently of different size fit into a particular granularity level of clusters appropriately. In addition, we have put links between clusters of different granularity if arbitrary two clusters found in different granularity level have their similarity larger than a threshold. This way, we have constructed a hierarchy of clusters which we call "cluster granularity hierarchy".

To cope with problem (2), we have run the clustering algorithm multiple times by changing the initial conditions, followed by applying a "cluster averaging algorithm" described later.

To alleviate problem (3), apparent noise (outlier) documents in each cluster are disposed. This smoothing algorithm is a part of cluster averaging algorithm. During query expansion, given an input query, "cluster granularity hierarchy" data structure (as depicted in Figure 1) is traversed from coarser level to finer level in sequel. Once there is a cluster whose similarity with the given query is higher than a threshold, we apply query expansion by considering the cluster average vector.

3.2 Cluster Averaging and Hierarchy Generation Algorithm

We have developed a method for query expansion based on the observation discussed in the previous section. The basic principle of our approach is to execute clustering multiple times with different initial conditions. Specifically, we first perform a clustering algorithm by changing granularity levels as $M_1, M_2, ..., M_k$. At each level, clustering is to be executed R times. In total, we run clustering Rk times. Our proposed algorithm consists of two parts; Part 1 is an averaging algorithm, given multiple granularity cluster levels. Part 2 is a cluster hierarchy construction algorithm.

● **Cluster Averaging Algorithm with Multiple Granularity Levels (Part 1)**

[step1] *Perform clustering with granularity level M ($M_1, ..., M_k$) R times by changing the initial seed of random variables. Denote the obtained document cluster by $\mathbb{D}^r = \{\mathbf{D}_1^r, \mathbf{D}_2^r, ..., \mathbf{D}_M^r\}$ ($r = 1, ..., R$).*

[step2] *Initialize a vector $\mathbb{H} = \{\mathbf{H}_1, \mathbf{H}_2, ..., \mathbf{H}_M\}$ (which we call "document cluster vector") by $\mathbb{D}^1$.*

[step3] *Apply cluster smoothing algorithm.*

In [step3], we perform "averaging" two similar vectors by taking their sum, followed by normalization. Applying this algorithm makes the resulting cluster less dependent upon the initial seed number of random variables and the granularity levels, we then construct a cluster hierarchy by applying **Cluster Hierarchy Generation Algorithm** as shown below.

● **Cluster Hierarchy Generation Algorithm (Part 2)**

[step1] *Compute the similarity between M_i and M_{i+1} with average cluster vectors.*

[step2] *If the similarity of document cluster $\mathbf{D}_i$ in $\mathbb{H}_i$ and document cluster $\mathbf{D}_{i+1}$ in $\mathbb{H}_{i+1}$ is larger than a threshold, add a link from $\mathbf{D}_i$ to $\mathbf{D}_{i+1}$.*

[step3] *Repeat* [step2] *until the granularity level reaches the finest document cluster set $\mathbb{H}_k$.*

Figure 1 illustrates a part of hierarchy obtained by applying cluster hierarchy generation algorithm. Clusters found in coarser granularity level are basically major clusters, and the number of elements is generally large. For example, at granularity level 16, we can find clusters labeled "Cell, Enzyme", "Fuel, Engine", and "Transmission, Brake". At granularity level 32, a categorically new cluster labeled "Board game, Pachinko" comes in, and some of clusters at granularity level 16 are divided into subclusters.

On getting "cluster granularity hierarchy", given a user's input query, we traverse the data structure to see if there is any cluster (i.e., an average cluster vector) that has higher similarity than a predefined threshold. If such a cluster is found, we perform query expansion with the formula as shown below. Otherwise we replace query expansion by ordinary similarity computation with the plain query vector.

$$\mathbf{q}' = \alpha\, \mathbf{q} + \sum_i w_i \mathbf{v_i}$$

Note that $\mathbf{v}_i$ represents an expanded word vector, w_i represents its weight, and α is a non-negative coefficient.

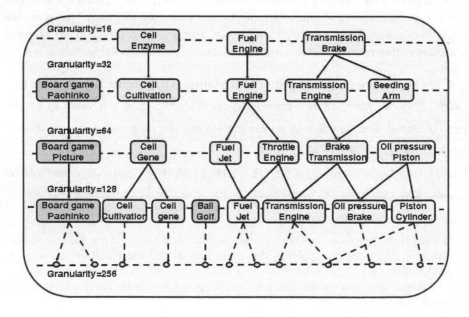

Fig. 1. Sample cluster hierarchy. Major clusters tend to be found at coarser granularity level, whereas medium to minor clusters tend to be observed at finer granularity level. For example, cluster with labels are "Ball" and "Golf" is detected only at granularity level 128 or finer.

4 Experimental Results

The data we used for experimentation is a collection of patents included in NTCIR-3 patent task [9]. The total number of patents is about 340,000, and we randomly sampled 40,000 documents. For the sake of comparison, we took naïve vector space model (VSM) and dimensionality reduction methods (LSI) with three different dimensions (k=128,256,512). In order to show the flavor of our algorithm's performance, we take a couple of examples as follows:

(1) "Rice-planting and Transplanting"
(2) "Vibration-proof architecture"

For input query (1), it fits into IPC subclass "A63F". The result in Figure 2 shows that our proposed method outperforms other methods. Three different dimensionality reductions with LSI have almost the same results.

For input query (2), it fits into multiple IPC subclasses, "E04H", "E04G", "F16F", "B32B", "H01L", "E02D", "E04F", "E01D, "B63B", and "E04C", where all of them have common descriptions on vibration-proof architecture of various devices and parts. The result in Figure 3 shows that our proposed method is superior to other methods. LSI with k=256 performs the second best result.

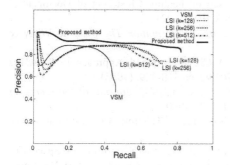

Fig. 2. Recall-precision graph for query with "Rice-planting" and "Transplanting

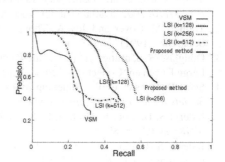

Fig. 3. Recall-precision graph for query with "Vibration-proof", and "Earthquake-proof" structure

During preprocessing, we extracted 38,400 keywords, and made document vectors for each patent document. Summing up document vectors, we obtained a matrix which can be fed into co-clustering. We selected 16, 32, 64, 128, 256, and 512 (i.e., 6 levels) granularity levels for clusters to be generated. Five different initial values for random variables were used. In total, 6 by 5 (30) times co-clustering was performed to construct a cluster hierarchical data structure.

Given user's input query, it was converted by morphological analyzer to a pseudo document vector. Taking advantage of the hierarchical data structure, we expanded the query, and sorted the search results in the descending order of similarity values.

5 Conclusion

We described a method for improving the retrieval performance using query expansion together with a "cluster granularity hierarchy" data structure constructed by applying multiple co-clustering algorithms with different initial conditions. Comparative experiments using patent data show that our method is a promising approach for improving retrieval performance. Because it is difficult to foresee what value k (dimension to reduce) is the best with a well-known dimensionality reduction method (LSI), we claim that our hierarchy data structure makes it possible to automatically choose a set of appropriate words for query expansion.

Although our hierarchical data structure was constructed by applying co-clustering algorithms, it might be possible to employ other clustering algorithms, since the data structure is inherently independent of clustering algorithms per se. Possible other future research work might include scalability enhancement, examination of the cases in which an input query fits into minor or outlier clusters, and application of our algorithm and data structure to a variety of data sets other than patent data.

References

1. Youjin Chang et al, "Conceptual Retrieval based on Feature Clustering of Documents," *Proc MF/IR 2002,* available at http://dcs.vein.hu/CIR/, (2002)
2. Thomas M. Cover and Joy A. Thomas, *Elements of Information Theory*, John Wiley & Sons, Inc., (1991)
3. Douglass R. Cutting, et al. "Scatter/Gather: A Clustering-based Approach to Browsing Large Document Collections," *Proc .ACM SIGIR'92*, pp.318-329, (1993)
4. Scott Deerwester et al., "Indexing by latent semantic analysis," *Journal of the American Society for Information Sciences*, vol.41, pp.391-407, (1990)
5. Inderjit S. Dhillon, S. Mallela, D. S. Modha, "Information-Theoretic Co-clustering", *Proc. SIGKDD '03*, pp. 89-98, (2003)
6. Inderjit S. Dhillon and Yuqiang Guan, "Information Theoretic Clustering of Space Co-Occurrence Data," *Proc IEEE ICDM'03,* Melbourne, Florida, USA, pp.517-520, November (2003)
7. Koji Eguchi, et al, "Adaptive Query Expansion Based on Clustering Search Results," *Transactions of Information Processing Society of Japan*, Vol.40, No.5, pp.2439-2449, May (1999)
8. Mei Kobayashi, Masaki Aono, H. Takeuchi, H. Samukawa, "Matrix computations for information retrieval and major and minor outlier cluster detection," *Journal of Computation and Applied Mathematics*, Vol.143, No.1-1, pp. 119-129, (2002)
9. NTCIR (NII-NACSIS Test Collection for IR Systems), http://research.nii.ac.jp/ntcir/

Chinese Question Classification from Approach and Semantic Views

Youzheng Wu, Jun Zhao, and Bo Xu

National Laboratory of Pattern Recognition, Institute of Automation
Chinese Academy of Sciences, Beijing P.O. Box 2728, 100080
{yzwu, jzhao, boxu}@nlpr.ia.ac.cn

Abstract. This paper presents a new Chinese question taxonomy respectively from approach and semantic viewpoints, and a SVM classification algorithm based on multiple features and hybrid feature weighting. The experimental results show that: (1) Lexical semantic features and structural features are the guarantee of high performance of question classification; (2) The contribution of dependency relation extracted from our current parser is no better than that of Bi-gram. (3) Our proposed feature weighting is effective for question classification.

1   Introduction

Question Classification(QC) is the basic and important module of question answering which task is to assign one or several classes to a given question. The errors of question classification will probably result in the failure of question answering. The experiments[8] show that about 36.4% of the errors of the open domain question answering result from the question classification module.

Handcrafted rules approach is commonly adopted by most question classification systems[1]. But it is time-consuming and labor-intensive. Recently, researches on question classification have been focused on the machine-learning approaches such as SVM[2,3], SnoW[4], Statistical LM[6], MEM[7], and etc[5].

In this paper, We presents a new Chinese question taxonomy respectively from the approach and semantic views, and a SVM classification algorithm based on multiple features and hybrid feature weighting. The experiments show that:

(1) Lexical semantic features and structural features are the guarantee of high performance question classification; (2) If we cannot get high accuracy dependency parser, Bi-gram features can replace the dependency relation without performance declining, which is inconsistent with our anticipation. (3) Our proposed feature weighting is effective for question classification.

2   Our Chinese Question Taxonomy

Numerous question taxonomies[1,4] have been defined according to question answering techniques, relevant resources and NLP tools available. Within in most

G.G. Lee et al. (Eds.): AIRS 2005, LNCS 3689, pp. 485–490, 2005.

Table 1. The Chinese Question Taxonomy

Question Type	#	Question Type	#	Question Type	#
Approach Categories					
ABBR	42	SYNONYM	190	LIST	234
CH-ABBR	11	BIRTHDAY	52	REASON	129
EN-ABBR	39	BIRTHDAY-PLACE	25	MANNER	90
ABBR-EX	92	BOOK-AUTHOR	71	CONTRAST	41
CH-ABBR-EX	6	REAL-NAME	41	FUNCTION	39
EN-ABBR-EX	7	CAPITAL-PLACE	48	DESCRIPTION	128
YES-NO	10	POPULATION	52	COMPONENTS	51
TRANS-TO-OTHERS	19	WHY-FAMOUS	79	CAUSE-OF-DEATH	41
TRANS-TO-EN	22	DEFINITION	257	OTHER-APPROACH	
TRANS-TO-CH	25				
Semantic Categories					
OTHER-TEMP	399	PARTY	20	MUSIC-INSTRU	35
DURATION	123	SPORTS-TEAM	35	BOOK-NAME	48
SEASON	28	UNIVERSITY	37	MOVIE-NAME	62
YEAR	206	MAGNEWS	18	PRODUCT	11
MONTH	37	BANK	26	PHONE-NUMBER	37
DATE	90	OTHER-ENTITY	641	ZIP-CODE	33
TIME	16	DYNASTY	48	EMAIL	4
AGE	48	LANGUAGE	56	URL	13
PERSON	769	ANIMAL	129	OTHER-NUMBER	426
OTHER-PLACE	606	PLANT	58	MONEY	67
CONTINENT	73	OCCUPATION	19	SPATIAL-NUMBER	209
COUNTRY	334	HUMAN-FOOD	50	SPEED	41
PROVINCE	99	BODY-PART	32	WEIGHT	44
CITY	189	DISEASE	26	ACCELERATION	25
BODY-OF-WATER	142	SPORT	36	ORDINAL	34
ISLAND	35	COLOR	51	PERCENTAGE	68
MOUNTAIN	45	UNIT	27	TEMPERATURE	56
SPHERE	72	MONETARY-UN	37	RANGE-NUMBER	19
OTHER-ORG	148	NATINOALITY	31		

of these question taxonomies, question types are defined from the semantic viewpoint of the answer for reducing the number of answer candidates. We think that the following principles should be abided in building question taxonomy.

1. Question category should be useful for selecting the approach of question answering. This is the approach classifier.

For example, pattern matching may be more effective to the questions such as questioning the author of book, someone's birthday and so on; while retrieval technique is more suitable for the questions querying about the description of something or somebody; but for other questions, the approaches based on natural language processing may be more competent than others.

2. Question category should be informative for determining the semantic category of the answer(such as PERSON, PLACE, TIME, etc), and thus restricting the space of answer candidates. This is the semantic classifier.

Because it's much more difficult or even infeasible to select correct answer from all of noun phrases than from some specific named entities.

3. The question taxonomy should be of good coverage and practicable based on current natural language processing resources and tools.

Table 1 shows our new Chinese question taxonomy which is based on the above principles and the observation of our question collection[10] (2800 questions of which are from HIT-IRLab).

In comparison with all other question taxonomies, the most obvious characteristic of our Chinese question taxonomy is that we have two parallel question categories which can make up their disadvantages, whereas other question taxonomies are hierarchical taxonomies which include coarse and fine categories. For example, given question 莫扎特是哪年出生的/In what year did Mozart born?, the approach class BIRTHDAY suggests that pattern matching approach is suitable for this question and semantic class shows that the semantic type of answer is YEAR. So we can use effective pattern matching approach while avoiding the mechanical string matching because of the semantic restriction of answer.

3   Feature Space and Feature Weighting

In this paper, three kinds of features, i.e. *basic features (word and POS), structural features (Bi-gram or dependency relation) and lexical semantic features (thesaurus and named entity types)*, are used. Intuitively, it is more reasonable if we replace the Bi-Gram features with the dependency relations.

Feature weighting is to seek the suitable measure to score the features according to their contribution to the classifier. As we know, TF×IDF is the classical weighting method. However, in QC task, TF is equal to 1 in most cases. Therefore, we need to find a more suitable measure to modify TF×IDF.

Two main factors should be considered when designing feature weighting. One is the local attribute of features like MI, CHI, DWF, the other is the global attribute of features like IG, DF. In this paper, we present a hybrid model of feature weighting which combines χ^2_{max} with TF×IDF. So the weight of a term

$$t_{ik} = \beta^d \times \sqrt[\lambda]{\chi^2_{max}} \times TF \times IDF \qquad (1)$$

where λ is the balance factor between χ^2_{max} and TF×IDF score, d is the distance between the interrogative and the other words, β denotes the distance penalty.

4   Experiments

In this paper, we will conduct experiments to answer the following questions. (1) Will the hybrid feature weighting be effective for QC Task? (2) Which feature has the biggest contribution to classifiers? (3) Will the precision of classifiers based on dependency relation be higher than that of classifiers based on Bi-gram?

We randomly select 700 questions for test and the rest 6350 questions are used for training, and conduct evaluations in terms of precision which is the proportion of the correctly classified questions among all test questions.

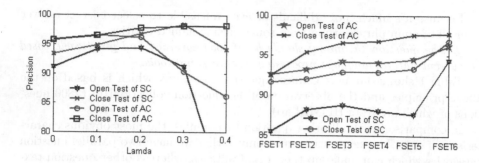

Fig. 1. The influence curve of local and global attribute of features for classifiers (Left Figure). The contribution of different features to classifiers (Right Figure). SC and AC denote semantic classifier and approach classifier respectively. FSET1~FSET6 represent the feature sets as follows. FSET1: word; FSET2: FSET1 + word Bi-gram; FSET3: FSET2 + named entities; FSET4: FSET3 + POS; FSET5: FSET4 + POS Bi-gram; FSET6: FSET5 + thesaurus.

Note that, all experiments make use of LibSvm[11].

Exp.1. Will the hybrid feature weighting be effective for QC Task?

The parameter λ in formula 1 is to balance local attribute and global attribute of features. The larger λ, the smaller contribution of local attribute. The smaller λ, the larger contribution of local attribute. The task of this experiment is to find the best value of λ^* which maximizes the precision of classifiers.

This experiment include basic features provided by [9], structural features(Bi-Gram only) and lexical semantic features. The results are shown in Fig.1.

From the left figure in Fig.1, we find that the idea that modifying the TF×IDF by χ^2_{max} is appropriate in QC task. In the early stage, the precisions of open and close test are improved with the increasing of λ. But the precisions decline in the ending. The precisions reach the top when λ^* is about 0.2.

This experiment shows that the feasible approach of getting high performance is to combine the different attributes of features.

Exp.2. Which feature has the biggest contribution to classifiers?

In the above experiment, we find that the best value of λ^* can be obtained through incorporating various kinds of features. In this experiment, we expect to compare the contributions of these features to the question classifiers which is shown in the right figure in Fig.1

The right figure in Fig.1 shows that it's very important to introduce lexical semantic features and structural features into the classifiers. The performance of the semantic classifier increases about 0.6% and 7% respectively after named entities and lexical semantic features are integrated. Meanwhile, Bi-gram feature is helpful not only to the approach classifier but also to the semantic classifier. However, the contribution of POS is very slight and even declines the precisions. The reason we speculate lies in that the helpful POS has been included in named entities, the rest POS such as nouns, verbs are not helpful to classification.

Exp.3. Will the precision of classifier based on dependency relation be higher than that of classifier based on Bi-gram?

In chapter 3, we speculate that the dependency syntactic relation may be better for classifiers than Bi-gram, because the dependency relation is not restricted by long distance. And this experiment is conducted to validate the above idea. Table 2 is the precision comparisons in detail.

Table 2. Comparison study of dependency relation and Bi-gram features. The feature sets are as follows. FSET6: word + POS + named entities + thesaurus; FSET6†: FEST6 + Bi-Gram; FSET6‡: FSET6 + dependency relation.

	Feature Set	Open Test	Closed Test
Semantic Classifier	FSET6	90.55%	96.15%
	FSET6†	94.37%	96.57%
	FSET6‡	93.27%	96.57%
Approach Classifier	FSET6	92.40%	94.58%
	FSET6†	96.20%	97.71%
	FSET6‡	94.05%	97.08%

From table 2, we find that the precisions of semantic classifier based on FSET6‡ and FEST6‡ are improved by 3.8% and 2.7% respectively compared to classifier that based on FEST6. While, the precision of approach classifier based on FSET6† and FEST6‡ are improved by 3.8% and 1.8% respectively compared to classifier based on FEST6. This shows that whether dependency relation or Bi-gram features has significant contribution to semantic and approach classifiers. However, the contribution of dependency relation extracted from our current parser is no better than that of Bi-gram. This phenomenon is inconsistent with our speculation, which can be explained as follows. *1.* The precision of the dependency parser for questions is about 90%, which means that it may output wrong dependency relation to the classifier. Therefore, these errors may result in the wrong classification for the question. *2.* Though Bi-gram features are less reasonable than features extracted by dependency parser, such "unreasonable" features may not consequentially result in misclassification.

This experiment shows that the contribution of dependency relation extracted by only high accuracy parser can achieve our anticipation; Otherwise, Bi-Gram can replace the dependency relation without performance declining.

5   Conclusion and Future Work

This paper puts forward a new Chinese question taxonomy from approach and semantic viewpoints. A support vector machine classification algorithm is also presented for question classification based on multiple features including basic features (word & POS), structural features (Bi-Gram & dependency relation) and lexical semantic features (named entity & thesaurus).

Empirically, we show that lexical semantic features and structural features are the guarantee of high performance of question classification. Regrettably, the contribution of dependency relation extracted from our current parser is no better than that of Bi-Gram which is inconsistent with our anticipation.

There exist many difficulties in question classification which is subject to error classification, wherever using machine learning algorithm or handcrafted rules. Three kinds of misclassifications in our current system are as follows: *1. Misclassifications resulting from inherently difficult questions. 2. Misclassifications resulting from mistakenly recognized Focus Words 3. Misclassifications resulting from the errors of word segmentation and Named entity recognition.*

In future, we will focus on the resolving the mistakes type 1 and 2 and apply the question classification in our Chinese Question Answering System.

Acknowledgement

This work was supported by the Natural Sciences Foundation of China(60372016) and the Natural Science Foundation of Beijing(4052027).

References

1. Hovy, E.H., U. Hermjakob, and D. Ravichandran: A Question/Answer Typology with Surface Text Patterns. In Proceedings of the Human Language Technology Conference. San Diego, CA. NIST, Gaithersburg, MD. (2002) 229-241
2. Dell Zhang, Wee Sun Lee: Question Classification using Support Vector Machines. In Proceedings of the 26th annual international ACM SIGIR conference on Research and development in information retrieval, Toronto, Canada. (2003) 26-32.
3. Jun Suzuki, Hirotoshi Taira, Yutaka Sasaki, et al: Question Classification using HDAG Kernel. In Proc. of 6th Information-Based Induction Sciences. (2003).
4. Xin.Li, D Roth: Learning Question Classification. In Proceedings of the 19th International Conference on Computational Linguistics, Taibai. (2002)
5. Thamar Solorio, Manuel Pérez-Coutiño, et al: A Language Independent Method for Question Classification. In the Proc. COLING2004, Switzerland. (2004) 1374-1380.
6. Wei Li: Question Classification Using Language Modeling. In CIIR Technical Report: University of Massachusetts, Amherst. (2002)
7. Krystle Kocik: Question Classification using Maximum Entropy Models. Available at http://www.it.usyd.edu.au/research/news/kocik_summary.pdf.
8. D. Moldovan, M. Pasca, S. Harabagiu, et al: Performance issues and error analysis in an open-domain question answering system. ACM Trans. Inf. Syst. (2002).
9. Youzheng Wu, Jun Zhao, et al: Chinese Named Entity Recognition Combining Statistical Model and Human Knowledge. In Proc. of Acl2003 Workshop. Japan.
10. Youzheng Wu, Jun Zhao, Xiaoyu Duan, Bo Xu: Building an Evaluation Platform for Chinese Question Answering Systems. In the Proc. of the First National Conference on Information Retrieval and Content Security, Shanghai, China. (2003).
11. Chih-Chung Chang, Chih-Jen Lin: LIBSVM - a Library for Support Vector Machines. Available at http://www.csie.ntu.edu.tw/~cjlin/libsvm/

GJM-2: A Special Case of General Jelinek-Mercer Smoothing Method for Language Modeling Approach to Ad Hoc IR

Guodong Ding and Bin Wang

Institute of Computing Technology, Chinese Academy of Sciences,
100080 Beijing, China
dingguodong@software.ict.ac.cn
wangbin@ict.ac.cn

Abstract. The language modeling approach to IR is attractive and promising because it connects the problem of retrieval with that of language model estimation. A core technique for language model estimation is smoothing, which adjusts the maximum likelihood estimator so as to correct the inaccuracy due to data sparseness. In this paper we propose a General Jelinek-Mercer method (GJM) by using a document-dependent mixture coefficient to control the influence of maximum likelihood model and the collection model. Utilizing the number of unique terms in the document to improve the accuracy of language model estimation, we further develop GJM-2 smoothing method as a special case of GJM. Experimental results show that using GJM-2 for the language modeling approach can achieve better retrieval performances than the existing three popular methods both on short and long queries.

1 Introduction

In the language modeling approach [1][2][3][4][5], a core technique for estimating document language model is smoothing, which adjusts the maximum likelihood estimator so as not to assign zero probability to unseen words in the document due to data sparseness. Zhai and Lafferty studied and compared three popular smoothing methods and their influences on retrieval performance: Jelinek-Mercer, Dirichlet and absolute discounting [5][6]. Their experimental results showed that the accuracy of smoothing is directly related to retrieval performance [5][6]. In this paper we develop a new smoothing method – GJM-2. Based on the analysis for Jelinek-Mercer method, we propose a general linear interpolated smoothing method – GJM, in which a document-dependent mixture coefficient is introduced. Analysis indicates that Dirichlet is a special case of GJM. Using the count of unique terms in current document rather than the document length, we further derive GJM-2 method, an improved version of GJM-1. Experimental results on several TREC testing sets show that the optimal retrieval performances of GJM-2 are better than the three popular methods both on short and long queries.

2 The Basic Language Modeling Approach to IR

Suppose we have a collection with total N documents, whose vocabulary is $V = \{w_1, w_2, ..., w_L\}$. Given a query $Q = q_1 q_2 ... q_m$ ($q_k \in V$, $1 \leq k \leq m$), the task is to rank the

G.G. Lee et al. (Eds.): AIRS 2005, LNCS 3689, pp. 491–496, 2005.
© Springer-Verlag Berlin Heidelberg 2005

documents according to the relevance of each document with the query. Based on the assumption of words independence, the language modeling approach views each document D as an observed sequence of words generated by a multinomial language model parameterized by $\theta_D = (\theta_{D1}, \theta_{D2}, ..., \theta_{DL}) \in [0,1]^L$, where $\theta_{D1} + \theta_{D2} + ... + \theta_{DL} = 1$ and $\theta_{Di} = p(w_i|\theta_D)$, the probability of observing word w_i under the multinomial generation model (i.e. unigram model) parameterized by θ_D. And the relevance of document D with the query Q is measured by the likelihood of Q according to the multinomial model θ_D:

$$P(Q|\theta_D) = \prod_{i=1}^{m} p(q_i|\theta_D) = \prod_{w \in Q} p(w|\theta_D)^{c(w,Q)} \tag{1}$$

where $c(w,Q)$ is the frequency of word w occurring in query Q.

Clearly, the retrieval problem is now essentially reduced to a multinomial language model estimation problem. The simplest method to estimate θ_D is to utilize the maximum likelihood estimator (MLE):

$$p(w|\hat{\theta}_D) = p_{ML}(w|\hat{\theta}_D) = \frac{c(w,D)}{|D|} \tag{2}$$

where $c(w,D)$ is the frequency of word w occurring in document D and $|D|$ is the length of D, i.e. $|D| = \sum_w c(w,D)$.

However, using MLE can cause serious zero probability problem due to data sparseness. A direct solution to the problem is smoothing, which adjusts the MLE so as to assign a nonzero probability to the unseen words and improve the accuracy of language model estimation. According to [5], there are three popular smoothing methods applied to the language modeling approaches to ad hoc IR: Jelinek-Mercer, Dirichlet and absolute discounting, summarized in Table 1. Notice that $|D|_u$ is the number of unique words in document D. The collection language model θ_C is typically estimated by MLE based on the whole collection, i.e.

$$p(w|\hat{\theta}_C) = p_{ML}(w|\hat{\theta}_C) = \frac{\sum_D c(w,D)}{\sum_w \sum_D c(w,D)} \tag{3}$$

Table 1. Summary of the three popular smoothing methods

Jelinek-Mercer	$p(w|\hat{\theta}_D) = \lambda p_{ML}(w|\hat{\theta}_D) + (1-\lambda)p(w|\hat{\theta}_C)$
Dirichlet	$p(w|\hat{\theta}_D) = \dfrac{c(w,D) + \mu p(w|\hat{\theta}_C)}{|D| + \mu}$
Absolute Discounting	$p(w|\hat{\theta}_D) = \dfrac{\max(c(w,D) - \delta, 0)}{|D|} + \dfrac{\delta|D|_u}{|D|}p(w|\hat{\theta}_C)$

3   Our Smoothing Method: GJM-2

Clearly, in the context of ad hoc IR, different documents have different statistical features, such as document length etc. However, Jelinek-Mercer method doesn't take this into account. An intuitive consideration is to make the coefficient λ dependent on the document. So we propose following general Jelinek-Mercer smoothing method (GJM):

$$p(w|\hat{\theta}_D) = \lambda_D p_{ML}(w|\hat{\theta}_D) + (1-\lambda_D)p(w|\hat{\theta}_C) \tag{4}$$

where λ_D is a document-dependent coefficient.

Ideally, GJM could make good use of the differences between the statistical features of documents and incorporate them into λ_D to improve the accuracy of the document language model estimation. However, the requirement for efficient computations over large collection make it impossible to set a completely different value of λ_D for each document. A reasonable tradeoff is to partition the collection into multiple "buckets" according to the commonness or similarity of statistical features between documents, and then to set the same value of λ_D to the documents in the same "bucket". So a crucial question for GJM method is: how to partition the collection, i.e. what statistical features of a document can be used to partition the collection?

From the statistical perspective longer document should put more trust in the maximum likelihood estimator $p_{ML}(w|\hat{\theta}_D)$. Therefore document length is maybe a good feature to partition the collection. By setting λ_D to be $\lambda_D = |D|/(|D|+\xi)$, we have the following GJM-1 smoothing method:

$$p(w|\hat{\theta}_D) = \frac{c(w,D) + \xi p(w|\hat{\theta}_C)}{|D|+\xi} \tag{5}$$

Clearly, GJM-1 is equivalent to Dirichlet, which indicates that Dirichlet is a special case of GJM. The excellent performance of Dirichlet showed in [5] validates that incorporating the document length into the coefficient λ_D does improve the quality of language model smoothing, which further testify the feasibility of the idea of GJM. Besides document length, is there any other statistical feature to help improve the accuracy of language model estimation?

Suppose there are two different documents D_1 and D_2. The length of D_1 is the same as that of D_2, i.e. $|D_1|=|D_2|$, but D_2 has a flatter distribution of words than D1, i.e. $|D_1|_u > |D_2|_u$, where $|D|_u$ is the number of unique terms in document D. According to GJM-1 method (i.e. Dirichlet method), the value of coefficient λ_D of D_1 will be the same as that of D_2, which implies that the maximum likelihood estimator of D_1 will get the same trust as that of D_2. This is not what we expect. From statistical perspective, the count of observed events in D_1 is larger than in D_2, which suggests it is more plausible to make D_1 get more trust in the maximum likelihood estimator than D_2.

On the other hand, a larger $|D|_u$ also implies a larger $|D|$ to some extent, so we think that $|D|_u$ will be more appropriate than $|D|$ as a statistical feature for partitioning collection in order to estimate language model more accurately. Similar to GJM-1, we set the coefficient λ_D to be: $\lambda_D = |D|_u/(|D|_u+\delta)$, where δ is a document-independent constant, $\delta > 0$. So we get the following GJM-2 smoothing method:

$$p(w|\hat{\theta}_D) = \frac{|D|_u}{|D|_u + \delta} p_{ML}(w|\hat{\theta}_D) + (1 - \frac{|D|_u}{|D|_u + \delta})p(w|\hat{\theta}_C) \tag{6}$$

On the surface, GJM-2 is a typical linear-interpolated smoothing method similar to Jelinek-Mercer except that the interpolation coefficient λ_D of GJM-2 is document-dependent: when using GJM-2 to smooth document language model, the larger the number of unique terms in the document, the more trust will be put in the maximum likelihood estimator. If compared to the linear-interpolated form of Dirichlet method, GJM-2 is highly similar to Dirichlet except that $|D|$ in Dirichlet method is substituted with $|D|_u$ in GJM-2. We think that when we adjust maximum likelihood estimator with smoothing strategy, $|D|_u$ will help to estimate language model of D more accurately than $|D|$, which will be testified in our experiments. Furthermore, from the point of view of computational efficiency, clearly GJM-2 is as efficient as the three popular smoothing methods, and it is very appropriate for the task of ad hoc IR.

4   Experimental Results

Our goal is to evaluate whether GJM-2 can improve retrieval performance when compared to the three popular methods. We use four data sets from TREC2, TREC3, TREC7 and TREC8 ad hoc task, respectively. Similar to [5], we construct two different versions of each set of queries: (1) short (title only) and (2) long version (title + description + narrative). The short queries are mostly two or three key words, whereas the long queries have multiple whole sentences. In all our experiments we only apply stemming with a Porter stemmer for tokenization. No stop words are removed. Table 2 gives the labels for all data sets, based on the collections and topics.

Table 2. Labels used for data sets

Collection	Topics101-150		Topics151-200		Topics351-400		Topics401-450	
	Short	Long	Short	Long	Short	Long	Short	Long
DISK1&2	TREC2S	TREC2L	TREC3S	TREC3L	N/A	N/A	N/A	N/A
DISK4&5-CR	N/A	N/A	N/A	N/A	TREC7S	TREC7L	TREC8S	TREC8L

In order to compare GJM-2 with the three methods, we follow the experimental methodology described in [5]: first we select a best run (in terms of non-interpolated average precision) for each method on each testing set, and then compare the average precision (AvgPrec), precision at 10 documents (P@10), and precision at 20 documents (P@20) of the selected runs. The results are shown in Table 3.

In spite of the unstable order among the old three methods, it is evident to see that: (1) On all testing sets the average precision (non-interpolated) of GJM-2 is better than the other three existing methods. (2) On most of testing collections P@10 and P@20 of GJM-2 are better than the three methods. (3) On average, GJM-2 is best among the four methods according to the three precision measures. Fig. 1 also shows their comparisons of average precision (non-interpolated) on short and long queries more intuitively.

Table 3. Comparisons of GJM-2 with the existing three popular methods. The left and right half are for short and long queries, respectively. JM denotes Jelinek-Mercer, Dir denotes Dirichlet and Abs denotes smoothing using absolute discounting. The last several rows show the mean of the three precision measures for short (left half) and long queries (right half). The best performance in each data set is shown in bold font.

Data	Method	Param	AvgPrec	P@10	P@20	Data	Method	Param	AvgPrec	P@10	P@20
TREC2S	JM	$\lambda = 0.4$	0.1629	0.378	0.367	TREC2L	JM	$\lambda = 0.2$	0.2713	0.526	0.493
	Dir	$\mu = 3000$	0.2022	0.444	0.426		Dir	$\mu = 3000$	0.2778	0.518	0.5
	Abs	$\delta = 0.8$	0.1749	0.428	0.392		Abs	$\delta = 0.6$	0.2399	0.526	0.495
	GJM-2	$\delta = 2500$	**0.2047**	**0.46**	**0.428**		GJM-2	$\delta = 2000$	**0.2828**	**0.526**	**0.503**
TREC3S	JM	$\lambda = 0.7$	0.2149	0.434	0.423	TREC3L	JM	$\lambda = 0.2$	0.3060	0.624	0.562
	Dir	$\mu = 2000$	0.2598	0.54	0.51		Dir	$\mu = 2000$	0.3190	0.636	**0.587**
	Abs	$\delta = 0.8$	0.2310	0.484	0.455		Abs	$\delta = 0.7$	0.2682	0.606	0.525
	GJM-2	$\delta = 1000$	**0.2637**	**0.548**	**0.525**		GJM-2	$\delta = 1500$	**0.3190**	**0.646**	0.581
TREC7S	JM	$\lambda = 0.7$	0.1656	0.354	0.31	TREC7L	JM	$\lambda = 0.2$	0.2171	0.458	0.397
	Dir	$\mu = 2000$	0.1857	0.424	0.355		Dir	$\mu = 3000$	0.2223	0.454	0.39
	Abs	$\delta = 0.7$	0.1704	0.378	0.339		Abs	$\delta = 0.7$	0.2001	0.432	0.396
	GJM-2	$\delta = 2000$	**0.1892**	**0.438**	**0.359**		GJM-2	$\delta = 2000$	**0.2340**	**0.49**	**0.419**
TREC8S	JM	$\lambda = 0.7$	0.2370	0.422	0386	TREC8L	JM	$\lambda = 0.2$	0.2551	**0.472**	**0.397**
	Dir	$\mu = 500$	0.2511	0.444	0.407		Dir	$\mu = 2000$	0.2517	0.448	0.388
	Abs	$\delta = 0.6$	0.2431	0.456	0.402		Abs	$\delta = 0.7$	0.2344	0.458	0.391
	GJM-2	$\delta = 500$	**0.2546**	**0.46**	**0.413**		GJM-2	$\delta = 2000$	**0.2594**	0.464	0.391
Average	JM	—	0.1951	0.397	0.371	Average	JM	—	0.2623	0.52	0.462
	Dir	—	0.2247	0.463	0.424		Dir	—	0.2677	0.514	0.466
	Abs	—	0.2048	0.436	0.397		Abs	—	0.2356	0.507	0.451
	GJM-2	—	**0.2281**	**0.477**	**0.431**		GJM-2	—	**0.2738**	**0.531**	**0.473**

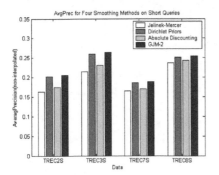
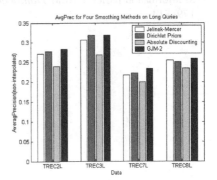

Fig. 1. Comparisons of the four methods on short and long queries in terms of non-interpolated average precision

5 Summary and Conclusions

In the language modeling approach to ad hoc IR, a central issue in language model estimation is smoothing, which adjusts the maximum likelihood estimator to compensate for data sparseness. By generalizing the Jelinek-Mercer smoothing method, we propose the GJM method, which uses a document-dependent coefficient to control the influence of the maximum likelihood model and the collection model. Analysis shows that Dirichlet method is equivalent to GJM-1, a special case of GJM. Using the number of unique terms in the document rather than the document length, we propose GJM-2 method, an improved version of GJM-1. Experimental results show that GJM-2 method can achieve better retrieval performances than the three existing popular smoothing methods both on short and long queries.

References

1. Ponte, J. M. and Croft, W. B. 1998. A language modeling approach to information retrieval. In *Proceedings of the 21st Annual International ACM SIGIR Conference on Research and Development in Information Retrieval*, Melbourne, 275~281.
2. Berger, A. and Lafferty, J. 1999. Information retrieval as statistical translation. In *Proceedings of the 22nd Annual International ACM SIGIR Conference on Research and Development in Information Retrieval*, Berkeley, 222~229.
3. Miller, D. R., Leek T., and Schwartz, R. M. 1999. A hidden Markov model information retrieval system. In *Proceedings of the 22nd Annual International ACM SIGIR Conference on Research and Development in Information Retrieval*, Berkeley, 214~221.
4. Hiemstra, F. and Kraaij, W. 1999. Twenty-one at TREC-7: Ad hoc and cross-language track. In *Proceedings of 7th Text Retrieval Conference (TREC-7)*. 227~238.
5. Zhai, C. and Lafferty, J. 2001. A study of smoothing methods for language models applied to ad hoc information retrieval. In *Proceedings of the 24th Annual International ACM SIGIR Conference on Research and Development in Information Retrieval*, New Orleans, 334~342.
6. Zhai, C. and Lafferty, J. 2004. A study of smoothing methods for language models applied to information retrieval. *ACM Transactions on Information Systems (TOIS)*, Vol. 2, No. 2: 179~214.

The Empirical Impact of the Nature of Novelty Detection

Le Zhao[1], Min Zhang[2], and Shaoping Ma[2]

[1] State Key Lab of Intelligent Tech. and Sys., Tsinghua University,
Beijing, 100084, China
zhaole@tsinghua.org.cn

[2] State Key Lab of Intelligent Tech. and Sys., Tsinghua University,
Beijing, 100084, China
{z-m, msp}@tsinghua.edu.cn

Abstract. Novelty detection systems aim at reducing redundant documents or sentences from a list of documents chronologically ordered. In the task, sentences appearing later in the list with no new meanings are eliminated. In an accompanying paper, the nature of novelty detection was revealed — Novelty as a combination of the PO (partial overlap) and CO (complete overlap) relations, which can be treated as two classification tasks; theoretical impacts were given. This paper provides what the nature of the task mean empirically. One new method — selected pool — implementing the nature of the task gained improvements on TREC Novelty datasets. New evaluation criteria are given, which are natural from the viewpoint of the nature of novelty detection. [1]

1 Introduction

Novelty detection asks the question, whether a sentence is new (compared to previously acquired knowledge). The first contribution to the study of large scale text novelty detection (experiments were performed on a document level novelty detection dataset) was made by [7]. After that, in the last three years, from 2002 to 2004 [1] [4] [3], there were three Novelty tracks held by the Text REtrieval Conference (TREC). The focus was on sentence level query-specific (intra-topic) novelty detection.

In Zhang Yi's pioneering work on Novelty [7], several questions (discrepancies between theory and observations) were raised regarding the redundancy measure and the novelty detection procedure: symmetric or asymmetric redundancy measure, sentence-to-sentence or sentence-to-multiple-sentences comparison model. We try to answer the questions both theoretically and empirically.

An outline for the rest of the paper is as follows: Section 2 starting from similarity, summarizes the widely used overlap method and one discrepancy between

---

[1] Supported by the Chinese National Key Foundation Research & Development Plan (2004CB318108), Natural Science Foundation (60223004, 60321002, 60303005) and the Key Project of Chinese Ministry of Education (No. 104236).

theory and experiments. Section 3 quickly reviews the two relations underlying novelty detection proposed by the accompanying paper. In section 4, we reveal more cases of discrepancy in evaluation of the experiments of the selected pool method. Furthermore, in section 5, we discuss the empirical importance of the evaluation methodologies for Novelty. Section 6 concludes the paper.

2 The Overlap Method

We know that if all the meanings of a sentence are the same as some known facts, the sentence is redundant. So a symmetric similarity measure between sentences can be used to estimate the symmetric "same" relation between meanings. A sentence sufficiently similar to a previous one is considered redundant. Taking a first look at the novelty task, anyone would probably come up with a similarity measure.

Although similarity has been proven to be effective experimentally [7] [5], if we think twice, when one sentence's meanings are covered by another, this relation is not necessarily symmetric, because sentences may contain different numbers of meanings. An asymmetric overlap measure should be used eventually, ([6] [7] mentioned such belief).

Surprisingly, in spite of the theoretical advantage of overlap, similarity is empirically better than asymmetric methods like the overlap method, as experimental results from [6] [7] indicated.

Table 1. Similarity and the overlap method

2004 task 2	#ret	Av.P	Av.R	Av.F	#novel
s0.4	986	0.688	0.977	0.790	627
o0.7	974	0.694	0.964	0.786	634
2003 task 2	#ret	Av.P	Av.R	Av.F	#novel
s0.4	13495	0.719	0.978	0.817	9962
o0.7	13303	0.719	0.972	0.815	9836

In all the tables we used the following abbreviations: o for overlap, s for similarity, p for pool, and sp for selected pool. In Table 1, "o0.7" is the overlap method with a threshold of 0.7; "s0.4" is the similarity method with threshold 0.4.

From the table, we can see that in F-measure (Av.F), similarity was better than overlap on both 03 and 04 TREC Novelty collections. The F-measure difference was small because overlap and similarity differ slightly.

3 The Two Relations

First, the partial order relation $>_{co}$, we called the *complete overlap relation (CO)*. One sentence A $>_{co}$ B, if A contains all the meanings of sentence B. This relation is a partial order relation. It is transitive and antisymmetric.

Second, the symmetric relation $>_{po}$, we called *partial overlap relation (PO)*. A $>_{po}$ B, if A and B have meanings in common. This relation is non-transitive and symmetric. As the PO relation is symmetric, we called the sentences that are PO related to one sentence its PO relatives. (e.g., for sentence A in {A: A $>_{po}$ B and A $>_{po}$ C}, B and C are called A's PO relatives, and similarly A is also B's and C's PO relative.)

4   The Selected Pool Method

Following the two relations, in the selected pool method, only sentences that are PO-related to the current sentence are included in the pool (approximating the PO relation), then, a pool-sentence overlap judgment (approximating the CO relation) follows. In the experiments, if the TFIDF [2] overlap score of the current sentence by a previous sentence exceeded a selection threshold, that previous sentence was considered PO-related to the current sentence. By setting the threshold to be 0, we include all previous sentences in the pool - the selected pool turns back into the simple pool method. Setting the threshold to be the threshold for pool-sentence overlap judgment, the selected pool becomes the overlap method. Experiments showed, in F-measure, selected pool (sp0.7s2.0) is significantly better than overlap (o0.7) by a paired t-test (0.620 vs. 0.608, significant at p=0.000006).The results are presented in Table 2.

Table 2. The selected pool method

Novelty04	#ret	Av.P	Av.R	Av.F	Difference
p0.7	5713	0.495	0.864	0.615	192 novel in
sp0.7s2.0	6205	0.487	0.911	0.620	492 extra
sp0.7s2.0	6205	0.487	0.911	0.620	80 novel in
sp0.7s3.0	6552	0.475	0.929	0.615	347 extra
sp0.7s5.0	6893	0.464	0.945	0.608	22 novel in
o0.7	6965	0.462	0.950	0.608	72 extra
Novelty03	#ret	Av.P	Av.R	Av.F	Difference
p0.7	9127	0.755	0.762	0.744	2763 novel
sp0.7s5.0	13250	0.720	0.969	0.815	4123 extra
sp0.7s5.0	13250	0.720	0.969	0.815	25 novel
o0.7	13303	0.719	0.972	0.815	53 extra

The last column of the table ("Difference") is the number of additional returned novel sentences in the totality of the extra sentences returned. In F-measure s2.0 is better than p0.7, and s5.0 is almost the same as o0.7. But for the additional returned sentences, only a small part (about 1/3 to 1/4) of the additional returned sentences were novel. Simple derivation showed that to increase the F-measure of a set of results, additionally returning a set with precision higher than P÷(P+R) is sufficient, where P and R are the precision and recall of the original result set. For example, if P=0.5 and R=0.9, including a set with precision greater than 0.36 already increases F-measure. This strange property of the F-measure can be misleading when we compare different Novelty methods only using F-measure, and this motivated us in devising new evaluation measures.

In the next section about evaluation, we could see how the question about the worse performance of the theoretically advantaged overlap measure (comparing to the similarity measure) arose.

5   Experimental Evaluations

As novelty detection could be treated as a two step classification task (PO and CO judgments). We propose an evaluation method, in which the error rate of the classifications is used, as in the following Pairwise Sentence Measure (PSM):

$$PSM = 1 - \frac{\#\text{misclassified pairs(system output)}}{\#\text{total pairs(judgment)}}$$

where, #misclassified pairs

$$= \#\text{missed pairs} + \#\text{false overlapping pairs.} \tag{1}$$

Here, by "#" we mean "the number of". In the second formula, the missed pairs and the false overlapping pairs are usually called misses and false alarms in the classification terminology (face detection for example), whereas the task here is to detect the overlapping pairs. We define the PSM more clearly; for a run A, suppose A_R is the set of redundant sentences judged by A, and A_N the novel sentences judged by run A (the sentences finally returned by A). Immediately, $A_R \coprod A_N = C$ (disjoint union), where C is the collection of all sentences. i is a sentence, $\Re$ is the set of redundant sentences by judgment (true redundant sentences), PO_i is the set of true PO relatives of sentence i, and SPO_i is the set of sentences run A judges as the PO relatives of i. For any X set of sentences, suppose, $|X|$ is the usual measure of X (the number of elements in X), $|X|_R$ is the redundancy measure of X (the number of redundant ones in X), and $|X|_N$ is the novelty measure of X (the number of novel ones in X). Here, we have $|X|_N + |X|_R = |X|$, $|X|_R = |X \cap \Re|$.

#misclassified pairs and #total pairs are further defined in equation (2):

$$\#\text{misclassified} = \sum_{i \in A_R - \Re} |SPO_i| + \sum_{i \in \Re - A_R} |PO_i|$$

$$+ \sum_{i \in A_R \cap \Re} |(SPO_i - PO_i) \cup (PO_i - SPO_i)| \tag{2}$$

$$\#\text{total pairs} = \sum_{i \in \Re} |PO_i|$$

In the experiments, unfortunately, as we were unable to determine all the correct pairs for PSM evaluation for all the 50 topics; there are thousands of sentences and tens of thousands of sentence pairs in the Novelty datasets (quite a tremendous task for the limited labor force available). Also, not all methods can return the PO relatives of a sentence, so we adopted an alternative that only made use of the human assessments currently available.

Simplified PSM (SPSM): since the *PO* and *SPO* are unknown, we assume every sentence has only one previous PO relative in the list, i.e.

$$\sum_{i \in A_R - \Re} |SPO_i| = |A_R - \Re|, \quad \sum_{i \in A_R - \Re} |PO_i| = 0$$

$$\sum_{i \in \Re - A_R} |PO_i| = |\Re - A_R|, \quad \sum_{i \in \Re - A_R} |SPO_i| = 0$$

Then, for a run A,

$$SPSM(A)$$
$$= (|\Re| - |A_R - \Re| - |\Re - A_R|)/|\Re|$$
$$= (-|A_R| + |A_R \cap \Re| + |A_R \cap \Re|)/|\Re|$$
$$= (|A_N| - |C| + 2|A_R|_R)/|\Re|$$
$$(since \; |A_R|_R = |\Re| - |A_N|_R = |\Re| - |A_N| + |A_N|_N)$$
$$= (2|\Re| - |A_N| + 2|A_N|_N - |C|)/|\Re|$$
$$= (|A_N|_N - |A_N|_R - (|C| - 2|\Re|))/|\Re|$$
$$= (|A_N|_N - |A_N|_R)/|\Re| + const$$

This simplification is intuitively proper; the SPSM is linearly related to the Redundancy-Mistake measure in [7] - an increase in SPSM always corresponds to a decrease in the Redundancy-Mistake. If a run A returns more novel sentences on the basis of B (i.e. $A_N \supset B_N$), $|A_N|_N - |B_N|_N = |A_N - B_N|_N$, then

$$SPSM(A) - SPSM(B) = (|A_N - B_N|_N - |A_N - B_N|_R)/|\Re|$$

#novel in $A_N - B_N$ (number of novel ones in the extra returned sentences) corresponds to the decrease in #false alarms, and #redundant in $A_N - B_N$ corresponds to the increase in #misses. This is shown in the last column of Table 2. Under SPSM, in Table 2, selected pool (sp0.7s5.0) on Novelty 03 dataset is slightly better than overlap, and simple pool is worse than both selected pool and overlap. For the 04 collection the improvement of selected pool is consistent under both SNM and SPSM.

Table 3. Evaluation with the Simplified PSM

2004 top 5 docs	$\lvert X_N\rvert_N$	$\lvert X_N\rvert_R$	SPSM
o0.7	634	340	294
s0.4	627	359	268
2003 all 25 docs	$\lvert X_N\rvert_N$	$\lvert X_N\rvert_R$	SPSM
o0.7	9836	3467	6369
s0.4	9962	3533	6429

In Table 3, results indicate that under SPSM, the overlap method is comparable to the similarity method. Actually, similarity is better than overlap on both

03 and 04 datasets under SNM because of the use of SNM. Till this point we have both theoretically and empirically answered the questions in the introduction proposed by [7]: symmetric or asymmetric measure (the SPSM evaluation for similarity and overlap pointed out where the problem truly lies: the evaluation method; symmetric measures are not always better under SPSM), one-to-one or one-to-multiple comparison (the selected pool method solved the mystery of this discrepancy between theory and practice). These questions arose because of the unclear perception of the nature of novelty detection.

6   Conclusions

The PO-CO framework and related discussions as the characteristics of novelty detection is important because they provide new insights into Novelty theoretically (detailed discussion provided in the accompanying paper) and empirically.

This nature of the novelty task has answered the questions (surprising discrepancies between theory and observation) proposed by [7]. This work has proposed a new approach to novelty detection (a new family of methods) – selected pool, which has been proved effective empirically. In the selected pool theme, not only can sentences be treated as sets of weighted terms like in section 4, but also can be treated as vectors or language models or sequences of terms. The nature of novelty detection takes effect independent of the representation of individual sentences. We leave the discovery of an optimal representation of sentence to the future work. In addition to the above empirical achievements, this paper provides as well insights into the characteristics of the datasets, and the evaluation methodologies. All these factors together contributed to the empirical impact of the nature of novelty detection.

References

1. D. Harman. Overview of the trec 2002 novelty track. In *Proceedings of TREC 2002*, 2003.
2. G. Salton and C. Buckley. Term weighting approaches in automatic text retrieval. *Information Processing and Management*, 24(5):513–523, 1988.
3. I. Soboroff. Draft overview of the trec 2004 novelty track. In *Proceedings of TREC 2004 (Notebook)*, 2004.
4. I. Soboroff and D. Harman. Overview of the trec 2003 novelty track. In *Proceedings TREC 2003*, 2004.
5. M. Zhang, C. Lin, Y. Liu, L. Zhao, and S. Ma. THUIR at trec 2003: Novelty, robust and web. In *Proceedings of TREC 2003*, pages 556–567, 2004.
6. M. Zhang, R. Song, C. Lin, Z. Jiang, Y. Jin, Y. Liu, L. Zhao, and S. Ma. Expansion-based technologies in finding relevant and new information: Thu trec2002 novelty track experiments. In *Proceedings of TREC 2002*, 2003.
7. Y. Zhang, J. Callan, and T. Minka. Novelty and redundancy detection in adaptive filtering. In *Proceedings of the 25th annual international ACM SIGIR conference on Research and development in information retrieval (SIGIR 2002)*, pages 81–88, 2002.

Song Wave Retrieval Based on Frame-Wise Phoneme Recognition

Yuuichi Yaguchi and Ryuichi Oka

The University of Aizu, Tsuruga, Ikkimachi,
Aizuwakamatsu-shi, Fukushima, 965-8580 Japan
{s1100217, oka}@u-aizu.ac.jp
http://iplpcx1.u-aizu.ac.jp

Abstract. We propose a song wave retrieval method. Both song wave data and a query wave for song wave data are transformed into phoneme sequences by frame-wise labeling of each frame feature. By applying a search algorithm, called Continuous Dynamic Programming (CDP), to these phoneme sequences, we can detect a set of similar parts in a song database, each of which is similar to a query song wave. Song retrieval rates hit 78% in four clauses from whole databases. Differences in each query from song wave data and speech wave data is investigated.

1 Introduction

This paper introduces a song wave retrieval system that is vocabulary independent and that uses frame-wise phoneme recognition. Our purpose is to show the
system's applicability from a song query tool to a continuous song database, and
find the most suitable threshold for retrieval dicisions in this system. In recent
years, computers have become capable of recognizing natural human voices from
the news or other television programs in real time and recording the speech of
many unspecified speakers in sentences and then retrieving them [1]. Related to
this is the great need for song wave recognition and retrieval applications that
can easily retrieve voices or songs for music businesses that sell CDs or karaoke
[2], [3]. However, research has not been conducted singing, that is one of voice in
comparison with speaking. One of the retrieval methods of song data with music
is this: pick up the melody and retrieve the database melody area using a query
melody [4], but there is little research about song wave retrieval that employs
phonological character [5].

2 Construction of a Vocabulary-Independent Song Retrieval System

Oka [6] proposed a speech retrieval system. This system converts frames of database and query wave data to phoneme labels by using a Bayesian method, and
retrieves intervals of the database, each of which are similar to the query by

G.G. Lee et al. (Eds.): AIRS 2005, LNCS 3689, pp. 503–509, 2005.

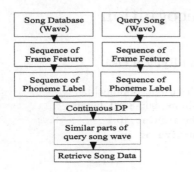

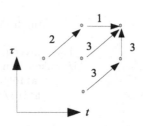

Fig. 1. Flow chart of song retrieval system

Fig. 2. Local path and skew weight of CDP

spotting, using CDP [7] the same way as a query. This retrieval method is completely vocabulary independent because this matching is not affected by words or sentences.

3 Frame-Wise Phoneme Labeling

3.1 Create the Feature Vector for Each Frame

A frame-wise sound retrieval system operates to create a feature vector for each frame of song data. This vector features sound directional patterns because this pattern method is more effective than the Cepstrum method [8]. First, this method makes 8-msec intervals and a 20-channel spectrum field from speech waveforms. Second, the spectrum field is extracted by gradients of a 4-direction pattern (up, down, left and right vector) from the middle 18 channels of the 20 channels ($4 \times 18 = 72$). Third, this 4-direction pattern is smoothed only in the time axis direction to seven frames from three frames before to three frames after a target. Fourth, the feature vector data can be set into 216-vector pattern data as a target frame from a target, 2 frames before and 2 frames after a target. This smoothing can reduce the range of speech melody and reduce the pitch distance in songs. Finally, these 216-vector patterns are converted to phoneme labels by using a Bayes calculation.

3.2 Frame-Wise Phoneme Recognition

Discriminate functions in this system were obtained from a collection of similar phoneme label frames by using the well-known Bayes estimation where every frame already has phoneme labels in speech waveforms.

$$g^l(x) = \sum_{i=1}^{k} \frac{\{\phi_{l,i}^T(x - \mu_l)\}^2}{\lambda_{l,i}} + \ln \prod_{i=1}^{k} \lambda_{l,i} - 2\ln p(\omega_l) \tag{1}$$

x : Will-identification input feature vector.
μ_l: Average of learned feature vector about phoneme l.

Table 1. Phoneme label list

/a/, /i/, /u/, /e/, /o/, /y/,
/w/, /r/, /n/, /m/, /nn/, /g/,
/j/, /z/, /f/, /h/, /s/, /sh/,
/b/, /d/, /k/, /p/, /t/, /ts/,
/ch/, /sp/

Table 2. Comparing frame-wise phoneme label translation rate from song waves using proposal technique. (Allow third place). Bayes function made by ATR SPEECH DATABASE.

	Level 1	Level 2	Level 3
Song DB	45.71	57.44	63.85

$\lambda_{l,i}$: ith eigen value of sample of learned feature vectors about phoneme l.
$\phi_{l,i}$: ith eigenvector of phoneme l.
k: total number of usable eigen values.
$p(\omega_l)$: Preliminarily incidence probability of phoneme l.

These discriminate functions are made of specific kinds of phonemes (26 kinds). In this paper, 26 types of Bayes estimation (Table 1) made by 5030 sentences of speech data in ATR Speech Database [9]. These 26 types of phonemes are chosen from common labels of 50 label types in the ATR Speech Database and 29 label types in the RWC Music Database [10]. Every frame of song waveforms, that is those in the database and query waves, is checked for these 26 phoneme labels used in the Bayes estimation. If one of the phoneme labels lies at a max value of some frame, that phoneme labels the frame.

3.3 Frame-Wise Phoneme Labeling of Database and Query Line

This phoneme label has not a small error (Table 2) but this phoneme labeling is thought of as a filter that picks up some feature quantity and converts other data types. Thus, the experiment in this research uses this labeling method because this phoneme labeling codes the database and query data that makes the same error [11].

4 Song Waveform Retrieval Algorithm

4.1 Application of Continuous Dynamic Programming

CDP [12] is used as the retrieval algorithm of the database for queries. Each frame is first expressed as the frame expression of a voice, and this is accomplished by labeling the phonemic symbol. In this research, we use the candidate in the first place in the database (input) line and the third place in the query (index) line. The database line expressed by $F(t) = (f_1(t))$. $f_1(t)$ is the phoneme label of the 1st candidate in the t frame. The parameter t indicates the time axis of the database, while τ indicates one of the query data. Then they are described by $F(t), t = 1, 2, 3, ...$ $G(\tau) = (g_1(\tau), g_2(\tau), g_3(\tau))$ $(1 \leqq \tau \leqq T)$.

The input pattern for this time is a phoneme row of the database. A phoneme row of a query is used for the reference pattern. This setup of the input is used to enable input of the data infinitely into the CDP algorithm when we obtain of minimum distance between the reference pattern and a suitable best interval database. The suitable interval is determined in a posterior way after detecting a local minimum in a stream of output of CDP.

There is the local distance between the input pattern and the reference pattern.

$$
d(t,\tau) = \begin{cases} 0.0: & f_1(t) = g_1(\tau) \\ 0.1: & f_1(t) = g_2(\tau) \\ 0.2: & f_1(t) = g_3(\tau) \\ 1.0: & (otherwise) \end{cases} \tag{2}
$$

The CDP recurrence formula that uses the local distance can be shown as follows.

Initial Condition:

$$
P(-1,\tau) = P(0,\tau) = \infty \tag{3}
$$

Iteration $(t = 1, 2, ...)$:
For $\tau = 1$

$$
P(t,1) = 3d(t,1) \tag{4}
$$

For $\tau = 2$

$$
P(t,2) = \min \begin{cases} P(t-2,1) + 2 \cdot d(t-1,2) + d(t,2) \\ P(t-1,1) + 3 \cdot d(t,2) \\ P(t,1) + 3 \cdot d(t,2) \end{cases} \tag{5}
$$

For $\tau = 3$

$$
P(t,\tau) = \min \begin{cases} P(t-2,\tau-1) + 2 \cdot d(t-1,\tau) + d(t,\tau) \\ P(t-1,\tau-1) + 3 \cdot d(t,\tau) \\ P(t-1,\tau-2) + 3 \cdot (t,\tau-1) + 3 \cdot D(t-\tau) \end{cases} \tag{6}
$$

Hence, the output is as follows:

$$
A(t) = \frac{1}{3 \cdot T} P(t,T) \tag{7}
$$

The local distance used with CDP and the weight are assumed to be that shown in Figure 2, and the weight shown in Figure 2 is asymmetric. The accumulation of weight steadies with $3T$, even the weight obtained from the best pass by accumulation distance $P(t,T)$ calculation. The logical conclusion is that this becomes easily performed as a regularized operation as in equation (7) to prevent the value of $A(t)$ from depending on the length of a standard pattern.

4.2   Extract Range of Retrieved Internal

This singing voice retrieval, the CDP value $A(t)$ at each time t, is output by applying CDP as in (Figure 5). Because the best pass that gives the output value at this time is decided, the starting point on the axis of the input time of the best pass is also decided. In this system, backtrace controls are applied at the starting point decision. Section N at $S(t)$ and the input time at each time

[Lyric] Female Singing			1st clause	/2nd clause	/3rd & 4th clauses
...		...	1. 夜中の3時	/目がさめて	/携帯にもメールが来ない
夜中の3時 目がさめて		Yonakanosanji Megasamete	(Yonakanosanji)	/(Megasamete)	/(Keitainimome-rugakonai)
携帯にもメールが来ない		Keitainimome-rugakonai	2. 今でも	/君が好きだと	/言っていいのかな
朝までずっと 待っている私		Asamadezutto Matteiruwatashi	(Imademo)	/(Kimigasukidato)	/(Itteiinokana)
結局は睡眠不足		Kekkyokuwasuiminbusoku	3. ちょっと待って	/不思議な	/ときめきあふれ出していく
あなたに会うと文句が言えない		Anataniautomonkugaienai	(Chottomatte)	/(Fushigina)	/(Tokimekiafuredasiteiku)
まるで飛べない鳥だね		Marudetobenaitoridane	4. 線路は続くよ	/どこまでも	/夢と希望のせどこまでも
...		...	(Senrohatuzukuyo)	/(Dokomademo)	/(Yumetokibounosedokomademo)
			5. きっと新しい	/気持ちを	/つれてくるから
			(Kittoatarashi)	/(Kimochio)	/(Tsuretekurukara)

Fig. 3. Example of Song Database Lyrics. Underlined parts of lyrics are targets of voice queries. (Japanese)

Fig. 4. Example of Voice Query Data Used in Experiment. (Japanese Script)

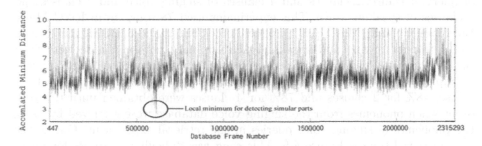

Fig. 5. Experiment in Retrieving Singing Voices with CDP: If script of is input as singing voice and retrieved as lyrics data, the length of Accumulated minimum distance becomes small in two places that adjust to input and reference

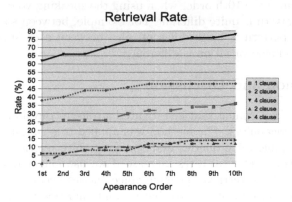

Fig. 6. Results of Song wave retrieval experiment

t can be decided as A with the starting point on the axis of the input time to give $A(t) \leq \alpha$.

$$N(t : A, \alpha) \stackrel{\text{def}}{=} [S(t), t] \tag{8}$$

If $N(t : A, \alpha)$ have a common section in $N(t' : A, \alpha)$, this system can select the N corresponding to the smallest one as compared with $A(t)$ and $A(t')$ because it never has a section that shares the same time as that of the retrieved sections. In general, the part of retrieval area that should not be retrieved increases, too, when this retrieval enlarges the value of A while the retrieval leakage decreases because the proportion of the section retrieved in the database grows. Moreover, the result is different from the evaluation for a singing voice recognition rate because this retrieval output is evaluated only of whether it resembles a query or not.

5   Song Wave Retrieval Experiment

We conducted an experiment to compare the results of retrieval with five types of query: 1 clause, 2 clauses and 4 clauses of singing voice and 2 clauses and 4 clauses of speaking voice. This experiment used 78 songs from RWC Music Database: Popular Music [10], Japanese solos but reduced BGM, and 4 men and 1 woman singing and speaking each 10 query phrase. Those were from the database and trimmed of query length (database example: Figure 3, query example: Figure 4). In the retrieval experiment, the retrieval rate of 36% for 1 clause, 48% for 2 clauses and 78% for 4 clauses were obtained until the 10th order when phonemes from the singing voice database were retrieved by using the phonemes of singing voice queries in the retrieval experiment. One of the miss-retrieved song is Figure 4-5. This song was difficult to express for query like a database phrase because this song had a strong echo and very high female voice. Some other songs had also weak or strong effects like delay and seleste, but these songs were obtained from the collecting area. However, the retrieval rate of speaking voices was quite low; 12% for 2 clauses and 14% for 4 clauses were obtained until the 10th order when using the speaking voice query because the phoneme pattern is quite different. For example, between song rhythm and speech rhythm pattern is quite different, also between each singing voice and speech voice phoneme variation is different.

6   Conclusion and Discussion

We described an experiment that investigated a voice retrieval method that does not depend on vocabulary. The method was applied to a singing voice that was retrieved by singing voice queries and speaking voice queries. In this experiment, singing voice retrieval rates increase if we use longer queries. However, this method could not retrieve speaking voice queries because it is quite different from singing voice in respect to rhythm and phoneme variation. Also some singing voice effects are made difficult to pick up collect area.

In the future, we will apply more proper weight and distance in CDP matching to improve singing voice recognition rates, investigate how much effect is added by vocals, what approaches exist for improving singing voice recognition rates by processing, research some noise reduction or noise free method for CD music retrieving with this retrieval method.

Acknowledgement: We wish to express our gratitude to Mr. Jian Xin Zhang (Media Drive) and Mr. Masanori Ihara (SHARP) who supported the advancement of this research.

References

1. A. Ando, *Real-time Speech Recognition*, The Institute of Electronics, Information and Communication Engineers, September 2003. (Japanese)
2. T. Sonoda et al., "A WWW-Based Melody Retrieval System", *IEICE Transcription*, vol. J84-D-II, no. 1, pp. 721-731, April 1999. (Japanese)
3. M. Goto, "F0 Estimation of Melody and Bass Lines in Musical Audio Signals",*IEICE Transcription*, vol. J84-D-II, no. 1, pp. 12-22, January 2001. (Japanese)
4. H. Hashiguchi et al, "Music Signal Spotting Retrieval by a Humming Query Using Model Driven Path Continuous Dynamic Programming", *IEICE Transcription*, vol. J84-D-II, no. 12, pp. 2479-2488, December 2001. (Japanese)
5. H. Wang, "Experiments in syllable-based retrieval of broadcast news speech in Mandarin Chinese", *Speech Communication*, vol. 32, nos. 1-2, pp. 49-60, September 2000.
6. R. Oka et al, "Vocabulary-free Speech Retrieval Based on Phoneme Symbol Labeling of Frame Feature", *IEICE Transcription*, vol. J86-D-II, no. 6, pp. 7 64-775, June 2003. (Japanese)
7. R. Oka, "Spotting Method for Classification of Real World Data", *The Computer Journal*, Vol.41, No.8, pp.559-565 (1998).
8. H. Matsumura et al, "Speaker-Independent Spoken Word Recognition by Using the Orientation Patterns Obtained from the Vector Field of Spectrum Pattern", *IEICE Transcription*, Vol. 72-D-II, No. 4, pp.487-498 1989. (Japanese)
9. ATR, *ATR SPEECH DATABASE, 503 Phonetically balanced sentences*, 1992. (Japanese)
10. M. Goto et al, "RWC Music Database: Popular Music Database and Royalty-Free Music Database", *IPSJ Transactions on MUS*, 2001-MUS-42-6, Vol.2001, No.103, pp.35-42, October 2001. (Japanese)
11. Y. Yaguchi et al, "Song Wave Retrieval Based on Frame-wise Phoneme Recognition", *Technical Report of IEICE*, SP2004-50, June 2004. (Japanese)
12. S. Furui, *Digital Speech Recognition*, Tokai university press, September 1985. (Japanese)

trackThem: Exploring a Large-Scale News Video Archive by Tracking Human Relations

Ichiro Ide[1,2], Tomoyoshi Kinoshita[3], Hiroshi Mo[2], Norio Katayama[2], and Shin'ichi Satoh[2]

[1] Nagoya University, Graduate School of Information Science,
Furo-cho, Chikusa-ku, Nagoya, 464-8603, Japan
ide@is.nagoya-u.ac.jp
[2] National Institute of Informatics,
2-1-2 Hitotsubashi, Chiyoda-ku, Tokyo, 101-8430, Japan
{ide|mo|katayama|satoh}@nii.ac.jp
[3] NetCOMPASS, Ltd.
#207, 5-17-8 Minami-Senju, Arakawa-ku, Tokyo, 116-0003, Japan
kino@netcompass.co.jp

Abstract. We propose a novel retrieval method for a very large-scale news video archive based on human relations extracted from the archive itself. This paper presents the idea and the implementation of the method, and also introduces the *trackThem* interface that enables the retrieval and at the same time track down the relations. Although detailed evaluations are yet to be done, we have found interesting relations through the exploration of the archive by making use of the proposed interface.

1 Introduction

There have been many works aiming to retrieve news video contents. However, not much has been reported on what can be done and what can be acquired from a very large news video archive. In other words, most of the works aimed at analyzing and/or retrieving the contents in an archive either from individual units (shots, stories, and so on), or simply within each independent program.

Recent technology has enabled us to archive video data in large quantities. We have built an automatic broadcast video archiving system [Katayama *et al.* 2004], which has up to now, archived approximately 700 hours of daily Japanese news video spanning over the past four years. Even without such a system, large scale news video archives have become available, for example by participating to the TREC-Video workshop [NIST]. This has encouraged some groups to start exploring a news video archive according to its contents as a whole, in the aspect of 'Question and Answering' [Yang *et al.* 2003], 'topic threading' [Ide *et al.* 2004, Duygulu *et al.* 2004], and so on.

In this paper, we propose a topic-based news video browsing interface which provides access to an archive based on human relations extracted from the archive itself. This approach is proposed since human activity is the core contents

G.G. Lee et al. (Eds.): AIRS 2005, LNCS 3689, pp. 510–515, 2005.

in news videos, and that interactions between the humans cause such activities. Therefore, we consider that extracting human relations from a news video archive is an essential foundation for the understanding of its contents.

2 Extracting Human Relations from a News Video Archive

2.1 Overview

Extracting human relations from a large quantity of data has been a hot topic in the data mining, the semantic web, and the social network analysis fields [Kautz *et al.* 1997]. Works in these fields have focused mainly on e-mail correspondence [Golbeck *et al.* 2004], web links [Matsuo *et al.* 2005], references in academic papers [Yoshikane *et al.* 2004], and so on. However extraction of social networks from multimedia data has not been sought.

We are working on human relation extraction from a news video archive, in order to realize a retrieval and browsing interface based on the relations. As this enables a user to track down news stories according to human relations, the interface is named *trackThem*. It is generally considered that the so-called '5W1H' (*i.e.* When, Where, Who, What, Why, and How) are essential components of a news text in journalism, where '4W' (*i.e.* When, Where, Who, and What) are especially important entities to describe a story. Most previous works in news video retrieval field retrieve similar stories based on what has happened

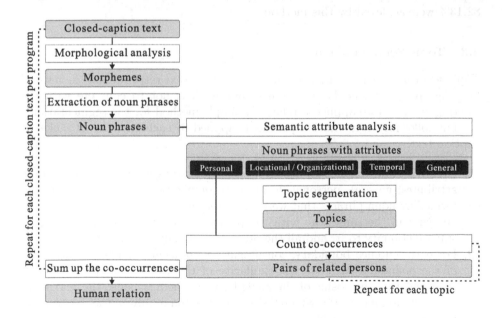

Fig. 1. Overall flow of the human relation extraction process

('What'), some new works consider the time order ('When') as an important factor [Ide *et al.* 2004, Duygulu *et al.* 2004], and some other work provides an ability to retrieve/browse by geographical location ('Where') [Christel *et al.* 2000]. According to this classification, our proposal can be considered as a method based on 'Who', which has not been sought deeply in previous works.

In this Section, we will briefly present the process of the human relation extraction. The overall flow of the process is shown in Fig. 1.

2.2   Detecting Noun Phrases with a Human Attribute

Since news videos not only talk about famous people, but they also refer to nameless people, we would like to detect noun phrases that indicate persons (hereinafter personal nouns), including but not limited to names with proper nouns, as in named entity analysis.

Basically in Japanese language, the suffix determines the attribute of a noun phrase. Based on this nature, we have collected nouns that may represent humans either individually or as a suffix of a noun phrase.

As a pre-process, each sentence of a closed-caption text (transcript of the audio speech provided from the broadcaster) is analyzed by a Japanese morphological analyzer. [1] Next, noun phrases are extracted according to the morphemes, followed by semantic attribute analysis based on the collected nouns.

Details on the composing of the dictionary and the method can be found in [Ide *et al.* 1999]. According to evaluations applied to 2,549 super-imposed captions that appeared in news videos, a precision of 72.47% and a recall of 82.13% were achieved by this method.

2.3   Topic Segmentation

Topic segmentation is a major research topic in the text retrieval and the natural language processing fields. The aim of our work is not to compete with the existing works, so we applied a relatively simple method for the segmentation.

The following segmentation process is applied to each sentence of a closed-caption text:

1. Create keyword vectors for each sentence. Keyword vectors for four semantic attributes; general, personal, locational/organizational, and temporal, are formed by noun phrases that were extracted in Sect. 2.1. The latter two are analyzed in the same way with the personal noun by applying a different suffix dictionary to it, and all the others are classified as general nouns.

2. For each sentence boundary, concatenate w adjacent vectors on both sides of the boundary. Measure the similarity of the two concatenated vectors by calculating the cosine of the angle between them. Choose the maximum similarity among all the window sizes: w. The maximum w was set to 10 in the following experiment.

---

[1] JUMAN 3.61 distributed from Kyoto University was used as the analyzer.

3. Combine the similarities in each semantic attribute and detect a topic boundary when it does not exceed a threshold. According to a training with 384 manually given topic boundaries, we have obtained an optimal weight of 0.23 for general, 0.21 for personal, 0.48 for locational/organizational, and 0.08 for temporal nouns, and a threshold of 0.17.
4. Concatenate over-segmented topics by measuring the similarity of the keyword vectors between adjacent topics.

Details of this method can be found in [Ide *et al.* 2004]. According to previous evaluations applied to 384 manually annotated topic boundaries as a ground-truth, a precision of 90.5% and a recall of 95.4% were achieved by this method when we allowed mis-judgments at a maximum of ±1 sentence.

2.4   Extracting Human Relations

We consider that persons that co-occur within a topic have some kind of relation. The relation $R(p_i, p_j)$ between two persons p_i and p_j is defined as follows:

$$R(p_i, p_j) = \sum_t f(p_i, t) f(p_j, t) \ , \tag{1}$$

where t represents a topic, and $f(p, t)$ the frequency of personal noun p in topic t.

It might be effective to put a higher weight when two persons co-occur within a sentence, and gradually release the weights according to their distance within a topic. However this is left for future investigation. Grouping of the same person with different representation is another issue needed to be solved. However, the solution to this issue may not be trivial since some representations may be ambiguous and change along time.

3   Exploring the Archive by Tracking Human Relations

Currently, the process in Sect. 2 is running fully automatically every night after the broadcast of the program. As of June 5, 2005, we have 17,468 topics ranging over 1,454 days. Within these topics, there were 150,238 noun phrases with a human attribute, of which 15,686 were different. There were 307,951 edges, or human relations, between the 15,686 noun phrases.

Fig. 2 shows a part of the human relation graph structure. The graph shows strong bilateral edges (relations) between the nodes (persons) and also strong unilateral nodes that link only the nodes that appeared in the bilateral structure. This structure was extracted automatically by referring to the top ten edges from each node, except for the merger of different representations of the same person.

In order to provide the extracted relations for video retrieval, we developed an interface that enables a user to retrieve and view news topics related to a selected pair of persons, while at the same time, track down the human relations. A snapshot of the interface, namely the *trackThem* interface, is shown in Fig. 3. We believe that this should provide a better understanding of news topics from the view point of human relations.

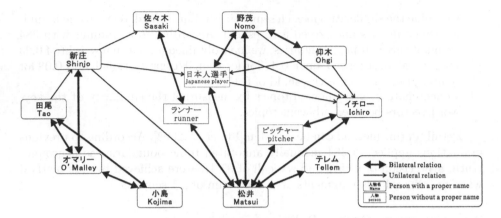

Fig. 2. A part of the human relation graph structure; the part mostly shows relations among Japanese baseball players playing in the US

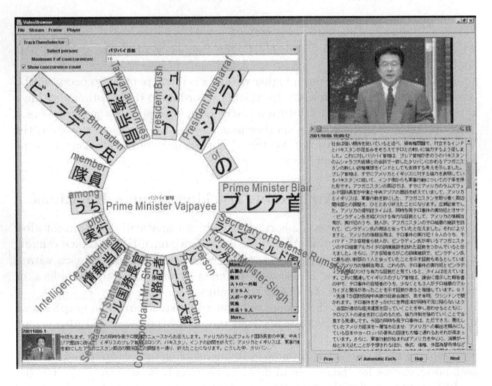

Fig. 3. The *trackThem* interface. The person in focus is encircled by related persons aligned in the order of their degrees of relation in proportional sizes. The person in focus may initially be selected from a list on the top. A single click on a related person enlists the topics that they co-occured at the bottom, while a double click switches the person in focus. A double click on a topic sets it on a video viewer on the right.

4   Conclusion

In this paper, we have proposed a novel approach for news video retrieval; retrieval and browsing according to human relations within a very large-scale archive. Future work includes the evaluation on the extracted relations and the efficacy of the interface. We are also considering to make use of co-occurrences of faces in the image, in order to extract relations that do not appear in the text.

Acknowledgements

This work was partly supported by a Joint Research program "Research on creating a large-scale video corpus" funded by the National Institute of Informatics.

References

[Christel *et al.* 2000] Christel, M.G., Olligschlaeger, M., and Huang, C.: Interactive maps for a digital video library. IEEE Multimedia **7(1)** (2000) 60–67

[Duygulu *et al.* 2004] Duygulu, P., Pan, J.-Y., and Forsyth, D.A.: Towards auto-documentary: Tracking the evolution of news stories. Proc. Twelfth ACM Intl. Conf. on Multimedia (2004) 820–827

[Golbeck *et al.* 2004] Golbeck, J. and Hendler, J.: Reputation network analysis for email filtering. Proc. First Intl. Conf. on Email and Anti-Spam (2004)

[Ide *et al.* 1999] Ide, I., Hamada, R., Sakai, S., and Tanaka, H.: Semantic analysis of television news captions referring to suffixes. Proc. Fourth Intl. Workshop on Information Retrieval with Asian Languages (1999) 37–42

[Ide *et al.* 2004] Ide, I., Mo, H., Katayama, N., and Satoh, S.: Topic threading for structuring a large-scale news video archive. Proc. Third Intl. Conf. on Image and Video Retrieval, Lecture Notes in Computer Science **3115** (2004) 123–131

[Katayama *et al.* 2004] Katayama, N., Mo, H., Ide, I., and Satoh, S.: Mining large-scale broadcast video archives towards inter-video structuring. Proc. Fifth Pacific Rim Conf. on Multimedia, Lecture Notes in Computer Science **3332** (2004) 489–496

[Kautz *et al.* 1997] Kautz, H., Selman, B., and Shah, M.: The hidden web. AI Magazine **18(2)** (1997) 27–36

[Matsuo *et al.* 2005] Matsuo, Y., Mori, J., Asada, Y., Hasida, K., and Ishizuka, M.: Mining large-scale social network of researcher from the web. Proc. Fifteenth Intl. Sunbelt Social Network Conf., (2005)

[NIST] National Institute of Standards and Technology: TREC Video Retrieval Evaluation. http://www-nlpir.nist.gov/projects/trecvid/

[Yang *et al.* 2003] Yang, H., Chaisorn, L., Zhao, Y., Neo, S.-Y., and Chua, T.-S.: VideoQA: Question and answering on news video. Proc. Eleventh ACM Intl. Conf. on Multimedia (2003) 632–641

[Yoshikane *et al.* 2004] Yoshikane, F. and Kageura, K.: Comparative analysis of coauthorship networks of different domains: The growth and change of networks. Scientometrics **60(3)**, Akadémiai Kiadó, Budapest / Kluwer Academic Publishers, Dordrecht (2004) 435–446

Topic-Independent Web High-Quality Page Selection Based on K-Means Clustering

Canhui Wang[1], Yiqun Liu[1], Min Zhang[2], and Shaoping Ma[2]

[1] State Key Lab of Intelligent technology & systems, Tsinghua University,
Beijing, 100084, China P.R.
{wangcanhui, liuyiqun}@tsinghua.org.cn
[2] State Key Lab of Intelligent technology & systems, Tsinghua University,
Beijing, 100084, China P.R.
{z-m, msp}@tsinghua.edu.cn

Abstract. One of the web search engines' challenges is to identify the quality of web pages independent of a given user request. Web high-quality pages provide readers proper entries to get more concentrated required information on the web. This paper focuses on topic-independent web high-quality page selection to reduce web information redundancies and clean noise. Different non-content features and their effects on high-quality page selection are studied. Then K-means clustering with these features is performed to separate high-quality pages from common ones. Experiments on 19GB (document size) TREC web data set (.GOV data) have been made. By this proposed approach, less than 50% of web pages are obtained as high-quality ones, covering about 90% key information in the whole set. Information retrieval on this high-quality page set achieves more than 40% improvement, compared with that on the whole data collection.[1]

1 Introduction

A lot of redundant or low-quality information is intermixed with useful information on the web, which brings the major problem to the development of modern search engines. Henzinger (et al) suggested that it should be extremely helpful for web search engines to be able to identify the quality of web pages independent of a given user request, which has been one of the search engines' challenges at this time [7].

Besides affording the most credible and best information on some topic, a high-quality page more usually offers many useful links to other high-quality informational pages regarding the topic, via which users can access more detailed information by just one click. That is the main difference between a high-quality page and a common one. The task of finding high-quality pages (also called key pages) regarding a certain topic is called "topic distillation" [4], which has been adopted as a major task in TREC Web Track for several years. Previous techniques [1][3][4][6] for the task were mostly carried out on the whole data collection, mainly to perform result

---

[1] This research is supported by the Chinese National Key Foundation Research & Development Plan (2004CB318108), Natural Science Foundation (60223004, 60321002, 60303005) and the Key Project of Chinese Ministry of Education (No. 104236).

G.G. Lee et al. (Eds.): AIRS 2005, LNCS 3689, pp. 516–521, 2005.

analysis. Improvements were achieved but results might have been hurt due to the noise caused by low-quality documents. High-quality pages take up only a small proportion of all pages. If they are found in advance independent of topics and used to retrieve information, both performance and efficiency of web information retrieval would be greatly improved.

In this paper, a topic-independent method of high-quality page selection is proposed. The selection of high-quality pages could be considered as a dividing process, which partitions all documents into high-quality pages and common ones. This process has to be treated with independent of topics because high-quality pages selected are used to retrieve with all possible topics and any topical affection should not be brought in before retrieval. In this case, contents of documents should not be added in as features because it is topic-concerned.

Previous research indicated that some non-content features could be used to carry out page finding work [8][9][10][12]. These features are applied here to implement selection of high-quality pages based on a K-means clustering approach, with which high-quality pages and common ones gather together respectively.

The remaining part of this paper is constructed as follows: Section 2 sets out statistical observations of comparing high-quality pages and common ones in non-content features. The method of high-quality page selection based on K-means clustering is proposed in section 3. Section 4 and 5 describe the high-quality page selection and retrieval experiments, followed by discussions and conclusions.

2   Non-content Features of Web Pages

Statistical characteristics of non-content features, namely in-degree, document length, URL-type, in-site out-link number and in-site out-link anchor rate, are observed and calculated, as shown in Fig. 1 below.

It is difficult to get a good sample of pages [7], so estimation is made to obtain a high-quality page set and a common page set. The high-quality page set used for statistics shown in Fig. 1 is composed of qrels of TREC11's topic distillation task, and we adopt .GOV corpus which includes about 19GB (document size) pages from .GOV domain as the common page set shown in Fig. 1. The .GOV corpus is a crawl of about

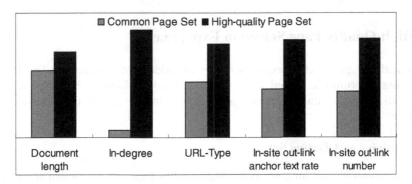

Fig. 1. Differences in non-content feature characteristics between common pages and high-quality ones

1,250,000 Web pages from .GOV domain. It is used in TREC web track task from TREC11 to TREC13.

In Fig. 1, in-site out-link is defined as the out-link pointing to another page at the same site. In-site out-link number is the number of in-site out-links in a page, and in-site out-link anchor text rate is defined as follows [12]:

$$rate = \frac{WordCount(in - site\ out - link\ anchor\ text)}{WordCount(web\ page\ full\ text)} \tag{1}$$

URL-types include ROOT, SUBROOT, PATH and FILE [8]. Different types are presented different values in the statistics as follows: ROOT=4, SUBROOT=3, PATH=2, FILE=1. The average type value of high-quality pages is 1.93, which tends to be a PATH value; though the value of common pages is 1.15, near to a FILE value.

3   High-Quality Page Selection Based on K-Means Clustering

Non-content features of web pages described in section 2 can be made good use of doing clustering which separates high-quality ones from common pages. The K-means clustering algorithm is a popular clustering method that minimizes the clustering error [11] and is widely used in statistical analysis because of its simplicity and flexibility [13].

In order to perform K-means clustering, every page in the document set is represented with a five-dimension vector, each dimension of which indicates a feature discussed in the previous section. Vectors are divided by their variance as a normalization to avoid the influence brought by numerical differences of dimensions.

K is set to 2 in our K-means clustering if we would like to get a high-quality page cluster and a common page cluster. A puzzled problem in the clustering is how to select initial mean vectors of the classes since performance depends on the initial starting conditions [5]. Statistical results in section 2 are utilized to help to select good mean vectors of two classes. Firstly, mean vector of the high-quality page set mentioned in section 2 is used as the initial mean vector of the high-quality cluster. Secondly, we get mean vector of the common page set mentioned in section 2 divided by a constant C (set to 2 in our experiments) as the initial mean vector of the common cluster.

4   High-Quality Page Selection Experiments

High-quality page selection experiments are introduced in this section. The K-means clustering algorithm described in section 3 is used to divide a big page set into a high-quality page set and a common page set, and metrics are brought to evaluate the result set.

4.1   Training and Testing Set

The classification's training set is the high-quality page set mentioned in section 2, which helps to select an initial mean vector of high-quality cluster, as mentioned in section 3.

The testing set is formed of the relevant qrels in TREC12's topic distillation task. They are all high-quality pages.

The testing set and the training set share no pages in common.

4.2 Evaluation Metrics

Traditional Recall metric can be presented to estimate how many high-quality pages the result set would cover.

Recall can be calculated by:

$$recall = \frac{\#((High \text{ - quality } Testing \ Set) \cap (Re\,sult \ Set))}{\#(High \text{ - quality } Testing \ Set)} \qquad (2)$$

4.3 High-Quality Page Selection Result

Carry out high-quality page selection using K-means clustering.

The result is laid out in Fig. 2 below, which shows the process of K-means clustering from left to right. As a result of the first iteration, a high-quality page set containing 16.7% of all pages covers nearly 70% of all testing high-quality pages. The clustering process converges after 17 iterations, bringing in a high-quality page set which is composed of 44.7% of all pages and covers 90% of all testing high-quality pages. This means that the clustering divides the whole document set into two page sets: one is the high-quality page set, which is smaller than half of the whole set in size but almost

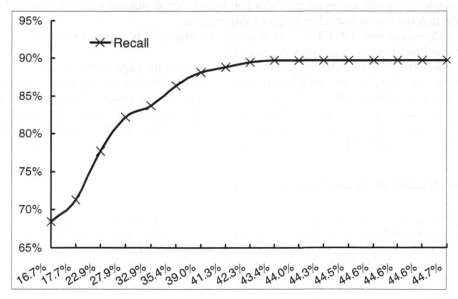

Horizontal axis: percentage of all pages in .GOV page set
Vertical axis: coverage of testing set

Fig. 2. High-quality page selection results using K-means clustering (*K*=2)

contains all useful pages in the whole set; the other is the common page set, which is mainly composed of useless pages.

5   Retrieval Experiments

The high-quality pages selected by proposed approach are used on topic distillation task in TREC12 to evaluate their effects on information retrieval. This task regards high-quality pages on a certain topic as its retrieval target. Retrieval results are shown in Table 1. All experiments are performed on our IR system named TMiner with BM2500 term weighting [2].

Table 1. Retrieval result comparison among the whole set, high-quality page set and TREC12 best result

	Precision@10	R-precision
Whole Set	0.0720	0.1145
High-quality Set	0.1240	0.1654
TREC12 Best [4]	0.1240	0.1636

As shown in Table 1, high-quality page set, which contains only half of all pages and covers 90% of testing high-quality pages, has attained a retrieval result with a promotion of 72% in Precision@10, 45% in R-precision, compared with the whole set result. This is because the high-quality page set has excluded a lot of low-quality pages which are actually noises for topic distillation task. It is easier and more effective to do the task upon such a small and high-quality page set.

Compared with TREC12's best result [4], the high-quality page set's result has the same Precision@10 and higher R-precision.

Results show that this topic-independent high-quality page selection gets rid of noises in a big page set, finds high-quality pages and obtains a smaller but better page set for information retrieve. Though K-means clustering is a converging process that costs a few hours to complete, it matters little since selection of high-quality pages is performed before retrieval topic-independently. This method improves both performance and efficiency of retrieval tasks.

6   Conclusions and Future Work

This paper introduces a topic-independent method of high-quality page selection using non-content features to improve performance and efficiency of web information retrieval. The selection of high-quality pages is considered as a clustering process in this paper, which divides all documents into high-quality pages and common ones. Non-content features are used to do the clustering, and K-means clustering algorithm is adopted.

Following conclusions can be made: Firstly, non-content features are helpful for finding high-quality pages topic-independently. Second, K-means clustering process converges and brings to us a high-quality page set that contains only half of the whole set but covers 90% of all key information. Finally, information retrieval result on generated high-quality page set has a big promotion in precision, compared with that on the whole collection of .GOV data in TREC12 web track.

The success brings us more problems to think about, and more and deeper research can be done in the future: Are there any other non-content features that can be used to perform the clustering? Can supervised learning be brought in to help separate high-quality pages from common ones? How will the performance, efficiency and result become if supervised learning is utilized?

References

1. B. D. Davison. Topical locality in the web. In W. B. Croft, D. J. Harper, D. H. Kraft, and J. Zobel, editors. Proceedings of the 23rd Annual International Conference on Research and Development in Information Retrieval (2000) 272-279
2. Min Zhang, Chuan Lin, Yiqun Liu, Le Zhao, Liang Ma, Shaoping Ma, THUIR at TREC 2003: Novelty, Robust, Web and HARD (2003)
3. D. Hawking and N. Craswell. Overview of the TREC-2002 web track. In Voorhees and Buckland (2002)
4. D. Hawking and N. Craswell. Overview of the TREC 2003 web track, 2003. In NIST Special Publication: SP 500-255, The Twelfth Text Retrieval Conference (2003)
5. J.A. Lozano, J.M. Pena, P. Larranaga, An empirical comparison of four initialization methods for the k-means algorithm, Pattern Recognition Lett. 20 (1999) 1027–1040
6. K. Bharat and M. Henzinger. Improved algorithms for topic distillation in a hyperlinked environment. In 21st International ACM SIGIR Conference on Research and Development in Information Retrieval, pages 104-111, Aug. (1998)
7. Monika R. Henzinger, Rajeev Motwani and Craig Silverstein, Challenges in Web Search Engines, in proceedings of the International Joint Conference on Artificial Intelligence (2003)
8. Nick Craswell and David Hawking. Query-independent evidence in home page finding. In ACM Transactions on Information Systems (TOIS) archive Volume 21 , Issue 3 (July 2003) table of contents (2003) 286-313
9. T. Westerveld, D. Hiemstra, W. Kraaij. Retrieving Web Pages Using Content, Links, URLs and Anchors. In Voorhees and Harman (2002) 663-672
10. W. Kraaij, T. Westerveld, and D. Hiemstra. The importance of prior probabilities for entry page search. In 25th annual international ACM SIGIR conference on research and development in information retrieval (2002) 27-34
11. A Likas, N Vlassis, JJ Verbeek, The global k-means clustering algorithm, Pattern Recognition (2003)
12. Yiqun Liu, Min Zhang, Shaoping Ma, Effective topic distillation with key resource pre-selection, Proceedings of the Asia Information Retrieval Symposium (2004)
13. T Kanungo, DM Mount, NS Netanyahu, C Piatko, The analysis of a simple k-means clustering algorithm, Symposium on Computational Geometry (2000)

Improving Text Similarity Measurement by Critical Sentence Vector Model

Wei Li[1], Kam-Fai Wong[1], Chunfa Yuan[2], Wenjie Li[3], and Yunqing Xia[1]

[1] Department of Systems Engineering, the Chinese University of Hong Kong,
Shatin, N.T., Hong Kong
{wli, kfwong, yqxia}@se.cuhk.edu.hk
[2] State Key Laboratory of Intelligent Technology and System, Tsinghua University,
Beijing 100084, China
ycf@tsinghua.edu.cn
[3] Department of Computing, Hong Kong Polytechnic University, Hung Hom, Hong Kong
cswjli@comp.polyu.edu.hk

Abstract. We propose the *Critical Sentence Vector Model (CSVM)*, a novel model to measure text similarity. The CSVM accounts for the structural and semantic information of the document. Compared to existing methods based on keyword vector, e.g. *Vector Space Model (VSM)*, *CSVM* measures documents similarity by measuring similarity between critical sentence vectors extracted from documents. Experiments show that CSVM outperforms VSM in calculation of text similarity.

1 Introduction

Text similarity is a hot topic, which has direct impact on applications such as text retrieval [2,3,4,5], text classification [6,7], document summarization [8], question and answering [9,10,11], etc. The predominating method for this purpose is Vector Space Model (VSM) [1], which converts a text document into a weighted vector and determines the similarity between two documents by the distances of the vectors. According to experimental results reported by [2,3], text retrieval systems based on VSM could achieve reasonable accuracy. However, VSM or keywords alone cannot capture the semantic information in the text leading to many redundant results [3].

We propose a novel model, *Critical Sentence Vector Model (CSVM)*, for text similarity calculation. CSVM attempts to capture the structural and semantic information embedded in selected sentences. In this model, critical sentence vectors are extracted from both documents, and the similarities of the two sentence vectors are measured. Compared with document, sentence is a smaller linguistic unit which also carries complete event description and the semantic associated information. Furthermore, it is easier to perform grammatical and semantic analysis on a sentence than on a document. Experiments show that CSVM outperforms VSM in calculation of text similarity.

The rest of this paper is organized as follows. In Sect. 2 we give a full description of CSVM. Experiments and result analysis are presented in Sect. 3. We conclude the paper in the last section.

G.G. Lee et al. (Eds.): AIRS 2005, LNCS 3689, pp. 522–527, 2005.

2 Critical Sentence Vector Model

2.1 Overview

Basically, a document consists of many sentences, in which only a few are important or related to the theme. According to the importance to the theme, we assign each sentence different *sentence weight*. In practice, sentences with weight higher than a predefined threshold are extracted and we term such sentences as *critical sentences*. In CSVM, similarity between two documents is calculated by summing all similarities between each pair of critical sentences within each document, shown as formula (1).

$$S(X,Y) = \sum_{i=1}^{M} \underset{j=1}{\overset{N}{Max}} \left(\frac{W(x_i)*W(y_j)}{W(x_i)^2 + W(y_j)^2} * Sim(i,j) \right) \tag{1}$$

$S(X,Y)$ denotes the similarity between document X and document Y. M and N are the number of critical sentences in two documents X and Y respectively. $Sim(i,j)$ denotes the similarity between the ith critical sentence within document X and j^{th} critical sentence within document Y. $W(x_i)$ and $W(y_j)$ denote the critical sentence weights measuring the significance of the critical sentences x_i and y_j related to the document X and Y respectively. Two technical questions arise in formula (1) regarding CSVM-based similarity calculation: critical sentence vector extraction and their weights calculation; similarity calculation between two critical sentences.

2.2 Critical Sentence Vector Extraction

We use certain classes of content words to calculate sentence weight. Classes of content words being used include title words, proper nouns (e.g. person name and place name), words with high occurrence frequency, and normal words. Sentence weight (W) can be calculated as formula (2).

$$W = f(i) * (W_T + W_H + W_P + W_N) \tag{2}$$

where W_T, W_H, W_P and W_N denotes weights of title words, high frequency words, proper nouns and normal words respectively. $f(i)$ is a factor measuring the significance of the position of the sentence to the sentence weight, ranging between 0 and 1. In general, the first and last sentences are generally more significant than the others in a news article. Thus, such sentences should have a higher value of $f(i)$. We use a quadric function to determine the value of $f(i)$ which is shown in formula (3).

$$f(i) = (i/N - 0.5)^2 + 0.75 \tag{3}$$

2.3 Critical Sentence Similarity Calculation

2.3.1 Method 1: Longest Common Word String

The longest common word string is extracted from two comparing sentences. Features of the common string, such as length, can be used to calculate the similarity between the two sentences. If word order is not considered, a common word string then degenerates into a common word array. Given two sentences $c_i^1 c_i^2 c_i^3 \Lambda c_i^n$ and $c_j^1 c_j^2 c_j^3 \Lambda c_j^m$ in which c denotes a word, and n and m are the numbers of words of the two sentences, respectively. The following formula takes the length of a common word array as the similarity measure. Note that we also assign different weights $W(c_i^u)$ to words with different word classes.

$$Sim(i,j) = \sum_{u=1}^{n}(W(c_i^u)*(1-\prod_{v=1}^{m}(1-I(c_i^u,c_j^v))))*\frac{1}{\sqrt{n*m}} \quad I(c_i^u,c_j^v) = \begin{cases} 1 & \text{if } c_i^u = c_j^v \\ 0 & \text{if } c_i^u \neq c_j^v \end{cases} \tag{4}$$

2.3.2 Method 2: Using Structural Information

Basically, a normal sentence comprises of a subject (S), a main predicate (V) and an object (O). We propose a fine-grained similarity measurement by calculating the SVO similarities between the two sentences, see formula (5):

$$Sim(i,j) = \sum_{\sigma\in\{S,V,O\}} b^\sigma Sim^\sigma(i,j), \quad \sum_{\sigma\in\{S,V,O\}} b^\sigma = 1 \tag{5}$$

where b^s, b^v and b^o are weights assigned to subject, main predicate, and object respectively. In practice, the significances of S, V, and O vary. It is reasonable to assume that S and O are more significant than V. The three similarities, i.e. Sim^S, Sim^V and, Sim^O are calculated with formula (4). To recognize S, V, and O, partial parsing [13,14] is required. In our implementation, we simplify the process of partial parsing with a manual rule set.

2.3.3 Method 3: Combined Method

Longest common word string and structural information of SVO are typical sentence features. We can generalize formula (5) to cope with other features such as number of nouns within sentence. These features can be combined to obtain the overall sentence similarity. The generalized formula is shown in formula (6).

$$Sim(i,j) = \sum_{k=1}^{n} b_k Sim_k(i,j), \quad \sum_{k=1}^{n} b_k = 1, b_k > 0 \tag{6}$$

$Sim_k(i,j)$ measures similarity of different features and b_k denotes different significance of the features. In our experiments, we employ five sentence features, namely, SVO, the number of common nouns, verbs, adjectives and proper names.

3 Experiments

3.1 Setup

We use accuracy and recall as the evaluation criteria, shown as formula (7).

$$accuracy = \frac{Nrc}{Nr}*100\% \quad recall = \frac{Nrc}{Nc}*100\% \tag{7}$$

where Nr denotes the number of similar news retrieved, Nrc denotes the number of correct ones in the retrieval result, and Nc denotes the total number of correct similar news in the collection.

10 articles were selected from a text collection containing 2,214 financial news articles. Different methods were deployed to retrieve news similar to the ten documents from the collection. The first two experiments were designed to choose appropriate weight vectors for the SVO and combined methods. We then evaluate the different

similarity calculation methods in CSVM and selected the best one for the comparison between the VSM-based and CSVM-based approaches. In our experiments, for simplicity, two articles are considered similar if their similarity is higher than 5%.

3.2 Significance of S.V.O.

We performed experiments with different weights assigned to SVO. Fig. 1 shows that the weight vector of (2/5, 1/5, 2/5) achieves the highest accuracy with a reasonable recall while the weight vector of (1/2, 0, 1/2) yields the worst result. Meanwhile, we find that the accuracy decreases as the weight of predicate increases from 1/5 to 1/2. This indicates that predicate should be less significant than the other two. We perform an experiment in which the predicate is completely ignored, i.e. with weight vector of (1/2, 0, 1/2), we find that the result worsens. Since the highest accuracy is achieved with weight vector of (2/5, 1/5, 2/5), we choose to use (2/5, 1/5, 2/5) to perform the remaining experiments.

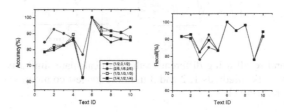

Fig. 1. Comparison of different weight assignment for SVO

3.3 Different Combined Methods

We evaluated three different combined methods in our experiments. The results are shown in Fig. 2. Method 1 achieves the highest accuracy and recall. In fact at most points all three methods achieve similar recall. This indicates that using more trivial features or increasing their weights have more impact on accuracy than recall. Weight assignment (0.6, 0.1, 0.1, 0.1, 0.1) achieves the best accuracy, which will be used for later experiments.

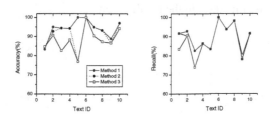

Fig. 2. Comparison of different combined methods. Methods 1 and 2 use five features with weight assignments (0.6, 0.1, 0.1, 0.1, 0.1) and (0.8, 0.05, 0.05, 0.05, 0.05), respectively. Method 3 uses three features: SVO, number of proper nouns and other nouns. Its weight assignment was (0.8, 0.1, 0.1).

3.4 Different Methods for Sentence Similarity Calculation

In Fig. 3, methods 1, 2 and 3 use the longest common word string, SVO and combined method for sentence similarity respectively. Method 3, the combined method, uses five features: SVO, number of common nouns, verbs, adjectives and proper nouns, and the $\vec{b}_k$ vector is (0.6, 0.1, 0.1, 0.1, 0.1). Method 3 achieves the highest accuracy but also the worst recall. This is not surprising for high accuracy often mistakenly neglects correct results leading to decreased recall. And this is also the reason why VSM-based method could achieve higher recall than CSVM at some points. Our goal is to balance between accuracy and recall. Therefore, we use SVO to calculate CSVM-based sentence similarity.

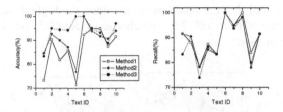

Fig. 3. Accuracy and recall using different methods to calculate similarity between sentences under CSVM framework. Methods 1, 2 and 3 used the longest common word string, SVO and combined method, respectively.

3.5 VSM Versus CSVM-Based Method

Fig. 4 presents the accuracy and recall of the two methods. For the CSVM-based method, we used SVO to determine the similarity between sentences. It shows that the CSVM-based method achieves higher accuracy than its VSM-based counterpart. The average accuracy of CSVM-based method is 90%. There is a significant improvement over VSM whose average accuracy is less than 80%. CSVM-based method also achieves reasonable recall. However, both methods produce low accuracy at some points, e.g. the fifth point. This is caused by high retrieval redundancy. At this point, Nc (number of correct similar news) is so small that even a small retrieval error caused significant loss in accuracy. This problem also renders a low recall, showed at point 4 for VSM-based method in the recall graph.

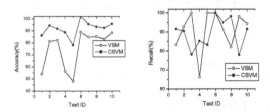

Fig. 4. Comparison of accuracy and recall between VSM-based and CVSM-based methods

4   Conclusion

Text similarity is often subjective and is even ambiguous sometimes. We show that the situation can be improved by utilizing more structural and semantic information. Combining with NLP techniques, the proposed CSVM provides a general framework for finer text similarity calculation. The experiments show that the CSVM-based method outperforms the traditional VSM-based method.

Acknowledgement

This project is supported by CUHK Direct Grant (No. 2050330), National Natural Science Foundation of China (NSFC No. 69975008), 863 project of China (No. 2001AA114210) and Hong Kong RGC CERG (Grant No. PolyU5181/03E).

References

1. Salton, G., Wong A., and Yang. C. S.: A Vector Space Model for Automatic Indexing. Communications of the ACM (1975) Vol.18, No.11, 613-620
2. V.V. Raghavan and S.K.M. Wong: A Critical Analysis of Vector Space Model for Information Retrieval. Journal of the American Society for Information Science (1986) 279-287
3. D.L. Lee, H. Chuang, and K. Seamons: Document Ranking and the Vector-space Model. IEEE Software (1997) 67-75
4. N. Maria and M. J. Silva: Theme-based Retrieval of Web News. Proceedings of the Third International Workshop on the Web and Databases (2000) 26-33
5. G. Salton, J. Allan, and C. Buckley: Approaches to Passage Retrieval in Full Text Information Systems. In ACM SIGIR conference on R&D in Information Retrieval (1993) 49-58
6. C.Y. Quek: Classification of World Wide Web Documents. Technical Report, Carnegie Mellon University (1996)
7. F. Sebastiani: Machine Learning in Automated Text Categorization. Technical Report, IEI-B4-31-1999, Consiglio Nazionale delle Ricerche, Pisa, Italy (1999)
8. H. Jing. Sentence Reduction for Automatic Text Summarization. In Proc. of the 6th Conference on Applied Natural Language Processing, pages 310--315, 2000.
9. K.C. Litkowski: Question-answering Using Semantic Relation Triples. TREC8 (1999)
10. S. Abney, M. Collins, and A. Singhal: Answer Extraction. In Proc. of the 6th ANLP Conference (2000) 296-301
11. Marius Pasca and Sanda Harabagiu: High Performance Question & Answering. Proc. ACM SIGIR, New Orleans (2001) 366–374
12. N. Friburger, D. Maurel: Textual Similarity Based on Proper Names, MF/IR (2002)
13. Steven Abney: Partial Parsing via Finite-state Cascades. In Workshop on Robust Parsing, 8th European Summer School in Logic, Language and Information, Prague, Czech Republic (1996) 8-15
14. Steven Abney: Partial Parsing. Tutorial at ANLP (1994)
15. Thomas H. Cormen, Charles E. Leiserson, and Ronald L. Rivest: Introduction to Algorithms, second edition.
16. Strehl, J. Ghosh and R. Mooney: Impact of Similarity Measures on Web Page Clustering, AAAI 2000 Workshop of Artificial Intelligence for Web Search (2000) 58-64

Audio Fingerprinting Scheme by Temporal Filtering for Audio Identification Immune to Channel-Distortion

Mansoo Park[1], Hoi-Rin Kim[1], Dong-Ho Shin[2], and Seung Hyun Yang[2]

[1] School of Engineering, Information and Communications University, Korea
{mansoo, hrkim}@icu.ac.kr
[2] Information Retrieval & Mining Research Team, Konan Technology Inc., Korea
{dhshin, yan}@konantech.com

Abstract. Channel-distortion in real-environment is at issue in music information retrieval system by content-based audio identification technique. As a matter of fact, audio signal is commonly distorted by channel and background noise in case of that it is recorded under real-situation. Recently, Philips published a robust and efficient audio fingerprinting system for audio identification. To extract a robust and efficient audio fingerprint, Philips applied the first derivative (differential) to the frequency-time sequence of perceptual filter-bank energies. In practice, however, it is not sufficient to remove the undesired perturbations. This paper introduces an extension method of the audio fingerprint extraction scheme of Philips that is more immune to channel-distortion. The channel-normalization techniques for temporal filtering are used to lessen the channel effects of real-environment.

1 Introduction

The beginning of most publications related to MIR (Music Information Retrieval) by content-based audio identification technique discussed the stochastic pattern modeling method based on pitch histogram or spectral envelope histogram which is organized by clustering spectral feature vectors with vector quantization [1]-[4]. However, it is still hard to apply into a very large database since it is no guarantee of scalability and quality adequate to commercial service. Thus, the techniques as mentioned above trend to apply into music classification such as genre or instrument. Since the number of music classes is not abundant in most cases, the stochastic pattern modeling method is easily applied into music classification. For that reason, recent issues focus on the guarantee of both scalability and quality at once for MIR by content-based audio identification technique in a large database.

Lately, content-based MIR has been worthy of notice as one of the state-of-the-art and attractive application services on the music portal market in wire/wireless communication. For example, many companies offer the application service to provide the information of a song greeted from a loudspeaker in any place, to monitor the broadcasting music, to prevent from sharing the unauthorized music files through peer-to-peer network, or to send a message when the song is being on the air [5][6]. The audio fingerprinting scheme of Philips, one of recent content-based audio identification techniques, is definitely pertinent to that purpose [7][8]. In real-

G.G. Lee et al. (Eds.): AIRS 2005, LNCS 3689, pp. 528–533, 2005.

environment, it still remains problems even so such as channel-effects, background noise, speed-change, arrangement, etc. Especially, the problem of channel effects should be firstly solved in sound recording condition just as speech recognition system [10][11]. Generally, an audio signal is easily distorted by channel-effects when it is recorded through a microphone. The recording audio signals may be distorted by the adverse effects of electrical devices such as microphones, sound devices, loudspeakers, etc. Figure 1 illustrates how distinct the spectrograms can be between the original and the recorded signal, where the left and right bottom spectrograms are recorded over a 2.1-channel and a poor quality laptop loudspeaker, respectively. A false of audio identification is mainly caused by the mismatch between the original audio and its recordings distorted by the channel-effects. Thus, the channel-normalization techniques as temporal filtering may be effective and useful to overcome this problem.

The next section describes a basic concept of the audio fingerprinting scheme of Philips and discusses the alternatives to temporal filtering to reduce the channel-effects. Section 3 evaluates the performance of the alternatives to temporal filtering for audio identification in real-environment.

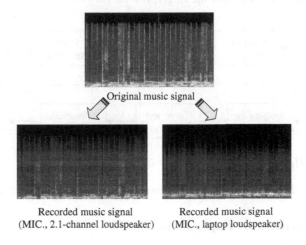

Fig. 1. The spectrograms of an original signal and its recordings

2   Audio Fingerprinting Scheme

2.1   The Audio Fingerprinting Scheme of Philips

The Philips fingerprinting scheme is based on a sign of differential sub-band energy of the perceptual audio spectrum. Overview of the audio fingerprint extraction scheme of Philips is depicted in Figure 2. Mel or bark scale filter-bank is commonly used to reflect perceptual characteristics of an audio signal. Sub-fingerprint for every frame is based on the sign of differentiated power spectrum simultaneously along the time and frequency axes. The derivatives of spectral parameters along frequency and time axes are to be a high-pass filtering. It may be possible to remove slowly varying components as the undesired perturbations. Also it is uncorrelated with its temporal and frequency neighbors. Generally, it is very robust to many kinds of audio processing [7][8]. Here, a sub-fingerprint is being a typically 32-bit code from perceptually divided 33 frequency bands. Also, it is directly being an addressing point for database lookup. The 32-bit sequence is usually referred to the hash value. As stated above, a sub-fingerprint can be hashing by a 32-bit code for every frame. The bit is assigned as

$$H(n,m) = \begin{cases} 1 & if \quad E(n,m) - E(n,m+1) - (E(n-1,m) - E(n-1,m+1)) > 0 \\ 0 & if \quad E(n,m) - E(n,m+1) - (E(n-1,m) - E(n-1,m+1)) \le 0 \end{cases} \quad (1)$$

where $E(n,m)$ is the energy of nth frame and m^{th} band [7][8].

This scheme can be very efficient for the database lookup since the hash value is highly unique and robust. For the fast database lookup, it checks only hash positions with the pre-determined Hamming distance. In other words, it is blockaded to match out of the checking positions. In this scheme, the similarity measure is based on a Hamming distance among hash values. That is, the best matched result is determined by the BER (Bit Error Rate) per the fingerprint block.

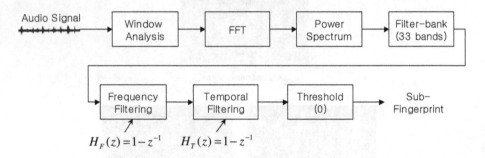

Fig. 2. Overview of the audio fingerprint extraction scheme of Philips

2.2 The Alternatives to Temporal Filtering

Temporal filtering of the FBEs (Filter-Bank Energies) is to remove its D.C. and slowly varying components as the undesired perturbations by linear distortion [9]-[12]. As mentioned above, the audio fingerprints would be much more robust to linear distortion if FBEs were uncorrelated with its temporal neighbors. Temporal filtering techniques have the effect of decorrelation of the FBEs that is somewhat verified in [9]-[12]. The typical temporal filtering techniques are defined as

$$H_{T1}(z) = 1 - z^{-1} \quad (2)$$

$$H_{T2}(z) = z - z^{-1} \quad (3)$$

$$H_{T3}(z) = \sum_{k=1}^{K} k(z^k - z^{-k}) \quad (4)$$

$$H_{T4}(z) = 0.1 \times \frac{2 + z^{-1} - z^{-3} - 2z^{-4}}{z^{-4} \times (1 - \alpha z^{-1})} \quad where \ \alpha = 0.94 \quad (5)$$

H_{T1} is high-pass type of a first-order FIR filter, H_{T2} is band-pass type of a second-order FIR filter, H_{T3} is a typical regression formula, and H_{T4} is the RASTA filter which is also a band-pass type of the IIR filter with a pole close to 1. H_{T3} is the general case of H_{T2}. H_{T3} when $K = 2$ is used in this work.

Main goal of this paper is to find the best relevant temporal filter to extract the audio fingerprints which are robust to channel-distortion regarding to real-situation. The high-pass filtering may be expected to suppress the effects of the convolutional noise by the channel, and the low-pass filtering may be expected to smooth out some of the fast spectral change. For that reason, the band-pass filter may be more relevant to temporal filtering in this work. Specially, the RASTA filter would be the best due to the filter slope or shape [11][12].

3 Experiments

3.1 Audio Data

For experiments regarding to real environment, an audio query clip was captured by using an inexpensive microphone such as a general pin or stand microphone which was apart from a 2.1 channel loudspeaker of mp3 player at a distance of 10 ~ 20 cm. The audio query has the 7~8 seconds' duration and is converted to standard PCM format which is sampled at 11.025 kHz and quantized with 16 bits in mono channel. Music items for references consist of 5,000 popular songs which have mp3 format (192 Kbps, 44.1 kHz, stereo) converted from audio CDs. The audio data are down sampled to 11.025 kHz for considering portable devices such as an mp3 player, a PDA, or a mobile phone. They include various genres such as rock/ballad, pop/dance, rap, folk, and so on. Audio query data were captured from the randomly selected 50 songs per each query set. And each song was played at randomly setting offset time several hundred times.

To evaluate the proposed techniques, the query data consist of 5 types of set according to the device and the recording environments. Only the query signal of Set IV has the 7 seconds' duration and the others have the 8 seconds' duration.

- ☐ Set I: Directly cropping mp3 file.
- ☐ Set II: Using a pair of stand microphone and 2.1-channel loudspeakers in very quiet environment.
- ☐ Set III: Using a pair of stand/pin microphones and 2.1-channel loudspeakers in noisy environment with TV sound and human voice.
- ☐ Set IV: Using a pair of stand/pin microphones and 2-channel laptop loudspeakers which makes poor sound in noisy environment with TV sound, human voice, and sporadic noise. In addition, some cases are overflow into the amplitude range of 16 bits PCM by very loud music sound.

☐   Set V: Directly extracting audio clips from the video file recorded from TV music show program. It consists of live songs mixed with background noise such as clapping, applauding, or cheering sound of audience.

To say nothing of, all microphones are omni-directional. Also, all cases of the distance between microphone and loudspeaker are apart around 10 ~ 20 cm, and the distance between microphone and noise source is around 2 ~ 5 meters.

In signal processing step, the audio frame was parameterized into 0.37 seconds rate and shifted at 11.6 ms rate to extract hash value. Considering human auditory system, the selected frequency bands lie in the range from 300 Hz to 3,000 Hz. This interval is the relevant spectral range at a sampling rate of 11.025 kHz.

3.2 Performance Evaluation

In ideal case sub-fingerprint is reliable that there is no bit error. However, it is not perfect when there is signal distortion by channel or noise. To improve this defect, the candidate positions for the database lookup expand into hash values with a Hamming distance of one bit error [8]. That is, one bit error per sub-fingerprint is tolerable in this work. Thus, it needs 33 times more lookup for audio identification. However, if the exact offset time location for playing the song is not required, it would be not checking all hash candidates by setting the threshold for breaking the database lookup. Empirically, it took only 3~4 times more lookup time when we set the threshold to 0.29 of the BER per the fingerprint block.

Table 1. Recognition performance evaluation according to the alternatives to temporal filtering when the checking positions for the database lookup are expanded or not (%)

Temporal Filter / Query	Database Lookup Candidates							
	Hamming Distance $= 0$				Hamming Distance ≤ 1			
	H_{T1}	H_{T2}	H_{T3}	H_{T4}	H_{T1}	H_{T2}	H_{T3}	H_{T4}
Set I	100	100	100	100	100	100	100	100
Set II	98.2	97.8	98.2	99.2	100	100	100	100
Set III	96.2	96.7	97.5	97.7	100	100	100	100
Set IV	78.7	79.6	79.1	86.3	97.2	97.5	97.2	99
Set V	56.3	55.9	58	63.1	92.8	94.1	94.5	95.8

As shown in Table 1, in the case of that the lookup candidates are expanded or not, the band-pass filters are generally superior to the high-pass filter type used in Philips. As was expected, the RASTA filter has the best results in this work. Especially, it is more effective in the case of the worse distortion as Set IV or Set V because the RASTA filter normalizes the channel-effects to be sure.

4 Conclusion

From the experiments, we observed that the alternatives to temporal filtering are generally effective in the case of recoding a query signal in real-situation. As was expected, the RASTA filter as a channel-normalization technique is much superior to the other temporal filtering techniques. In this work, even if we had no regard for out-of-set materials, it could be easily solved by setting the threshold to verify whether acceptance or rejection. Empirically, there is no false acceptance when the threshold is set to 0.41 of BER. But a false rejection is added to the above results. In case of Set V, the additional false rejection rate is below 0.63 % when the checking positions are expanded. Since there is a trade-off relation between a false rejection and a false acceptance, it should be adjusted as the case may be.

For the further study, we will consider not only the alternative to temporal filtering but also the alternative to frequency filtering which is robust to real-noise for commercial service. Also, we will seek for the best combined filter with frequency and temporal filter to have the better synergy effect.

References

1. Mansoo Park et al., "Content-based Music Information Retrieval using Pitch Histogram of Band Pass Filter Signal," *Proc. of AIRS2004*, pp. 245-248, Oct. 2004.
2. J. Herre, E. Allamanche, and O. Hellmuth, "Robust matching of audio signals using spectral flatness features," *Proc. of Workshop on Applications of Signal Processing to Audio and Acoustics 2001, IEEE*, pp. 127-130, 2001.
3. E. Allamanche, J. Herre, and O. Hellmuth, "Content-based Identification of Audio Material Using MPEG-7 Low Level Description," *Proc. of ISMIR 2001*, pp. 197-204, 2001.
4. Jonathan T. Foote, "Content-Based Retrieval of Music and Audio," *Proc. of SPIE*, Multimedia Storage and Archiving Systems II, Vol. 3229, pp. 138-147, 1997.
5. AudibleMagic, http://audiblemagic.com.
6. Shazam Entertainment, http://www.shazam.com.
7. Haitsma J., Kalker T. and Oostveen J., "Robust Audio Hashing for Content Identification," *Proc. of the Content Based Multimedia Indexing 2001*, September 2001.
8. J.A. Haitsma and T. Kalker, "A Highly Robust Audio Fingerprinting System," *Proc. ISMIR 2002*, pp. 144-148, Oct. 2002.
9. C. Nadeu, D. Macho, and J. Hernando, "Time and Frequency Filtering of Filter-Bank Energies for Robust HMM Speech Recognition," *Speech Communication*, vol. 34, pp. 93-114, 2001.
10. S. Young, The HTK BOOK (for HTK Version 3.0), 2000.
11. Rosenberg A. et al., "Cepstral channel normalization techniques for HMM-based speaker verification," *Proc. ICSLP -94*, pp. 1835-1838, 1994.
12. Hermansky H. et al., "Compensation for the effect of the communication channel in the auditory-like analysis of speech (RASTA-PLP)," *Proc. EUROSPEECH-91*, pp. 1367-1370, 1991.

On the Chinese Document Clustering Based on Dynamical Term Clustering

Chih-Ming Tseng[*], Kun-Hsiu Tsai, Chiun-Chieh Hsu, and His-Cheng Chang

Department of Information Management,
National Taiwan University of Science and Technology
Department of Information Management,
Jin-Wen Institute of Technology, Taipei, Taiwan
tseng@jwit.edu.tw, arshu@ms56.hinet.net,
cchsu@cs.ntust.edu.tw, hcchang@cc.hwh.edu.tw

Abstract. With the rapid development of global networking through the network, more and more information is accessible on-line. It makes the document clustering technique more dispensable. With the clustering process we can efficiently browse the large information. In this paper, we focus on Chinese document clustering process, which uses data mining technique and neural network model. There are two main phases : preprocessing phase and clustering phase. In the preprocessing phase, we propose another Chinese sentence segmentation method, which based on data mining technique of using a hash-based method. In the clustering phase, we adopt the dynamical SOM model with a view to dynamically clustering data. Furthermore, we use term vectors clustering process instead of document vectors clustering process. Our experiments demonstrate that the term clustering results in better precision rate, and the term clustering will be more efficiently when the amount of documents grows gradually.

1 Introduction

With the rapid development of global networking through the network, the explosion of information has resulted in an information overload problem. However, to find users' desired information is not an easy task.

Document clustering is an important technology to solve the information overload problem [4,6]. But, document clustering is a complex job because different language or different domain will cause different problems. Considering the urgent need to promote Chinese information retrieval. In this paper, we propose new methods based on SOM (Self Organization Maps) [1,2,3] technique to solve Chinese document clustering problems.

First, we gather Chinese news from several news documents websites and segment the sentences of the news documents into meaningful words. In order to overcome the shortcoming of traditional Chinese sentence segmentation process, we propose a new method to combine the segmentation with the thesaurus and the compound words detection. Next, we use term vectors clustering process instead of document vectors

---

[*] Corresponding author.

G.G. Lee et al. (Eds.): AIRS 2005, LNCS 3689, pp. 534–539, 2005.

clustering process. Finally, we design a dynamical clustering process based on SOM technique to solve high dimensionality of clustering, and unpredicted cluster number problem. Via this model, we get a better clustering result and do the clustering more efficiently.

The rest of this paper is organizing as follows: Section 2 introduces our proposal methods. Section 3 gives the experiments results. Section 4 contains conclusions and future works.

2 Proposed Methods

2.1 Chinese Sentence Segmentation

We use the Chinese Knowledge Information Processing (CKIP) system that is developed by ACADEMIA SINICA. CKIP system is a Chinese sentences segmentation system based on the thesaurus. For example, CKIP segments the sentence "台灣科技大學論文口試" into "台灣 科技 大學 論文 口試". But, the right result should be "台灣科技大學 論文 口試". Obviously, there is a serious drawback that the system can't tell a term correctly if the thesaurus lacks the information of the term. In order to overcome this drawback, we propose a compound words detection process that based on DHP algorithm [5]. Our compound words detection process contains four steps.

Step1. Give each term a unique number that it used to speed up the compare process.

Step2. Make a hash table. First, we create a database is store all document's terms as shown in Fig. 1. Second, to find out all possible compound words of two terms from each document as shown in Fig. 2. Finally, convert terms into addresses by a hash function and accumulate the number in the hash table as shown in Fig. 3.

TID	Items
001	123412
002	23513
003	1235
004	25

001 {1 2} {2 3} {3 4} {4 1}
002 {2 3} {3 5} {5 1} {1 3}
003 {1 2} {2 3} {3 5}
004 {2 5}

Fig. 1. Database D represent all document, TID represent different document number, and items represent different term number

Fig. 2. Represent all possible compound word of two terms from each document

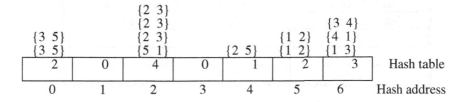

Fig. 3. In Fig. 2, the compound word of two terms from each document and via hash function in equation (1) to produce result

$$H(\{x, y\})=((\text{order of } x) * 10 + (\text{order of } y)) \bmod 7. \tag{1}$$

Step3. Delete impossible compound words that their possible maximal occurrences don't exceed the minimal confidence

Step4. Generate all possible compound words as shown in Fig. 4.

$$\left.\begin{array}{l}\{1, 2\} \\ \{2, 3\} \\ \{3, 5\}\end{array}\right\} \longrightarrow \left.\begin{array}{l}\{1, 2, 3\} \\ \{2, 3, 5\}\end{array}\right\} \longrightarrow \{1, 2, 3, 5\}$$

Fig. 4. From the compound words of two terms, we can produce all possible compound words

2.2   Term Vector Generation and Dynamical Term Clustering Mode

2.2.1   Term Vector Generation
We convert each term into a vector through three steps.

Step1. Generate identification of each term. We produce term vectors is called identification whose dimension value is produced with randomly real number between 0 and 1 to represent terms such as following example in Table 1.

Table 1. Different term has different identification

terms	identification
寬頻	(0.1, 0.1, 0.2□
頻寬	(0.2, 0.2, 0.3□
網路	(0.7, 0.7, 0.7□

Step 2. Calculate similarity between terms. We calculate similarity between terms by following measure as shown in equation (2).

$$Similarity_{A,B} = \frac{C(A,B)}{C(A)+C(B)-C(A,B)}. \tag{2}$$

C (A, B)-- Number of document simultaneously containing term A and term B
C (A)+C (B)-C (A, B)-- Total number of document containing term A or term B

Table 2. The address of each term by a hash function

hash function	h(t)=(order of term) mod 3	
Number of term	Term	address
0	寬頻	0
1	頻寬	1
2	網路	2

Step 3. Owing to three terms "寬頻"、"頻寬" and "網路" have high similarity with each other. So, there three identification can be combined into a term vector of "

寬頻" that it based on hash technique as the method of combination. First, we give each term a unique number and calculate the address of each term by a hash function, as shown in Table 2. Then we accumulate the identification into the address as shown in Table 3.

Table 3. Three identifications can be combined into a term vector

Term	寬頻		
Address	0	1	2
Term vector	(0.1, 0.1, 0.2	0.2, 0.2, 0.3	0.7, 0.7, 0.7)

2.2.2 Dynamical Term Clustering

Here we design the dynamical clustering based on measuring the quality of clustering. First, we adopt the measure of intra-similarity to evaluate the quality of clustering in each cluster as shown in equation (3).

$$Intra\_similarity(c_i) = \frac{\sum S(x_i, c_i)}{|cluster_i|}. \tag{3}$$

S -- Measure of distance: $S(d_i, d_j) = (d_i \cdot d_j) \times (|d_i| \times |d_j|)$

x_i -- Data of cluster i

c_i -- Centroid of cluster I

di-- document i

$cluster_i$ -- Number of data in cluster i

Second, our dynamical clustering method is trying to improve the quality of clustering by adding clusters step by step. The dynamical clustering method can be done during two processes. The first process is growing clusters in the same level and the second process is generating hierarchical structure.

Process 1. Algorithm of growing clusters

Step1.	Calculate initial quality of cluster. View original data as one cluster and calculate the centroid by averaging all data. Then calculate the quality of cluster.
Step2.	Start clustering. Start SOM clustering with 2 clusters. And calculate the quality of cluster.
Step3.	Growing phase. Set threshold of growing between 0 and 1. If present quality of cluster is not satisfied initial quality of cluster * growing threshold, then generate one cluster from the cluster with worst intra-similarity.
Step4	Repeat Step3 until stop growing.

Process 2. Algorithm of growing hierarchical clusters

Step1.	Growing phase. Set threshold of growing hierarchical cluster between 0 and 1. If intra-similarity of cluster is not satisfied initial quality of cluster multiply by growing threshold, then generate hierarchical cluster.
Step2.	Set next level with 2 clusters then restart the process of Growing clusters.

3 Experiments

We evaluate the performance of our dynamical clustering method and compare our proposed method with K-means and Bisecting K-means. We experimented with our designed data sets containing topics and documents. The data set has ten topics and each topic has fifty documents. In our proposed method, we select the α percentage terms of the higher TF*IDF value from each document. We using α= {2%, 10%, 20%, 50%} and experiment result shows that 2% and 10% are better than others. Next, the generation of term vector with the size of identification equal to {5, 10, 15, and 20} and the size of hash table equal to {31, 41, and 53, 101}. Experiment results show that these combinations are resulting in good precision rates. Finally, experiment result show the precision rate about 70%, when the parameter growing cluster threshold between 0.4 and 0.6. In Fig. 5 show that experiment. Especially, when α is 10% , the precision rate is highest.

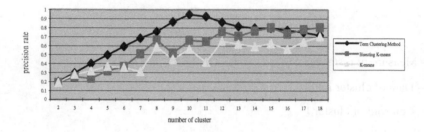

Fig. 5. Comparison with other algorithms

Fig. 6. Clustering result representation of second data set

Finally, we show our clustering result. For each cluster, we select ten representative terms as the label. In the first data set, we set the threshold of growing cluster equal to 0.55 and set the threshold of growing hierarchical cluster equal to 0.9. The clustering result is as shown in Fig. 6. According to the SOM, similar cluster was clustered into adjacent area

4 Conclusion and Future Works

In this paper, we us this preprocess that have analyzed the characters of the Chinese language and have proposed the novel process of Chinese sentences segmentation.

We can improve the precision rate usefully and give the cluster result more meaningful labels. In the clustering, the dynamical term clustering was demonstrated that it is useful. Furthermore, it is more efficiently to cluster terms than to cluster documents because the amount of terms will not grow rapidly with the growth of documents. And through SOM, the result is more readable for users.

In the future, we should apply our system in more network services such as the personal summary and the personal service.

References

1. T. Kohonen, Self Organizing Maps, Third Edition, Springer (2001)
2. T. Kohonen, S. Kaski, K. Lagus, J. Salojarvi, J. Honkela, V. Paatero, and A. Saarela, "Self Organization of a Massive Document Collection", IEEE Transactions on Neural Networks, Special Issue on Neural Networks for Data Mining and Knowledge Discovery, vol. 11 (2000) 574-585
3. T. Kohonen, "Self-organization of very large document collections: State of the art", Proceedings of ICANN, volume 1 (1998) 65-74
4. Gerald Kowalski, Information Retrieval System—Theory and Implementation, Kluwer Academic Publishers (1997)
5. J.S. Park, Ming-Syan Chen, and Philip S. Yu, "Using a Hash-Based Method with Transaction Trimming for Mining Association Rules", IEEE Transactions On Knowledge And Data Engineering, Vol. 9, NO. 5 (1997) 813-825
6. C.J. van Rijsbergen, Information Retrieval, Butter-worths, London, 2nd edition (1979)

Integrating Heterogeneous Multimedia Resources

Seong Joon Yoo and Chull Hwan Song

School of Computer Engineering, Sejong University, 98 Gunja, Gwangjin,
Seoul, Korea 143-747
sjyoo@sejong.ac.kr, peternara@naver.com

Abstract. This paper proposes a new multimedia metadata that will support integrating non-standard multimedia metadata as well as the standard multimedia metadata. The metadata is defined by integrating MPEG-7 MDS and TV-AnyTime metadata. We also designed and implemented a framework for integrating multimedia databases. Retrieving multimedia data from heterogeneous resources described in MPEG-7 MDS and TV-AnyTime metadata is faster than retrieving multimedia data from homogeneous resources.

1 Introduction

This paper aims at defining integrated metadata for ubiquitous multimedia information retrieval, which can search various types of metadata in distributed heterogeneous environments. Defining this integrated metadata starts from ensuring compatibility with the current international multimedia metadata standards. In other words, it is necessary to ensure compatibility mainly with MPEG-7 Multimedia Description Scheme (MDS) [1] and TV Anytime metadata [2]. These two standards include the widest range of elements and attributes related to multimedia-related metadata that have emerged so far, so that they can be a useful basis for defining integrated metadata information retrieval. This integrated metadata will be used for the basis of designing federated multimedia information system on the semantic web.

For this purpose, MPEG-7 MDS and TV-Anytime metadata were compared and analyzed to identify commonness and differences between these two standards. Based on the results, metadata made up of a union of these two standards was created. Investigating these two standards revealed that some definitions were expressed in different terms even though they have the same meaning. In this case, either ones were used or third terms were selected. In another case, an element or an attribute of a definition in one standard included the entire elements or attributes of a definition of the other standard, which was easily integrated. When two elements had an intersection with some differences, the intersection was defined with a newly adopted term while the remnants were defined with the terms originally used in the standard.

2 Related Works

Roantree[3] describes a metadata management scheme for federated multimedia systems. He adopted an object oriented common model for integrating metadata and

G.G. Lee et al. (Eds.): AIRS 2005, LNCS 3689, pp. 540–545, 2005.
© Springer-Verlag Berlin Heidelberg 2005

proposed a high-level query interface for the ODMG schema repository. This scheme does not propose a specific metadata for the multimedia information retrieval from multimedia information retrieval systems. Most recent research [4][5][6][7][8] proposes ontology based approach for multimedia information systems. Specially, Tsinaraki et al.[7][8] proposes a framework which allows transforming OWL ontology to MPEG-7 and TV-Anytime. However, they have not showed an integrated metadata with which access MPEG-7 and TV-Anytime metadata. Tsinaraki et al. transforms OWL to MPEG-7 and OWL to TV-Anytime respectively. The approach of transforming OWL to each metadata is not flexible enough to support non-standard metadata. This paper proposes a universal metadata that will support non-standard multimedia metadata as well as the standard multimedia metadata.

3 MPEG-7 MDS and TV-Anytime Metadata

MPEG-7 MDS (ISO/IEC JTC1/SC29/WG11) is an international standard for multimedia contents, which enables efficient storage, retrieval and transmission of multimedia data by effectively expressing them. On the other hand, TV-AnyTime metadata was designed to fit the digital TV broadcasting environment. Therefore, most multimedia data deals with motion images. MPEG-7 MDS expresses much more information in XML schema format, in comparison to TV-AnyTime Metadata.

Of these two standards, MPEG-7 MDS deals with all digital contents such as image information, audio, video, and 3D as well as motion images, unlike TV-AnyTime Fig. 1 shows the relationship between MPEG-7 MDS and TV-AnyTime. Most elements of TV-AnyTime metadata correspond to some elements of MPEG-7 MDS.

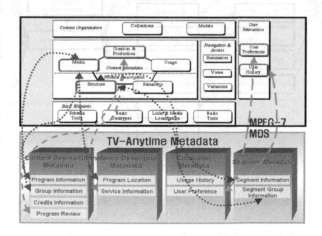

Fig. 1. Relationship of MPEG-7 MDS and TV-AnyTime Metadata

4 UMA Metadata

This chapter describes a part of a UMA(unified multimedia access) metadata that have been newly defined by integrating MPEG-7 and TV-AnyTime metadata. Even though we have derived a larger set of integrated metadata elements, we describe one of them to show the principle of metadata integration.

The CreationType element of MDS is related with the BasicDescription element of TVA metadata as shown in Fig. 2. The relationship between descendents of these two elements is summarized in Table 3. Since MPEG-7 and TV-AnyTime have a same name for "title", UMA metadata accept this name for the meaning of "title". However, since these two standards have two different names for "media title", we need to choose one word for "media title". Here we take the element name of MPEG-7 for the new metadata. Similarly, several new element names are defined for the elements common to the two standards even though we describe only one element in this paper.

Table 1. Common Metadata for CreationType and BasicDescription

MPEG-7	Relationship	TVA	UMA
Title	Is equivalent to	Title	Title
TitleMedia	Is equivalent to	MediaTitle	TitleMedia
Abstract	Is equivalent to	Synopsis	Synopsis
CreationCoordinates	Is equivalent to	CreationCoordinates	CreationCoordinates
Creator	Is equivalent to	CreditsList	Creator

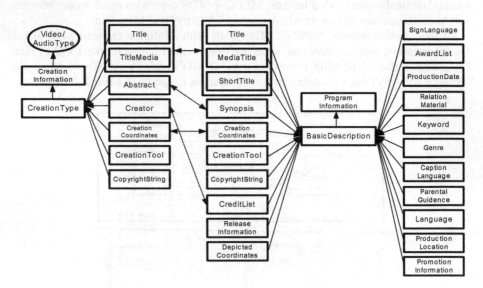

Fig. 2. The Relationship of CreationType and BasicDescription

5   Implementation and Experiment

This section describes the architecture of the web service based multimedia integration system that we have implemented for experimenting the applicability of UMA metadata. Since the integration system is implemented using web services technology, it gives users more flexibility than previous multimedia integration systems. The integration system is composed of three layers: application layer, mediation layer, and resource layer. The web service API provided by the mediation layer and the resource layer are used for data transfer between layers.

5.1 Application Layer

In Application Layer, a user or an upper module transfers query and receives the results. For example, a user can generate in simple and general query such as name, genre, ID, or keyword. Application Layer calls the web service API provided by Mediation Layer. This API transfers the query to Mediation Layer in XML format using SOAP protocol. Also, this API transfers the results of query to Application Layer in XML format.

5.2 Mediation Layer

Mediation Layer is composed of Query Processor, Rule Manager, and Global Schema Manager. Query is transferred from Application Layer to Mediation Layer using the API methods. Since the mediator functions are implemented using web services, users can connect a mediator and wrappers using API. Users may compose this relationship using a graphical user interface.

5.3 Resource Layer

Resource Layer is connected to Local DB through wrappers. This layer retrieves relevant data from Local DB. Resource Layer is composed of a wrapper manager and multiple wrappers. Since the major functions are provided with web services API, users can build their own wrapper with ease.

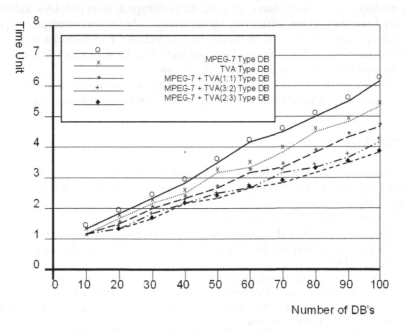

Fig. 3. Response Time of Retrieving Data from Several Types of Multimedia Databases

5.4 Experiment

The proposed integration framework and metadata work well for retrieving multimedia data in heterogeneous resources. However, it is slower retrieving multimedia data from homogeneous resources. The simulation is performed on one computer system and the simulation program calls wrappers N times. The result shows relative comparison of response time for several cases: retrieving data from databases described with MPEG-7 MDS only, from databases described with TV-AnyTime metadata and from databases described with MPEG-7 and TV-AnyTime. Retrieving data from MPEG-7 described databases takes longer than any other cases. Retrieving data from TV-AnyTime described databases takes shorter than retrieving data from MPEG-7 databases. The system shows better performance in retrieving data from databases with MPEG-7 and TV-Anytime description. This is illustrated in Fig. 3.

6 Conclusion

This paper introduced a new metadata for multimedia contents. In order to define and construct the new metadata, two standards, which are internationally recognized to have the most multimedia information, were compared to investigate their relationship. In order to prove the effectiveness, we have implemented a prototype system for integrating multimedia databases. We have tested UMA data by integrating databases tagged with five different standards and found that the mapping tool enables defining the relationship between UMA and the five standards semi-automatically. In addition, users can build their own wrappers and compose the relationship between wrappers and a mediator more easily than ever since the prototype system provides web service API. We have showed this efficiency by showing easily implemented prototype system in the previous section. In the future, this metadata for multimedia contents will be used in defining multimedia ontology language, like RDF or OWL [9][10], so that it can be used for context aware multimedia access.

We are going to measure the response time by simulating concurrent access of multiple databases. This will show more realistic comparison of performance.

References

1. Martinez, J. M.: Overview of the MPEG-7 Standard (version 5.0): ISO/IEC JTC1/SC29/WG11 N4031, Singapore, March (2001), http://www.cselt.it/mpeg/standards/mpeg-7/mpeg-7.htm
2. TV-Anytime Forum, http://www.tv-anytime.org/
3. Roantree, M.: Metadata Management in Federated Multimedia Information Systems: Proceedings of the thirteenth Australasian Conference on Database Technologies. Vol. 5 (2002) 147-155
4. Hunter, J.: Adding Multimedia to the Semantic Web-Building an Mpeg-7 Ontology: International Semantic Web Working Symposium (SWWS), Stanford, (2001) 261-283
5. Chotmanee, A.; Wuwongse,V., Anutariya,C.: A Schema Language for MPEG-7: LNCS 2555, Vol. 2555 (2002) 153-164

6. Troncy, R.: Integrating Structure and Semantics into Audio-visual Documents: In 2nd International Semantic Web Conference (ISWC'03), LNCS 2870, Sanibel Island, Florida, USA, Vol. 2870 (2003) 566-581
7. Tsinaraki, C., Polydoros, P., Christodoulakis, S.: Integration of OWL ontologies in MPEG-7 and TVAnytime compliant Semantic Indexing: In the proceedings of the 3rd HDMS, Athens, Greece, Vol. 3084 (2004) 398-413
8. Tsinaraki, C., Polydoros, P., Christodoulakis, S.: Interoperability Support for Ontology-Based Video Retrieval Applications: LNCS 3115, Vol. 3115 (2004) 582-591
9. OWL Web Ontology Language Reference, http://www.w3.org/TR/2004/REC-owl-ref-20040210/#EnumeratedDatatype
10. Ferdinand, M., Zirpins, C., Trastour, D.: Lifting XML Schema to OWL : in Web Engineering - 4th International Conferences, Vol. 3140 (2004) 354-358

Calculating Webpage Importance with Site Structure Constraints

Hui-Min Yan[1,3,*], Tao Qin[2,3,*], Tie-Yan Liu[3], Xu-Dong Zhang[2], Guang Feng[2,3,*], and Wei-Ying Ma[3]

[1] Dept. Computer Science & Engineering, Shang Hai Jiao Tong University, Shanghai, 200030, P.R. China (8621)62932564
bellylaugh@sjtu.edu.cn
[2] MSPLAB, Dept. Electronic Engineering, Tsinghua University, Beijing, 100084, P.R. China (8610)62789944
{qinshitao99, fengg03}@mails.tsinghua.edu.cn
zhangxd@tsinghua.edu.cn
[3] Microsoft Research Asia, No. 49, Zhichun Road, Haidian District, Beijing, 100080, P.R. China (8610)62617711
{t-tyliu, wyma}@microsoft.com

Abstract. PageRank is one of the most popular link analysis algorithms that have shown their effectiveness in web search. However, PageRank only consider hyperlink information. In this paper, we propose several novel ranking algorithms, which make use of both hyperlink and site structure information to measure the importance of each web page. Specifically, two kinds of methodologies are adopted to refine the PageRank algorithm: one combines hyperlink information and website structure information together by graph fusion to refine PageRank algorithm, while the other re-ranks the pages within the same site by quadratic optimization based on original PageRank values. Experiments show that both two methodologies effectively improve the retrieval performance.

1 Introduction

Typical search engines today use hyperlink information to measure the importance of a page for producing better search results. PageRank [7] and HITS [6] are two of the most popular link analysis algorithms for calculating the importance of web pages. Most link analysis algorithms such as [3,5,6,7] mainly focus on hyperlink information. The underlying assumption is that the Web is a flat graph, where all pages are identical and their importance is only determined by the link connections. However, it is clear that the structure of the Web is not as simple as such. Simon [10] argued that all the system, including the Web, are likely to be organized with a hierarchical structure. If having a macro look, we can find that domains, sites and pages form a hierarchy. Symmetrically, if having a micro look, we will find that each website is also organized hierarchically (as shown in Figure 1). In this paper, our goal is to study if we could improve the link analysis algorithms by introducing site hierarchy.

---

* This work was performed at Microsoft Research Asia.

G.G. Lee et al. (Eds.): AIRS 2005, LNCS 3689, pp. 546–551, 2005.
© Springer-Verlag Berlin Heidelberg 2005

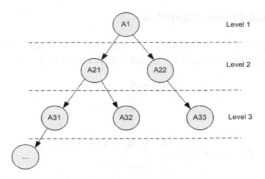

Fig. 1. Hierarchical structure in a website

From the view of website administrator and the view of web user, we can get the following two rules:

Rule 1: The more important a parent page is, the more likely its children will be important. In other words, a parent endorses its children pages. Similarly, the more important a child page is, the more likely its parent will be important. That is, a child page also endorses its parent. This rule displays the parent-child endorsement relationship.

Rule 2: Generally speaking, a parent page would be more important than its child pages, since the website administrator uses children pages to support the parent page while he is constructing the website. Since the level of parent page is less than its children, this rule displays the level priority in the site structure constraints.

The above constraints reflect the goal of the website administrator when he/she constructs the site, and they are also consistent with the users' browsing behaviors. Thus, we have the confidence that page importance computation with site structure constraints will improve the effectiveness and precision of Web information retrieval system. The rest of this paper is organized as follows. In Section 2, we propose how to combine hyperlink graph and site structure graph together to refine PageRank algorithm. In Section 3, we describe the optimization based PageRank algorithm with site structure constraints. Experimental results are reported in Section 4. And last, we give the concluding remarks and future work in Section 5.

2   PageRank with Site Structure Constraints

As well known, PageRank algorithm simulates a random walk on the hyperlink graph, and it assumes that hyperlinks represent human endorsement. According to the Rule 1 in Section 1, parent and child pages also endorse each other. Similar to the hyperlink graph, we can construct a site structure graph. In such a way, we will get two graphs. Let A and A^* represent the adjacency matrix of the hyperlink graph and site structure graph separately. To integrate the site structure information for Web page ranking, we need to fuse these two graphs for the random walk model.

2.1 Additive Graph Fusion Algorithm

One of the simplest fusion methods is to add the two graphs directly. That is, we merge the adjacency matrix A and A^* to get a new adjacency matrix B

$$B = A + A^* \tag{1}$$

where

$$B_{ij} = A_{ij} + A_{ij}^* = \begin{cases} 1, & if\ A_{ij} = 1\ or\ A_{ij}^* = 1 \\ 0, & otherwise \end{cases} \tag{2}$$

For the new graph with adjacency matrix B, we can follow the standard PageRank algorithm to compute the PageRank for each page in the Web. We call it by additive graph fusion algorithm (AGF for short).

2.2 Multiplicative Graph Fusion Algorithm

In the additive graph fusion algorithm, we get a new graph by adding hyperlink graph and site structure graph together. In this sub section, we fuse the two graphs by multiplication. This is the so-called multiplicative graph fusion algorithm algorithm (MGF for short).

Different from the additive graph fusion algorithm, we do not multiply the two adjacency matrices directly. Instead, we first convert the adjacency matrix of each graph to a probability transition matrix, and then multiply the two transition matrices together to get a new graph for random walk model. The details of this algorithm are shown as follow:

Same as the standard PageRank algorithm, we first normalize each row of the adjacency matrix A with its sum, and then get a probability matrix $\overline{A}$. Similarly, we get a row-stochastic matrix $\overline{A^*}$ from the adjacency matrix A^*. Then we get a matrix $\overline{C}$ for the new graph by multiplication:

$$\overline{C} = \overline{A^*}\,\overline{A} \tag{3}$$

It is easy to get that $\overline{C}$ is also a row-stochastic matrix. And the stationary distribution of $\overline{C}$ is used to measure the importance of each web page.

3   Optimization Based Algorithm

As mentioned in Rule 2 in Section 1, from the view of website administrator, most of the parent pages should be more important than their child pages because the children are the supports of their parent. However, the standard PageRank can not guarantee this level priority naturally. To make PageRank better suited to the site structure constraints, we need to refine the importance of pages within the same site by optimization. We call this algorithm OB for short.

Suppose there are k pages in a website, whose levels are l_1, l_2, ... , l_k, and the importance scores calculated by standard PageRank algorithm are $\pi_1, \pi_2, \cdots, \pi_k$. Let L denote the maximal level in the site, and $\bar{\pi}$ represent the mean PageRank of all the pages in that site. Define $w=(w_1, w_2, ..., w_L)$ as a L-dimensional weight vector, and then we refine the importance scores by adding a constant value to those pages in the same level of the site. The so-refined importance score are denoted by $\pi_1^*, \pi_2^*, \cdots, \pi_k^*$, where $\pi_i^* = \pi_i + w_{l_i} \bar{\pi}$.

During this refinement process, on one hand, we try to make those pages in the same site consistent with the level priority; while on the other hand, we do not want to make too much change for the original PageRank. Note that the change of the original PageRank depends on the weight vector w. The smaller the module of w, the less the change of the original PageRank is. So as a result, we can formulate the optimization problem as below.

$$\min \ \|w\|^2 \tag{4}$$
$$\text{s.t. } \pi_i^* \geq \pi_j^* \text{ if } i \text{ is the parent of } j$$

Considering that the level priority shown in Rule 2 is true for general sense, but it may be unsatisfied for some special cases, we introduce relaxation variables μ_{ij} to the optimization model of (4) as follows,

$$\min \ \|w\|^2 + C\sum \mu_{ij} \tag{5}$$
$$\text{s.t. } \pi_i^* + \mu_{ij} \geq \pi_j^* \text{ if } i \text{ is the parent of } j$$
$$\mu_{ij} \geq 0, i = 1, ..., k, j = 1, ..., k.$$

where C controls the trade-off between the modification to original PageRank and the violation of level priority. If $C=+\infty$, the model focuses on level priority: it does not allow any violation of the level priority, and the model of (5) degenerates into the simple model of (4). In the other extreme, if $C=0$, the model neglects the level priority and the PageRank remains unchanged.

It is clear that the models in (4) and (5) take the forms of typical quadratic optimization problems. We can use the algorithms in [1] to fulfill this task. We will not list further deductions of the dual problem and the details of the solution due to the limitation of paper length.

4 Experiments

To compare our new PageRank algorithms with the standard PageRank (PR) [7], we chose the topic distillation task in Web track of TREC 2003 as the benchmark. To generate the hierarchical structure for each website in the data corpus, we adopt the method in [4]. We use BM2500 [8] for the relevance weighting function and get the baseline with the precision at 10 (P@10) of 0.104.

For each query, we first use BM2500 to get a relevance list. We then choose the top 2000 pages from the relevance list, and combine the relevance score with importance score as follow:

$$score_{combination} = \alpha \times score_{relevance} + (1-\alpha) \times score_{impro\tan ce} \qquad (6)$$

The P@10 of all algorithms under investigation is shown in Figure 2. All the four curves converge to the baseline while α=1. From this figure, we can see that all our three algorithms outperform the standard PageRank algorithm, which shows the effectiveness of considering site structure information. Particularly, OB significantly boosts the retrieval accuracy than any other algorithms. The success of OB directly shows the validation of the site structure constraints mentioned in the introduction. In both AGF and MGF, we integrate site structure information by modifying the random walk graph. However, we do not know clearly how much site structure contributes to the final importance score. Therefore we are not sure whether the final importance score is consistent with the site structure constraints. However, in OB, we treat the site structure constraints explicitly in the optimization formulation. So the final importance score will most possibly follow the site structure constraints. As a result, we can say, OB makes the best use of site structure information among all the algorithms in Figure 2.

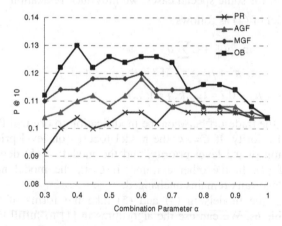

Fig. 2. Comparison of P@10 on TREC2003

5   Conclusions and Future Work

In this paper, we pointed out that site structure information should be considered while ranking web pages, which was neglected by traditional link analysis algorithms. Based on this motivation, we modified the standard PageRank algorithm from two different aspects: one modified the transition graph for the random walk model, and the other post-optimized the importance score according to site structure constraints. We developed three new algorithms with site structure constraints for page importance analysis: additive graph fusion algorithm, multiplicative graph fusion algorithm and optimization-based algorithm. Experiments on the topic distillation task of TREC2003 showed that all the new algorithms outperform the standard PageRank algorithm. Particularly the optimization-based algorithm significantly boosted the retrieval accuracy.

HITS [6] is another popular link analysis algorithm. For the future work we would like to apply site structure constraint to modify HITS algorithm.

References

1. Boyd, S., and Vandenberghe, L. Convex optimization. Course notes for EE364, Stanford University, 2003.
2. Brin, S., and L. Page, L. The anatomy of a large-scale hypertextual Web search engine, In The Seventh International World Wide Web Conference, 1998.
3. Chakrabarti, S., Joshi, M., and Tawde, V. Enhanced topic distillation using text, markup tags, and hyperlinks, In Proceedings of the 24th annual international ACM SIGIR conference on Research and development in information retrieval, ACM Press, 2001, pp. 208-216.
4. Feng, G., Liu, T. Y., Zhang, X. D., Qin. T., Gao, B., Ma, W. Y. Level-Based Link Analysis, in the 7th APWeb, 2005.
5. Haveliwala, T.H. Topic-sensitive pagerank. In Proc. of the 11th Int. World Wide Web Conference, May 2002.
6. Kleinberg, J. Authoritative sources in a hyperlinked environment, Journal of the ACM, Vol. 46, No. 5, pp. 604-622, 1999.
7. Page, L., Brin, S., Motwani, R., and Winograd, T. The PageRank citation ranking: Bringing order to the web, Technical report, Stanford University, Stanford, CA, 1998.
8. Robertson, S. E. Overview of the okapi projects, Journal of Pageation, Vol. 53, No. 1, 1997, pp. 3-7.
9. Salton, G. and McGill, M. J. Introduction to Modern Information Retrieval. McGraw-Hill, 1983.
10. Simon, H. A. The Sciences of the Artificial. MIT Press, Canbridge, MA, 3rd edition, 1981.

Gene Ontology Classification of Biomedical Literatures Using Context Association

Ki Chan and Wai Lam

Department of Systems Engineering and Engineering Management,
The Chinese University of Hong Kong,
Shatin, Hong Kong
{kchan, wlam}@se.cuhk.edu.hk

Abstract. The functional annotation of gene products from biomedical literatures has become a pressing issue due to the huge human efforts involved and the evolving biomedical knowledge. In this paper, we propose an approach for facilitating this functional annotation to the Gene Ontology by focusing on a subtask of annotation, that is, to determine which of the Gene Ontology a literature is associated with. This subtask can be formulated as a document classification problem. A feature engineering approach using context association conveyed in the biomedical literatures, in particular, utilizing the proximity relationship between target gene(s) and term features is proposed. Our approach achieves an F-score of 60.24%, which outperforms the submission runs of TREC Genomics 2004 annotation hierarchy subtask. We show that incorporation of context association can enhance the performance of the annotation hierarchy classification problem.

1 Introduction

The rapid development of online resources of the biomedical community provides huge amount of valuable research data, such as the sequencing data and the biological literatures published. The data raises issues on managing this massive amount of information. How to fully utilize the information to have a more complete picture of the current understanding of the biomedical world becomes a pressing issue.

The Gene Ontology (GO) [1] project attempts to address such goal by providing three controlled vocabularies for describing molecular function, biological process, and cellular component of gene products. The Gene Ontology is used for collaborating databases of the gene products, which can be annotated to these three ontologies. Databases, such as MGI Genome databases[1] are member organizations of the GO Project. They provide annotation association with information, such as, gene sequence, protein structures, and also association of biomedical publications with the gene products and evidence statement on how the linkage is made.

---

[1] Mouse Genomics Informatics http://www.informatics.jax.org

G.G. Lee et al. (Eds.): AIRS 2005, LNCS 3689, pp. 552–557, 2005.

The annotation process requires huge human efforts. Curators have to review and analyze the literatures, discover encoded information conveyed with other resources, in order to provide the annotation. This has become a challenging task because of the evolving size of the gene products and amount of literatures available. As a result, there is the pressing need for techniques to facilitate the determination of appropriate function or annotation with gene products.

Many research activities on the annotation of biological documents have been pursued, such as Critical Assessment of Information Extraction Systems in Biology (BioCreAtIvE) and Text retrieval Conference (TREC) Genomics Track. One task of the BioCreAtIvE Workshop focuses on the automatic functional annotation of proteins using the Gene Ontology (GO) classes, which is to assign the GO term's codes inside the gene ontology hierarchies. The low precision in performance illustrates that actual GO term annotation is considerably more difficult. Most participated groups [11,4] adopted text categorization methods, such as support vector machines and other supervised machine learning methods.

The TREC Genomics Track in 2004 introduced an information extraction task exploring the annotation of gene function according to Gene Ontology [6]. It involved the identification of documents having experimental evidence warranting annotation with GO codes, and the identification of the GO hierarchies (Biological process, Cellular component, Molecular function) that the article have the functions within, given the article and gene names. Most groups adopted a classification approach. Indiana University [12] achieved a top F-score 0.561, using variants of k-nearest neighbor model with weighted aggregated scores, MeSH terms, and gene names recognition. University of Wisconsin [13] achieved F-score 0.514 using a two-tier statistical machine learning system of "zone"-level and document-level predictions with Naive Bayes classifier and maximum entropy model respectively. Others used information retrieval approach [5] and statistical heuristic models [2,9].

Some researches investigated the annotation of GO codes to genes or the association of GO terms with function and protein annotation [8]. Raychaudhuri, et al. studied the use of different classification methods, maximum entropy, naive Bayes, and nearest neighbor classifications, with GO codes from biological process [10], and achieved 72% accuracy using maximum entropy.

In this paper, we investigate the gene ontology annotation problem using a document classification approach, which encapsulates the idea of context organization characteristics in articles. A feature engineering approach using context association pervaded in documents is employed. We exploit the proximity relationship of the features and the corresponding genes. The features having stronger proximity relationship with the corresponded genes will be regarded as having a higher significance. By assessing the underlying affinity of the features and the genes in the articles, a more effective way for capturing the characteristic of the problem is established. Our approach outperforms the submission runs of TREC Genomics 2004 annotation hierarchy subtask. Among all the submissions, the F-score of the best run and mean F-score of all 36 submissions were 56.11% and 38.24% respectively, while our approach achieved an F-score of 60.24%.

2   Our Approach

When an author writes, he or she would normally have an organization in mind to present their information [3] and context information, such as statistical information, is beneficial for text processing [7]. In particular, context organization is usually pervaded in biomedical literatures for expressing concepts and relations [14]. Both explicit and implicit organizations may exist. Explicit ones are section organizations of the texts, such as abstract, introduction, methods, results, and discussion. These section organizations have explicit indicators or boundaries inside the texts. Implicit organizations refer to structure(s) without explicitly specified boundaries. They are the hidden structures, which may or may not correspond to section boundaries. Therefore, they cannot be easily identified, and advanced methods are required to automatically discovering those hidden organizations. As an example, an author may express an idea or a concept within a certain context window and in which with some keynotes are closely adjoined together. We believe that by adopting feature engineering approach, this kind of organizations will have stimulating effect towards modeling.

Gene Name Annotation. In function annotation, the key concept is the gene and all other features are associated to it in different extents. Hence, the first step is to identify the gene's appearances inside the article, which we refer as the target gene. A tag, *target_name* is used to substitute each matched target gene name. In addition to identifying the target gene for context association analysis, gene name annotation has the advantage of normalizing the mentions of a gene. This can reduce the burden of classification by refraining it from taking on redundant gene names, and focusing on capturing the concept of function annotation to the target gene.

To locate all variants of the target gene names given, we combine the dictionary-based and rule-based approaches. For the dictionary-based approach, we construct synonym lists of genes from the MGI database of mouse, human, and rat, as synonyms from other species may also indicate the existence of the function relation. To capture the variations in the full name and abbreviation name of genes, we construct a set of rules to expand the synonym list to tackle the orthographical and morphological variations.

Feature Extraction. The context association can provide clues for locating the correct gene and hierarchy association among all possible gene-hierarchy correlations. We employ the proximity relationship between the context words and the target gene for measuring the context association, since features appearing more distant to the target gene tend to be less closely related with it.

For each feature, an association weight is added to the feature frequency for computation of weight for feature extraction. Let f_{k_i} be the k-th feature, f_k, at position i, and g_j is the target gene of document j. The association weight, $pos(f_{k_i}, g_j)$, depends on the absolute distance between a term and the target gene of the document. The formula is shown in Equation 1. Equation 2 finds the absolute value of the closest distance between feature f_{k_i} and g_j where $position(x)$ represents the position of a feature in a document. win_size is the number of terms appeared before and after the target gene. M and N represent the upper bound and the lower bound for the association weight, $pos(f_{k_i}, g_j)$. The value of this association weight lies inside the range of $(M - N)$. The implication of Equation 1 is that a feature being closer to the target gene indicates that it has a stronger association to the target gene, and therefore has a higher association weight. One constraint is that the features should be within a context window around the target gene; otherwise, no association weight will be added.

$$pos(f_{k_i}, g_j) = \begin{cases} M - \frac{(M-N)dist(f_{k_i}, g_j)}{window\_size} & if\ f_{k_i}\ and\ dist() \leq window\_size \\ 0 & otherwise \end{cases} \quad (1)$$

$$dist(f_{k_i}, g_j) = |position(f_{k_i}) - position(g_j)| \quad (2)$$

With the association weight, the feature weight for each feature in the jth document, d_j, is calculated by Equation 3, where $tf(f_k)$ is the term frequency of feature f_k in the document; $sec(f_{k_i})$ is the score of explicit organization of the document. This score can be a pre-assigned value for different position or section of the document, such as the introduction, method, etc. The section weight contributes to the importance on the association weight.

A final weight for a feature in a document is computed by Equation 4, where $df(f_k)$ is the document frequency of feature, f_k, and D is the total number of document in the training dataset. Since both the feature weight and inverse document frequency can vary quite a large range of values depending the terms. The logarithm transformation is used for both the feature weight and the inverse document frequency for stabilizing the variance in them.

$$feat\_wgt(f_k, d_j) = tf(f_k) + \sum_{i \in d_j} pos(f_{k_i}, g_j) \times sec(f_{k_i}) \quad (3)$$

$$final_weight(f_k, d_j) = log(feat\_wgt(f_k, d_j) + 1) \times log(\frac{D}{df(f_k) + 1}) \quad (4)$$

Classifier Learning. After retrieving the context associations of the features and target gene, the representation transformation of each document-gene pair can be used for classifier learning and classification. To capture the similarity of context association across all the training articles, the supervised learning approach, k-nearest neighbor classifier is adopted. kNN is able to look for the highest similarity of context association across the training data. A 4-fold cross validation is used for tuning the parameters such as the number of features, the number of neighbors (k), and the threshold used for classifying a document, to obtain the best set of parameters for classification. The set of parameters that achieves the highest averaged performance over all the folds will be selected. The classifier will then be retrained using the whole training data set.

3   Experiments and Discussions

The TREC Genomics 2004 annotation task dataset is used for the evaluation of our approach. The dataset contains 1,418 and 877 document-gene pairs for

Table 1. Performance of our approach and TREC official runs

Overall Performance	win-size	M	N	Precsion	Recall	F-score
Baseline(words)	-	-	-	80.40%	37.02%	50.70%
Annotated target gene	0	0	0	78.38%	45.12%	57.27%
Annotated target gene	5	5	0	78.79%	45.72%	57.86%
Annotated target gene	5	20	0	79.39%	47.12%	59.14%
Annotated target gene (hybrid: GO definition features for CC)	5	20	0	80.81%	48.02%	60.24%
Annotated target gene	10	1	0	78.38%	45.38%	57.48%
Annotated target gene	10	30	0	82.02%	45.82%	58.80%
Best TREC Genomics official runs						56.11%
Median of TREC Genomics official runs						35.84%

training and testing respectively which indicates the associated gene of each document assigned by MGI. An updated version of the data is also released with a total of 58 articles removed. However, the original dataset is used for comparative study of our approach with the TREC Genomics 2004 submission runs. Three kNN models correspond to the three GO hierarchies are developed using 4-fold cross validation. An overall evaluation of the 3 hierarchies is calculated using the evaluation program provided by TREC Genomics 2004.

We have conducted extensive experiments by adjusting the values of the 3 parameters namely, the window size, the upper bound, M and the lower bound, N, to evaluate their effects on the classification. An experiment using only bag of words as features and the classic TF-IDF feature weighting is carried out as the baseline for our evaluation. The results are shown in Table 1. With target gene annotated, there is an increase of 6.6% on F-score, which shows that the classification is largely benefited by the identification of target gene. It is also observed that as the value of M increases, the performance increases from 50.7% to 59.14% in F-score. This shows that our approach performs better as we put more emphasis on features having stronger context association with the target gene. All our runs outperform significantly the median of the official runs in TREC Genomics 2004 subtask and the F-scores of our approach exceed the best official run.

Also, each of the hierarchies has different characteristics in respect to their association of target genes and GO related terms. Hybrid approach can be employed to pinpoint the characteristics of the GO hierarchies. For example, GO terms and definition feature list can be adopted to the CC hierarchy together with the context association weight. The F-score achieved using the hybrid approach is 60.24%, which shows that the GO terms and the terms in their definition are informative.

References

1. Ashburner, M., Ball, CA., Blake, JA., Botstein, D., Butler, H., Cherry, JM., Davis, AP., Dolinski, K., Dwight, SS., Eppig, JT., Harris, MA., Hill, DP., Issel-Tarver, L., Kasarskis, A., Lewis, S., Matese, JC., Richardson, JE., Ringwald, M., Rubin, GM., Sherlock, G.: Gene Ontology Consortium: Gene Ontology: tool for the unification of biology. Nature 25:25-29, 2000.

2. Aronson, A.R., Demner, D., Humphrey, S.M., Ide, N.C., Kim, W., Liu, H., Loane, R.R., Mork, J.G., Smith, L.H., Tanabe, L.K., Wilbur, W.J., Xie, N.: Knowledge-intensive and Statistical Approaches to the Retrieval and Annotation of Genomics MEDLINE Citations. The Thirteenth Text Retrieval Conference: TREC 2004. Gaithersburg, MD: National Institute of Standards and Technology.

3. Chan, K., Lam, W.: Extracting causation knowledge from natural language texts. International Journal of Intelligent Systems, 20(3), 327-358, 2005

4. Ehrler, F., Ruch, P.: Preliminary Report on the BioCreative Experiment: Task Presentation, System Description and Preliminary Results. BioCreAtIvE 2004, Granada, Spain.

5. Eichmann, D., Zhang, Y., Bradshaw, S., Qiu, X.Y., Zhou, L., Srinivasan, P., Sehgal, A.K., Wong, H.: Novelty, Question Answering and Genomics: The University of Iowa Response. The Thirteenth Text Retrieval Conference: TREC 2004. Gaithersburg, MD: National Institute of Standards and Technology.

6. Hersh, W. R., Bhuptiraju, R.T., Ross, L., Johnson, P., Cohen, A.M., Kraemer, D.F.: TREC 2004 Genomics Track Overview. The Thirteenth Text Retrieval Conference: TREC 2004. Gaithersburg, MD: National Institute of Standards and Technology.

7. Lam, W., Chan, K., Radev, D.R., Saggion, H., Teufel, S.: Context-based generic cross-lingual retrieval of documents and automated summaries. Journal of the American Society for Information Science and Technology, 56(2): 129-139, 2005.

8. Lu, Z., Hunter, L.: GO Molecular Function Terms are Predictive of Subcellular Localization. Pacific Symposium on Biocomputing 2005, Hawaii, January.

9. Nakov, P.I., Schwartz, A.S., Stoica, E., Hearst, M.A.: BioText Team Experiments for the TREC 2004 Genomics Track. The Thirteenth Text Retrieval Conference: TREC 2004. Gaithersburg, MD: National Institute of Standards and Technology.

10. Raychaudhuri, S., Chang, J.T., Sutphin, P.D., Altman, R.B.: Associating Genes with Gene Ontology Codes Using a Maximum Entropy Analysis of Biomedical Literature. Genome Research 12:203-214, 2002

11. Rice, S.B., Nenadic, G., Stapley, B.J.: Protein function assignment using term-based support vector machines - Biocreative Task Two 2003. BioCreAtIvE 2004, Granada, Spain.

12. Seki, K., Costello, J.C., Singan, V.R., Mostafa, J.: TREC 2004 Genomics Track experiments at IUB. The Thirteenth Text Retrieval Conference: TREC 2004. Gaithersburg, MD: National Institute of Standards and Technology.

13. Settles, B., Craven, M.: Exploiting Zone Information, Syntactic Features, and Information Terms in Gene Ontology Annotation from Biomedical Documents. The Thirteenth Text Retrieval Conference: TREC 2004. Gaithersburg, MD: National Institute of Standards and Technology.

14. Shah, P.K., Perez-Iratxeta, C., Bork, P., Andrade, A.: Information extraction from full text scientific articles: Where are the keywords?. BMC Bioinformatics, 4:20, 2003

An Examination of Feature Selection Frameworks in Text Categorization

Bong Chih How and Wong Ting Kiong

Faculty of Computer Science and Information Technology,
94300 Kota Samarahan,
Sarawak, Malaysia
{chbong, wongtingkiong}@gmail.com

Abstract. Feature selection, an important task in text categorization, is used for the purpose of dimensionality reduction. Feature selection basically can be performed locally and globally. For local selection, distinct feature sets are derived from different classes. The number of feature set is thus depended on the number of class. In contrary, only one universal feature set will be used in global feature selection. It is assumed that the feature set should preserve the characteristic of all classes. Furthermore, feature selection can also be carried out based on relevant feature set only (local dictionary) or both relevant and irrelevant feature set (universal dictionary). In this paper, we explored the different frameworks of feature selection to the task of text categorization on the Reuters(10) and Reuters(115) datasets (variants of Reuters-21578 corpus). We then investigate the efficiency of 7 different local or global feature selections corresponds the use of local and universal dictionary. Our experiments have shown that local feature selection with local dictionary yields optimal categorization results.

1 Introduction

Features selection is used for the purpose of dimensionality reduction by selecting significant terms from text. It can be performed basically in two ways: local and global feature selection. Furthermore, feature set can be seen in another perspective: local dictionary and universal dictionary. In this paper, we intend to answer the following questions with empirical evidence on the 7 feature selections:

- Which feature selection framework is optimal in text categorization?
- To what. extend the performance of local feature selection compared to global one?
- Is combining positive and negative feature yields better classifier reading?

Feature selection in text categorization has enjoyed rich literatures in the past 2 decades, especially on local and global feature selection, plus small number of works on local and universal dictionary. However, there is no work reporting the correspondence effect of local and global feature selection on the different dictionary.

G.G. Lee et al. (Eds.): AIRS 2005, LNCS 3689, pp. 558 – 564, 2005.

2 Feature Selection

Feature selection basically can be performed in two distinct ways: local and global selection [4]. Say, for a set of training examples $D=\{d_1, d_2, ..., d_n\}$, where each of them is tagged with category label, $C=\{c_1, c_2, ..., c_m\}$.

Local Feature Selection – feature set f_1, is extracted from each category of interest (positive class) of which the specific classifier will operate. Feature set extracted from c_1 thus will be differed from feature set derived from category other than c_1. The study of the feature selection using local feature set can be seen in [5]. There are 2 conditions when performing local feature selection: local feature size cannot be fixed at a pre-defined quantity. Rather, it can be seen as threshold (cut-off point), it will therefore never choose more features than there are unique terms in training documents of that category. This is usually happened to populated categories. The second condition proposes if there are training documents where their distinct features is smaller than threshold; for example, the distinct feature size will make the threshold, no matter how high the threshold is. For smaller training data with smaller unique term, it tends to has smaller feature set. Local feature selection is operated under the category of interest where it capable of capturing more descriptive feature and give more information to classifier. Hence, it can be smarter [2][4]. Somehow, for scarcely populated category, it turned out to be less robust [1].

Global Feature Selection – selects terms from the documents under all categories. In order to specifically weight the term globally, at class independent sense, a globalization technique is applied to obtain a global score relatively to each category. The most common technique likes sum, averaged or selecting the maximum value of the category-specific value can be seen in [2][3][5]. Global feature selection by definition has no idea on what classification task is going to be required of the features. They must preserve and obtain if possible every category-specific significant feature that may be important to classification task and can only safely remove features that will not be relevant to classification task. At its best, a feature set f_2, extracted from all the classes $C=\{c_1, c_2, ..., c_m\}$. Sometime, this is a very difficult job as because it has so little information to work with, especially working on small size training documents, where it is very likely to over-generalize feature set. Beside, it is tough, as to what extend the number of feature is needed to characterize each category in order to capture the characteristics of all categories in order to produce the best classification result.

3 Feature Set

After looking at "how" features can be selected, we shift our attention to "what" kind of features can be obtained. Research on text categorization suggests two possible ways in which the term features can be harvested: document within the positive class (local dictionary), or combination of both the positive and negative classes (universal dictionary). We can treat that the whole feature space is divided into 2 parts: relevant (positive) category, c_1 and irrelevant (negative) categories other than c_1, where the idea of closed-world assumption is applied. Features can be chosen between class c_l and class c_l', where $c_l \subset C$. c_l' here indicates all classes in C except c_l. Usually the size of c_l' is $1 \leq c_l' \leq m$.

Local Dictionary – choses only significance terms from the interested class to train the classifier. Various criteria can be used to measure the amount of good it does to include or exclude the term from consideration in examining whether a document belongs to c_l or c_l'. Literatures have reported that local dictionary gives better performance. In particular, results from our study show that local dictionary gives considerably better performance [6]. For local dictionary, the term's weight for each category is computed based on the relevant document in the category only. Local dictionary can be seen either in local or global feature selection [2]. In local feature selection, only features from the interested category are taken into account. In global feature selection, features from each category of interest are collected and normalized by gradually summing or averaging the weights of a feature among the categories.

Universal Dictionary – is made up of both relevant and irrelevant documents. If a feature set is being derived for a class c_l classifier, it is considered positive class when working with it, and the training documents for the rest of the classes are labeled as c_l'. Feature set, f_3, can be collected from either c_l only or combination of c_l and c_l'. It is possible that no terms from c_l could be chosen but only terms from c_l' (negative categories) are chosen where this will be the best set of terms to use in order to make such a decision. Note that all of these methods can keep terms that occur only in c_l' if they are very telling of the category c_l'. However, there are special cases where a term can occur in many categories carries different weights in different category. In this case, we end up having 2 feature sets: positive, F+ and negative, F-; it is always true that {F+}<{F-}, as F- constitutes from categories other than c_l. We intend to pick up high weight F+ and low F+ to be the good indicators of the positive and negative category . The larger (smaller) the value is, the more likely the term to positive (negative) category, universal dictionary will be the union of the two. Universal dictionary for global feature selection is build by combining universal dictionary from all categories into one single global feature set. Global score is computed by sum, averaged or selecting the maximum value of the category feature set.

4 Experimental Setting

There are 7 feature selection measures being examined in our study: Correlation Coefficient (CC) [7][8], Chi-Square (CC)[4][5][7][8], Categorical Term Descriptor (CTD)[9], Gain Ratio (GR)[7], Information Gain (IG)[4][5][8], and Mutual Information (MI)[5]. For the sake of brevity, we have omitted their definition and justification. Their detailed can be obtained in the respective literatures. We employed Reuters-21578 as benchmarking dataset in our experiments. In our study, it was divided into subsets of the 10 most populous categories and original 115 categories, which we refer them as Reuters(10) and Reuters(115) respectively. The reason of dividing Reuters-21578 into 2 subsets is to examine the feature selection methods' effectiveness in choosing feature terms from uniform and scattered distributed categories. Feature selection on Reuters(10) is assumed to be easier when compared to Reuter(115). On the other hand, Reuters(115) is seen to be more difficult because it contains scattered document in high number of categories. Theoretically, it tends to generate higher misclassificaïion rate. We employed Multinomial Naïve Bayes [10] here as the control classifiers to compare various feature selection measures. To evaluate the performance we use FMeasure [3][4]. As we run the experiments with Reuters(10) and Reuters(115), it is crucial that the readings do not to be affected by the large gap of category and document size between them. For this reson, we report only mirco-averaged FMeasure.

5 Result and Analysis

Overall, we could notice in Table 1 that local feature selection always outperforms global feature selection in both local and universal dictionary. Our finding is aligned with [2][4]. This has suggested that local feature set is informative and better at describing categories. At the same time, we also discovered that categories with high number of document tend to generate more descriptive feature set. On the other hand, the performance of global feature selections is rather pessimistic, especially on the scarcely distributed Reuters(115). There are many repeated features among the feature set; an evidence of over-generalization. The poor performance of global feature selection is very likely caused by improper normalization, such as averaging and selecting of maximum score. We believe that averaging the score of a feature could reduce significantly the high relevancy of the term to the specific category as the score might be dispersed to other category. This is rather true if we are dealing with dataset with high number of category. Moreover, selecting maximum score may literally favor of rare term which is not significant; it biases toward the category which gives more weight to the term, tends to perform unfair selection when dealing with imbalanced data where it ends up high proportion of the feature set are nominated from the highly populated categories. From our study, the performance of averaged-global feature selection is identical to maxed-global feature selection.

Table 1 also indicates that the universal dictionary in either local or global feature selection does not perform as well as the local dictionary. Local dictionary is the better descriptor for the category; incorporating negative feature does not optimize the categorization results as claim in [3][7]. Our partial finding has suggested that the negative features can be the noise in disguise. It occurs when the negative features dominate the universal dictionary, increasing misclassification rate.

Our intuition also suggested that the imbalanced division of dataset into positive and negative category is another factor of poor performance of universal dictionary Our preliminary study suggested that if a dictionary does not take into account of negative features, the chances of them appear to be the noise to classifier is thus reduced. However, [7] in their study has contrary finding in which incorporating of negative feature can remarkably improve categorization performance. In addition, balanced dataset such as Reuters(10), always has better reading than Reuters(115).

Table 1. Micro-averaged FMeasure for Reuters(10) and Reuters(115) of 7 feature selections at the feature size of 2000

	Local Feature Selection				Global Feature Selection							
	Local Dict.		Universal Dict.		Local Dict (AVG)		Universal Dict (AVG)		Local Dict (MAX)		Universal Dict (MAX)	
Reuters	10	115	10	115	10	115	10	115	10	115	10	115
CC	0.71	0.67	0.71	0.5	0.71	0.45	0.66	0.41	0.66	0.46	0.65	0.41
CHI	0.69	0.68	0.68	0.48	0.66	0.48	0.69	0.41	0.66	0.48	0.66	0.42
CTD	0.70	0.68	0.67	0.47	0.65	0.46	0.66	0.43	0.66	0.48	0.66	0.42
GSS	0.71	0.68	0.69	0.51	0.65	0.39	0.66	0.41	0.66	0.44	0.65	0.41
IG	0.70	0.67	0.67	0.44	0.65	0.42	0.71	0.51	0.65	0.42	0.64	0.54
MI	0.69	0.68	0.59	0.43	0.65	0.43	0.47	0.43	0.66	0.47	0.47	0.43
OR	0.68	0.64	0.69	0.55	0.67	0.44	0.58	0.41	0.67	0.35	0.48	0.33

Table 2. Averaged of positive and negative feature nominated from each category in earn, crude, corn, trade, acq, grain, ship, interest, wheat and money-fx with universal dictionary at the feature size of 2000

	Average number of term			
	+ve	-ve	% of -ve	Micro-avg.
IG	2000	0	0.0	0.71
CHI	1996	5	0.2	0.69
CC	1506	492	24.6	0.66
GSS	1327	493	27.1	0.66
CTD	1333	667	33.4	0.66
OR	1888	112	5.6	0.58
MI	599	1402	70.1	0.47

Table 3. Averaged of feature size nominated from each category in earn, crude, corn, trade, acq, grain, ship, interest, wheat and money-fx with local dictionary at the feature size of 2000

	Average term	Duplicated term (%)
CC	643	32.1
CHI	1146	57.3
CTD	1162	58.1
GSS	740	37.0
IG	1643	82.1
MI	1663	83.1
OR	498	24.9

We find that some feature selection metrics tend to incorporate high number of negative feature (see Table 2). This is especially true to MI and CTD. The negative feature in MI dominates the global feature set, average 70%. Looking at its categorization efficiency, it has recorded merely 0.47 and is the worst performer among the 7 feature selection we have studied. On the other hand, IG and CHI contain no and least negative feature in average, both are the top performers. However, it would be unfair arguing that negative feature is harmful for classifier. In the table, we notice to that CC, GSS, and CTD consist of high number negative feature but produce decent result whereas OR has worse result though having small number negative feature. The negative feature accrues in the universal dictionary able to negate opposite document; however, it is bound to the nature of feature selection.

Table 3 implies that with global feature selection, some categories only capable of contributing small portion of positive features in the 2000 features. By investigating the term distribution pattern, we found high ratio of duplicated term in the categories. In other words, terms appear in local feature set can appear in other local feature set. In the worst case, we even came across with a number of terms which appear in all of the 10 categories. Global feature selection leads to a situation where the feature set made up by irrelevance terms in respective categories. There is high number of over-lapped terms among categories. The inconsistent feature size from each category is because the limited number of unique term in each category can result high rate of misclassification, which is very likely to be overrun by the negative features.

6 Conclusion

In this paper, we discussed local and global feature selection with two different dictionaries: local and universal dictionary, with Reuters-21578 variations as dataset. We concluded that:

- Local feature selection with local dictionary is the best performer among all. Local feature manages to preserve better category information as it uses as many feature as possible. It works particularly well with local dictionary.
- Global feature selection tends to leave out some significant terms at the same time consists of high number of repeated term. This may be caused by the improper normalization of global feature set. We also concluded that normalization like averaging and maximizing score does not make significant differences.
- Universal dictionary does not work well with most of the local and global feature selection. It introduces insignificant and high overlapped term (noise). In most cases, it is over-generalized and dominated by irrelevant feature from opposite categories.

In addition, we also reported that CTD[9], which derived from term weighting scheme can perform equally well compared state-of-the-art feature selections like CHI and IG. It is a mild performer in local and global feature selection, works well with local dictionary.

References

1. D, Franca and Sebastiani, F. (2003). Supervised term weighting for automated text categorization. Proceedings of SAC-03, 18th ACM Symposium on Applied Computing, Melbourne, US, 2003, pp. 784--788.

2. Ng, H. T., Goh, W. B. and Low, K. L. (1997), Feature Selection, Perception Learning, and a Usability Case Study for Text Categorization, in 'SIGIR '97: ACM Press, pp. 67–73.
3. Z. Zheng, X. Wu and R. Srihari, (2004). Feature Selection for Text Categorization on Imbalanced Data, ACM KDD Explorations Newsletter, 6(1), June 2004, pp.80-89.
4. Sebastiani, F. (1999). A tutorial on automated text categorisation. Proceedings of ASAI-99, 1st Argentinian Symposium on Artificial Intelligence, Buenos Aires, AR, 1999.
5. Yang, Y., and Pedersen, J. (1997). A comparative study on feature set selection in text categorization. In Proc. of the 14th International Conference on Machine Learning, pages 412--420, Nashville, TN. Morgan Kaufmann.
6. Debole, F. & Sebastiani, F., Supervised term weighting for automated text categorization. Text Mining and its Applications, ed. S. Sirmakessis, Physica-Verlag, Heidelberg, DE, Number 138 in the "Studies in Fuzziness and Soft Computing" series, pp. 81–98, 2004.
7. Zheng, Z., Srihari, R,. (2003). Optimally Combining Positive and Negative Features for Text Categorization. ICML 2003 Workshop.
8. Forman, G. (2003) An Extensive Empirical of Feature Selection Metrics for Text Categorization. Journal of Machine Learning Research 3 (2003) 1289-1305.
9. Bong C. H. and Narayanan K. (2004). An Empirical Study of Feature Selection for Text Categorization based on Term Weighting Scheme. IEEE/WIC/ACM International Joint Conference on Web Intelligence (WI'04), Beijing, September 2004.
10. D. D. Lewis. (1995). Evaluating and optimizing autonomous text classification systems. In Proceedings of SIGIR-95, 18th ACM International Conference on Research and Development in Information Retrieval, pages 246{254, Seattle, US, 1995.

Query Transitive Translation Using IR Score for Indonesian-Japanese CLIR

Ayu Purwarianti, Masatoshi Tsuchiya, and Seiichi Nakagawa

Department of Information and Computer Science, Toyohashi University of Technology
ayu@slp.ics.tut.ac.jp, tsuchiya@cc.tut.ac.jp,
nakagawa@slp.ics.tut.ac.jp

Abstract. We combined the mutual information score and TF×IDF score (IR score) in order to select the best keyword translation in our transitive translation. The transitive translation used bilingual dictionaries to translate Indonesian query into Japanese keywords. The Japanese keywords are then used as the input to retrieve Japanese documents. The keyword selection is done in two steps. The first step is to sort translation candidates according to their mutual information scores calculated from a monolingual target language corpus. The second step is to select the best candidate set among 5 top mutual information scores based on their TF×IDF scores. The experiment against NTCIR-3 Web Retrieval Task data shows that the keyword selection based on this combination achieved higher IR score than a direct translation method using original Indonesian-Japanese dictionary and also higher than the machine translation result using Kataku (Indonesian-English) and Babelfish (English-Japanese) engines.

1 Introduction

Using a pivot language in the query translation of a Cross Language Information Retrieval (CLIR) system has been an effective method where the language's pair has a limited data resource [2][10]. This approach is called transitive translation[2]. In this research, we translated Indonesian query into Japanese keyword list through English as the pivot language. Because Indonesian has limited data resources, we used a bilingual dictionary in the transitive translation.

A transitive translation based on a bilingual dictionary usually produces many irrelevant translation candidates. These irrelevant words will lead to a low retrieval score where many unintended documents are retrieved. A statistical query filtering has been done in some researches such as in [3][9][16]. In [3], the co-occurrence frequencies are analyzed to disambiguate phrase translations. The co-occurrences score is called *em* score. Each set is ranked by *em* score and the highest ranking set is taken as the appropriate translation. The selection is to select best English translation in Spanish-English translation. In [9], it selected the best Chinese translation from English sentence by the coherence score. They used EMMI weighting measure [17] by taken into account the distance between words to calculate the coherence score. In [16], it selected the best Spanish-English and Chinese-English translation by using

G.G. Lee et al. (Eds.): AIRS 2005, LNCS 3689, pp. 565–570, 2005.

English corpus. The coherence score calculation was based on 1) web page count; 2) retrieval score; 3) mutual information score. In this paper, we combined the mutual information score taken from monolingual corpus and TFxIDF score to select the best translation.

The transitive translation results are compared to the direct translation result using Indonesian-Japanese dictionary and also compared to a transitive translation based on machine translation. The rest of the paper is organized as technique description, experiment result, and conclusion.

2 Overview of the Query Translation System

There are two sub systems in the Indonesian-Japanese query translation: (1) Keyword Translation, (2) Query Filtering. Keyword translation's aim is to get the target translation for each keyword using a bilingual dictionary. The keyword translation system includes word matching and stop word elimination process.

Indonesian queries usually consist of native (Indonesian) words and borrowed words. For example, Indonesian query "Saya ingin mengetahui siapa yang telah menjadi peraih Academy Awards beberapa generasi secara berturut-turut" which means "I want to know who have been the recipients of successive generations of Academy Awards" includes a borrowed word "Academy Awards". The word "Academy Awards" is borrowed from English in its original spelling. Using only Indonesian-English and English-Japanese dictionaries will not be able to translate the borrowed words which are usually hold important role in the query. Therefore to translate the borrowed words, we used English-Japanese dictionary. English-Japanese dictionary is used to translate borrowed words because most of borrowed words in our query translation system are come from English.

The keyword translation system resulted in many irrelevant translation candidates. Therefore, to get better translation, it needs the query filtering or keyword selection system. Aim of this process is to select most relevant terms among all translation candidates. This keyword selection system is described in the next section.

3 Keyword Selection System

In the keyword selection system, rather than choosing the highest TFxIDF score or the highest mutual information score among all sequences, we combined both scores by selecting the highest TFxIDF score among 5 top mutual information scores which are calculated iteratively. To avoid the calculation of all sequences, we calculated the mutual information score per word pair. First, we selected the 50 (or less) best mutual information score sequences among the translations of first 2 Indonesian keywords. These 50 best sequences joined with the 3rd translation set are recalculated to get the mutual information score and reselected to get the 50 best sequences for the 3 translation sets. This step is repeated until all translation sets are covered.

For a word sequence, the mutual information score is:

$$I(t_1 \ldots t_n) = \sum_{i=1}^{n-1} \sum_{j=i+1}^{n} I(t_1, t_2) \tag{1}$$

$I(t_1 \ldots t_n)$ means the mutual information for a sequence of words t_1, $t_2, \ldots t_n$. $I(t_1, t_2)$ means the mutual information between two words (t_1, t_2). Here, for a zero frequency word, it will have no impact on the mutual information score of a word sequence.

The next step is re-rank the sequence of the 5 best mutual information score based on the TF×IDF score. The TF×IDF score used here is the relevance score   (Equation (2) taken from [8]) between the document and the query. For the final output, we selected 1 query among the 5 best mutual information scores with the highest TF×IDF score.

$$\sum_t \left(\frac{TF_{t,i}}{\frac{DL_i}{avglen} + TF_{t,i}} . log \frac{N}{DF_t} \right) \tag{2}$$

$TF_{t,i}$ denotes the frequency of term t appears in document i. DF_t denotes the number of documents containing term t. N denotes the total number of documents in the collection. DL_i denotes the length of document i (i.e., the number of characters contained in i), and $avglen$ denotes the average length of documents in the collection.

4   Experiments

4.1   Experimental Data

Our CLIR experiments are done on NTCIR-3 Web Retrieval Task data (100 Gb Japanese documents). In the NTCIR-3 data, the Japanese queries and English queries were prepared. The Indonesian queries (47 queries) are manually translated from English queries. The IR system[8] is borrowed from Atsushi Fujii (Tsukuba University). The query translation system used resources below:

- Indonesian-English dictionary (KEBI[13], 29,054 Indonesian words)
- English-Japanese dictionary (Eijirou[5], 556,237 English words)
- English stop word list, combined from [7] and [19]
- English morphology rule, implement WordNet[18] description
- Indonesian morphology rule, restricted only for word repetition, posfix –nya and –i
- Chasen[4], Japanese morphological analyzer
- Mainichi Shinbun newspaper corpus[15]
- Indonesian-Japanese dictionary (online dictionary [12], 14,823 Indonesian words)

4.2   Experimental Result

In the experiment, we compared our proposed method with 2 other translation methods as higher target. The compared methods are direct translation using Indonesian-Japanese dictionary and transitive translation using machine translation

(MT). In the direct translation, there are 2 schemas, with and without using the English-Japanese dictionary to translate the borrowed words. In the transitive translation using MT, we used Kataku engine [11] to translate the Indonesian query sentence into English and Babelfish[1]/Excite[6] to translate the English translation result to the Japanese. For the baseline, we choose the transitive translation using a bilingual dictionary without any keyword selection.

Fig. 1 shows the IR score achieved in the Indonesian-Japanese CLIR. The IR scores shown are in Mean Average Precision (MAP) scores. There are 4 MAP scores: RL (highly relevant document as correct answer with hyperlink information used), RC (highly relevant document as correct answer), PL (partially relevant documnt as correct answer with hyperlink information used), PC (partially relevant document as correct answer).

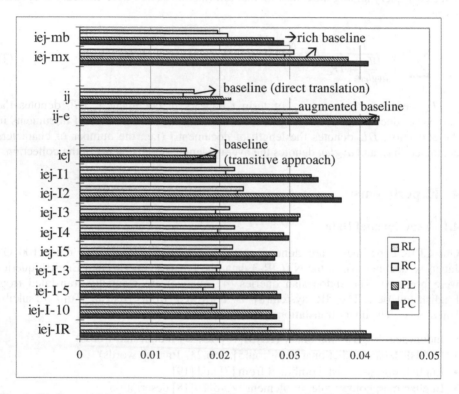

Fig. 1. IR Score of Indonesian-Japanese CLIR (iej: Indonesian-English-Japanese transitive translation using bilingual dictionary, ij: direct translation using bilingual dictionary, iej-mb: transitive translation using Kataku and Babelfish machine translations, iej-mx: transitive translation using Kataku and Excite machine translations, iej-X: X key word sequences with highest mutual information score as the keyword selection, iejX: X[th] key word sequence with highest mutual information score, iej-IR: combine the mutual information and TF×IDF score in the keyword selection)

Fig. 1 shows that using keyword selection in the query translation enhanced the IR score achieved by the baseline method (iej). Using 3 highest mutual information score sequences (iej-I-3) achieved higher IR score compared to the 5 or 10 highest mutual information score. Using only 1 sequence (iej-I1) achieved better IR score than using some sequences (iej-3, iej-5, iej-10). And using the combination of mutual information and TF×IDF score (iej-IR) achieved higher IR score than both schema using the mutual information score only. By using the combination of mutual information and TF×IDF score in keyword selection, it enhanced the baseline method (iej) by 114%.

Compared to the direct translation with a middle sized Indonesian-Japanese dictionary (14,823 words), iej-IR showed different result. Direct translation (ij) that only used Indonesian-Japanese dictionary got lower IR score than the iej-IR for about 103%. This low IR score is caused by that there are many OOVs yielded by using only Indonesian-Japanese dictionary. If the borrowed words are translated by using English-Japanese dictionary (ij-e), the IR score is almost the same as iej-IR.

Compared to the machine translation result, iej-IR achieved higher IR score. Compared to the Kataku and Babelfish machine translation result, iej-IR gained higher IR score about 39%. And compared to the Kataku and Excite machine translation result, iej-IR also achieved almost the same IR score.

One of the main reasons of the low MAP score is the quality of the bilingual dictionary. The important words in queries for an IR system are proper nouns. Unfortunately, not all of proper nouns in the queries are covered in the bilingual dictionary, including the English-Japanese dictionary. Among 47 queries, there are about 12 queries with proper nouns or OOV such as "norse", "yggdrasil", "miyabe", "miyuki", "sanguozhi", "kyoto", "ozoni", "shiba inu", "nara", "heian", etc.

5 Conclusion

The main point concluded from the experiments that using a combination of mutual information and TF×IDF score can improve IR score significantly in comparison with the baseline method. It is even get higher IR score than other translation systems such as direct translation and transitive translation using Kataku (Indonesian-English) and Babelfish (English-Japanese) machine translation. The keyword selection is quite effective for a transitive translation method which yielded many translation candidates. This method is also applicable for language with limited data resources or surprised language such as Indonesian language.

Another conclusion is that the importance of the proper noun translation in an IR system. These proper nouns usually hold as important keywords. Using only bilingual dictionaries could not handle the proper noun problems. Therefore, for our future work, we will address the proper noun problems in our query translation system.

Acknowledgement

We would like to give our appreciation to Dr. Atsushi Fujii (Tsukuba University) to allow us to use the IR Engine in our research. This work was partially supported by The 21st Century COE Program "Intelligent Human Sensing".

References

[1] Babelfish English-Japanese Online Machine Translation, http://www.altavista.com/babelfish/, April 2004.

[2] Ballesteros, Lisa A., "Cross-Language Retrieval via Transitive Translation", *Advances in Information Retrieval*, Kluwer Academic Publisher, 2000, pp. 203-230.

[3] Ballesteros, Lisa A., W. Bruce Croft, "Resolving Ambiguity for Cross-Language Retrieval", *ACM Sigir*, 1998.

[4] Chasen, http://chasen.naist.jp/hiki/ChaSen/, February 2004.

[5] Eijirou, Alc Co., http://www.alc.co.jp/, 2002

[6] Excite English-Japanese Online Machine Translation, http://www.excite.co.jp/world/, April 2004.

[7] Fox, Christopher, "A Stop List for General Text", *ACM Sigir*, Vol 24, Issue 2 Fall 89/Winter 90, pp. 19-21

[8] Fujii, Atsushi, Tetsuya Ishikawa, "NTCIR-3 Cross-Language IR Experiments at ULIS", in *Proc. Of the Third NTCIR Workshop*, 2003.

[9] Gao, Jianfeng, Jian-Yun Nie, Endong Xun, Jian Zhang, Ming Zhou, Changning Huang, "Improving Query Translation for Cross-Language Information Retrieval using Statistical Model", in *Proc. Sigir*, 2001.

[10] Gollins, Tim and Mark Sanderson, "Improving Cross Language Information Retrieval with Triangulated Translation", in *Proc. Sigir*, 2001.

[11] Indonesian-English Online Machine Translation, http://www.toggletext.com/kataku_trial.php, May 2004.

[12] [12]Indonesian-Japanese Online Dictionary, http://ml.ryu.titech.ac.jp/~indonesia/tokodai/dokumen/ kamusjpina.pdf, May 2004

[13] KEBI, Kamus Elektronik Bahasa Indonesia, http://nlp.aia.bppt.go.id/kebi/, February 2004.

[14] Kishida, Kazuaki and Noriko Kando, "Two-Stage Refinement of Query Translation in a Pivot Language Approach to Cross-Lingual Information Retrieval: An Experiment at CLEF 2003", CLEF 2003, LNCS 3237, pp. 253-262, 2004.

[15] Mainichi Shinbun CD-Rom data sets 1993-1995, Nichigai Associates Co., 1994-1996

[16] Qu, Yan, G. Grefenstette, D. A. Evans, "Resolving Translation Ambiguity using Monolingual Corpora", *Advanced in Cross-Language Information Retrieval*, vol. 2785 of LNCS, pages 223-241. Springer Verlag, 2002.

[17] van Rijsbergen, D.J. , "Information Retrieval", 2nd ed., Butterworths, London, 1979.

[18] WordNet, http://wordnet.princeton.edu/, February 2004..

[19] Zu, Guowei, Wataru Ohyama, Tetsushi Wakabayashi, Fumitaka Kimura, "Automatic Text Classification Techniques", *IEEJ Trans EIS*, Vol. 124, No. 3, 2004.

Development of a Meta Product Search Engine
with Web Services

Wooju Kim, Daewoo Choi, Jongmyong Kim, and Bonggyun Jin

Department of Information and Industrial Engineering, Yonsei University,
134 Shinchon-dong, Seoul, South Korea
wkim@yonsei.ac.kr, qorwkr@nate.com, zzang94@daum.net
Web Services Center, K4M Inc, 192-19 Nonhyeon-dong, Seoul, South Korea
bgjin@k4m.com

Abstract. The research goal of this paper is to develop an advanced product
search agent framework where personalized agents can meet consumer's information needs more effectively and accurately based on the Web Services, Semantic Web technologies and AI techniques. These days, one of the major bot-
tlenecks in E-commerce is that it is not easy for consumers to find the relevant
information about the products they want. Such a situation is caused mainly by
inaccurate representation of consumer's search intent, and absence of appropriate product information filtering and retrieval mechanism. To resolve these
problems, we developed an ontology-based personalized product search query
representation methodology, an information extracting methodology specialized
for semantic web-based product information, and a multi-attribute-based product scoring methodology. Furthermore, we implemented the proposed methodologies as a prototype system and validated its performance by connecting our
system to the well-known Amazon.com and Buy.com.

1 Introduction

Generally, web information search is defined as a process of searching for web resources holding desirous information. For information search, a user utilizes information portal search engines or specific site-dependent engines, or searches for information by clicking hyperlinks by oneself. These search results are heterogeneous web
resources, which need to be compared to get more precise results.

As e-commerce search systems, various search engines and evaluation systems
with methods of limited product information search or product category base are
currently available [1,2]. But the Boston Consulting Group says that 48% of all users
have experienced not being able to satisfactorily search a desired product and 28% of
all product purchase tryouts could not reach purchase because of research failure [3].

The main causes of dissatisfactory search are as follows. (1) Most product information search engines cannot reflect a user's search intent exactly because of their keyword-based search method. (2) Product information evaluation cannot reflect a user's
real preference completely. (3) Most product information search engines and evaluation systems are developed as lower applications of shopping sites, and each shopping
site has its own search service, criteria for evaluating search results, and product classification category [4].

G.G. Lee et al. (Eds.): AIRS 2005, LNCS 3689, pp. 571–576, 2005.
© Springer-Verlag Berlin Heidelberg 2005

Brand new technologies of Web Services and Semantic Web will furnish existing Internet-based applications with new opportunities. Especially, product information search and comparison systems in e-commerce will become killer applications.

Web Services technologies will provide smart alternatives on developing meta-search engines in product information search and comparison fields. Amazon.com offers Web Services technologies, and an increasing number of shopping sites will follow. These sites will facilitate the development of meta-search engines.

Although structured product information is extracted easily by Web Services, there are still critical problems that remain [5]. Each shopping mall or site uses its own classification and terminology to represent its product information. Ontology mapping technology will be utilized to resolve this problem [6], and researches on adopting this product information search technology have been progressing [7,8]

To search and compare product information, we developed *ProMetas* with three methodologies based on the Web Services, Semantic Web, and Ontology mapping technologies: (1) the configuration of a user's search purpose, (2) Product Category mapping, and (3) multi-attribute-based product information scoring.

2 Overview of the *ProMetas* System

Along with the development of Web Services and Semantic Web, there will be an increasing number of shopping malls providing not only information about their products through the web services but also taxonomy with RDF, OWL, etc. such as the Open Directory Project [9]. Each Web Services' WSDL is described in each shopping mall, and Meta Search Engine can search and use appropriate Web Services. So if a shopping mall's product classification taxonomy, which is described with Semantic Web languages, can be mapped to the product classification taxonomy of *ProMetas*, it can get all structured product information within the matched category of each shopping mall.

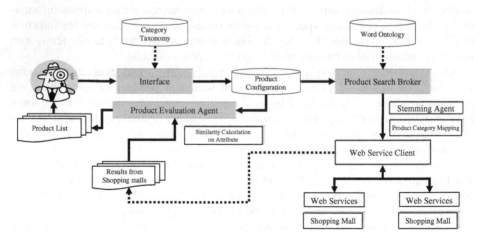

Fig. 1. Architecture of *ProMetas*

Under this environment, *ProMetas* can search and compare product information by not only selecting product classifications but also inputting product attributes. We will, therefore, suggest a meta-search and comparison framework *ProMetas* consisting of three main modules (See Fig. 1).

In *ProMetas*, a user inputs his or her search intent in a structured format to the *Interface*. Then, the *Product Search Broker* transforms the user's configured product category into the product category of each shopping mall and requests the product information to shopping malls through Web Services. The *Product Evaluation Agent* evaluates and compares the results, and shows a user the list of selected products with ranking, attributes, and their values.

3 Personalized Product Information Search Procedure

In this section, we explain the three product information search methodologies for *ProMetas*: Configuration of a User's Search Intent and Preference, Product Classification Mapping, and Product Information Evaluation.

3.1 The Configuration of a User's Search Purpose

To grasp user's intent accurately and reflect relative importance of each attribute, we suggest a personalized product search intent and preference representation methodology, which explains user's search intent by inputting three kinds of information (search context, feature/attribute information, and relative importance).

First, a user selects the desired product (Search Context) from the categories of ODP, input attribute name of selected category, attribute value, measurement unit and range operator (Feature Information), and indicate one's own weight of attributes.

Feature information consists of four terms: attribute name, value, measurement unit, and operator. The attribute name and value fields are mandatory and the others are optional. We formally denote feature information as a set notation {attribute, value, measurement unit, range operator} and call this ADS (Attribute Description Set). Furthermore, each ADS should have a different weight of importance in user's purchase decision making. To reflect the different weight of each attribute, we also allow a user to express preference by assigning an appropriate relative weight to each ADS.

3.2 Product Category Mapping

After configuring a user's search purpose, a product information request is made to the Web Services of shopping malls. However, there are some remaining problems. Each shopping mall has its unique product classification. So, to find the product category in a taxonomy most relevant to a given product category from a different taxonomy, we implement three consecutive steps. (1) Since each term that appears in the category path usually has various semantics, we narrow the consideration range of semantics of each term by using the product category hierarchy information. Also, since different terms can have the same semantics, we expand a given term to a set of synonyms. Both tasks basically use WordNet. (2) The second step collects prospective categories from the taxonomy of a product information provider by a proposed filtering procedure based on the product category information preprocessed in the previous step. (3) The last step evaluates the relevancy of each prospective category using a similarity measure and chooses the product category most relevant to the category provided by a user. Then we can have a set of alternative products that reside in the chosen category of a specific Internet shopping mall.

3.3 Multi-attribute-Based Product Information Scoring Methodology

Multi-Attribute-Based Product Information Scoring Methodology evaluates all product information of the selected Category by Product Category Mapping Methodology through Web Services, and consists of two steps: (1) to select the product information suitable for each attribute and (2) evaluate the product information with the method.

First, a methodology similar to existing text mining is utilized to extract product information. If there are ADS attribute names used in XML tag, the tag values are extracted. Otherwise, if there are no matched names, values are extracted by data type, unit, or ADS attribute value.

In the next step, the similarity calculation module integrates every distance of the attributes to calculate the similarity of each product. We used a general similarity calculation method to evaluate the products. The customer's priorities for each attribute are changed to attribute weights. We calculated the weighted sum of distances with the distances and weights of every attribute. Finally, we ranked products by their similarities to the customer's configuration.

4 Implementation and Experimental Result

We developed the *ProMetas* prototype of intelligent shopping malls using Web Services and category ontology with the information from Buy.com. We also used the Web Services of Amazon.com, and constructed a category ontology with the information from Amazon.com. Therefore, users can search for and compare products at Amazon.com and Buy.com with *ProMetas*.

We implemented *ProMetas* depicted in Fig. 1 into a working prototype using Java. Fig. 2 shows an illustrative screen of the main window of the prototype system.

For comparison and evaluation of *ProMetas*, we built product category taxonomies of Amazon.com and Buy.com. *Table1* shows a comparison of search results from *ProMetas* with keyword-based search results from the shopping malls.

ProMetas needs to input just one search condition and it gets 100% result. With existing product search engines, sometimes even 4 user inputs cannot produce satisfactory results. Without a direct visit to the existing shopping mall sites, *ProMetas* can assist users with purchase decision-making. Moreover, it is very convenient to input search condition to *ProMetas*, and it cuts down the time required for various keyword-based search trials to acquire accurate results. On the other hand, there was no attempt to prove that *ProMetas* system was more accurate and efficient than the traditional keyword-based meta-search engines because the experiment was limited. The experiment only presented an example of a better result. We are planning to conduct a more precise experiment to prove the advantages of the *ProMetas* system.

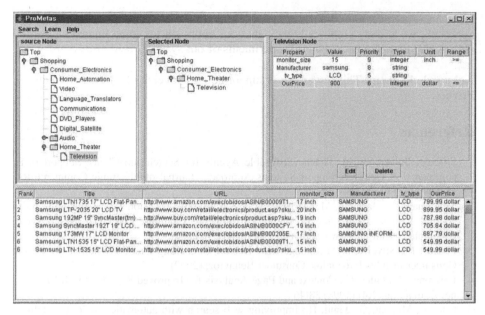

Fig. 2. An illustrative screen shot of *ProMetas*

Table 1. *ProMetas vs.* Amazon.com & Buy.com

Result from *ProMetas*		Result from Amazon.com		Result from Buy.com	
Precision (%)	Recall (%)	Precision (%)	Recall (%)	Precision (%)	Recall (%)
100	100	27.1	43.8	30.8	66.7

5 Conclusions

We proposed a semantic web-based personalized product meta-search agent approach to achieve two important and complementary goals: (1) allow users more expressive power in utilizing their Web searches for products, and (2) improve the relevancy of search results based on the user's real purchase intent. In contrast to the previous research, we focused not only on the search problem itself, but also on the decision-making problem that motivates users to search the Web.

Our contributions are briefly summarized as follows.

First, we proposed a product search intent representation scheme through which users could express their real search intent by specifying domain-specific product search context, expressing feature information of products using *ADS* concept, and assigning appropriate weights to each *ADS* concept. Second, to enhance the *precision* of the retrieved information, we presented a hybrid rating mechanism which considers both the user's search intent represented by the context information, that is, category path, and the user's search preference represented by a multi-*ADS* list and the corresponding weights. Third, we designed and implemented a meta-search agent system called ***ProMetas*** that cooperates with WordNet for concept retrieval, and with most well-known internet shopping malls such as Amazon.com and Buy.com for electronic goods. This open and extensible architecture will allow new Internet shopping malls to be incorporated into *ProMetas* at any time. For the empirical validation of our approach, we already empirically validated our approach for some limited cases, and we are also doing some real world experiments of our system.

Acknowledgement. This research was supported by University IT Research Center Project.

References

1. Sproule, S., Archer, N.: A Knowledgeable Agents for Search and Choice Support in E-commerce: A Decision Support Systems Approach. Journal of Electronic Commerce Research. 1(4) (2000) 152-165
2. Silverman, B., Bachann, M., Al-Akharas, K.: A Markov Decision Processing Solution to Natural Language Querying of Online e-Commerce Catalogs: The EQUIsearch Agent. Available at < http://www.seas.upenn.edu/~barryg/mdp.pdf>
3. Pecaut, D., Silverstein, M., Stanger, K.: Boston Consulting Group.: Winning the Online Consumer Insights Into Online Consumer Behavior. (2000)
4. Lawrence, S., Giles, C.: Context and Page Analysis for Improved Web Search. IEEE Internet Computing, 2(4) (1998) 38-46
5. Gal, A., Modica, G., Jamil, H.: Improving web search with automatic ontology matching. Available at <http://citeseer.ist.psu.edu/gal03improving.html>
6. Kalfoglou, Y., Schorelmmer M.: Ontology mapping: the state of the art. The Knowledge engineering review, 18(1) (2003) 1-32
7. The ARTEMIS project web site.: <http://islab.dico.unimi.it/artemis/d2i/>
8. Mena, E., Illarramendi, A., Kashyap, V., Sheth, A.: OBSERVER: An approach for query processing in global information systems based on interoperation across pre-existing ontologies. Conference on Cooperative Information Systems, (1996)
9. Open Directory Project.: <http://www.dmoz.com>

An Automatic Code Classification System by Using Memory-Based Learning and Information Retrieval Technique

Heui Seok Lim[1], Won Kyu Hoon Lee[2], Hyeon Chul Kim[2]
Soon Young Jeong[2], and Heon Chang Yu[2]

[1] Dept. of Software, Hanshin University, Korea
limhs@hs.ac.kr
http://nlp.hs.ac.kr
[2] Dept. of Computer Science Educatoin, Korea University, Korea
lee{hkim, jsy, yuhc}@comedu.korea.ac.kr
http://comedu.korea.ac.kr

Abstract. This paper proposes an automatic code classification for Korean census data by using information retrieval technique and memoory-based learning technique. The purpose of the proposed system is to convert natural language responses on survey questionnaires into corresponding numeric codes according to standard code book from the Census Bureau. The system was trained by memory based learning and experimented with 46,762 industry records and occupation 36,286 records. It was evaluated by using 10-fold cross-validation method. As experimental results, the proposed system showed 99.10% and 92.88% production rates for level 2 and level 5 codes respectively.

1 Introduction

There have been several researches on automated coding systems since early 1980s in U.S., France, Canada, Japan[1], [3], [5], [10]. AIOCS(Automated Industry and Occupation Coding System) was developed and used for the 1990 U.S. Census [1], [5]. Since then, the AIOCS has been improved with new approaches: Eli Hellerman algorithm, a self-organizing neural network, the holograph model, nearest neighbor and fuzzy search techniques, etc. [1], [5]. Memory Based Reasoning system was one of the successful system among the efforts to improve the AIOCS [4]. The ACTR(Automated Coding by Text Retrieval) system is the generalized automated coding system developed by Statistics Canada. It is based on the Eli Hellerman Algorithm[10], similar to AIOCS and is also designed for a wide range of coding application. ACTR is however unsuitable for Census Bureau industry and occupation coding since it is designed to assign a code to a single text string and weighting scheme cannot be altered. At this time, many of the systems are at preliminary stages and the Census Bureau is conducting research on a wide range of different automated coding and computer-assisted coding systems.

G.G. Lee et al. (Eds.): AIRS 2005, LNCS 3689, pp. 577–582, 2005.
© Springer-Verlag Berlin Heidelberg 2005

While there have been many researches on automated coding system as described above, researches on automated coding system for Korean have been rarely studied. Since Korean is agglutinative language and very different from foreign languages like English, research on developing an automated coding system considering Korean characteristics is very important.

In this paper, we propose an Automated Korean Industry and Occupation Coding System(AKIOCS) using information retrieval and memory-based learning(kNN) techniques. The proposed system consists of three main modules: Indexing module, candidate codes generator module, and code generation module. The indexing module extracts index terms by using morphological analyzer and noun extractor[8], calculates weight of each term using conventional TF/IDF weighting scheme and makes an index database of which structure is inverted file. The Candidate codes generator retrieves a set of candidate codes by selecting several similar codes with input record. The code generator module selects more than one final codes from the candidate set by using a code generation function defined in this paper. The details of each module are explained in the following sections.

2   Training and Weighting

The standard code book provided by the KNSO describes each classification code with four fields: code name, short description of the code, several examples and exceptional cases. Each code is treated as a document in conventional information retrieval system. Unfortunately, the description of code book is not enough to represent each code completely. The current code description for each code provides very limited information of only 40 to 50 word size. Another problem with the standard code book is that many individual responses usually contain ambiguous, incorrect and ill-formed data. Variability of the terms and expressions between many respondents is also very serious: a equivalent occupation can be described in so many different ways with so many different terms while the standard code description contains very small number of fixed terms. To alleviate the problem of limited information available in the standard code book, it is desirable to use Korean thesaurus which is not available for the present. Instead, we propose to augment code description by adding nouns and phrases in the records of which classification code were manually assigned in the past census.

The indexing module extracts index terms by using morphological analyzer and noun extractor[8] and calculating weight for each indexing term. Then, it makes an inverted file including code ID, starting position of the posting file, and the number of the posting files. Code ID is a classification code in a code book. The posting file includes the code ID in which a term is occurred, weight for the term. The starting position of the posting file is a starting address in the posting file for a term.

Weight for a term indicates how the term is discriminative and it is calculated by the following modified TF/IDF weighting scheme[2], [9].

$$w_{ij} = \frac{f'_{ij}}{max_l f_{lj}} \times log \frac{N}{n_i} \tag{1}$$

where w_{ij} is the weight of the ith term in the jth code, N is the total number of codes in a code book, and n_i is the number of code descriptions in which the term appeared. Modified frequency, f'_{ij} is equal to $5 \times f_{ij}$ if term i occurred in past census data[1], otherwise, equal to the conventional term frequency, f_{ij}. Through indexing and weighting terms, each code is represented as vector in the n-dimensional term space. The dimension of the code vector is the total number of the valid terms. Value of each component of the vector is the weight of the corresponding term. Later in code generation step, input record is also represented as a vector and distance between the vectors is calculated as a measure of similarity.

3   Code Generation

The individual response is converted into query which is set of nouns of the company name, business type and job description. The candidate code generator retrieves a set of relevant codes with input query by using *vector space model*. The vector space model uses vector representation for each code description and user query, and retrieves codes by calculating cosine similarity between the code vectors and query vector. Cosine similarity between a jth code vector, $\vec{C_j} = (w_{1j}, w_{2j}, \ldots, w_{tj})$ and query vector, $\vec{Q} = (w_{1q}, w_{2q}, \ldots, w_{tq})$ is defined in equation 2.

$$sim(C_j, Q) = \frac{\vec{D_j} \cdot \vec{Q}}{|\vec{C_j}| \times |\vec{Q}|} = \frac{\sqrt{\sum_{i=1}^{t} w_{ij} \times w_{iq}}}{\sqrt{\sum_{i=1}^{t} w_{ij}^2} \times \sqrt{\sum_{i=1}^{t} w_{iq}^2}} \tag{2}$$

In the equation (2), $\sqrt{\sum_{i=1}^{t} w_{ij}^2}$ is calculated in indexing time for each code and $\sqrt{\sum_{i=1}^{t} w_{iq}^2}$ is not calculated because it is same for all the codes.

The code generator module select one or more classification codes by corresponding classification modes: fully automated mode and semi-automated mode. The proposed system assigns a classification code in fully automated mode. In semi-automated mode, it assigns p classification codes and human expert selects a final code among them. The human export can assign a correct code with less difficulty by only searching p classification codes than fully manual coding. We define two target functions, DVF(discrete-valued function) and SF(similarity-based function) as in equation 3 and 4.

$$\bar{f}(candidateset, l)_p = argmax_{c \in C_l} \sum_{i=1}^{k} \zeta(c, candidate_i) \tag{3}$$

---

[1] The constant 5 is acquired heuristically through many experiments

$$where\ \zeta(a,b) = 1\ \ if\ a_l = b_l,\ \ 0\ otherwise$$

$$\bar{f}(candidate\,set, l)_p = argmax_{c \in C_l} \sum_{i=1}^{k} \zeta(c, candidate_i) \tag{4}$$

$$where\ \zeta(a,b) = sim(\overrightarrow{(q}, \overrightarrow{candidate_i})\ if\ a_l = b_l,\ \ 0\ otherwise$$

In euations 3 and 4, *candidate set* is the result of the candidate code generator and l indicates classification level, 1-5. a_l or b_l represents a substring consisting of l digits from the first digit of string a or b. For example, 12345_3 means string 123. p indicates the number of codes made by code generator. If p is 1, the system operates as a fully automated system while it makes m final codes as a semi-automatic system when p is m. DVF of equation 3 assigns the most common c_l code in the candidate set. Although the DVF is simple and easy to implement, it rarely uses similarity information between code vector and query vector and it is not robust to noisy data. The SF is an alternative way to consider the similarity information, it selects classification codes by sum of similarities between query vector and code vectors which have the sam c_l.

4   Experimental Results

We used 46,762 records of which industry code were manually assigned and 36,286 records for occupation records to evaluate our proposed system. Performance of the system is evaluated by 10-fold cross-validation.

We defined a evaluation measure, *production rate* as in equation 5. We assume a code is correctly assigned in p mode if the system makes p best candidate codes which include correct code for the input case.

$$PR_p = \frac{\sharp\ of\ correctly\ assigned\ cases}{\sharp\ of\ input\ cases} \times 100 \tag{5}$$

Table 1 shows results with some different p value. The results of *after augmenting* represent the efficacy of using past census data as to alleviate term inconsistency problem between code book and respondents.

As we can see in table 1, using past census data is very effective to improve production rate. In fully automatic mode, production rate for classifying level 2 code was 87.08% and 66.08% for level 5 code. Though the performance of fully automatic mode is not very high, the system showed very promising performance in semi-automatic mode($p \geq 2$). It showed 99.10% and 92.88% production rate for level 2 and level 5 code classification in semi-automated mode.

Table 2 shows results with some different p value. The production rate of job code is rather lower than that of industry code for most cases. This is because the average number of words included in input records for job code is more smaller than that for industry code. This means the input for industry code has many distinguishable index terms and information between different codes in

Table 1. Production rate of Industry Code in p mode(%)

	p	level2	level3	level4	level5
before augmenting	1	70.03	66.16	60.23	57.08
	2	81.04	80.91	75.02	67.23
	3	83.52	81.10	77.02	72.98
	10	84.55	83.02	80.70	78.38
after augmenting	1	87.08	82.46	73.12	66.08
	2	95.16	90.91	85.14	77.01
	3	97.22	94.16	90.03	82.65
	10	99.10	98.22	95.80	92.88

Table 2. Production rate of Job Code in p mode(%)

	p	level2	level3	level4	level5
before augmenting	1	66.03	60.25	55.83	47.30
	2	71.04	65.72	58.45	57.23
	3	73.52	70.84	62.71	61.72
	10	74.55	73.99	78.80	73.27
after augmenting	1	75.08	71.36	68.12	64.08
	2	84.67	78.56	85.14	77.01
	3	89.14	83.65	90.03	82.65
	10	96.20	94.86	93.29	92.88

industry code classification. It is very promising that the production rate after augmenting code set are also much improved. This means that our proposed method to alleviate inconsistency between sets of index terms from code book and respondents are very effective.

Most failure of classification of the system resulted from spacing errors of input records and 1-syllable sized noun. There were much spacing errors in input records made in entering descriptions of respondents into computer. Most of errors resulted from spacing errors would be addressed, if there were Korean word-spacing system which could deal with spacing errors in short phases or short sentences. Most of current Korean word-spacing system works well on normal sized sentences which have enough context information. The another problem of 1-syllable sized noun resulted from noun extraction system of indexing module. Most of 1-syllable sized Korean syllables are nouns. So, usual Korean noun extractor extracts nouns of which size are more than 2 syllables. It is one of future works to address the problem.

5   Conclusions

This paper describes development of the automated industry and occupation coding system for Korean using information retrieval and automatic document classification technique. We used 46,762 manually assigned records of industry code and 36,286 records for occupation records to evaluate our system. The 10-fold cross-validation is used to evaluated the system. The experimental results shows that using the past census data is very successful in increasing production rate and target function, SF is more effective than DVF to increase performance. Although production rate of the proposed system as a semi-automatic system is pretty good, the performance as a fully automated coding system is not satisfactory yet. This unsatisfactory result resulted from variability of the terms and expressions used to describe same code and spacing errors in input data. The system has much room to be improved as a fully automated system such as in dealing with spacing errors in input records and 1-syllable sized noun problem. Nevertheless, we expect that the system is very successful and enough to be used as a semi-automate coding system which can minimize manual coding task or as a verification tool for manual coding results.

References

1. Apeel, M. V. and Hellerman, E.: Census Bureau Experiments with Automated Industry and Occupation Coding. Proceedings of the American Statistical Association, 32-40, 1983.
2. Baeza-Yates and Ribeiro-Neto.: Modern Information Retrieval. Addison-Wesley, 1999.
3. Chen, B., Creecy, R. H., and Appel, M.: On Error Control of Automated Industry and Occupation Coding. Journal of Official Statistics, Vol. 9, No. 4, 729-745, 1993.
4. Creecy, R. H., Masand, B. M., Smith, S.J., and Walts, D. L.: Trading MIPS and Memory for Knowledge Engineering. Communications of the ACM, Vol. 35, No.8, 48-64, 1992.
5. Gilman, D. W. and Appel, M. V.: Automated Coding Research At the Census Bureau. U.S. Census Bureau, http://www.census.gov/srd/papers/pdf/rr94-4.pdf
6. Korean Standard Industrial Classification. National Statistical Office, January 2000
7. Korean Standard Classification of Occupations. National Statistical Office, January 2000
8. Lee, D.G.: A High Speed Index Term Extracting System Considering the Morphological Configuration of Noun. M.S. Thesis, Dept. of Computer Science and Engineering, Korea Univ., Korea, 2000.
9. Salton, G. and McGill, M.J.: Introduction to Modern Information Retrieval. McGraw-Hill, New York, 1983.
10. Rowe, E. and Wong, C.: An Introduction to the ACRT Coding System. Bureau of the Census Statistical Research Report Series No. RR94/02 (1994)

Finding New News: Novelty Detection in Broadcast News

Georgina Gaughan[1] and Alan F. Smeaton[2]

[1] Centre for Digital Video Processing, Dublin City University,
Glasnevin, Dublin 9, Ireland
[2] Adaptive Information Cluster, Center for Digital Video Processing,
Dublin City University, Glasnevin, Dublin 9, Ireland
{Georgina.Gaughan, Alan.Smeaton}@computing.dcu.ie

Abstract. The automatic detection of novelty, or newness, as part of an information retrieval system would greatly improve a searcher's experience by presenting "documents" in order of how much extra information they add to what is already known instead of how similar they are to a user's query. In this paper we present a novelty detection system evaluated on the AQUAINT text collection as part of our TREC 2004 Novelty Track experiments. Subsequent to participation in TREC, the algorithm has been evaluated on another collection with its parameters optimized and we present those results here. We also discuss how we are extending the text-only approach to novelty detection to also include input from video analysis.

1 Introduction

In 1999 Hal Varian, an economist, suggested that from an economists viewpoint *"the value of information is that it is only new information that matters"* [7]. The context of his statement was a challenge to the established tradition in information retrieval whereby documents are ranked in response to a query by their similarity to that query. This approach to document ranking is firmly established partly because it can be implemented in a computationally efficient manner which was important in the early days of information retrieval. Nowadays it remains prevalent because it allows search engines like Google to implement sub-second response time when searching billions of web pages for millions of users daily.

Yet despite its computational efficiency and scalability, ranking by query similarity is merely one tool which we use as part of our broader information seeking tasks in which we engage in many times daily. When we search we formulate a query in our mind, input some keywords, browse the resulting list of summaries, select a document and view it, maybe go back to our search ranking and view some more documents. In doing this we may clarify our information needs so that we may reformulate our query and issue another search. This generates another document ranking which includes the documents we've seen and viewed, and the ones we've seen before and don't want to see again ! The

G.G. Lee et al. (Eds.): AIRS 2005, LNCS 3689, pp. 583–588, 2005.

search function, is helping us because it is fast, but it is not intelligent and it still leaves us to do all the interpretation of search outputs. Over time we have grown tolerant to the fact that IR searching is actually a low-level function in the broader picture of information seeking.

Recent trends in IR reveal a more questioning approach to the established tradition and includes developments like document summarisation, clustering of the outputs of search results and emergence of attempts to capture users' contexts in search. All these try to ease the cognitive load on searchers by making the interpretation of search output more digestible. One other technique for doing this which we are interested in is the automatic detection of novelty in search output. Novelty in search output is defined as the incremental information added to a document based on what the user has already learned from looking at previous documents in the document ranking. It assumes that a user views a ranked list of documents and as he/she views documents their information need changes or evolves, and their state of knowledge increases as they learn new things from the documents they see. At any point in the ranking the technique of *relevance feedback* can be used to help reformulate the query to take account of shifting information needs, and this is commonplace in information retrieval. However, little work has been done on taking account of what the user has already seen from documents viewed, i.e. there is little work in the automatic detection of *novelty* in the documents being presented to users. It follows that if we use relevance feedback to account for shifting information needs we should use each document's novelty value as a factor in determining where it should appear in a document ranking.

Our experiments have been carried out using the AQUAINT collection of text news data from both the 2003 and 2004 TREC novelty tracks [5,6]. We have developed a text novelty detector which has been tested in the TREC novelty track where it was one of the best-performing systems, and which has been further extended and optimised as presented here. We also introduce our work that brings novelty detection into the increasingly important field of video IR by actually using elements from the video itself. The rest of this paper is organised as follows. In the next section we give a brief overview of related work and we follow that with a description of our technique for novelty detection. The collection of news broadcasts we used and our experimental results obtained are presented in section 4. In section 5 we outline our plans for applying novelty detection to news stories in live broadcast TV news and we finish with a concluding section.

2   Related Work

The detection of new information and the subsequent re-ranking of documents based on their degree of "newness" is a relatively new area. Carbonell and Goldstein [3] proposed the Maximal Marginal Relevance (MMR) algorithm which uses Cosine similarity to detect new information used for multi-document summarisation. It focused on finding a balance between relevancy and novelty rather than concentrating on thresholds that are needed by the Novelty Track task. Allan, Gupta and Khandelwal [1] have investigated novelty detection on a TDT corpus through the use of different language models. Their work involves developing a language model to estimate the probability that a sentence is novel to its predecessors using both individual and clusters sentence models.

Zhang, Callan and Minka [8] focused on topic novelty detection in adaptive filtering, examining models previously applied to other areas and adapting them to detect novel information, such as the cosine distance metric and a metric based on a mixture of language models. Finally, Allan, Wade and Bolivar [2] have investigated various models used for novelty detection using the TREC Novelty 2002 data. These range in complexity from simple word counts, set differences and Cosine distance measures to language models using KL divergence with different smoothing techniques.

For the last three years (2002-2004) the annual Text REtrieval Conference (TREC) [5,6] has run a novelty track task to explore and evaluate methods of locating novel information. The data used in the TREC novelty track in 2004 was the AQUAINT collection, containing sources of news articles from three different newswires, the Xinhua News Service, the New York Times News Service and the Associated Press, all taken from an overlapping time period (1996-2000) [6]. The reason for using three sources of material was to increase the likelihood of near-duplicate or redundant news articles occurring across the different newswires thereby increasing the realism of the experiment. One aspect of the novelty track in 2004 required participants to identify text documents that provided novel information to the user, given a topic and an ordered list of documents known to be relevant to that topic. The track used fifty standard TREC topics containing a title, description and narrative which were evenly divided into two types, *events* where topics were about a particular event that occurred within the time period, and *opinions* where topics were about different points of view on particular issues. For the purpose of the novelty track experiments, each document in the AQUAINT collection is split into sentences. Each sentence of approximately twelve words was given a unique identifier and referred to as a document, on which participants carried out their experiments. From this point forward will use sentences as the units for novelty detection.

3   Novelty Detection

It is assumed that the user has no prior knowledge of the topic at the beginning of the search and all knowledge about the topic is acquired during the search. This is not quite reflective of the real world but it is an assumption that allows us to address novelty issues directly. As defined by Zhang et al. [8], novelty and redundancy are treated as opposite ends of a continuous scale. For each relevant sentence in a returned list, we calculate its novel score based on the importance value of each unique word found in the current sentence when compared to an accumulated set of previously seen words (the History Set) for a particular topic. The following notation is defined with respect to each topic and used to explain the method used.

d_c : Current sentence under investigation
u_w: Unique word i.e. this word has not appear in *any* sentence seen so far
U_h: Set of Unique words encountered to this point (History Set)
tf_u: Term Frequency of the unique word
idf_u: Inverse Document Freq of the unique word
N: Number of Words in current sentence d_c
IV_{d_c}: ImportanceValue Score of the current sentence d_c (i.e Novelty Score)

The *Importance Value* measure (1) is a variation of TF-IDF. It exploits the properties of a word from both within the current sentence d_c and the overall collection of sentences for each topic. It models the assumption that a word with a high term frequency (tf) and a high inverse document frequency (idf) would most likely be valuable in providing new and valuable information about a topic. A sentence that is assigned a novel score, higher than a predefined threshold (set to different values for different collections), is considered a novel sentence. As novelty is determined on a single pass of the results list we use a fixed threshold which was set on the training data.

$$IV_{d_c} = \left(\sum_{i=1}^{n} tf_{u_{w_i}} \cdot \sum_{i=1}^{n} idf_{u_{w_i}} \right) \cdot \frac{1}{N} \tag{1}$$

Given a sentence d_c in the ordered list of known relevant sentences, we determine the number of unique words u_w that occur in that sentence, against an accumulated list of all unique words U_h encountered to this point. The *Importance Value* (1) takes as input each unique word u_w of the current sentence d_c. The output/novelty score is then assigned to the current sentence d_c. If the score for the current sentence d_c is above the predefined threshold, all the of unique words u_w from that sentence are added to the accumulating history set U_h. The current sentence d_c is then added to the list of novel sentences to be returned to the user.

4   Experimental Results

Experiments were carried out using TREC guidelines, on the AQUAINT collection from the 2003 and 2004 novelty tracks. The standard performance measure for the Novelty Track is the F-measure [6]. A key aspect of utilizing our *Importance Value* measure is the threshold above which we assume the sentence to be novel. We examined a range of threshold values using the 2004 data, as shown in Figure 1. Our previous official TREC novelty run had been the highest performing TREC run in 2004 [6] with an F-score of 0.622, where the threshold value was determined from the training data. Optimizing the threshold did not provide a significant improvement (F-score 0.623). Although we had not participated in TREC2003, we carried out the same procedure on that data with an optimised threshold for 2003 (Figure 2) yielding an F-score of 0.807. In 2003 there were forty five runs submitted to the Novelty task. This F-score would have placed us sixth highest among novelty runs. The F-score from our runs on the 2003 data at 0.807 is much larger than that obtained on the 2004 data with an F-score of 0.622. Although the data for 2003 and 2004 came from essentially the same resource this variation in thresholds is certainly not unexpected. It has been shown in other TREC tracks, such as TRECVid that even though data may come from the same source two years in succession, optimization for different years produces different best parameter values and different best performances. There are a number of possible reasons for this including the fact that topics for each of the years are different, with the topics for 2004 proving more difficult overall. The average F-measure on all topics for 2003 was .731 and for 2004 it was .597. The average precision for each topic for 2003 was .652 whereas for 2004 it was .46. Another possible reason for the differences could be that there are on average more relevant documents for topics in year 1 than in year 2 though we are not sure exactly how this impacts performance.

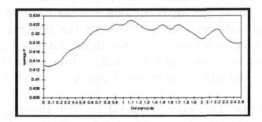

Fig. 1. *ImportanceValue* F-scores vs. threshold on 2004 data

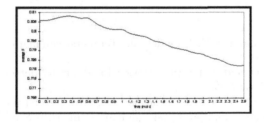

Fig. 2. *ImportanceValue* F-scores vs. threshold on 2003 data

5   Novelty in Video

We have concentrated our work on novelty detection using the dialogue or closed captions from broadcast TV news as the genre of text on which we experiment. A typical broadcast TV news program is usually a very rich source of information on a variety of diverse news topics. However it is also rife with repetition as video footage, story elements and developments in stories and even story introductions within the same broadcast are re-used. Here we seek to organise broadcast news retrieval results based on the degree of "newness" to the topic rather than the traditional ranking by degree of relevance, thereby reducing a user's time to locate new and interesting content. Within our group, we have much experience of developing Interactive Video Retrieval Systems [4]. Leveraging this experience and our preliminary experiments described above, we are in the process of developing a novel video retrieval system which uses more than just text from spoken dialogue. This is not a simple problem as novelty detection over the text and video domains differ greatly (video does not necessarily correspond to the spoken audio track). We are currently looking at methods that allow us to accurately and consistently analyse a video sequence to detect repetition and similar sequences, and use that as part of our novelty detection.

6   Conclusion

Hal Varian has highlighted the problem that traditional ranked list approaches to IR fail to favour novel documents. This paper presented our text based Novelty Detection which we ran on both 2003 and 2004 data for TREC novelty detection. The optimal performance values for the ImportanceValue measure differ substantially for both years, even though the data used is very similar. We are now working on incorporating video analysis from repetitive new broadcast footage from CNN and ABC from an overlapping time period.

Acknowledgements. This work is funded by Irish Research Council for Science Engineering and Technology and gratefully acknolowledged and supported by Science Foundation Ireland under grant 03/IN.3/I361.

References

1. J. Allan, R. Gupta, and V. Khandelwal. Temporal summaries of new topics. In *ACM SIGIR 2001*.
2. J. Allan, C. Wade, and A. Bolivar. Retrieval and novelty detection at the sentence level. In *ACM SIGIR 2003*.
3. J. Carbonell and J. Goldstein. The use of MMR, diversity-based reranking for reordering documents and producing summaries. In *ACM SIGIR 1998*.
4. G. Gaughan, A. Smeaton, C. Gurrin, H. Lee, and K. NcDonald. Design, implementation and testing of an interactive video retrieval system. In *ACM MIR 2003*.
5. I. Soboroff and D. Harman. Overview of TREC2003 novelty track. In *TREC 2003*.
6. I. Soboroff and D. Harman. Overview of TREC2004 novelty track. In *TREC 2004*.
7. H. R. Varian. Economics and search. *SIGIR Forum*, 33(1):1–5, 1999.
8. Y. Zhang, J. Callan, and T. Minka. Novelty and redundancy detection in adaptive filtering. In *ACM SIGIR 2002*.

Named Entity Tagging for Korean
Using DL-CoTrain Algorithm

Byung-Kwan Kwak[1] and Jeong-Won Cha[2]

[1] Samsung Advanced Institute of Technology,
San 14-1, Nongseo-ri, Giheung-eup, Yongin-si, Gyeonggi-do, Korea
bk21.kwak@samsung.com
[2] School of Computer information & Communication,
Changwon National University 9 Sarim-dong,
Changwon Gyoungnam, Korea 641-773
jcha@changwon.ac.kr

Abstract. Our approach to solve the problem of Korean named entity classification adopted a co-training method called DL-CoTrain. We use only a part-of-speech tagger and a simple noun phrase chunker instead of a full parser to extract the contextual features of a named entity. We will discuss the linguistic features in Korean which are valuable for named entity classification and experimentally show how large a labeled corpus and which unlabeled corpus is necessary for the better performance and portability of a named entity classifier. With only about a quarter of the labeled corpus, our method can compete with its supervised counterpart.

1   Introduction

In MUC-6 [8], MUC-7 [9] and IREX [10], various supervised learning methods for named entity task were applied and they gave a somewhat satisfactory performance. However, a large labeled corpus and named entity dictionaries or handwritten rules are generally needed for these supervised named entity recognition approaches. Moreover, practical and domain specific information extraction and question answering systems require the domain portability of a named entity recognition.

These reasons naturally make us try to utilize a relatively small labeled corpus, dictionaries or hand-written rules and a large unlabeled corpus which is easily obtainable. [3] satisfied these requests to some degree. However, they used a dependency-based full parser [4] to extract contextual features of a named entity, and current state-of-the-art parsing still causes some limitations of robustness and practicality in named entity recognition systems, especially for Korean. Further, they did not empirically show how large a labeled corpus and which unlabeled corpus and seed rules are actually needed for practical named entity recognition.

This paper is organized as follows. We will explain feature extraction and a learning algorithm for Korean named entity recognition in chapter 2 and 3 in detail. Our experimental results are given in chapter 4 and conclusions are in chapter 5.

G.G. Lee et al. (Eds.): AIRS 2005, LNCS 3689, pp. 589–594, 2005.

2 Robust Feature Extraction

We first detect named entities using a Korean POS tagger [2] and a LSP (Lexico-Syntactic Patterns) database. Then we extract two distinct views (lexical and contextual features) of named entities as input to both DL-CoTrain learner and a classifier, using a rule-based simple noun phrase chunker.

2.1 Detecting Named Entities

The detection of a named entity uses LSP's composed of POS tags and lemmas. As Korean does not have capitalization, Korean named entities are harder to detect than English, and can be made of diverse sources such as ''(MP/, Kim Dae-Jung), proper nouns together with common nouns ' '(MP/ MC/ MC/, Inchon International Airport).[1]

The LSP database is composed of three different types: (1) only lemmas('', Republic of Korea), (2) tags and lemmas('&MP '), and (3) only proper noun tags('&MP &MP). The named entity detecting module first normalizes morphemes within the maximum length [2] of a named entity with their POS tags and lemmas, and looks up the LSP database to find an LSP entry matching the normalized form. In this procedure, the matching order is following the above three entry types.

2.2 Lexical Features

Lexical features are internal attributes of named entities for classification. We extract the following eight lexical features from the named entities, e.g. (Inchon International Airport)' and '(Mr. Kim Dae-Jung)':

- Full lexical (full_lexical: ' ', '')
- Beginning word of a named entity for multiple words (beginning_word: '', N/A)
- Ending word of a named entity for multiple words (ending_word: '', N/A)
- Beginning 2 or 3 syllables of first word (beginning_2syllables: N/A, '')
- Ending 2 or 3 syllables of last word (ending_2syllables: N/A, '')
- Suffix attached to a named entity (suffix: N/A, '')

2.3 Contextual Features

Contextual features are external attributes of a named entity. They are extracted within the left and right 15 window size around the named entities in a sentence using a rule-based simple noun phrase chunker. We add contextual rules to the seed rules of DL-CoTrain, unlike [3] which only uses lexical rules as seed rules. The following are contextual features and their examples:

---

[1] '+' means boundary between morphemes inside a word.

[2] We set the maximum length of a named entity to 5.

- Left common noun directly attached to a named entity instance (left_noun) e.g. left_noun = '*MC/*' for 'T/ *MC/ MP/*(my *friend* <u>Yeong-Cheol</u>)'
- <u>Head</u>, a common noun, of noun phrase including a named entity (right_noun)[3] e.g. right_noun = '*MC/*' for '<u>MP/</u> *MC/*(*President* Kim Dae-Jung)' <u>*MC/*</u> (<u>Yeong-Cheol</u>'s *arm*')'
- <u>Particle</u> attached to a named entity (particle) e.g. particle = '*j/*' for '<u>MP/</u>+*j/*(*in* <u>Japan</u>) '
- <u>Right</u> nearest predicate (verb and adjective) of a named entity (predicate) e.g. predicate = '*D/*' for '<u>MP/</u>+j/ *D/*+eGE/.(*come back* from <u>Japan</u>.)'
- Combination of above <u>two</u> features (particle_predicate) e.g. particle_predicate = '*j/ D/*' for '<u>MP/</u>' and particle_predicate = '*j/ D/*' for '<u>MP/</u>' in '<u>MP/</u> MC/+j/ <u>MP/</u>+j/ <u>*D/*</u>+eGE/.(President <u>Kim Dae-Jung</u> *comes back from* <u>Japan</u>.)'

3   Learning and Classification of Korean Named Entity

We adapted DL-CoTrain of [3] as our learning algorithm. We stop iteration when the rules are not generated any longer.

3.1   Decision List Learning

The decision list has rules sorted according to their strength in descending order, and each rule has a pair of collocation x and its decision ω, or class and its strength. We regarded the strength of each rule as an estimate of conditional probability $P(\omega|x)$ like [3], such as

$$P(\omega|x) = \frac{C(x,\omega) + \alpha}{C(x) + k\alpha},$$

where $C(x,\omega)$ is the number of times that a collocation x and a class ω appears together in training data, $C(x) = \sum_{\omega \in \Omega} C(x,\omega)$ indicates the number of times that x shows up in training data, k is the number of classes, and α is a smoothing parameter.

3.2   Classification of Named Entity

The classification function of decision list, $f : X \rightarrow \Omega$, can be formalized as follows:

$$f(x) = \arg\max_{x \in X, \omega \in \Omega} P(\omega|x),$$

where X is a set of possible collocation and Ω is a set of classes.

---

[3] In Korean, head of noun phrase is mostly located in its right end.

3.3   DL-CoTrain Algorithm

DL-CoTrain is performed with decision list (learning rules) and co-training (feature-split setting and augmenting pseudo-labeled data) frameworks. The input to the learning algorithm comprises seed rules extracted from a small set of labeled training corpus and pairs of lexical and contextual features of a large set of unlabeled named entity instances (candidates) detected automatically. During learning, lexical and contextual rules are increased with respect to each category, and unlabeled instances are pseudo-labeled by intermediate-generated rules. The output of DL-CoTrain is a final decision list obtained from the instances last pseudo-labeled.

4   Experiments and Discussions

4.1   Experiment Environment

We used the same labeled training and test corpus of [11][4] and 3.5 million POS-tagged corpus of [6][5] as an unlabeled corpus. Table 1 and table 2 show the details of the corpora.

Table 1. Details of Labeled Corpus

	news domain			non-news domain		
	P	L	O	P	L	O
Training	337	133	994	677	591	344
Test	26	44	193	102	72	57

Table 2. Details of Unlabeled Corpus

Corpus	NEs
News domain 1 (A)	26,394
News domain 2 (B)	51,318
Non-news domain 1 (C)	50,555
Non-news domain 2 (D)	91,127
Mixed domain (E)	76,949

The non-news domain corpora (C, D) are heterogeneous ones including various genres, such as novels, essays, encyclopedia and travel sketches. The mixed domain corpus (E) consists of mixed news and non-news corpus to make it balanced.

---

[4] Courteously provided by NLP Lab. in Sogang University.
[5] Courteously provided by the National Academy of the Korean Language.

4.2   How Large a Labeled Corpus Should Be?

We first try to find out how large a labeled corpus should be for competitive performance. We extract seed rules from a quarter, a third, a half, and a full labeled training corpus in these experiments respectively, and use the corpus B for the news domain and the corpus E for the non-news domain as the unlabeled corpus, which showed the best performance in each domain. Figure ?? shows the overall results. In brief, using only a quarter of a labeled corpus without any named entity dictionary can give a performance comparable to the supervised one. Unlike [5] and [12], the performance is not always proportional to the size of the seed rule. Seed rules with ambiguous named entities (like country names) caused a lower performance in using a half or full of labeled corpus in non-news domain. By contrast, ambiguous named entities like country names in the specific news domain have a consistent category.

4.3   How Large and Which Unlabeled Corpus Is Necessary?

We now extract seed rules (news domain: 30, non-news domain: 27) using only a quarter of labeled instances in these experiments. The performance with each corpus type (news vs. non-news) and that of the supervised counterpart [11] are given in table 3.

Table 3. Performance with each corpus type (news vs. non-news) and that of the supervised counterpart [11]

	news			non-news		
	Precision	Recall	F-measure	Precision	Recall	F-measure
Supervised	*80.21*	*86.31*	*83.26*	*83.94*	*79.22*	*81.58*
Corpus A	81.12	76.81	78.91			
Corpus B	**83.01**	**81.75**	**82.38**			
Corpus C				83.33	80.09	81.68
Corpus D				81.22	80.52	80.87
Corpus E	79.54	78.33	78.93	**87.28**	**86.15**	**86.71**

While our method without a named entity dictionary produced a performance almost similar to the supervised one using dictionaries in the news domain, a better performance was delivered in the non-news domain. These results show that the effect of the co-training in general domain is larger than that in specific domain.

5   Conclusion

We presented a semi-supervised method for Korean named entity recognition. We do not use any named entity dictionary, but use a small set of labeled training corpus to extract seed rules, a large set of POS-tagged unlabeled corpus and a few LSP to detect the named entities. We use only a POS tagger and a simple noun phrase chunker, not a full parser, to extract more robust contextual features of a named entity. As a result, our method is more robust and practical than ones using a full parser or a named entity dictionary. This paper experimentally shows how large a labeled corpus and which unlabeled corpus is necessary for our method to compete with the supervised method. With only a quarter of labeled corpus, we could produce performance comparable to the supervised methods.

References

1. Avrim Blum and Tom Mitchell: Combining Labeled and Unlabeled Data with Co-training. Proceedings of the Workshop on Computational Learning Theory(COLT), Morgan Kaufmann Publishers. (1998)
2. Jeongwon Cha and Geunbae Lee and Jong-Hyeok Lee: Generalized Unknown Morpheme Guessing for Hybrid POS Tagging of Korean. Proceedings of the Sixth Workshop on Very Large Corpora. (1998) 85–93
3. Michael Collins and Yoram Singer: Unsupervised Models for Named Entity Classification. Proceedings of the Joint SIGDAT Conference on Empirical Methods in Natural Language Processing and Very Large Corpora. (1999)
4. Michael John Collins: A New Statistical Parser Based on Bigram Lexical Dependencies. In Arivind Joshi and Martha Palmer, editor, Proceedings of the Thirty-Fourth Annual Meeting of the Association for Computational Linguistics, Morgan Kaufmann Publishers, San Francisco. (1996) 184–191
5. Silviu Cucerzan and David Yarowsky: Language Independent Named Entity Recognition Combining Morphological and Contextual Evidence. Proceedings of Joint SIGDAT Conference on EMNLP and VLC. (1999)
6. Hung-Gyu Kim and Beom-Mo Kang: 21st Century Sejong Project - Compiling Korean Corpora. Proceedings of the 19th International Conference on Computer Processing of Oriental Languages. (2001)
7. Jee-Hyub Kim and Byung-Kwan Kwak and Seung-woo Lee and Geunbae Lee and Jong-Hyeok Lee: A Corpus-Based Learning Method of Compound Noun Indexing Rules for Korean. Information Retrieval, Vol 27 Num 4. (2001) 115–132
8. MUC-6: Proceedings of The Sixth Message Understanding Conference (MUC-6). Morgan Kaufmann Publisher. (1995)
9. MUC-7: Proceedings of The Seventh Message Understanding Conference (MUC-7). (1998)
10. Sekine Satoshi and Isahara Hitoshi: IREX: IR and IE Evaluation Project in Japanese. Proceedings of the 2nd International Conference on Language Resources & Evaluation. (2000)
11. Choong-Nyoung Seon and Youngjoong Ko and Jeong-Seok Kim and Jungyun Seo: Named Entity Recognition using Machine Learning Methods and Pattern-Selection Rules. Proceedings of the Sixth Natural Language Processing Pacific Rim Symposium. (2001) 229–236
12. Takehito Utsuro and Manabu Sassano: Minimally Supervised Japanese Named Entity Recognition: Resources and Evaluation. Proceedings of the 2nd International Conference on Language Resources & Evaluation. (2000)

Semantic Categorization of Contextual Features Based on Wordnet for G-to-P Conversion of Arabic Numerals Combined with Homographic Classifiers

Youngim Jung[1], Aesun Yoon[2], and Hyuk-Chul Kwon[1]

[1] Pusan National University, Department of Computer Science and Engineering,
Jangjeon-dong Geumjeong-gu, 609-735 Busan, S. Korean
{acorn, hckwon}@pusan.ac.kr
[2] Pusan National University, Department of French,
Jangjeon-dong Geumjeong-gu, 609-735 Busan, S. Korean
asyoon@pusan.ac.kr

Abstract. Arabic numerals show a high occurrence-frequency and deliver significant senses, especially in scientific or informative texts. The problem, how to convert Arabic numerals to phonemes with ambiguous classifiers in Korean, is not easily resolved. In this paper, the ambiguities of Arabic numerals combined with homographic classifiers are analyzed and the resolutions for their sense disambiguation based on KorLex (Korean Lexico-Semantic Network) are proposed. Words proceeding or following the Arabic Numerals are categorized into 54 semantic classes based on the lexical hierarchy in KorLex 1.0. The semantic classes are trained to classify the meaning and the reading of Arabic Numerals using a decision tree. The proposed model shows 87.3% accuracy which is 14.1% higher than the baseline.

1 Introduction

Currently, TTS technologies for naturalness have improved dramatically and have been applied to many unlimited domain systems. However, improvement in the accuracy of TTS products has been relatively static. According to the accuracy test results of 19 TTS products by Voice Information Associates, the weakest area of the TTS products is in number processing of which average accuracy is 55.6% among the ambiguity-generating areas [7]. In the modern Korean language, numerals have three different origins—Korean, Chinese and English—and they show a variety of variants. Their distribution largely depends on context. For example, a single numeral '3' can be read in five different ways depending on its following classifier or its preceding morpheme (Ex 1-a~e).

(Ex 1)   a. 3*geuru*[*se/ seog/ seo/ sam/ seuli*][2] "three stumps"
b. 3*nyeon* [*se/ seog/ seo/**sam**/ seuli*] "three years"
c. *big* 3 [*se/ seog/ seo/ sam/**seuli***] "Big 3"

---

[1]   *Geuru* is "a unit of trees" and *nyeon* means "year". *Doe* and *mal* are Korean units of volume for measuring liquid or grain; one *doe* is about 1.8ℓ, and one *mal* is about 18ℓ.
[2]   In this paper, letters in italics stand for G-to-P conversion of Korean. Phrases in quotation marks or brackets are the interpretation of each example phrases.

G.G. Lee et al. (Eds.): AIRS 2005, LNCS 3689, pp. 595–600, 2005.

d. 3*doe* [*se*/**seog**/ *seo*/ *sam*/ *seuli*] "5.4ℓ"

e. 3*mal* [*se*/ *seog*/**seo**/*sam*/*seuli*] "54ℓ"

f. 3*gu*   [**se**/ *seog*/ *seo*/**sam**/ *seuli*] "three bodies/three boroughs or the third ballℓ"

In (Ex 1), classifiers following Arabic numerals play an important role for determining the reading of Arabic numerals. However, a homograph classifier following an Arabic numeral, multiple readings are acceptable for an Arabic numeral as shown in (Ex 1-f). Thus, contextual features or patterns are required to resolve the ambiguity in reading of Arabic numerals, and to be learned in order to cover new data.

The other parts of this paper are as follows. In Section 2, related work on WSD is studied. In Section 3, one approach to WSD by learning the semantic categories of contextual features extracted from corpora is suggested. Categorization of the semantic classes based on the lexical relations in KorLex1.0 is illustrated. Experimentations are performed in this section. Conclusions and future work of this paper are followed.

2 Related Studies Word Sense Disambiguation

Because of the strong dependencies of contextual features, a decision tree algorithm has been adopted, which is an efficient classifier for handling complex conditional dependencies and non-dependencies [2, 5]. Efficiency deteriorates when the classifier handles very large parameter spaces, such as the highly lexicalized feature sets. Thus, work on grouping similar individual words as semantic categories was studied based on established semantic categories contained in Roget's thesaurus [8]. The method achieves high accuracy in disambiguating word sense when thesaurus categories and senses align well with topics. Twenty-four semantic categories in WordNet1.5[3] have been applied for WSD, in the respect of sense granularity, semantic categories in WordNet are finer than that of Roget thesaurus [1].

3 Word Sense Disambiguation of Homographic Classifiers

Ambiguities in reading Arabic numerals can be resolved using context as shown in (Ex 1-a~e). Homographic classifiers, however, cause ambiguities and need additional contextual features as to determine the reading of an Arabic numeral combined with the classifier. For the purpose of analyzing the ambiguities caused by homographic classifiers and resolving the ambiguities by learning contextual features, the training data were randomly sampled from news articles issued for two years (January 1st, 2000 to December 31st, 2001) from 10 major newspapers in Korea. The size of corpora is 15,196 *eo-jeol*'s. All instances of Arabic numerals combined with homographic classifiers are collected and then the correct RFA tags are labeled[5].

---

[3] WordNct groups noun senses in 24 lexicographer's files [4].

[4] *Eo-jeol* is a morpheme cluster of continuous alphanumeric characters and symbols with space on either side in Korean. In general, symbols are placed between the two paralleled items without spacing. In most cases an *eo-jeol* is composed of several morphemes of different parts of speech [9].

[5] The process of labeling RFA tags is semi-automated, using the rule-based transliteration system of Arabic Numerals Expressions (ANEs) developed by [9]. Hand-craft correction has been followed for accurate RFA tagging by authors.

3.1 Ambiguities Caused by Homographic Classifiers

Since many Chinese homographic classifiers are combined with Arabic numerals, precedent analysis on the senses of the classifiers is required for selecting the correct Reading Formulae of Arabic numerals (RFA). [Table 1] shows each sense of homographic classifiers and the RFA as an example.

Table 1. Senses of a Homographic classifier '*gu*'

Classifiers		Example	RFA[6]
Pron	Sense		
gu	1	unit of a dead body	*ideul-eun sache 3gu-e year uibog, cheolmo deung yupum-eul balgulhaessda.* "They exhumed six bodies and then the relics such as clothes and helmets."	[se] Kca_b
	2	borough	*gangnam-gu(0.08%), songpa-gu(0.05%), seocho-gu (0.04%) deung 'gangnam 3gu'neun pyeonggyun-eul mitdol-assda.* "'Gangnam 3gu' such as Gangnam-gu (0.08%), Songpa-gu (0.05%) and Seocho-gu (0.04%) were below average."	[sam] Cor_b(+D)
	3	pitch	*imyeonghoneun seonballo naseon choesangdeog-ui 3gujjae jigguleul tongtahaessda.* "Lee, Myoungho hit the sixth fastball thrown by a starting pitcher, Choi, Sangdeok."	[sam] Cor_b(+D)

Other homographic classifiers such as '*gi1* (unit of rockets, tombs), *gi2* (unit of a stage, a session)', '*dae1* (unit of auto- mobiles, machines or bicycles), *dae2* (the biggest item), *dae3* (the time of life or persons in the time of life)', '*dan1* (unit of bundled vegetables), *dan2* (level)', '*dong1* (unit of container for liquid), *dong2* (unit of village)', '*byeong1* (a bottle), *byeong2* (level of a soldier)', '*chuk1* (unit of ships), *chuk2* (Korean measurement of height)', '*bak1* (musical time), *bak2* (unit of stay)', '*bun1* (honorific form of persons), *bun2* (a minute)', '*su1* (a move in baduk game), *su2* (a piece of poems), *su3* (sou)', '*guan1* (Korean measurement of weight), *guan2* (unit of halls)', '*jib1* (a series), *jib2* (a house)' have been analyzed.

3.2 Homographic Sense Disambiguation Based on Corpus and KorLex

Since RFA is determined depending on the sense of homographic classifiers and the ambiguities of homographs are resolved by the semantic correlation with neighboring words in turn, words around the Arabic numerals and homographic classifiers can be used as distinctive features to predict the correct RFA. The steps of the extraction of contextual features will be outlined, using a homographic classifier '*gu*' in [Table 1], as an example.

---

[6] The sub-categorization of RFA suggested by [9] is adopted in this paper. The abbreviations representing the sub-categories of RFA are as follows; K=Korean, C=Chinese, E=English, ca=cardinal, or=ordinal, b=base form, v=variants, n=noun, D=DSM (Decimal Scale Marker). The abbreviations can be combined. For example, 'Kca_b' is consisted of 'K', 'ca', and 'b', which means 'Korean cardinal adjective numeric in base-form', altogether. 'Cor_b[+D]' means 'Chinese ordinal adjective numeric in base-form with DSM'.

Step 1: Morphological Analysis
In Korean, content words and function morphemes such as case markers, postpositions, or endings come in one *eo-jeol*. Content words are separated from function morphemes and be lemmatized through morphological analysis.

Step 2: Contextual Feature Extraction and Semantic Categorization
Among the lemmatized content words, nouns are extracted as shown in [Table 2].

Table 2. Left and right contextual features of homographic classifier *'gu'* (excerpted)

Classifiers	Sense	W[-3]	W [-2]	W [-1]	W [+1]	W [+2]	W [+3]
gu	1			sache	uibog	cheolmo	balgul
	2	Songpagu	Seochogu	Gangnam	pyeonggyun		
	3	seonbal	naseo-	choesangdeog	jiggu	tongtaha-	

Words proceeding (-3, -2, -1) or following (+1, +2, +3) the combination of Arabic numerals and homographic classifiers are clustered into semantic categories based on lexical hierarchy in KorLex 1.0 [3]. The process for semantic categorizing contextual features is described as follows:

Step 2-1: Mapping lemmatized words used as contextual features-extracted from the tagged corpus- to KorLex hierarchy. For example, words {*cheinji-eob* (change-up), *bol* (ball), *jiggu* (fastball), *samjin* (putout)} used as contextual features for disambiguating *'gu3* ("pitch")' are mapped to the hierarchy in KorLex.

Step 2-2: Listing all common hypernyms of synset nodes mapped from contextual features. Common hypernyms are {*haengwi* (act)} as shown in [Figure 1].

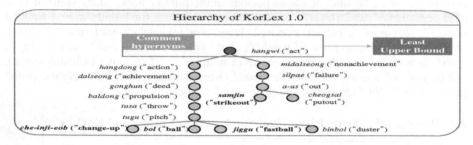

Fig. 1. Automatic selection of Least Upper Bound

Step 2-3: Finding the Least Upper Bound (LUB) of synset nodes mapped from contextual features. Here, { *haengwi*} is selected as LUB.

Step 2-4: Selecting the LUB as a semantic category for the contextual features. The selected {*haengwi*} becomes the generalized semantic category of {*cheinji-eob, bol, jiggu, samjin*}. Following the same procedure, {*sache* (dead_body)} has been reassigned for the semantic category of {*sache* (dead_body), *siche* (corpse)}, which are contextual features for disambiguating *'gu1*(unit of dead body)' and {*haengjeong_gu-yeog* (administrative_district)} for {*gangnam-gu* (Gangnam-gu), *songpa-gu* (Songpa-gu), *seocho-gu* (Seocho-gu), *seongeogu* (election_district)}, which are contextual features for '*gu2* (borough)', respectively. By application of the procedure to the training corpus, 54 semantic categories have been obtained.

Step 3: Extraction of Pattern and Arithmetic Features
The other learning features are combined patterns of Arabic numerals and text symbols, arithmetic features and the individual homographic classifiers as in [Table 3].

Table 3. Learning Features and values

Features	Subcategories	Value
Pattern features	No. of groups in an ANE	NA1: one group of numeral in an ANE NA2: more than 2groups
	No. of text symbols in an ANE	NT0: no text symbols in an ANE NT1: one text symbols NT2: more than two text symbols
	Types of text symbols	T1 : '-', T2 : '~', T3 : '.', T4 : ',', T5 : ':' T6 : '/'
Arithmetic features	Size of Arabic numeral	S1: $1900<x<2100$, $0<y<12$, $0<z<32$ (x, y, z are integers appeared in one ANE), S2: the rest
	Difference between two numerals	B1: $(y-x)10^n=1*10^n$ ($n\geq1$, x, y, n: integers), B2: the rest
	1st place of an ANE	FP0: '0', FP1: the rest (not '0')
	Places of Arabic numeral	P1: 1places, P2: 2places, P3: 3places, P4: more than 4places

Input ANEs are converted to patterns, for example, '3' is converted to 'N', and 'NA1, NT0' are obtained for its pattern features. Once the pattern features are obtained, the corresponding arithmetic features such as the size of Arabic numerals or the 1st place of Arabic numerals are extracted to distinguish same token having different meanings.

Step 4: Training Learning Features and Testing Performance
Since semantic categories of contextual features affect each other and arithmetic features largely depend on patterns, a decision tree has been adopted as the learning algorithm [6]. The performance of the model is tested using a 10-cross validation checking method. Baseline accuracy has been measured by adopting one rule-if the number of groups in the target ANEs is 'NA1', then RFA is 'Cca_b[+D]', which is the most frequent class (MFC). The result is shown in [Table 4].

Table 4. Comparison of WSD accuracies

	Baseline	Application of KorLex 1.0
Accuracy (%)	73.2	87.3

The proposed model shows 87.3% accuracy, which is 14.1% higher than that of the baseline determined by MFC. Though the result is good, two problems still remain to be resolved:

First, contextual features which are homographs or polysemies cause their own ambiguities. For example, a homograph {*gageog*} can be mapped to {*gageog* (shot)} and {*gageog* (monetary_value)}. In addition, there are many synsets having multiparents-or having lattice structure-, which make difficult for a word to be assigned to a single semantic category in KorLex. For resolving this problem, scoring algorithm to select the correct sense of *gageog* among other senses should be considered. Second, since KorLex 1.0 based on WordNet2.0 has not been refined completely, numerous Korean words or concepts which do not exist in WordNet are missing in KorLex1.0.

4   Conclusions and Future Work

In this paper, the ambiguities of Arabic Numerals combined with ambiguous classifiers are analyzed and the resolutions for their sense disambiguation based on KorLex 1.0 are proposed. Nouns proceeding or following the ANEs are categorized into 54 semantic classes based on the lexical hierarchy in KorLex1.0. The semantic categories of contextual features are trained to decide the meaning and the reading of ANEs using C4.5 algorithm. The experimentation results show that the proposed model is efficient and accurate. For the future work, WSD for ambiguous contextual features by adopting scoring algorithm should be continued. Since KorLex1.0 has not been refined completely yet, continuous studies on WSD for other applications with the refined KorLex are promising.

Acknowledgement

This work was supported by the National Research Laboratory Program M10400000279-05J0000-27910 of Korea Science and Engineering Foundation.

References

1. Agirre, Eneko et al. (1996), "Word Sense Disambiguation using Conceptual Density", *Proc. COLING'96*, pp.16~22.
2. Jung, Youngim et al. (2004), "Learning for Transliteration of Arabic-Numeral Expressions Using Decision Tree for Korean TTS", *Proc. ICSLP2004* Vol. III, pp. 1937~1940.
3. Lee, Eunryoung et al. (2004), "Construction of Multilingual Lexico-Semantic Network", *French Culture and Art*, Vol.12, pp.1~33.
4. Miller, George et al.(1998), *WordNet -An electronic lexical database*, Cambridge: MIT Press.
5. Olinsky, Craig et al. (2000) "Non-Standard Word and Homograph Resolution for Asian Language Text Analysis," presented at ICSLP2000, Beijing, China.
6. Quinlan, J. Ross. (1993), *C4.5: programs for machine learning*, San Francisco: Morgan Kaufmann Publishers.
7. Tetschner, Walt "Text-to-Speech - Naturalness and Accuracy", *ASR News,* July, 2003 http://www.asrnews.com/ttsap/ttspap11.htm (referred to on June 7, 2004).
8. Yarowsky, David (1997), "Homograph Disambiguation in Text-to-speech Synthesis", *Progress in Speech Synthesis*, pp.159~174, New York: Springer
9. Yoon, Aesun et al. (2003) "An Automatic Transcription System for Arabic Numerals in Korean", *Proc. 2003 NLP-KE*, pp.221~226.
10. Yu, Ming-Shing et al.(2003), "Disambiguating the senses of non-text symbols for Mandarin TTS systems with a three-layer classifier", *Speech communication*, Vol.39, No.3/4, pp.191-229
11. Tool: Weka 3 : http://www.cs.waikato.ac.nz/ml/weka/

Robust Matching Method for Scale and Rotation Invariant Local Descriptors and Its Application to Image Indexing

Kengo Terasawa, Takeshi Nagasaki, and Toshio Kawashima

School of Systems Information Science, Future University-Hakodate,
116-2 Kamedanakano-cho, Hakodate-shi, Hokkaido, 041-8655, Japan

Abstract. Interest point matching is widely used for image indexing. In this paper we introduce a new distance measure between two local descriptors instead of conventional Mahalanobis distance to improve matching accuracy. From experiments with synthetic images we show that the error distribution of local jet is gaussian but the distribution of the descriptors derived from local jet is not gaussian. Based on the observation, we design a new distance measure between two local descriptors and improve accuracy of point matching. We also reduce the number of candidate points and reduce the computational cost by taking into account the characteristic scale ratio. Experimental results confirm the validity of our method.

1 Introduction

Appearance-based image indexing can be roughly divided into two approaches: global method and local method. Local appearance describes the characteristics of small area around some specific points. This approach has advantage of robustness to partial occlusions and background changes. Furthermore, this technique is appropriate to multiple object search and pose recognition because it matches corresponding features in images and is consequently able to recover the structure of images.

Usually, this approach begins with the extraction of points where image information is concentrated: such points are called interest points. After the extraction of interest points, the characteristics of local area around each extracted interest point is described by a local descriptors vector. Finally, the interest points are matched according to the similarity of local descriptors. At every step of these processes, a lot of studies for improvement have been proposed and evaluated.

There are many way to extract interest points. Most commonly used methods are a corner detector based on Harris function [4] and a blob detector based on Laplacian. Both of them use the responses of Gaussian derivative filters for implementation and a problem is that Gaussian derivatives are dependent on image scale. Scale-space theory introduced by Lindeberg [6] normalize these

G.G. Lee et al. (Eds.): AIRS 2005, LNCS 3689, pp. 601–615, 2005.

derivatives and generalizes interest points. Based on his scale normalized differentiation, many type of scale invariant interest point detectors are derived in the past few years [7,8,9].

Local feature of these interest points are described by a feature descriptor. Local jet [5] is often used to describe the characteristics of local feature. It is a set of the responses of Gaussian derivative filters which describes the neighborhood of a point. Unfortunately, it again poses a problem that Gaussian derivatives are dependent on image orientation and scale. To avoid the rotation dependency, rotation invariant vectors based on local jet components are devised [11,13,15]. Another approach to obtain rotation invariance is to normalize local jets to dominant direction [1,9]. This normalization is implemented by applying steerable filter [3] to the gradient direction of that point. Scale invariance is realized by describing local descriptor of interest points at multiple-scales [2,13] or by using characteristic scale to determine a radius of neighbor region [1,9]. Alternative approaches also exist, such as: SIFT descriptors proposed by Lowe [7,8] and complex filters proposed by Schaffalitzky and Zisserman [12]. Mikolajczyk and Schmid [10] reported that SIFT shows the best performance among of them, and the steerable filter follows it.

In interest point matching implementation, Mahalanobis distance is commonly used as a similarity measure of two local descriptors. This distance measure has an advantage of simplicity in computation, however, it also has some disadvantages. One such is that it uses a single covariance matrix to all the points — this hypothesis is inadequate for some cases. Another problem is that they hypothesize error distribution as Gaussian normal without verification.

In this paper, we investigate the error distribution of local descriptors by observing synthetic images with controlled displacements such as small translations, small stretches, and random noises. According to the observation, we design a new distance measure for the rotation invariant local descriptors. The distance definition improves the precision of point matching.

In addition, we refine indexing process by taking into account the characteristic scale ratio information. Experimental result shows effectiveness of our methods.

2   Local Jet and Its Scale Invariant Formulation

In this paper we use local jets both in interest point detection and in description of its local neighborhoods. The following is brief introduction to local jets and its normalization to scale. Local jets are the responses of Gaussian derivative filters, and are written as

$$L_{i_1 \ldots i_n}(\boldsymbol{x}, \sigma) = G_{i_1 \ldots i_n}(\boldsymbol{x}, \sigma) * I(\boldsymbol{x}), \tag{1}$$

where $I(\boldsymbol{x})$ is image intensity, $G(\boldsymbol{x}, \sigma)$ is Gaussian distribution function, and subscripts represent partial differentiation. These $L_{i_1 \ldots i_n}$ are dependent on image resolution and Gaussian parameter σ. They are, therefore, inconvenient to use for image indexing with different scale.

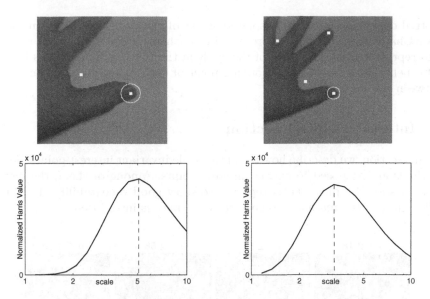

Fig. 1. Two images of different scale and the characteristic scale of corresponding point (the top of the thumb)

To be robust to scale change, normalized Gaussian derivatives and characteristic scale are often used [6,9]. The normalized Gaussian derivatives of m-th order is written as

$$D_{i_1 \dots i_m}(\boldsymbol{x}, \sigma) = \sigma^m L_{i_1 \dots i_m}(\boldsymbol{x}, \sigma). \tag{2}$$

To prove that $D_{i_1 \dots i_m}$ is normalized for scale, consider two images of different scale, I and I', which are connected with $I(\boldsymbol{x}) = I'(\boldsymbol{x}')$, where $\boldsymbol{x}' = t\boldsymbol{x}$. Applying Gaussian derivatives to this equation, we obtain

$$\sigma^m G_{i_1 \dots i_m}(\boldsymbol{x}, \sigma) * I(\boldsymbol{x}) = t^m \sigma^m G_{i_1 \dots i_m}(\boldsymbol{x}, t\sigma) * I'(\boldsymbol{x}'), \tag{3}$$

so that we have

$$D_{i_1 \dots i_m}(\boldsymbol{x}, \sigma) = D'_{i_1 \dots i_m}(\boldsymbol{x}', t\sigma). \tag{4}$$

This equation indicates that the values of D are independent of the scale of image, if σ is properly chosen. In practice, since the scale ratio between two images is unknown, it is not clear how to choose appropriate σ. It should satisfy $\sigma' = t\sigma$.

The use of characteristic scale solves this problem. Characteristic scale can be obtained by examining some kind of function of normalized Gaussian derivatives, e.g. squared gradient, Laplacian, Harris function, and so force. The function should be chosen depending on the purpose. The characteristic scale is defined as the scale σ where a function of normalized Gaussian derivatives takes a peak value as shown in Fig. 1. The characteristic scale is proportional to image scales, therefore we can make local jet invariant to scale by substituting characteristic scale for σ in (2). The bottom row of Fig. 1 represents the Harris function value plotted over σ at the points displayed center of circles in the images in the top row. Characteristic scale is represented as dashed line in the bottom row, and also represented as the radius of the circle in the top row. It indicates that the ratio between two σ at corresponding point of each image gives the scale ratio between two images.

3   Interest Point Detection

In this section, we describe how to extract scale invariant interest points. Several methods are proposed to extract interest points. Among of them, the method of Harris and Stephens [4] is reported to show good repeatability [14]. In the followings, Harris method extended to scale space is introduced.

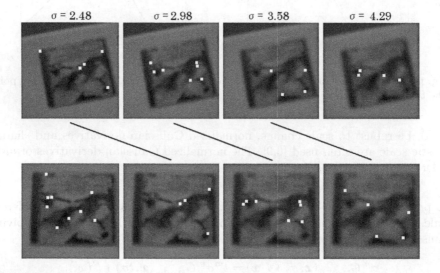

Fig. 2. Scale invariant interest points of two images with different scale and orientation. Interest points have 3D coordinates (x, y, σ).

The idea is to search for maxima in the 3D space of x, y and σ. Here again σ represents the Gaussian parameter. For implementation, all coordinates should be represented in discrete domain. x and y are the location of a pixel, and σ is the scale sampled at exponential intervals, $\sigma_n = k^n \sigma_0$. In this 3D grid space, we calculate the 2×2 matrix:

$$M = \exp\left(-\frac{x^2 + y^2}{2\widetilde{\sigma}^2}\right) \otimes \begin{bmatrix} D_x^2 & D_x D_y \\ D_x D_y & D_y^2 \end{bmatrix}, \tag{5}$$

where $\widetilde{\sigma}$ must be proportional to σ. In this study, we set $\widetilde{\sigma} = \sigma$.

Next, we calculate Harris function R:

$$R = \det(M) - k\,\mathrm{trace}(M)^2, \tag{6}$$

where k is a constant. In this study, we set $k = 0.06$, which is commonly used value. This R is invariant to rotation and scale. Scale invariant interest point is defined as coordinates (x, y, σ) where the function gives local extrema of R. In practice, certain threshold value t is set to avoid the clutters. Summarizing above, point (x_n, y_m, σ_l) is extracted as scale invariant interest point if it satisfies

$$R(x_n, y_m, \sigma_l) \geq R(x_{n+i}, y_{m+j}, \sigma_{l+k}), \quad \forall i, j, k \in \{-1, 0, 1\} \qquad (7)$$
$$R(x_n, y_m, \sigma_l) \geq t.$$

In this paper, we set threshold value $t = 4000$. As a result, the average number of extracted point per image is about 50 to 200.

In this way, we can extract interest points that is invariant to image rotation and scales. Figure 2 is an example. This figure shows interest points of two images with different scale and rotation. Interest points are represented as white dot in the figure. Each point has 3D coordinates, x, y, σ-coordinates. If they are compared in each same row respectively, they do not correspond at all. However, they do correspond if taken as point group in 3D space.

4   Description of Local Neighborhoods

In this section, we consider how to describe the characteristics of the region around each interest point. It is desirable that this descriptor is robust to illumination change, camera position, camera noise, etc.

One idea is to use local jets introduced in Sect. 2. If we set characteristic scale to σ in (2), it obtains invariance to scale. There are several candidates for function to determine the characteristic scale as described before. In this study, we already calculated Harris function to extract interest points, so we use this again. In this case, characteristic scale is the same as σ-coordinate of interest point. This local jets are invariant to scale but not to rotation. To obtain the invariance to rotation, combine the components as:

$$\nu[0...8] = \begin{bmatrix} D \\ D_i D_i \\ D_i D_{ij} D_j \\ D_{ii} \\ D_{ij} D_{ji} \\ \varepsilon_{ij}(D_{jkl} D_i D_k D_l - D_{jkk} D_i D_l D_l) \\ D_{iij} D_j D_k D_k - D_{ijk} D_i D_j D_k \\ -\varepsilon_{ij} D_{jkl} D_i D_k D_l \\ D_{ijk} D_i D_j D_k \end{bmatrix}, \qquad (8)$$

where $\varepsilon_{xy} = -\varepsilon_{yx} = 1$, $\varepsilon_{xx} = \varepsilon_{yy} = 0$. This vector ν is invariant to rotation [11,13].

Furthermore, to get robustness to illumination change, substitute $D_{i_1...i_m}$ to $D_{i_1...i_m}/D$. By this substitution (so we don't use $\nu[0]$), the vector becomes invariant to linear illumination change. We use this 8-dimensional vector ν as the interest point descriptor.

In this time, only components up to third order are used. Higher order derivatives may provide more accurate descriptor and may improve the precision of point matching, however, higher order term is likely to make descriptors more sensitive to noise, and have disadvantage that increase computational cost. For this reason, we use terms up to third order derivatives.

5   Interest Point Matching

5.1   Test for Normality of Error Distribution

Owing to the local descriptor derived in the last section, interest point matching based on their local features is now available. Matching candidates are determined by measuring similarity between descriptors, i.e. the point whose descriptor gives the smallest distance from the descriptor of query point in the feature space is considered as a matching candidate. To implement this process, the distance measure between two descriptors must be defined. In existing method, Maharanobis distance

$$d_M^2(\boldsymbol{\nu}_i, \boldsymbol{\nu}_j) = (\boldsymbol{\nu}_i - \boldsymbol{\nu}_j)^T \Lambda^{-1} (\boldsymbol{\nu}_i - \boldsymbol{\nu}_j) \qquad (9)$$

(where Λ^{-1} is inverse of covariance matrix) is used frequently [13,9]. This method has advantage that it can be calculated easily, but it also has disadvantage or incompleteness. One incompleteness is caused by the fact that it ideally requires covariance matrix for each and every cluster, where in this case cluster means the set of interest points that should be regarded to correspond. In the real situation, since there exist infinite variety of interest point, it is impossible to know all covariance matrices in advance. Ordinary implementation uses only one global covariance matrix as a substitute for such covariance matrices. Another incompleteness is that it is based on the assumption that the error of descriptors should follow normal distribution, but this assumption is verified neither theoretically nor experimentally.

To know the characteristics of error distribution, we executed an experiment as follows. We define the error as the difference between true value and observed value for each local descriptor of the interest point. Observed value is the summation of true value and observation noise.

We suppose that the noise comes mainly from imaging sensor and digitization process. To simulate these two noise artificially, we employ the function

$$I(\boldsymbol{x}) = \frac{1}{1 + e^{-(\boldsymbol{x}^T A \boldsymbol{x} - r^2)}}, \qquad (10)$$

which gives ellipse image (Fig. 3). We modify this image by slight translation (less than one pixel), and slight scale change, and adding 10% white noise, i.e.

$$I'(\boldsymbol{x}) = I(a\boldsymbol{x} + \boldsymbol{u}) + w, \qquad (11)$$

where a represents stretch ratio, $\boldsymbol{u}$ represents small translation, and w represents white noise. Numerous I' are made, and the statistics of local descriptors

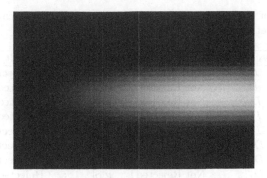

Fig. 3. Synthetic image used in our experiment

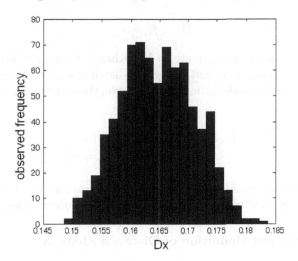

Fig. 4. Distribution of D_x

observed in whole these images are considered as the error distribution of local descriptors under noise. Figure 4 is the result of D_x. This distribution is symmetric, has a single peak, forms a bell curve, looks like a normal distribution. To verify the normality of distributions, we also apply the Kolmogorov-Smirnov test for normality. Table 1 represents the result. The result indicates that it is adequate to regard the distribution of original local jets have normality, but it is not adequate to regard the distribution of rotation invariant descriptors constructed by combination of local jets have normality.

The non-normality of rotation invariant descriptors can be understood by following discussion. The observation error of rotation invariant descriptors e is expressed as:

$$\widetilde{\nu[i]} = \nu[i] + e[i], \qquad (12)$$

where ν represents true value, $\widetilde{\nu}$ represents observed value, and $\nu[i]$ represents the i-th element of vector ν. On the other hand, the error of local jet ε_* is defined as

Table 1. Result of Kolmogorov-Smirnov test for normality to local descriptors. Level of significance is set at 0.05.

descriptor	:	result	descriptor	:	result
D_x	:	Not Rejected	$\nu[1]$	:	Not Rejected
D_y	:	Not Rejected	$\nu[2]$	:	Rejected
D_{xx}	:	Not Rejected	$\nu[3]$	:	Rejected
D_{xy}	:	Not Rejected	$\nu[4]$	:	Rejected
D_{yy}	:	Not Rejected	$\nu[5]$	:	Not Rejected
D_{xxx}	:	Not Rejected	$\nu[6]$	:	Not Rejected
D_{xxy}	:	Not Rejected	$\nu[7]$	:	Not Rejected
D_{xyy}	:	Not Rejected	$\nu[8]$	:	Rejected
D_{yyy}	:	Not Rejected			

$$\widetilde{D}_* = D_* + \varepsilon_*. \tag{13}$$

As mentioned above, it is adequate to hypothesize that ε_* follows normal distribution. If we hypothesize that, the error distribution for the combination of some D_* is obtained by calculation. For example, the error of $\widetilde{D}_x\widetilde{D}_x$ is calculated as:

$$\begin{aligned}
\widetilde{D}_x\widetilde{D}_x &= (D_x + \varepsilon_x)(D_x + \varepsilon_x) \\
&= D_xD_x + 2\varepsilon_xD_x + \varepsilon_x^2
\end{aligned} \tag{14}$$

This equation indicates that errors expand proportional to the values of D_x. It derives the non-normality of $\boldsymbol{\nu}$, corresponding to our observation.

5.2   The Arranged Definition of Distance Measure

Since we have found that the error of $\boldsymbol{\nu}$ does not follow normal distribution, we should rearrange distance measure according to this speculation.

Assuming that ε_* follows normal distribution $N(0, \sigma)$, the error of $\nu[1]$ is evaluated as

$$\begin{aligned}
e[1] &= \widetilde{\nu[1]} - \nu[1] \\
&= (\widetilde{D}_x\widetilde{D}_x + \widetilde{D}_y\widetilde{D}_y) - (D_xD_x + D_yD_y) \\
&\approx 2\varepsilon_xD_x + 2\varepsilon_yD_y \\
&= 2D_xN(0,\sigma) + 2D_yN(0,\sigma).
\end{aligned} \tag{15}$$

Using the additivity of variance of independent variable, the variance of this equation is evaluated as $4\sigma^2(D_x^2 + D_y^2)$. Therefore, if we divide this equation by $\sqrt{4(D_x^2 + D_y^2)}$, the variance of error is normalized to constant value, σ^2. (In practice, since the true value of D_x, D_y is unknown, the maximum likelihood estimate $\widetilde{D}_x, \widetilde{D}_x$ is used instead). Same calculation is made to the rest element of $\boldsymbol{\nu}$, and we obtain

$$e[2] \approx 2\varepsilon_x(D_{xx}D_x + D_{xy}D_y) + 2\varepsilon_y(D_{yy}D_y + D_xD_{xy}) \tag{16}$$
$$+ \varepsilon_{xx}D_x^2 + \varepsilon_{yy}D_y^2 + 2\varepsilon_{xy}D_xD_y,$$

$$e[3] \approx \varepsilon_{xx} + \varepsilon_{yy},$$

$$e[4] \approx 2\varepsilon_{xx}D_{xx} + 4\varepsilon_{xy}D_{xy} + 2\varepsilon_{yy}D_{yy},$$

$$e[5] \approx \varepsilon_{xxx}D_y^3 - 3\varepsilon_{xxy}D_xD_y^2 + 3\varepsilon_{xyy}D_x^2D_y - \varepsilon_{yyy}D_x^3$$
$$- 3\varepsilon_x(D_{xxy}D_y^2 - 2D_{xyy}D_xD_y + D_{yyy}D_x^2)$$
$$+ 3\varepsilon_y(D_{xxx}D_y^2 - 2D_{xxy}D_xD_y + D_{xyy}D_x^2),$$

$$e[6] \approx \varepsilon_{xxx}D_xD_y^2 + \varepsilon_{xxy}(D_y^3 - 2D_x^2D_y) + \varepsilon_{xyy}(D_x^3 - 2D_xD_y^2) + \varepsilon_{yyy}D_x^2D_y$$
$$+ \varepsilon_x(D_{xxx}D_y^2 - 4D_xxyD_xD_y + 3D_{xyy}D_x^2 - 2D_{xyy}D_y^2 + 2D_{yyy}D_xD_y)$$
$$+ \varepsilon_y(2D_{xxx}D_xD_y + 3D_{xxy}D_y^2 - 2D_{xxy}D_x^2 - 4D_{xyy}D_xD_y + D_{yyy}D_x^2),$$

$$e[7] \approx \varepsilon_{xxx}D_xD_y^2 + \varepsilon_{xxy}(2D_xD_y^2 - D_x^3) + \varepsilon_{xyy}(D_y^3 - 2D_x^2D_y) + \varepsilon_{yyy}D_xD_y^2$$
$$+ \varepsilon_x(2D_{xxx}D_xD_y + 2D_{xxy}D_y^2 - 3D_{xxy}D_x^2 - 2D_{xyy}D_xD_y - D_{yyy}D_y^2)$$
$$+ \varepsilon_y(D_{xxx}D_x^2 + 2D_{xxy}D_xD_y + 3D_{xyy}D_y^2 - 2D_{xyy}D_xD_y - 2D_{yyy}D_xD_y),$$

$$e[8] \approx \varepsilon_{xxx}D_x^3 + 3\varepsilon_{xxy}D_x^2D_y + 3\varepsilon_{xyy}D_xD_y^2 + \varepsilon_{yyy}D_y^3$$
$$+ 3\varepsilon_x(D_{xxx}D_x^2 + 2D_{xxy}D_xD_y + D_{xyy}D_y^2)$$
$$+ 3\varepsilon_y(D_{xxy}D_x^2 + 2D_{xyy}D_xD_y + D_{yyy}D_y^2).$$

These equations lead us to normalization of error variance for each coordinate of $\boldsymbol{\nu}$.

Our new measure is summarized as follows. The distance measure between two local descriptor vector $d(\boldsymbol{\nu}_i, \boldsymbol{\nu}_j)$ is defined as

$$d^2(\boldsymbol{\nu}_i, \boldsymbol{\nu}_j) = \sum_k \frac{(\nu_i[k] - \nu_j[k])^2}{\alpha_i[k] + \alpha_j[k]}, \tag{17}$$

where α is

$$\alpha[1] = 4(D_x^2 + D_y^2),$$
$$\alpha[2] = 4(D_{xx}D_x + D_{xy}D_y)^2 + 4(D_{yy}D_y + D_xD_{xy})^2 + D_x^4 + D_y^4 + 4D_x^2D_y^2,$$

and so force (omitted $\alpha[3..8]$ are easily derived from (16)). α_i is calculated by the derivatives correspond to $\boldsymbol{\nu}_i$, and α_j is calculated by the derivatives correspond to $\boldsymbol{\nu}_j$.

5.3   Experimental Verification of Arranged Distance Measure

We also made a experiment to verify the effect of our new definition of distance measure. First, we extract 1306 interest points from 21 test images, and then calculate distance for all combinations ($1306 \times 1305/2 = 852165$ pairs), and sort

Table 2. Rank of corresponding point with noise

	4dim Mahalanobis	8dim Mahalanobis	4dim arranged	8dim arranged
worst	194556	180447	53913	28502
mean	22561	20744	3641	380

it in increasing order. In following experiment, this sorted distance table is referred to evaluate how small the distance is. On the other hand, we calculate distance between each pair of corresponding point of synthetic images. In this time synthetic modification are made by

$$I'(\boldsymbol{x}) = I(aR\boldsymbol{x} + \boldsymbol{u}) + w, \tag{18}$$

where R represents rotation matrix. The descriptor $\boldsymbol{\nu}$ is ideally robust to such modifications. At last, we evaluate how small the distances of two $\boldsymbol{\nu}$ with different modification is, by use of ranked distance table obtained above. In the evaluation, we use the largest distance (worst) and average distance (mean). Same experiment are executed in four cases, that is, the dimensions of vector $\boldsymbol{\nu}$ is set either 8-dimension (it means up to third order derivatives are used) or 4-dimension (up to second order derivatives are used), and ordinary Mahalanobis distance and our arranged distance is applied respectively. In ordinary Mahalanobis distance case, Λ is covariance matrix of all 1306 descriptors.

Table 2 represents the result. In mean distance evaluation, it is found that if we use the Mahalanobis distance measure of 4-dimension, corresponding point stand at rank 22561 of 852165, it means that the correct matching stand inner of about 2.6%. On the other hand, if we use our arranged distance measure of 4-dimension, the correct match stand at rank 3641 of 852165, it means that stand inner of 0.43%. Furthermore, if we use arranged measure of 8-dimension, the result is improved moreover. These result represents the advantage of our method.

In addition, we have made same experiment for descriptors normalized to dominant direction by steerable filter. However, this type of descriptor needs highly precise dominant direction estimation. We found it difficult to obtain sufficient repeatability and distinctiveness if the dimension of descriptor is relatively low as this experiment.

6   Elimination of False Matching

Since the characteristic scale is proportional to image resolution, the proportion of characteristic scale of corresponding point in two image should be constant. By using this properties, we can roughly guess the scale proportion between two images. It leads to elimination of false matching. In this section, according to this consideration, we propose a new modification to image indexing method.

At the first step, for each interest point of query image, calculate the distance for all interest points in the database. For each point in query, the nearest

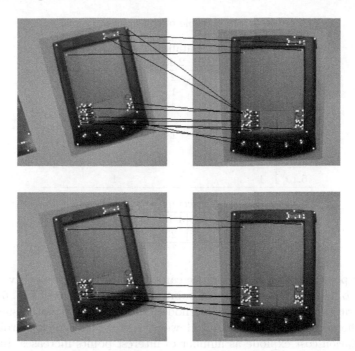

Fig. 5. Improvement of point-to-point matching. The top row is the result of simple nearest neighbor method, and the bottom row is the result after elimination of false matching.

neighbor point (the point which gives minimum distance) in the each image of database is set as first candidate for corresponding point (top of Fig. 5).

The second step is the estimation of scale proportion between two images. This estimate is obtained by voting method based on the first candidates for corresponding point obtained in the last step. Table 3 is the example. As plotting candidate of corresponding point on the table, we may find the diagonal area where much votes concentrates if two image is corresponding (as top of Table 3). In the case of this example, we can find diagonal line one block upper from main diagonal line acquires much votes. This is the good estimate of scale proportion of two images. In practice, we accumulate the number per scale ratio (as bottom of Table 3), and the proportion with maximum vote is taken as estimate for scale proportion. In this example, the proportion 1:1.2 acquires the maximum vote, therefore we can estimate the scale proportion of two images as 1:1.2.

As we can estimate scale proportion according to this method, we can eliminate false positive matching candidates. It is, if the candidate combination is off the line of Table 3, it is likely to false matching. It should be discarded and new candidate should be taken among the on-line combination. That is to say, we choose a first candidate of corresponding point as the nearest neighbor point in the whole points in the database at first, and after the estimation of scale between two images, the candidate point is re-chosen as the nearest neighbor point in the limited points which has estimated proportion of characteristic scale to

Table 3. Match table of characteristic scale

Query Image	Database Image							
	1.44	1.72	2.07	2.48	2.98	3.58	4.29	5.15
1.44	3	2	1	2			1	
1.72			3	1			3	
2.07			1	4				
2.48					4			
2.98					1		4	1
3.58							4	
4.29								2
5.15	1						1	

Diagonally accumulated count

⋯	1.44:1	1.2:1	1:1	1:1.2	1:1.44	1:1.72	⋯
	1	1	4	23	3	2	

the query point. By this operation, we can eliminate the false positive matches, and able to improve the accuracy of point matching (bottom of Fig. 5).

In literature, there exist other method to eliminate false match such as geometric coherence check or RANSAC. However test of such type has problem that the calculation cost explode as number of interest points increases. In contrast to it, the cost of elimination method proposed in this section is linear to the number of interest points. Furthermore, we may also apply geometric elimination method after proposed elimination method with far lower computational cost. The reduction of the number of candidate points is experimentally verified in the next section.

7   Experiment

In order to verify the effect of our method for indexing, we made an image retrieval experiment for an image database consists of 852 images. The database contains scanned picture postcards published in our city in the last hundred years. Parts of them are shown in Fig. 6.

In the retrieval test, we use 32 image pairs; each pair consists of images of same scene but with different scale and camera angle. For each pair, one image is used as the query image, and the other is included in the database. Among these pairs, 9 pairs are taken from publicly available database provided by Mikolajczyk's website [16], and 10 pairs are photoshots taken near our laboratory with different camera angle, and the rest 12 pairs are a scanned picture image and its transformed one. Applied transformations are 20 degree rotation and scale changes. Parts of them are shown in Fig. 7.

Our implementation goes as:

0. Extract interest points and calculate local descriptors for all images in the database. Images are 256-level grayscale, 256×256 pixels, and discrete σ is 10 step ($\sigma = 1.2^n$, $n = 1, 2, ..., 10$). The threshold value of Harris function

Fig. 6. Parts of images in our database

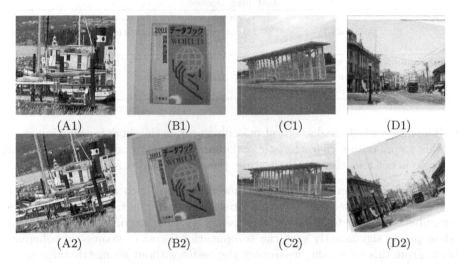

(A1)   (B1)   (C1)   (D1)

(A2)   (B2)   (C2)   (D2)

Fig. 7. Parts of images used in our experiment. A1 and A2 are provided by Mikolajczyk, B1,B2,C1 and C2 are photoshots taken near our laboratory, D1 and D2 are scanned postcards.

for interest point extraction is set as $t = 4000$. Descriptors are 8-dimensional rotation invariant descriptors, where up to third order local jets are used.

1. In the same way, extract interest points and calculate local descriptors for query image.
2. Calculate distance for each pair of interest points between query image and database image. For each interest point of query image, the nearest neighbor point in each database image is chosen as first candidate of corresponding point.
3. According to first candidate, estimate image scale ratio by voting method. The scale ratio which acquire the maximum vote is chosen as estimate.
4. Re-choose the candidate point as its characteristic scale correspond to that of query point. In this step, only ± 1 step error is allowed.
5. If the distance between query point and final candidate point is under certain constant, determine them as the corresponding point (this constant is adjusted experimentally: in this case we choose 0.04 for arranged measure, and 0.20 for Mahalanobis measure). The number of determined corresponding point is regarded as matching score of the two images.

Table 4. Results of image indexing. 'our method with elimination' is the result after all step(1–6) executed, and 'our method without elimination' is the result without step 3 and 4

Recognition Rate

Method	recognition rate
Mahalanobis distance based method	21.9%
our method without elimination	56.3%
our method with elimination	81.3%

Matching Scores

Method	average score for correct image (a)	average score for incorrect image (b)	(a)/(b)
Mahalanobis distance based method	34.2	26.9	1.27
our method without elimination	37.1	20.4	1.82
our method with elimination	28.3	8.0	3.53

6. The image which marks highest matching score is chosen as indexed image. In this step, because characteristic scale found at minimum scale or maximum scale is not true characteristic scale, they are excluded for calculation.

In usual image retrieval system, some refinement such as geometric coherence check is processed after above process, but its computational cost explode as number of candidate matching increases. The reduction of the number of candidate points significantly save the computational cost of geometric coherence check. From this viewpoint, we display the result without geometric refinement. Table 4 is the result. In the table, the recognition rate and average matching score of correct image and incorrect image is represented.

By comparing these result, we can verify the advantage of our method. Our indexing method without elimination choose true image in 56.3% cases, it is higher that of Mahalanobis method, 21.9%. It shows the effect of our distance measure arrangement. Furthermore, by use of our false match elimination method, the recognition rate of our method grows above 80%. Remark that this refinement cost is proportional to the number of corresponding point, in contrast to cost of geometric refinement method explode as the number increases.

It is also observed that our method can eliminate false matching significantly. Although the matching score of correct image decline only 24%, the matching score of incorrect image decline 61%. It leads to save the computational cost of geometric coherence check, if applied.

8   Conclusion

In this paper, we proposed two ideas which improve image indexing based on local descriptors. The first idea is a new distance measure for local descriptors which improves the accuracy of point-to-point matching. The other idea reduces the number of matching candidates by voting characteristic scale ratio. The experimental result has proved the effectiveness of our method.

For further improvement of our method, a promising approach is to use higher dimensional local descriptors, or to add the constraints of semi-local coherence. In case of these arranged implementation, the advantage of our method still exist as the reduction of computational cost, because of its contribution to the reduction of candidate point.

References

1. O. Chomat, V.C. de Verdière, D. Hall, and J.L. Crowley, "Local scale selection for Gaussian based description techniques," *In ECCV, LNCS 1842*, vol. 1, pp. 117–133, 2000
2. Y. Dufournaud, C. Schmid, and R. Horaud, "Matching Images with Different Resolutions," *Proc. of the Conference on Computer Vision and Pattern Recognition, CVPR '00*, vol. 1, pp. 612–618, South Carolina, Jun.2000.
3. W.T. Freeman, E.H. Adelson, "The Design and Use of Steerable Filters," *IEEE Trans. Pattern Analysis and Machine Intelligence*, vol. 13, No. 9, pp. 891–906, Sep.1991
4. C. Harris and M. Stephens, "A Combined Corner and Edge Detector," *Alvey Vision Conf.*, pp. 147–151, 1988.
5. J.J. Koenderink and A.J. van Doorn, "Representation of Local Geometry in the Visual System," *Biol. Cybern.*, vol. 55, pp. 367–375, 1987.
6. T. Lindeberg, "Feature detection with automatic scale selection," *International Journal of Computer Vision*, vol. 30, No. 2, pp. 77–116, 1998
7. D.G. Lowe, "Object Recognition from Local Scale-Invariant Features," *Proc. of the International Conference on Computer Vision, ICCV '99*, vol. 2, pp. 1150–1157, Kerkyra, Corfu, Greece, Sep.1999.
8. D.G. Lowe, "Distinctive image features from scale-invariant keypoints," *International Journal of Computer Vision*, vol. 60, No. 2, pp. 91–110, Nov.2004
9. K. Mikolajczyk and C. Schmid, "Indexing based on scale invariant interest points," *Proc. 8th IEEE International Conference on Computer Vision, ICCV '01*, vol. 1, pp. 525–531, Vancouver, B.C., Canada, Jul.2001.
10. K. Mikolajczyk and C. Schmid, "A performance evaluation of local descriptors," *Proc. of the Conference on Computer Vision and Pattern Recognition, CVPR '03*, vol. 2, pp. 257–563, Madison, Wisconsin, Jun.2003.
11. B.M. ter Haar Romeny, L.M.J. Florack, A.H. Salden, M.A. Viergever "Higher order differential structure of images," *Image and Vision Computing*, 12(6), pp. 317–325, 1994.
12. F. Schaffalitzky and A. Zisserman, "Multi-view matching for unordered image sets, or "How do I organize my holiday snaps?"," *In ECCV, LNCS 2350*, pp. 414–431, 2002.
13. C. Schmid and R. Mohr, "Local grayvalue invariants for image retrieval," *IEEE Trans. Pattern Analysis and Machine Intelligence*, vol. 19, No. 5, pp. 530–534, May.1997
14. C. Schmid, R. Mohr, and C. Bauckhage, "Comparing and Evaluating Interest Points," *IEEE Proc. of the 6th International Conference on Computer Vision, ICCV '98*, pp. 230–235, Bombay, India, Jan.1998
15. N. Sebe, M.S. Lew, "Comparing salient point detectors," *IEEE International Conference on Multimedia and Expo*, Tokyo, Japan, Aug.2001.
16. http://www.inrialpes.fr/lear/people/Mikolajczyk/

Image Feedback Retrieval Based on Vector Space Model Transformation

Luo Xin[1], Shiro Ajioka[1], Masami Shishibori[1], and Kenji Kita[2]

[1] Faculty of Engineering, Tokushima University, Tokushima, 770-8506, Japan
[2] Center for Advanced Information Technology,
Tokushima University, Tokushima, 770-8506, Japan
{luoxin, bori, kita}@is.tokushima-u.ac.jp

Abstract. In recent years, the employment of user feedback information to improve the image retrieval precision has become a hot subject in the research field. But in traditional relevance feedback methods, both relevant and irrelevant user assigned information was required for the retrieval system. For the sake of practicality and convenience, the present paper advances that users only need to choose their inquired image files, which generate a new index vector as relevant information. Through the feature vector space transformation, the index is moved towards the user's inquiry intention. Meanwhile, the analysis of the user's inquiry intention together with relevant forecast of index target in the database make it possible for the less similar vectors to get closer to the demanding vectors and thus increasing index precision. In this paper, a prototype system is introduced of image database and experimental illustration to 51138 image files. Compared with the traditional relevance feedback technique, the suggested method is shown to obviously improve the retrieval function.

1 Introduction

In recent years, with the rapid development of computer technology and the popularity of digital image equipments, there is an increasing number of digital image files. Thus how to get quickly and accurately image files has become an imperative problem to be solved. Therefore, image retrieval has become one of the hot subjects in research field.

Traditional keyword-based retrieval is difficult to realize key-word automatic retrieval. With the emergence of large-scale image databases, artificial annotation is found to be a sealy hard job. Meanwhile the increasing number of image files and the influence of a marker's subjective consciousness also makes difficult assigning correct annotations to each image file. In order to solve this problem, researchers put forward the CBIR (Content Based Image Retrieval). However, the chosen image features with CBIR are the basic visual characters of color, texture, shape, etc., which are unable to discern the real object, i.e, unable to convey the high level of semantic meanings in the images. For example, the retrieval of a sunset image will be followed by images of red color and round shape. In addition, the users' subjective

G.G. Lee et al. (Eds.): AIRS 2005, LNCS 3689, pp. 616–625, 2005.

consciousnesses, their interested objects, and feelings vary accordingly, which requests the correspondingly changing index. Thus it is considered that the present CBIR system based on basic visual features can not meet the practical requirement of the common users.

To make up the deficiencies of CBIR, the user's relevance feedback retrieval is suggested. As a mutual retrieval process between a person and a computer, the relevance feedback technique enables the user to evaluate the retrieval results and to point out whether the results are relevant (positive examples or feedback) or not (negative examples and feedback) to the index destination. Based on this evaluation, an adjustment, which can be repetitive, is made for further retrieval until a satisfying retrieval result appears.

Two strategies are adopted in this relevance feedback retrieval: moving inquiry vector and modulating re-weighing [1].The famous Rocchio[2] formula successfully realizes the relevance feedback retrieval through moving the inquiry point with the increase of the relevant features of positive feedback and the decrease of those of negative feedback. Through generating the image feature vectors similar to text vectors, MARS (Multimedia Analysis and Retrieval System) employs this formula for image feedback retrieval [3].

Rui[4] and other researchers provide a hierarchically modulating re-weighting method, which observes the individual weighting arrangement of a feedback vectors in various dimensions of feature space. The distributed feature vectors of a feedback vector on i-th dimension are measured by its standard deviation r_i. If the r_i is bigger, then the degree of relevance between the weighing and the retrieval, then it becomes lower. The weighting should accordingly be reduced. Otherwise it would be increased.

Ishikawa [10] and others who have employed ellipsoid distance to presume the distance function of a user's inquiry intention and the central location of the inquiry vector, have ameliorated the efficiency of feedback retrieval when the inquiry samples are insufficient. Recent combination of SVM and relevance feedback technique further advances retrieval accuracy [11].

On the basis of the analysis to the user's intentions, this paper is to present a kind of feedback technique based on vector model transformation for the sake of higher image retrieval accuracy. According to this technique, the user's intended retrieval image will be regarded as the relevant information and turned into a new inquiry vector model. In the vector database, the vector model is taken as the basic point. The transformation of feature vectors moves relevant feature vectors more closely to the inquiry basic point, furthers the spatial distance between irrelevant feature vectors and the inquiry point, and then reaches a better retrieval accuracy. A prototype system of the image database index is implemented. Compared with the relevant traditional methods, this retrieval technique is proved through experiments to have obviously improved the analogical retrieval of image.

This paper puts forth the background and purpose of our study at the very beginning. Then the method of image feedback retrieval based on vector model transformation is introduced in section 2. Section 3 focuses on the experiment results and analysis report. The final section is devoted to the conclusion and our future work.

2 Image Feedback Retrieval Based on Vector Model Transformation

2.1 Basic Ideas

No matter what kind of features a content-based image retrieval technique may have or no matter what kind of distant testing strategy is used, semantic meanings of images can not actually be represented. In addition, the user's different emphases result in changing responses towards the retrieval objects, and the result is completely determined by the retrieval. Thus, retrieval systems need to automatically meet the inquiry demand and then improve the inquiry results based on the forecast of the user's inquiry intentions.

Nakajima [5] and others have put forward a difference amplification feedback retrieval. There exists a kind of difference between the user chosen positive images and some similar positive images that are not chosen by the user. Modulation of this difference can create new retrieval vectors corresponding to the user's inquiry intentions. This technique requires the feature vectors to be clustered as a part of the organization of the database.

With the application of user feedback information the documents transfigure the feature space, drawing positive feature vectors to and widening negative feature vectors from the inquiry vector. Thus the feedback retrieval of 3D model image is realized[6].

Grounded on these two ideas, a retrieval system is designed in which the user only needs to choose their intended image samples. Then, based on those positive samples the system will automatically produce an inquiry vector similar to the user's inquiry intention. Furthermore, we amend the equation for the document in the retrieval system and change the feature vector spaces of the images of relevant positive feedback. In this way the relevant images' feature vectors move gradually to the inquiry vector. Conversely the vector spaces of irrelevant images are more and more distant from the inquiry basic point. Then a clustering of vector spaces based upon the inquiry vector is realized.

Our retrieval system runs according to the following processes.

1) The user appoints an inquiry sample in the general CBIR system.
2) Relevant retrieval is conducted on the basis of the user's appointed inquiry sample.
3) If the result is satisfying, the retrieval ends; if not, the user chooses one or more image samples among the retrieval results.
4) The user's choice is exploited to create another new inquiry vector and then to transform the feature vector space model.
5) Skip to step 2).

2.2 Reproducing the Inquiry Vector

In CBIR, if a suitable inquiry sample is chosen, then an ideal effect can be achieved. Hence, the choice of samples is most important. What's more, in each retrieval step, even if the user chooses the comparatively suitable sample, the index result may not be satisfactory. At the same time, many experiments illustrate that user chosen positive feedback images bear strong similarities in semantic meaning and usually belong to the same semantic category, though they can be different in content. Therefore, inquiry vectors based on the user's retrieval intention can produce better results.

By improving on the former equation for inquiry movement, we use the user's feedback samples to generate a new inquiry vector which can represent in some degree the user's retrieval intention. For the user's convenience, only vector feature data of positive feedbacks are considered. In this way, the user only needs to choose their intended inquiry sample (as a positive sample) rather than give the relevant and irrelevant information as well as the qualifying degree, etc. in the retrieval.

Reproduction of inquiry vector can be achieved by application of the following formula.

$$q' = \sum_{i=1}^{M} (\ln(s_i \pi) d_i) \bigg/ \sum_{i=1}^{M} \ln(S_i \pi) \tag{1}$$

Where, d_i is the order of feedback samples provided by the user. s_i is the similarity parameter of the relevant positive feedback samples and the target image. M is the sum of the chosen sample images.

2.3 Transformation of Vector Model

Though the inquiry vector generated by the above formula can make, to a certain extent, the inquiry features vector close to target retrieval destination, the moving scope of the feature vector will reduce spontaneously with comparatively low similarities of the user's chosen feedback images. For example, the user chooses some flag images as the feedback samples among the suggestive ones. But these images may bear low similarities in content in spite of their semantic relevance. Thus, a satisfying effect can not be achieved by the adoption of common arithmetic similarities for retrieval.

Therefore, we adjust the feature vectors in the database of relevant images changing their direction towards that of the inquiry vector. The relationship among inquiry vector q, feedback vector f_j and relevant vector d_i is illustrated in Fig. 1.

Where, $f = \{f_1 \dots f_j\}$ is a feature vector of the relevance feedback. $d = \{d_1 \dots d_i \dots\}$ presents feature vector in the database. Transformation from vector d_i to inquiry vector can be described in the following formula.

$$d_i = k v_{iq} \tag{2}$$

$$k = \alpha \sum_{j=1}^{M} u_i \exp(-c_i^n \sqrt{|v_{ij}|}) \tag{3}$$

In formula (3), parameter α and $-c$ are two standard factors. Parameter u_i is the similarity guideline, and parameter n is a punishment coefficient. In the process of mutual communication with the user, the retrieval accuracy of the system can be improved through constant change of these parameters. This hypothesis is proved by our experiment a results. $j = 1...M$ in the formula is the number of user's feedback vectors. v_{ij} is the vector from vector d_i to vector, v_{iq} is the vector from vector d_i to inquiry vector q'.

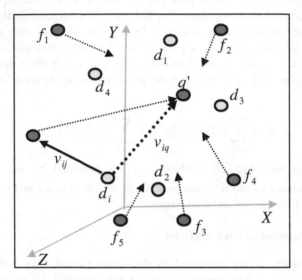

Fig. 1. Vector Transformation Model

2.4 Similarity Measurement

In CBIR, the Euclidean or weighted Euclidean distance is usually applied to similarity measurement of feature vectors. However, experiments prove that only through certain sum of positive feedback samples can Euclidean ameliorate retrieval result.

Ishikawa[10] and others have achieved the relevance feedback retrieval through utilization of elliptical distance measure function. This distance measurement can handle some special situations. Therefore, in our feedback retrieval system the elliptical distance function is adopted for the similarity measurement of features vectors. (Illustration by the right picture of Fig. 2.)

It can be observed in Fig. 2 that Euclidean equidistance is a spherical surface and that weighted Euclidean distance is an ellipse, though its principle axis and coordination's axis are parallel. Equidistance surface of elliptical distance can be distance measurement of bevel or even of arbitrary directions.

The measurement of elliptical distance is described with the following formula:

$$D(x, y) = \sqrt{(x-y)^T A(x-y)} \tag{3}$$

Where, $x = [x_1,...,x_n]^T$, $y = [y_1,...,y_n]$ is vector of n dimension; $A = [x_{ij}]$ is the positive symmetry rank of $n \times n$.

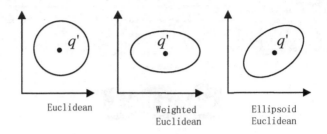

Fig. 2. Equidistance plan of distance functions

3   Experiments and Comments

3.1   Construction of the Image Database

Based on previous ideas, a prototype system of image retrieval is constructed. In our image database 51138 images of various kinds are collected and classified according to key words. There are a total of 512 key words in the database - for example, building, scene, sunset, car, flag, antique, etc. Nevertheless, the visual difference among the same sort of images still exists in the terms of content.

Two feature data of images are introduced: color and texture.

As the distance between colors counted by RGB color space can not represent the actual difference between the two colors sensed by the user, an L*u*v color scheme is thus adopted to accord the definition of color distance with the user's visual features. A description on how to transform RGB to L*u*v can be found at [7].

As for texture features, as introduced by Tamura [9] and used by QBIC [8], they basically correspond to the degree of finish and orientation of textures in an image.

With these two types of features combined, 48 dimensions of color features and 48 dimensions of texture features, we have adopted a total of 96 dimension features for our retrieval implementation.

3.2   Experiment Results and Evaluation

During the experimental phase of reproducing the inquiry vector, the scope of s_i in formula (1) is set [2, 0] within $(0 < s_i \le 2)$. Based on automatic digression of the user's selection order, a relatively ideal retrieval result is acquired when the digressive extent is 0.2. In the experiment of formula (2), the ideal index effect will be obtained under the following conditions: $\alpha = 0.3 ; c = 2 \times \pi ; n = 2$. The data scope of u_i is between [0, 1] $(0 < u_i \le 1)$.

Recall and Precision are adopted to judge the retrieval function:

$$recall = |relevant \cap retrieved| / |relevant|$$

$$precision = |relevant \cap retrieved| / |retrieved|$$

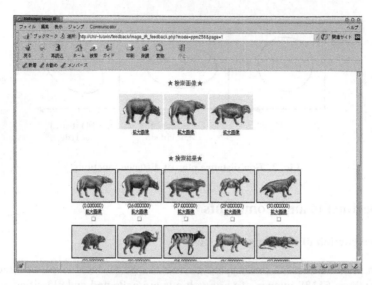

Fig. 3. The Retrieval Results after the Relevance Feedback

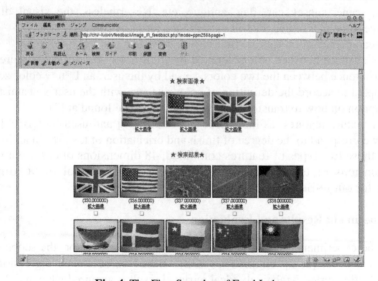

Fig. 4. The Flag Samples of Feed Index

Where, retrieval donates collection of the returning retrieval objects from the system; relevant indicates collection of the actually relevant objects in the database.

For each retrieval, the retrieval accuracy is the aggregate of the actual relevant images among the first 100 images. From Fig. 3 and Fig.4, screenshots of practical retrieval in the system, it can be observed that the retrieval accuracy is improved to a great extent especially that of the retrieval of flag (Fig. 3).

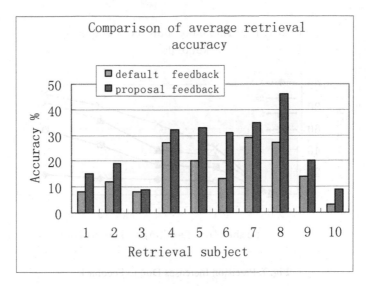

Fig. 5. Comparative Plot of Maximal Index Precision

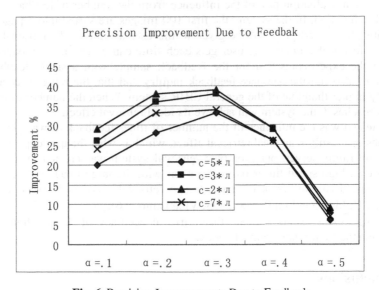

Fig. 6. Precision Improvements Due to Feedback

A comparison is made between the traditional retrieval methods and the technique described in this paper. Each experiment sub-catalog is retrieved ten times and the feedback is gained correspondingly. The comparative study of the average maximal retrieval accuracy is illustrated in the vertical square plot in Fig. 5.

And Fig. 6 is a comparative plot of retrieval precision based on the changes of parameters in formula (2).

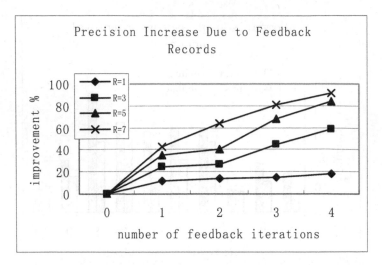

Fig. 7. Precision Increases Due to Feedback

Fig. 7 is an evaluation plot of the influence from the number of feedback samples over index function. In the system, the first 100 images are sorted into 5 pages. Each page with 20 reduced plots will be given to the user as clue of the retrieval results. Thus, the feedback samples the user gets each time can be as many as twenty. It is found in the experiments that for the feedback sample with a single feedback the system can also run the relevance feedback inquiry and that the retrieval accuracy is relatively higher than that of the general CBIR system. When the number of feedback samples reaches 7, the system will achieve its ideal retrieval effect.

Also tested was the influence of the number of times feedback. It was given that 3 or 4 times can result in an ideal retrieval effect, which is what the user expects to get.

Built on Linux server, our prototype retrieval system was created in C and PHP and it uses a high-speed linear index. So even with the large image database a high retrieval speed can still be kept. The average retrieval speed is 1.2 seconds on the whole (CPU: Intel Pentium III 800, OS: Vine Linux 2.6).

The experiment results indicate that retrieval accuracy of this method is much higher than the traditional feedback index.

4 Conclusions

This paper proposed a technique of transforming the characteristic vector space on the basis of a newly-generated inquiry vector. This technique can bring relevant feature vectors close to the inquiry feature vector even if there are only a few similarities. Contrasted with the traditional retrieval method, this one has the benefit of self-study and makes retrieval correspond to the user's inquiry intentions. The retrieval prototype system designed in this way, shows that the suggested method can obviously improve the efficiency of relevant feedback retrieval.

Henceforth, based on its prototype further expansion of this system's function will be conducted, which will mainly include the following aspects: (1) To summarize the visual characteristic of images and to make inquiry more suitable to the user. (2) To implement better self-study and self-adoption; to reduce the noisy images among retrieval results, and to further improve the index precision.

References

1. Wei-Ying Ma and HongJiang Zhang: Content-based image indexing and retrieval [A].Handbook of Multimedia Computing[C]. US: CRC Press LLC, (1999) 227-254
2. J.J.Rocchio: Relevace Feedback in Information Retrieval. in G.Salton ed., The SMART Retrieval System-Experiments in Automatic Document Processing, Prentice Hall, Englewood Cliffs,N.J.,(1971) 313-323
3. Y.Rui, T.S.Huang, and S.Mehrotra: Content-based Image Retrieval with Relevance Feedback in MARS. In Proc. Of IEEE Int, Conf. On Image Processing '97,Santa Barbara,CA,Oct.1997
4. Rui Y,Huang TS:A novel relevance feedback technique in image retrieval. In Proc. Of the 9th ACM Int'1. Multimeedia Conf.Ottawa: ACM Press, (2001) 107-210
5. Shinsuke Nakajima, Shinichi Kinoshita, and Katsumi Tanaka: Image Database Retrieval Based on relevance Feedback By Difference Amplification. IEICE.Vol.J87-D-I No2.(2004) 164-174
6. Hoon Yul and Tsuhan Chen: Feature Space Warping: An Approach to Relevance Feedback. ICIP, Rochester, NY, Sept 2002
7. http://anipeg.yks.ne.jp/color.html
8. C.Faloutsos, R.Barber,M. Flickner,J.Hafner,W.NiblackmD.Petkovic,and W.Equitz: Efficient and effective querying by image content. Journal of Intelligent Information Systems, 3(3/4), July (1994) 231-262
9. H.Tamura,S.Mori,and T.Yamawaki: Texture features corresponding to visual perception. IEEE Trans.Syst Man Cybern. SMC-8(6), (1978) 460-473
10. Y.Ishikawa, R.Subramanya,and C.Faloutsos . Mindreader: Querying databases through multiple examples. In Proc. Of VLDB, New York, NY,Aug, Morgan Kaufmann. (1998) 218-227
11. Tong S,Chang E. Support vector machine active learning for image retrieval. In:Proc. Of the 9th ACM Int'1.Multimedia Conf. Ottawa: ACM Press, (2001) 107-119

Indexing Structures for Content-Based Retrieval of Large Image Databases: A Review

He Ling, Wu Lingda, Cai Yichao, and Liu Yuchi

Institute of Information System & Management,
National University of Defense Technology, Changsha 410073
heling6159@163.com

Abstract. Content-based image retrieval is a focused problem in current multimedia domain. To obtain better searching results more efficiently in some applications, a proper indexing structure is indispensable. This paper reviews the typical indexing structures in content-based image retrieval at first. Then based on the comparison of their different performance, the paper uncovers the problems in those structures and points out the development direction to improve the performance of CBIR in the future.

1 Introduction

With the progress of multimedia techniques and computer networks, we are faced with more and more digital images. Undoubtedly, in order to make a perfect use of the interesting information implied in the disordered data, there should be some image retrieval techniques which can search and access the corresponding images in time. At the same time, with the emerging of large image databases, the traditional text-based image retrieval techniques which depend on manual annotations can't meet users' increasing needs. Thus content-based image retrieval (CBIR) emerges as the times require.

In CBIR, we usually construct a feature database using the extracted features at first, and transform an image object in the original image database into a corresponding point in the vector space, which is the so called feature vector. Since image features are always high dimensional vectors, the content-based image retrieval is then transformed into the nearest neighbor searching of high dimensional data points in feature databases.

For a large scaled image database, the corresponding feature database is also large. So the linear scan is not competent for users' research, and a valid indexing scheme must be needed to support the searching and improve the performance of it. Most traditional indexing methods degrade when the dimension of target data exceeds 5, even being outperformed by linear scan, which is the well known "curse of dimensionality". Originating from it, this paper makes an analysis and a comparison of current typical indexing techniques in CBIR, summarizes the problems in them, and points out the direction in the future development.

The remainders of the paper are as the followings. Section 2 reviews existing indexing researches from five aspects. Section 3 gives the performance analyses of those indexing structures and uncovers the problems. As the conclusion of the whole paper, section 4 directs the development of indexing techniques in CBIR.

G.G. Lee et al. (Eds.): AIRS 2005, LNCS 3689, pp. 626–634, 2005.

2   Indexing Structures in CBIR

The basic function of an indexing structure is to organize feature vectors, manage the procedure of searching and speed up the final querying. An important difference between multimedia indexing structures and those general structures is that the former is confronted with the influence of curse of dimensionality. To solve this problem, there emerge many methods applied in various situations. We classify those methods into five categories, which are multidimensional indexing method, dimension reduction method, approximate nearest neighbor method, multiple space-filling curves method and filter-based method.

2.1   Multidimensional Indexing Method (MIM)

MIM works by partitioning the data space, clustering data according to partitions, and using the partitions to prune the search space for querying. While MIM generally performs well at low dimensional data spaces, their performances degrade rapidly with the increasing of dimensionality, even being outperformed by linear scan. The most successful MIM is the tree-based indexing structure. Those methods group the data points in the database into clusters using some strategies at first, then they represent each cluster by a certain bounding object, and all those bounding objects are organized by corresponding tree structure. During a searching, these bounding objects will provide the lower bound from points in clusters to the query object. Actually, the above mentioned lower bound is the one that from the bounding object to the query object, so the bounding object is the approximation of a corresponding cluster.

Furthermore, MIM can be divided into two classes, one is derived from the K-D-tree, and the other is from the R-tree. The main difference between them lies in the partitioning of data spaces. The former uses space-partitioning, which splits the data space along a pre-defined hyperplane regardless of the data distribution. The regions formed by this strategy are mutually disjoint, with their union being the complete space. Instead, the latter uses data-partitioning according to the data distribution, and there may be some overlapping after this partitioning. Besides these two approaches, there also exist some other techniques with a combination of multiple methods.

The R-tree structure and its variants are most commonly used for spatial data, and they are also the early attempts to high dimensional data indexing. Guttman proposed the concept of R-tree in 1984[1]. It is the generalization of the B+-tree to high dimensional spaces, which represents the data by the minimal bounding rectangles(MBRs). Some experiments show that the performance of R-tree degrades when the dimension of data exceeds 5.

SS-tree[2] is similar with the R-tree, except that it uses the minimal bounding spheres(MBSs). Though the use of spheres reduces the overlapping of regions and thus the performance of the SS-tree outperforms the R*-tree, there still exist some overlapping in high dimensional spaces.

SR-tree[3] is the improvement to the SS-tree with the combination of the SS-tree and the R*-tree[4], which uses both MBRs and MBSs as an approximation in the directory. By this means, the regions spanned by a node are the intersections of the MBRs and MBSs associated with that node, thus it reduces region overlap among sibling nodes. This structure is better than both the R*-tree and the SS-tree.

X-tree[5] is the generalization of the R*-tree to high dimensional data. The X-tree uses two techniques to deal with high-dimensional data. First, it introduces an overlap-free split algorithm, which is based on the split history of the tree. Second, where the overlap-free split algorithm would lead to an unbalanced directory, the X-tree omits the split and the according directory node is enlarged becoming a super-node. The X-tree outperforms both the R*-tree and the TV-tree[6].

Henrich proposed the LSD[h]-tree[7] as an improvement to the LSD-tree in 1998. It combines the low fanout from the K-D-tree with the advantage that the R-tree has in not covering empty. This structure is slightly better than the X-tree.

The pyramid technique[8] which is proposed by Berchtold uses a special partitioning strategy optimized for high dimensional data. The basic idea is to perform a dimension reduction allowing the use of efficient uni-dimensional index structures to store and search data. The pyramid technique divides the data space into 2D pyramids whose apexes lie at the center point. In a second step, each pyramid is cut into several slices parallel to the basis of the pyramid forming the data pages. The pyramid technique associates each high dimensional point to a single value, which is the distance from the point to the top of the pyramid, according to a specific dimension. This value is later used as a key in the B+-tree. The pyramid technique outperforms the X-tree and the sequential scan using uniformly distributed data. However, this structure is not good for the nearest neighbor searching, instead it is proper for range querying[1].

After this, Chakrabarti proposed Hybrid-tree[9]. It combines the advantages from space-partitioning structures and data-partitioning structures. The Hybrid-tree splits a node using a single dimension to guarantee that the fanout is independent of data dimension. This method allows overlapping regions as data-partitioning structures do. This structure outperforms both the SR-tree and the hB-tree.

Recently, Sakurai proposed the A-tree[10], which is an index structure for high dimensional data that introduces the notion of relative approximation. The basic idea of the A-tree is the use of virtual bounding rectangles to approximate minimum bounding rectangles or objects. Thus, on one node of the tree we have information about the exact position of the region MBR and an approximation of the relative position of its sons. The A-tree outperforms the VA-File[11] and the SR-tree.

As for the above mentioned MIMs, there is not a fixed taxis among them. Moreover, when the data dimension is relatively high, all of them degrade rapidly, which is a common shortcoming among them.

2.2 Nearest Neighbor Method

For images, the features are approximations of images per se. The nearest neighbors of feature vectors are not that of images, so we can't guarantee to have exact results even using exact searching. For reasons of it, researchers propose many methods based on the approximate nearest neighbor (ANN) searching to solve the curse of dimensionality[12]. The idea behind the ANN approach is to retrieve k ANNs faster within a given error bound ε instead of retrieving exact k NNs. Given a query point q and distance error $\varepsilon > 0$, a point p is a $(1+\varepsilon)$-ANN of q such that for any other database

---

[1] Given a d-dimensional interval, $[q0_{min}, q0_{max}],\ldots,[qd-1_{min},qd-1_{max}]$, determine the points in the database which are inside the range, which is range query.

point p', $\|q - p\| \le (1+\varepsilon)\|q - p'\|$. The dimension reduction and multiple space-filling curves that will be introduced later are both belonging to the approximate nearest neighbor approach.

2.3 Dimension Reduction Method

The dimension reduction is one of the most direct methods to deal with curse of dimensionality. This approach first condenses most of information in a dataset to a few dimensions by applying the singular value decomposition (SVD), the discrete cosine transform (DCT), or the discrete wavelet transform(DWT). Then it applies traditional multidimensional indexing schemes to the processed data. The QBIC system uses the primary component analysis (PCA) to reduce the 20-dimension shape feature based on the moment to form the indexing of images. Furthermore, the Fastmap algorithm[13] proposed by Faloutsos and Lin is also a typical dimension reduction method. It uses multidimensional scaling (MDS) to realize the indexing and visualization of multimedia databases.

In 2002, Yu proposed iMinMax(θ)[14], which maps points in high-dimensional spaces to single-dimensional values determined by their maximum or minimum values among all dimensions. By varying the tuning "knob", θ, users can obtain different families of iMinMax structures that are optimized for different distributions of data sets. The transformed data can then be indexed using existing single-dimensional indexing structures such as the B+-tree. iMinMax is mainly developed to address range queries. However it also supports the nearest neighbor search at the cost of much more running time to obtain higher accuracy. In range queries, this method outperforms both the VA-file and the pyramid technique.

2.4 Multiple Space-Filling Curves Method

The multiple space-filling curves approach orders the d-dimensional space in many ways, with a set of space-filling curves such as Hilbert curves, each constituting a mapping from $R^d \to R^1$. This mapping gives a linear ordering of all points in the data set. Therefore, when a query point is mapped to the space-filling curve, one can perform a range search for nearby points along the curve to find near neighbors in the data space. However, due to the nature of the $R^d \to R^1$ mapping, some near neighbors of the query point may be mapped far apart along a single curve. To make sure that these points are not overlooked, multiple space-filling curves are used, based on different mappings from $R^d \to R^1$. Thus the efficiency obtained from approximate nearest neighbor searching will be greatly reduced.

2.5 Filter-Based Method

The filter-based approach overcomes the dimensionality curse by filtering the vectors so that only a small fraction of them must be visited during a search. It can be realized by various ways.

Clustering, classification and latent semantic analysis are all commonly used filter methods. Besides, we can narrow the search range using some simple structured attributions in relational databases.

The triangle inequality $d(i,q) \geq |d(i,k) - d(q,k)|$ is another efficient filter approach[28]. In the formula, d is a kind of measure, i, q and k are feature vectors. Using this formula, we won't omit the right solutions. And this method can be used in all retrieval techniques the distance measures of which are metrics.

In image searching based on the color histogram, we can use a particular filter method. Since the basic idea of this searching is to compute the distances from each images in the database to the query object and regard the distance as the corresponding histogram distance, the computation can be simplified by reducing the number of the bins or selecting a subset of the image database only.

More idiographic, the VA-File and its variants are all belonging to this kind of method. And only this class of structure is the accurate nearest neighbor searching method in contrast to the approximate nearest neighbor searching.

The VA-File divides the data space into 2^b rectangular cells where b denotes a user specified number of bits. For each dimension i, a small number of bits b_i is assigned, and 2^{b_i} slices along the dimension i are determined in such a way that all slices are equally full. Let b be the sum of all b_i, i.e. $\sum_{i=1}^{d} b_i = b$, where d is the dimension of data sets. Then the data space is divided into 2^b hyperrectangular cells, each of which can be represented by a unique bit-string of length b. Each data point is approximated by the bit-string of the cell into which it falls. In addition to the basic vector data and the approximations, only the boundary points along each dimension must be stored. Depending upon the accuracy of the dada points and the number of bits chosen, the approximation file is 4 to 8 times smaller than the original vector file. Thus, storage overhead ratio is very small, on the order of 0.125 to 0.25. When searching, the entire approximation file is scanned at first, then the exact file is retrieved with some look-ups if necessary. Though the VA-File provides a solution to the dimensionality curse and outperforms the sequential scan and most MIMs in high dimensions, it has some drawbacks. The major drawbacks lies in two aspects. One is that more bits are needed for the approximations in proportion to the dimensionality to enhance the filtering power. The other is that the filtering power decreases severely for clustered data, such as image data.

Berchtold proposed IQ-tree in 2000[15]. This tree has a three-level structure. The first is a flat directory consisting of minimum bounding rectangles, the second level contains the approximations and the third level contains real points. As a significant development of the VA-File, it uses different compression schemes on each partition depending on the density of data. This structure outperforms both the X-tree and the VA-File.

As another perfect improvement, Guang-Ho Cha proposed GC-tree in 2002[16]. Different from the IQ-tree, the GC-tree maintains the hierarchical directory corresponding to the partition hierarchy.

Being the only structure that is better than sequential scan by far, there are many other variants based on the VA-File. Aiming at skewed data distribution, Manjunath fitted the marginal distribution of data sets using Gaussian mixture model on each dimension[17]. Then it partitions each dimension independently based on the model parameters. Ferhatosmanoglu also proposed VA+-File to deal with ununiform data sets in 2000[18]. This method removes the relativities among dimensions using Karhunen-Loeve transform at first. Then it makes an unbalanced assignment according to each dimension's energy after the transform. Besides, Guang-Ho Cha proposed the

local polar coordinate file(LPC-File)[19] . The basic idea is to enhance the discrimina-
tory power of the approximation by adding polar coordinate information of the vector
to the approximation.

3   Comparisons of Typical Indexing Structures

From the above summarizations, we can conclude that each structure has its advantages and disadvantages. In other words, the performance of an indexing structure is
in close correlation with the searching algorithm used in the application. So we can
only give some comparison results based on certain given conditions and some similar structures to some extent.

Table 1. comparison results of typical index structures.

Reference	Comparison results	Conditions and comments
20	R-tree with splitting strategy of Z-Hashing > R-tree	The former needs less seek operations, and the average storage utilization is higher.
4	R*-tree>Variants of the R-tree R*-tree has best storage utilization and insertion times.	For all data list and queries, only number of disk ac-cesses is measured.
21	Skd-tree>R-tree The former requires more space.	The performance is in term of number of page accessed per search operation.
22	KDB-tree>R-tree	Compared with the query times.
23	Buddy tree with tansformation >R-tree, Buddy tree with overlapping regions> Buddy tree with transformation>R*-tree	Not for large query regions.
23	Buddy tree with clipping is better	For uniform data sets.
24	Hilbert R-tree slightly better than R*-tree.	
25	Cell tree with oversize shelves > R*-tree and hB-tree	Oversize shelves lead to great improvements for access methods clipping.
3	SR-tree > R*-tree, SS-tree and VA-File	For ununiform data sets.
5	X-tree > R*-tree and TV-tree	
8	Pyramid-tree > X-tree and Sequential scan	For range query of ununi-form data sets.
9	Hybrid-tree > SR-tree and hB-tree	
10	A-tree > VA-File and SR-tree	
14	IMinMax(θ) > VA-File and Pyramid-tree	For range query.
15	IQ-tree > X-tree and VA-File	For ununiform data scts.

In this table, ">" means "better than".

Anyway, researchers have proposed many methods to solve the curse of dimensionality. Some of them have certain improvements, and obtains faster searching speed than sequential scan. But on the other hand, we are still in a primary stage studying high dimensional data indexing. And there also exist some problems to be solved. They can be summarized as the followings.

(1) Most of the indexing structures degrade rapidly when the dimension of data exceeds 10.

(2) During the partitioning of high dimensional data, there always exist some assumptions, such as the uniform distribution of the data et al.. But these assumptions are usually far from the real data sets.

(3) Most of the structures can't support the dynamic update of data sets, or the overhead is high.

(4) The computation complexity of most structures, especially the high dimensional indexing structures, is very high.

(5) Most of the indexing structures can deal with only fixed dimension data.

(6) Generally speaking, a newly proposed indexing scheme is aiming at only one or one class of existing scheme, without the considering of the efficient combination with various schemes.

(7) To improve the efficiency of CBIR, most work focus on the improvement of indexing structures, but few of them focuses on the improvement of searching algorithms.

Besides the research results shown in the above sections, the comparisons of some other typical indexing structures can be seen in table1.

4   Conclusion

Till now, we have summarized current researches of indexing techniques in CBIR, compared the performance of them and pointed out the existing problems.

Due to the high dimensionality, complexity and dynamic of multimedia data feature, we conclude that an indexing scheme for multimedia databases should satisfies the following main requirements.

(1) The overlap among data regions using the indexing structure should be minimum. At the same time, the utilization ratio should be as high as possible.

(2) The indexing structure can deal with various types of queries, including range query, nearest neighbor query, et al..

(3) The indexing structure can track the dynamic changes of a database efficiently, and deal with those changes perfectly.

(4) The indexing structure should be scalable. Besides, it should support the management of auxiliary memory efficiently.

(5) The indexing structure should be independent of the order of input data.

In conclusion, the curse of dimensionality is a major problem that lies in the research of indexing schemes of CBIR all the times, and it is also an impetus to drive the research in this domain in progress. By far, there are various methods proposed by many researchers. Those methods do solve some problems in some particular applications to some extent[26,27]. Since the evaluation of indexing schemes are relied on the performance of corresponding searching algorithms, and various applications have various searching algorithms, we don't have a common model to evaluate existing indexing structures by far, which is also an open problem in this research field.

On the other hand, the combination with various indexing techniques to form a new indexing structure is also an inevitable trend in the improvement of indexing schemes in CBIR.

Furthermore, from the summarization ahead we can see that most of the researches focus on the construction of the optimal indexing structure, but few of them commit themselves to the introduction of parallel searching algorithms to improve the performance of searching. However, we would obtain much better results with the combination of a proper indexing scheme and a parallel searching algorithm than only using certain indexing structure. So it is also another important research branch in the future.

References

1. Antomn Guattman. R-tree:a dynamic index structure for spatial searching.[A]ACM Sigmod Int.Conf.on Management of Data[C].Boston:MA (1984)47-57
2. David A. White,Ramesh Jain. Similarity indexing with the SS-tree[A]. Proc.of the 12th IEEE Int.Conf.on Data Engineering[C] (1996)
3. Norio Katayama,Shin'ichi Satoh. SR-tree:An index structure for high dimensional nearest neighbor queries[A]. Proc. of the Int. Conf. on Management of data[C] (1997)
4. Norbert Beckmann,Hans-Peter Kriegel,Ralf Schneider. The R*-tree:An Efficient and robust access method for points and tectangles[A].Proc.1990 ACM SIGMOD Int.Conf. management of Data[C].AtlanticCity,NJ (1990) 322-331
5. Stefan Berchtold, Daniel Keim,Hans-Peter Kriegel.The X-tree: An Index Structure for High-Dimensional Data.[A] Proc. of the 22nd Int. Conf. on Very Large Data Bases[C].Mumbai(Bombay):India (1996)
6. King-Ip Lin,H.V.Jagadish,Christos Faloutsos. The TV-tree:An index structure for high dimensional data[J]. VLDB, Vol, 3 (1994) 517-549
7. A. Henrich. The LSDh-tree: An access structure for feature vectors[A].Proc. 14th Int. Conf. Data Engineering[C] (1998) 362–369
8. Stefan Berchtold, Christian Bohm, Hans-Peter Kriegel. The Pyramid Technique: Towards Breaking the Curse of Dimensionality [A]. Proc. of the Int. Conf. on Management of Data [C]. ACM Press (1998)
9. Kaushik Chakrabarti,Sharad Mehrotra. The Hybrid Tree: An index structure for high dimensional feature spaces[A]. Proc. of the 15th Int. Conf. on Data Engineering[C] (1999) 440–447
10. Yasushi Sakurai, Masatoshi Yoshikawa, Shunsuke Uemura. The A-tree: An Index Structure for High-Dimensional Spaces Using Relative Approximation[A]. Proc. of the 26th Int.Conf. on Very Large Data Bases (VLDB'00)[C] (2000)
11. Roger Weber, Hans-J. Schek, Stefan Blott. A quantitative analysis and performance study for similarity-search methods in high-dimensional spaces[A]. Proc. of the 24th Int. Conf. on Very Large Data Bases (VLDB'98)[C]. NewYork, USA (1998) 194–205
12. Paolo Caicca,Marco Patella. Approximate similarity queries:a survey[R].University of Bologna,Italy (2001)

13. Christo Faloutsos,King-Ip Lin. Fastmap:a fast algorithm for indexing,data mining,and visualization of traditional and multimedia database[A]. Sigmod Record,Proc.'95 ACM SIGMOD Int.Conf.on Management of data[C] (1995)

14. Cui Yu, Stephane Bressan, Beng Chin Ooi. Querying high dimensional data in single dimensional space[J]. VLDB Journal (2002)

15. Stefan Berchtold, Christian Bohm, H. V. Jagadish.Independent quantization: An index compression technique for high-dimensional data spaces[A].Proc. of the 16th Int.Conf. on Data Engineering (ICDE'00)[C]. San Diego,USA (2000)577–588

16. Guang-Ho Cha,Chin-Wan Chung.The GC-tree: a high dimensional index structure for similarity in image databases[J]. IEEE Transactions on multimedia, vol,4 (2002)

17. Peng Wu,B. S. Manjunath. An Adaptive Index Structure for Similarity Search in Large Image Databases[A]. Proceedings of SPIE [C].Vol. 4519 (2001)

18. Hankan Ferhatosmanoglu,Ertrem Tuncel,Divyakant Agrawal.Vector approximation based indexing for non-Uniform high dimensional data sets[A]. ACM International Conf. on Information and Knowledge Management [C] (2000)

19. Guang-Ho Cha, Xiaoming Zhu, Dragutin Petkovic.An Efficient Indexing Method for Nearest Neighbor Searches in High-Dimensional Image Databases[J].IEEE Transactions on multimedia, Vol, 4 (2002)

20. Hutflesz, A., H.W. Six, P. Widmayer .Globally order preserving multidimensional linear hashing[A]. Proc. 4th IEEE Int. Conf. on Data Eng.[C] (1988) 572-579

21. Ooi, B.C. Efficient Query Processing in Geographic Information Systems. Number 471 in LNCS. Berlin/Heidelberg/New York (1990)

22. Oosterom P. Reactive Data Structures for GIS. Ph.D. thesis, University of Leiden, The Netherlands (1990)

23. Seeger B..Performance comparison of segment access methods implemented on top of buddy tree[A]. Advanced in Spatial Databases[C]. Number 525 in LNCS, Berlin/Heidelberg/New York (1991) 277-296

24. Kamel I.,C. Faloustsos. Hilbert R-tree: An improved R-tree using fractals[A].Proc. 20th Int. Conf. On Very Large Data Bases[C] (1994)500-509

25. GaedeV., O. Günther. Survey on Multidimensional Access Method[R]. Department of Economics and Business Administration, Humboldt University Berlin, revised version (1997)

26. Jianling Xu, Baihua Zheng, Wang-Chien Lee, Dik Lun Lee. The D-Tree:An Index Structure for Planar Point Queries in Location-Based Wireless Services. IEEE Transactions on Knowledge and Data Engineering. Vol.16 (2004) 1526-1542

27. Gang Qian, Qiang Zhu, Qiang Xue, Sakti Pramanik. The ND-Tree: A Dynamic Indexing Technique for Multidimensional Non-ordered Discrete Data Spaces. In: Proceedings of the 29th VLDB Conference, Berlin, Germany (2003)

28. Guojun Lu. Techniques and Data Structures for Efficient Multimedia Retrieval Based on similarity. IEEE Transactions on Multimedia, vol.3 (2002) 372-384

Document Similarity Search Based on Generic Summaries

Xiaojun Wan and Jianwu Yang

Institute of Computer Science and Technology,
Peking University, Beijing 100871, China
{wanxiaojun, yangjianwu}@icst.pku.edu.cn

Abstract. Document similarity search is to find documents similar to a query document in a text corpus and return a ranked list of documents to users, which is widely used in recommender systems in library or web applications. The popular approach to similarity search is to calculate the similarities between the query document and documents in the corpus and then rank the documents. In this paper, we investigate the use of document summarization techniques to improve the effectiveness of document similarity search. In the proposed summary-based approach, the query document is summarized and similarity searches are performed with the new query of the produced summary instead of the original document. Different retrieval models and different summarization methods are investigated in the experiments. Experimental results demonstrate the higher effectiveness of the summary-based similarity search.

1 Introduction

Document similarity search is to find documents similar to a query document in a text corpus and return a ranked list of documents to users. The typical kind of similarity search is K nearest neighbor search, namely K-NN search, which is to find K documents most similar to the query document. Similarity search is widely used in recommender systems in library or web applications. For example, *Google* can perform an advanced search with "related" option to find similar web pages with a user-specified web page and *CiteSeer.IST* provides a list of similar papers with the currently browsed paper.

Document similarity search is in fact a text retrieval process with a long query. In current search engines, the queries users input are usually short and include only a few keywords. The popular retrieval models used in current IR systems include the Okapi BM25 function (abbr. Okapi), the Smart's vector space model with length normalization (abbr. Smart) and the standard Cosine measure (abbr. Cosine), among which the standard Cosine measure is considered as the best model for document similarity search because of its good ability to measure the similarity between two documents.

When the query is short and contains only several words, search engines can handle this kind of search effectively, as shown in popular web search engines (e.g. *Google*, *MSN Search*, etc.) and full-text search engines (e.g. *Lucene*, etc.). While for document similarity search, the query is a full document consisting of hundreds of

G.G. Lee et al. (Eds.): AIRS 2005, LNCS 3689, pp. 635–640, 2005.
© Springer-Verlag Berlin Heidelberg 2005

words. Long query (i.e. full document) contains more redundant and ambiguous information and even greater noise effects stemmed from the presence of a large number of words unrelated to the overall topic in the document. This observation might deteriorate the retrieval effectiveness and this kind of search might not be handled well by current search engines.

A well known method for improving the quality of similarity search in text is to transform the original data space into a new small concept space and perform similarity search in this new space. Brants and Stolle [2] use Probabilistic Latent Semantic Analysis to find similar documents in a small corpus of 1,321 texts. But this process is based on SVD in linear algebra and is time-consuming. The large amount of documents cannot be indexed effectively through this process. Aggarwal and Yu [1] provide conceptual search among documents by creating a representation in terms of conceptual word-chains which contain sets of closely correlated words. The document indexing and searching are all based on the conceptual space. However, the conceptual space (i.e. a set of conceptual word-chains) needs to be created beforehand based on a given text corpus, which is inefficient and inapplicable in real domains.

In this paper, we investigate the use of document summarization techniques to improve document similarity search. The query document is summarized and similarity searches are performed with the new summary-based query instead of the original document-based query. A generic summary of a document should contain the main topics of the document while keeping redundancy to a minimum, which is expected to reduce noisy information in the query and improve the retrieval effectiveness. In the experiments, we compare two approaches for similarity search, i.e. similarity search based on documents and similarity search based on summaries. We explore the influences of different retrieval models and different summarization methods. Experimental results show that the Cosine measure is indeed the best model for both document-based similarity search and summary-based similarity search, and a high-quality-summary-based similarity search can improve the search effectiveness. On the other hand, document similarity search can be considered as an extrinsic task for evaluating text summaries.

The rest of this paper is organized as follows: Summarization techniques are described in Section 2. Experiments are performed and results are analyzed in Section 3. Lastly, we present our conclusion in Section 4.

2   Generic Summarization Techniques

A generic summary should contain the overall topic of the document and convey the most "important" information within the document. Recent studies have investigated the usefulness of generic summaries for several particular tasks, such as document indexing in information retrieval [6], term selection in relevance feedback [5], text categorization [4], etc. We employ simple extraction-based summarization methods in this paper. Extraction-based methods usually assign each sentence a score based on different features and then rank the sentences in the document.

Four summarization methods are employed in the experiments:

1. Lead Method: It takes the first sentences in the document as the summary.

2. Frequency & Position-based Method: The sentences in the document are ranked by their scores calculated based on a linear combination of the following two feature weights and top sentences are taken to form the summary.

1) TF*IDF. The weight of a sentence is calculated as the sum of the weights of words in the sentence. The weight of a word in the sentence is calculated based on *tf*idf* method. If a word appears in the title of the document, its weight is promoted.

$$W_{TF*IDF}(s) = \sum_w tf(w) * idf(w) = \sum_w tf(w) * (1 + \log(N/n(w))),\qquad(1)$$

where *tf(w)* is the normalized frequency of word w in the document. If the word w appears in the title of the document, the value of *tf(w)* is doubled. N is the number of documents in the collection and $n(w)$ is the number of documents in which the word w exists.

2) Sentence Position. The leading several sentences of a document are usually important and so we calculate for each sentence a weight reflecting its position priority as follows:

$$W_{position}(s) = 1 - \frac{i-1}{n},\qquad(2)$$

where i is the sequence of the sentence s and n is the total number of sentences in the document. Obviously, i ranges from 1 to n.

After all the above weights are calculated for each sentence, we sum all the weights and get the overall score for the sentence as follows:

$$W(s) = \alpha * W_{TF*IDF}(s) + \beta * W_{position}(s),\qquad(3)$$

where α, β are parameters reflecting the importance of different features and in the experiments $\alpha = 0.3$, $\beta = 0.7$.

3. MMR-based Method: Sentences are ranked by the maximal marginal relevance (MMR) method [3], which strives to maximize relevant novelty in summarization. A sentence is selected into the summary as follows:

$$MMR \underset{def}{=} Arg \max_{s_i \in D \setminus S} \left[\lambda(sim_1(s_i, q) - (1 - \lambda) \max_{s_j \in S} sim_2(s_i, s_j)) \right],\qquad(4)$$

where q is a query representation; D is the set of sentences in the document; S is the set of sentences in the summary, which is a sub set of D; $D \setminus S$ is the set difference, i.e. the set of as yet unselected sentences in D; sim_1 is the similarity metric for calculating the similarity between the query q and a sentence s_i. sim_2 is the similarity metric for calculating the similarity between two sentences s_i and s_j. λ is a weighting parameter.

In the experiments, we use top 20 words with the largest *tf*idf* values in the document as the query representation. The similarity metrics sim1 and sim2 are the standard Cosine measure and the parameter λ is set to 0.7. The terms are weighted by *tf*idf* value.

4. Hierarchical Method: This method is composed of two steps: First the frequency & position-based method is employed to select a few candidate sentences. Then the MMR-based method is employed to re-rank the candidate sentences and top sentences are selected to form the summary. The second step is considered as a redundancy removing process.

Note that the length of summary is an important parameter to be appropriately set in the experiments. The length of summary will directly influence the retrieval efficiency. In the following experiments, the summaries are 100-words long. The number of candidate sentences for the hierarchical method is set to 12.

3 Experiments

3.1 Experimental Setup

In the experiments, we explore the use of different kinds of summaries for document similarity search based on different retrieval models. The three retrieval models include the standard Cosine model and the popular Okapi model and the Smart model. The four summarization methods described in Section 2 are employed for similarity search respectively and their corresponding performance is compared. The baseline run is the traditional document-based similarity search. Each query is compared with the documents in the collection and a ranked list of 200 documents.

To perform the experiments, a ground truth data set is required. We build the ground truth data set from the TDT-3 corpus, which has been used for evaluation of the task of topic detection and tracking (TDT) in 1999 and 2000. 120 topics are defined and about 9, 000 stories are annotated over these topics with an "on-topic" table presenting all stories explicitly marked as relevant to a given topic. According to the specification of TDT, the on-topic stories within the same topic are relevant. Stories within a topic are similar to each other and stories across different topics are dissimilar to each other. After removing the stories written in Chinese, we use 50 topics as a test set, while the others are used as a training set. For each topic, the first document is considered as the query and all other within-topic documents are considered as the answer documents. For each query, a ranked list of 200 documents is returned.

We use typical 10-NN search and 20-NN search for evaluation in our experiments. The evaluation metric for K-NN search is the precision in the retrieved K documents, which is defined as follows:

$$P = \frac{|C \cap R|}{|R|}, \tag{5}$$

where R is the set of retrieved K documents, and C is the set of similar documents defined above for a given query document. The precision is calculated for each query and then the values are averaged across all queries.

3.2 Experimental Results

Table 1 shows the precision values for document-based similarity searches with different retrieval models, which are the baseline results. It can be observed from Table

1 that the Cosine retrieval model outperforms the other two models, which validates the fact that the Cosine model is the best model for document similarity search.

Table 1. K-NN precisions for document-based similarity search (baseline)

Retrieval Model	10-NN Precision	20-NN Precision
Cosine	0.630	0.530
Smart	0.586	0.481
Okapi	0.594	0.474

Table 2. K-NN precisions for summary-based similarity search

Retrieval Model	Summarization Method	10-NN Precision	20-NN Precision
Cosine	Lead	0.614	0.523
	Frequency & Position-based	0.628	0.534
	MMR-based	0.632	0.524
	Hierarchical	**0.648**	**0.539**
Smart	Lead	0.586	0.496
	Frequency & Position-based	0.596	0.503
	MMR-based	0.602	0.509
	Hierarchical	**0.629**	**0.520**
Okapi	Lead	0.592	0.491
	Frequency & Position-based	0.598	0.490
	MMR-based	0.598	0.496
	Hierarchical	**0.602**	**0.498**

The precision values for the proposed summary-based similarity searches are demonstrated in Table 2. Different retrieval models and different summarization methods are compared. Given a retrieval model, different summaries have different influences on the retrieval effectiveness. The following comparisons are performed based on the same retrieval models. The lead baseline summaries usually get the worst results, which are worse than the corresponding results of the baseline document-based similarity searches based on the Cosine model and the Okapi model. The frequency & position-based summaries and MMR-based summaries achieve almost the same performance, which is either the same as or a little better than the performance for the corresponding baseline document-based similarity searches. The hierarchical summaries always achieve the best performance for all retrieval models, which is better than the performance for the corresponding baseline document-based similarity searches.

We can summarize that the summary-based similarity search does improve the performance only if the summaries are of high quality, regardless whatever the retrieval model is. A high-quality summary is able to reduce the redundant and ambiguous information in the query document and make the query more concise and indicative, so as to improve the search performance. In fact, the frequency & position-based summarization method may produce summaries with redundant sentences and the MMR-based summarization method may produce summaries with some sentences unrelated to the overall topic, while the hierarchical summarization method both focuses on the overall topic of the document and diversifies the sentences in the summary. In the similarity search task, the hierarchical summarization method is proved to be able to produce high-quality summaries.

4 Conclusion

In this paper, we have explored the use of document summarization techniques for document similarity search. The proposed summary-based similarity search can improve the search effectiveness. We will consider extracting salient words as pseudo-summary for similarity search in future work.

References

1. Aggarwal, C. C., Yu, P. S.: On effective conceptual indexing and similarity search in text data. In Proceedings of the 2001 IEEE International Conference on Data Mining, San Jose, California, USA (2001) 3-10
2. Brants, T., Stolle, R.: Finding similar documents in document collections. In Proceedings of the Third International Conference on Language Resources and Evaluation (LREC-2002), Workshop on Using Semantics for Information Retrieval and Filtering, Las Palmas, Spain (2002)
3. Carbonell, J., Goldstein, J.: The Use of MMR, Diversity-based Reranking for Reordering Documents and Producing Summaries. In Proceedings of the 21st Annual International ACM SIGIR Conference on Research and Development in Information Retrieval (1998) 335-336
4. Kolcz, A., Prabakarmurthi, V., Kalita, J.: Summarization as feature selection for text categorization. In Proceedings of the Tenth International Conference on Information and Knowledge Management (2001) 365-370
5. Lam-Adesina, A. M., Jones, G. J. F.: Applying summarization techniques for term selection in relevance feedback. In Proceedings of the 24th Annual International ACM SIGIR Conference on Research and Development in Information Retrieval (2001) 1-9
6. Sakai, T., Jones, K. S.: Generic summaries for indexing in information retrieval. In Proceedings of the 24th Annual International ACM SIGIR Conference on Research and Development in Information Retrieval (2001) 190-198

KNM: A Novel Intelligent User Interface for Webpage Navigation*

Shiguang Liu[1], Hua-Jun Zeng[2], Zheng Chen[2], Chuangbai Xiao[1],
and Wei-Ying Ma[2]

[1] College of Computer Science and Technology, Beijing University of Technology,
Chaoyang District, Beijing, 100022, P.R. China
martinliu@emails.bjut.edu.cn
cbxiao@bjut.edu.cn
[2] Microsoft Research Asia, 49 Zhichun Road, Haidian District,Beijing, 100080, P.R. China
{hjzeng, zhengc, wyma}@microsoft.com

Abstract. In order to help readers grasp key information from web pages within limited time, a novel intelligent user interface for webpage navigation: Keyphrase Navigation Map (KNM) is proposed in this paper, which presents a map to the readers, assisting them to navigate their webpage. First, the key phrases are generated from the webpage and ranked by the keyphrase extraction engine, then they are clustered by keyphrase relevancy, and finally they are shown on the thumbnail according to their relative coordinates in the full page. The usability test proves that the KNM which presents an overview of the corresponding web page to readers can really help them to find information they are interested in effectively.

1 Introduction

With the explosion of the amount of web pages, readers do not have enough time to navigate the full page but they do not want to lose key information in them either. Automatic text summarization [6], which can extract the key phrases or sentences from the webpage, has become an effective tool to solve such a problem. Recently, Some research works of summarization are on how to organize the key phrases extracted from the webpage in order to make them better assist reader navigation [1],[4]. Many research works are on how to present and organize the location information of the text in document, such as scrollbar [2], and profileskim [3] etc. Therefore, we believe that the positions of the key phrases in a page are rather significant for readers to search their interested information. And We propose a novel user interface called the Keyphrase Navigation Map (KNM) in order to help readers understand the result generated by automatic summarization system.

The inspiration of designing KNM is from the overview map in some battle computer games, such as Ages of Empires. The overview map of the game can help player rapidly realize the runtime development of enemy and friend army, and it can also

---

* This work is done at Microsoft Research Asia.

G.G. Lee et al. (Eds.): AIRS 2005, LNCS 3689, pp. 641–646, 2005.
© Springer-Verlag Berlin Heidelberg 2005

help player control his army out of the main window. From this idea, to construct a keyphrase map is a good way to present the position information of keyphrase to readers (see Fig. 1). The map can be pasted with a background of the thumbnail of the original webpage, and the keyphrase tags are located on the map according to its relative position in the original webpage. The reader can select his/her interested keyphrase by virtue of the position of the keyphrase in the page and the background thumbnail. From the map readers can build an overview of the webpage content not only from keyphrase itself but also from keyphrase positions and the background. In essence, the KNM which lets reader participate in the selec-tion of the results of summarization, is a trade-off between time and accuracy.

Fig. 1. This is the user interface of the KNM. The left sub-window is the normal web browser, while the right smaller window is used to display the navigation map.

2   The Structure of KNM

The architecture graph of KNM is shown in Fig. 2. The beginning of data flow is Webpage, and the end of the flow is readers' browser. The core components of KNM are three engines: (1) KEX engine, which is the main engine of them, can extract the keyphrases from the webpage by statistical method. KEX engine can not only extract keyphrases but also rank these keyphrases by their score. (2) Cluster Engine, which clusters the keyphrases by phrase relevancy into several topical groups. The phrases relevancy is determined not only by the component words of the phrases but also the position information of phrase. (3) Map Engine, which receives the clustered keyphrases and position of the phrases, draws the salient keyphrases from the topical group on the thumbnail in suitable position.

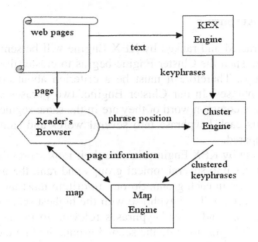

Fig. 2. The architecture graph of KNM

3 Algorithms

3.1 Kex

Keyphrase Extraction is a task in which a set of words or phrases are extracted from a given webpage, which are most indicative of the content of the webpage. There are three components in the Keyphrase Extraction algorithm:

(1) Webpage content acquisition. Keyphrase extraction algorithm directly works on the structuralized data. However, webpage is not structuralized, so it needs to transform it from unstructured to structure. First, a text parser is applied to extract some useful information from webpage, including page title, meta descriptions, hyperlinks, as well as page content, including font size, color and style. At the same time, a simple text preprocessing module is applied to tokenize the full-text feature into a bag of words, as well as stop-word removal and word stemming [5].

(2) Keyphrases generation. This component is to generate candidate keyphrases based on the information which has been obtained from the component of Webpage content acquisition. The candidate keywords can be generated from four sources: (1) Statistical Keyphrases Extractor (2) Query-log based Extractor (3) Structure-based Extractor (4) Title and keyphrases in metadata. Several different informative features are synchronously generated with the candidate keyword in each source.

(3) Ranking. A Candidate Key Phrase Set (CKS) consists of all selected Keywords or phrases from the above four sources. In our KEX, there are 10 features used to describe each candidate keyphrase. We could use a single formula to combine the 10 features and calculate a salience score for each candidate key phrase. We utilize training data to learn a Linear Regression model.

3.2 Clustering of Keyphrase

The keyphrases extracted and ranked by KEX Engine will be sent to Cluster Engine with their hot score. Then the Cluster Engine begins to cluster those keyphrases into several topical groups. Therefore it must be a criterion about how to evaluate the relevancy between phrases. In our Cluster Engine, two phrases are relevant if two phrases have the same common word or they are in the same segment of the webpage. Cluster Engine splits each keyphrase into several words and stems [5] these words before they are compared.

Each keyphrase sent by KEX Engine all have their rank scores. The Cluster Engine is to cluster keyphrases into several topical groups and rank the groups according to the scores of keyphrases in each group. So our algorithm must take the rank order of the keyphrases into account. The keyphrase with the highest score must be in the first keyphrase topical group, and other keyphrases relevant to the keyphrase are added into the group. Then it begins to build the second group, the first element added to the group is the keyphrase which has the highest score in the set of key-phrases have not been added to other groups.

3.3 Keyphrase Position

Because the more frequently the phrase appears in the webpage the more probability it become a keyphrase. Therefore, the unique position of each keyphrase must be configured before clustering and displaying. It is obvious that the KNM needs to select the most representative position for each keyphrase. The strategy in KNM is : if the keyphrase appears in the title of a webpage or segment, the postion of the title will be selected as the Representative Position(RP) of the keyphrase; if the keyphrases occurs in title twice or above, then compare the times of keyphrase occurrence in each segment, the higher one will be selected as RP of the keyphrases; if there is no title containing the keyphrase, then it will select the position of the segment of which the keyphrase occurrence is the highest as the RP of the keyphrase. If the absolute RP of the keyphrase in webpage is (x_0 , y_0), the width and height of the webpage are W_D and H_D , the width and height of the map are W_M and H_M, then the relative position of is: $(\dfrac{x_0 W_M}{W_D} , \dfrac{y_0 H_M}{H_D})$.

4 Protoype and Experiments

In order to testify the feasibility of KNM, we build a prototype system of KNM on English webpage navigation. The initial user interface of KNM is shown in the Fig. 1. For example, when the KNM navigates the portal website of BUC, the sub-window of web browser will display the webpage but it won't display the full web page because of the limited size of the browser window. Then the Navigation Map in the right sub-window will display the thumbnail of the full page and some key-phrases tags after keyphrases extraction and clustering. The Fig. 3 is an enlarged picture of the Navigation Map. There are four keyphrase tags shown in the Fig. 3 namely, "undergrad", "campus", "student", "prospective students". These keyphrases are the salient keyphrases of each topical group. The KNM selects four or five groups to display on the thumbnail according to their precise phrase position and each topic always contains not more than 5 keyphrases because the keyphrases tag will be easily overlapped if there are too many keyphrases displayed at the same time. Then readers can select their interesting topic keyphrases. Fig. 4 displays the three keyphrases tags ("current students", "prospective students", "international students") in the same group when reader clicks the keyphrase tag "prospective students" in the Fig. 3. When readers click the "back" below the map in the Fig 4, the map will trace back to the Fig 3 in order to help readers navigate the keyphrases of other groups.

Fig. 3. The Navigation Map   **Fig. 4.** Three Keyphrases in the Same Group

Usability test is regarded as a key step in user-centered design. There are 20 college participants (consists of 7 male and 13 female English Department students) in the usability test of KNM. The 20 participants use three different interfaces of web navigation to navigate 10 webpages selected from web randomly: (1) the web browser without any summarization (NB); (2) Keyphrases Navigation List (KNL), which does not contain the navigation map, and the keyphrases are arranged as a phrases list by their keyphrase salience score; (3) Keyphrases Navigation Map (KNM).

Each time when a participant finishes reading a webpage, he or she will be asked to give a score to the inter-face he or she just has used in navigating the webpage. The score is from 1 to 5, and the more the better. From the Fig. 5, it is obvious that the average score of the KNM is better than that of the KNL, and this result proves that the position information given by the map can indeed help readers understand the keyphrases by summarization more effectively. And we also find that the average score of the KNM and KNL are better than that of NB, which proves that the KEX algorithm is workable. Further study the rating result of KNM, we find that the KNM will work more effectively when it navigates the webpage with long text segment than that of Homepage.

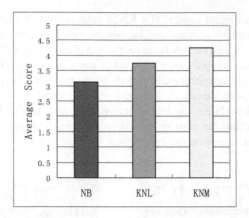

Fig. 5. The result of the usability test

5   Conclusion and Future Work

In this paper, a novel model of user interface: Keyphrase Navigation Map(KNM) is proposed. The KNM is mainly composed of KEX engine, Cluster engine and Map engine. The usability test proves that the KNM which presents an overview of the corresponding web page to readers can really help them to find information they are interested in effectively.For the future work of the KNM, we plan to do further research on the key-phrase position selection, we want to know whether showing double or more position of the keyphrase can give reader more information when the keyphrase appeared in the webpage twice or more needs future research; and we also plan to add zooming support to our present user interface.

References

1. Boguraev, B., Kennedy, C., Bellamy, R., Brawer, S.,Wong. : Dynamic Presentation of Webpage Content for Rapid On-Line Skimming. Spring Symposium, AAAI, 1998.
2. Byrd,D.: A scrollbar-based visualization for webpage navigation. Proceedings of the fourth ACM conference on Digital libraries, 1999.
3. Harper, D.J., Koychev, I., Sun Y., Pirie I.: Within-webpage Retrieval: A User-Centred Evaluation of Relevance Profiling. Information Retrieval, Kluwer Academic Publishers.Issue: Volume 7, Numbers 3-4. 2004 .Pages: 265 – 290.
4. Lam, H. , Baudisch, P.: Summary Thumbnails: Readable Overviews for Small Screen Web Browsers. In Proceedings of CHI 2005, Portland, OR, 2005, pp. 681-690.
5. Porter M.F. : An algorithm for suffix stripping. Program 1980.
6. Witten, I.H., Paynter,G.W., Frank, E.: KEA: practical automatic keyphrase extraction. Proceedings of the fourth ACM conference on Digital libraries, August 1999.

Towards Construction of Evaluation Framework for Query Expansion

Masaharu Yoshioka

Graduate School of Information Science and Technology, Hokkaido University,
N-14 W-9, Kita-ku, Sapporo 060-0814, Japan
yoshioka@ist.hokudai.ac.jp

Abstract. Query expansion is an important technique for achieving higher retrieval performance. However, a good framework for evaluating this technique in isolation does not exist because the effect of query expansion depends on the quality of the initial query. Feature quantities that characterize the quality of the initial query are defined in this study. Correlations between these quantities and retrieval performance were analyzed using the NTCIR-4 web test collection.

1 Introduction

It is very difficult for many users of Information Retrieval (IR) utilities to select appropriate query terms for representing the information need. Because query terms are often imprecise and inappropriate, the documents selected may contain only some of the query words and be irrelevant to the user's needs.

To reduce the mismatch between query terms and information need, many IR systems use query expansion techniques to find better query terms. However, the effectiveness of a query expansion technique depends on the quality of query terms in the initial query. Cronen-Townsend et al. [1] used a query clarity score based on a language model for deciding if the query terms contain enough relevant information for the query expansion; this approach was shown to be effective.

The Reliable Information Access (RIA) Workshop [2] conducted a failure analysis [3] for a set of topics using seven different, popular IR systems, and proposed a topic categorization based on the types of failures that they encountered. They also conducted a relevance feedback experiment using a different IR system [4]. This study, however, did not examine the relationship between topic difficulty based on the mismatch and the effect of relevance feedback. Because the relevance feedback technique is used for reducing the mismatch between the initial query and information need, it is important to determine the effectiveness of relevance feedback when used with query expansion.

In this study, various statistical features were selected for evaluating topic difficulty, and the correlations between these features and the effectiveness of retrieval performance were investigated. A retrieval experiment with different relevance feedback settings was conducted to select statistical features that were

G.G. Lee et al. (Eds.): AIRS 2005, LNCS 3689, pp. 647–652, 2005.

good representations of topic difficulty. The NTCIR-4 web test collection [5] was used with our IR system [6] in this experiment.

2   Estimating Mismatch Between Query Terms and Information Need

2.1   Feature Quantities for Predicting Topic Difficulty

There are two approaches for evaluating the difficulty of a query defined for the test collection. One is human evaluation using the topic description, and the other is a statistical evaluation based on the distribution of the topic terms in the documents.

In TREC-6, Voorhees et al. [7] analyzed topic difficulty based on topic descriptions. However, they could not find a good correlation between human-defined difficulties and difficulties for IR systems. BMIR-J2 is a human evaluation approach that uses function-based topic categorization. [8]. This categorization is similar to the categorization from failure analysis used in [3]. However, Eguchi et al.[9] could not show a significant correlation between these categories and topic difficulties using NTCIR-1 test collection [10].

Because the human evaluation approach fails to predict topic difficulties, the statistical evaluation approach is used for defining topic difficulty. Cronen-Townsend et al. [1] proposed a query clarity score that predicts query performance. This score is based on language modeling for IR and has weak correlation with the average of IDF(Inverted-Document Frequency). Eguchi et al.[9] analyzed the correlations between topic difficulty and various statistical measures of the query terms in a document database and average of document frequency correlate with topic difficulty.

2.2   Feature Quantities for Estimating Mismatch Between Query Terms and Information Need

The previous section briefly reviewed research on predicting topic difficulty. However, previous research was primarily focused on evaluating topic difficulties using the given set of topic query terms and the their frequency in an entire document database.

The objective of this study is to evaluate topic difficulty using the mismatch between the query terms and the user's information need. However, it is difficult to estimate this using only the information in the query terms. The information in a set of relevant documents is a resource used to estimate what information is needed. Comparisons between those documents and the query terms are useful for estimating the mismatch between query terms and information need.

In order to estimate this mismatch, a Boolean IR model was used to define a set of feature quantities. To simplify the feature quantities, simple Boolean queries that consisted of sets of terms and sets of "or" terms combined with the "and" operator of the form (A and (B or C)), were employed.

First, I must define some variables and functions.

$topic_i, andSet_{ij}, relevant_i, allDoc$ a Boolean formula for i-th topic , j-th "or" Boolean formula in "and" Boolean formula in i-th topic, a set of relevant documents for i-th topic, a set of all documents, respectively (e.g., when $topic_i =$ (A and (B or C)), $andSet_{i1} =$ (A), $andSet_{i2} =$ (B or C)).

$Select(aBooleanFormula, aDocSet)$ A set of documents that satisfies a Boolean formula ($aBooleanFormula$) from a given document set ($aDocSet$).

$SizeOf(aDocSet)$ A number of documents in a given document set (aDocSet)

$Coverage(aBooleanFormula, aDocSet)$
$= SizeOf(Select(aBooleanFormula, aDocSet))/SizeOf(aDocSet)$
A ratio between the number of documents that satisfies a Boolean formula ($aBooleanFormula$) from a given document set ($aDocSet$) and a number of documents in a given document set ($aDocSet$).

Each topic was evaluated with the following feature quantities.

$$Candidate_i = SizeOf(topic_i, allDoc)$$
$$Relevant_i = SizeOf(relevant_i)$$
$$CoverageRel_i = Coverage(topic_i, relevant_i)$$
$$FocusAppropriateness_i = \frac{SizeOf(Select(topic_i, relevant_i))}{Candidate_i}$$
$$CoverageRelMax_i = max\{Coverage(andSet_{ij}, relevant_i)|j \in J_i\}$$
$$CoverageRelMin_i = min\{Coverage(andSet_{ij}, relevant_i)|j \in J_i\}$$
$$CoverageRelAvg_i = \sum_{j \in J_i} Coverage(andSet_{ij}, relevant_i)/|J_i|$$

J_i is a set of integer between 1 to a number of and set in i-th Boolean formula. The characteristics of proposed quantities are as follows.

$CoverageRel_i$ and $FocusAppropriateness_i$ represent the appropriateness of a Boolean formula from the view point of recall and precision respectively. When the user constructs an appropriate Boolean formula to represent their information need, $CoverageRel_i$ and $FocusAppropriateness_i$ equals 1.0. Values of $CoverageRel_i$ less than 1.0 mean that there are alternative terms for representing the information need. Ones of $FocusAppropriateness_i$ less than 1.0 mean that constraints is not good at excluding irrelevant documents.

$CoverageRelMax_i, CoverageRelAvg_i, CoverageRelMin_i$ decomposes the characteristics of $CoverageRel_i$ into each term or set of "or" terms. $CoverageRelMax_i$, and $CoverageRelAvg_i$ represent the possibility of finding relevant documents by using partial matching. $CoverageRelMin_i$ represents the existence of a bad keyword that prevents exact matching.

3 Experiments

3.1 The IR System Used for the Experiments

Correlations between the feature quantities described above were determined using IR systems with different relevance feedback strategies.

The Appropriate Boolean query Reformulation for Information Retrieval (ABRIR) [6], combined the probabilistic IR model, Okapi [11], with a Boolean IR model. Because the ABRIR achieved the highest retrieval performance in NTCIR-4 Web retrieval task [5], it was used as a baseline system for evaluating topic difficulty.

The NTCIR-4 Web test collection [5] was also used. This collection consists of 100 GBytes of web documents from jp (Japan) domain web servers, with 35 survey topics and 45 target topics. The difference between the survey and the target types is the number of documents available. Because fewer target documents were used in the collection than survey documents, a retrieval task for target documents may miss more of the relevant documents than a task directed to survey documents. Therefore, only survey type topics were used for the experiment [1].

An expression similar to the query terms used in real Web search engines, <TITLE>, was used for the retrieval tests on the NTCIR-4 web test collection. <TITLE> has two or three terms coupled with Boolean operators.

The assessors for the NTCIR-4 web test scored documents as highly relevant (S), fairly relevant (A), partially relevant (B), or irrelevant (C) - the "Multi grade relevance" score. Both "S" and "A" documents were classified as relevant in the evaluation used in the experiments reported here.

Two IR experiments with different query expansion methods were conducted. Five pseudo-relevant documents were used in the first experiment for calculating the Okapi probability score. In the second experiment, in addition to the pseudo-relevance feedback from the first experiment, ABRIR selects 300 terms with higher significance in relevant documents from the first five pseudo-relevant documents retrieved (please refer to [6] for detail).

In each experiment, ABRIR retrieved up to 1000 documents for each topic and calculated the number that were relevant, the mean average precision and precision at rank 5 documents.

3.2   Results

Table 1 shows an overview of the experimental results (average of 34 topics: 3851 relevant documents in total). The results show that query expansion improves query performance. However, there are cases that query expansions deteriorate their performance. In order to analyze this deterioration, I assume it is necessary to take into account into account topic difficulty based on the mismatch between query terms and information.

The relationship between the feature quantities described in the previous section and the retrieval performance was evaluated by analyzing the correlations between those quantities and retrieval results for each topic.

Because the feature quantities do not have a normal distribution, Spearman's correlation coefficient by rank test was used for this analysis.

---

[1] Because some quantity variables cannot be calculated for the topic $Candidate_i = 0$ (topic 84), this topic is removed from the evaluation.

Table 1. Retrieval Results of the Experiments

	With Query Expansion	No Query Expansion
Retrieved Relevant Documents	2736	2383
MAP	0.258	0.177
Prec@5	0.406	0.300

Table 2. Spearman's Correlation Coefficient by Rank Test

	With Query Expansion			No Query Expansion		
	Retrieved	MAP	Prec@5	Retrieved	MAP	Prec@5
Candidate	-0.067	*-0.320*	*-0.359*	-0.105	*-0.320*	-0.176
Relevant	**0.927**	**0.557**	**0.610**	**0.899**	**0.464**	**0.675**
CoverageRel	0.024	-0.011	-0.186	0.027	0.025	0.049
FocusAppropriateness	**0.668**	**0.655**	**0.568**	**0.680**	**0.611**	**0.493**
CoverageRelMax	*-0.364*	*-0.311*	*-0.408*	*-0.312*	-0.210	*-0.305*
CoverageRelMin	0.046	0.040	-0.138	0.042	0.033	0.053
CoverageRelAvg	-0.126	-0.123	*-0.330*	-0.120	-0.060	-0.098

Table 2 shows the results of this analysis. Numbers in bold and italic face represent high correlations (larger than 0.3) and numbers in bold face represent correlations that are significant at the 0.01 level for the two-sided test.

This analysis shows that Relevant and FocusAppropriateness have higher correlation coefficients with query performance than other feature quantities. In almost cases, the absolute value of the correlation coefficient is larger for the query expansion than without the query expansion. The explanation for this result may be that these correlate with the quality of pseudo-relevant documents. The selection of good pseudo-relevant documents supports to select good query expansion terms.

CoverageRelMax has negative correlation coefficients with query performance and the absolute value of the correlation coefficient is larger for the query expansion than without the query expansion. This may imply initial query term (or "or" term sets) with higher CoverageRel is good enough to retrieve most of the relevant documents and expansion of the term may deteriorate retrieval performance.

4   Conclusions

In this paper, feature quantities were defined to characterize topic difficulty. These were used to analyze the mismatch between the query terms and information needed for topic difficulty. The correlations between these quantities and retrieval performance were obtained. This analysis confirmed that relationship between the relevant document set and document set that satisfies the initial Boolean query is useful for judging topic difficulty.

Future work should include failure analysis and an investigation into the relationships between this analysis and the proposed quantities to establish the evaluation framework for query expansion.

Acknowledgments

I thank the National Institute of Informatics (NII) for permission to use the NTCIR test collection. This research was partially supported by a Grant-in-Aid for Scientific Research on Priority 16016201 from the Ministry of Education, Culture, Sports, Science, and Technology, Japan.

References

1. Cronen-Townsend, S., Zhou, Y., Croft, W.B.: Predicting query performance. In: Proceedings of the 25th Annual International ACM SIGIR Conference on Research and Development in Information Retrieval. (2002) 299–306
2. Harman, D., Buckley, C.: Sigir 2004 workshop: Ria and "where can ir go from here?". SIGIR Forum **38** (2004) 45–49
3. Buckley, C.: Why current ir engines fail. In: SIGIR '04: Proceedings of the 27th annual international conference on Research and development in information retrieval, New York, NY, USA, ACM Press (2004) 584–585
4. Warren, R.H., Liu, T.: A review of relevance feedback experiments at the 2003 reliable information access (ria) workshop. In: SIGIR '04: Proceedings of the 27th annual international conference on Research and development in information retrieval, New York, NY, USA, ACM Press (2004) 570–571
5. Eguchi, K., Oyama, K., Aizawa, A., Ishikawa, H.: Overview of the informational retrieval task at ntcir-4 web. In: Working Notes of the Fourth NTCIR Workshop Meeting. (2004) http://research.nii.ac.jp/ntcir-ws4/NTCIR4-WN/WEB/NTCIR4WN-OV-WEB-A-EguchiK.pdf.
6. Yoshioka, M., Haraguchi, M.: Study on the combination of probabilistic and boolean ir models for www documents retrieval. In: Working Notes of the Fourth NTCIR Workshop Meeting, Supplement Volume. (2004) 9–16 http://research.nii.ac.jp/ntcir-ws4/NTCIR4-WN/WEB/NTCIR4WN-WEB-YoshiokaM.pdf.
7. Ellen Voorhees, D.H.: Overview of the Sixth Text REtrieval Conference (TREC-6). In: Proceedings of TREC-6. (1997) 1–24
8. Sekine, S., Isahara, H.: IREX: IR and IE evaluation-based project in japanese. In: Proceedings of the Language Resource and Evaluation Conference. (2000)
9. Eguchi, K., Kuriyama, K., Kando, N.: Sensitivity of ir systems evaluation to topic difficulty. In: Proceedings of the 3rd International Conference on Language Resources and Evaluation (LREC 2002). (2002) 585–589
10. Kando, N., Koyama, T., Oyama, K., Kageura, K., Yoshioka, M., Nozue, T., Matsumura, A., Kuriyama, K.: NTCIR : NACSIS test collection project. In: The 20th Annual Colloquium of BCS-IRSG. (1998)
11. Robertson, S.E., Walker, S.: Okapi/Keenbow at TREC-8. In: Proceedings of TREC-8. (2000) 151–162

An Efficient Incremental Nearest Neighbor Algorithm for Processing k-Nearest Neighbor Queries with Visal and Semantic Predicates in Multimedia Information Retrieval System*

Dong-Ho Lee[1] and Dong-Joo Park[2]

[1] Department of Computer Science and Engineering, Hanyang University,
Gyeonggi-Do 426-791, Korea
dhlee72@cse.hanyang.ac.kr

[2] School of Computing, Colleage of Information Science, Soongsil University,
Seoul 156-743, Korea
djpark@computing.ssu.ac.kr

Abstract. Recently, advanced multimedia applications, such as geographic information system, and content-based image/video retrieval system, require the efficient processing of k-nearest neighbor queries with semantic predicates as well as visual predicates. In this paper, we propose an integrated index structure, so-called SPY-TEC+, that provides an efficient method for indexing visual and semantic feature information at the same time using the SPY-TEC and the signature file. We also propose an efficient incremental nearest neighbor algorithm for processing the k-nearest neighbor queries with visual and semantic predicates on the SPY-TEC+.

1 Introduction

In recent years, most of current multimedia information retrieval systems have come to require the efficient process of k-nearest neighbor queries with visual and semantic properties as depicted in Fig. 1. This query, represented in an extended SQL language, is similar to Fagin's multimedia query (Artist = 'Beatles' $\wedge$ Color = 'red') [1], that means "retrieve k albums whose artist is Beatles

```
SELECT *
FROM DISC
WHERE Artist = 'Beatles'
ORDER BY distance(Color, red)
STOP AFTER k
```

Fig. 1. Example of the k-nearest neighbor query with visual and semantic predicate

---

* This work was supported by the research fund of Hanyang University(HY-2004).

G.G. Lee et al. (Eds.): AIRS 2005, LNCS 3689, pp. 653–658, 2005.

and cover colors best match red". It involves the semantic predicate (i.e., `Artist = 'Beatles'`) as well as the visual predicate (i.e., `distance(Color, red)`) that means the cover colors of albums having to be similar to red. In this query, the semantic predicate is represent by plain text, while the visual predicate is usually represent by a high-dimensional feature vector (e.g., color histogram). For processing it efficiently, it is necessary to browse through a collection of color vectors on the basis of their distances from a given query object `red`[1] until k query answers are obtained [2]. Up to date, Hjaltason and Samet's incremental nearest neighbor algorithm is know as the best choice [3].

Hjaltason and Samet's algorithm, using a hierarchical multidimensional index structure like the R-tree [4], has the following advantage: when the upper operator (e.g., the select operator for `Artist = 'Beatles'`) needs another tuple with the next neighbor, their algorithm can provide it for the upper operator without restarting the algorithm from scratch [3,5]. However, their algorithm may generate a large number of tuples that will turn out not to fulfill the remaining semantic predicates. In [2], to overcome this drawback, the authors proposed a new index structure, so-called the RS-tree, that is able to index the visual and semantic feature together by using the R-tree and the S-tree [6]. However, the R-tree used in the RS-tree does not perform sufficiently well on high-dimensional data spaces even though it provides good result on low-dimensional data spaces.

In this paper, we propose an efficient index structure, so-called SPY-TEC+, that integrates the S-tree and the SPY-TEC [5] which was proposed for indexing high-dimensional data. We also propose an efficient incremental nearest neighbor algorithm (hereinafter, called the *INNonSPY-TEC+*) for processing k-nearest neighbor queries with semantic predicates on the SPY-TEC+.

2   SPY-TEC+

The key idea of the SPY-TEC+ is based on the observation that the SPY-TEC will be better than the R-tree, as the underlying index structure for processing the k-nearest neighbor query with semantic predicates because the SPY-TEC provides a better performance than the R-tree in high-dimensional data spaces.

2.1   Structure of the SPY-TEC+

The SPY-TEC+ is a hybrid of the SPY-TEC and the S-tree that are used as data structures for the visual attribute and the semantic attribute, respectively. Fig. 2 shows the construction of the SPY-TEC+ from the `DISC` table with both `Color` and `Artist` attributes. Fig. 2(b) shows a signature table for `Artist`. And, Fig. 2(c) shows the structure where several d-dimensional feature vectors for `Color` are distributed by the partitioning strategy of the SPY-TEC. Fig. 2(d) is the structure of the SPY-TEC+ for indexing `Color` and `Artist` attributes at the same time. The left tree of Fig. 2(d) shows the structure of the B$^+$-tree

---

[1] Although it really means a d-dimensional feature vector for red color, we use this in the same context.

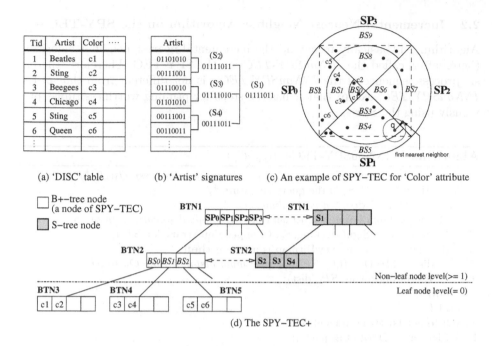

(a) 'DISC' table   (b) 'Artist' signatures   (c) An example of SPY–TEC for 'Color' attribute

(d) The SPY–TEC+

Fig. 2. The Construction of the SPY-TEC+

for the SPY-TEC, while the right tree shows the structure of the S-tree for the signature table. The S-tree has a hierarchical index structure similar to the B^+-tree, and its node and entries are symmetric with those of the B^+-tree in the SPY-TEC. Each node of the S-tree contains an array of (*key, pointer*) entries where *key* is a signature (representing a set value) which bounds all the semantic values in the subtree pointed at by *pointer*.

The construction of the S-tree is classified into two types according to the level of the S-tree, i.e., $l = 1$ and $l > 1$. In case where $l = 1$, a signature of each entry in the S-tree node is created by superimposing (ORing) [7] all the signature of the semantic values in the subtree of its corresponding B^+-tree entry. For example, in Fig. 2(d), the S-tree node STN2 corresponds to BTN2, and the entry S_2 in STN2 corresponds to BS_0 that is the entry of BTN2. The signature for S_2 is created as follows: Since the subtree of BS_0 (i.e., BTN3) contains c1 and c2, the generator of the S-tree first gets the semantic values of the Artist attributes 'Beatles', 'Sting' for c1 and c2, and then generates their signatures (i.e., 01101010 for 'Beatles' and 00111001 for 'Sting') using a signature hashing function. Finally, the generator creates the signature for S_2, that is 01111011, by superimposing these two signatures on a bit-by-bit basis. At the higher level than 1, a signature of each entry in the S-tree node is created by superimposing all the signatures in the child node pointed at by *pointer*. For example, the signature for S_1 in STN1 is created by just superimposing all the signatures (i.e., S_2, S_3, and S_4) in its child node (i.e., STN2).

2.2   Incremental Nearest Neighbor Algorithm on the SPY-TEC+

Algorithm 1 is basically to extend the incremental nearest neighbor algorithm (hereinafter, called the *INNonSPY-TEC*) on the SPY-TEC. Therefore, the basic process sequence of the *INNonSPY-TEC+* is not different from that of the *INNonSPY-TEC*, except that it has the steps for pruning worthless tuples previously using the S-tree.

Algorithm 1. INNonSPY-TEC+ (Q_v, Q_s)

   /* Q_v and Q_s denote a visual and semantic query value, respectively */
1: S_q = Hash(Q_s); /* S_q is the query signature */
2: **for** i = 0 **to** 2d-1 **do** /* d is the dimension */
   /* ChoppedSignArray is filled with the $f(l)$ chopped signatures in the S-tree */
3:    NewBitmap = SignChecking(S_q, ChoppedSignArrary for SP_i);
4:    **if** at least one bit in NewBitmap is not zero **then**
5:       dist = MINDIST(Q_v, SP_i); /* minimum distance from Q_v to SP_i */
6:       ENQUEUE(queue, SP_i, dist);
7:    **end if**
8: **end for**
9: **while** not ISEMPTY(queue) **do**
10:   Element = DEQUEUE(queue);
11:   **if** Element is a spherical pyramid **then**
12:      **for** each bounding slice in a spherical pyramid **do**
13:         NewBitmap = SignChecking(S_q, ChoppedSignArray for BS_l);
14:         **if** at least one bit in NewBitmap is not zero **then**
15:            dist = MINDIST(Q_v, BS_l);
16:            ENQUEUE(queue, BS_l, dist);
17:         **end if**
18:      **end for**
19:   **else if** Element is a bounding slice **then**
20:      **for** each object in a bounding slice **do**
21:         **if** the semantic value of a object equal to Q_s **then**
22:            dist = Dist_Query_to_Obj(Q_v, object);
23:            ENQUEUE(queue, object, dist);
24:         **end if**
25:      **end for**
26:   **else** /* Element is a object */
27:      Report an element as the next nearest object;
28:   **end if**
29: **end while**

In the *INNonSPY-TEC*, the distances of each spherical pyramid from the query point are first calculated, and each spherical pyramid with its distance are inserted into the priority queue. However, in the *INNonSPY-TEC+*, it is not necessary to calculate the distance between the query point and all of the spherical pyramids. Before calculating the distances from the query point to

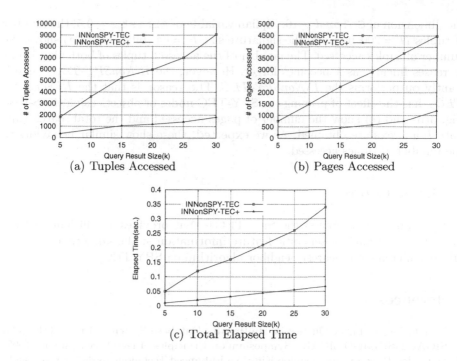

(a) Tuples Accessed   (b) Pages Accessed

(c) Total Elapsed Time

Fig. 3. Performances with varying the query result size

each spherical pyramid, it first performs the "inclusion test" for each signature in the S-tree nodes that correspond to the B^+-tree nodes for each spherical pyramid. And then, it calculates the distances between the query point and only the spherical pyramids whose corresponding signatures pass the signature checking, and enqueues them into the priority queue with their distance. Passing of the signature checking means that there may be some values equivalent to the semantic query value in the subtree rooted at the corresponding B^+-tree node. Lines $3 \sim 7$ of Algorithm 1 show these steps. Similarly, in lines $13 \sim 17$, the *INNonSPY-TEC+* performs the signature checking for each signature in the S-tree nodes that correspond to the B^+-tree nodes for each bounding slice. The other steps of Algorithm 1 are similar to those of *INNonSPY-TEC*.

3   Experimental Evaluation

For the experiments, we defined a simple DISC table that our test queries are performed over and have a simple schema (i.e., DISC(Artist, Color)).

For semantic attributes, we generated only synthetic datasets from Zipfian distribution [7] with the Zipfian value $z = 0.5$. As visual attributes, we used 16-dimensional Fourier points used in a CAD-model, which correspond to feature vectors of Color. Fig 3 shows the performance of the two algorithms for different query result sizes (i.e., $k = 5 \sim 30$) with the following experimental parameters:

the dimension of Color $d = 16$, Zipfian variable of Artist $z = 0.5$, the number of tuples $N = 200,000$, and the signature size $F = 64$ (bits). Fig. 3(a) shows the number of tuples accessed. The number of the accessed tuples of both algorithms increases linearly as k becomes larger. However, the *INNonSPY-TEC+* significantly outperforms the *INNonSPY-TEC*. The reason is that the *INNonSPY-TEC+* has the effect of pruning the SPY-TEC nodes or objects using the S-tree. Fig. 3(b) and (c) show the number of pages accessed and the total search time until k answers are obtained. As we expected, these show similar behaviors to the number of tuples accessed.

4   Conclusions

In this paper, we proposed the SPY-TEC+ that provides an efficient method for indexing visual and semantic feature information at the same time, and the efficient incremental nearest neighbor algorithm on SPY-TEC+.

References

1. Ronald Fagin: Fuzzy Queries in Multimedia Database Systems. Proc. 16th ACM SIGACT-SIGMOD-SIGART Symposium on Principles of Database Systems (1998)
2. Dong-Joo Park and Hyoung-Joo Kim: An Enhanced Technique for k-Nearest Neighbor Queries with Non-spatial Selection Predicates. Multimedia Tools and Applications **19** (2003) 79–103
3. G. R. Hjaltason and H. Samet: Distance Browsing in Spatial Databases. ACM Transaction on Database Systems **24** (1999) 265–318
4. A. Guttman: R-trees: A Dynamic Index Structure for Spatial Searching. Proc. ACM SIGMOD Int. Conf. on Management of Data (1984) 47–57
5. Dong-Ho Lee and Hyoung-Joo Kim: An Efficient Technique for Nearest-Neighbor Query Processing on the SPY-TEC. IEEE Transactions on Knowledge and Data Engineering **15** (2003) 1472–1486
6. U. Deppisch: S-Tree: A Dynamic Balanced Signature Index for Office Retrieval. Proc. of the ACM Conf. on Research and Development in Information Retrieval (1986) 77–87
7. C. Faloutsos and S. Christodoulakis: Optimal Signature Extraction and Information Loss. ACM Transaction on Database Systems **12** (1987)

Generating Term Transliterations Using Contextual Information and Validating Generated Results Using Web Corpora

Jin-Shea Kuo

Chung-Hwa Telecommunication Laboratories, Taiwan
jskuo@cht.com.tw

Abstract. Transliterating foreign entities into Chinese is usually done through direct-style approach. The direct-style approach transliterates each syllable rendered from foreign terms into Chinese directly. Not every syllable can be rendered. An approach utilizing contextual information for term transliteration is proposed in this paper to attack this problem. Traditionally, evaluating transliteration performances always uses character and word error rates. However, many transliteration variants of the same term always found. Validating the generated results using Web corpora is more suitable and is proposed in this paper. Using the proposed evaluation method, experiments on term transliteration were conducted. From the experimental results show that taking contextual information is helpful to term transliteration and validating the generated results using Web corpora can provide more concrete evidences to transliteration evaluation.

1 Introduction

Machine transliteration plays an important role in machine translation, cross-language information retrieval and named entity recognition. Term transliteration in machine transliteration addresses the problem of converting terms in one language into their phonetic equivalents in the target language via spoken form using character or phonetic units. Many papers work on transliterating foreign terms into Chinese [1][5][6][7][8]. [1] and [5] are two typical works on this issue using phoneme-based and character-based approaches, respectively.

Gao [1] used a direct transliteration model for transliterating out-of-vocabulary foreign names. A statistical learning algorithm was used to generate basic pronunciation units from 1,500 cognate pairs. These units consisting of chunks of phonemes do not always compose of meaningful combinations of consonants or vowels. This will result in high possibilities of data loss in finding suitable units in transliteration. Li [5] proposed an n-gram direct orthographical mapping for converting basic pronunciation units in English characters into Chinese counterparts. This model uses character-based syllables as units and does not involve any letter-to-phoneme

G.G. Lee et al. (Eds.): AIRS 2005, LNCS 3689, pp. 659–665, 2005.
© Springer-Verlag Berlin Heidelberg 2005

system. The problem of this model is it requires a very large training corpus to mitigate the data sparseness problem. For example, "knew" and "new" may be pronounced the same. They have the same pronunciation units in phoneme level, but have ones in character level. This will also result in losses of finding mapping units in term transliteration.

To overcome the data sparseness problem, a huge training corpus may be used to achieve this goal. Such a huge corpus may not always available. An approach using phonemes is proposed in this paper to alleviate this problem. Firstly, using phoneme information can reduce the combinations of different terms with the same phonemes. Secondly, combining both syllables and sub-syllables can compose of almost all the syllable-based pronunciation units. In transliteration, when the syllable-based units are not available, the sub-syllable-based units can be used to generate candidates of syllables. Generally, using syllables can achieve a higher precision in mapping basic units. This is similar to use n-gram as index terms in information retrieval. "Information Retrieval" in a document implies "Information" and "Retrieval" in that document; however, "Information" and "Retrieval" in a document does not imply "information retrieval" in that document.

Character and word error rates are always used to evaluate their performances [1][5][7]. Evaluating the transliteration performances using these criteria does not reflect the real usages of transliterations. For example, if the standard transliteration to the source term "Smith" is "史密斯" (shi-mi-si). "時宓思" (shi-mi-si) may be a better transliteration than "使密斯" (shi-mi-si) even if the character error rate of "時宓思" is higher than that of "使密斯". In addition to that, a foreign term may be transliterated into Chinese in various forms. For example, the "Bush" of "the President Bush" may be rendered into "布希 (bu-xi)", "布殊 (bu-shu)" and "布什 (bu-she)" in Taiwan, Hong-Kong and Mainland China, respectively [1]. Taking these regional transliteration variants into account will be helpful to boost the performances of term transliteration and cross-language information retrieval. Therefore, an evaluation method taking the real cases of transliterations into consideration using Web corpora is proposed to measure transliteration performances.

The remainder of the paper is organized as follows. Section 2 describes the proposed approach. Experimental results are presented in Section 3. Conclusions are drawn in Section 4.

2   The Proposed Approach

In transliteration, terms need to be decomposed into basic pronunciation units. Then, basic units are aligned and converted cross-linguistically. Finally, a transliteration model using contextual information is proposed to incorporate the variations in pronunciations or characters. From the extraction results reported in [4], some of the isolated pronunciation units, such as /r/ and /l/, may be elided in transliteration. Therefore, contextual information is used to boost the performance of transliteration.

A simple text-based syllabification algorithm for English terms is available in the literature [8]. This algorithm is applied to letters to convert letters into phonemes on the fly using heuristic mapping rules. EM algorithm has been used widely in alignment and obtaining basic pronunciation units [1][5]; however, not all the chunks of phonemes consist of basic linguistic components. A letter-to-sound system using machine-learning techniques can reduce complicated combinations of characters to a limited set of phonemes; therefore, each foreign term can be converted into phonemes using such a system in this paper. The phoneme-based syllabification approach used here is very similar to the classic one described in [2]. Traditionally, an English syllable is composed of an initial consonant cluster followed by a vowel and with the option of a final consonant cluster. However, in order to converting English syllables into Chinese syllables, all consonants in the final consonant cluster are then segmented into isolated consonants. Such a syllable may be viewed as the basic pronunciation unit in transliteration. Combining syllable and sub-syllable information can alleviate data sparseness and hence achieve a better performance.

From an analysis on our training corpus shows that 70% of cognate pairs are with equal syllable numbers. This feature can be utilized to align basic units. Firstly, the alignment the basic pronunciation units of English and Chinese terms can be generated by adopting equal syllable numbers. Then the obtained statistical information can then be used to align other cognate pairs with unequal syllable numbers. Correspondences between basic pronunciation units of English and Chinese terms are shown in Table 1. One point worthy of noting is that some isolated syllables may or may not be elided from training corpus. For example, the /er/ in "Carlo" is elided when the term is rendered into Chinese; on the other hand, the /er/ is "Carson" has been reserved. Another point also observed is that two the same syllables may be transliterated into different targets. For example, "Ca"s in "Carlo" and "Carson" have been mapped to /ka/ and /ke/, depending on neighboring syllables, respectively.

Table 1. The syllable correspondences between English and Chinese terms

English Terms	English Phonemes	Chinese Terms	Chinese Syllables
Carlo	/ka/ /er/ /lo/	柯羅	/ke/ /-/ /luo/
Carson	/ka/ /er/ /son/	卡爾森	/ka/ /er/ /sen/

One of the most important factors that affect term transliteration is pronunciation variation. Pronunciation variation is a phenomenon of pronunciation ambiguity. Some phonemes in source language terms may be pronounced swiftly, quietly or strongly in many different situations according to speakers' speaking habits. Elision is one of the important problems. For example, elision is quite common in English speech. /t/ and /d/ are often elided before consonants or when they are parts of a sequence of two or three consonants. Another type of isolated pronunciation units, such as /l/ of "boulder", may or may not be transliterated into Chinese depending on the translators.

A generative framework using finite state-machine has been proposed for English-Japanese term transliteration [3]. This learning algorithm decomposed the transliteration process into many subsystems. Each subsystem can perform a transformation independently. Following this framework, suppose that the possible transliterated-token pair is denoted by $\hat{J} = (\check{S}, \check{T})$ to indicate that there is a transliteration equivalent, $\check{T}$, in target language with the largest probability can be selected for each token $\check{S}$ in the source language. Each $\hat{J}$ can be determined by means of equation (1).

$$\hat{J} \approx \arg\max_{W_t} p(H_s^i \mid W_s^i) p(H_t \mid H_s^i) p(W_t \mid H_t) , \tag{1}$$

where H_s^i and H_t are phonemes converted from terms in source language and target language, respectively. If an existing source language letter-to-sound system is used and in order to simplify the explanation, let the target language phoneme-to-text conversion be deterministic, then the cross-linguistic phoneme-to-phoneme conversion is the main focus in this algorithm. Taking the elision of isolated unit into considera-

tion, the source language syllables, $H_s^i = \{(H_s^{i11},...,H_s^{i1n_1}),...,(H_s^{iU1},...,H_s^{iUn_U})\}$, may

contain of many different combinations in which isolated syllables may or may not be silent in transliteration. There are k syllables and U sub-sets of syllables in H_s^i in total and the items in each sub-set are sorted in descending order in indexes. Each sub-set of the source-language syllables is a basic unit used to transliterate into a term in the target language. The syllable-to-syllable probability then can be estimated by a set of context-dependent syllables trained from the transliteration lexicon directly. The main focus of equation (1) can be expressed by means of equation (2):

$$\arg\max_{H_t} p(H_t \mid H_s^i) \tag{2}$$

$$\approx \arg\max_{H_t^j H_s^{iu}} \prod_{w=1}^{M_{iu}} (p(H_t^{jw} \mid H_s^{i(m-1)}, H_s^{im}, H_s^{i(m+1)}) + \varepsilon),$$

where $M_{iu} = \left| H^{iu} \right|$ is the window size of each sub-set and m is the absolute syllable index of w in H_s^i and ε is a very small constant used to avoid any zero probability. A null syllable is attached for the cases of those syllables at the beginning and end of the pronunciation units.

3 Experimental Results

The fast growing Internet is one of the largest distributed databases in the world. Though the World Wide Web is not systematically organized, much invaluable information can be obtained from this huge text corpus. A large quantity of transliteration terms have been devised personally and used on the Web. For example, "Paxton" can be transliterated into "派克司頓 (pai-ke-si-dun)", "派克斯頓 (pai-ke-si-dun)", "帕士頓 (pa-shi-dun)", "派斯頓 (pai-si-dun)" and "佩斯頓 (pei-si-dun)". Most of these terms have not been registered to be transliterated terms of the source term in the dictionary. This information can be used to evaluate the transliteration performances.

If a cognate pair can be found on the Internet with sufficiently large instances meaning that the transliteration can be regarded as correct. Two formal definitions are given to evaluate the transliteration performances. The first one defines what a possible cognate pair is when incorporating pronunciation variation. Those cognate pairs verified according to the first definition are then validated by the second procedure. The second one defines the automatic validation proposed in this paper.

Definition 1. A cognate pair generated by a transliteration process is qualified if $|t|/|s| > m$, where m is a dynamically determined threshold, $|s|$ is the number of the syllabified basic pronunciation units of the source language term and $|t|$ is the characters of the transliterated terms.

Definition 2. A transliteration term, t, can be validated to be a correct cognate of the source language term, s, if the co-occurrences, $f(s, t)$, of this cognate pair exceed some specified threshold in a sentence on text snippets obtained from search engines.

According to the above criteria, four different approaches using phoneme-based direct transliteration with language model (PDTM-LM), syllable-based direct transliteration model with language model (SDTM-LM), direct orthography-based model (DOM) and the proposed approach, context-based model (CM), are compared. The training data composed of about 30,000 cognate pairs are used in the experiment. Many terms in source language are not originating from English in this corpus. The test data set is composed of one hundred entries selecting the least popular fifty girls' names and fifty boys' names from the USA top-1000 popular baby names[1]. Names in this data set are not frequently used as that of top-ten ones in the list. They may have chances to be found on the Web. If a name is used too frequently, it has a chance to be collected and registered in a lexicon.

Table 2. The occurrences of cognate pairs larger at least 3 times and 2 (the gray part) using the proposed evaluation approach

Methods	1-best	3-best	5-best	10-best	1-best	3-best	5-best	10-best
PDTM-LM	1	1	2	3	5	17	21	43
SDTM-LM	6	12	13	16	10	25	40	65
DOM	6	10	13	22	8	19	30	58
CM	6	12	21	32	13	27	42	70

[1] http://www.socialsecurity.gov/OACT/babynames/

The results of the top-one, top-three, top-five and top-ten transliterations generated by transliteration systems are validated and shown in Table 2 with instances at least three times and. For those cognate pairs co-occur only once in a sentence cannot be viewed as qualified because the instances are too small within top-100 snippets in a query. From the experimental results show the context-model (CM) achieved a better result than others on the average.

Several points can be observed from the experimental results. DOM achieves a relatively good performance with only slightly worse than that of syllable-based approaches. Examining the basic units required in the transliteration, it discloses that most of the character-based basic units can be found; however some complex cases such combinations of one consonant cluster and one vowel cluster haves higher possibilities of being able to lose. These cases impact the transliteration performance. The performance achieved by phoneme-based direct transliteration model is worse than those syllable-based models. The reason is that converting a syllable cross-linguistically is easier and precisely than mapping the combinations generated from a group of sub-syllables, although, syllable-based approaches have problems in obtaining sufficiently large syllables without huge training data. The main reason that the proposed approach achieved a better performance than the syllable-based direct transliteration model is because sub-syllable information can be used when any syllable unit is not available. The other reason is taking the elision of isolated syllables into account.

4 Conclusions

A syllable-based model utilizing contextual information and combining different levels of phoneme information for term transliteration is proposed in this paper. Experiments on term transliteration using phoneme-based and character-based direct transliteration approaches and the proposed approach were also conducted. Using an objective evaluation method, which in turn utilizing Web corpora can reflect the term usages of the real world, the results achieved by different methods are evaluated. The experimental results showed that taking contextual information into account is helpful to term transliteration and validating the generated results using Web corpora can provide more concrete evidences to transliteration evaluation.

References

1. Gao, W., K. F. Wong and W. Lam 2004, Phoneme-based Transliteration of Foreign Names for OOV Problem, In *Proceedings of 1st International Joint Chinese Natural Language Processing*, pp. 374-381, Hainan, China.
2. Jurafsky, D. and J. H. Martin 2000, Speech and Language Processing, pp. 102-120, Prentice-Hall, New Jersey.
3. Knight, K. and J. Graehl 1998, Machine Transliteration, Computational Linguistics, Vol. 24, No. 4, pp. 599-612.

4. Kuo, J. S. and Y. K. Yang 2005 Incorporating Pronunciation Variation into Extraction of Transliterated-term Pairs from Web Corpora, In *Proceedings of International Conference on Chinese Computing*, pp. 131-138, Singapore.
5. Li, Haizhou, M. Zhang and J. Su 2004, A Joint Source-Channel Model for Machine Transliteration, In *Proceedings of 42nd ACL*, pp. 159-166, Barcelona, Spain.
6. Meng, H., W. K. Lo, B. Chen and K. Tang 2001 Generating Phonetic Cognates to Handle Named Entities in English-Chinese Cross-Language Spoken Document Retrieval, In *Proceedings of the Automatic Speech Recognition and Understanding Workshop*, pp. 311-314.
7. Virga, P. and S. Khudanpur 2003 Transliteration of Proper Names in Cross-Lingual Information Retrieval, In *Proceedings of 41st ACL Workshop on Multilingual and Mixed Language Named Entity Recognition*, pp57-64.
8. Wan, S. and C. M. Verspoor 1998 Automatic English-Chinese Name Transliteration for Development of Multilingual Resources, In *Proceedings of 17th COLING and 36th ACL*, pp.1352-1356, Montreal Quebec, Canada.

Handling Orthographic Varieties in Japanese IR: Fusion of Word-, N-Gram-, and Yomi-Based Indices Across Different Document Collections

Nina Kummer[1,2], Christa Womser-Hacker[1], and Noriko Kando[2]

[1] Universität Hildesheim, Germany
[2] National Institute of Informatics, Tokyo, Japan
{nina, kando}@nii.ac.jp
womser@uni-hildesheim.de

Abstract. Orthographic varieties are common in the Japanese language and represent a serious problem for Japanese information retrieval (IR), as IR systems run the risk of missing documents that contain variant forms of the search term. We propose two different strategies for handling orthographic varieties: pronunciation or yomi-based indexing and "Fuzzy Querying", comparing katakana terms based on edit distance. Both strategies were integrated into our multiple index and fusion system [1] and tested using two different test collections, newspaper articles (Mainichi Shimbun '98) and scientific abstracts (NTCIR-1), to compare their performance across text genres.

1 Introduction

A serious problem in Japanese IR, although rarely discussed outside the major difficulty of correct word segmentation, is the high degree of orthographic variety in the Japanese language. Traditional IR systems, which compare terms according to their written representation, run the risk of missing documents that contain variant forms of search terms.

One possible solution for the automatic handling of orthographic variety would be lexicon-based disambiguation, as suggested by Halpern [2, 3]. However, a disambiguation dictionary is costly to compile and requires constant maintenance, as the language is evolving quickly. Therefore, we argue that a more flexible strategy for automatic handling of orthographic varieties is needed.

2 Background

2.1 Orthographic Variety in the Japanese Language

Owing to the combined usage of four different scripts within one writing system (kanji, hiragana, katakana, and Roman characters), orthographic variety is very frequent in the Japanese language. The most common forms of orthographic varieties comprise cross-script variants (words which can be represented in different scripts), okurigana

G.G. Lee et al. (Eds.): AIRS 2005, LNCS 3689, pp. 666 – 672, 2005.

variants (differing in the number of syllables expressed in hiragana in addition to a kanji stem), hiragana variants (irregularities in the use of hiragana), kanji variants, phonetic substitutes, and katakana variants. A comprehensive overview of the types of orthographic variety can be found in Halpern [2] and Kummer et al. [4].

From the information retrieval point of view, we can classify orthographic varieties in Japanese into two groups:

1. Variants originating from a different written representation of the same phoneme (cross-script variants, okurigana variants, hiragana variants, kanji variants, and phonetic substitutes).
2. Variants originating from a different interpretation of the sound structure to be represented (katakana variants).

Variants in the first group share the same pronunciation. This fact can be exploited for information retrieval, if the terms are matched using their pronunciation instead of their written representation. Variants of the second type only differ in minor aspects, i.e. usually only one character. We suppose that matching terms based on their editing distance may be an effective means of retrieving documents that contain katakana variants of a search term.

2.2 Yomi-Based Indexing

Yomi-, or pronunciation-based, indexing is not a new strategy for use in Japanese IR. In contrast, it is a rather old technique, which used to be employed before the introduction of double-byte processing on computers, when information processing systems used the katakana syllabary to represent Japanese text phonetically. The yomi-based index has been abandoned since the introduction of double-byte character handling, as the Japanese language is very rich in homophones and the kanji characters convey important information for disambiguation.

Although a yomi-based index may incur losses in precision through ambiguous homophones, we suppose that it may be valuable for the handling of orthographic varieties. The advantage of a pronunciation-based index is that it is insensitive to orthographic variants (*e.g.*, okurigana, kanji, or kana variants), as it is independent from the written form of a word. Fusion with other index types may help to reduce the negative influence of ambiguous homophones.

2.3 Fuzzy Querying for Katakana Terms

As our basic retrieval engine, we used the open source IR library Lucene, which is licensed by Apache Software (http://lucene.apache.org). Lucene offers a query option denoted as "FuzzyQuery", which matches terms similar to a specified term. If a query term is defined as "fuzzy", the similarity between terms in the index and a specified target term is determined using the Levenshtein distance algorithm. The edit distance affects the scoring, such that terms with lower edit distances are scored higher. Equation 1 shows how the FuzzyQuery distance is calculated [5]. The variable "targetlen" refers to the length of the target term.

$$1 - \frac{dis \tan ce}{\min(textlen, t \arg etlen)} \tag{1}$$

We decided to use Fuzzy Querying for katakana terms to determine if it could prove helpful for the handling of katakana variants. Fuzzy Querying was implemented with a word-based index and added to our fusion approach as a fourth system.

2.4 Fusion in Japanese IR

The evaluations of the NTCIR Workshop series have not produced a clearly superior indexing approach, but rather, show systems performing equally well using very different indexing approaches. The two basic approaches are word-based indexing, which requires Natural Language Processing (NLP) techniques, and N-gram indexing, which is language independent. Both strategies lead to similar results, but their effectiveness varies case-by-case [6, 7]. To take maximum advantage of the strengths of the individual approaches, while at the same time minimizing their disadvantages, a number of enhanced approaches have been suggested. Among these are the "combination-of-evidence", or fusion approaches. These approaches merge the result lists obtained using more than one index type, usually by coupling word-based and N-gram-based indices. The results show that ranking documents based on a multiple index search is a promising strategy in Japanese information retrieval [8, 9, 10].

Jones *et al.* [8] used coupled word-based and character-based indexing, and found that the use of a combination showed marginally better results. Sakai *et al.* [9] employed character-based and morpheme-based matching to avoid matching problems caused by nonexplicit word boundaries. Vines and Wilkinson [10] tried several different indexing strategies (*e.g.*, character-based, word-based, and bi-gram-based with unsegmented English strings), and subsequently combined the two best approaches: words without English, and bi-grams without English, obtaining an improvement of 1.2 percentage points in the average precision. The document score was calculated using the simple formula of $sim_{new} = 0.5 \cdot sim_1 + 0.5 \cdot sim_2$.

3 Methods

3.1 Test Collections

Our experiments were carried out using two different test collections in order to compare the effectiveness of our approach across text genres. We chose part of the NTCIR-4 collection, the Mainichi Shimbun articles from 1998, as an example of a rather standardized collection. Major news companies, including Mainichi Shimbun, have strict usage guidelines concerning vocabulary and orthography for contributors. The second test corpus used was the NTCIR-1 collection of scientific abstracts. About half the documents were from the fields of electronic engineering and computer sciences, where new concepts are created frequently and rapidly, and the terminology is mostly borrowed from English. The frequency of katakana terms is therefore much higher than in the newspaper test collection (14.5% in the NTCIR-1 collection versus 10.0% in the Mainichi '98 collection). Additionally, we expected more variation in vocabulary and orthography in this collection because of the heterogeneity of the authorship.

Search requests were generated from all fields of the topic descriptions, *e.g.* title, description, narrative, and concept. For the experiments with the newspaper genre, we used the 46 NTCIR-4 topics with more than five relevant documents in the Mainichi '98 collection. For the experiments with the NTCIR-1 collection, we used the official test Topics 31 to 83. The calculation of the average precision for each run was based on the relaxed relevance judgments provided by the NTCIR-1 and NTCIR-4 workshops, respectively.

3.2 Indices

Three different indices were created: a bi-gram-based index, a word-based index, and a yomi-based index. For the bi-gram-based index, the hiragana characters were discarded, the katakana and roman character strings were left in their original forms, and the kanji character strings were divided into overlapping bi-grams. The morphological analysis for the word- and yomi-based indices was carried out using the Japanese morphological analyzer ChaSen (http://chasen.aist-nara.ac.jp/hiki/ChaSen/). Out-of-vocabulary words, *i.e.* words not recognized by ChaSen, were divided into bi-grams. This can be called a hybrid approach [11, 12]. For the yomi-based index, in the case of more than one suggested reading for a term, the readings were indexed as separate terms (*e.g.*, ナマモノ and セイブツ for 生物). Stoplists were used to discard the most frequent terms per index type and per collection.

3.3 Fusion Strategy

To determine the influence of the yomi-based index on the retrieval effectiveness, we carried out experiments using a triple index: word-based, bi-gram-based, and yomi-based, and added Fuzzy Querying as a fourth system. After initial test runs to determine the performance of the individual systems, we adapted their weights manually to obtain an optimum fusion result. The fusion strategy we adopted was Z-Score, which was successfully employed by Savoy [13] in the NTCIR-4 data, and yielded the best results in our earlier study [14].

Z-score fusion allows for a normalized linear combination of the search results. The contribution of the individual systems is controlled using a weight represented by the parameter α (*see*. Equation 2).

$$Z-ScoreRSV_k = \alpha \cdot \left[\frac{RSV_k - Mean^i}{Stdev^i} + \delta \right] \qquad \delta = \frac{Mean^i - Stdev^i}{Stdev^i} \qquad (2)$$

Key: RSV = "Retrieval Status Value", i.e., the score assigned to a retrieved document.

4 Results

4.1 Performance of the Individual Systems

As a first step, we evaluated the performance of our four individual systems for both document collections. Table 1 shows the mean average precision (MAP) per system.

Table 1. The MAP obtained using the individual systems

	Mainichi '98	NTCIR-1
Yomi-based index	.3707	.2776
Word-based index	.3634	.2775
N-gram-based index	.3819	.3072
Fuzzyword Querying	.3572	.2392

The marked difference in retrieval performance across the two collections is probably owing to the fact that our system had originally been designed to handle newspaper articles. However, we can observe the same order of performance for the four individual systems. The best-performing system in both cases was the bi-gram-based approach. Surprisingly, the yomi-based approach slightly outperformed the word-based approach for both collections.

Fuzzy Querying clearly performs the worst. However, we found a number of cases where Fuzzy Querying clearly outperformed the other approaches. An analysis of the NTCIR-4 Topic 54 used with the Mainichi'98 collection revealed that one of the katakana query terms was ファイバ (faiba = fiber). However, the index contained only its variant ファイバ− (faibaa). The variant was contained in 407 abstracts, 96 titles, and 203 keyword fields, while not a single document contained the original search term.

4.2 Performance of Fusion Runs

For our fusion experiments, we first carried out a test run, assigning the same basic weight of unity to each of the indices. We then manually tuned the weights, using the heuristic that indices that performed better in the single runs should be assigned a higher weight. It turned out, however, that the best performance for both test collections was yielded by the non-tuned runs. Tables 2 and 3 show the percentage improvement reached in the fusion runs relative to the best single run, the single bi-gram-based system. Results marked with "*" are statistically significant (T-Test, confidence level = 95%). Comparing the fusion runs with the best single run helps to see how much increase in retrieval performance can be achieved with fusion at the cost of having several indices and taking longer time for query processing.

The results show that the additional yomi-based index leads to a significant improvement in retrieval effectiveness over the single bi-gram-based index using the NTCIR-1 collection of scientific abstracts. It also led to an increase in the MAP using the Mainichi '98 collection. However, this increase was not significant. The precision can be improved further by adding Fuzzy Querying as a fourth system.

Table 2. The MAP of the fusion runs (NTCIR-1 collection)

Weights				Avg. Prec.	Improvement
N	W	Y	fW		
1	1	0	0	.3094	0.71%
1	1	1	0	.3276*	6.64%
3	1	1	0	.3193*	3.93%
2	1	1	0	.3230*	5.14%
1	1	1	1	.3278*	6.69%
3	3	3	2	.3278*	6.68%

Table 3. The MAP of the fusion runs (Mainichi '98 collection)

Weights				Avg. Prec.	Improvement
N	W	Y	fW		
1	1	0	0	.3798	–0.56%
1	1	1	0	.3947	3.35%
3	1	2	0	.3910	2.38%
2	1	1	0	.3899	2.11%
1	1	1	1	.3953	3.50%
3	3	3	2	.3952	3.50%

Key: N=N-gram-based index, W=word-based index, Y=yomi-based index, fW=fuzzy word

5 Conclusion

We tested two strategies for the handling of orthographic varieties in Japanese: yomi-based indexing, and Fuzzy Querying. Integrating a yomi-based index system and merging the results obtained with a bi-gram-based, a word-based, and the yomi-based system led to a significant improvement in precision for the NTCIR-1 collection of scientific abstracts, and to a slight improvement in precision for the Mainichi Shimbun '98 collection. Fuzzy Querying was not effective as a single approach. However, it led to a minor improvement of precision within our fusion system.

References

[1] Womser-Hacker, Christa (2005): An Information Retrieval Prototype for Research and Teaching. To appear in: Eibl, Maximilian; Wolff, Christian; Womser-Hacker, Christa (eds.): Designing Information Systems. Festschrift für Jürgen Krause. Konstanz: Universitätsverlag [Schriften zur Informationswissenschaft].

[2] Halpern, Jack (2002): Lexicon-Based Orthographic Disambiguation in CJK Intelligent Information Retrieval. In: Proceedings of the 19th Conference on Computational Linguistics, COLING-2002, August 24–September 1, 2002, Taipei, Taiwan.

[3] Halpern, Jack (2000): The Challenges of Intelligent Japanese Searching. Working paper (www.cjk.org/cjk/joa/joapaper.htm), The CJK Dictionary Institute, Saitama, Japan, revised 2003.

[4] Kummer, Nina; Womser-Hacker, Christa and Kando, Noriko (2005): Handling Orthographic Varieties in Japanese Information Retrieval: Fusion of Word-, N-gram-, and Yomi-Based Indices across Different Document Collections. NII Technical Report.

[5] Gospodnetić, Otis and Hatcher, Eric (2004): Lucene in Action. Manning, Canada.

[6] Yoshioka, Masaharu; Kuriyama, Kazuo and Kando, Noriko (2002): Analysis of the Usage of Japanese Segmented Texts in NTCIR Workshop 2. In: Proceedings of the Second NTCIR Workshop on Research in Chinese and Japanese Text Retrieval and Text Summarization, National Institute of Informatics, Tokyo, Japan, pp. 291–296.

[7] Ozawa, Tomohiro; Yamamoto, Mikio; Umemura, Kyoji and Church, Kenneth W. (1999): Japanese Word Segmentation Using Similarity Measure for IR. In: Proceedings of the First NTCIR Workshop on Research in Japanese Text Retrieval and Term Recognition, August 30–September 1, 1999, Tokyo, Japan, pp. 89–96.

[8] Jones, Gareth J.F.; Sakai, Tetsuya; Kajiura, Masahiro and Sumita, Kazuo (1998): Experiments in Japanese Text Retrieval and Routing Using the NEAT System. In: Proceedings of the 21st Annual International ACM SIGIR Conference on Research and Development in Information Retrieval, Melbourne, Australia, pp 197–205.

[9] Sakai, Tetsuya; Shibazaki, Yasuyo; Suzuki, Masaru; Kajiura, Masahiro; Manabe, Toshihiko and Sumita, Kazuo (1999): Cross-Language Information Retrieval for NTCIR at Toshiba. In: Proceedings of the First NTCIR Workshop on Research in Japanese Text Retrieval and Term Recognition, August 30–September 1, 1999, Tokyo, Japan, pp. 137–144.

[10] Vines, Phil and Wilkinson, Ross (1999): Experiments with Japanese Text Retrieval Using mg. In: Proceedings of the First NTCIR Workshop on Research in Japanese Text Retrieval and Term Recognition, August 30–September 1, 1999, Tokyo, Japan, pp. 97–100.

[11] Chow, Ken C.W.; Luk, Robert W.P.; Wong, Kam-Fai and Kwok, Kui-Lam (2000): Hybrid Term Indexing for Different IR Models. In: Proceedings of the Fifth International Workshop on Information Retrieval with Asian Languages. Hong Kong, China, pp. 49–54.

[12] Luk, Robert W.P.; Wong, Kam-Fai & Kwok, Kui-Lam. (2001): Hybrid Term Indexing: An Evaluation. In: Proceedings of the Second NTCIR Workshop on Research in Chinese and Japanese Text Retrieval and Text Summarization, National Institute of Informatics, Tokyo, Japan, pp. 130–136.

[13] Savoy, Jacques (2004): Report on CLIR Task for the NTCIR-4 Evaluation Campaign. In: Proceedings of the Fourth NTCIR Workshop on Research in Information Retrieval, Automatic Text Summarization and Question Answering, pp.178-185.

[14] Kummer, Nina; Womser-Hacker, Christa and Kando, Noriko (2005): Re-Examination of Japanese Indexing: Fusion of Word-, N-gram- and Yomi-Based Indices. In: Proceedings of the 11th Annual Meeting of The Association for Natural Language Processing, March 14–18, 2005, University of Kagawa, Kagawa Prefecture, Japan, pp. 221-224.

A Term Weighting Approach for Text Categorization

Kyung-Chan Lee, Seung-Shik Kang, and Kwang-Soo Hahn

School of Computer Science, Kookmin University & AITrc, Seoul 136-702, Korea
{sskang, kshahn}@kookmin.ac.kr
http://nlp.kookmin.ac.kr/

Abstract. It is common that representative words in a document are identified and discriminated by their statistical distribution of their frequency statistics. We assume that evaluating the confidence measure of terms through content-based document analysis leads to a better performance than the parametric assumptions of the standard frequency-based method. In this paper, we propose a new approach of term weighting method that replaces the frequency-based probabilistic methods. Experiments on Naïve Bayesian classifiers showed that our approach achieved an improvement compared to the frequency-based method on each point of the evaluation.[1]

1 Introduction

The goal of text categorization is to classify the documents into a fixed number of predefined categories [1,2]. One of the most commonly investigated applications of text categorization is a topic spotting for news articles. Current researches on text categorization have been focused on the method of computation by classifier models and the extraction of learning features [3,4]. For classifier models, there are statistical approaches, machine learning approaches, and information retrieval techniques. As for the representation of categories and input documents, one of the basic assumptions in probabilistic model is that a set of terms frequently occurring in a document would be the representation of a document. Classifiers are represented in document vectors and the most significant feature of a classifier is a weighting value of terms in the category.

Probabilistic learning methods are the most dominant techniques to build a classifier. Basically, text categorization system estimates the generation probability of input document by the classifiers of pre-defined categories. The generation probability is calculated by the terms that are extracted from input document. Through the machine learning techniques like NB, SVM, kNN, and LLSF, the pre-classified documents are trained and the representative terms are selected for the classifiers. The standard approaches have so far been using a document representation in a word-based document vector together with frequency-based statistics [5,6,7].

A large number of classification models have been explored, together with feature selection and reduction [8,9,10]. Despite the numerous attempts to explore more so-

---

[1] This work was supported by the Korea Science and Engineering Foundation (KOSEF) through the Advanced Information Technology Research Center (AITrc).

G.G. Lee et al. (Eds.): AIRS 2005, LNCS 3689, pp. 673–678, 2005.

phisticated document representation techniques, the simple 'bag-of-words' assumption remained very popular. This assumption has been used to distinguish the categories together with the number of words that occur in training documents. As an effort to improve the performance of text categorization, feature distribution and topic difference factors have been explored. These approaches are to capture the discriminating capability of the classifiers [11,12].

One of the important issues of text categorization is to extract good terms and to est imate the term probabilities on the document. The first step to text categorization is to extract the classifiers from the documents, which typically are a sequence of words or terms. And then, classifiers are trained by categorization model. In statistical models, t erm frequency and inverse document frequency are used to calculate the weight value s of classifiers, and features are automatically trained by machine learning methods. F eature learning system is based on the terms and term frequencies. Because of the co mmon terms of high frequency, both *tf* and *idf* measure is combined as a weighting sc heme of the terms.

Though frequency-based term weighting is a common technique, it is not sufficient for the representation of the document. Also, in the text categorization problem, the ef forts to improve the performance of the categorization algorithm have a limitation on t he frequency-based weighting scheme. The standard frequency-based estimation of te rm probabilities may not the best solution of document representation and it would be better if more sophisticated document representation techniques are introduced. We fe el that making unwarranted parametric assumptions on standard frequency-based term weighting will not lead to better performance than the knowledge engineering approa ch. Furthermore, making prior assumptions about the similarity of documents is not w arranted either. In this paper, we give a further evidence to the usefulness of a more so phisticated text representation method, which is based on the content-based term weig hting with a smoothing technique, that we improved the accuracy of the text categoriz ation system.

2   Term Weighting Method

Naïve Bayesian(NB) classifier is to use the joint probabilities between terms and categories to determine categories for input documents. Naïve Bayesian model assumes that the conditional probability of a word is assumed to be independent from other words. We complement the weakness of the word independence assumption by combining term weighting method to estimate the probabilities of terms.

2.1   Term Weighting Algorithm

In general, the construction of a document vector depends on both term frequency and inverted document frequency. We introduced a content-based term weighting method for the Korean language [13]. It is an analytic approach that analyses the contents of a document to extract a keyword list from the document and term weights are evaluated by considering thematic factors as a keyword. Term weighting method is based on the relative importance of terms in a document. As for assigning relevance values to terms, terms are identified by term-type, term-length, thematic role in a sentence, location, and frequency count. The weight value of a term is calculated by combining all these term-weighting factors, and terms are ordered by the scores.

Term scoring features are identified through the word-level, sentence or phrase level, and document level analysis of the document. Sentence-level features are the type of a phrase or a clause, sentence location, and sentence type. From the rhetoric word in a sentence, the importance of a sentence is computed and weight is added to the corresponding terms in the sentence. Also, weighting scheme of a term in the subjective clause is not equal to the terms that occur in auxiliary clauses or modifying clauses. That is, term weighting results are affected by the type of words, sentences, phrases, and clauses in which terms are extracted. Initial weight by term type is 0.0~1.0 that is given by intuition: compound noun 0.9, common noun 0.5, and verbalized noun 0.2.

```
Algorithm TermWeighting(text)
begin
  for (each sentence in text) {
    GetTermsFromSentence(sentence);
    for (each term in a sentence) do {
      score = InitialWeightByTermType(term);
      Adjust weight by sentence location;
      Adjust weight by term length;
      Adjust weight by thematic role;
      Adjust weight by noun chunking;
    }
  }
  Calculate term weight by sorting and unifying terms;
end
```

For each term, base score is assigned by the term-type, and then weighting factor is multiplied to the base score according to term features that are captured from the analysis of a document. Content analysis is performed through the morphological analyser and base-noun chunking. Base noun chunking is needed for identifying multi-word compound nouns and assigns the same scores for component nouns. Relative scores for term features are heuristically assigned by intuition. After the term scoring process, term score is converted to a weight value of 0 to 1.

Term weighting is a more sophisticated method of assigning weight values to terms. Terms and their weight values represent a document and document vector for input document or classifiers for categorization are extracted in the same manner. The term ranking method considers term and document features such as term locations and the role of words in a sentence, which is based on the surface-level analysis by morpho-syntactic analyser. So, there is a possibility to improve the term weighting through deep analysis of a document and the document type features like title-abstract-conclusion in a research paper.

2.2 Probability Estimation of Terms

The probability estimation of terms is the core part of categorization system. We have been explored a term weighting schemes that is a combination of weighting metrics with smoothing and inverse category frequency. First three methods of TF-1, TF-2, and TF-3, are the variants of frequency-based techniques. The only differences of them are the smoothing technique (TF-2) and inverse category frequency (TF-3). TF-1 is a standard Naïve Bayesian model with a smoothing technique by collection frequency. In TF-2, smoothing value was fixed to a constant α that is the minimum probability over the collection. Inverse category frequency $icf(t)$ was applied to the probabilities of terms in TF-3.

$$\text{TF-1.} \quad P(t\,|\,c) = \begin{cases} \dfrac{tf\,(t,c)}{\sum_i tf\,(t_i,c)} & \text{if } tf\,(t,c) > 0 \\[2mm] P(t\,|\,G) & \text{otherwise} \end{cases}$$

$$\text{TF-2.} \quad P(t\,|\,c) = \begin{cases} \dfrac{tf\,(t,c)}{\sum_i tf\,(t_i,c)} & \text{if } tf\,(t,c) > 0 \\[2mm] \alpha & \text{otherwise} \end{cases}$$

$$\text{TF-3.} \quad P(t\,|\,c) = \begin{cases} \dfrac{tf\,(t,c)}{\sum_i tf\,(t_i,c)} \times \dfrac{1}{cf\,(t)} & \text{if } tf\,(t,c) > 0 \\[2mm] \alpha & \text{otherwise} \end{cases}$$

As a new approach of applying term-weighting model, two methods are proposed. One of them is the replacement of frequency-based metric with term weighting (TW-1). In this method, term weight $w(t,c)$ has been applied only to the representation of input document. That is, term probabilities in category learning process of TW-1 is the same one as that of TF-3. The other one is to apply the term weighting metric both in the category learning process, together with the representation of input document (TW-2).

$$\text{TW-1.} \quad P(t\,|\,d) = \begin{cases} \dfrac{w(t,d)}{\sum_i w(t_i,d)} \times \dfrac{1}{cf\,(t)} & \text{if } tf\,(t,d) > 0 \\[2mm] \alpha & \text{otherwise} \end{cases}$$

$$\text{TW-2.} \quad P(t\,|\,c) = \begin{cases} \dfrac{w(t,c)}{\sum_i w(t_i,c)} \times \dfrac{1}{cf\,(t)} & \text{if } tf\,(t,c) > 0 \\[2mm] \alpha & \text{otherwise} \end{cases}$$

$$P(t\,|\,d) = \begin{cases} \dfrac{w(t,d)}{\sum_i w(t_i,d)} \times \dfrac{1}{cf\,(t)} & \text{if } tf\,(t,d) > 0 \\[2mm] \alpha & \text{otherwise} \end{cases}$$

3 Evaluation on Text Categorization

We performed an experiment to evaluate the effects of content-based term weighting on the selection of terms and text categorization. Through the experiment, we tried to get a better solution of improving the text categorization system. We evaluated the term weighting method for text categorization with the feature selection method of χ^2 statistics. Base-line model is Naïve Bayesian classifier. Test data in this experiment are news group data collection. This data collection consists of 10,331 documents for 15 categories [14]. We used 7,224 articles for training data and 3,107 articles for test data.

Table 1. Performance evaluation in F-measure

Model # terms	TF-1	TF-2	TF-3	TW-1	TW-2
10000	0.714	0.780	0.812	0.820	0.823
20000	0.733	0.798	0.831	0.840	0.844
30000	0.746	0.816	0.844	0.847	0.853
40000	0.755	0.823	0.846	0.854	0.858
50000	0.767	0.833	0.857	0.859	0.866
60000	0.777	0.837	0.861	0.867	0.868
70000	0.791	0.848	0.863	0.862	0.869
80000	0.804	0.857	0.864	0.867	0.873

The goal of the experiment is to evaluate the effect of the term weighting method with feature selection. In this experiment, about 90,000 features have been extracted from the training data and we pruned the terms with low probabilities by χ^2 statistics. The result showed that the combination method of content-based term weighting and inverted category frequency with a smoothing of minimum value achieved the best performance. The performance of the hybrid method TW-2 achieved 6.9%~11.1% improvement in F_1-measure compared to the base-line model (TF-1). The performance is monotonically increasing according to the number of features in the experiments. TF-1 and TF-2 are pure Naive Bayesian classifiers with collection frequency smoothing (TF-1) and minimum value smoothing (TF-2), respectively. TF-2 of minimum value smoothing achieved 5.3%~6.8% improvement compared to the collection frequency smoothing. When we adopted term weighting and inverted category frequency to the probabilities of terms in TF-3 resulted in 0.8%~4.2% improvements.

4 Conclusion

It is common that information retrieval model is designed and implemented on the probability estimation by frequency-based metrics that is one of the important factors for term weighting. In this paper, we explored a new approach of term weighting method, which will overcome the limitation of frequency-based weighting scheme. Term weighting is performed by content analysis of the document. It is based on the combination of term importance metrics in a sentence or paragraph together with frequency-based metrics. Term weights are calculated considering several factors such as location information, grammatical roles in a sentence, and type of terms.

We applied term-weighting model to Naïve Bayesian model of text categorization and evaluated the results. Experimental results showed that term weighting approach to Naïve Bayesian model outperformed the standard frequency-based model. Also, we found that smoothing and inverted category frequency have a great role for performance improvement, and we also showed that term weighting in document representation technique is an important factor for performance enhancement of the text categorization system.

References

1. Sebastiani, F.: Machine Learning in Automated Text Categorization. ACM Computing Surveys, Vol.34, no.1 (2002) 1-47
2. Yang, Y., Zhang, J., Kisiel, B.: A Scalability Analysis of Classifiers in Text Categorization. SIGIR'03 (2003) 96-103
3. Yang, Y., Liu, X.: A Re-examination of Text Categorization Methods. Proceedings of Int. Conference on Research and Development in Information Retrieval (1999) 42-49
4. Bennett, P.: Using symmetric Distributions to Improve Text Classifier Probability Estimates. SIGIR'03 (2003) 111-118
5. Yang, Y., Pedersen, J. P.: A Comparative Study on Feature Selection in Text Categorization. Jr. D H. Fisher(eds.), Proceedings of the 14th Int. Conference on Machine Learning (1997) 412-420
6. Lam, W., Lai, K.: A Meta-Learning Approach for Text Categorization. SIGIR'01 (2001) 303-309
7. Robertson, S.: The Probability Ranking Principle in IR, Morgan Kaufmann Publishers (1997) 281-286
8. Bekkerman, R., El-Yaniv, R., Tisshby, N., Winter, Y.: On Feature Distributional Clustering for Text Categorization. SIGIR'01 (2001) 146-153
9. Kawatani, T.: Topic Difference Factor Extraction between Two Document Sets and its Application to Text Categorization. SIGIR'02 (2002) 137-144
10. Rijsbergen, C., Harper, D., Porter, M.: The Selection of Good Search Terms. Information Processing and Management, Vol. 17 (1981) 77-91
11. Lai, Y., Wu, C.: Meaningful Term Extraction and Discriminative Term Selection in Text Categorization via Unknown-Word Methodology. ACM Transactions on Asian Languages Information Processing, Vol. 1, no.1 (2002) 34-64
12. Yang, Y.: A Study on Thresholding Strategies for Text Categorization. Proceedings of SIGIR'01 (2001) 137-145.
13. Kang, S., Lee, H., Son, S., Hong, G., Moon, B.: Term Weighting Method by Postposition and Compound Noun Recognition. Proceedings of the 13th Conference on Korean Language Computing (2001) 196-198
14. Ko, Y., Park, J., Seo, J.: Automatic Text Categorization using the Importance of Sentences. Journal of Korean Information Science Society: Software and Application (2001) 417-423

A LF Based Answer Indexing Method for Encyclopedia Question-Answering System

Hyeon-Jin Kim, Ji-Hyun Wang, Chang-Ki Lee, Chung-Hee Lee,
and Myung-Gil Jang

161 Gajeong-dong, Yuseong-gu, Daejeon,
305-350, Korea
{jini, jhwang, leeck, forever, mgjang}@etri.re.kr
http://km.etri.re.kr/index.php

Abstract. This paper proposes a fast and effective question-answer system for encyclopedia domain using a new answer indexing method. We define about 160 answer types. The indexer generates AIU(Answer Index Unit) structures between answer candidates and content words within LF(Logical Form) and sentence boundary. We select essential terms among question terms using syntactic information for ranking the answer candidates. Experiments show our new method is good for the encyclopedia question-answering system.

1 Introduction

Question-Answering(QA) processing has been attracting a great deal of attention recently[1]. Many researches on question answering have been carried out to make up for the weak points in IR systems.[2,3]. We have implemented AnyQuestion2.0(http://anyQ.etri.re.kr) which is a encyclopedia question-answering system following AnyQuestion1.0 in 2003[4]. AnyQuestion1.0 is a question-answering system that extracts a short-answer for user's question only in the person category of encyclopedia domain. The method for finding answers is 3-step answer process(which is the combination of IE-supported QA technique and passage extraction method). However, it takes long time to extract an answer in AnyQuestion1.0 on account of passage extraction method.

In AnyQuestion2.0, we adopt answer indexing method instead of passage extraction method to solve this problem and improve IE-supported QA method. Moreover, we extend category from only person to entire domain of encyclopedia and add up techniques to be able to process descriptive answer(for questions that ask for definition, reason, method, objective etc.) as well as short answer. In this paper, we focus on the question answering technique using answer indexing method among techniques of AnyQuestion2.0. This paper is structured as follows: In the second section, we review the related works. Section 3 describes answer indexing technique and section 4 explains our answer processing method. Results of our evaluation test are presented in section 5. Finally, we draw our conclusions.

G.G. Lee et al. (Eds.): AIRS 2005, LNCS 3689, pp. 679–684, 2005.
© Springer-Verlag Berlin Heidelberg 2005

2 Related Works

In current techniques for QA, there are IE(Information Extraction)-supported QA technique[5], passage extraction method based on IR system[6], the technique of answer indexing[7,8], and so on. [5] is a typical IE-supported QA system. They define templates about each entity(for example: person entity) and then fill up template values using IE techniques. In a closed domain such as encyclopedia texts or newspapers, IE-supported method is successful[6,9] but is an impractical solution in open-domain due to the dependency of IE systems on domain knowledge. Therefore, passage extraction methods have been the most commonly used ones by many QA systems. In the passage extraction methods, sentences or passages which are the most relevant to the question are extracted and then answers are retrieved by using lexico-syntactic information or NLP techniques[6]. However, it takes a long time to extract an answer in these QA systems because rules should be applied to each sentence including answer candidates on the retrieval time[7]. To overcome this problem, [7,8] uses a method for indexing answer candidates in advance. In [7,8], they define answer types(they called QA token or semantic category) and identify answer candidates in a text and then index them. Especially, [7] uses a predictive answer indexer based on 2-pass scoring method. However, [7,8] uses not high-level information(grammatical role or dependency structure etc.) but low-level information like the term frequencies and the distances.

3 Answer Index

For the indexing module, we rely on natural language processing techniques including morphological process, word sense disambiguation, answer type tagging (similar to the extended named entity recognizer) and syntactic analysis. We define about 160 answer types in consideration of user's asking points for finding answer candidates. They have 15 top levels and each top node consists of 2 or 4 layers. The base set of such types is; PERSON, STUDY_FIELD, THEORY, ARTIFACTS, ORGANIZATION, LOCATION, CIVILIZATION, DATE, TIME, QUANTITY, EVENT, ANIMAL, PLANT, MATERIAL, and TERM. The AT-tagging engine annotates with answer types(AT) for each sentence and then the indexer generates AIU(Answer Index Unit) structures using the answer candidates(the AT annotated words) and the content words which can be founded within the same context boundary. We adopt LF(Logical Form) and sentence as the context boundary.

First, the LF-based method extracts the AIU structures within the same LF relations. We defined LF(logical form) as the syntactic relation between a verb and other predicate arguments in the same dependency structure[4]. (e.g. verb(x, y, z,...)). We classify these predicate arguments and verbs into three sets; answer candidate word set(the AT annotated words), verb set and content word set(noun, compound noun, adverb, genitive phrase etc). We construct AIU structures based on the following formula and then add up LF information(S:subject, O:object, V:verb, A:adverb) for each AIU structures.

$$C \text{ (content words set)} = \{c_1, c_2, c_3 \dots c_l\}$$
$$V \text{ (verb set)} = \{v_1, v_2, v_3 \dots v_m\}$$
$$A \text{ (answer candidate words set)} = \{a_1, a_2, a_3 \dots a_n\}$$

(1)

$$AnswerIndexUnit = (c_i, a_j) \quad c_i \in C, \ a_j \in A$$
$$AnswerIndexUnit\_forVerb = (c_i, v_j, a_k) \quad c_i \in C, \ v_j \in V, \ a_k \in A$$

Second, the sentence-based method constructs the AIU structures within a same sentence. In other words, we adopt AIU structures between answer candidate word set and content word set within a sentence boundary with the exception of same AIU structures which is extracted from the first method. In addition, we exclude verb set in this method because verbs produce side effects even if they appear with the answer candidates within the same sentence, so verb set is restricted in LF-based method. We also prevent effectively over-generation of AIU structures. We append distance information between answer candidates and content words to AIU structures. Fig.1 contains as example of the data structure passed from the indexing module.

[example sentence]
The Nightingale Award, the top honor in international nursing, was established at the International Red Cross in 1912 and is presented every two years (title: Nightingale)

[AT-tagging process]
<The Nightingale Award:CV_PRIZE>, the top honor in international nursing, was established at <the International Red Cross:OGG_SOCIETY> in <1912:DT_YEAR> and is presented every <two years:DT_DURATION> (title: <Nightingale:PS_NAME>)

[answer candidates]
The Nightingale Award:CV_PRIZE
the International Red Cross:OGG_SOCIETY
1912:DT_YEAR
two years:DT_DURATION
Nightingale:PS_NAME

[LF structures]
· establish (<subj: The Nightingale Award:*CV_PRIZE* >,
   <adv: the International Red Cross:*OGG_SOCIETY*>,
   <adv: 1912:*DT_YEAR*>)
· present (<subj: The Nightingale Award:*CV_PRIZE* >,
   <adv: two year:*DT_DURATION*>)

<LF-based AIU structures >

AnswerIndexUnit	(the International Red Cross, The Nightingale Award):Object-Subject (1912, The Nightingale Award):Adverb-Subject (two year, The Nightingale Award)Adverb-Subject etc.
AnswerIndexUnit_Verb	(the International Red Cross, establish, The Nightingale Award):Verb-Subject (1912, establish, The Nightingale Award):Verb-Subject etc.

<sentence-based AIU structures>

AnswerIndexUnit	(1912, two year):distance info. (two year, the International Red Cross):distance info etc.

Fig. 1. Example of index processing

4 Answer Processing

The answer processing module searches the relative answer candidates from index DB using question analysis and calculates the similarities and then extracts answers. This module is composed of question term- weighting part and answer-ranking part. First, the question term weight module assigns weight to each question terms to get potential answers. We choose essential terms among question terms according to the following equation.

$$ScoreE(Se_i) = \sum_i w_i * sf_i$$

$sf_1 = Title\ point\ (\ title\ of\ encyclopedia)$

$sf_2 = LF\ point \in \{subject\ point, object\ point, adverb\ point\}$ (2)

$sf_3 = AT\ point \in \{PLO\ point, notPLO\ point\}$

$w_i = each\ feature\ weight$

Equation 2 shows three features; title point(if question term is title of encyclopedia), LF point(if term is LF arguments(Subject, Object, Adverb)) and AT point (if term is answer type). Especially, in case of AT point, if the term is PLO type(Person, Location, Organization), it will be added to more points than not PLO type. Essential term is a question term which has the highest scores. After selection of essential term, we assign term weight as in the following equation. After assigning term weight, we calculate the similarities between query terms and answer candidates. To compute similarities, we use AND operation of a p-Norm mode.

$if\ essential\ terms$

$$Q(Weight) = extra\_each\_weight + extra\_plus\_weight * (\frac{1}{max\_score\_count})$$

$else$

$$Q(Weight) = extra\_each\_weight - extra\_plus\_weight$$

$max\_score\_count : count\ of\ essential\ terms$
$total\_query\_count : total\ count\ of\ question\ terms$
$total\_verb\_query\_count : total\ count\ of\ verbs$ (3)
$verb\_weight = (total\_verb\_query\_count\ /\ total\_query\_count) * Wv$
$Wv : constant\ value\ for\ verb\ weight$
$extra\_total\_weight : 1 - verb\_weight$
$extra\_each\_weight = extra\_total\_weight\ /\ total\_query\_count$
$extra\_plus\_weight = max\_score\_count\ /\ total\_query\_count$

Second, the input to the answer ranking part is results of relative answer candidates searched from index DB. The answer candidates are ranked accordingly to the following equation. In this system the final score is combination of first score(W_i)and second score($Score(R_i)$). First score is calculated from sum of $Q(weight)$ described in previous section. Second score($Score(R_i)$) has following tree types of weight.

- Document matching weight : existence weight of title information recommended from question analysis. Ex) where was Gauss born? (recommended title is '*Gauss*'. If answer candidate exists in 'Gauss' document, this weight is added.)

- Distance weight : distance weight between query term and answer candidate. (LF boundary > within 1 or 3 words boundary > 3 words over boundary)
- Occurrence weight : number of appearing counts of the same answer candidate in high rank set (In this system, we assign scores to candidate answer according to their frequency in 30 ranked answers.)

$$Score(A_i) = \alpha * w_i + (1 - \alpha)Score(R_i)$$
$$Score(R_i) = \sum_i sw_i * sf_i$$
$$w_i = \sum_i Q(w_i)$$

$sf_1 = Document\ matching\ weight$
$sf_2 = Distance\ weight$
$sf_3 = Occurrence\ weight$
$sw_i = feature\ weight$

(4)

5 Experiments

To experiment on our system, we use ETRI QA Test Set[5] which consists of 402 pairs of question and answer in encyclopedia. Our encyclopedia currently consists of 163,535 entries, 13 main categories, and 41 sub categories in Korean. For each question, the performance score is computed as the reciprocal answer rank(RAR) of the first correct answer. To compute the overall performance of AnyQuestion2.0, we use the Mean Reciprocal Answer Rank(MRAR). We consider 5 answers in the highest ranks as the answer candidates. For this experiment, we used 402 pairs of the evaluation set. Table1 shows the result of AnyQuestion1.0(using passage retrieval system). The performance of the proposed method in this paper is shown in Table2. Table3 summarizes the result of another AnyQuestion2.0 except for LF based method.

Table 1. Result of AnyQuestion1.0

	1	2	3	4	5
Number of correct answer	188	25	13	3	2
MRAR			0.51		

Table 2. Result of AnyQuestion2.0 (using LF)

	1	2	3	4	5
Number of correct answer	185	25	10	3	1
MRAR			0.50		

Table 3. Result of AnyQuestion2.0 (not using LF)

	1	2	3	4	5
Number of correct answer	149	38	15	4	5
MRAR			0.43		

As shown in Table1 and Table2, the performance of AnyQuestion2.0(using LF, Table3) is similar to that of AnyQuestion1.0(using passage retrieval system, Table1). The problem of AnyQustion1.0 is that the average response time of this system exceeds 5 second, while AnyQuestion2.0 takes less than the maximum 0.5 second. This result means AnyQuestion2.0 is more useful. Moreover we tested performance of LF-based indexing method. From Table2 and 3, we see that the accuracy of AnyQuestion2.0 using LF method is higher than that of AnyQuestion2.0 excluding LF method. The fact shows that the proposed method in this paper is good for the encyclopedia question-answering system.

6   Conclusion

We presented a fast and effective question-answer system for encyclopedia domain. We focus on answer indexing method based on syntactic relation in this paper. For answer indexing method, we classified user's asking points into 160 answer types. We explained how our system generated AIU(Answer Index Unit) structures within LF and sentence boundary in indexing process. For ranking the answer candidates, we chose essential terms using syntactic information. We have shown that our proposed method is more useful with some experiments. While these methods have improved our previous QA system, we note that more improvements may be pursed in future work. We have to construct more practical QA system not only for the encyclopedia domain but also for other domain. Further work includes the fine-tuning of current system and we plan to expand our AnyQuestion system to be able to process list type questions.

References

1. Toru Takaki : NTT DATA TREC-9 Question-Answering Track Report, TREC 2000
2. Ellen M, Voorhees: Overview of TREC 2003 Question Answering Track. The Proceedings of the twelfth Text REtreival Conference(TREC-12), November 2003.
3. Harabagiu S., Moldovan D., Pasca M., et al.: FALCON: Boosting Knowledge for Answer Engines TREC-9, 2000.
4. H. J. Kim, H. J. Oh, C. H. Lee., et al.: The 3-step Answer Processing Method for Encyclopedia Question-Answering System: AnyQuestion 1.0. The Proceedings of Asia Information Retrieval Symposium (AIRS) (2004) 309-312
5. Wei Li, Rohini K. Srihari : Extracting Extract Answers to Questions Based Structural Links, Coling-2002
6. Sanda M. Harabagiu, Steven J. Maiorano: Finding Answers in Large Collections of Texts: Paragraph Indexing + Abductive Inference, AAAI-1999.
7. Harksoo Kim, Jungyun Seo: A Reliable Indexing Method for a Practical QA System, Coling-2002.
8. Prager J., Brown E. and Coden A.: Question-Answering by Predictive Annotation, The proceedings of SIGIR 2000.
9. Julian Kupiec: MURAX: A Robust Linguistic Approach for Question Answering Using On-line Encyclopedia, SIGIR 93

Approximate Phrase Match
to Compile Synonymous Translation Terms
for Korean Medical Indexing

Jae Sung Lee and Hye Mi Yun

Department of Computer Education,
Information and Computer Education Major,
Chungbuk National University, Korea
jasonl@cbu.ac.kr, janpooh@chol.com

Abstract. The medical thesaurus, MeSH, has been used to index medical documents. A Korean MeSH also has been developed, but it does not include many of the synonymous translations for the English terms. The coverage of synonymous translation is important to index medical documents correctly. In this paper, we propose an approximate phrase match method to extract synonymous translations from Korean medical documents, where parentheses are used to include English terms, or English keywords are used in the keyword field. The approximate phrase match is to handle the unregistered terms in a bilingual dictionary. The empirical evaluation showed that the proposed methods are very effective to compile translation phrase pairs.

1 Introduction

In medical information retrieval, manual indexing has been preferred and used for a long time. MeSH (Medical Subject Heading) has been used to map non-controlled vocabulary to controlled vocabulary: i.e. mapping synonymous or related terms (Entry terms) to standard terms (Subject Headings) [1]. It is a thesaurus which groups all the medical terms with the same meanings into one concept and provides the hierarchy of the concepts.

Korean MeSH (hereafter K-MeSH) has been developed as a translation of MeSH [2]. It includes not only the English translations but also Korean specific synonyms and variations. It can be used for indexing Korean medical documents [3, 4]. One of the problems in developing K-MeSH is translating the English terms and gathering synonym lists. Because one English term can be translated into many different Korean terms, finding corresponding translations is the same as gathering a synonym list for the word.

In this paper, we propose a method to extract translation pairs from the English phrase used in the parentheses and in the keyword field in Korean medical documents; Korean is used as a major language and English is used as an auxiliary language within parentheses; for the document retrieval of foreigners, English keywords are used in keyword fields and their corresponding Korean words usually appear in the abstract texts.

G.G. Lee et al. (Eds.): AIRS 2005, LNCS 3689, pp. 685–690, 2005.
© Springer-Verlag Berlin Heidelberg 2005

Bilingual alignment methods are used for the large size of corpus to extract automatically translation word pairs. There are many approaches for the alignment; a pure statistical approach without using a dictionary from raw corpora [6, 8], a statistical approach using a dictionary in the initial stage [7], a statistical approach using spelling similarity in the same language family [9] and so on.

Because the alignment of the translation pairs enclosed within parentheses or in keyword fields is limited to a sentence or a few paragraphs, a pure statistical approach, which needs a large corpus for reliable probability calculation, is not appropriate for this problem. In this paper, we use a base bilingual dictionary to align Korean words and English words. For the unregistered terms, approximate phrase matching method is proposed, which utilizes the transliteration probability, the syllable similarity between Korean words, and partial matching probability for compound words.

2   Translation Pair Extraction

2.1   Parentheses Translation Pair Extraction

The phrase enclosed within parentheses is used for various purposes. We focus on the case in which the phrase is used to represent the same meaning in different language, either English or Korean, in this paper. We define English phrases as EP and Korean phrases as KP. Either EP or KP may be enclosed within parentheses. Figure 1 shows an example of the KP(EP) case, where '퇴행성' is the translation of 'degenerative', '뇌' is that of 'brain' and '질환' is that of 'disorder'.

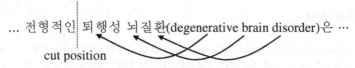

Fig. 1. A translation phrase enclosed within parentheses, KP(EP) example

In order to extract the translation pairs, the translation relation between EP and KP should be recognized first. Matching EP with KP is not always direct even though we use a bilingual dictionary, because all the phrases are not registered. Therefore approximate phrase matching is needed, which is described in section 3. In case of KP(EP), as shown in Figure 1, KP starts from the cut position and ends before the open parenthesis. The cut position is the point that makes the maximum probability of APM (approximate phrase match) between KP and EP. If the probability of APM is lower than cut-off value in any positions, we assume that the KP and EP is not a translation pair. In case of EP(KP), finding the cut position is relatively easy because of a different character set. If EP within parentheses is used with other words like acronyms, it should be removed in the preprocessing step.

2.2   Keyword Translation Pair Extraction

Keyword translation pairs can be extracted by using as a sub-method the parentheses translation pair extraction method described in section 2.1. That is done by trying to put temporarily the English keyword, EP, into every word in the abstract and find the best matching KP among all possible KP candidates. Because Korean is an agglutinative language and Korean phrases are actually noun phrases, EP should be inserted between the noun part and the suffix part by using a morphological analyzer [10]. Figure 2 shows some hypothetical insertion points to find the keyword translation pair. If no noun part is found in a word phrase, the approximate phrase matching skips to the next word phrase.

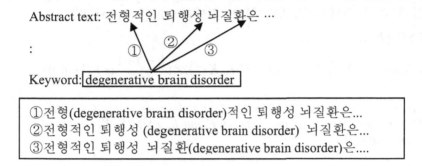

Fig. 2. Hypothetical keyword translation insertions for parentheses uses

3 Approximate Phrase Matching (APM)

3.1 Word Matching Probability

We use a bilingual dictionary to calculate a word matching probability. If the source words and the translation words in the documents are matched with one entry word and one of the corresponding translation words in the dictionary, the probability is 1. Otherwise, it is 0.

In reality, a bilingual dictionary does not include all the translation words used in documents. In order to solve the unregistered translation word problem, syllable similarity and phonetic similarity are used. Syllable similarity is to match lexically similar words, which are usually similar in meaning. For Korean translation words, word similarity is calculated, based on the percentage of the number of common syllables over the number of unique syllables in two words. Phonetic similarity between two words can be learned from English-Korean transliteration word pairs. Each English word and Korean transliteration can be divided into pronunciation units, and the units may be aligned with best probability. The total product of the units' probability normalized by the number of units is the phonetic similarity between the two words [11, 12].

3.2 Compound Word Match Probability

While the spacing in English text is relatively firm, a Korean compound noun can be spaced in many ways. Therefore, one Korean compound word can be partially matched with one English word. We propose a compound word partial matching method as a sub-method for approximate phrase match. It is calculated by the matching probability between an English word and a subpart of a Korean word. The matching probability is calculated with both syllable similarity and phonetic similarity, and the partial matching is reflected by the weight factor α where $0 \le \alpha \le 1$. Formula (1) is the compound word match probability, in which $K_{j,k}$ is the substring of Korean word K starting from j-th syllable to k-th syllable. When 'working' and '작업메모리' (cakepmeymoli) are given to match, all possible substrings of KP are generated and are tried to match with 'working'; they are '작', '작업', 작업메', '작업메모', '작업메모리', '업', '업메' '업메모' ... '모리', and '리'.

$$CSIM(E, K)$$

$$= MAX_{j,k}(\ SSIM(E, K_{j,k}), PSIM(E, K_{j,k}))\times(\frac{k-j+1}{|K|}\alpha+(1-\alpha))) \qquad (1)$$

where $|K|$ is the length of K and α is a balancing factor for partial matching. SSIM(E, K) is syllable similarity between E and K. PSIM(E, K) is phonetic similarity between E and K.

3.3 Approximate Phrase Match Probability

The phrases, EP and KP, are composed of a word or several words. The alignment of the words is not always 1:1 and it can be across [5]. For the calculation of alignment probability, we borrowed the idea of Model 2 in [8], which simply uses both lengths of the phrases and positions of the corresponding word pairs. The approximate phrase matching probability is the normalized value of the product of each English word's compound word match probability multiplied by the alignment probability. The formula is in (2).

$$APM\ (EP, KP)$$

$$= MAX_m \sqrt[l]{\beta^k \times \prod_{i=1}^{l}(CSIM(E_i, K_j)\times A(i|j, l, m))} \qquad (2)$$

where E_i is a word in EP and K_j is a word in KP, l is the number of E_i and m is the number of K_j. And $A(i \mid j, m, l)$ is alignment probability of i for given j, m, l. β is the penalty for unmatched K_i and k is the number of the unmatched K_i.

4 Experimental Results

The experiment was done against a set of medical article summaries within home doctoring field, extracted from a Korean medical database (KMBASE) [2]. For the evaluation, 100 summaries from the collection were tested. A medical multilingual dictionary for Korean, English and Japanese, was used as a base dictionary, which was compiled from a Korean medical terminology dictionary [13] with about 14,900 entries and an average of 1.3 translation words per entry word. As training data for transliteration probability calculation, we used the 1,500 English-Korean transliteration pairs used in [11]. And for the calculation of alignment probability shown in (2), we extracted the training data from 100 summaries in KMBASE.

We used 2 evaluation criteria: 1. Exact Extraction (EE), which counts only the exactly matching pairs, 2. Recognition of Pairs (RP), which counts both Exact Extraction and other translation pairs extracted with incorrect cut position. The measures are recall, precision and f-measure that combine recall and precision equally weighted. As a baseline method, we used dictionary matching for the component words matching in phrases.

The parameters are approximately optimized by trying every 0.1 intervals for best performance. The parameters, however, were not so sensitive in this experiment. The results are shown in Table 1 and 2 when □ = 0.5 and □ = 0.1; Table 1 shows the result of parentheses translation pair extraction (PTP extraction) and Table 2 shows the result of keyword translation pair extraction (KTP extraction). The baseline method was very low in both results. That means the entry words, both English and its translations, are not same as words used in real text. As we can see, APM method's performance was much better. The EE of KTP extraction is much lower than that of PTP extraction, but the RP of KTP extraction is close to the RP of PTP. The performance of PTP is better than that of KTP; KTP has more possibility to match incorrectly or cut incorrect position of the corresponding phrase, because KTP tries to search every possible phrase in the text while PTP searches only the word sequences in front of parentheses.

Table 1. Parentheses translation pair extraction performance (%)

	baseline method (PM)			APM method		
	Recall	Precision	F	Recall	Precision	F
EE	3.70	100.00	7.14	62.96	87.93	73.38
RP	3.70	100.00	7.14	83.95	90.67	87.18

Table 2. Keyword translation pair extraction performance (%)

	baseline method (PM)			APM method		
	Recall	Precision	F	Recall	Precision	F
EE	10.53	83.72	18.70	19.01	59.09	28.76
RP	12.87	86.27	22.39	70.47	84.27	76.75

5 Conclusion

We have presented an approximate phrase match method to recognize and extract translation phrases from English phrases enclosed within parentheses or in keyword field, using a bilingual alignment method based on a base bilingual dictionary. The approximate phrase match method improved significantly the performance of translation pair compilation, because it handles unregistered translation words by combining syllable similarity, phonetic similarity, and a compound word partial matching method. The method can be used not only for medical translations but also for other general field translations.

References

1. MeSH http://www.nlm.nih.gov/mesh/
2. KMBASE: http://kmbase.medric.or.kr
3. Lee, J. S., Kim, M. S., Lee, Y. S.: Spacing Variant Effect on Automatic Cross Lingual MeSH Keyword Suggestion. Proceedings of Asia Information Retrieval Symposium (2004) 253-256
4. Aronson, A. R., Mork, J. G., Gay, C. W., Humphrey, S. M., Rogers, W. J.: The NLM Indexing Initiative's Medical Text Indexer. MedInfo (2004) 268-272
5. Shin, J.: Aligning a Parallel Korean-English Corpus at Word and Phrase Level, Master's thesis, KAIST (1996) (in Korean)
6. Brown, P. F., Lai, J. C., Mercer, R. L.: Aligning Sentences in Parallel Corpora, In Proceedings 29th Annual Meeting of the Association for Computational Linguistics, Berkeley, CA (1991) 169-176
7. Wu, D., Xia, X.: Learning an English-Chinese Lexicon from a Parallel Corpus. Association for Machine Translation in the Americas, Columbia, MD (1994) 206-213
8. Brown, P. F., Pietra, S. A. D., Pietra, V. J. D., Mercer, R. L.: The Mathematics of Statistical Machine Translation: Parameter Estimation, Computational Linguistics, 19(2) (1993) 263-311
9. Church, K. W.: Char_align: A Program for Aligning Parallel Texts at the Character Level, in Proceedings of the 31st Annual Meeting of the Association for Computational Linguistics, Ohio, (1993) 1-8
10. Kang, S. S.: HAM version 5.00a at http://nlp.kookmin.ac.kr
11. Lee, J. S., Choi, K.: English to Korean Statistical Transliteration for Information Retrieval. Computer Processing of Oriental Languages, 12(1) (1998) 17-37
12. Lee, J. S., Choi, K.: A Statistical Method to Generate Various Foreign Word Transliterations in Multilingual Information Retrieval System. In Proceedings of the 2nd International Workshop on Information Retrieval with Asian Languages-1997, Oct. (1997) 123-128
13. KMA (Korean Medical Association): Medical Terminology (2001)

Protein Function Classification Based on Gene Ontology

Dae-Won Park[1], Hyoung-Sam Heo[2], Hyuk-Chul Kwon[1], and Hea-Young Chung[3]

[1] Department of Computer Science & Engineering, Pusan National University,
30 Jangjeon-dong Geumjung-gu, Busan, 609-735, Korea
[2] Interdisciplinary Program of Bioinformatics, Pusan National University,
30 Jangjeon-dong Geumjung-gu, Busan, 609-735, Korea
[3] Department of Pharmacy, Pusan National University,
30 Jangjeon-dong Geumjung-gu, Busan, 609-735, Korea
{bluepepe, hsheo, hckwon, hyjung}@pusan.ac.kr

Abstract. Most proteins interact with other proteins, cells, tissues or diseases. They have biological functions and can be classified according to their functions. With the functions and the functional relations of proteins, we can explain many biological phenomena and obtain answers in solving biological problems. Therefore, it is important to determine the functions of proteins. In this paper we present a protein function classification method for the function prediction of proteins. With human proteins assigned to GO molecular function terms, we measure the similarity of proteins to function classes using the functional distribution.

1 Introduction

Many biology databases such as PubMED, Genbank, SWISS-PROT, and InterPro provide various kinds of data: proteins, genes, gene sequences, research articles, and others. This data is being used as a useful knowledge resource for subsequent research. To utilize biological databases and the knowledge they contain, methods to integrate and analyze different kinds of information are needed. Research based on text data is especially necessary. In text-based genome research, information extraction, information retrieval, and classification methods are applied and used as useful methods.

Proteins play important roles in biological phenomena and many cellular processes. A protein interacts with other proteins, organs, or cells in an organism. These interactions are related to the functions of proteins. Revealing the functions of proteins is one of the most important issues in the post-genomic era. For the discovery of new proteins by genome research, many methods for protein function annotation are presented. The reliable method of function annotation is a manual approach. Biological experts search the functional information of a protein from several databases and annotate the functions of the protein. The manual approach is reliable but it is time-consuming. Most systematic approaches use the homologies of protein sequence, structures, or protein-protein interactions.

In this paper we present a protein function classification method for the function prediction of human proteins. Our method is for proteins in biological texts. We experiment with human proteins assigned to the GO molecular function terms.

G.G. Lee et al. (Eds.): AIRS 2005, LNCS 3689, pp. 691–696, 2005.

2 Related Work

2.1 Protein Annotation and Function Classification

Proteins are one of the important elements for revealing the secrets of various biological phenomena. Protein functions are considered to be one of the basic factors in biological research. The first approach to determining protein function used sequence assignment [1, 11]. By sequence comparison, proteins with similar gene sequences are classified into a similar function category. This method uses sequence assignment tools such as Blast and Blast-T. Another approach is using the structural homologues of proteins [4]. There are also approaches using protein-protein interactions. Proteins act alone or interact with other proteins. Proteins in interaction are functionally related. According to these interactions, the functions of proteins are predicted [2, 5, 10].

Many techniques with supervised learning algorithms have shown reasonable performance in text classification. C.Z. Cai used a support vector machine for the classification of proteins into functionally distinguished classes [1]. In his experiment, for each protein sequence, feature vectors were assembled from encoded representations of tabulated residue properties. Hans-Peter introduced the FUNCLASS system, which uses a nearest neighbor algorithm to classify unknown proteins [7]. The system was designed to use the SWISS-PROT databank. The classification algorithm requires a BLAST output as input. The common approach to classifying protein functions is to extract characteristic keywords for each of the functional classes from a set of proteins classified by experts.

2.2 Gene Ontology

Ontology is an explicit specification of a conceptualization. The GO consortium uses ontology to describe the attributes of gene products in three domains of molecular and cellular biology [3]. The three domains do not overlap each other and each domain describes biological processes, cellular components, and molecular functions in a species-independent manner. GO molecular function terms describe the activities of gene products and form a hierarchy. GO molecular function terms support 'is-a' and 'part-of' relationships.

According to the functions of proteins, proteins are assigned to GO molecular function terms by GO curators or systematic approaches [3, 4]. Most proteins have one function. But, some proteins have more than one function. Assignment of proteins to GO molecular function terms can be used to predict the functions of proteins [8, 9].

3 Features for Protein Function Classification

3.1 Protein and Features

Protein is one of the most important elements for explaining biological phenomena that occur in organisms. A protein acts alone or interacts with other proteins, and most proteins have biological roles in organisms. The relations among proteins and the biological processes of each protein in the human body are strongly related to their molecular functions. To extract proper information related to the proteins of organisms, it is important to know which functions proteins have.

In text-based research, terms are used as important features in handling documents. Biological texts show us the many research results such as sequence, protein structures, protein-protein interactions, and others. Keywords extracted from those biological texts are used as important features in obtaining useful information [6]. Generally, a protein name consists of several terms. Terms in protein names represent amino acids, biological processes, tissues, cells, or diseases. We use terms in protein names as features for protein function classification.

3.2 Feature Extraction

Term features of human proteins are extracted by following two steps. The first step of feature extraction is tokenizing. In this step, a protein name is divided into several words and candidates of term features are selected from among those. Some adjacent words are separated by delimiters, but they should be treated as single terms representing specific meanings. For instance, the protein 'B-cell lymphoma 6 protein' is tokenized as follows: { 'B', 'cell', 'lymphoma', '6', 'protein'}. 'B-cell' is a cell in the human body. To detect candidates of term features from adjacent words, we use a knowledge-base and apply the local alignment method for sequence comparison. Important terms of cellular components and diseases are established as a knowledge-base. The second step is filtering. In protein names, there are important terms which can be used as features and non-informative terms which include numerals and stopwords. We filter the non-informative terms. Even though numerals are used to indicate specific proteins, we remove them in order to reduce the dimensions of feature vectors.

4 Protein Function Classification

According to the functional characteristics, each feature is distributed into function classes on the basis of the functions of the protein. A protein's functions are predicted by the classification method derived from the learning method.

4.1 Feature Weight

Most protein names are composed of several term features. Each feature has a different weight in the function prediction of proteins. The functional characteristics of each feature are derived from the functions of the protein. The function probability of each feature in a particular function class is calculated by analysis of features extracted from function-known proteins. The functional probability of each feature is affected by occurrence in the function classes and by the number of function classes including the feature. The feature with a high frequency in a particular function class has a higher functional probability than in other function classes. The functional importance of a feature among features is also affected by the total frequency and the number of function classes including that feature. Functional importance is inversely proportional to the total frequency of the feature and the number of function classes.

Let $freq(f_i, C_k)$ be the frequency of a feature f_i in function class C_k and let icf_i be the inverse of class frequency; then, the weight of feature f_i in C_k is the following.

$$W(f_i | C_k) = (freq(f_i, C_k) / \textstyle\sum_{(j=1,N)} freq(f_i, C_j))* (icf_i)^2$$

where f_i is the i-th feature
$\quad\quad C_k$ is the k-th function class   (1)
$\quad\quad N$ is the number of function classes, and
$\quad\quad icf_i$ is the inverse of class frequency

Not all function classes include all features. Some features do not belong to some function classes. According to Equation (1), if a feature's occurrence is zero in a function class, the probability of that feature is zero. This shows that the feature cannot be used to represent the function. However, according to the data sparseness problem, the probability of a feature can be zero. Therefore, we assign a small value of less than 1 to each function class and modify the probability of the feature in the function class that the feature does not occur. We set a different smoothing value for each feature. The λ_k is a small value that is determined by the total frequency of the feature and the class frequency. The following equation calculates the smoothing value λ_k.

$$\lambda_k = icf_i * \textstyle\sum_{(j=1,N)} freq(f_i, C_j) * \alpha$$

where, icf_i is the inverse of class frequency for f_i (2)
$\quad\quad \alpha$ is 1   if $min(freq(f_i, C_j)) > 1$ and
$\quad\quad\quad 0.5$ otherwise

As can be seen in Equation (2), the smoothing value λ_k is calculated by the inverse class frequency icf_i and the total feature frequency $\sum_{(j=1,N)} freq(f_i, C_j)$. $\sum_{(j=1,N)} freq(f_i, C_j)$ is greater than the class frequency of feature f_i. Therefore, $icf_i * \sum_{(j=1,N)} freq(f_i, C_j)$ is always greater than 0 and is equal to or less than 1. Each feature is assigned a value between 0 and 1 as a function probability. The weight of each feature is calculated by Equation (3). Using the function probability, each feature's weight for the function class is adjusted to the classification model.

$$W(f_i | C_k) = ((freq(f_i, C_k)+\lambda_i) / \textstyle\sum_{(j=1,N)}(freq(f_i, C_j)+ \lambda_j))* (icf_i)^2$$ (3)

4.2 Similarity Measure

To determine the functions of proteins, we use a mixture model derived from information theory and the naïve Bayesian method with feature collocation. We assume that the function of a protein is determined by the functional probability of its features. Each feature has an affect on the determination of protein functions. A protein is described as a set of feature weights. The similarity of a protein and a function class is measured by information theory and the naïve Bayesian method. We multiply the similarity value of information theory and the similarity value of the naïve Bayesian with collocation.

$$Sim(P, C_i) = \textstyle\sum_{[j=1..t, f_i \in Vp]} W(f_j | C_i) * (\Pi_{[j=1..t, f_j \in Vp]} W(f_j | C_i) + \alpha)$$

where, P is an input protein and   (4)
$\quad\quad C_i$ is the i-th function class

5   Experimental Data and Results

5.1   Experimental Data

The European Bioinformatics Institute (E.B.I.) provides assignments of gene products to the Gene Ontology resource. A controlled vocabulary is being applied to a non-redundant set of proteins described in the EBI's core genome and proteome databases. We use 565 human proteins, which are related to one of 39 tissues and cells, as experiment data. Proteins assigned to GO terms are classified into the function classes based on the GO molecular function. For the experiment, labeled data are divided into two groups. The first is a training dataset including 90 percent of the learning proteins. By the learning task, we obtain the probability distribution of features. The second group is a testing dataset. The performance of our approach is estimated using 10 percent of the proteins. We experiment using 5-fold cross-validation for estimation.

5.2   Experimental Results

We compared the results of our approach with those of the Naïve Bayesian approach and Information Theory. Table 1 shows the experimental results of the function classification. For the training data, the hit ratio is 98.42% in the case of the mixed method. For the test data, the hit ratio of our method is 74.41%. Compared with the Naïve Bayesian approach and Information Theory, our method is superior in the case of the test data. There was 3.22% and 2.17% of improvement in the test data.

Table 1. Experimental Results of Function Classification

	Information Theory (A)		Naïve Bayesian with Collocation (B)		Mixture of A and B	
Hit	Training	Test	Training	Test	Training	Test
Ratio	97.68%	71.19%	98.47%	72.24%	98.42%	74.41%

6   Conclusion and Future Work

In this paper we presented a protein function classification method for the function prediction of proteins. Our method uses the functional distribution of features in the GO molecular function classes. Similarity is measured by the mixed model (information theory and naïve Bayesian method) with feature collocation. The mixed model shows better performance than either Information Theory or the naïve Bayesian method. In this study, we classified proteins into function classes based on the GO molecular function terms. Classifying proteins the lower-level function classes will provide more reliable function classification. By combining lower-level function classes into upper-level function classes, the performance accuracy can be improved.

Acknowledgement

This work was supported by the National Research Laboratory Program M10400000279-05J0000-27910 of Korea Science and Engineering Foundation.

References

1. Cai C.Z., Wang W.L., Sun L.Z., et al.: Protein function classification via support vector machine approach, Mathematical Biosciences 185, 2003, 111-122
2. Alexei Vazquez, Alesandro Flammini, Amos Maritan, *et al.*: Global protein function prediction from protein-protein interaction networks, Nature Biotechnology Vol. 21 June 2003
3. Evllyn C.: The Gene Ontology Annotation (GOA) project – application of GO in SWISS-PROT, TrEMBL and InterPro, Comparative and Functional Genomics, 2003
4. Federico A., Alfonso V.: Automatic Annotation of Protein Function Based on Family Identification, PROTEINS: Structure, Function, and Genetics, 53, 2003
5. Minghua D., Kui Z., Shipra M., *et al.*: Prediction of Protein Function using Protein-Protein Interaction Data, IEEE CSB, 2002
6. Goran N., Simon R., Irena S., *et al.*: Selecting Text Features for Gene Name Classification: from Documents to Terms. Proceeding of ACL, 2003
7. Hans-Peter K., Thomas W.: Functional Classification of proteins using a nearest neighbour algorithm, In Silico Biology 3, 2003
8. Jensen LJ., Gupta R., Staerfeldt HH., *et al.*: Prediction of human protein function according to Gene Ontology categories, Bioinformatics, March 2003
9. Hanqing Xie, Alon Wasserman, Zurit Levine, *et al.*: Large-scale Protein Annotation through Gene Ontolgy, Genome Research, 2002
10. Letovsky S., Kasif S.: Predicting protein function from protein/protein interaction data: a probabilistic approach, Bioinformatics, July 2003
11. Tamames J, Ouzounis C, Casari G, *et al.*: EUCLID: automatic classification of proteins in functional classes by their database annotations, Bioinformatics, 1998

Extracting and Utilizing of IS-A Relation Patterns for Question Answering Systems

Bojun Shim[1], Youngjoong Ko[2], and Jungyun Seo[3]

[1] Diqust.Inc, Seocho-dong, Seocho-gu, Seoul, 137-070, Korea
simbj@diquest.com
[2] Dept. of Computer Engineering, Dong-A University, 840 Hadan 2-dong, Saha-gu,
Busan, 604-714, Korea
yjko@dau.ac.kr
[3] Dept. of Computer Science and Interdisciplinary Program of Integrated Biotechnology,
Sogang University, Sinsu-dong, Mapo-gu, Seoul, 121-742, Korea
seojy@sogang.ac.kr

Abstract. Most of existing open domain question answering systems predefine the conceptual category to which answers can belong. So, they cannot generate appropriate answers in every case or must use a strategy that handles exceptions when the concept requested in the question is not prepared in the system. In this paper, we suggest a flexible strategy that can generate the candidate answers which correspond to any nominal target concepts. The proposed question answering system is equipped with general patterns that can extract hyponyms of the nominal target concept with their confidence scores. Therefore, it can create a set of candidate answers from the dynamically generated ontology when a user requests any nominal concept.

1 Introduction

Although open domain question answering systems provide essential information to seek general knowledge, it has not been widely used yet. In this paper, we remark that most existing question answering systems have concentrated on improving the ability of dealing with limited and typical target concepts.

In many question answering systems, the finite conceptual categories of expected answers are previously prepared and named entity recognizers are widely used for capturing the answer candidates which have semantic hyponym relations with the typical categories. In the case of these systems, if a question has a target concept not to be prepared in the systems or the target concept cannot be captured by named entity recognizers, they must operate a module for handling the exception to generate answer candidates. For example, if a system does not have the target concept 'book' as an expected target category, it is highly difficult to extract answer candidates that are semantically hyponyms of 'book'.

"What **book** did Rachel Carson write in 1962?"

In this paper, we suggest a flexible strategy that can extract answer candidates for the questions with general and untypical target concepts. It is obvious that there are

G.G. Lee et al. (Eds.): AIRS 2005, LNCS 3689, pp. 697–702, 2005.
© Springer-Verlag Berlin Heidelberg 2005

always 'is-a' relations between answer candidates and target concept. Thus we extracted Lexico-Semantic Patterns (LSP) [1][2] of 'is-a' relations from the World Wide Web documents and assigned a confidence score to each pattern. Using these 'is-a' relation patterns, we can extract answer candidates corresponding to the general and untypical nominal concepts. And we exploited bootstrapping algorithm of Ravichandran [3] and Riloff [4] in the proposed system.

2   Extracting Answer Candidates Using 'is-a' Relation

In this paper, we only focus on the questions whose expected answers are nominal concepts. Table 1 shows a categorization method for typical nominal answer types which is used in many question answering systems.

Table 1. The examples of answer type categorization in typical methods

Question	Answer Type
What **actress** has received the most Oscar nominations?	PERSON
What **beach** was "I Dream of Jeannie" filmed on?	LOCATION
What **book** did Rachel Carson write in 1962?	Cannot recognize

In such method, it is important not only to properly categorize the answer type but also to thoughtfully predefine the categories of answer type. To answer to the questions with an unexpected category of concepts, the system must add a new category to the set of expected concepts. The proposed method makes use of nominal concepts that are directly specified in a question as the question's answer type. Table 2 shows the proposed method of answer type categorization. By using the method, answer types of all questions can be automatically classified without exception.

Table 2. The examples of answer type categorization in the proposed method

Question	Answer Type
What **actress** has received the most Oscar nominations?	ACTRESS
What **beach** was "I Dream of Jeannie" filmed on?	BEACH
What **book** did Rachel Carson write in 1962?	BOOK

3   Extracting and Utilizing of 'is-a' Relation Patterns

In this section, we describe the autonomous method of extracting 'is-a' relation patterns, assigning them confidence scores, and using them to find answer candidates.

3.1   Extracting 'is-a' Relation Patterns and Assigning Confidence Scores

In order to represent the patterns of the phrase with a 'is-a' relation, we use the Lexico-Semantic Pattern (LSP). In LSP, we use a lexical tags, a part of speech tags, and a named entity tags. We also use the snippets returned by the Google web search engine[1] in the stages for extracting 'is-a' relation patterns, assigning confidence scores to those patterns, and constructing an answer candidate set with the patterns.

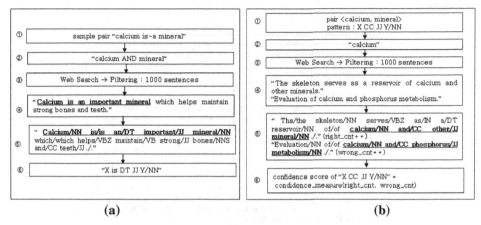

(a)   **(b)**

Fig. 1. An example of extracting patterns and assigning confidence scores to them

The first step to extract patterns is to select the pairs of seed words which obviously have 'is-a' relationship. We manually picked out 110 <answer(X), target-concept(Y)> (e.g. <Iberia, Peninsula>, <Napoleon, Ruler>) pairs from the question answering in TRECs from 1999 to 2002. In the next step, patterns with these <X, Y> pairs are extracted from snippets of the web search engine. Fig. 1. (a) shows an example of the process to extract a pattern for the word pair of <'calcium', 'mineral'>.

The extracted patterns can have the various levels of confidence scores. Fig. 1. (b) shows an example of assigning a confidence score to each pattern.

The confidence score of this pattern is calculated by the following formula.

$$C.S(Pattern) = \frac{right\_cnt}{right\_cnt + wrong\_cnt} \times \frac{\log(right\_cnt)}{\log(sample\_cnt)} \qquad (1)$$

where Riloff (1996)'s RlogF measure scheme is used in the formula (1) and *sample_cnt* means the count of total sample pairs which produce the same pattern.

The following example shows a pattern and the corresponding confidence scores of the pattern generated by processes of Fig. 1. (a) and Fig. 1. (b).

Pattern: X is the RBS JJ NN/Y, Confidence Score : 0.962
Example(*X* is-a **Y**): ***calcium*** is the most abundant **mineral**

We extracted the 'is-a' relation patterns using the selected pairs and pruned patterns with the confidence scores of 0.0. Finally, we used 26 patterns in our method.

3.2 Extracting Answer Candidates Using the Patterns

Now we can extract hyponyms of given target concepts by using the patterns constructed in the previous section. In this process, we also use web search engine. The

---

[1] We use Google Web Api, http://www.google.com/apis

process is similar to Fig. 1 (b) but there is one significant difference. Fig. 1 (b) assumes that we already know what an X term of the "X is-a Y" relation is, but we just know what Y as a target concept is. Fig. 2 shows the process of extracting answer candidates.

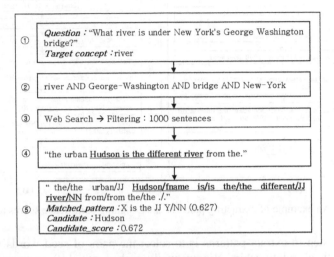

Fig. 2. Extracting answer candidates

3.3 The Hybrid Methods

In general, the coverage of the propose method using patterns is wider than methods using a named entity recognizer (NE). However, each method has the weak points in different cases of target concepts. The following examples show the cases that only one method can find the correct answer.

"What **gas** is 78 percent of the earth's atmosphere?" (Only the Pattern method)
"What **president** served 2 nonconsecutive terms?" (Only the NE method)

In the first example, the target concept, 'gas', can be easily detected by patterns while it cannot be covered by the named entity recognizer, and 'president' as the target concept of the second example can be easily captured as a 'PERSON' by the named entity recognizer. If two methods can be efficiently combined, their strong points can compensate for their weak points. Therefore, we constructed the hybrid methods as follows:

Hybrid 1: if the NE method can detect answer candidates, the pattern method extracts answers from the previously detected answer candidates. Otherwise, only the pattern method is applied to select answer candidates such as 'movie' or 'gas'. And then we assign the confidence score of the pattern to the answer candidate.

Hybrid 2: we combine the confidence scores from two methods (pattern and NE) by a linear combination as the following formula:

$$S(ans_i) =$$
$$S_p(ans_i) \times \log(cnt_p^{ansi} + 1) + S_{ne}(ans_i) \times \log(cnt_{ne}^{ansi} + 1) \qquad (2)$$

where $S(ans_i)$ is the score of the answer candidate ans_i, S_p is the answer score by the pattern method, and S_{ne} is simply 1.0 if ans_i extracted by the NE method, otherwise 0.0. The cnt_p^{ansi} and cnt_{ne}^{ansi} are the counts of ans_i to be extracted as the answer by pattern and NE methods respectively.

4 Empirical Evaluation

In the experiments, we focused on only questions with the pattern of "What Noun-Phrase Verb-Phrase". These questions can be regarded as the equivalent form of "What Verb-Phrase Noun-Phrase". However, we merely consider the questions whose the noun phrase follows 'What' because finding the target concept is not the main research area of this paper. In such a pattern, the head noun of a noun phrase is obviously resolved as the target concept.

Among 413 factoid questions in TREC 2003, there are 150 questions with the "What NP VP" pattern. In addition, we removed 8 questions of which the judgement set has no correct answer. Finally, we experimented with 142 questions. To apply the proposed method to question answering tasks, the head noun of each noun phrase is considered as the target concept. And then we constructed the answer candidate set through the process of Fig. 3.

As performance measures, we followed the standard definition of MRR and Accuracy measures for TREC evaluations. According to the TREC 2003 judgement set, we determined whether the extracted candidate answer is a correct answer.

4.1 Experimental Results

We conducted experiments for NE, Pattern, and two hybrid methods. Table 3 shows the result of each experiment. The measure of accuracy means the proportion of the correct answers when the system submits only one answer per each question.

In this experiment, the pattern method performed better than the NE method and the hybrid 2 showed the best performance among all the methods. This result means our proposed pattern method works properly to capture the hyponyms of the target concept and the hybrid strategies for making up for the weak points of both NE and pattern methods are also useful.

Table 3. Experimental results of each method

Method	MRR	Accuracy
NE	0.202	0.127
Pattern	0.258	0.218
Hybrid1	0.356	0.324
Hybrid2	0.427	0.359

5 Conclusions and Future Works

In this paper, we proposed the flexible method which can easily find answers with any nominal target concept. As shown in our experiments, the 'is-a' relation patterns with confidence scores are useful instruments when a user queries a question with untypical answer type which can be hardly captured by the named entity recognizer.

This study awaits several further researches. First of all, the strategy for avoiding noise data is essential to increase the confidence of the system. And the additional study to discover the target concepts of questions with a complicated type is also needed for practical applications.

Acknowledgement

This research was performed for the Intelligent Robotics Development Program, one of the 21st Century Frontier R&D Programs funded by the Ministry of Commerce, Industry and Energy of Korea.

References

[1] Harabagiu, S., Moldovan, D., Paşca, M., Mihalcea, R., Surdeanu, M., Bunescu, R., Gîrju, R., Rus, V., and Morărescu, P.: The Role of Lexico-Semantic Feedback in Open-Domain Textual Question-Answering, In Proceedings of ACL 2001 (2001) 274-281
[2] Lee, G.G., Seo, J., Lee, S., Jung, H., Cho, B., Lee C., Kwak, B., Cha, J., Kim, D., An, J., Kim, H., Kim, K.: SiteQ: Engineering High Performance QA system Using Lexico-Semantic Pattern Matching and Shallow NLP, In Proceedings of TREC 10 (2001)
[3] Ravichandran, D. and Hovy, E.: Learning surface text patterns for a question answering system, In Proceedings of ACL 2002 (2002) 41-47
[4] Riloff, E.: Automatically Generating Extraction Patterns from untagged text, In Proceedings of the Thirteenth National Conference on Artificial Intelligence (1996)

An Iterative Approach for Web Catalog Integration with Support Vector Machines

Ing-Xiang Chen, Jui-Chi Ho, and Cheng-Zen Yang

Department of Computer Science and Engineering,
Yuan Ze University, Taiwan, R.O.C.
{sean, ricky, czyang}@syslab.cse.yzu.edu.tw

Abstract. Web catalog integration is an emerging problem in current digital content management. Past studies show that more improvement on integration accuracy can be achieved with advanced classifiers. Because Support Vector Machine (SVM) has shown its supremeness in recent research, we propose an iterative SVM-based approach (SVM-IA) to improve the integration performance. We have conducted experiments of real-world catalog integration to evaluate the performance of SVM-IA and cross-training SVM. The results show that SVM-IA has prominent accuracy performance, and the performance is more stable.

1 Introduction

Web catalog integration is an emerging problem in current digital content management [1,6,7,8]. For example, a B2C company such as Amazon may want to merge catalogs from several on-line vendors into its catalog to provide customers versatile contents. As noted in [1], catalog integration is more than a classification task because if some implicit source information can be exploited, the integration accuracy can be highly improved. In [1], an enhanced Naive Bayes classifier (NB-AS) is proposed and its improvements are justified.

Recently, several studies [2,3,4,5] have shown that Support Vector Machine (SVM) achieves better classification accuracy on average. In [2], a *cross-training* SVM (SVM-CT) approach is proposed to improve the accuracy by extracting the implicit relationships between the source and the destination catalogs. However, SVM-CT outperforms SVM in only nearly half the cases. In addition, the cross-training process is very time-consuming. In [4], a *topic restriction* approach is proposed to improve NB and SVM by restricting the classification of any document to a small set of candidate destination categories. A candidate category is decided if more than a predefined number of common documents appear in both source and destination categories. Although this approach can significantly improve the performance of NB, it only slightly improves the performance of SVM. In [5], Zhang and Lee propose a *Cluster Shrinkage* approach in which the documents of the same category are shrunk into the cluster center. The conducted transductive SVM called CS-TSVM can consistently outperform NB-AS. However, because the shrinking process is applied to all documents, it suffers from tentatively misclassifying a document into an improper destination category.

In this paper, we propose an iterative-adapting approach on SVM called SVM-IA for catalog integration with pseudo relevance feedback. In SVM-IA, the training set

G.G. Lee et al. (Eds.): AIRS 2005, LNCS 3689, pp. 703–708, 2005.

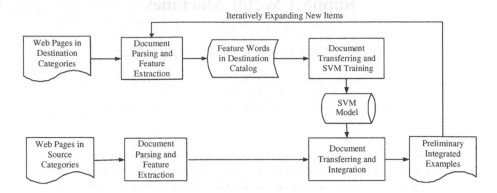

Fig. 1. The integration process of SVM-IA

is iteratively expanded with newly integrated items to retrain the SVM classifier. With these adapted hyperplanes, the integration accuracy is thus improved. Since the expended features are classified first, the possibility of misclassification is reduced.

We have conducted several experiments with real-world catalogs from Yahoo! and Google. We have also compared SVM-IA with SVM and SVM-CT. The results show that SVM-IA outperforms SVM-CT on average, and the performance of SVM-IA is very stable in most cases.

2   Iterative-Adapting SVM

In SVM-IA, the flattened source catalog S with a set of m categories $S_1, S_2, \ldots, S_m$ is intended to be merged into the flattened destination catalog D with a set of n categories $D_1, D_2, \ldots, D_n$. Since a binary SVM can solve only two-class classification problems, we adopt a "one-against-all" strategy to decompose a multi-class problem into a set of binary SVM problems. Positive training data are composed of the feature information extracted from the destination class, and negative training data from other non-destination classes as in [9]. A set of binary SVM classifiers are then trained for the integration process of each destination category.

2.1   Iterative Integration Process

Figure 1 shows the catalog integration process of SVM-IA. The set of documents in the destination catalog is parsed first to extract the feature words as the training input of the SVM. In feature extraction, the stopwords are removed and the remaining words are the features for training. The SVM classifier is trained with the positive and negative training examples extracted from the target category and other destination categories. After the training process, a cutting hyperplane is formulated for future classification tasks. When the classification is finished, an integration iteration is completed.

The integration process can be repeated to find a more suitable hyperplane. The adaptation is performed by iteratively adding the newly integrated source documents

Table 1. The experimental categories

Category	Yahoo!	Y-G	Y Test	Google	G-Y	G Test
Autos	/Recreation/Automotive/	1732	436	/Recreation/Autos/	1090	451
Movies	/Entertainment/Movies_Film/	1801	211	/Arts/Movies/	612	222
Outdoors	/Recreation/Outdoors/	7266	1346	/Recreation/Outdoors/	5184	1381
Photo	./Visual_Arts/Photography/	1921	710	/Arts/Photography/	5721	727
Software	/Computers_Internet/Software/	1637	221	/Computers/Software/	2392	227
Doc Sum		14357	2924		14999	3017

into the training set. Since these integrated source documents may have implicit information of the source catalog, the hyperplane can be adapted to have better separation performance. In our study, the well-known linear kernel function was used in the SVM classifier. SVM^{light} [11] was used as our SVM tool.

2.2   Feature Expansion

In the integration phase, the feature words of the source documents that have been integrated are incorporated as the implicit catalog information to re-train the SVM classifiers. There are two thresholds to control the number of expanded feature words. One is the term frequency, the number of term occurrences in the integrated source documents. Another is the document frequency, the number of documents in which the term appears. If two documents belong to the same category in S, they may have strong semantic relationships and are more likely to belong to the same category in D. Therefore, iteratively expanding new features from the source documents will be beneficial for the SVM classifiers to learn the semantics between feature information and enhance the classifiers in the destination catalog.

An SVM-IA classifier constructs a hyperplane that separates the positive and negative examples by iteratively training new items from the source catalog with a maximum margin. After new items are iteratively added into the classifier and retrained, new support vectors are created to adjust the hyperplane. Since the hyperplane is supported by the combination of new source documents, the cutting hyperplane is automatically adjusted by the new support vectors and would be beneficial for catalog integration.

3   Experiments

We have conducted experiments with real-world catalogs from Yahoo! and Google to study the performance of SVM-IA with SVM^{light}. The experimental results show that SVM-IA consistently improves SVM in all cases, and outperforms SVM-CT on average.

3.1   Data Sets

Five categories from Yahoo! and Google were extracted in our experiments. Table 1 shows these categories and the number of the extracted documents after ignoring the documents that could not be retrieved and removing the documents with error messages. As in [1,2], the documents appearing in only one category were used as the destination

Table 2. The accuracy of catalog integration from Google to Yahoo!

	SVM	CT1	CT2	CT3	IA1	IA2	IA3
Autos	89.43%	90.11%	90.80%	89.43%	93.79%	93.79%	93.79%
(435)	(389)	(392)	(395)	(389)	(408)	(408)	(408)
Movies	85.73%	90.09%	88.97%	87.98%	86.23%	85.95%	86.30%
(1423)	(1220)	(1282)	(1266)	(1252)	(1227)	(1223)	(1228)
Outdoors	91.16%	91.63%	90.70%	87.44%	94.42%	94.42%	94.42%
(215)	(196)	(197)	(195)	(188)	(203)	(203)	(203)
Photo	65.40%	63.29%	69.62%	63.71%	78.48%	81.01%	80.59%
(237)	(155)	(150)	(165)	(151)	(186)	(192)	(191)
Software	93.35%	95.05%	89.96%	94.06%	95.33%	95.47%	95.33%
(707)	(660)	(672)	(636)	(665)	(674)	(675)	(674)
Average	93.35%	95.05%	89.96%	94.06%	95.33%	95.47%	95.33%

Table 3. The accuracy of catalog integration from Yahoo! to Google

	SVM	CT1	CT2	CT3	IA1	IA2	IA3
Autos	80.96%	88.30%	85.78%	86.70%	84.86%	85.78%	85.78%
(436)	(353)	(385)	(374)	(378)	(370)	(374)	(374)
Movies	93.39%	91.83%	88.11%	92.05%	95.54%	95.62%	95.62%
(1346)	(1257)	(1236)	(1186)	(1239)	(1286)	(1287)	(1287)
Outdoors	82.81%	91.40%	87.33%	90.50%	86.43%	86.43%	86.43%
(221)	(183)	(202)	(193)	(200)	(191)	(191)	(191)
Photo	81.52%	94.79%	82.94%	92.89%	86.73%	87.20%	88.15%
(211)	(172)	(200)	(175)	(196)	(183)	(184)	(186)
Software	90.28%	96.06%	96.20%	95.77%	93.80%	93.94%	93.94%
(710)	(641)	(682)	(683)	(680)	(666)	(667)	(667)
Average	89.12%	92.51%	89.30%	92.10%	92.20%	92.44%	92.51%

catalog D, and the common documents were used as the source catalog S. The number of distinct common documents is 2870. However, because some documents may appear in more than one category of the same catalog, the number of test documents may slightly vary in Yahoo! and Google. Thus, we measured the accuracy by the following equation.

$$\frac{\text{Number of docs correctly classified into } D_i}{\text{Total number of docs in the test dataset}}$$

In the processing, we used the stopword list in [10] to remove the stopwords.

3.2 Experimental Settings

In our experiments, both the cross-training and iterative-adapting techniques were employed on SVM to test how much they can enhance a purely text-based SVM learner. In [2], the label attributes extracted from the D_A catalog are considered useful predictors for the D_B catalog by adding extra $|A|$ labels. Therefore, in the SVM-CT implementation, a document $d \in D_B - D_A$ is submitted to the SVM ensemble $S(A, 0)$, which gives a score $w_{c_A} \cdot d + b_{c_A}$ for each class $c_A \in A$. These scores are inserted into the $|A|$ columns as label attributes. To convert the scores into the term attributes, ordinary term attributes are scaled by a factor of f ($0 \leq f \leq 1$) and label attributes are scaled by $1 - f$. We followed the origin SVM-CT settings with $f = 0.95$ and $1 - f = 0.05$. After

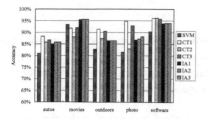

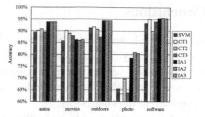

Fig. 2. The accuracy performance from Google to Yahoo!

Fig. 3. The accuracy performance from Yahoo! to Google

the transformation of label attributes, every document $d \in D_A - D_B$ gets a new vector representation with $|T| + |A|$ columns where $|T|$ is the number of term features. Then, these new term vectors are trained as $S(B, 1)$ to classify the test documents. As the algorithm reported in [2], the cross-training process can be repeated like a ping-pong way.

3.3 Results

Table 2 lists the experimental results of integrating Google's pages into Yahoo!'s categories. Table 3 lists the experimental results of reversely integrating Yahoo!'s pages into Google's categories. As listed in the two tables, we have measured the accuracy achieved by the following classifiers: SVM, cross-training SVM (SVM-CT), and iterative-adapting SVM (SVM-IA). IA1, IA2, and IA3 separately represent the result by first, second, and third iterations of adding new features from the source catalog and retraining. Similarly, CT1 is the result of first cross-training with the label attributes extracted from the source catalog. The result of CT2 is based on the SVM-CT1 classifiers proceeding with the second cross-training, and so is the result of CT3 based on the SVM-CT2 classifiers.

Table 2 and Table 3 both show that SVM-IA consistently improves SVM after three iterations. In Table 2, the SVM-IA classifiers not only have sustaining improvements but also outperform SVM-CT in most categories. In /Recreation/Outdoors and /Arts/Photography, SVM-CT is even worse than pure SVM and the improvements are very unstable. Although in Table 3 SVM-CT have effective improvements in most categories after CT3, the overall improvements are not stable, and the accuracy in /Entertainment/Movies_Film is even worse than pure SVM. Figure 2 and Figure 3 further indicate that the accuracy of SVM-IA is stably improved, but SVM-CT has unstable accuracy performance. The reason of vastly unstable performance is that a large number of label attributes are altered in the subcategories of /Entertainment/Movies_Film in Yahoo! after cross-training process. The same situation also happened in /Recreation/Outdoors and /Arts/Photography in Google. These label changes resulted in wrong mappings between the subcategories, and would thus decreased the accuracy. Moreover, we found that the cross-training process was very time-consuming. This makes SVM-CT less feasible for large catalog integration.

4   Conclusions

In this paper, we have studied the effects of iterative-adapting approach to enhance the integration accuracy. We compared our approach with SVM and SVM-CT. The experimental results are very promising. It shows that our approach consistently achieves improvements on SVM classifiers and is on average superior to cross-training that has been proposed to improve SVM.

Several issues still need to be further discussed. First, generalizing the flat catalog assumption to the hierarchical catalog model is of the major interest for the catalog integration because hierarchical catalogs are more practical in real cases. Second, how to construct a systematical mechanism combining effective auxiliaries to enhance the power of SVM is a more difficult problem but needs further investigation. To conclude, we believe that the accuracy of catalog integration can be further improved with the assistance of more effective auxiliary information.

Acknowledgement

We would like to especially thank S. Godbole for his great help in our SVM-CT implementation.

References

1. Agrawal, R., Srikant., R.: On Integrating Catalogs. Proc. the 10th WWW Conf. (WWW10), (May 2001) 603–612
2. Sarawagi, S., Chakrabarti S., Godbole., S.: Cross-Training: Learning Probabilistic Mappings between Topics. Proc. the 9th ACM SIGKDD Int'l Conf. on Knowledge Discovery and Data Mining, (Aug. 2003) 177–186
3. Chen, I.-X., Shih, C.-H., Yang, C.-Z.: Web Catalog Integration using Support Vector Machines. Proc. 1st IWT, (Oct. 2004) –
4. Tsay, J.-J., Chen, H.-Y., Chang, C.-F., Lin, C.-H.: Enhancing Techniques for Efficient Topic Hierarchy Integration. Proc. the 3rd Int'l Conf. on Data Mining (ICDM'03), (Nov. 2003) (657–660)
5. Zhang, D., Lee W. S.: Web Taxonomy Integration using Support Vector Machines. Proc. WWW2004, (May 2004) 472–481
6. Kim, D., Kim, J., Lee, S.: Catalog Integration for Electronic Commerce through Category-Hierarchy Merging Technique. Proc. the 12th Int'l Workshop on Research Issues in Data Engineering: Engineering e-Commerce/e-Business Systems (RIDE'02), (Feb. 2002) 28–33
7. Marron, P. J., Lausen, G., Weber, M.: Catalog Integration Made Easy. Proc. the 19th Int'l Conf. on Data Engineering (ICDE'03), (Mar. 2003) 677–679
8. Stonebraker, M., Hellerstein, J. M.: Content Integration for e-Commerce. Proc. the 2001 ACM SIGMOD Int'l Conf. on Management of Data, (May 2001) 552–560
9. Zadrozny., B.: Reducing Multiclass to Binary by Coupling Probability Estimates. In: Dietterich, T. G., Becker, S., Ghahramani, Z. (eds): Advances in Neural Information Processing Systems 14 (NIPS 2001). MIT Press. (2002)
10. Frakes, W., Baeza-Yates, R.: Information Retrieval: Data Structures and Algorithms. Prentice Hall, PTR. (1992)
11. Joachims, T.: Making Large-Scale SVM Learning Practical. In Scholkopf, B., Burges, C., Smola, A. (eds): Advances in Kernel Methods: Support Vector Learning. MIT Press. (1999)

Fuzzy Post-clustering Algorithm for Web Search Engine

Younghee Im, Jiyoung Song, and Daihee Park

Dept. of computer & Information Science, Korea Univ., Korea
{yheeim, songjy, dhpark}@korea.ac.kr

Abstract. We propose a new clustering algorithm satisfying requirements for the post-clustering algorithms as many as possible. The proposed "Fuzzy Concept ART" is the form of combining the concept vector
having some advantages in document clustering with Fuzzy ART known
as real-time clustering algorithms.

1 Introduction

Web-document clustering methods could be divided into pre-clustering methods and post-clustering methods; the former are off-line clustering of the entire
document collection, and the latter are on-line clustering of the retrieved document set by Web search engines [1] [2] [3]. The post-clustering algorithms have
different requirements from both conventional clustering algorithms and pre-
clustering algorithms. Zamir et al. [4] have identified some key requirements for
the post-clustering algorithms as follows: 1) Relevance; 2) Browsable Summaries;
3) Overlap; 4) Snippet-tolerance; 5) Speed; 6) Incrementaility.

   We intend to devise a new clustering algorithm satisfying requirements for the
post-clustering algorithms as many as possible. To devise a new post-clustering
algorithm, we borrow two important concepts such as a concept vector [5]
and Fuzzy ART [6]. The proposed one, which is named by "Fuzzy Concept
ART(FCART)", is the form of combining the concept vector that have some advantages in document clustering with Fuzzy ART known as real-time clustering
algorithms. FCART is satisfied with all of requirements for the post-clustering
algorithms. Besides, we expect that it may be the alternative model to circumvent some drawbacks of Fuzzy ART such as sensitivity to the order of input
sequence, time-complexity, and true meaning of fuzzy set theory [8].

2 Document Representations and Concept Vector

2.1 Document Representations

In the vector space model, each document is represented as the weighted term-
frequency vector. According to the relevant researches [4], composing document
vector with the snippets returned by Web search engine can reduce the search
space significantly keeping the precision of clustering. Also, since the title of

G.G. Lee et al. (Eds.): AIRS 2005, LNCS 3689, pp. 709–714, 2005.

document stands for the whole content of document, we use only both snippets and title in constructing document vector instead of using the entire document to improve the speed of clustering. In addition, design of loading the clustering tool in the client machines may take an advantage of reducing overload of Web search engine's server.

2.2   Concept Vector

The concept vector [5] is the normalized centroid of the cluster to have unit Euclidean norm. The concept vector of a certain cluster is guaranteed to be closest in cosine similarity (in an average sense) to all document vectors in the corresponding cluster. In particular, the concept vectors are sparse and localized in the word space. The sparsity of concept vectors simplifies the computation of cosine similarity and cluster's coherence [5]. Hence the computational complexity of post-clustering can be remarkably decreased.

Furthermore, the locality of concept vectors is extremely useful in labeling the latent concepts for clusters. If it is provided users with well-represented labels of cluster, they can select the cluster containing the information that they want, by seeing the labels alone.

The keywords of cluster π_j are represented as a word cluster $\mathbf{Word_j}$. it is defined as follows [5]

$$\mathbf{Word_j} = \{k\text{th word}: 1 \leq k \leq d,\ \mathbf{c_{k,j}} \geq \mathbf{c_{k,m}},\ 1 \leq m \leq c,\ m \neq j\} \quad (1)$$

where d is total number of terms. Since the concept vectors are local to each word cluster, the word cluster $\mathbf{Word_j}$ provides good keywords for the corresponding cluster. Also among the document vectors in the cluster, the summary of cluster may be thought of as the document vector that is closet in cosine similarity to the concept vector. It is possible to understand the contents of cluster intuitively. So, in FCART, the cluster's summary of cluster π_j, $\mathbf{Summary_j}$ is defined as follows

$$\mathbf{Summary_j} = \arg \max_{\mathbf{x} \in \pi_j} \{\cos(\theta(\mathbf{x},\ \mathbf{c_j}))\} \quad (2)$$

3   FCART(Fuzzy Concept ART)

The basic idea of FCART is that the weight vector of cluster unit becomes concept vector of the corresponding cluster. FCART performs fuzzy clustering in the true sense of the word by applying the fuzzy set theory: it represents the degree of input pattern's membership for each cluster by relative fuzzy membership values(context-sensitive) and determines which of the input pattern is noise or outlier by absolute fuzzy membership value(context-insensitive). Also it updates not the weights of the cluster that is the most similar to input pattern(WTA strategy), but also the weights of every cluster according to the relative fuzzy membership values(soft-competitive learning). Therefore, the document which contains many topics can belong to many clusters. Now, Fuzzy Concept ART are now presented in details:

Initialization. The number of cluster,c, is initialized to be one. Input patterns are normalized to have unit L_2 norm. And initial weight vector is initialized to be the first input pattern:

$$\mathbf{w}_1^{(0)} = \mathbf{x_1} \tag{3}$$

Since the matching degree between input pattern and weight vector is measured by cosine similarity, FCART guarantees that the first pattern is assigned the first category without regard to the value of vigilance variable.

Activation Function(AF). The activation function is defined as the relative fuzzy membership function:

$$AF(\mathbf{w}_j^{(t)}, \mathbf{x_i}) = R_{ij} = \frac{A_{ij}}{\sum_{h=1}^{c} A_{ih}} \tag{4}$$

where the absolute fuzzy membership function, A_{ij}, is defined as the cosine similarity between the input pattern and the weight vector:

$$A_{ij} = \cos(\theta(\mathbf{w}_j^{(t)}, (\mathbf{x_i}))) = \mathbf{x_i} \cdot \frac{\mathbf{w}_j^{(t)}}{||\mathbf{w}_j^{(t)}||} \tag{5}$$

The weight vector of cluster π_j, $\mathbf{w}_j^{(t)}$, is defined as sum of the input patterns which are classified to cluster π_j:

$$\mathbf{w}_j^{(t)} = \sum_{x_i \in \pi_j} \mathbf{x_i} \tag{6}$$

Then the concept vector of cluster π_j, $\mathbf{c}_j^{(t)}$, is defined as follows

$$\mathbf{c}_j^{(t)} = \frac{\mathbf{m}_j^{(t)}}{||\mathbf{m}_j^{(t)}||} = \frac{\mathbf{w}_j^{(t)}}{||\mathbf{w}_j^{(t)}||} \tag{7}$$

where the mean vectors, m_j, contained in the cluster π_j is

$$\mathbf{m_j} = \frac{1}{n_j} \sum_{x \in \pi_j} \mathbf{x} \tag{8}$$

where n_j is the number of document vectors in π_j. Note that the mean vector $\mathbf{m_j}$ need not have a unit norm. In FCART, the concept vectors are computed by normalizing the corresponding weight vectors to have unit norm without computing the mean vectors.

Matching Function(MF). The matching function which is applied to vigilance test is defined as the absolute fuzzy membership function:

$$MF(\mathbf{w}_j^{(t)}, \mathbf{x_i}) = A_{ij} \tag{9}$$

Step0. **Normalize input pattern with L_2 norm.**
      Initialize Weights and the number of cluster:
         $$\mathbf{w}_1^{(0)} = \mathbf{x}_1, \quad c = 1$$
Step1. **While Stopping Condition is false, do Step 2-7**
      Step2. **For each training input, do Step 3-6**
            Step3. **Set activation to zero**
            Step4. **Compute Activation Function:**
                  $$AF(\mathbf{w}_j^{(t)}, \mathbf{x}_i) = \frac{A_{ij}}{\sum_{h=1}^{c} A_{ih}}, \quad 1 \leq j \leq c$$

            where $A_{ij} = \cos(\Theta(\mathbf{w}_j^{(t)}, \mathbf{x}_i)) = \mathbf{x}_i \cdot \dfrac{\mathbf{w}_j^{(t)}}{\|\mathbf{w}_{ij}^{(t)}\|}$

            Step5. **Find $j*$ with max activation**
            Step6. **Test for reset:**

                  If, $MF(\mathbf{w}_j^{(t)}, \mathbf{x}_i) = A_{ij} = \mathbf{x}_i \cdot \dfrac{\mathbf{w}_j^{(t)}}{\|\mathbf{w}_{ij}^{(t)}\|} \geq \rho$ **then**

                  $$\mathbf{w}_j^{(t+1)} = \mathbf{w}_j^{(t)} + (R_{ij})^m \cdot \mathbf{x}_i, \quad 1 \leq j \leq c$$
                  else   new processing element allocation:
                        $$c = c + 1$$
                        $$\mathbf{w}_c^{(t+1)} = \mathbf{x}_i$$
Step7. **Test for stopping condition**

Fig. 1. FCART Algorithm

From the above definitions, the activation function and the matching function are satisfied with the following condition [7].

$$MF(\mathbf{w}_1, \mathbf{x}_i) > MF(\mathbf{w}_2, \mathbf{x}_i) \Leftrightarrow AF(\mathbf{w}_1, \mathbf{x}_i) > AF(\mathbf{w}_2, \mathbf{x}_i) \tag{10}$$

That is, when best-matching template $\mathbf{w}_{j*}^{(t)}$, selected according to $AF(\mathbf{w}_j^{(t)}, \mathbf{x}_i)$, does not satisfy the vigilance criterion, a new processing unit can be immediately allocated to match the input pattern $\mathbf{x}_i$. And the corresponding input pattern is assigned to weight vector of the new cluster. This means that no mismatch reset condition and search process are required to detect the resonance domain. Hence, in speed, FCART has an additional advantage for post-clustering.

Detection of resonance unit. To select resonance unit, the vigilance test is

$$MF(\mathbf{w}_{j*}^{(t)}, \mathbf{x}_i) = \rho \tag{11}$$

where the best-matching cluster $j*$ is $\arg\max_{j=1,\cdots,c}\{AF(\mathbf{w}_j^{(t)}, \mathbf{x}_i)\}$.

That is, the value of activation function means the degree of the current input pattern's credit for the corresponding cluster and the value of matching function determines whether the input pattern is an outlier for the cluster or not.

Updating Weights. In FCART, input patterns have the degree of the membership for each cluster by equation (4). So, when the weights are updated, input patterns have effect on the weight vectors of each cluster according to the relative membership value

$$\mathbf{w}_j^{(t+1)} = \mathbf{w}_j^{(t)} + (R_{ij})^m \cdot \mathbf{x}_i, \quad 1 \leq j \leq c \tag{12}$$

where $m \in (1, \infty)$ is weighting exponent for the degree of membership. By equation (12), FCART updates not only the weight of the best-matching cluster but also the weights of any other clusters. The algorithm of the FCART is summarized at fig.1

4   Experimental Results

We sampled the title and snippet of 185 high-ranked documents which are returned by Web search engine, Google, for a query "guinea". First, we removed

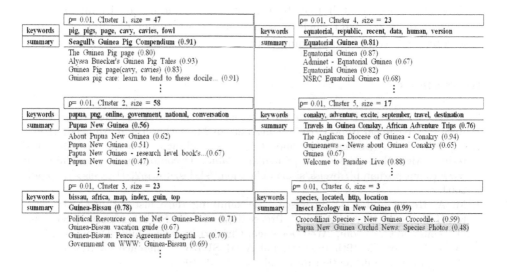

Fig. 2. Clustering result of FCART(= 0.01)

HTML tags, then we eliminated non-content-bearing stopwords and terms which occurred in less than 2 documents. The documents set, GUINEA consists of 159 dimensional document vectors which are sparse (96 % sparsity). To validate the performance of FCART, we cluster the GUINEA and fig.2 gives the result of clustering. In this experiment, we set vigilance parameter to $0.01(\rho = 0.01)$ and weighting exponent to 2($m = 2$). The value lying next to the document's title means the relative fuzzy membership value for the corresponding cluster.

As far as the incrementality is concerned, whenever a new pattern comes in, FCART can learn the pattern without relearning the entire system. Especially FCART can perform fuzzy clustering. For example, the document, "Papua New Guinea Orchid News" which is member of the Cluster 6 in fig.2, belongs to not only Cluster 6 (for species) but also Cluster 2 (for Papua New Guinea). fig.3 gives the relative fuzzy membership values of that document for each cluster.

Papua New Guinea Orchid News						
Cluster 1	Cluster 2	Cluster 3	Cluster 4	Cluster 5	Cluster 6	Cluster 7
0.03	0.23	0.06	0.03	0.12	0.05	0.48

Fig. 3. Fuzzy membership for document "Papua New Guinea Orchid News"

5   Conclusions

In this paper, we have proposed a novel clustering algorithm satisfying all of requirements for the post-clustering algorithms. Particularly, the proposed FCART is the form of combining the concept vector that have some advantages in document clustering with Fuzzy ART known as real-time clustering algorithms. Besides, we expect that it may be the alternative model to circumvent some drawbacks of Fuzzy ART such as sensitivity to the order of input sequence, time-complexity, and true meaning of fuzzy set theory [8].

References

1. A. Leouski and W. B. Croft, "An Evaluation of Techniques for Clustering Search Results", Technical Report IR-76, University of Massachusetts at Amherst, 1996.
2. S. Osinski, J. Stefanowski, and D. Weiss, "Lingo: Search Results Clustering Algorithm Based on Singular Value Decomposition", avalilable at www.cs.put.poznan.pl/dweiss/site/publications/slides/iipwm2004-dweiss-lingo.pdf, 2004.
3. M. A. Hearst and J. O. Pedersen, "Reexamining the Cluster Hypothesis: Scatter/Gather on Retrieval Results", Proceedings of ACM SIGIR '96, pp. 76-84, 1996.
4. O. Zamir and O. Etzioni, "Web Document Clustering: A Feasibility Demonstration", Proceedings of the 19th International ACM SIGIR Conference on Research and Development in Information Retrieval, pp. 46-54, 1998.
5. I. S.Dhillon and D. S. Modha, "Concept Decomposition for Large Sparse Text Data using Clustering", Technical Report RJ 10147(9502), IBM Almaden Research Center, 1999.
6. G. A. Carpenter, S. Grossburg, and D. B. Rosen, "Fuzzy ART: An Adaptive Resonance Algorithm for Rapid, Stable Classification of Analog Patterns", Proceedings of International Conference on Neural Networks, Vol. II, pp. 411-416, 1991.
7. A. Baraldi and E. Alpaydin, "Simplified ART: A New Class of ART Algorithms", International Computer Science Institute, TR 98-004, 1998.
8. Y. H, Im, "Fuzzy Concept ART: Post-Clustering Algorithm for Web information Retrieval", M.Sc. Thesis, University of Korea, Korea, 2001.

A Relational Nested Interval Encoding Scheme for XML Storage and Retrieval[1]

Gap-Joo Na and Sang-Won Lee

Dept. of Computer Engineering, Sungkyunkwan University,
Suwon, Kyunggi-do, 440-746, Korea
{factory, swlee}@skku.edu

Abstract. The XML data is a typical kind of tree-data. However, the XML research community has given little attention to the traditional Relational database Management System(RDBMS) based encoding schemes for tree-data. In this paper, we will investigate one of the traditional RDBMS-based encoding schemes, called Nested Interval, for storage and retrieval of XML data. Especially, our approach is very robust for updating XML data, including insertion of new nodes. In fact, the existing RDBMS-based XML storage and indexing techniques work very poorly against XML data updates because they should be rebuilt from the scratch when any update occurs in XML data. In contract, our scheme does not require re-encoding. In this respect, our approach is a viable option for storing and querying update-intensive XML applications.

1 Introduction

As XML is rapidly becoming the de-facto standard for data representations and exchanges in the Internet age, much research has been done on how to store XML data in relational database management system(RDBMS) and how to query/process the XML data in RDBMS. The existing works have mainly focused on how to store and how to query XML data efficiently in native XML DBMS(database management system), object-relational DBMS(ORDBMS), or pure RDBMS. In particular, previous studies[1][2][3] are about the technique which defines an element in tree-structured XML document to one node, and index the node. In case of [1][2][3], they show good performance to insert and to query a single XML document. But, they have problems that they must re-index partial document or whole document when a new XML document insert or a new element insert.

In most case, by the way, the XML data is a kind of tree data. However, the XML research community has given little attention to the traditional RDBMS-based encoding schemes for tree data. In this paper, we will investigate one of the traditional RDBMS-based encoding schemes, called Nested Interval[6], for storage and retrieval of XML data. Especially, our indexing technique can efficiently insert new XML data into the RDBMS that has been already stored XML document, which is impossible or

---

[1] This work was supported by grant No.(R05-2003-000-11943-0) from Korea Science & Engineering Foundation.

G.G. Lee et al. (Eds.): AIRS 2005, LNCS 3689, pp. 715–720, 2005.

very inefficient in the existing approaches, because the encoding and indexing should be rebuilt from the scratch when any update occurs in XML data.

In this paper, we apply a relational nested interval encoding scheme for XML storage & retrieval. Nested interval encoding scheme does not need to re-index when a new XML document or data insert, update and delete, so we show that this scheme has good performance for storing and querying XML data in RDBMS. This scheme is valid only in tree-structured data, not applicable to the general graph-structured data.

This is the very limitation of our scheme. However, we believe that most XML data is currently represented as tree, thus our approach has wide applications.

The remainder of this paper is organized as follows. In Section 2, we briefly review the related works on how to store and to query a tree-structured data in RDBMS. In section 3, we describe the nested interval encoding scheme. Section 4 describes an implementation of the nested interval encoding scheme. Finally, section 5 concludes with some future studies.

2   Related Works

This paper is to study how to store and how to query XML data efficiently. In most case, an XML data is tree-structured, so, we introduce related studies how to store and query a tree-structured data in RDBMS, and we will compare a recent well-known RDBMS-based XML encoding scheme, called XPath Accelerator. For the lack of space, in-depth descriptions are omitted, see the technical report version of this paper[10].

- *Adjacency List Model* [5] : This model is the method to store a current node key and a parent node key to store tree-structured data.
- *Materialized Path Model* [5] : In this model, each node stores the whole path to the root. Each node has a key value and the whole path to the root.
- *Nested Set Model* [5] : In this model, each node indexed (lft, rgt) segment and these values stored in a table. Using this technique, we can know that total node number equals (root node's rgt)/2, and the difference between the (lft, rgt) values of leaf nodes is always 1, and the descendants of a node can be found by looking for the nodes whose (lft, rgt) numbers are between the (lft, rgt) values of their parent node.
- *XPath Accelerator* [3]: XPath Accelerator, an indexing model to store XML document in RDBMS, index a node to pre-ordered value and post-ordered value. Using this model, we can find ancestor, following, preceding and descendant nodes in the pre/post plane.

These indexing models have good performance in common, but they must re-index partial document or whole document when a new XML document or element inserted.

3   Nested Interval and Materialized Path

In this section, we suggest how to apply Nested Interval Model[6] to store XML data into RDBMS. Nested intervals generalize nested sets. Thus, from Nested Interval encoding, we can easily calculate Materialized Path. Consequently, we can exploit the advantage of each model.

3.1 Basic Structure

A basic structure of Nested Interval is similar to Nested Set, but the difference is to represent a node by a rational expression in Nested Interval. We must represent infinity number for (lft, rgt) value, so this model uses rational number set.

3.2 The Mapping

Fig.1 shows mapping segments (lft, rgt) of nested interval on two-dimensional plane. Rgt is a horizontal axis and lft is a vertical one-y. As shown in Fig.1, a parent node '1.1' has a child node '1.1.1'. X-position of a node '1.1.1' is smaller than x-one of a node '1.1' (rgt(1.1.1) < rgt(1.1)) and y-position of a node '1.1.1' is bigger than y-one of a node '1.1' (lft(1.1.1) > lft(1.1)). We can find relationships among the nodes and figure specific. Now, we decide the point of root nod (1,0) in Fig.1. This means that all nodes except root node locate between 0 and 1. And child node '1' of the root node map into (1,1/2), '1.1' is (1,3/4), and '1.2' is (3/4, 5/8). The rules are as follow.

- *RULE 1* **:** First child node (cx1, cy1) of a node (x,y) ; mid-point between (x,y) and (x,x) => (x+x/2, x+y/2)
- *RULE 2 :* Next sibling node (fx1, fy1) of a node (x,y) ; mid-point between (x,y) and (py1, py1) of parent node (px1, py1) of (x,y) => (x+py1/2, y+py1/2)

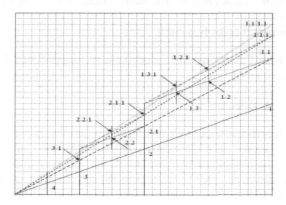

Fig. 1. The Mapping of Nested Interval

We can map all nodes into the two dimension plane with Rule (1), (2). As Nested Set model use (lft, rgt), a node (x,y) is (rgt, lft) in this model. So, we take the same advantages of nested set. Because all node have unique value (x,y) in nested interval model, we can consider only current node to insert, update, delete and we do not need to re-index any other node. And, Nested Interval can convert into Materialized Path easily. Moreover, because the sum of lft, rgt has a unique value, we can store numerator and denominator of the sum into RDBMS.

4 Implementation and Experiment

Now, we describe how to implement Nested Interval indexing model in a commercial RDBMS. Also, we describe the experiment result. For this, we run the typical XML queries such as Xpath, and insert new XML data and new elements into existing XML document. All experiments were run on an 2.0GHz Pentium IV processor with 1GB of physical memory running Windows XP Professional. We used Oracle 10g for our experiments. Our XML data used [9] (The Plays of Shakespeare in XML).

4.1 XML Document Parsing

We parsed XML document using JAVA SAX Parser[8] to Materialized Path. To store XML document, node information stores in NIXML table and contents of each node store in XDATA table like [3].

4.2 Mapping Functions

We implement some functions that maps Materialized Path into Nested Interval with an XML document to store RDBMS. Each function was coded using Java Class, and they are called from Oracle PL-SQL. Followings are functions of each group. The details of description are found in [10].

- *Storing function group* : x_numer, x_denom, y_numer, y_denom
- *Relation function group* : parent_numer, distance, child_numer, ...
- *Path function group* : path, path_numer, path_denom, sibling_number

4.3 Table Scheme and Data Insertion

We create two tables for storing XML document in RDBMS and Fig.2 shows table schemes and insert query.

4.4 Inserting XML Document

It takes the fixed time because our indexing technique has the advantage that it does not need to re-index when we insert additional nodes into RDBMS. Table.1 shows a result that the total time increases linearly as we insert new nodes. For this experiment, first we deleted mid-nodes of an XML document in [8] and parsed it. And then, we stored XML document in RDBMS and inserted a new node that had been deleted like, we could obtain the result that the inserting time per each node is increase linearly.

Table 1. Total elapsed time vs. Number of nodes

Number of node	100	500	1000	2000	3000	4000	5000
Total Elapsed Time(ms)	96	510	997	1992	3013	4101	5078

XIXML table for node description :	XDATA table for node contents :
create table NIXML	create table XDATA
(	(
doc_num integer, // document number	doc_num integer, // document number
doc_name varchar2(30), // document name	node_num integer, // node(element) number
node_num integer, // node(element) number	val varchar2(4000) // node(element) content
node varchar2(40), // node(element) name	);
attr varchar2(10), // attribute	
numer varchar2(2000), // numerator of a node	
denom varchar2(2000), // denominator of a node	
y_numer varchar2(2000), // numerator of y	
y_denom varchar2(2000), // denominator of y	
x_numer varchar2(2000), // numerator of x	
x_denom varchar2(2000), // denominator of x	
path varchar2(100), // materialized path	
depth integer // depth of node	
);	

SQL for node inserting :
INSERT INTO NIXML VALUES (1, 2, 'ITEM', 'false', path_numer('1.1'), path_denom('1.1'),
y_numer(path_numer('1.1'), path_denom('1.1')), y_denom(path_numer('1.1'), path_denom('1.1')),
x_numer(path_numer('1.1'), path_denom('1.1')), x_denom(path_numer('1.1'), path_denom('1.1')),
'1.1', distance(path_numer('1.1'), path_denom('1.1'), 3, 2));

Fig. 2. The Mapping of Nested Interval

4.5 Converting Xpath Queries into SQL

Now we describe how XPath queries translate into SQL. Nested Interval index model can easily convert to Materialized Path. So, we can use advantages of each model. In this paper, we show typical XPath query to find parent node. For lack of space, the other Xpath queries are presented in the technical report version of the paper [10].

"//TITLE/parent::ACT" (XPath) => SELECT n1.* FROM NIXML n1, NIXML n2
- SQL(Using Materialized Path) : WHERE n1.node='ACT' and n2.node='TITLE' A
ND n2.depth = n1.depth +1 AND n2.path like n1.path || '.%'
- SQL(Using Nested Interval)   :   WHERE n1.node='ACT' and n2.node='TITLE'
 AND distance(n2.numer, n2.denom, n1.numer, n1.denom) = 1

In this indexing model, some queries don't have good performance. Because this technique encode nodes with Binary Rational Number. But, binary encoding grows exponentially, both in breadth and depth. To avoid numeric overflow, we store each numerator and denominator value as text type. So, we can not calculate (numerator/denominator), if numerator and denominator number is very big. Unfortunately, as all commercial RDBMS are not support big integer(over 64bit), we should study alternative. We describe an alternative of this problem.

5 Conclusion and Future Work

In this paper, we exploited the nested interval model for encoding tree data in RDBMS into XML storage to avoid re-indexing as updates occur in XML document. The Nested Interval model generalizes nested set so it provides the same advantages of both Nested Set and Materialized Path. The key advantage of Nested Interval is that we do not need to re-index partial or whole document as additional nodes inserted in RDBMS and we can find easily position values of each node by calling some functions. And we can find a position value of parent or child node without access RDBMS. In conclusion, Nested Interval model, which is proposed to store tree-structure data, can be used for XML storage as we have shown in section 4.

However, our model encodes each node with Binary Rational Numbers and thus the size of binary encoding data grows exponentially. It can cause overflow in RDBMS. In this paper, we solved this problem using BigInteger class (produced by JAVA). Another alternative is Nested Intervals with Farey Fractions [7], but it can not convert to Materialized Path. To overcome the Binary Rational Number problem, how to store big integer into RDBMS is the next step in our research direction.

References

1. D.Floresce, D.kossman, "Storing and Querying XML data Using a RDBMS", IEEE Data Engineering Bulletin, Vol.22, No 3, 1999
2. I. Tatarinov et al., "Storing and Querying Ordered XML Using a Relational Database System", Proc. ACM SIGMOD Int'l Conf. on Management of Data, 2002
3. Torsten Grust, "Accelerating XPath Location Steps", ACM SIGMOD, Madison, June, 2003
4. W3C, XML Path Language(XPath), Version 1.0, W3C Recommendation, November 1999
5. CELKO.J, "Joe Celko's Trees & Hierarchies in SQL for Smarties", Morgan Kaufmann, 2004
6. TROPASHKO, V. 2003a. Trees in SQL:Nested Sets and Materialized Path. http://www.dbazine.com/tropashko4.shtml
7. TROPASHKO, V. "Nested Intervals with Farey Fractions.", eprint arXiv:cs/0401014, 2004
8. http://www.saxproject.org/
9. The Plays of Shakespeare in XML. (http://www.xml.com/pub/r/396)
10. Gap-Joo Na, Sang-Won Lee, "A Relational Nested Interval Encoding Scheme for XML Storage and Retrieval" (Technical Report Version). (http://vldb.skku.ac.kr/pdf/ninterval.pdf)

The Design of Webservices Framework
Support Ontology Based Dynamic Service Composition

Seungkeun Lee[1], Sehoon Lee[2], Kiwook Lim[3], and Junghyun Lee[1]

[1] Department of Computer Science and Engineering
Inha University, Inchon, Korea
sglee@nlsun.inha.ac.kr, jhlee@inha.ac.kr
[2] School of Computing and Information Systems
Inha Technical College, Inchon, Korea
seihoon@inhatc.ac.kr
[3] Department of Industry Engineering of Knowlege and Information
Sunmoon University, Asan, Choongnam, Korea
rim@sunmoon.ac.kr

Abstract. The coupling of webservices and semantic web technology provides the ability to automatically discover, compose and execute webservices. Most importantly, automatic composition can provide access methods for all activities on the WWW. As a result of this popularity, a number of people are researching this area. However, the composition of webservices is generally static because these webservices are usually described using BPEL4WS or WSFL, restricting dynamic operation because the composite service only has a sequence execution plan. This dynamic composition cannot generate a parallel execution plan for many Internet business applications. In this paper, we design an ontology based framework for dynamic webservice composition. Also, we present a semantic webservice framework using dynamic composition model. This dynamic composition model can generate a parallel execution plan. These plans are calculated using QoS model, hence the best execution plan is selected.

1 Introduction

Webservices are a core technology in e-Business and are researched by a number of people by a spread using of XML(eXtensible Markup Language), WSDL(Web Service Definition Language), SOAP(Simple Object Access Protocol). However, because a webservice is composed only by syntactic information described by in XML, the structure cannot process semantic of contents. Due to this issue, efforts toward the adaptation of the Semantic Web to webservices are gaining momentum. This enables webservices to be accessed by contents rather than by keywords. Webservices can be discovered, selected and composed automatically by other services[1].

This composition is very important because it presents approaches for all kinds of WWW activities. A static composition has problems in a dynamic WWW environment. If a webservice is modified once, all composition plans having the modified webservice must be redesigned. It is largely an ad-hoc, time-consuming and error prone process. The dynamic composition of webservices is noticed by many researchers [2]. These researchers' studies have not been completed yet and therefore

G.G. Lee et al. (Eds.): AIRS 2005, LNCS 3689, pp. 721–726, 2005.
© Springer-Verlag Berlin Heidelberg 2005

suitability in the diversity of a business environment cannot be determined. Dynamic composition generates an execution plan with webservices, IOPE(Input/Output/ Precondition/Effect). This execution plan is a sequence list of executions of simple webservices. But, there is no relationship between the Input/Output two webservice, so an execution plan including two services cannot be made dynamically. These services are executed in parallel and are composed as a composition service.

This paper presents an ontology-based framework for dynamic composition of webservices. This ontology is designed by an extension of OWL-S[3]. A presented framework can generate an execution plan having a sequence or parallel execution plan of webservices automatically and selecting the best execution plan. A selected plan is translated into an OWL-S ServiceProcess model. This framework has some benefits which are not described previously. (1) It can create an execution plan having a sequence plan and a parallel plan. (2) It can select the best execution plan, using the QoS model presented by the designed ontology. (4) A selected execution plan is used in various execution environments, supporting OWL-S[4,5].

2   Dynamic Composition Model Using Ontology

The dynamic composition of semantic web services creates proper execution plans of composite webservices and selects a best execution plan using the QoS properties of a composite webservices. In this section, we propose the ontology for execution plan creation, and the evaluation of an execution plan for best execution plan selection. It is based on extensions of OWL-S[3].

2.1   Ontology Model

We proposed an ontology model, the extension of OWL-S for this framework. Fig 1 describes this ontology model. The QoS ontology is composed of three properties. These are a response time, a execution cost, and the reliability of webservice. Each property has three values, min/average/max. A response time describes the time from calling an operation to getting a response from a webservice. An execution cost describes the total cost in terms of resources utilization. Reliability describes the rate in which webservices are executed correctly. A connection between webservices is achieved by exchanging message. A message describes datatype, name, unit and role. The business role gives the semantics of the corresponding parameter. It takes its value from a predefined taxonomy for business roles. In order to connect between two webservices the mapping between messages of two webservices must be completed. The functionalities provided by a webservice are accessible through operation invocations. We consider four operation modes. 'one-way', 'notification', 'solicit-response', and 'request-response'. A composite service is treated as a logical webservice. This service is executed using transaction methods. We designed properties for a transaction. A state of transaction is defined with 'commit', 'executing', 'compensate', and 'abort' properties. An activity is defined with 'started', 'completed', 'running', and 'blocked'. This ontology is not within the scope in this paper. It will be published in a subsequent paper.

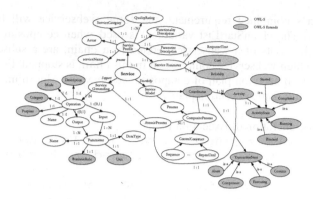

Fig. 1. The Extends of OWL-S Ontology

2.2 Webservice Composability

In this section, we describe how the framework can decide whether two webservices can be composed together. A composition of two webservices is achieved by an operation of one webservice call to an operation of another webservice. A calling of operation call is achieved by a sending a message. In order to decide whether two webservices can be composed, message compatibility and operation compatibility are verified.

Message Compatibility
Interoperation is achieved by exchanging messages. A message could be composed of parameters, having specific datatypes. A sending parameter must be interoperable with a receiving parameter. Every parameter would have well-defined semantics according to that taxonomy. We consider two primary data-type-compatibility methods: direct and indirect compatibility. Two parameters are directly compatible if they have the same data type. A parameter p is indirectly compatible with a q if the type of p is derived from the type q. We extend the notion of data type compatibility to messages as follows: A message M is a datatype compatible with a message N if every parameter of M is directly or indirectly compatible with a parameter of N. Note that not all parameters of M need to be mapped to the parameters of N.

Operation Compatibility
In order to be compatible with other operations, these operations have a "dual" mode. For example, if an operation mode of one webservice is "one-way" then the other operation mode must be "notification". Also, two operations have the same purpose properties and category properties. A detailed algorithm is omitted because of a restricted coverage in this paper.

Automatic Creation of Execution Plan

In this section, we describe how an execution plan can be created automatically. First, chainStartList is generated from user requirements. If a webservice can satisfy a user's requirements, there is one element within chainStartList. If a webservice can satisfy a user's combined requirement, the some webservice will be elements of chainStartList. The chainStartList variables, is used when composing a sequence of webservices. If inputs of a webservice, added to a chain, are a subset of user's inputs(weHave) then webservice composition in this chain is stopped. Finally, all chains are eturned for an xecution plan of composite webservices Algorithm 1 describes the creation of an automatic execution plan.

Algorithm 1. Generation of Execution Plans.

```
Input: weHave = {inputs provided by User Requirement};
Output : weWant = {outputs desired by User Requirment};
Begin
  chainStartList = findServiceChainStart(weWant);
  while nextChainStart(chainStartList) do
    chainList.add(new chain(chainStart));
    MakeServiceChain(chain, chainStart.input,
                                   chainStart.output);
  End While
  Function MakeServiceChain(chain, input, output)
  Begin
    svcs = getServicesHavingOutput(chainLast.input);
    if svcs.count = 1 then chain.add(svcs);
    else if
      foreach service in svcs
        chain.add(new chain(service));
        MakeServiceChain(chain, service.input,
                                     service.output);
      end foreach
    if input in weHave then return chain;
    return null; // no chain found
  End function
End
```

3   Design of Framework

In this section, we designed an ontology-based framework for composing semantic webservices. This framework supports dynamic composition of webservices and selects best execution plan using QoS properties. Finally, it is translated to OWL-S for execution engine. Fig 2 describes an overview of this framework. It consists of WebService Registrator, Composition Plan Generator and OWL-S Translator. In order to interpret the ontology, we use an OWL inference engine. This engines specifies are not within the scope of this research. WebService Register converts webservice description to PSO TRIPLE. The proposed ontology is based on OWL-S, therefore, it is a subset of RDF(Resource Definition Framework)[6]. Conversion to TRIPLE elements are stored in a knowledgebase and used for matchmaking and selection of the execution plan. The OWL-S translator translates a best execution plan into OWL-S.

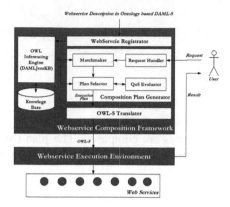

Fig. 2. An Overview of Framework

4 Experiment

In this section, we describe how a designed framework creates a best execution plan. For this experiment, we assume that some webservices are registered in a repository using properties. Assume user's input message has parameter a b and user' requirement is r q.

Service	Operation	Input	Output	QoS (Max/Avg/Min)		
				Time	Cost	Reliabilty
S1	Op1	A, b	d	10/12/13	8/10/11	71
S2	Op2	A, b	c	11/13/14	12/13/14	83
S3	Op3	C	s	12/14/15	13/14/15	62
S4	OP4	B	i	8/9/10	13/14/17	94
S5	Op5	F	c, e	5/7/8	20/24/28	83
S6	OP6	e, g, h	J, h	10/11/12	6/8/10	72
S7	OP7	A	d, e	13/14/15	11/13/14	81
S8	Op8	D	f	20/21/24	15/16/18	57
S9	Op9	C, e	r	15/17/19	12/16/17	84
S10	Op10	S	q	13/15/16	8/10/11	95

By using Algorithm 1, chainStartList is composed {S9, S10} because there is no webservice to satisfy output r, q. (Line 4 in Algorithm 2). A composite webservice has a parallel execution plan having two sequences of webservices. Using S9 and S10 as chainStart, each execution plan are generated. (Line 7 in Algorithm 1) S9 can be connected with a composition of S2and S7 and S5. Two composition plans are generated (Line 15~18 in Algorithm 1) and a best execution plan among two compositions is selected.

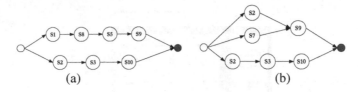

Fig. 3. Execution Plans

Fig 3 shows how webservices are composed. The plan (b) is selected using QoS properties and is translated to OWL-S for executing in webservice composition engine.

5 Conclusion

We designed the ontology based framework for the dynamic composition of webservices and a model for dynamic composition and calculation for finding the best execution plan. This framework has some merits. (1) It can generate a best execution plan dynamically using ontology and QoS properties. It can be adapted to a variety of business applications. (2) This plan can be translated to OWL-S, for usage in any execution environment supporting OWL-S. In the future, we will extend this framework using a transaction model. This will achieve execution, monitoring, and fault handling of composite webservices.

Acknowledgements

This work was supported by an INHA UNIVERSITY Research Grant

References

1. M. Paolucci, K. Sycara, "Autonomous Semantic Web Services", IEEE Computer Society, 2003.
2. D. J. Mandell, S. A. McIlraith., "A Botton-Up Approache to Automating Web Service Discovery, Customization and Semantic Web Translation, KSL Lab, Stanford University, 2003.
3. The DAML Service Coalition., OWL-S:Semantic Markup for Web Service, http://www. daml.org/services/dalm-s
4. M. Paolucci, A. Ankolekar, N. Srinivasan, Katia P. Sycara: The DAML-S Virtual Machine. International Semantic Web Conference 2003: 290-305
5. DAMLJessKB, http://edge.cs.drexel.edu/assemblies/software/damljesskb/damljesskb.html.
6. RDF Primer, http://www.w3.org/TR/rdf-primer/, 2004

Privacy Preserving Decision Tree in Multi Party Environment

Eakalak Suthampan and Songrit Maneewongvatana

Department of Computer Engineering,
King Mongkut's University of Technology Thonburi,
91 Prachauthit Road, Bangmod, Thung Kharu, Bangkok 10140, Thailand
s6450014@st.kmutt.ac.th
songrit@cpe.kmutt.ac.th

Abstract. Recently, there have been increasing interests on how to preserve the privacy in data mining when source of data are distributed
across multi parties. In this paper, we focus on the privacy preserving on
decision tree in multi party environment when data are vertically partitioned. We propose novel private decision tree algorithms applied to
building and classification stages. The main advantage of our work over
the existing ones is that each party cannot use the public decision tree to
infer the other's private data. With our algorithms, the communication
cost during tree building stage is reduced compared to existing methods
and the number of involving parties could be extended to be more than
two parties.

1 Introduction

Privacy preserving data mining is a relatively new research area in data mining
and knowledge discovery. The main goal of privacy preserving data mining is
to preserve the privacy during data mining operations and this can be done by
modifying the traditional data mining algorithms, which were not considered, so
that the private raw data like identifiers, names, addresses, etc. remain private
for the data owner even after the mining processes. The algorithms for privacy
preserving data mining depend on the data mining tasks(association rule, classification, clustering) and how the data are distributed among parties(*centralize*
where all attributes and transactions locate in one party, *horizontally* where
transactions are distributed to involving parties but each party has only a subset of transactions attributes, *vertically* where transaction attributes are distributed to involving parties but each party has only a subset of attributes). In
this paper, we particularly focus on applying privacy-preserving method on the
decision tree-based classification on vertically partitioned data. There are considerable amount of applications that use decision tree in classification, whereas
the attributes are distributed across several parties, e.g. a collection of depart-
mental databases on number of products sold. Each product is a column in the
table, different departments offer different products. Some department requires
that individual data should not be revealed to other parties.

G.G. Lee et al. (Eds.): AIRS 2005, LNCS 3689, pp. 727–732, 2005.

The contributions in this paper are: 1. New algorithms for building the decision tree and to classify a query transaction. The privacy is preserved through both building and classification stages. 2. Our algorithms could extend the number of involving parties while the communication cost is reduced when compared to existing methods.

In the next section, we give an overview of related work in privacy preserving data mining. The inference problem in decision tree classification is discussed in Section 3. Section 4 presents our work private decision tree both in tree building and classification stages to protect the inference problem. Conclusion is given at the last section.

2   Related Work

In recent work of privacy preserving data mining. The *secure multi party computation* (SMC) techniques [4] such as secure sum, secure scalar product, secure intersection, are utilized in the algorithms. Two privacy preserving algorithms proposed by Clifton [1] and [2] are based on an SMC technique. They were designed to find association rules on horizontally and vertically partitioned data, respectively. Both use secure scalar product of the vectors as a primary tool. Secure scalar product allows two parties to collaboratively compute the scalar product without revealing their own vector to the other party.

Du et al. presented an algorithm to build the decision tree on vertically partitioned data in [3]. They introduced an SMC-based protocol which improves performance of secure scalar product but their algorithm requires the use of a third party. However, their decision tree may still reveal some sensitive data due to the *inference problem*. Moreover, it is difficult to extend the number of involving parties when secure scalar product is used. In [7], Vaidya proposed another algorithm to build the decision tree. However, the tree on each party does not contain information that belongs to other parties. The drawback of this method is that the resulting class can be altered by a malicious party. Moreover, the communication cost is rather high due to the heavy use of SMC operations.

3   Inference Problem

In decision tree-based classification with vertically partitioned data scheme, the *inference problem* can be derived from the use of *public decision trees*. Public decision tree is a traditional decision tree which does not have any feature to protect privacy. After the training stage, all parties can access full information of the public decision tree. Such information can be used to infer the private data of other parties both in tree building and classification stages. Let us consider the following example where two parties, *Alice* and *Bob* are involved. Suppose that Alice and Bob have collaboratively built a public decision tree shown in Fig. 1 without explicitly exchanging any sensitive data. After the tree is built, both parties have complete knowledge of the structure of the tree. Now they want to classify a new transaction T_i=(Outlook = Sunny; Temperature

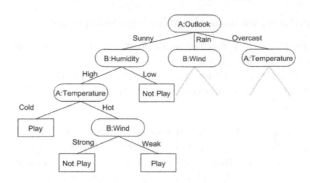

Fig. 1. Public decision tree

= Cold; Humidity = High; Wind = Strong) which Alice holds only attributes 'Outlook = Sunny; Temperature = Cold' and Bob holds the other attributes. After T_i is classified, both parties know that 'Play' is the outcome and thus they can use the structure of the tree to trace all possible paths that lead to 'Play'. There might be many paths that result in 'Play' but since each party knows some attribute values of Transaction T_i, it can narrow down the possibilities. In the example below, both parties can trace to the path 'Outlook = Sunny; Humidity = High; Temperature = Cold'. Hence Alice can use this path to identify the value of 'Humidity', which is Bob's private attribute. However, Alice cannot obtain Bob's 'Wind', because it is not a part of the outcome path. Bob can perform the same analysis and discover the values of both of Alice's private attributes. The inference of the outcome path can also be applied to the training data set that was used during the tree building stage too.

4   Proposed Algorithms

In this section, we describe our algorithms that build and classify decision tree and at the same time preserve the privacy of the data of each party. Our tree building algorithm is based on ID3 algorithm [6], but it can easily be modified to accommodate other decision tree construction algorithms.

4.1   Tree Building

Let $P = P_1, \ldots, P_k$ be a set of k parties involved in the operations. Any transaction, t, contains a set of $m + 1$ attributes $A_S = A_1, \ldots, A_m, C$ where C is the class attribute. The set of training transactions, T, is vertically partitioned into k partitions, $T_1, \ldots, T_k$, such that T_i is accessible from P_i only. Each T_i has attribute set AS_{P_i}, where $AS_{P_i} \subset A_S$ and $AS_{P_i} \cap AS_{P_j} = \emptyset$ when $i \neq j$.

All k parties would like to collaborate in building a public decision tree DT from T without revealing their own data to other parties. In order to do so, we introduce private decision tree, DT_i, for each party P_i. DT_i is known to P_i only. Full DT could be built from all DT_i's combined.

In our algorithms, we make the following assumptions:

1. Every party $P_1, \ldots, P_k$ has the same number of transactions.
2. AS_{P_i} is not empty for all i's.
3. Domain of the class attribute C is known to all parties.
4. Attributes of query transactions are distributed in the same manner as training transactions.

For each node N in the decision tree, P_i calculates the best local information gain similar to the original ID3 algorithm [6] and compares with the best information gain received from other parties. If its best local information gain is the best among all parties, the node is labeled with the attribute A which belongs to its best local information gain. The party P_i then notifies other parties that the node belongs to P_i but it does not give any information related to the attribute A such as the attribute name and its values. Then the party P_i partitions T into m partitions $T_{a_1}, \ldots, T_{a_m}$ such that attribute associated with the maximum information gain A of every transaction in T_{a_i} has value a_i. Then the party P_i broadcasts each partition associated with each of new m nodes and also broadcasts sets of transaction IDs $ID(T_{a_i})$ associated with each partition T_{a_i}. Finally, each party updates its unselected attributes AS_{P_i} along the new nodes.

After the private decision tree for each party is built. All parties collaborate using these trees to classify new coming query transactions. Let us consider the example in Fig. 2 Alice's private decision tree (left side in Fig. 2) contains only the information for Alice. Similarly, Bob's private decision tree (right side in Fig. 2) contains only the information for Bob. To classify a new coming transaction (Outlook = Sunny; Temperature = Hot; Humidity = High; Wind = Strong) which Alice holds only attributes 'Outlook = Sunny; Temperature = Hot' and Bob holds the rest attributes. Alice creates its candidate paths set $A = Path1, Path3, Path4$. Bob creates its candidate paths set $B = Path2, Path3$ then both parties use the normal intersection protocol such as in [5] to find the result of $A \cap B = Path3$ which is the predicted outcome (class).

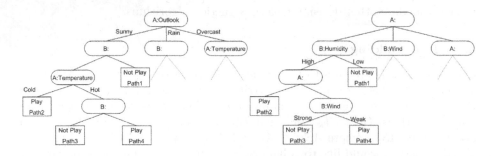

Fig. 2. Alice and Bob's Private Decision Trees

4.2   Privacy Analysis

During the tree building, the following information have been disclosed

- Sets of transaction IDs associated with each tree path. This can be used to imply the distribution of each node's attributes.
- The information gain associated with each node.
- The owner and cardinality of each node which can be derived from the tree structure.

Although many types of information have been revealed, they can not be combined together to derive private data of other parties. This is mainly because the attribute associated with each node is undisclosed. However, if a malicious party is aware of the distribution of an attribute or each party has very few attributes, it might be possible to guess the value of private data. Moreover, the malicious party cannot guess the data values in the same transaction by using the knowledge in public decision tree as described earlier. Therefore, the inference problem cannot occur during tree building stage.

During classification stage, the information about candidate paths of each party is encrypted in the intersection protocol [5]. Candidate path IDs will be guarded. Only the number of candidate paths is disclosed. After classification, all parties know the outcome path ID. This combined information cannot be used to reconstruct the public decision tree. Therefore, the inference problem cannot occur during classification. Moreover, in order to get the correct result in classification, each party cannot alter its own set of candidate paths. This removes the drawback of the algorithm in [7], which allows a malicious party to notify other parties with the wrong classification results.

Although sending the set of transaction IDs may create some weakness in terms of protecting the data privacy but it reduces the computation and communication costs and improves the efficiency.

4.3   Computation and Communication Analysis

The computation and communication costs depend on the following parameters: the number of parties k, the number of nodes on the tree N. Two major steps contribute to the communication cost. The first one occurs while it finds the best information gain at each node. k parties broadcast their $bestGain$ to compare to other parties, thus the communication needed is $k*sizeofbestGain*N$ bits. The second communication requires broadcasting a set of transaction IDs $ID(T_{a_i})$ to every node. The communication cost for this is $sizeofID(T_{a_i})*N$ bits. Actually, $sizeofID(T_{a_i})$ linearly decreases with the depth of the node in the tree. Therefore, the total communication cost for tree building is $O(k*sizeofbestGain*sizeofID(T_{a_i})*N^2)$ bits. For computation cost it needs no extra SMC algorithm like [3,7] since each party computes its private decision tree locally. Therefore, the computation cost is comparable to the original ID3 algorithm [6].

In classification stage, Each party has to create its set of candidate paths S_{path} then uses the intersection protocol from [5] to find the solution path. The intersection protocol requires that the set of each party needs to be encrypted by all other parties. Assume that the average number of elements in set of candidate paths is n and average size of each element is $sizeofn$ bits. The computation and communication costs are $O(nk^2)$ and $O(nk^2 * sizeofn)$ respectively. Compared to the computation and communication costs in [7], we need to involve the intersection protocol only once in the classification stage to find the predicted class while the algorithm in [7] needs to involve the intersection protocol in tree building stage every time the information gain of each attribute is computed.

5   Conclusion

In this paper, we have investigated the problem of privacy preserving classification based on decision tree on vertically partitioned environment. We have shown that information in the public decision tree can be used to infer private data of other parties both in the tree building and classification stages. Therefore, we propose a new set of classification algorithms using private decision tree to avoid the inference problem. Another advantage of our approach is that the number of involving parties can be easily extended while the communication cost is reduced.

References

1. M. Kantarcioglou and C. Clifton, *Privacy-preserving Distributed Mining of Association Rules on horizontally Partitioned Data*, ACM SIGMOD Workshop on Research Issues in Data Mining and Knowledge Discovery (2002), 24–31.
2. J. Vaidya and C. Clifton, *Privacy, Preserving Association Rule Mining in Vertically Partitioned Data*, ACM SIGKDD Int. Conf. Knowledge Discovery and Data Mining (2002), 639–644.
3. W. Du and Z. Zhan, *Building Decision Tree Classifier on Private Data*, IEEE ICDM Workshop on Privacy, Security and Data Mining (2002), 1–8.
4. A. C. Yao, *Protocols for Secure Computations*, IEEE Symp. Foundations of Computer Science (1982).
5. R. Agrawal, A. Evfimievski, and R. Srikant, *Information Sharing Across Private Databases*, ACM SIGMOD Int. Conf. Management of Data (2003), 86–97.
6. J. Rose Quinlan, *Induction of Decision Trees*, Machine Learning 1(1986):81–106.
7. J. Shrikant Vaidya, *Privacy Preserving Data Mining Over Vertically Partitioned Data*, Ph.D Thesis of Purdue University, August 2004, 28–34.

Author Index

Lecture Notes in Computer Science

For information about Vols. 1–3652

please contact your bookseller or Springer